THE PUBLICATIONS

OF THE

Selden Society

περὶ παντὸς τὴν ἐλευθερίαν

VOLUME 78

FOR THE YEAR 1960

ii

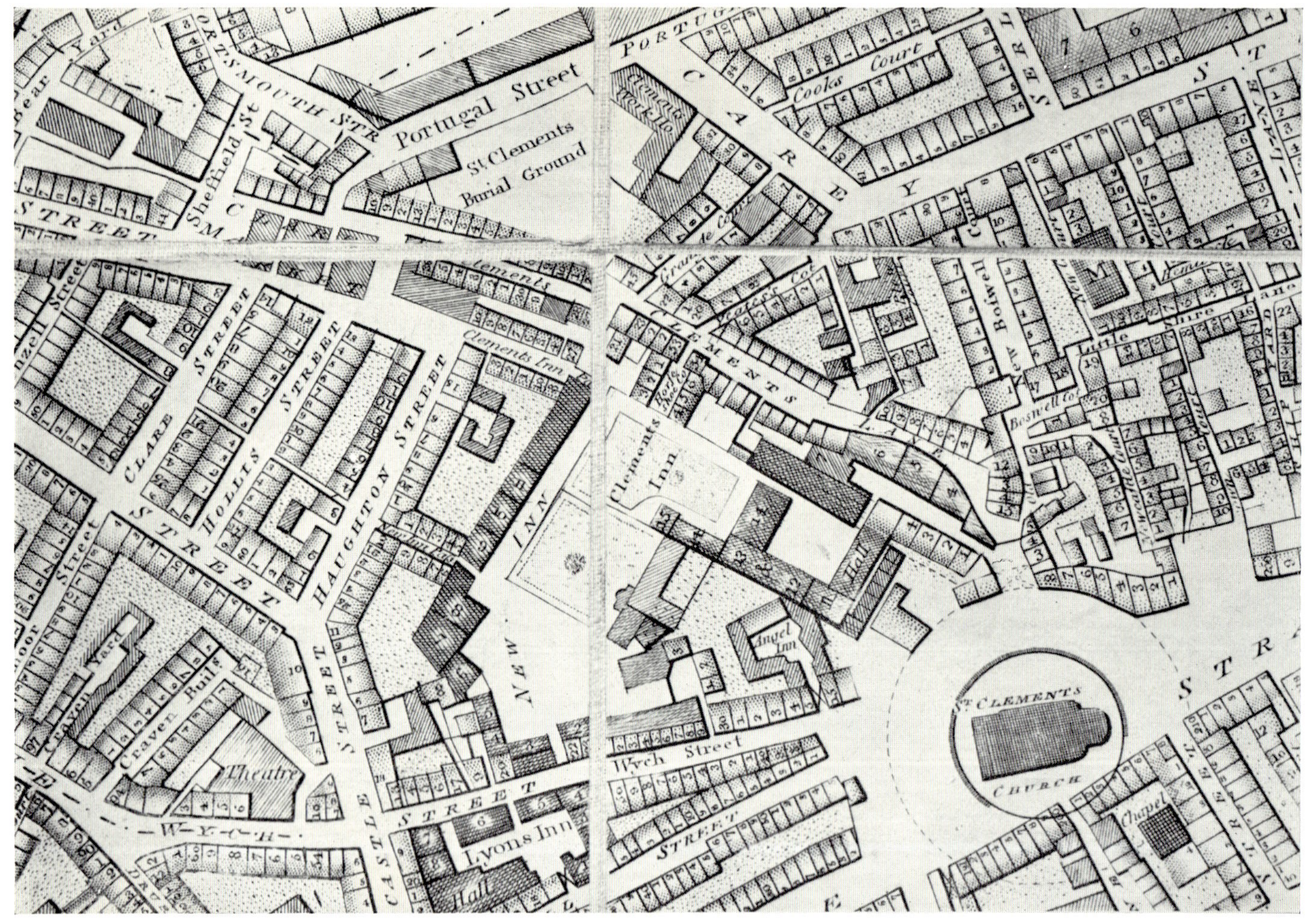

Part of Horwood's map of London (2nd. ed., 1807), showing Clement's Inn in the centre with New Inn adjoining on the south west: see pp. xliii-xlv below.

Selden Society

PENSION BOOK OF CLEMENT'S INN

EDITED

FOR THE SELDEN SOCIETY

BY

SIR CECIL CARR

K.C.B., Q.C., F.B.A.

LONDON

BERNARD QUARITCH 11 GRAFTON STREET W.1

1960

Printed in Great Britain
SPOTTISWOODE, BALLANTYNE & CO. LTD.
London and Colchester

CONTENTS

INTRODUCTION   PAGE

    Preface vii

    List of the Taylor Papers in the Public Record Office xi

    Abbreviations xi

   I. The Manuscript xiii

  II. Inns of Court and of Chancery xvi

 III. The Ancient Amity and Union xxii

 IV. Exercises of Learning xxvii

  V. Dues and Arrears xxxii

 VI. Finance xxxv

 VII. The Establishment xxxvii

VIII. Chambers xlii

 IX. Building Leases xlv

  X. The Kellett Affair xlvii

 XI. Earlier History l

 XII. Constitutions and Orders li

XIII. Admission Books liv

XIV. End of the Inns of Chancery lxi

TEXT

The Clement's Inn Pension Book (1714–50) 1

The Constitutions and Orders 218

APPENDIX

List of Members Admitted (1656–1883) 249

INDEX OF PERSONS 311

INDEX OF MATTERS 339

PREFACE

"THAT which in the Two Temples is called a Parliament, in Lincoln's Inn a Council, in Gray's Inn is called a Pension, that is, an Assembly of the Members of the Society to consult of the Affairs of the House."[1] At Clement's Inn, as at Gray's Inn and Barnard's Inn, such an assembly was a "Pension", and the business there transacted by the Principal and Ancients was entered in a Pension Book.

A manuscript Pension Book of Clement's Inn, covering the period from November 1714 to March 1749/50, was presented to the Inner Temple, shortly before his death, by the late George James Turner whose devoted services to the Selden Society are on record.[2] Himself a member of Lincoln's Inn, he decided that this relic of a defunct Inn of Chancery should find a home in the Inn of Court to which Clement's Inn had belonged. How, when or where the manuscript had come into his possession Turner was unable to recall. All he would say was that its occasional references to the visits of a Reader from the Inner Temple might make their modest contribution to the history of legal education. If he had ever contemplated editing the Pension Book, this was one of the tasks he postponed until too late.

Accident and apathy have lost us too many records of our ancient Inns of Chancery. Three Minute-Books of Clifford's Inn for instance, dating from 1609, perished when the Inner Temple Library was wrecked by enemy action in the late war.[3] On the other hand, a valuable manuscript, containing details of Furnival's Inn in the 15th and 16th centuries, in the possession of the Middle Temple, has lately been made available for study by Mr. D. S. Bland, its editor and commentator.[4] Although no other Pension Books of Clement's Inn may ever come to light, a rewarding collection of memorials of that Inn fortunately survives in the Public Record Office, the generous gift of Richard Stephens Taylor [5] who had

---

[1] Blunt, *Law Dictionary* (1670), s.v. "Pension".

[2] See Sir Percy Winfield's tribute in *Year Book of 5 Edward II* (1947), p. vii, and Professor Plucknett's *Brevia Placitata* (1951), p. vii. And see *British Academy Proceedings* (1954), xii, pp. 208–10, 214, 216–17.

[3] A so-called "Minute-Book of Clifford's Inn (1738–84)", mostly consisting of accounts, is in the Public Record Office (Lord Chamberlain's Papers, 9/344). Three Pension Books of Barnard's Inn (1620–1893), with an Admission Book (1800–69), survive in the possession of Gray's Inn.

[4] *Early Records of Furnival's Inn* (1957).

[5] Four of that name were partners in a London firm of solicitors in successive generations. The second in the series was admitted to Clement's Inn in 1867, the third (his eldest son) in 1882: see pp. 309–10 below. After the death of the third, the fourth, who left the firm in 1939 and died in 1950, presented the papers to the P.R.O.

inherited them from his father, one of the Society's last members. A list of these Taylor papers follows this preface. With the permission of the Keeper, and the unfailing help of his expert staff, full use has been made of this material. The names of the members admitted from 1656 onwards, taken from the two original Admission Books (items 1 and 2 in that list), are added in an Appendix at p. 249 below. A text of the "Constitutions and Orders of Clement's Inn", printed at p. 218 below, has been compiled from items 4 and 5; it includes dated extracts from Pension Books of a period from 1620 to 1781.

Besides the manuscript of this 18th-century Pension Book, the Inner Temple possesses two other objects formerly the property of Clement's Inn. One is the statue of the Black Boy,[1] once the central ornament of the latter Inn's garden, now to be seen in the south-east corner of the Inner Temple lawn. The other is a portrait of Sir Randolph Crewe, Chief Justice of the King's Bench in 1625, one of the pictures given to Clement's Inn in 1726 by Edward Halsted.[2] Other relics, two volumes of Principals' accounts and a cellar-book,[3] were listed in the sale catalogue of a firm of London booksellers in 1932, but have vanished without trace.

The Selden Society is indebted to the Inner Temple for permission to publish the Pension Book (and also for a special contribution towards the cost of this volume) and to the Keeper of the Public Record Office for like permission to reproduce material from the Taylor papers.

The editor desires to thank the Treasurers and Benchers of all four Honourable and Learned Societies of the Inns of Court for leave to quote from their records and, in the case of Gray's Inn, to study the manuscript Pension Books of Barnard's Inn. Sweet and Maxwell Ltd. have allowed free reference to *Early Holborn and the Legal Quarter of London*, the erudite work of the late Elijah Williams.

Miss Helen Wallis of the Map Room at the British Museum gave expert advice on plans of 18th-century London, and Mr. J. F. Kerslake of the National Portrait Gallery and Mr. R. A. Riches of the Royal Courts of Justice in connection with pictures formerly at Clement's Inn. Dr. Nelly J. M. Kerling skilfully carried out considerable tasks of transcription and verification.

To consult the archivists and librarians in charge of local and institutional records—to inquire, for instance, what, if anything, is known of the men named in the list of persons admitted to the Inn—has been to realise how generously these scholars will contribute their knowledge and their time to help an amateur historian. To name only a few of them,

[1] See the late Sir Frank MacKinnon's *Inner Temple Papers* (1948), pp. 106–7.
[2] See p. 126 below.
[3] See pp. xxxvi n., lx. below.

Mrs. E. Cottrill (Hants), Miss Ida Darlington (London County Council), Miss Joyce Godber (Beds.), Miss Joan Sinar (Devon), Mrs. John Varley (Lincs.) and Messrs. D. Charman (Ipswich and East Suffolk), Eric J. Davis (Bucks.), F. G. Emmison (Essex), Irvine Gray (Glos.), R. I. King (Northants.), L. A. Parker (Leics.) and John R. Wild (Derbyshire) took far more trouble to answer questions than he had any right to ask. The Revd. J. Gerald Holbeche of Solihull, Miss A. W. Richardson of Camblesforth, Selby, Mr. L. Smith of Doncaster and Miss Dorothy Yarde of Torquay furnished interesting genealogical details of former members of Clement's Inn. Comdr. W. E. May, R.N., of the National Maritime Museum, traced all those who served in East Indiamen.

Finally, the editor has particular reason to be grateful to Professor S. E. Thorne (whose authority and learning in matters of legal history are well known to members of the Selden Society) and, amongst other friends, to Mr. E. R. Timings of the Public Record Office, Canon G. W. Addleshaw, Sir Eric de Normann and Mr. G. D. Squibb, Q.C.

Some sixty years ago Maitland wrote of the serious gap in our knowledge of medieval England which should be filled by the tale of the Inns of Court. Every scrap of information obtainable about them, he said, should bear a high value in the eyes of all who care for English history. The present volume concerns one Inn only, and that an Inn of Chancery already in decline and now extinct. Although the scrap be immaterial, it may help to link afresh the four great *hospicia* which survive, and especially John Selden's own Inn, with the Society which bears Selden's name.

LIST OF THE TAYLOR PAPERS IN THE
PUBLIC RECORD OFFICE

P.R.O. 30/26/74/—

1. April 1656–April 1790	Admission Book (1 vol.)	
2. June 1790–January 1883	,, ,, (1 vol.)	
3. 1586–1652	Agreements for erection of chambers, &c. (Entry book with signatures)	
4. [late 15th century] to [1632–1650]	Constitutions and Orders Nos. 1–62 (1 vol.)	
5. [late 15th century] to 1687	Constitutions and Orders. Translation and transcript of preceding and of a lost vol. covering Nos. 63–84 (A.D. 1650–1687) (1 vol.)	
[1683–1781]	Pension Book entries	
1661–1780	Abstract of deeds	
6. Early 19th century	Subject Index to the Constitutions and Orders (1 vol.)	
7, 8.	Deeds relating to the Boar's Head (2 deeds) [1]	
9. 21 June 1682	Deed relating to the Inn (1 deed) [2]	
10. 1815 ?–1866?	Oaths taken on admission, with signatures (1 file)	
11. 1631–1763	Papers and accounts (1 packet)	

[1] Indentures of April 5 and 6, 1669, by which Gilbert, Earl of Clare, demises to Thomas Halfpenny of St. Martin's in the Fields, farrier, the Boar's Head (next Clement's Inn fore-gate): Halfpenny pays £280 and is to pay 5s. annually "in the Great Dining Hall of the Mansion House of the Rt. Hon. Elizabeth Countess Dowager of Clare commonly called Clare House in Drury Lane".

[2] A deed on vellum, not signed or witnessed. It is Francis Kellet's demise to Robert Dodsworth, of the Inner Temple, esquire, of "All that Inn or Hostell commonly called Clement's Inn in the County of Middlesex adjoining to the Lamb Inn in part south, the Angell Inn and New Inn Garden west, Mr Pettyes and Mr Markelands houses in part north and Clement's Lane and the houses built there in part east".

ABBREVIATIONS

Denton–Bacon–Cary report	Report of Thos Denton, Nicholas Bacon and Robt Cary to Henry VIII on the best form and order of study in the Houses of Court, printed by Edw. Waterhous in *Fortescutus Illustratus* (1663) at pp. 543–6.
Dugdale, *Origines*	*Origines Juridiciales*, by Sir Wm Dugdale, 3rd edn. (1680).
Williams, *Early Holborn*	*Early Holborn and the Legal Quarter of London*, by Elijah Williams (1927).

I. THE MANUSCRIPT

THE manuscript Pension Book, which occupies most of the text of the present volume, consists of 196 numbered pages, mostly with writing on both sides, and a further 38 unnumbered. The script is in many hands; when the entries begin in 1714, one seems to recognise the neat calligraphy of Thomas Callowe, the clerk or steward; as the Principal and Ancients sometimes subscribe their characteristic signature to a decision, it is possible to guess at the identity of other writers. After 1733, though Parliament had sought to encourage greater legibility,[1] the clerkly hand degenerates.

At Gray's Inn all orders of Pension had to be taken down at the time by a Bencher and perused and allowed in the same term by two or three senior members; after such approval, they were copied into the book by the steward; from 1794 the Minutes of each Pension had to be read at the next meeting.[2] Had similar directions operated at Clement's Inn during our period, a few obvious slips of the pen would doubtless have been corrected.[3]

Among the matters most frequently recorded are the collection of arrears owed by members to the Inn, the disposal of chambers and the audit of the Principal's accounts. These will be further discussed presently. Three other topics gradually become familiar: the election of a Principal (from 1725 onwards); the attendance of the Reader sent from the Inner Temple (from 1730) and the calling up of Companions to the Ancients' Table (from 1734). The records are the domestic annals of a cloistered fellowship. We hear of the public "comotions" of 1688 only because P. 241 they cause an interruption of commons. The brutal murder of John Penny, an ex-Principal, in his chambers in the Inn is not mentioned, though it probably explains the engagement of a watchman. The work of the Society P. 197 of Gentlemen Practisers and the drastic regulation of attorneys in 1729[4] are ignored. Fortunately the formal routine of the record is occasionally varied. St. Clement Danes Church served as the Chapel of the Inn; we Pp. 14, 87, can note the contributions of the House to the repair of the steeple and 130, 243 the organ and to the re-lining of the pews (to some of which the Inn claims an exclusive right), as well as the gifts made (with a cautious Pp. 18, 62, caveat that nothing is legally due) to the rector. Subscriptions also &c. provide for a dial for the clock outside the Hall, for a porter's gown Pp. 56, 140, 153

---

[1] See 4 Geo. II. c. 26, made perpetual by 21 Geo. II. c. 3.

[2] *Pension Book of Gray's Inn*, ii, pp. v, 371.

[3] *E.g.* the repetition of "And Desireing", at p. 102 below (Coates' arrears), and the duplication of Webb's composition on pp. 170–1. See also pp. xl, 68, 107, 118, 141.

[4] See 2 Geo. II. c. 23.

P. 104

P. 186

P. 126

Pp. 11, 244

P. 234

P. 246

and staff, for fire-fighting equipment, and, on his retirement from the Principalship, for the portrait of Joshua Blackwell.[1] We learn of the processional arrangements for a call of Serjeants (a ceremony that could provoke problems of precedence), of Edward Halsted's gift of pictures, of the sometimes unneighbourly actions of New Inn and of occasional disputes over ancient lights and nuisances. It is thought worth while to chronicle the dismissal of John Tidy, the gardener (who is not to be re-employed in any capacity), the permission to the butler to apply for a warrant against Mr. Middlemore who has been assaulting him, or (on one occasion only) the closing of the access from Horseshoe Court on Ascension Day.[2] A few entries affirm the extra-parochial character of the premises[3]; there is, however, no mention of those "dropt children" whose benevolent adoption by other Inns (whence came their surnames of Temple, Lincoln or Gray as the case might be[4]) betokened not only the kindliness of the benchers but also the assertion of immunity from interference by parish officers.

Clement's Inn consisted of a Principal, a limited number of Ancients and a residue of Companions. The Pension consisted of the Principal and Ancients: some of the earlier orders refer to the governing body as the Graund Councell[5] or Graund Company.[6] During our period the Pension met most often on Fridays, less frequently on Wednesdays and once only on a Monday or Tuesday. More than a quarter of the meetings took place in February, more than a sixth in November; there were none in September or October. The number present varies between five and twelve; once, when only five attend, no business is recorded.[7] Companions, though they may subscribe to some common object,[8] have no share in the administration except to vote at the election of a Principal. The result of

---

[1] The Barnard's Inn Pension Books (possessed by Gray's Inn) show that an outgoing Principal usually received a piece of plate suitably inscribed and (until 1839) the chair in which he had presided.

[2] At Barnard's Inn the closing of the gates on Ascension Day is recorded in the Pension Book annually.

[3] Cf. *Black Books of Lincoln's Inn*, iii, 474; *I.T.R.*, v, 285; *Pension Book of Gray's Inn*, i, p. xli; ii, pp. 318, 320. And see p. 242 below.

[4] See "The Temple Family" in Sir Frank MacKinnon's *Inner Temple Papers* (1948), p. 24, and for other examples the *Inner Temple* and *Middle Temple Records*, the *Black Book of Lincoln's Inn* and *Pension Book of Gray's Inn*, *passim*. The Clifford's Inn Minute-Book in the P.R.O. shows that babies were sometimes abandoned in an Inn of Chancery.

[5] See pp. 223–4 below (Orders 33–5, 37–8).

[6] See pp. 226–7 below (Orders 51–2). At Gray's Inn the last call to the degree of Ancient, carrying membership of the "Grand Company", was in 1709—*Pension Book of Gray's Inn*, ii, p. ix. The expression "Grave Company" was in use at Barnard's Inn as late as the eighteen-seventies.

[7] There was no quorum rule except under Order 33 (see p. 223 below).

[8] The subscribers in 1718 were Companions only; in 1727, Ancients only: see pp. 56, 130 below.

these Polls must usually have been a foregone conclusion, but there was a close vote in 1742, when John Green was chosen with a majority of one[1]; even then there were no more than thirteen votes. We do not know the total of members, but in 1721 we have an alphabetical list of 130 in connection with the subscription towards the repair of St. Clement Danes Church. Only 62 subscribed; the list doubtless included the name of several who had died or left the Society, but it gives us a maximum figure. The legal *hospicia* were voluntary societies—so voluntary indeed that in 1533 some recalcitrant members threated to secede from the Inner Temple and found another Inn of Court.[2] As Maitland more than once observed, the Inns exemplified the value of the trust as an alternative to incorporation. Corporateness could have given them such "incidents" as perpetual succession and the power to purchase and hold land, to make bylaws or statutes for better government, to sue and to enter into contracts. They managed well enough without this supposed advantage. They placed their property with feoffees in trust—in the case of Clement's Inn in trust for the Society and the Principal and Ancients present and future, "to be disposed of in such manner as the Principal for the time being with any five Ancients for the time being in Pension assembled should from time to time direct and appoint".[3] The periodical renewal of trustees, though tiresome, worked adequately.[4] Every *hospicium* enacted its own regulations and every member knew he had to obey them. Contracts were made by representative members on the authority of a recorded resolution. At Clement's Inn the fire insurance was effected in the name of the Principal or the Deputy Principal or some other Ancient.[5] Members were authorised to settle claims against the Inn or to collect money due. If it was necessary to sue a member or his surety on an admittance bond, the Principal or the steward found no difficulty in taking action.[6] The three experts whom Henry VIII invited to recommend reforms in legal study proposed a new corporation, to be named "the Governor, Vice-Governor and King's Students".[7] The proposal, however, was not carried out; the legal Inns retained their unincorporated independence.

P. 87

[1] P. 198 below. His opponent voted for him: in the circumstances he declined to serve and paid the prescribed fine.

[2] *I.T.R.*, i, 103.

[3] See, for example, p. 4 below. It has been noted (Williams, *Early Holborn*, 29) that unincorporated feoffees, suing for rent, could not proceed at common law, but had to apply to the Chancellor for a remedy.

[4] The Abstract of Deeds among the Taylor papers show that more than once the renewal was arranged when only one surviving trustee was left.

[5] See pp. 29, 108 (where Halsted has to distinguish his personal interest), 109 and 158 below.

[6] At Gray's Inn in 1629 the Treasurer gave the steward a letter of attorney to sue in his name—*Pension Book of Gray's Inn*, i, 288.

[7] See the report printed by Waterhous, *Fortescutus Illustratus* (1663), p. 544.

II. INNS OF COURT AND OF CHANCERY

In introducing a manuscript of the seventeen-hundreds it is rash to blunder into the unsolved mysteries of the 13th and 14th centuries. If, despite the researches of scholars, our knowledge of the origins and the mutual relations of the Inns of Court and of Chancery is incomplete, it may be worth while to indicate some of the gaps.

Legal historians from Dugdale onwards have made us familiar with certain formative events of the 13th century[1]—the fixing of the Court of Common Pleas *in aliquo certo loco* (at Westminster), the banishment of law schools from the City of London, the abandonment by the clergy of the work of advocates and judges in civil courts, the direction to Sir John de Metingham and his judicial colleagues to recruit the more worthy and teachable as *apprenticii*[2] for the better service of the court and the people, and the City authorities' selective registration of practising lawyers. The legal profession has begun to be organised in specialised grades; lawyers are wanted and men want to be lawyers; the judiciary will prescribe the qualifications for practice (a responsibility which they are presently presumed to have delegated[3] to the four Inns of Court, though each of the four seems to be calling men to the bar of its Inn *ex proprio vigore* and thereby conferring a prospective right of audience) and will exercise a visitatorial control.

At this stage we embark on guesswork. "The original institution of the Inns of Court nowhere precisely appears", observed Lord Mansfield[4]— a cautious understatement equally applicable to Inns of Chancery. Groping in the dark, we might follow up Sir William Holdsworth's suggestion that bodies of would-be practitioners may have cohered round some distinguished master of the law.[5] Certainly some legal Inns grew up under the care of an eminent lawyer. Or, with Sir Frederick Pollock, we could envisage groups of students gathering, as at the medieval universities in Paris and elsewhere, to "constitute themselves into regular permanent societies with something of the common life and discipline of a gild, something of the systematic teaching and discussion of a university, and governing bodies of Ancients who may present suitable candidates to the

---

[1] See, generally, Pollock and Maitland, *History of English Law* (2nd edn., 1898), c. vii (the Age of Bracton); Holdsworth, *History of English Law* (4th edn., 1936, ii, 311, 484, 494, &c.; Maitland, *Collected Papers* (1911), iii, 78–86.

[2] For the transition from *apprenticii* to "barristers" see Bolland in *Law Quarterly Review* (1908), xxiv, 399.

[3] Lord Mansfield asserted the delegation in *R. v. Gray's Inn* (1780), 1 Dougl. 353. See also Bolland, *ubi sup.*, p. 392.

[4] *R. v. Gray's Inn, ubi sup.*

[5] Holdsworth regarded legal education as the principal *raison d'être* of the legal Inns (see *Law Quarterly Review* (1928), xliv, 384). If so, Serjeant's Inn would be an exception.

King's judges to be approved and licensed advocates."[1] Or again, we may take note, and await the fuller development, of the theory tentatively outlined by Professor S. E. Thorne,[2] who inclines to regard the Inns' function of professional instruction as an afterthought or second stage. Recalling the brevity of the legal terms (four periods of less than a hundred days in the year),[3] he points out that, as soon as the Courts had been fixed at Westminster, the practitioners would want permanent accommodation in the vicinity. They would occupy *hospicia*[4] (a word we may translate as inns or hostels) which would form a combination of hostel, club and professional chambers but not a school. These would be sparsely and uneconomically tenanted during the intervening vacations. To get more subscribing members and to make fuller use of otherwise empty buildings, the legal Inns would presently have an incentive to undertake the teaching of younger men. When the surviving Black Books of Lincoln's Inn begin, some early entries indicate the growth of a practice or a requirement that members resident in London and Middlesex paid commons dues not only in term-time but also in vacation.[5] Fellows would have to attend as teachers in the weeks which became known as the Learning Vacations, when senior members would be selected to serve as Lent and Autumn Readers.

Never having received or even asked for charters of incorporation, the legal Inns had no rival anniversaries to celebrate. Although dates have been named for their beginnings,[6] they themselves appear unconscious of one another's birthdays; otherwise there need have been no dispute over seniority between Clement's and Clifford's Inns.[7] Clement's Inn, presumably unable to specify the year of its foundation, took pride in having been recognised in 1480 as already *et diu antea* "a Society of men of the

---

[1] See *Origins of the Inns of Court*, an address to Canadian guests at Lincoln's Inn, July 1, 1931; see also *For my Grandson* (1933), cap. 5.

[2] In a lecture on Gray's Inn delivered there in June 1959, printed in *Graya*, (1959), L, p. 79.

[3] Spelman, *Original of the Four Terms of the Year* (1614), remarked that the annual calendar of *dies fasti* and *nefasti* had allowed the Roman praetor only 28 days for pronouncing his edicts, "whereas we have in our terms above 96 days in court".

[4] *Hospicium*, observed Professor T. F. Tout, is only a rather grand name for a house. The primary meaning of "inn" is a dwelling-house, according to the *N.E.D.* (which rejects any special connotation of "town house" or nobleman's residence). At Cambridge there were several *hospicia* and at least one *deversorium* (Oving's Inn, absorbed into Trinity College): see Willis and Clark, *Architectural History of Cambridge* (1886), i, p. xix; ii, pp. 403–4. Our legal *hospicia* were not to be *deversoria*; they were to be hostels, not hostelries: see p. xx below.

[5] See *Black Books*, i, 2 (1428); see also *ibid.*, 6–7 (1436) and 12 (1442) for the voluntary offer and subsequent requirement. An early order at Clement's Inn (No. 4, p. 219 below) may fit into this context.

[6] Dates are assigned, for instance, by Underdown, *Six Lectures on the Inns of Court and Chancery* (1912), p. 65, and by Williams, *Early Holborn*.

[7] See *I.T.R.*, i, 228 (1563), and see p. xxvi n. below.

Court of the Temporal Law and of Counsellors of the same Law".[1] The description is apt for a stage at which, with counsellors and attorneys living in commons together, the inmates of the legal Inns do not yet exhibit differences of function but stand all at one level.

When, *circa* 1470,[2] Fortescue wrote his panegyric of the laws of England, he graded the legal *hospicia* as either *majora* or *minora*.[3] The *majora*, he says, are four; they are called *Hospicia Curie*, Inns of Court; each has some two hundred members. The *minora* are ten *et quandoque vero plura*,[4] called *Hospicia Cancellarie*; each has a hundred students at least.[5] Personally connected with four Inns,[6] Fortescue wrote with knowledge and authority, though his deliberately limited scope left open several questions to which he might have offered answers. At what approximate date, for instance, did the four Inns of Court emerge as *majora*? Had it happened in his life-time? Were they evolved as a new type, "second thoughts", due to the need of firmer and more formal discipline?[7] If not so evolved, how came they to be upgraded while the Inns of Chancery remained inferior? Was it perhaps that some Inns provided more attractive amenities or more fashionable teachers than others? Their superiority, it seems, was not parental; there are persistent hints to the contrary.[8] What Fortescue does tell us is that the members of the Inns of Chancery are the *juvenes*; they study the originals and the elements of the law; as they become proficient in these and as they grow up, they are admitted into the *hospicia majora*. His commentator, Edward Waterhous, elaborates this; the Houses of Chancery were "preparatory Lodges of Freshmen, for none were to be admitted of an Inn of Court but such as first have been in an Inn of

---

[1] See below, pp. 218, 232; and see Dugdale, *Origines*, p. 187.

[2] Between 1467 and 1471: see S. B. Chrimes, *Sir John Fortescue* (1944), pp. xxxvi–xxxviii.

[3] *De Laudibus Legum Anglie*, c. clix.

[4] See the list given by Prof. Chrimes, *ubi sup.*, p. 197. Some legal Inns did not survive the death of their founder: see Williams, *Early Holborn*, 1466.

[5] Figures given for Clement's Inn in 1586 (see E. Williams, *Staple Inn*, p. 105) show 100 present in term-time and 20 during vacation. On Fortescue's words here (*centum studentes ad minus*) Waterhous comments, "they resided not therein always nor had Commons therein but in Term-time when the Attorneys and other Members of them came up to the Term to follow their Clyents' Business, yet were contributory to the charge and submissive to the Government of them and there had their Chambers and were in Judgment of Law abiding (*Fortescutus Illustratus*, p. 527). See the early order (No. 4, p. 219 below) requiring some attendance in vacation.

[6] He was a Governor of Lincoln's Inn (where he had been admitted before 1420), and a feoffee of Clement's Inn, St. Mary's (afterwards Strand) Inn, and Angel Inn (later a common hostelry): see Williams, *Early Holborn*, 24, 26, 1466, and, as to Angel Inn, 1474–5; and Chrimes, *ubi sup.*, p. xxi.

[7] As suggested by R. J. Fletcher, *Pension Book of Gray's Inn*, i. pp. xiii–iv.

[8] The two Temples, it was said, had been established by men from Thavies Inn: see *I.T.R.*, i, pp. xi, &c. The Principal of Clifford's Inn did not admit the seniority of the Inner Temple: see *R. v. Allen* (1834), 110 E. R. 1055.

Chancery"; the four Inns of Court "received not the Gudgeons and Smelts but the Polypuses and Leviathans, the Behemoths and Gyants of the Law".[1] When Waterhous published his commentary in 1663, the rule that a student entered an Inn of Court after passing through an Inn of Chancery had long been broken. It cannot have been rigidly enforced. The Houses of Chancery were petitioning the Houses of Court in the reign of Edward VI not to admit anyone who could not produce a certificate that he had studied in the former for the prescribed time.[2] Coke said that the young student "most commonly cometh from one of the universities" and enters one of the Houses of Chancery "to learn there the elements of the law".[3] He himself went to Clifford's Inn in 1571, as did Selden in 1602, on the way to the Inner Temple; but Matthew Hale went from Magdalen Hall at Oxford to Lincoln's Inn in 1629 *per saltum*.

To Fortescue, then, the difference between the inmates of the two types of *hospicia* was the difference between seniors and juniors. To later generations the Inns of Court meant societies of barristers whereas the Inns of Chancery meant societies of attorneys and solicitors. But what were finally classified as Houses "of Chancery"[4] originally included barristers and apparently called their students to the bar of their Inn. References to utter (or outer) and inner barristers are embedded in the ancient Constitutions and Orders of Clement's Inn[5] and Clifford's Inn[6]; Furnival's Inn and Thavies Inn contained utter barristers even in the Elizabethan era[7]; Clifford's Inn, which in 1344/5 had been let to the *apprenticii de banco*,[8] produced a Serjeant in William Skrene sixty years later, though the event was noted as exceptional.[9] The stratified Orders of Clement's Inn contain fossilised references to mootings and readings, revels and Christmas celebrations,[10] which suggest that the pattern of life in the early days of that Inn was much like that in the early days of an Inn of Court.

[1] *Fortescutus Illustratus*, p. 526.

[2] See Bland, *Early Records of Furnival's Inn*, p. 43, and, for the order of 1557 and the 17th-century certification, p. xxiv below.

[3] 3 Rep. xxxv.

[4] For possible variations in the classification see Williams, *Early Holborn*, 15–16.

[5] See No. 13 at p. 220 below; the phrase "call to the Barr to moot" in No. 12 is a reminder of the physical features of the Hall. The modern "call to the bar", with its implication of a right of audience, is still a call to the bar of a particular Inn: see Manning, *Serviens ad Legem* (1840) p. 328: *Law Quarterly Review* (1913), xxix, 23.

[6] After half a year the admittee was to be entitled to all the "learning" belonging to an inner barrister, and after a year and a day all that belonging to an outer barrister (Ordinance No. 46). Did Lyon's Inn "call" a man (see p. xxix n. below) in 1734?

[7] Dugdale, *Origines*, pp. 242, 270–1.

[8] See Williams, *Early Holborn*, 970; the apprentices, he suggests, had probably been in occupation already.

[9] A. R. Ingpen, *Middle Temple Bench Book* (1st edn., 1912), pp. 2–3, citing Brerewood. Skrene became Serjeant in 10 Henry IV and King's Serjeant in 1 Henry V.

[10] See pp. 219–20 below.

Half-way through the 16th century the attorneys were ordered to quit the Inns of Court and get back to their Inns of Chancery.[1] They had failed, it seems, to bear their share in the exercises of learning. Perhaps their presence created difficulties of professional discipline or convention. The accommodation, anyhow, was limited; as was presently emphasised, the Inns were not intended for the lodging of gentlemen from the country, "which, if it should be suffered, were to disparage the said Societies and to turn them from *hospicia* to *deversoria*"; there was to be no room for knights, gentlemen, foreigners and discontinuers.[2] Presently one reason for banishing common attorneys and solicitors is bluntly stated. They are to be excluded because "there ought always to be preserved a difference between utter barristers, Readers in Court, apprentices at law—which are the principal persons next to the Serjeants at Law and Judges in administration of justice—and attorneys and solicitors which are but ministerial persons and of an inferior nature".[3] Although the gentlemen of the long robe have never attained a pinnacle in popular esteem, the attorneys suffered for centuries a special obloquy as the "lower branch" of the legal profession.[4]

The frequent renewal of the order excluding attorneys from the Inns of Court[5] indicates laxity of enforcement. Be that as it may, as attorneys were thrust forth from the *majora hospicia*, barristers disappeared from the *minora*; the Inns of Chancery became "inexplicably"[6] monopolised by attorneys; special chambers were no longer reserved for students, despite the attempt under Charles II to restore the old system.[7]

Of the integration of particular Inns of Chancery with particular Inns of Court something will be said on a later page. Meanwhile why, it may be asked, Inns "of Court" and "of Chancery"? Fortescue wrote of the Inns of Court almost as though they were Inns of courtiers; their members,

---

[1] See *I.T.R.*, i, 190 (1557), &c., and Bellot's full study of the exclusion of attorneys in *Law Quarterly Review*, xxvi (1910), 137. To keep out the attorneys and solicitors and to secure the admission of none but students, certificates from an Inn of Chancery (see p. xxiv below) had in 1639 to be attested by the Reader to that Inn; see *I.T.R.*, ii, 249.

[2] See *I.T.R.*, ii, 33–4 (1614); iii, 30 (1664). In 1596 no one was to be admitted to an Inn of Court unless he had a chamber in it; meantime he was to be in some Inn of Chancery; *ibid.*, i, 413. A Clement's Inn man could not expect to keep his chamber there if he joined an Inn of Court: see p. 223 (Order 32) below.

[3] *I.T.R.*, ii, 84 (1614); *Pension Book of Gray's Inn*, i, 213, &c. Dugdale shows the even less kind substitution of "immaterial" for "ministerial" when the order is repeated in 1684: see *Origines*, p. 322. Can this be a misprint? In *I.T.R.*, iii, 32, the word is "ministerial".

[4] E. B. V. Christian, *Short History of Solicitors* (1896), prints a wide selection of adverse comments—from the Commons' petition of 1402 to Sir George Stephen's astringent criticisms (before the Select Committee of 1846) of his own profession.

[5] In 1574, 1615, 1633, 1665 and 1684: see Christian, *ubi sup.*, *passim*.

[6] See *Edinburgh Review* (1871), p. 489; the reviewer is less than sympathetic towards attorneys.

[7] See below, p. 226, n.

besides studying law, learnt singing and dancing and all the social accomplishments of the royal household, so that, in Dugdale's words, "these Hostells, being Nurseries or Seminaries of the Court, taking their denomination of the end wherefore they were so instituted, were called therefore the Innes of Court".[1] The Inns of Chancery, said Fortescue less conclusively, were so called because the members were young men studying the first elements. Dugdale preferred the explanation that "they were antiently *hospicia* for the Clerks of Chancery",[2] thus presenting us with yet another mystery. The administrators of a medieval king were part of his household. When the Chancellor grew to be more than a domestic officer, his clerks became separated from the royal clerks and formed a society acting directly under his orders. Professor Tout observed[3] that, as early as the middle of the 13th century, *hospicium Cancellarie* occurs as the name of the household of the Chancery clerks.[3] These clerks are not to be confused with the students in the Inns of Chancery described by Fortescue. Indeed the Chancellor enjoined his clerks to keep themselves to themselves and not to dwell *inter apprenticios legis attornatos aut alios extraneos*. The training of the Chancery officials in the knowledge of writs, largely acquired by copying common forms, was just as essential to the common lawyer; it was the link between the administrative officer and the would-be practitioner. "Students of law who did not want to be clerks of Chancery could well begin their education at the same point." The Chancery clerks within their *hospicia Cancellarie* had been ordered not to mingle with the *extranei* who wanted to join their household *propter doctrinam et scripturam*—to learn their vocation by copying the forms of writs or otherwise and perhaps by acquiring the art of reading and writing the court hand. Somehow the prospective practitioner succeeded in an infiltration which grew into exclusive occupancy. There is "a chaos of silence as to the process by which Chancery clerks' lodgings in the 14th century became preparatory schools for common lawyers less than a century later".[4] We find no solid evidence that any of Fortescue's *minora hospicia* occupied the site of such lodgings. The title of "Principal", common in the structure of Inns of Chancery, may be a tenuous link, perhaps the only one, with the older technical schools for clerical work.

[1] Dugdale, *Origines*, p. 141. Besides the study of the law, wrote Waterhous, the Inns of Court promoted "exercises of manhood, of ornament and delicacy, of Learning and activity": *Fortescutus Illustratus*, p. 532.

[2] *Origines*, p. 143.

[3] See, for the whole of the passage above, *Collected Papers of Thomas Frederick Tout* (1934), ii, 143 ("The Household of the Chancery and its Disintegration"). And see B. Wilkinson, *The Chancery Under Edward III* (1929), pp. 87 ff.

[4] *Collected Papers of T. F. Tout, ubi sup.*, p. 167.

III. THE ANCIENT AMITY AND UNION

By the middle of the 16th century the Inns of Chancery are seen to be parcelled out among the four Inns of Court. Furnival's Inn and Davy's (or Thavies) Inn "belong" to Lincoln's Inn; Clement's, Clifford's and Lyon's Inns "belong" to the Inner Temple; New Inn and Chester (or Strand) Inn "belong" to the Middle Temple, Barnard's Inn and Staple Inn to Gray's Inn. These appropriations, sometimes confirmed by the relationship of landlord and tenant,[1] are variously manifested in the practice whereby an Inn of Court sent a Reader to conduct and supervise legal education at each of its Inns of Chancery, in the preferential admission of men from an Inn of Chancery to its linked Inn of Court, and in certain long-enduring social or ceremonial contacts. The linkages carried an element of visitatorial jurisdiction akin to that exercised by the judges over the Inns of Court; it was natural for a House of Chancery to submit its constitutional disputes (where, for example, the election or authority of its Principal was challenged) to the arbitration of the Benchers of its Inn of Court. This jurisdiction must have grown up long before those formal directions for such submission which are recorded in Tudor and Stuart times. In 1574, we know, "the reformation and order of the Inns of Chancery" were "referred to the consideration of the Benchers of the Inns of Court whereto they are belonging"; and in 1614 and 1644 the Inns of Chancery were bidden to "hold their government subordinate" to their Inns of Court.[2] The instances of the exercise of this jurisdiction, marshalled by Bellot from the published records, take us back no earlier than 1561.[3] *Circa* 1503 a dispute over the election to the principalship of Furnival's Inn had been submitted to the Lord Chancellor who asked Moore of Lincoln's Inn and Pigott of the Inner Temple to look into the facts.[4] A generation later Furnival's Inn would surely have put this *magna contentio* up to Lincoln's Inn direct. Somehow and at some date in the first third, or the first quarter, of the 16th century the alliances or linkages between particular Inns of Chancery and particular Inns of Court were formed. Exactly how or when we do not know.

Topographical propinquity may have had its influence. The Denton-

---

[1] Thus Lincoln's Inn acquired Furnival's Inn in 1547 and Davy's Inn in 1549: see Bland, *Early Records of Furnival's Inn*, pp. 42, 55; *Black Books of Lincoln's Inn*, i, 286, 297. The Inner Temple acquired Lyon's Inn in 1583: see *I.T.R.*, i, 315, 363, 467, and Williams, *Early Holborn*, 1460, 1477, 1479. The Middle Temple acquired New Inn in 1608: see *ibid.*, 43.

[2] See *I.T.R.*, i, 278; ii, 83; iii, 30.

[3] *Law Quarterly Review*, (1910) xxvi, p. 384.

[4] See Bland, *Early Records of Furnival's Inn*, p. 39.

Bacon-Cary report on legal studies, presented to Henry VIII in 1540, states that, of the existing Inns of Chancery, four "being in Holborn" are "read of" (*i.e.* receive a Reader from) Gray's Inn and Lincoln's Inn; the other five "which are within Temple Bar are of the two Temples".[1] The procedure for appointing Readers is a compromise between dependence and independence. "At the Election of Readers for Inns of Chancery", says Dugdale when writing of the Inner Temple, "the order is that the late Reader of the Inn of Chancery, near the time of Reading, delivers to the Bench at Dinner the names of six Utter Barristers that have not yet read, out of which number the Bench makes choice of three and sends the names of those three to the Inns of Chancery, who choose one of them to be their Reader, only to Lions Inne they send the whole six."[2] It looks as though Lyon's Inn had originally made a separate bargain; the linkings between Inns of Court and their Inns of Chancery may not all have been simultaneously agreed or decreed.

The practice of sending a Reader from an Inn of Court to its Inns of Chancery must have arisen because the latter could not themselves produce a properly qualified teacher from their own ranks. How long had this inferiority existed? Would not the Autumn Reader at Furnival's Inn in 1408[3] have been a Furnival's Inn man? If so, when did Lincoln's Inn take over the task of providing the Reader? The records show that the Inner Temple nominated Master Beaumont and Master Caryll senior for Reader to Clement's Inn and Lyon's Inn respectively in 1529/30.[4] How much earlier had it been staffing these readerships? The order in each case is that the nominee is to be Reader and to be presented to the Inn of Chancery "according to the decree made by the Chancellor of England and the King's justices". If this decree could be identified, it might throw light upon our problem.

An established alliance seems indicated when in 1521 the Inner Temple admits to membership the Principal of Clement's Inn "according to ancient custom".[5] In 1507 it had admitted the Principal of Barnard's Inn

---

[1] See Waterhous, *Fortescutus Illustratus*, p. 545.

[2] Dugdale, *Origines*, p. 161. After 1772 only three names are sent to Lyon's Inn: see *I.T.R.*, v, 278, 291, 309, &c. See *Black Books of Lincoln's Inn*, ii, 23, for a failure to present names (1662).

[3] See Bland, *Early Records of Furnival's Inn*, p. 23.

[4] *I.T.R.*, i, 93, 95. The Middle Temple is said to have sent a Reader to New Inn in 1503: see p. 1 below.

[5] *I.T.R.*, i, 65. The extent of the custom is uncertain. Other Clement's Inn Principals were admitted in 1532 (John Payn "for divers causes and for a fine of 20s.") and 1577 (John Bradshaw "in consideration of the good will of old time borne to this House and accounted as a particular member of the same"): *ibid.*, i, 101, 288. A Principal of Furnival's Inn was admitted at Lincoln's Inn in 1513 and 1516: see *Black Books of Lincoln's Inn*, i, 172, 178.

with special favour, "because he was a particular friend of the Society before his coming".[1] Moreover, in 1524/5 the Inner Temple excused Master Barnardiston from serving as steward because he had executed the office of Principal at Davy's Inn "at the instance of this Society for two years".[2] Barnard's and Davy's Inns never "belonged" to the Inner Temple. May we not infer from these last two entries that in the initial decades of the century the alliances were not yet solid?

The same inference might be drawn from the Inner Temple registers of admissions, though here the evidence is imperfect because the clerks do not consistently record the Inn of Chancery from which an admittee has come. In the years from 1507 to 1521 eight men entered the Inner Temple from its three Inns of Chancery, while eighteen entered from Inns of Chancery linked with other Inns of Court. In the next fifteen years the preponderance is reversed. From 1522 to 1537 the Inner Temple received thirteen men from its own three Houses of Chancery as against only four from other Houses.[3] There seems to be no record before 1557 of entrants from those three Houses obtaining any concession in respect of admission fees. In that year it was ordered that none be admitted "without the certificate of the Principal and two Ancients of the Inn of Chancery from whence he cometh of his honesty and that he is a good learner and a mooter and that he hath continued in the same Inn of Chancery one year and a half at the least"; the admittee was to pay 40s.[4] Soon afterwards the liability for the fee was limited to "such persons as come from such Houses of Chancery as this House doth not read unto"; the men from Clement's, Clifford's and Lyon's Inns were to be "received at a general admission gratis".[5]

We might cautiously propound the year 1530 as the date by which the alliances between Houses of Court and Houses of Chancery had been finally settled.[6] Whatever the year or decade, however, we might be surprised—were it not that "time immemorial" has an artificial significance

---

[1] *I.T.R.*, i, 8.   [2] *Ibid.*, i, 81.

[3] Much later, in 1571, when the clerk begins once more to register the admittee's House of Chancery regularly, thirty six out of a total of forty new entrants join the Inner Temple from Clement's, Clifford's and Lyon's Inns; no one enters from any other Inn of Chancery. During that year, however, ten men from those three Inns of Chancery entered the Middle Temple; was there perhaps no room for them at the Inner?

[4] *I.T.R.*, i, 194. Three such certificates from Clement's Inn and four from Clifford's Inn (1623–4) survive among the Croome Court papers in the Birmingham Reference Library. It was necessary to punish false certification: see *I.T.R.*, i, 337. See also p. xxix n. below.

[5] *Ibid.*, i, 196–7 (1557/8): see also i, 234 (1564/5) and ii, 68, 70 (1612). Cf. *Black Book of Lincoln's Inn*, i, 363 (1568).

[6] Williams, *Early Holborn*, 43, takes 1528 as the date before which no Inn of Chancery had become an appanage of an Inn of Court.

for lawyers—to find that in 1561 (less than a century after Fortescue had written his book) the Inner Temple was claiming to have "had, used and enjoyed the readings" of Clement's Inn, Clifford's Inn and Lyon's Inn "by all the time whereof no memory of man is to the contrary". The occasion was the attempt of the Middle Temple, which had been left with only one Inn of Chancery,[1] to level matters by appropriating one of the three belonging to the Inner. The Inner Temple protested that its three Houses of Chancery had "ever been accepted and taken as members united and annexed to the body of this our House". "By all the same time" it had ministered and imparted to those three Houses "the learnings and knowledge of the law by readings, moots and other kinds of learning", and had shown "a great zeal and tender care to the preservation, further-ance, good government, increase and continuance of the same Houses of Chancery". "By reason of this their ancient amity and union" it had at all times been ready to nourish them as "loving members . . . united to us by this ancient and long continued friendship". The intercession of Robert Dudley, afterwards Earl of Leicester, still gratefully remembered in the Inner Temple Hall, secured the frustration of the Middle Temple's attempt.[2]

The language of this protest, even if the claim of antiquity be dis-counted, indicates the high value placed by an Inn of Court upon its Chancery readerships. Mere prestige was not the only motive. The reader-ship to a House of Chancery (though not, of course, so important as the readership within the Inn of Court itself) was a recognised rung on the professional ladder. By his office, onerous rather than lucrative,[3] the Reader discharged his Inn's traditional responsibility for promoting legal educa-tion "abroad" (in the Inns of Chancery); he was the liaison officer available to convey instructions from headquarters[4]; he could help recruits and re-cruitment.[5] Thanks to that reiterated "unity and ancient friendship", said the Inner Temple in 1561, "the number of students, as well in this House as in the said Houses of Chancery, doth much increase, whereof

[1] Owing to the demolition of Strand Inn in 1549 to make room for the Protector Somerset's projected palace.

[2] See *I.T.R.*, i, 215–19 and Dugdale, *Origines*, p. 150. By purchasing the freehold of Lyon's Inn (see p. xxii n. above) the Inner Temple made itself landlord, as well as legal superior, of the Inn which the Middle had sought to take over.

[3] The Reader had to pay something at Clifford's Inn: see *I.T.R.*, v, 232. For his fee earlier at Furnival's Inn see Bland, *Early Records of Furnival's Inn*, pp. 23, 28, &c., also below, p. xxxii. For the readership as a stage in the *cursus honorum* see p. xxxi.

[4] In 1557 the Houses of Chancery were to be thus informed of the orders about apparel, weapons and study gowns: see *I.T.R.*, i, 193. See also above, p. xx n. and *Black Books of Lincoln's Inn*, i, 360 (report on candidates for call).

[5] See pp. 251 (Cropley), 253 (Lane) and 255 (Goodwyn) below for signs of Readers' influence. Is the puzzle of Legrange in 1744 (p. xxix n. below) soluble as a survival of their ancient authority to select men for " call "?

there is great hope and likelihood that as many learned men shall proceed as have in any one age before this time".[1]

In early days, when the legal Inns were all young together, they must have felt themselves united as members of one vocational brotherhood. In the reign of Henry VI a Furnival's Inn man was amerced for not having attended the burial of one of the fellows of Gray's Inn.[2] Later, after alliances had become crystallised, the loyalties of ancient amity and union displayed themselves at such traditional ceremonies as the call of a Serjeant. The Inns of Court and their Inns of Chancery paraded in procession. The rites needed to be written down to preserve the relative rights of procedence. Our Clement's Inn Pension Book records the routine at a call of Serjeants in 1736[3] just at the moment when the Inner Temple was seeking to assert (against the Middle) the privilege of walking last of all the Inns of Court, "the place of greatest honour and respect in all such public processions".[4] One Friday night the gentlemen of the Bar, the students and the Inns of Chancery are ordered to meet in the Inner Temple Hall in their gowns at 8 a.m. next day, to attend the call of Serjeants from the Middle Temple Hall to Westminster.[5] They meet and are "treated with Wine and Bisketts".[6] Clement's Inn and Lyon's Inn walk together[7]; Clifford's Inn follows behind. Clement's Inn takes the right hand; "the next time Lyon's Inn must have it". And so to Westminster. Gray's Inn and its two Inns of Chancery have no part in the procession because there is no new Serjeant from Gray's Inn.[8]

The ancient amities lived on longest in this context of social observance. "Our only connection with Gray's Inn", said the Principal of Staple Inn in 1854, "is that, when a Serjeant is called from Gray's Inn, they ask us to breakfast."[9] The Barnard's Inn records show its Principal laying before the Ancients in 1816 an invitation from Gray's Inn to come "in your gowns, attended by your Porter in his robes, according to the ancient custom of

---

[1] *I.T.R.*, i, 215.

[2] See Bland, *Early Records of Furnival's Inn*, p. 29.

[3] P. 186 below. Cf. the Inner Temple butler's memorandum of the similar formalities in 1724, *I.T.R.*, iv, 114–16.

[4] *Ibid.*, iv, 319–20, 326–30. The Inns of Chancery had to go first: see the note on the procession of Mr. Justice Coventry to Westminster in 1605/6, *ibid.*, ii, 14. For a dispute between "two of the junior Inns of Chancery" (perhaps also arising at the call of Serjeants in 1724), cannily settled by directing the rivals to "walk intermixed," see *ibid.*, iv, 328, and footnote 7 below.

[5] *I.T.R.*, iv, 319.

[6] In 1724 they had been served with "brisket" (? bisket), "sack, burnt wine and cool tankards": *ibid.*, iv, 114.

[7] Were these the two Inns directed to "walk intermixed" (see footnote 4 above)? The juniors had to walk first, then the next in seniority: see *I.T.R.*, iv, 115.

[8] See p. 187 below.

[9] Royal Commission of 1854, Q. 938.

your Society, to meet the Benchers and Members of Gray's Inn to receive John Hullock esquire, a barrister of Gray's Inn, who will be present to take leave of the Society, being about to receive the Degree of Serjeant at Law". An invitation in the same terms is reported when in 1842 and 1845 Alfred Septimus Dowling and Robert Allen are respectively being called to be Serjeants. After each occasion a common-form entry embodies the Principal's report that he duly attended, along with the Ancients then in town and the clerk, "all of whom were received with great respect by the Treasurer and the Society of Gray's Inn and breakfasted at a table placed in the centre of Gray's Inn Hall and appropriated for that purpose". In 1882, when there are no more Serjeants, the Principal tells his fellow-members that, on the invitation of the Treasurer, he dined with the Benchers of Gray's Inn "and was very cordially welcomed and most hospitably entertained". Gray's Inn, we see, honoured the ancient amity to the last.[1]

IV. EXERCISES OF LEARNING

A FEW undated but obviously early items in the Constitutions and Orders of Clements' Inn give us a glimpse of the traditional system of legal education—in Maitland's familiar phrase "an academic scheme of the medieval sort, oral and disputatious".[2] There are lectures and moots in the two vacations; law cases are put to the various tables in the Hall every working day; a writ is read every working day during term or vacation; the Principal calls men to the bar to moot; there are fines for allowing the moot to cease or be "quashed", and for failing to moot or report "perfectly without book".[3] Whether the daily reading of a writ involved memorising a formula or discussing the remedy we are not told; absence therefrom was seemingly a venial fault, carrying a fine of only a penny at Clement's Inn and only a farthing at Clifford's Inn. Of the mooting in Inns of Chancery in the Tudor period the Denton–Bacon–Cary report gives a brief account—the Reader comes from the Inn of Court, bringing with him two learners of that Inn, "and there meet them for the most part two of every House of Court, who, sitting as Benchers doe in Court at their Motes, hear and argue such Motes as are brought and pleaded by

---

[1] For another "ancient amity" still happily enduring between Gray's Inn and the Inner Temple see F. D. MacKinnon, *Inner Temple Papers* (1948), p. 68.

[2] *English Law and the Renaissance* (1901), p. 26.

[3] See pp. 219–20 below.

the gentlemen of the same Houses of Chancery".[1] If the mooting was like that performed in Houses of Court, "the Readers and Benchers sit down on the bench at the end of the Hall whereof they take their name, and, on a forme towards the midst of the Hall sitteth down two Inner Barresters, and of the other side of them on the same forme two Utter Barresters, and the Inner Barresters doe in French openly declare unto the Benchers (even as the Serjeants doe at the barr in the King's Courts to the Judges) some kinde of Action, the one being as it were retained with the plaintiff in the Action and the other with the Defendant, after which things done the Utter Barresters argue such questions as be disputable within the Case (as there must always be one at the least) and, this ended, the Benchers doe likewise declare their opinion how they think the law to be".[2] The procedure must have simulated that of an actual hearing in a court of law. Exactly how a moot came to be "quashed"—whether through nonattendance, inappropriate choice of subject, irrelevant argument, inadequate preparation or otherwise—remains obscure.[3] The exercise of "case-putting" was probably conducted at Clement's Inn as in other Houses. After dinner, before the company rose, someone would propound a case to which the Reader had possibly referred earlier in the day; "which Case is debated by them all in like forme as the Cases are used to be argued at his reading, and like order is observed at every messe at the other Tables and the same manner always observed at supper when they have no Motes".[4] We know that Lord Keeper Guilford valued case-putting for its stimulus to readiness in argument and reasoning; "he used to say", wrote Roger North, "that no man could be a good lawyer that was not a put-case". The account of an "imparlance", as performed at the Inner Temple as late as 1735,[5] seems to justify the assumption that all these observances retained much obsolete or obsolescent ritual.

When the medieval exercises of learning began to decline in the post-Tudor era, the Readers of the Houses of Chancery had repeatedly to be admonished. They were enjoined to read in person and not (unless with leave of the Benchers) by deputy.[6] They were to continue their full time of

---

[1] Waterhous, *Fortescutus Illustratus*, p. 545. For the neglect of Inner Temple students to attend the Reader in 1701 see *I.T.R.*, iii, 361.

[2] Waterhous, *ubi sup.*, p. 545.

[3] At Furnival's Inn, *temp.* Henry VI, there was no moot *pro defectu benchsitters*: one moot fails, *temp.* Edward IV, because it falls on a saint's day, another *in defectu Lectoris*: several members are fined, *temp.* Henry VIII, for absence from moots or "for failinge a Moot within the Barre—Bland, *Early Records of Furnival's Inn*, pp. 29, 42. See also *Black Books of Lincoln's Inn*, i, 126–7 (1502).

[4] Waterhous, *Fortescutus Illustratus*, p. 545. See also Dugdale, *Origines*, pp. 194–5, for the method at the Middle Temple.

[5] *I.T.R.*, iv, 310.

[6] *Ibid.*, iii, 84 (1614). See i, 143, 226 for the earlier rule.

reading, at least a fortnight a time, even if the Reader in the House of Court gave over earlier.[1] They were to continue their readings for two years "according to ancient custom", and not ask to be discharged any sooner.[2] The "great neglect of Readers in Chancery in keeping their "petitt moots" in term-time had to be censured[3]; they were to keep them "as anciently they were to be kept".[4] Better care was to be taken in the Inner Temple in 1635/6 for the performance of grand moots abroad at the Houses of Chancery.[5] Both at the Inner Temple and at Lincoln's Inn small committees had been set up to find out what was wrong.[6] Perhaps the fault lay at the receiving end; in 1630 the Reader went twice (with students) to Furnival's Inn without finding an audience.[7] Readings, it appears, had been falling out of favour. Coke at one moment praised the exercises of learning as "most excellent and behooveful" for attaining knowledge of the law. At another he disparaged readings, likening them to riddles and the Readers to lapwings "who seem to be nearest their nests when they are furthest from them".[8] A conservative profession would be easily convinced that the training was not what it used to be. In 1546 it had been necessary to limit moot cases to "two points argumentable".[9] In 1594/5 Readers had to be told to make their cases short "and as much uppon the statut readd over as may be".[10] In the seventeenth century students might find in printed books a substitute for oral methods, and prospective Readers were perhaps more ready to yield to the demands of private practice.[11] The substantial fine for omitting to read was evidence of the reluctance which had to be overcome. The savage treatment of John Selden for the "wilfulness and contempt" of his refusal to read at Lyon's Inn in 1624 jeopardised his whole career.[12] Yet the ancient discipline was dying hard. The students who, just at this time, were passing from Clement's and Clifford's Inns into the Inner Temple were still being certified as having duly performed their exercises of learning.[13] And presently, after the legal

---

[1] *I.T.R.*, ii, 94 (1615/6).   [2] *Ibid.*, ii, 100 (1616).

[3] *Pension Book of Gray's Inn*, i, 193–4 (1611).   [4] *Ibid.*, ii, 332 (1638).

[5] *I.T.R.*, ii, 229.   [6] *Ibid.*, ii, 191; *Black Books of Lincoln's Inn*, ii, 87.

[7] *Black Books of Lincoln's Inn*, ii, 293.   [8] Co. Litt. 280.

[9] *I.T.R.*, i, 192.   [10] *Black Books of Lincoln's Inn*, ii, 33.

[11] See *Pension Book of Gray's Inn*, i, 20 (1575); *Black Books of Lincoln's Inn*, ii, 87 (1605), for early instances.

[12] Mitigated next year, it was remitted in 1632; he became a Bencher in 1638: see *I.T.R.*, ii, 145–6, 157, 203, 208.

[13] Certificates (see p. xxiv n. above) from Clement's Inn in 1624 declared that the student "hath performed all exercises and Motes of learning", those from Clifford's Inn that he "hath mooted without the Bar". Among many 17th and 18th-century certificates in the Inner Temple from other Inns one (of 1744) from Lyon's Inn states that Andrew Legrange has been at Lyon's Inn for 23 years and "hath bin called an Utter Barrister, having duly performed his Exercise of Mooting on the 23rd Day of November, 1734, Edward Mills Esquire being then Reader."

curriculum had been disrupted by the Civil War, the Inns of Court still held men who clung to the traditional methods which, when the monarchy was restored, vigorous efforts were made to revive.[1] Francis North, entering the Middle Temple in 1655 and called to the bar in 1661, was scrupulous in those time-honoured "preparatives" which led him to the Lord Keepership. "He was not called to the bar *ex gratia* or for favour, as when the person is not of standing or hath not performed his exercises, but, being early admitted, his time was fully run out and he performed all his moots both in the Inns of Chancery . . . and also in the Hall, and not perfunctorily as of latter times the use is by way of *opus operatum* as for tale and not for weight, but in well studied arguments." He was "an attendant (as well as exerciser) at the ordinary moots in the Middle Temple and at New Inn". In those days, says Roger North, the moots were carefully performed; "they are not so now".[2] The "tale" of exercises required for call to the Inner Temple in 1614 had included "twelve term moots in the Inns of Chancery belonging to the House" within three years next before call[3]; the would-be barrister, besides having been eight years at his Inn of Court and most of that time in commons "and a painful and sufficient student", must have "usually frequented and argued grand and petty moots in the Inns of Chancery".[4] These minimum conditions could not be maintained, although even as late as 1738 the Inner Temple purported to insist on "six petty moots done at the Inns of Chancery".[5]

Of all this range of exercises of learning our 18th-century Pension Book of Clement's Inn has little to tell us. The Inner Temple, as its records show, had regularly been forwarding lists of three names from which the Principal and Ancients could choose their Reader[6]; it had been discharging the chosen Readers when their task was performed[7] or amercing them for non-performance.[8] In 1728/9, after fining William Jefferies the usual £20 for not reading at Lyon's Inn, it ordered the Principals of its three Inns of

---

[1] See *I.T.R.*, iii, 22, 30–3 (1663/4). In 1671 requirements were reduced because it had been impossible to perform exercises in the Inns of Chancery: see *Pension Book of Gray's Inn*, ii, 16. There was complaint at the Inner Temple that, after call, members immediately left and seldom appeared in the House to do their exercises: see *I.T.R.*, iii, 146–7, 152.

[2] Roger North, *Lives of the Norths* (ed. Jessopp, 1890), i, 21, 29, 39.

[3] *I.T.R.*, ii, 78.

[4] *Ibid.*, ii, 101 (1616/17); and see *ibid.*, 161, 178.

[5] *Ibid.*, iv, 382.

[6] See p. xxiii above. For the rules at Furnival's Inn see *Black Books of Lincoln's Inn*, ii, 99 (1675).

[7] And when they had paid their duties: see *I.T.R.*, iv, 2 (1714). How much were these duties? The more important Reader of the Inn of Court paid £50: see *ibid.*, 12, 23, 26, &c.

[8] Among Readers of Clement's Inn in the seventeen-twenties, Ambrose Holbech (perhaps also Wm. Bellamy) was fined £20: see *ibid.*, iv, 87, 139.

Chancery to certify annually in writing how often the Readers it sent to them had done their duty.[1] This order explains the entry in our Pension Book by Principal Penny, one day in 1730, that James Jenyns esquire has come from the Inner Temple, bringing with him two students of that Inn, and has read upon the statute cap. 12 of 8 Henry VI. This is the book's first mention of an exercise of learning.

P. 155

Of the series of seventeen Readers thus recorded as attending at Clement's Inn between 1730 and 1749 six were substitutes for the barrister originally chosen.[2] In nearly half the instances we are told merely that they "brought a case to read upon"; in the rest the topic is stated; sometimes it is an old enactment like *De Donis*, the Reader perhaps using the commentary of a predecessor[3]; once it is a quite recent statute.

P. 194

P. 197

The readings of Jenyns and his successors at Clement's Inn are performed, we note, at a single visit on one day of the year. Such is the languor that has descended upon legal societies in the 18th century as elsewhere upon the Church and the universities. There is evidence *aliunde* of the limited observance of exercises of learning in Inns of Chancery at about this period. Publishing his *New View of London* in 1708, Edward Hatton reports that there are mootings at Clement's Inn sometimes twice a term, at New Inn once or twice a term, at Lyon's Inn once in four terms, at Thavyes Inn once in about two years, at Barnard's Inn and Staple Inn none, at Furnival's Inn "no mooting by Utter Barristers of Lincoln's Inn of late". In 1800 Clement's Inn is given the credit of keeping up the custom of mooting longer than these other societies.[4] In 1846 a Select Committee of the House of Commons was informed that the Inns of Court sent a lecturer to the Inns of Chancery not for purposes of instruction "but to enable the Reader himself to be qualified in his progress to the Bench".[5]

Later, in 1854, when a Royal Commission was investigating *inter alia* the activities and resources of the Houses of Chancery, the testimony was mainly negative. The Treasurer of the Inner Temple was asked if Readers were still sent to those Houses; "Yes", he replied; "they were rebellious for some years, but the rule of our Society is that we choose the three

---

[1] *I.T.R.*, iv, 193, 204. There was probably an earlier order: see *ibid.*, iv, 143. See also the inquiry whether Thomas Jenner had read, *ibid.*, 503–4 (1746) and see v, 108, and 232, where the "ancient and usual custom" is re-asserted.

[2] When Thomas Edlyne Tomlins was proxy for Thomas Mott in 1787, the Principal and Ancients were not present; this raised doubt whether the reading would count: see *I.T.R.*, v, 493, 501.

[3] Apparently a well precedented practice: see Professor S. E. Thorne, *Readings and Moots at the Inns of Court* (1952), i, p. lxvii.

[4] Ireland, *Picturesque Views of the Inns of Court* (1800), p. 105.

[5] A Select Committee to inquire into the present state of legal education in England and Ireland. The witness was Robert Maugham, secretary and solicitor to the Incorporated Law Society.

senior barristers in rotation and send them to the Inn and they take one
. . . This year we sent the name of a gentleman to Clement's Inn whom
afterwards we could not find, and therefore he could not read." The
steward of Clement's Inn confirmed this statement, adding "we make no
payment to the Reader; on the contrary he pays something, I think, to
our porters. The Reader explains some new Act of Parliament very often
or any alteration in the law that has taken place; only the Principal,
Ancients and commoners come, no students, no strangers; there was a
reading last year, and this year they were to read; the few members that
there are are always there, but they are only six."[1] A New Inn witness
said that readings there had ceased in 1846—he thought it was because the
Middle Temple sent no more Readers.[2] Staple Inn had none for the last
sixty years, Barnard's Inn none for the last two hundred.[3] Lyon's Inn said
"we have no students and therefore we require no lecture"; no Reader had
visited them since 1832; only two members of its society were now left,
both of them Ancients; one of these thought he could remember seeing a
Reader once in 1815, when a schoolboy home for the holidays; his father
had told him that the last Reader who came "had burlesqued the thing so
greatly that they were disgusted and never asked for another".[4]

V. DUES AND ARREARS

ON admission at Clement's Inn, as at other legal Houses, the entrant
signed a bond, with one or more sureties or "pledges",[5] to be of good
behaviour and to pay his dues. His engagement to be "in commons"
(which meant taking his share in the obligations as well as the advantages
of the life of the community and coming under the discipline of the House)
and to pay all dues punctually is emphasised in several of the Standing
Orders printed on a later page.[6] If to be "cast into commons" created a
liability, to be "put out of commons" could be a heavy penalty.[7] Not long
before our Pension Book begins, all attorneys and solicitors had received

---

[1] Royal Commission of 1854, Report and Evidence, Qq. 248 (Inner Temple), 831–41
(Clement's Inn).

[2] *Ibid.*, Qq. 740–5.   [3] *Ibid.*, Qq. 949–52, 989–91.

[4] *Ibid.*, Qq. 248, 666, 675, 685, 688, 694. For a Lyon's Inn mooting in 1734 see
p. xxix n. above.

[5] See p. liv below.

[6] See below, Orders 9, 23, 25, 29, 51, 60, 81 at p. 219 onwards, and the 1682 Order at
p. 240.

[7] See Orders 12 and 13, p. 220 below.

fresh orders to belong to some legal Inn and "duly keep commons there".[1] The rule at Clement's Inn that a new member was not cast into commons for his first year was modified in 1729.[2] Nobody was cast into commons while the rebuilding of the Hall interrupted the normal provision of meals.[3] The Principal and Ancients, at any rate from 1767, had their commons free.[4]

The member's dues, as we shall presently see, were twofold. His "pension" (his regular payment towards the overhead expenses of the House) was charged at 2s. per term, his "absent commons" (a minimum subscription required of each member) at 5s. per term.[5] Described as "the only support of the Society",[6] these two levies look much alike; but there was this difference—the liability for "pension" was never remitted, but the charge for "absent commons" could be "abated" (it was usually halved) for any term in which the member had not been in town. If he thus applied for abatement, he had (from 1717) to pay an additional 6d. per term for the "servants' rolls".[7] The Pension Book shows members repeatedly asking for abatement; their request seems always to have succeeded; their statement of the number of terms during which they had been absent was apparently never challenged.

The frequency of the applications attests both the amount of absenteeism and the laxity of collection. Term-time occupying but a few weeks in the year,[8] members could be practising their profession or holding legal appointments in the provinces. Some, when applying for abatement, say they have not been in town for over twenty—in one case for as many as thirty—of the terms for which they are charged. Others say they come to town only one term in the year. Despite the orders inculcating prompt payment, the arrears accumulate. The book-keeping is unsystematic. When money is wanted in 1715 for the reconstruction of the Hall, the admittance bonds are scrutinised and "abstracted", county by county, so that any Ancient who has contacts with a particular locality can report on the circumstances of debtors there. It turns out that one defaulter had died insolvent some twenty-five years earlier; another had been for some years a member of Lincoln's Inn. A third, sued for rent for a period ending in

P. 143
(Hardwick)

P. 15

P. 22
(Gartrell and
Dixon)

---

[1] See p. lvii below.

[2] See below, pp. 35 (Benett) and 143.

[3] See below, pp. 15, 23, 27. On grounds of economy in 1728 commons were cut down for the "issuable terms"; see p. 138 below.

[4] See below, p. 146, and, for "absent commons", pp. 205, 245.

[5] See note to p. 2 below. See also *Black Books of Lincoln's Inn*, iii, p. xxxi. For repastors (members privileged to come in for a meal) see p. 242 below.

[6] See p. 229 below (Order 60). Cf. *Black Books of Lincoln's Inn*, i, 292 ("of whome only ryse ower profett"), and see *ibid.*, ii, p. xxxi.

[7] See p. 43 below. They were sometimes called the "porters' rolls": see pp. 194, 216.

[8] See p. xvii above.

P. 19
(Slack)
P. 24
(Pennell)

P. 44
(Millward)

1696, had died "leaving little or no assetts"; a fourth, "some time since deceased", had entered into his bond in 1661 before the penalty was raised from £10 to £20, and there had been "a long neglect" in claiming against his executors. Yet another "hath for many years been gone into parts beyond the seas and hath not been heard of whether living or dead for above fifteen years past". One man had long ago joined the Customs service; he had not apprehended that, on leaving the law, he would be liable for dues, and anyhow he had not been asked to pay. In one instance

P. 20
(Jefferys)

it was "a very stale debt, he not having been resident in the Inn or had any

P. 80
(Stretehay)

demand made of him for the money for 30 or 40 years". The desire to compound for arrears often arose from a wish to resign membership; the member, or perhaps his surety, would be seeking the cancellation of the admittance bond. A common statement is that the member has ceased to practise and now lives altogether in the country or is now a householder in London or Westminster.[1] Or perhaps he has gone, or is going, abroad.[2]

P. 181
(Wood)

In one case an attorney gives up practice in order to be clerk to a counsel. There are pleas *in misericordiam*; the member is "ancient and infirm" or has "met with misfortunes" or is "troubled with the gout" or "in very mean

P. 40
(Stanton)

circumstances". One man pleads poverty and "the miserable condition of his wife (being big with child)"; another's widow and executrix is "left

Pp. 207–8
(Bridges)

in low circumstances with a large family of children and not well able to pay the whole". Although mercy is allowed at times to season justice, the Society looks strictly to the bond. The member will be sued or "prosecuted"; sometimes "vigorous" prosecution or prosecution "with effect" is specifically ordered; the costs of suit, with the bailiffs' and sheriffs' charges, will be added to the bill. One debtor is already in the Fleet;

P. 90
(Bulstrode)
P. 41
(Richmond)

Pp. 236–7,
240

another is in custody. If someone omits to discharge "the King's taxes", the Inn may have to pay and will recover the money from him.[3] If the Inn's claim is for rent, it may direct that the defaulter's chamber be "padlockt up"; striking off the padlock is a grave matter.

[1] See p. lvii below for the significance of such statements. A celibate community was willing to make some concession to those who had their wives in town: see pp. 222, 225 below (Orders 23, 24, 42).

[2] See below, pp. 72 (Benson), 174 (Doyley), 182 (Winder).

[3] See below, pp. 2 (Lowth), 10 (Clerk), 19 (Sherratt); see also pp. 33 (Tilden), 43 (Jolland).

VI. FINANCE

FINANCIALLY Clement's Inn lived from hand to mouth. It was a familiar story that the House "runneth contynyally in arrerage and dett and of late Tyme hath had no stock to defraye the reparations and other necessaries P. 225 which daylie increase more and more". Our Pension Book occasionally refers to "the stock" or "the stock and other rents and profits" of the Society,[1] but the Inn possessed no standing funds or endowments; there is no mention of a banking account.[2] When money was wanted, loyal members took the risk (if risk it was) of advancing it, or it was borrowed from outside sources. The Inn's premises could be mortgaged as security. A Pp. 209, 211 lender got interest at 5 or 6 per cent on his investment; payment of interest apparently required an *ad hoc* resolution of Pension. His executors would want the capital repaid some day; if so, Pension would order the Principal to repay it out of moneys coming in.[3] Sometimes another member made the repayment; sometimes the loan had been assigned; in one case it reached the hands of a goldsmith-banker, a partner in Child's Bank.[4]

The expense of erecting or reconstructing chambers was a constant drain upon the Society's resources. Much was achieved by building leases,[5] which cost the House nothing and promised an ultimate profit, though exceptionally the Ancients thought it better to undertake their own build- Pp. 65–6 ing. The reconstruction of staircase 18 was financed by reviving temporarily P. 144 the practice of granting assignments[6] "instead of running into further debt or borrowing money at interest". For the removal of buildings at the fore-gate and the provision of a new gate and porter's lodge, as also for a Pp. 94–8, 209 new staircase, 14 subscribers came forward. The repair of the kitchen and the "house of office" was paid for by a general levy on members. Pp. 232–4

The Principal—or in minor matters the Steward—received sums "for the use of the Society" and made payments on its behalf. Once a year, occasionally at longer intervals, there was the prescribed audit of the

---

[1] See pp. 66, 95, 210, 246 below.

[2] Within our period Lincoln's Inn (1743) and Gray's Inn (1744) had recourse to the House of Child: *Black Books of Lincoln's Inn*, iii, 330; *Pension Book of Gray's Inn*, ii, 246–7, 264, 346. Later, in 1782, Gray's Inn opened an account with Messrs. Hoare of Fleet Street (*ibid.*, p. 338). In 1822 Barnard's Inn had an account with Messrs. Brooks and Dixon of Chancery Lane.

[3] See below, pp. 54 (Carter), 84 (Wrightson), 117 (Evans), 118 (Gregg), 124 (Fuller). In Fuller's case the Principal paid the importunate widow in advance of sanction.

[4] Henry Rogers (see p. 110 below). Apprenticed in 1693 to Sir Francis Child, the first banker to give up the goldsmith's business, Rogers was a partner in Child's bank by 1707; he died in 1735; it is unlikely that he practised as a goldsmith; there is no record of his mark having been registered.

[5] See p. xlv below.

[6] See p. xlii below.

Principal's accounts by two Ancients and two Companions. The auditors struck a balance between the gross receipts and gross disbursements and certified the result[1]; his accounts were then approved as just and true and he was formally "discharged". If the report disclosed a deficit, he had to recoup himself out of future income from rent, dues, fines or other profits. Among the Principals of our period Joshua Blackwell was so unlucky as to encounter a deficit at all seven of his audits[2]; Dovey was on the right side almost every time; Penny was over £500 to the bad at his first audit and over £500 to the good at his second. Some reports by the auditors expressly state that the previous year's balance has been carried forward. In one case the Pension had found itself obliged to order an outgoing Principal to hand over his surplus to his successor.

Pp. 136, 142

P. 257 (No. 80)

This system of accounting, unless punctiliously operated, invited suspicion and dispute. At Clifford's Inn in 1615 some 65 members petitioned the Inner Temple because, they said, their Principal had been in office for over forty years, yet had produced accounts in two years only[3]. The Inns of Court found that the election of a new Treasurer every twelve months did "much conduce to the ascertaining the revenue and other benefits of the Society".[4] At Gray's Inn in 1672 two recent Treasurers were challenged to explain what they had done with money lately in their hands.[5] In 1695 petitioners from Clement's Inn cited as precedent an order obtained from the Inner Temple seven years earlier to compel Edward Gerrard, lately Principal, to render a fuller account, "there being a surcharge of the summe of £480 10s. on his former account". And now, they alleged, Michael Wrightson, late a Principal, was similarly at fault "notwithstanding he received great summes of money for the use of the House during his time and particularly of Mr Holbech his predecessor in the year 1682 the sum of £375 6s. 4d. which remained in his hands at the end of his Terme of three years, he [presumably Holbech] being the only person that has

---

[1] The detailed materials available to the auditors are illustrated by a fragmentary bundle of receipts among the Taylor papers (item 11, p. xi above), mostly of 1757 (when Chapone was steward) and 1759. They include payments for bricks, paintwork and coals, the cook's bills for beef, potatoes, horse radish and celery, the butler's account for Grand Day expenses (wine, candles, washing of table-cloths, scouring plates, etc.), five guineas to Blackwell, the rector of St. Clement Danes, one guinea to the lecturer and something for the parish clerk. The original accounts of the Principal's receipts and payments from 1757 to 1785 and from 1809 to 1823 emerged momentarily in 1932 in a bookseller's catalogue, but have not been traced.

[2] Apparently he let the adverse balance accumulate against him. Eventually he released the interest due thereon; see p. 115 below. A Principal might have certain perquisites: see Hay-Edwards, *History of Clifford's Inn* (1912), pp. 80–1.

[3] *I.T.R.*, ii, 88–90.

[4] *Ibid.*, iii, 274 (1691). For the Middle Temple arrangements and the easing of its Treasurer's task of debt-collecting see *Calendar of M.T. Records* (1903), xiv, xix.

[5] See *Pension Book of Gray's Inn*, ii, 21–2; see also *ibid.*, 326.

passed any publique Account these many yeares". The Inner Temple Benchers ordered Gerrard's auditors to report at the Table after dinner, Gerrard and the then serving Principal to attend. The petitioners recalled that in Merrifield's principalship, when the Bench ordered him to produce his accounts, arrears of £170 were shown, which sum Gerrard had received. In Merrifield's time, they said, there were ninescore men in the House; there were probably as many in Gerrard's time; suppose, however, that there were no more than 150. Their pension payments and essoigns at £52 10s. each, would bring in £367 10s. for Gerrard's seven years. Adding further estimates of commons payments, specific fines for chambers, ground rents and other rents and receipts, the petitioners arrived at a grand total of nearly £1700 as the sum for which Gerrard had to account.[1] The Inner Temple referred the dispute to a committee of three benchers, Johnson, Bowyer and the hard-worked William Petyt. The parties were summoned to attend with William Callow and to bring their books, rolls and abstracts.[2] There is no record of the sequel. Gerrard apparently admitted the figures of his receipts and disbursements. Perhaps the petitioners had not known the whole story; in 1684 Wrightson and Gerrard had paid up £400 apiece towards a settlement of the Kellett business.[3]

VII. THE ESTABLISHMENT

THE foregoing pages have shown us the three-tiered composition of Clement's Inn—Principal, Ancients and Companions. The Principal serves his term and may be re-elected. He and the other Ancients constitute the Grand Company which forms the Pension. The Companions choose P. 231 the Principal from a panel of three names propounded by the Grand Company; one of the three will probably be that of the out-going Principal. The choice, when made, will be formally approved by the Ancients in commons.[4] The Principal, whenever he deems it necessary, announces that fresh Ancients are wanted because there are "scarce enough to make a Pension to transact the affairs of the House". He specifies the number and the persons he thinks proper. The Pension agreeing, the nominees are

---

[1] A copy of the petition is in the file of Taylor papers forming item 11 in the list at p. xi above.

[2] *I.T.R.*, iii, 278–80, 282–4. A copy of the accounts produced by Callow is in the file mentioned in the previous note.

[3] See pp. xlix, 238–9 below.

[4] See below, pp. 137, 179, 190. Later their approval, if given, is not recorded.

B

called up to the Ancients' table with strict regard to their seniority,[1] and, publicly in Hall, they take the oaths of allegiance, supremacy and abjuration. An early Elizabethan statute had required allegiance to be sworn by, amongst others, the "Benchers, Readers, Auncientes in any House or Houses of Courte and all Pryncypall[s], Treasurers and such as bee of the Grande Company in every Inne of Chauncerye".[2] The oaths subscribed by eighteen members of Clement's Inn between 1799 and 1866 survive among the Taylor papers.[3] Their language, if a digression be permitted, recalls bygone strains and stresses in the country's history. Thus we find William Broughton Flexney (admitted to the Inn in 1803[4]) promising allegiance to King George and afterwards to King William the Fourth, and, in another oath, declaring:

> I do from my heart abhor, detest and abjure as impious and heretical that damnable Doctrine and Position that Princes excommunicated or deprived by the Pope or any Authority of the See of Rome may be deposed or murdered by their Subjects or any other whatsoever, and I do declare that no foreign Prince, Person, Prelate, State or Potentate hath or ought to have any Jurisdiction, Power, Superiority, Pre-eminence or Authority Ecclesiastical or Spiritual within this Realm.

Flexney takes yet another and even longer oath, stating that—

> I do believe in my conscience that not any of the Descendants of the Person who pretended to be and took upon himself the Style and Title of King of England by the name of James the Third or of Scotland by the name of James the Eighth or the Style and Title of King of Great Britain hath any Right or Title whatsoever to the Crown of the Realm or any other the Dominions thereunto belonging.

He renounces and refuses allegiance or obedience to any such, swears to defend His Majesty against all traitorous conspiracies, promises to disclose all treasons and undertakes to maintain the succession as limited by the Act of 1700 to the Princess Sophia Electress and Duchess Dowager of Hanover and the heirs of her body, being Protestants.[5] James Glenie Price, too, admitted to Clement's Inn as late as 1866,[6] still has to swear that none of the descendants of the Pretender has any right to the throne; he, too, promises disclosure of all treasons and traitorous conspiracies. These cumbrous precautions, swept away in 1868,[7] are in line with much older suspicions that "ill subjects" and "dangerous persons" found sanctuary in the Inns of Court and Chancery, "being privileged and exempted places" needing periodical search.[8]

---

[1] See below, pp. 192, 201–2, 214.
[2] 5 Eliz. c. 1. s. 4.
[3] Item 10 in the list at p. xi above.
[4] See below, p. 303.

[5] 12 & 13 Will. III. c. 2.
[6] See below, p. 309.
[7] See 31 & 32 Vict. c. 72.
[8] See the 1614 orders, *I.T.R.*, ii, 83.

But we must return to the establishment of Clement's Inn. The primary need of the *hospicium* (next to the finding of accommodation) would have been the appointment of someone "to provide the victual of the House"[1] and to collect the cost. This would have been the task of the Steward. The early orders of Clement's Inn show that he was at first selected merely by rotation, that youth was no disadvantage and that his duties lasted no longer than a week.[2] No qualifications were required except that he must have been a member of the House for at least a year and must find sureties for his satisfactory accounting. The appointment was compulsory, though some members would probably buy themselves off by paying the fine of 12*d.* for refusing office.[3] It ran the round of the staircases; "the youngest in every chamber shall be first chosen". The steward was in charge of the buttery.[4] He had to "attend the Eating Times and Times of Learning". He kept the commons roll; members were to pay him punctually; he had to "answer to the House for the Profit he shall make of the Provision of the House during his week"; he could be amerced for his "superfluous expence during his week"; he was not to "cheat the House or seek his own profit in his Office of Steward on pain of Expulsion".   P. 219   Pp.219, 224

These arrangements, the haphazard appointment, brief tenure and constant change of office-holder, were too primitive for a more progressive era. At some date unknown the seven-day steward of Clement's Inn became the permanent officer, acting also as clerk, whom we meet in the pages of our 18th-century Pension Book. As clerk he might perhaps relieve the Principal of some of his administrative burdens, just as the Under-Treasurer, first appointed in 1694, could help the Treasurer at the Inner Temple.[5] Our Pension Book shows us a "Steward or Clerk", engaged by the Ancients, holding office during good behaviour, entering into a bond with a penalty of £200 and finding sureties. He gets the "ancient fees and perquisites"[6] and a small salary; his chamber rent may be fixed indulgently. His post, at any rate, was attractive enough for the Ancients still to

---

[1] Denton–Baron–Cary report: see Waterhous, *Fortescutus Illustratus*, p. 546.

[2] See Orders 5–10, 17, 40, 42, at pp. 219, 221, 224–5 below. At Clifford's Inn the steward at Christmas was to be changed at the end of the week as in other times of the year (Order 13).

[3] At Furnival's Inn, *temp.* Edw. IV, fifty-three members at one time were amerced 12*d.* for refusing the stewardship: Bland, *Early Records of Furnival's Inn*, p. 30. At Clifford's Inn the price of exemption was the same.

[4] At Clifford's Inn the steward, who had to produce the money for bread and service for his week, was expressly given charge of the buttery cloths, cups, saltcellars, &c., and had to hand them over to his successor on the Saturday (Orders 3 and 4).

[5] *I.T.R.*, iii, 175–6; iv, p. xxxiii.

[6] P. 199 below. At Gray's Inn the steward's perquisites included fees on an admission or an assignment of chambers: see *Pension Book of Gray's Inn*, ii, 335 (1782). See also *Black Books of Lincoln's Inn*, i, p. xxiii.

stipulate that it should not go to an outsider.[1] His duty was still to collect
the dues. He would have to press members who were in arrear; if they must
be sued on their bonds, he would have to take the action, afterwards presenting a bill for the law charges; he might be authorised to distrain upon
debtors' goods. His books would sometimes be examined; the Ancients
would want to know the Inn's financial position and the efficiency of the
debt-collecting. Matters demanding decision at a higher level would be
delegated to some specially experienced member, or to a small committee
of Ancients, for inquiry or settlement. Even if restricted to the transaction
of the Inn's routine business, the "steward or clerk" would need to use
care and intelligence and to display some clerical aptitude. At the Inner
Temple, as late as 1673, even the third, fourth and puisne butlers had to
learn the court hand.[2] Whether or no the "steward or clerk" at Clement's
Inn always wrote up the Pension Book himself, there are (as already noted)
inevitable slips of the pen[3]; nor is it surprising to find such surnames as
Shepherd or Benett spelt inconsistently, even in a single entry.

When our Pension Book begins in 1714, the "steward or clerk" is
Thomas Callow, who had been admitted in 1692 a member of a family
long connected with the Inn.[4] He dies in 1718 and is replaced by Thomas
Tufton. When Tufton gives up, Joseph Barras is appointed. Barras dies
in 1727, leaving a widow whose claim against the House for services
rendered or money paid by him is presently settled. Brightwell Smith,
husband of the executrix of Barras, succeeds him. On Smith's retirement
William Gofton gets the post but is dismissed within a year, "having
spent a considerable Summe of the House's money, as well as money
received for the Land Tax". Gofton and his sureties are sued upon their
bonds and the Principal is desired to find the money for the tax lest the
Society be prosecuted. Maybe it was felt that the pay for the post was not
high enough to keep the occupant out of temptation; when Thomas Perkins was a successful applicant soon afterwards, the rate of remuneration
was specified and perhaps increased.

Below the steward, who was also clerk, came the butler, who was also
porter. The latter's "severall offices or places of butler and porter of the
foregate" were separately rewarded; in 1776 he got £4 a year as butler and
£20 a year as head porter. He had to give a bond of £50 for his good
behaviour. The rent of £6 which he paid for his ground-floor chamber at

Pp. 141, 189

P. 177

P. 199

P. 246

---

[1] See p. 199 below. So also at the Inner Temple the Under-Treasurer had to be chosen
from the existing members (*I.T.R.*, iv, iii). As such he could be expected to have the
interests of the House at heart.

[2] *I.T.R.*, iii, 94.

[3] See above, p. xiii n., and below, pp. 68 n., 107 n., 118 ("Brewer"), 141 ("Mills"),
182 ("Blackenbury").

[4] For Thomas Callow the elder (admitted in 1669), see pp. 58, 287 below.

No. 2, deemed in 1742/3 to be too high, was retrospectively reduced to 20s. The butler's wife made herself useful about the House, and, if left a widow "in bad circumstances" might receive a gratuity. The butler, who Pp. 203-4 was not to be knocked about with impunity, had a dignified part to play Pp. 221, 240 on ceremonial occasions, walking bare-headed before the Principal; it P. 187 may have been he who would attend at St. Clement Danes Church to P. 14 prevent strangers from intruding into the pews reserved for senior members of the Inn. He had to shut the gate every evening; his pay would be cut if Pp. 223, 228 the door was left unlocked after the appointed hour; there were careful rules for the custody of the keys. We read in 1720 of a butler who is also porter of the foregate, in 1736 of a butler and two porters, and in 1776 of a Pp. 79, 187, head porter and an under-porter who earns an additional stipend as 246 gardener. There was, of course, a porter at the back gate next Clare Market. In 1729 his lodge there was declared to be "so close and dark that itt is not fitt for him to lay in it"; he was therefore allowed to have the ground-floor P. 143 room at No. 8 "which the joyner now uses". He could hope to be promoted, if a vacancy occurred, to the foregate portership. He too would appear at ceremonies, with the silver-headed staff and cloth tufted gown for which the Companions had subscribed. P. 56

The Ancients had constantly to guard against outbreaks of fire; they wanted also to keep undesirable characters out of the premises. In 1740, after a murder in the Inn,[1] two night watchmen were engaged at £15 a year, a suitable watch-house being provided. As in the Temple, their P. 197 charge was a code more definite than Dogberry's. The watchmen were to come upon the watch with candle, lanthorn and staff, for the hours of P. 202 darkness; as soon as the Inn gates were shut, and once afterwards every night, they were to go up each staircase and into the boghouse "to see that doors, lamps and everything else be safe". If sleep was interrupted in Clement's Inn by the watchman's duty to cry the hours in each of the three courts from 11 p.m. till daylight, the residents were better off than those in the Temple where he had also to knock on the door of every chamber twice in the night.[2] The watchman was not to go into the lodge; the porter whose turn it was to sit up at the gate was not to leave it. There was a general instruction to "take care to remove all beggers and other disorderly persons".[3] Neglect of duty would involve stoppage of pay and

---

[1] See above, p. xiii, and below, pp. 197, 267n.

[2] *I.T.R.*, iv, 18 (1715/6, after the murder of Langford): see also iv, 5 (knocking at any lighted chamber after midnight). Cf. *Pension Book of Gray's Inn*, ii, 239-40 (crying the hours and the weather).

[3] In the Inner Temple the criers of old clothes were also to be excluded (*I.T.R.*, iv, 158, 163) and the watchmen were to examine all suspicious baskets and bundles brought in after dark, to prevent the "dropping" (see p. xiv above) of children who might be chargeable to the House (*I.T.R.*, v, 225).

P. 203

dismissal. The premises had to be kept clean; the foregate porter was made responsible for the First Court, the back-gate porter for the Garden Court, one night watchman for the Middle Court and the other for the boghouse. Menial as some of these employments might be accounted, the servants who performed them could be conscious of a share in the prestige and dignity of the House. At the Inner Temple the establishment included panniermen, turnspits and washpots; all of these were liable for their turn (at 12*d.* a night) in the night watch[1]; all of them also, when the Inner Temple mustered its membership in public at a call of Serjeants, took their place in the procession.[2] So too, with surely no less pride, did the butler and porters of Clement's Inn.

P. 187

VIII. THE CHAMBERS

P. 30
(Drury)

THE frequent entries about the disposal of chambers follow a formal pattern. A purchase for life meant a 99-year term, if the purchaser should so long live, "with the usual covenants and provisions", one of which would be a stipulation that he remained a member of the Society.[3] Two types of transaction became familiar. X, having a 99-year lease, agrees with Y for the purchase of X's chambers; X surrenders his lease, Y gets a new lease and is admitted to the chambers, the Society receiving a small fine. Y, of course, must be admitted to membership of the Inn[4]: non-admitted tenants run the risk of having their chambers padlocked up[5]; the legal Inns had a right to know who was occupying their premises.[6] Or again X, having a 99-year lease, desires to buy an assignment for one life after the expiration of his own, he pays the Inn a fine of perhaps £30 and obtains his wish, nominating the life within a time-limit.[7] His nominee may be an infant; if so, "some sufficient person" must guarantee performance of the covenants.[8] Assignment for a fresh life would obviously postpone the date

---

[1] *I.T.R.*, iv, 4.

[2] *Ibid.*, iv, 115.

[3] For special covenants, see below, pp. 32, 47, 81–2, 91, 100 (painting, wainscoting, &c.), 92 (ancient lights), 246 (breaking walls, &c.), 247 (letting, &c., to strangers).

[4] See p. 230 below; see also pp. 37, 47 (Trott and others), 94 (Monger), 173 (Obrian and Limbrey), 189, 202 (Roper and Marshall), 204 (Parke, Heekford and Worth).

[5] See pp. 94, 189, 202, 208, 212–13 below.

[6] See Order 75, p. 235 below. Cf. *Pension Book of Gray's Inn*, ii, 79 (1684).

[7] See p. 174 (Peart) below.

[8] See below, pp. 84 (Dobson), 131 (Grove). For a plea of infancy see p. 70 (Owen). At the Inner Temple minors were admitted to chambers, but not allowed to come into commons under 16: *I.T.R.*, v, 503 (1788).

when the chambers would, to the Society's advantage, fall in. In 1717/8 it P. 57
was decided to grant no more assignments after a specified date which a
few Ancients hastened to anticipate. Presently, in 1729, the need of money P. 144
to rebuild No. 18 staircase led to a short-term lifting of the ban, ten such
assignments bringing in about £600. Again in 1730/1 another relaxation was
sanctioned to finance the new building at No. 12. A practice ascribed to P. 160
several Principals of the Society of granting chambers in reversion had
caused "great impoverishing" and had therefore been abolished in 1655; P. 235
thenceforth all grants of chambers were to be made by the Principal and
Ancients within a week of the end of term; but the new arrangement was
afterwards found "too narrow a confinement" of the power to make P. 242
leases and contracts. A few members managed to hold several sets of
chambers.[1] This, being deemed a detriment likely to diminish the numbers of
the Society, led to an order in 1716/7 that separate pension liability should
attach to each set[2]; the order, however, was disregarded and found
inconvenient; it was therefore revoked in 1734. P. 180

Tradesmen who had shops in the Inn had to be content with short
leases—Hinder, the vintner, for the vaults and cellars at the back gate,
Hale for the fruitshop there, and Wilkins for the stationer's shop at the
fore-gate.[3] If a member was nominated lessee for a non-member, he had to
pay dues as if he were owner of the chambers.[4]

The plan of Clement's Inn and its surroundings which forms the frontispiece to this volume does not establish the location of the courts and
staircases to which our Pension Book refers. It is an enlargement of a
part of the second edition of Horwood's map.[5] In the middle of the plan
is an open space marked "Clement's Inn", rectangular in shape except at
its south-east corner. This space is the Clement's Inn garden; at its upper
end it is entered from the north-west by a passage marked "Clement's
Inn Pa." This point of entry is the "back gate" of the Inn, sometimes
called the "Clare Market gate".

Stow and his successors describe Clement's Inn as consisting of three

---

[1] Halsted was a conspicuous pluralist; see pp. 25, 37, 80–1, 88, 97, 100, 110, 112,
116, 119 below.

[2] P. 31 below; and see pp. 38, 81, 87, 91, 100 for the express insertion in the deed.

[3] See pp. 40, 97, 119 (Hinder), 98 (Wilkins), 101 (Hale). Cf. the case of Tibson, the
peruke-maker of Tanfield Court, whom the Inner Temple would not allow to purchase
chambers for his life: *I.T.R.*, v, 54, 347–8, 361. "Mr Burton the Taylor", mentioned at
p. 125 below, was presumably in arrear for rent as a tenant and not for dues as a member.

[4] See p. 245 below.

[5] Horwood's second edition is dated 1807; the first had appeared some ten years
earlier. John Rocque's large-scale plan of London (*c.* 1750) is thought to be less accurate
than Horwood's. John Ogilby's map of 1677 contains hieroglyphics to which the unique
copy of his "Explanation" in the British Museum affords no adequate key. Rocque's
and Ogilby's plans are reproduced in *Maps of Old London* (1908).

courts opening into one another. A right of way through the Inn was, we know, reserved in the Earl of Clare's conveyance.[1] The progress of pedestrians exercising this right can be followed on the Horwood map. They would enter at the "back gate", proceed in a straight line down the north-east edge of the garden (passing on their left the entrance into Horseshoe Court[2]) and find themselves in a square court of which the south-east side was occupied by the Hall built in 1715. Just before reaching the Hall, they would turn sharp left under an arch[3] and come out into the south-west side of a long narrow court; then, turning right-handed, they would emerge from its jaws by way of the "fore-gate", leaving the Inn at a point north of the circle enclosing St. Clement Danes Church.[4]

The garden buildings, the square court and the long, narrow court give us the three courts mentioned by Stow. Contemporary map-makers, however, omit to label the courts,[5] and our Pension Book speaks confusingly of a First, Second and Third Court, a Garden Court, a Middle Court and a Hall Court. Of these the Third Court, Middle and Hall Court seem to be identical[6]: the names are those of the square court of which the Hall forms the south-east side. The lay-out of the Garden Court is plain enough; it comprised staircase 21 and 22, both built by Wheatley in the south-east corner of the garden, and 23 and 24 which were "Kellett's Buildings at the Upper End of the Garden". No. 24 was "next adjoining New Inn" whose garden bordered on that of Clement's Inn. Under No. 23 was the passage whence began the thoroughfare between the back gate and the fore-gate.

The other courts and their chambers are less easy to plot, even with the guidance of the numerals on Horwood's map; the rate-books give little help. The First Court included the staircases from No. 1 near the fore-gate to No. 7 at the upper end of the court, fronting the gateway

P. 148

Pp. 28, 31, etc.

Pp. 131, 155

Pp. 161–4, 183

---

[1] See pp. xlvii, 239 below.

[2] See p. 246 below.

[3] ? the "new passage" mentioned in the 1715 order for paving (p. 22 below).

[4] If they then turned right, along the outer circumference of the church outlined by Horwood, they would pass the entrance to the unnamed enclosure of the Lamb Inn, for which see p. 100 below. Arriving in Wych Street, they would pass the Angel Inn (which he names), for which see pp. 247–8 below.

[5] Exceptionally Ogilby labels the square court "Elm Court". This name, nowhere else found in connection with Clement's Inn, he must have transplanted from the Temple by mistake.

[6] Staircase 17, Maydwell's Building, was in the Third Court (pp. 8, 151 below) and in the Middle Court (pp. 156, 168). No. 20 Dobbs' Building, was in the Third Court (pp. 6, 134), "in the Hall Court", over the arch leading into the garden (p. 52), and "in the Court formerly called the Third Court, now the Middle Court" (p. 159). Horwood's plan shows the site of the post-1714 Hall; the Hall Court, north-west of it, must be that illustrated in the books of Ireland, E. Williams, Bellot and others; their drawings, looking south-east, show the spire of St. Clement Danes Church above the Hall roof.

south and the Talbot Alehouse yard north and abutting on Clement's
Lane east. No. 8, "in the now First Court", was in the north-west
corner; No. 9 "over the arch near the Hall" was in the First, but in 1701
had been in the Second, Court. For the rest, No. 11 had in 1687 been in
the Middle Court, No. 12 in the corner was variously assigned to the
First, Second and Middle Courts,[1] and Nos. 14–18 and 20 are referred to as
either in the Middle or the Third Court or both. Periodical reconstructions
may have altered access and frontages.[2] In 1731, there being no longer any
staircase numbers between 10 and 17,[3] it was decided that Nos. 17 to 24
should be renumbered 11 to 18.

Pp. 116, 122
Pp. 45, 119, 161
P. 168

IX. BUILDING LEASES

A COLLECTION of Clement's Inn building agreements, dating from the
reign of Elizabeth I, survives among the Taylor papers.[4] Thus during that
reign there are articles between "Richard Stretton Principal and the
Ancients of the House whose names are underwritten" and "George
Readinge and Richard Page Companyons of the same House". They recite
that Readinge and Page, with the consent of the Principal and Ancients,
have built "one newe chamber with two new Studyes in the same and one
Gallerye over the said Chamber and Studyes" at their great charge and
expense. In consideration thereof it is agreed that the two, their executors,
administrators and assigns, shall have, hold and enjoy the premises for
forty-one years. There are the usual concise undertakings on both sides.
Readinge and Page promise not to grant to anyone unless he be first
admitted to membership of the Society; the grantee is to be liable for his
pension payments and for observance of the orders of the House. The
Principal and Ancients agree that any admission to the premises during
the specified period shall be void if it has not the consent of Readinge and
Page. In witness to the agreement the Principal and Ancients and the two
Companions subscribe their signatures.

In Tudor and Stuart times there were frequent attempts to restrict new

---

[1] See below, pp. 70 (First), 46, 112 (Second), and 166–7 (Middle).

[2] The front of No. 19, for instance, was pulled down, and in 1715 there was a new
passage between two courts; see pp. 22, 139 below.

[3] The new Hall replaced Nos. 15 and 16 and apparently also 14 (pp. 1, 21 below).
The Pension Book does not refer to 10 or 13; one of these may have been the house of
office (see pp. 166–7 below). What was described as "the building No. 14" was ruinous
in May 1744, when steps were taken to get the occupants out: see pp. 206, 208.

[4] Item 3 in the list at p. xi above.

3*

P. 230

housing in the London suburbs. Clement's Inn objected to building development in its vicinity because of the distraction to its students. It managed to frustrate Thomas Ford's project of a bowling green, though it failed to prevent Gervas Hollys from constructing fifteen dwelling-houses, with necessary out-houses and a chapel, in Clement's Inn Field.[1] In the reign of Elizabeth there was particular concern at overcrowding and "new erections" in the Inns of Court[2]; yet in Clement's Inn building was continuously going forward. During that reign Christopher Pegge and William Browne the younger, two Companions, built an upper chamber and William Dilke got a forty-one-year lease[3] for "one building which he ys mynded presently to sett up in the gardeyne of Clement's Inn aforesaid". In the 17th century the builders must have been constantly at work. In 1606 Christopher Thacker, an Ancient, built four new chambers with seven new studies. In 1620 Godfrey Maydwell undertook to erect within a year a new building of eight chambers with cellars and windows, "to the great enlarging and beautifying" of the Inn, in the Clement's Inn garden near the Angel and New Inn: he was to hold it for fifty-nine years and to give the Society "one double silver salt of the value of five pounds". In 1626 Thomas Dobbes similarly undertook to erect a new building with nine double chambers and garrets over them, with convenient studies; six of the chambers were to be at the end of the old buildings of Clement's Inn garden and three others "to cross over the said garden adjoining the said new buildings".[4] He was to give two silver bowls and have a sixty-one-year lease. He got a fresh lease two years later, giving one silver bowl and undertaking not to erect any other building in the garden without consent. Presently when Maydwell was Principal, there were several agreements for chambers separately undertaken in "the new brick building in the Middle Court".[5] A building lease of 1637, when Thomas Holbech was Principal, contains an additional stipulation "that there shall be two in every chamber in the said new building except it be an Antient's chamber".[6]

[1] Copies of the petition asking the Lord Keeper (1641/2) not to seal the patent for Hollys and of the licence granted to Hollys are among the Taylor Papers (item 11, p. xi above). The petitioners said the Court of Chancery had stopped one Collinson from building a carpenter's shop near them. For an earlier success see *I.T.R.*, i, 390 (1593).

[2] *Ibid.*, i, pp. lxxix, 277, 300.

[3] The agreement, dated in 1586, was not entered in the book of leases till he requested it in 1613, when twenty-seven years had already expired. See also p. 228 below.

[4] There was an arch under the cross building; see p. 235 below.

[5] The undertakers included John Staffin, Michael Emerson, John Mason, Rafe Gregg, Thomas Bateman, William Wolrich, George Healey, John Dand, John Bold and Martyn Holbeche.

[6] Shortage of accommodation in Elizabethan times had caused a direction that two be housed in each chamber: *I.T.R.*, i, pp. xxviii–ix, 277. For an Ancient's privilege see p. 225 below.

Besides furnishing the names of Principals[1] and other members at a period earlier than that of our Admission Books, these records explain the origin of such descriptions as Dilke's, Maydwell's or Dobbs' Building.[2] Our Pension Book shows us, in the case of the premises erected by John Lawes, how the disposal of chambers was worked out between the Society, the builder and the approved occupiers. The Inn reserved a ground rent and, at the end of the agreed term, acquired the chambers.[3] In 1718/9 the Society decided for once to be its own builder, in order to replace a timber building in which Maurice Johnson and Arthur Squire had long ago been granted chambers. It employed William Seabrooke, a bricklayer, who, as its "surveyor" for several years, would be engaged in "making Draughts, contriving the Buildings, contracting with the Workmen and seeing the Work done as it should be". His accounts and vouchers would be examined and certified. Sometimes a responsible member of the House would have exercised supervision.[4]

Pp. 12–13, 15, 25

Pp. 65–6

Pp. 107, 152–153

P. 83

X. THE KELLETT AFFAIR

DEALINGS with Seabrooke were amicable. When his work was done, he was admitted a member of the Inn, the Principal being his surety. The building agreement with Francis Kellett made a less happy story. Kellett, who married a daughter of the Thomas Dobbes already mentioned, got a building lease in 1673 and erected the premises which bore his name. But he took in, as he was afterwards forced to confess, more ground than his agreement allowed him, and, in the dispute which followed, he refused to take his lease of the premises or to pay the agreed rent of £12. By a counterstroke which his fellow-members must have thought unpardonable, he went behind their backs to the Earl of Clare, and in 1677 purported to acquire for £350 the Earl's estate in the chambers, buildings, courts, gardens, lights and water-courses in the Inn,[5] subject only to the right of way through it from Clare Market. Actions and cross-actions in the Court

P. 273

---

[1] Thus, confirming or supplementing the details in Pension Book extracts (p. 228 below, onwards), we can identify the principalships of Richard Stretton (1558, 1562), Richard Edwards (1617), Anthony Langston (1625), Thomas Style (1626, 1628), Godfrey Maydwell (1632) Rowland Fryth (1634), Thomas Holbech (1637/8), Richard Keylway (1639/40), Richard Williams (1648) and James Prescott (1649).

[2] Cf. *I.T.R.*, i, p. lxxiv. At Clement's Inn Maydwell's Building was No. 17 (p. 69 below), Dobbs' near No. 20 (p. 134), Wright's was No. 2 (p. 147), Lawes' No. 5 (p. 12), Kellett's Nos. 23 and 24 (pp. 17, 131), and Wheatley's Nos. 21 and 22 (p. 148).

[3] Cf. *I.T.R.*, i, p. lxxiv; *Pension Book of Gray's Inn*, i, 2.

[4] See, for example, Matthew Evans's case, p. 39 below.

[5] See p. li below.

of Chancery ensued during the principalships of Thomas Sturmy and Ambrose Holbech,[1] and there are significant references to the culprit as "late a Companion". Whether or no composed before his expulsion, Kellett drew up a "Case against Clement's Inn to free him from the aspersions that are daily cast upon him as though he intended the dissolution of the Society and to lett the world know that he is not so unreasonable and perverse as the Society do in all places make him to be and that what Kellett hath done hath been for his preservation and not out of perverseness, being willing to do anything for the good of the Society so as he may be paid what he is bona fide out of purse for his building".[2]

Details of the controversy emerge from this report of a committee of five Benchers of the Inner Temple to whom the dispute had been referred.

> First we find that an agreement [was made] between the Principal and Antients of the said Society and the said Mr Kellett that the said Mr Kellett should build a brick building within the said Society three floors in height besides garrets and cellars being the second rate of building according to the Acts of Parliament for building the City of London and that Mr Kellett proceeded in the said building and allegeth that he hath expended the sume of £1900 or £2000 in the said building but it doth not appear to us that the said Mr Kellett either did or really needed to have expended above £1400 or thereabouts in the building thereof.
>
> Item that by the said Agreement the said Mr Kellett was to have a term of 40 years as a recompense for his charge of building under the rent of £12 per annum and we do certify that by reason of Mr Kellett's complaint of his great loss and charge therein we did propose to the Principal and Antients that they would add 20 years to the said term of 40 years and abate six pounds per annum part of the twelve pounds per annum rent so agreed upon as aforesaid which the said Principal and Antients consent unto.
>
> Item upon examination of the numbers of chambers in the said building and the value thereof that a term of 60 years at 6 pounds per annum will be a considerable recompense for so much monie as Mr Kellett did lay out or was necessary to be laid out upon the said building.
>
> Item that Mr Kellett built the building of a bigger dimension than was agreed by and between the said parties which hath made the chambers of a better value and so for Mr Kellett's advantage, that the Principal and Antients do not insist upon the strictness of the agreement with them therein, neither do they insist upon the agreement to compel him to make the garden even or level as it was before, but have made it decent and handsome at the charge of the said Society which they say have cost them £150.
>
> Item there was a large brick wall thrown down by Mr Kellett's workmen and the brick employed in the building which for quietness sake the said Principal and Antients are contented to waive their recompense and satisfaction for.
>
> Lastly we do find that Mr Kellett hath been guilty of miscarriage in coming into Council in the Hall when expeld by the Principal and Antients to the evil example of others in that and other Societies.

[1] See the entry in the note at p. 218 below.
[2] The document is among the file of Taylor papers which form item 11, p. xi above.

The five benchers sign the report, and the benchers order that both parties may have copies of it "and may be heard thereon".[1]

Kellett, needing money for his building and now no doubt heavily "out of purse", found James Rogers willing to accommodate him with various sums as shown by the 1713 "Abstract of Deeds and Writings relating to Clement's Inn".[2] The largest amount was £1600, secured on a mortgage of properties which had come to him partly as executor of his father, partly as son-in-law of Thomas Dobbs senior and partly on his own account. They included "Dobbes' building" and the controversial "Kellett's building", both within the Inn. James Rogers died leaving his widow as his executrix and two daughters—Anne, married to Richard Brawne, and Frances, a spinster. Richard Brawne died, leaving a widow and two daughters, Elizabeth and Anne. Deeds comprised in the Abstract, Pp. 237–9 as well as references in Orders Nos. 82 to 84, reveal that five Ancients together subscribed £825 8s. 6d. towards the dependants of James Rogers, that two of the five (Michael Wrightson, Principal, and Edward Gerard) later put up another £812, and that the Principal and Ancients paid Kellett £463 6s. 6d. "in full of the £350 paid by him to the Earl and the interest". This last-mentioned payment is recorded in a deed executed by Kellett which recites admissions that in his building he "took in more ground out of the said garden than by his agreement he was to have had" and that, in his application to the Earl of Clare, he had "pretended a title in the Earl of all the House Inn and Hostel known as Clement's Inn". By this deed, executed in part performance of a Decretal Order in Chancery made on November 15, 1681, and in consideration of the payment to him of the £463 6s. 6d. already mentioned, Kellett conveys to trustees all Kellett's estate in Clement's Inn and the other properties in trust for the Society and the Principal and Ancients and their successors, to be disposed of as the Principal and Ancients or the major part might appoint. Thus Francis Kellett disappears from the scene[3] and the Inn remained vested on behalf of its unincorporated Society in trustees whom it was necessary periodically to renew.

[1] The document, certified "true copy" among the Taylor Papers (item 11, p. xi above) must be the copy obtained by Clement's Inn. The report is dated February 1673/4. The Benchers were Thomas Robinson, Richard Powell, Edward West, Thomas Farrar and R. Hampson.

[2] See item 5 in the list of Taylor Papers, p. xi above.

[3] A Francis Kellett was admitted at the Inner Temple in 1680/1 (on certificate from Clement's Inn) and his sons Maurice and Edward in 1684. This Francis Kellett was in trouble for permitting strangers to lodge in his chambers there. Maurice, called to the bar in 1689, received charity from the Inn as a "decayed barrister". See *I.T.R.*, iii, *passim.*

XI. EARLIER HISTORY

WHATEVER title had been "pretended" in the Earl of Clare, the Society thereafter derived its right to the Inn from his conveyance to Kellett in 1677 and from the decree in Kellett's subsequent Chancery action against the Principal and Ancients; "that", said the Inn's steward in his evidence before the Royal Commission in 1854, "is where we commence our claim from".[1] The patient scholarship of the late Mr. E. Williams has disinterred the earlier history.[2] He shows the site as coming into the possession of Richard Barre, citizen of London, whose daughter and heir married William Cantelow. Barre and Cantelow were owners but not occupiers; they let the property, it seems, to legal occupiers who had their own feoffees, one of whom, as already mentioned, was Sir John Fortescue. Within two years of Fortescue's departure into exile in 1461, Clement's Inn is found to be held directly from its owner Sir William Cantelow who himself held it of the Chapter of St. Paul's and the Hospital of St. Giles. His grandson, Sir John Cantelow, leased the Inn[3] for eighty years from 1487 at a rent of £4 6s. 8d. to two brothers, William and John Elyot. It was at about this date that the House was declared to have been for a long time a *hospicium* of men of the law.[4]

John Elyot may well have been Principal of the Inn, for, when he died in 1492, he desired to be buried in the Chapel of Our Lady in St. Clement Danes Church "there afore Clements pewe"; he bequeathed to his wife his household possessions in his chambers and in the Hall and to the Company of the Inn twenty pence "to make them to drink the day of my burying". William Elyot, the other lessee, died in 1507, leaving *inter alia* his law books to All Souls and his leasehold of the Inn to his brother Richard who had been made a Serjeant in 1503 and was then Reader from the Middle Temple to New Inn.[5] Later a Justice of the Common Pleas, Richard died in 1522, leaving the leasehold to his son Thomas. Thomas, admitted to the Clerks' Commons at the Middle Temple in 1510 and already clerk of assize in the west country, was made Clerk of the King's Council in 1519 on Wolsey's recommendation and at the age of 42 was

---

[1] Q. 827 (Gregory). The witness asserted no great knowledge; "some documents have been burnt, some of them we cannot read" (Q. 282).

[2] *Early Holborn and the Legal Quarter of London*, 1465–9.

[3] The lease gives some details of the site which lies between Cantelow's tenement in the tenure of John Elyott and Tykettsfield on the east and the Inn and garden of New Inn and the Inn and garden of Sir John Fortescue on the west: see H. B. Wheatley, *London Past and Present* (1891), i, 416.

[4] See p. 218 below.

[5] Williams, *Early Holborn*, 1472.

sent by the King as his special ambassador to Charles V. Before leaving England he sold his lease of the Inn (with twenty-nine years still to run) to William Holles, alderman and later Lord Mayor of London. The ultimate heir of Sir William Cantelow was Margaret Wood; in 1531 she married as her second husband Sir William Hawte: he in the same year sold the freehold of Clement's Inn to William Holles who already had bought the lease. Holles soon afterwards demised the Inn, to a body of students then occupying it, for a term of ninety-nine years. He died in 1543, leaving the Inn (subject to his wife's life interest) to his son Francis. Francis dying without issue, the property came to his eldest surviving brother William, who died in 1591. In 1629 when the ninety-nine-year lease was near expiration, Sir John Holles, Earl of Clare, grandson of Sir William Holles, decided to re-enter upon the premises and refused to renew the lease. The Society of Clement's Inn went to the High Court pleading fixity of tenure; the Lord Keeper ordered that the Inn of Chancery should remain as such to the professors of the law for ever at the then customary rent, subject to one chamber being reserved for someone of the Earl's name and kin and another for the Earl's solicitor. A copy of a petition from the Inn to the Earl dated February 10, 1647/8, survives among the Taylor papers.[1] The Earl had demanded his two chambers; the Principal and Ancients say they are willing to give him satisfaction "notwithstanding that the said order had for many years slept and never been putt in execucion". They say they had assigned him the stipulated accommodation but he has entered on a chamber "adjoining to the Lambe Gate" for which the Inn has for forty years been receiving rent from a tenant. They beg him to be content with the chambers allotted to him "without infringinge the Priviledge of the House, itt being a very Ancient House founded for Educacion of Students and Learninge". The sequel is unknown, but the document illustrates afresh the claim to an undated antiquity.

XII. CONSTITUTIONS AND ORDERS

WE know of three versions or instalments of the Constitutions and Orders of Clement's Inn. The first and third are among the Taylor papers in the P. xi Public Record Office.

The first version is the original "Book bound in Calves Skin with

---

[1] In item 3 of the list at p. xi above.

Clasps", described on a later page[1]; it contained Orders 1 to 62. Nos. 1 to 41 are in French, 42–46 in English, 47 to 52 in French again, and the last ten in English except that 61 is in Latin. This Latin order is the writ of nuisance to restrain Thomas Ford from constructing, on ground north of the Inn, a bowling green which might distract the Inn's students from their studies.[2] The earlier orders, grouped in some degree by subject, may represent an attempt at a code. No. 53 begins a merely chronological sequence of extracts from Pension Books dating from 1620 to perhaps 1649.

The second version, "the Book of Orders 1650 Bound in a Book with a Parchment Cover, beginning No. 63", is missing. It carried on the numbered sequence to No. 84 which belongs to the year 1684. Its disappearance matters the less because the third version (which survives), the "Translation of Clement's Inn Old Orders", reproduces (in English) the contents of the first and second. The compiler of this cumulative edition, after he has copied No. 84 and added a note of the right of way through the Inn, writes "Here Ends the Books of Orders—All since are in the Pension Books". He then completes his record with supplementary extracts ending with one of 1781.[3] The remaining blank pages are thriftily occupied by an "Abstract of the Deeds and Writings relating to Clement's Inn taken 8 April 1713", running backwards from the end of the book.

The Taylor papers also include an index, ascribed to the early part of the 19th century,[4] covering Orders 1 to 83 so comprehensively as to include under "Forfeitures" a list of nearly sixty different fines which a member could have incurred.

The comparable Statutes and Ordinances of Clifford's Inn (in the possession of the Inner Temple), framed in French throughout, declare themselves to have been made in the reign of Henry VII and newly written down in the 20th year of Henry VIII.[5] They contain one order (regulating the election of marshal, constable and steward at Christmas) which dates

---

[1] See note to p. 232 below. If, in the cipher (there mentioned) embossed on the front and back covers, the vertical initials "C.I." stand for Clement's Inn, the horizontal initials "M.H." may be those of Martin Holbeche of Fillongley, Warwickshire, father of the Thomas Holbeche, whose name appears on the front page (see p. 218 below).

[2] The order to the sheriff (8 Charles I.) is filed among the *Placita de Banco*, C.P. 40/2312, file 1667 dors.

[3] In 1880, when the Inn was near its end, the Constitutions and Orders (down to No. 83) were reproduced in a handsome volume "Privately printed for the Society, C. J. Mander principal."

[4] The Inner Temple indexed its orders in 1740 (*I.T.R.*, v, 46), Lincoln's Inn in 1770 (*Black Books of Lincoln's Inn*, iii, 404), Gray's Inn in 1793 (*Pension Book of Gray's Inn*, ii, 369).

[5] At Furnival's Inn new orders and statutes were drawn up *temp.* Henry VII: Bland, *Early Records of Furnival's Inn*, p. 35.

itself to the reign of Edward III. At Clement's Inn the first fifty-two Orders bear no date except that No. 47 purports to have been published in the 19th P. 226 year of "the late King", who may—if we have to guess—be the seventh or eighth Henry or indeed some much earlier sovereign. The fact that forty-seven of these fifty-two (reprinted below in the later English translation) have come down to us in French may be no proof of great antiquity. Roger North tells us that his brother, Lord Keeper Guilford (born in 1637), habitually and from choice made his notes in law French. William Style, when "in obedience to authority" he published his reports in English in 1658, doubted if the language would make them more generally useful. Whatever their original date, many of the Clement's Inn orders must have seemed archaic to the Principal and Ancients of our Pension Book period. The references to noble pensioners, solemn revels, grand Christmas, royal nobles and marshal marks[1] must have lost their significance. What could the provisions which contemplate the weekly appointment of a junior member as steward[2] have conveyed to later generations Os. 5–9, p. when the office was held by some responsible officer for years at a time? 219 What did the list of numbered rooms for students mean to members O. 48, p. 226 whose chambers were identified by numbered staircases? Did the 18th century appreciate the description of barristers as "outer" and "inner", the former not necessarily entitled yet to practise, the latter still mere students? Did the Principal still read the Inn's statutes "openly in the O. 36, p. 224 Hall" twice a year? Did he read a writ "every working day" in term-time O. 14, p. 220 and vacation?

Apart from these vestigial survivals the orders for decent behaviour inside and outside the Inn (28, 30, 33), for brotherly conduct (18, 20, 30), for respect towards the Society's senior members (27) and for religious observance (24) are such as one might expect to find in a medieval gild. Those for regulating the buttery (17, 26), for protecting the butler and the cook (21), the furniture (22) or the trees and flowers in the garden (22), for closing the gates at night (31, 57) and forbidding anyone to climb in thereafter (31), for prohibiting unlawful games and incontinence (19) and for elementary hygiene (31, 77), were such as any collegiate body might have imposed. Several orders deal with the punctual payment of pension money and commons, the collection of arrears, the office and powers of the Principal, his election and the audit of his accounts, and the need to

---

[1] See p. 219 n. below. There is presumably some connection with the King and Marshal of the Christmas revels. In 5 Edward IV one member of Furnival's Inn was amerced 6*s.* 8*d. pro eo quod renuit Officium Regale* and another *quia renuit Officium Marescalli: Early Records of Furnival's Inn*, (ed. Bland, 1957), p. 30. At Clifford's Inn the amercement for refusing the office of Marshal, Constable or Steward for Christmas was 20*s.*

[2] See p. xxxix above.

O. 45, p. 225

keep the chambers fully occupied, while allowing an Ancient to choose his own room-mate. Misbehaviour by servants was visited upon the heads of their employers (76, 77).

Regulations were sometimes dictated from above, as when the judges directed that the gentlemen of the Inns of Court should not wear beards above a fortnight's growth.[1] Otherwise each legal Inn made its own orders. There is a general similarity, but there are local variants. At Clifford's Inn, for instance, it was forbidden to take usury for a loan or to keep a greyhound, mastiff or spaniel. At Gray's Inn it was ordered "That no Fellow of the Society should stand with his back to the Fire,"[2] and that firearms should not be discharged from the windows.[3] Under the draft scheme propounded to Henry VIII for a corporation of the King's law students the keeping of concubines and the stealing of books from the library were to have been punished.[4]

XIII. ADMISSION BOOKS

At the Inner Temple it was ordered in 1546/7 that the chief butler should enter on a parchment roll the names, surname, habitation and county of every fellow, his special or general admittance, the day and year thereof and his pledges.[5] There is no evidence of a similar direction at Clement's Inn, but the two surviving Admission Books supply exactly that information. Here is the first entry in the earlier of the two:

P. xi

> *Cornub* Bernard Kendall of Lanlivery in the county aforesaid gent was specially admitted the nyne and twentieth day of Aprill in the yeare of our Lord 1656.
>   Mr Sloper pledge by bond

The final entry in the second of the two shows how faithfully the formula had been followed:

> *Middlesex* Mortimer Rooke of 13 Clement's Inn was specially admitted the 2nd day of January 1883.
>   Thos Henry Carew Hunt of 1 Lincoln's Inn Fields gent. pledge

---

[1] See *Black Books of Lincoln's Inn*, i, 321 (1557); Dugdale, *Origines*, p. 311.
[2] Dugdale, *Origines*, p. 291.
[3] *Pension Book of Gray's Inn*, ii, 329 (1778).
[4] Waterhous, *Fortescutus Illustratus*, p. (?) 545.
[5] *I.T.R.*, i, 148: "special" admission, carrying certain privileges or exemptions and involving a higher entrance fee, was in some legal Inns recorded in their minutes. The Clement's Inn admissions from which the list at p. 249 below is compiled were all "special".

We do not know whether these two books were the first of their series.[1] The earlier one bears on its title-page the words, "The Booke of Admittances of Clement's Inn beginning Easter Terme in the yeare of our Lord one thousand sixe hundred fifty and five". The later, beginning in Easter term 1740, has the single word "Admissions".

As already stated, the legal Inns naturally required security for the new entrant's good behaviour and for the payment of his dues. At the Inner Temple, where admittance (except from its Inns of Chancery) was "at the instance" of a member,[2] the surety or pledge was usually someone already himself admitted; he often signed personally; at Clement's Inn the surety did not sign the book, but would, of course, have signed the bond.[3] Normally each entrant to Clement's Inn had one surety[4]; exceptionally there were two[5] or even three; it was not uncommon for two new members to be pledges for one another. In a very few cases, perhaps because the admittee was the kinsman of a member or was otherwise sufficiently known, no pledge is recorded.   O. 1, p. 218

At first the entries in our two Admission Books are in that uncial script which Roger North likened to pigs' ribs. The language at first is English, as prescribed in 1650,[6] but it loyally relapses into Latin at the restoration of the monarchy, when also the regnal years reappear. From 1733 the record obeys the statute which forbade the use of an unknown tongue and required such documents to be "written in a common legible hand and not in any hand called court hand".[7] An occasional muddle over the relative priority of admittees suggests that the clerk was posting up his register intermittently.[8] Did he sometimes omit an entry altogether? A dozen or more persons whom our Pension Book names as Companions of the Society seem not to have been entered in the Admission Books.[9]

---

[1] The Inner Temple Parliament had ordered a separate register of admissions as early as 1510/1 (*I.T.R.*, i, 22). The surviving Staple Inn Admission Books date from 1716, that of Barnard's Inn from 1800.

[2] At Barnard's Inn a candidate's name was before the Society for a probationary period before formal admission.

[3] A few such bonds survive: see below, pp. 250 n. (Kecke), 255 n. (Ball).

[4] At Furnival's Inn two pledges *pro securitate de bono gestu* began to be required in 27 Henry VI.: Bland, *Early Records of Furnival's Inn*, p. 29. At the Inner Temple the pledges' names are recorded down to *c.* 1620 and intermittently until 1628. Gray's Inn decided in 1794 that pledges' names should be added in the Admission Book: *Pension Book of Gray's Inn*, ii, 371.

[5] Two pledges are not unusual where one is a namesake (presumably a kinsman) of the admittee.

[6] *Acts and Ordinances of the Interregnum*, ii, 455; and see 12 Car. II. c. 3. s. 4.

[7] 4 Geo. II, c. 26.

[8] See the interpolations at pp. 278–9, 282, 288, 294–6 below.

[9] *E.g.* Wm. Adams, Brayfield, Jas. Bridges, Nich. Cooper, Thos. Dymoke, Noah Curtis and Thos. Pryor. Also apparently omitted, but presumably either Ancients or Companions, are Grew, Leigh Langley and Sturgis.

At first, save for a sprinkling of "esquires", every admittee is described as "gentleman". Among all the hundreds of entries "attorney" occurs once only,[1] "solicitor" not at all. "Whosoever studieth the lawes of the realme . . . shall be taken for a gentleman", wrote Sir Thomas Smith during the reign of the first Elizabeth.[2] Dr. Robson has shown us the attorneys climbing the road of respectability in 18th-century England[3]; the new members of Clement's Inn must have thought they had already arrived. "Gentleman" is their synonymous label for "attorney" or for any student of the laws, whether he intended to practise professionally or, like Master Robert Shallow (himself of Clement's Inn), merely to combine a little learning with prospective memories of the chimes of midnight London.

The Clement's Inn admittances, as might be expected, furnish evidence of local and hereditary links. Some counties—Lincolnshire and Warwickshire, for example—make a bigger contribution than others. In the sixteen-sixties the Plague and the Great Fire have little effect upon the volume of admissions.[4] Waterhous, whose commentary on Fortescue had been published just before these two events, noted belatedly a change in the character of the entrants into the legal Inns.

> Although most men now repair thither for fashion and to spend money, yet of old they thither went and there resided to acquire parts of virtue and action and to compleat themselves as good Christians and stout Gentlemen.[5]

Another observer remarked soon afterwards the altered composition[6] of the Inns of Chancery.

> They were heretofore preparatory Colledges for younger Students and many were entred here before admitted into the Inns of Court. Now they are for the most part taken up by Attorneys, Solicitors and Clerks who have here their chambers apart and their Diet at a very easie Rate in a hall together.[7]

The Tudor glory had departed. In 1619 the Inns of Chancery were bewailing the scarcity of students; they were no longer the preparatory lodges of

---

[1] For Tobias Stapleton, surety for Hinde in 1788, see p. 296 below.

[2] *De Republica Anglorum*, I, cap. 20. For the juristic basis of gentility see G. D. Squibb, *High Court of Chivalry* (1959), pp. 60, 139–40, 170–7. Christian, *Short History of Solicitors* (1896), p. vii, glances at the legend that solicitors were gentlemen by Act of Parliament; for this no more solid basis has been suggested than the unlikely misreading of *generosum* for *generalem* in Statute of Westminster II (power to appoint attorney).

[3] R. Robson, *The Attorney in 18th-Century England* (1959), cap. x.

[4] See pp. 254–5 below.

[5] *Fortescutus Illustratus*, p. 527.

[6] See *I.T.R.*, ii, 113. Cf. the lament, long afterwards, of Furnival's Inn for the good old days—"at those times country attornies and solicitors made a point of being admitted to the Inns of Chancery (from the fees on which admissions a considerable revenue arose to the Society) which is seldom or never the case now": *Black Books of Lincoln's Inn*, iv, 105 (1807).

[7] Chamberlayne, *Present State of England* (1684 edn.), Part I, Bk. iii.

freshmen. Towards the end of the 17th century the numbers were falling away. During the decade which begins in 1693 the annual intake averaged less than five. In June 1705 the *London Gazette* published an order of the iudges of the Courts of Queen's Bench, Common Pleas and Exchequer[1] which might have stimulated recruitment. It directed—

> that all Attornies and Clerks of the said Courts not admitted of one of the Inns of Court or Chancery shall be admitted before the end of Trinity Term next and take Chambers there or Lodgings near and leave Notice in Writing with the Butler or Porter of the Inn to which they belong: And that none shall be sworn Attornies for the future or admitted Clerks till they are first admitted of one of the said Inns and produce a Certificate thereof.

No attorney or clerk was to put himself out of such Society till he brought a certificate that he was admitted of some other Society, unless he had "totally left off the practice of the law".[2] Attorneys and clerks "shall duly keep commons in such Society of which they are admitted". Anyone offending against any part of this order was, if an attorney, to be put out of the Roll, and, if a clerk, to be displaced and discharged from his office. A list of the offenders was to be delivered to the Chief Justices and Chief Baron.

In so far as the order intended all attorneys to have an ascertainable address for service, it was ultimately superseded by the system under which every London solicitor has such an address within three miles of the Law Courts and every country solicitor has a London agent. In so far as it was driving all attorneys into a legal Inn, the judges must have known of the previous reluctance of Inns of Court to accept an attorney, not to mention also the absence of any power to compel any Inn, whether of Court or of Chancery, to admit anybody. Be that as it may, the Clement's Inn Admission Books exhibit no consequent acceleration of recruiting; for the five years from 1710 the average annual intake was less than four.

Presently the legal "gentlemen" are seen to be diluted by an infusion of laymen. In 1742 a stationer and a brewer are admitted, in 1743 another brewer, in 1748 a periwig-maker.[3] After these four intruders the sequence of gentlemen and esquires is resumed until the seventeen-sixties when we come upon a builder, two merchants, a doctor of physic, an apothecary, a

---

[1] *London Gazette*, 1705, June 14 and 21.

[2] Thus our Pension Book is careful to mention that members leaving for another Inn have produced a certificate: see below, pp. 76 (Hussey), 93 (Hope), 99 (Allen), 103 (Pavey), 118 (Madgwick). Later the fact is omitted: see pp. 146 (Turner), 184 (Miller and Burrell), 194 (Burton), 217 (Elers). And, when a member wants to have his bond up and leave the Inn, it is usually stated that he is giving up practice.

[3] Wm. Room, who left the Inn in 1734, soon after admission, is described as "no lawyer nor practicer of it" (p. 181 below). Does this mean that he was a layman? See pp. 196, 276 for the subsequent admission and departure of one of that name.

clerk (presumably someone in Holy Orders), two plumbers, a cheese-maker, a cook and a musical-instrument-maker. The Inn attracts a few notables from the theatrical world near by. These, if the identifications are not at fault, include Benjamin Griffin (1734), actor and dramatist: Christopher Mosyer Rich (1758), interested, like his father and brother, in theatre management: John Moody (1766 or 1779), the comedian who often appeared at Drury Lane: James Aickin "of the Drury Lane Theatre, esquire" (1782), for whom Moody stood surety, the Irishman who played heavy parts in Edinburgh and in London and who fought a duel with John Kemble: and, finally, Joseph Shepherd Munden (1796), well known on the stage of the Covent Garden and Haymarket theatres.

Admissions in the seventeen-seventies give us a student from Cambridge, an undertaker, a watchmaker, a shoemaker, two musicians, two surgeons and a painter. There is also the first of a little band of six sea-faring men, surgeons, pursers or other officers aboard East Indiamen, doubtless glad of a *pied à terre* in London between voyages.[1] The seventeen-eighties produce a broker, two captains (one in the Dragoons, the other in H.M. Marine Forces), a sugar refiner, a grocer, a coal merchant, a pawnbroker and a pianoforte-maker. Although clergymen of the Church of England have been refused admission to an Inn of Court, Clement's Inn accepted several between 1771 and 1795; the last in the series was the rector of St Clement Danes, the church in which the Society had its special pews and to which it made contributions. Other admissions in 1795 include a Madeira merchant and a Fleet Street "chymist and druggist". The Inn had often accommodated officials, men from the Six Clerks' Office or from the Exchequer Office in the Inner Temple; in the seventeen-nineties there are entrants from the Excise Office and the India House, as well as from the Navy Pay Office and the Auditors' Office, both in Somerset Place. In 1796 a member of the Stock Exchange joins the Inn, together with someone from the Bank of England. The entry of "Jane Frith of Sloane Street, Chelsea", in the previous year, with no description, "gentleman" or otherwise, offers a choice between rival improbabilities: is this a man with a feminine Christian name, or has a woman really been admitted to membership of an essentially masculine society? Or is it just an error?

Among notable entrants in this decade is Isaac d'Israeli, merchant and author, father of a more famous son.[2] Two others made their mark in contemporary literature—Robert Pallock, author of *Peter Wilkins*, a romance which Scott and Lamb praised, and John Wolcot, doctor,

---

[1] Details of their ships and sailings, courteously furnished by the National Maritime Museum, are given in footnotes to pp. 289, 292, 295, 298–300 below.

[2] The future Lord Beaconsfield entered Lincoln's Inn, but withdrew in 1831, "his health not permitting him to follow the law": *Black Books of Lincoln's Inn*, iv, 182.

parson and satirist, Boswell's "contemptible scribbler" who wrote as "Peter Pindar".[1] Certain other admittees bring us into touch with Dr. Johnson himself,[2] of whose worship at St. Clement Danes on more than one Good Friday we know from his biographer.

Within the period covered by our Pension Book the addresses of new members, recorded on their admission, are given with increasing frequency as "Clement's Inn": The clerk may be saving himself trouble by applying the principle of *nunc pro tunc*, or it may be that fewer men are coming up from the provinces now that the old system of legal education has lapsed. Laymen must have been joining the Inn for residential, rather than for business, purposes; but it is noteworthy that in 1775 the Society had to forbid the exhibition of trade advertisements.[3] In the Victorian age Thackeray's picture of the squalor of his "Shepherd's Inn" in *Pendennis* (confidently stated by Bellot to have been drawn with an eye on Clement's Inn)[4] portrayed a solitary solicitor driving down to his chambers there two or three times a week. The Royal Commission of 1854 heard the steward of Clement's Inn say "there are so many other better chambers that we cannot get solicitors to come and live there". He believed there were five solicitors practising in the Inn. Asked what class of persons occupied the chambers other than attorneys, he replied "they are men holding public situations, one in the Tithe Office perhaps, others in banks"; there were no students for the bar; "they would consider it derogatory to live in our Inn; no Counsel reside there".[5]

As the 19th century approached, the rate of admittances had changed abruptly. For the decade beginning in 1787 the average annual intake was about seventeen; the years from 1798 to 1802 together produced only eight new members. Only one entered in 1804, none at all in the following three years. The stiff increase in the stamp duty[6] had brought discouragement

[1] For his biography see T. Girtin, *Doctor with Two Aunts* (1958). See p. 296 below.

[2] See footnotes, below, to pp. 280 (Robinson, Chapone and Rolt), 284 (Dr. Brocklesby), 285 (Hoole), and 292 (Fielding).

[3] See p. 246 below. In that year Gray's Inn had to forbid sales and auctions in its chambers: *Pension Book of Gray's Inn*, ii, 317, 322. Cf. *I.T.R.*, v, 50 (1754). Clifford's Inn had, in Tudor times, visited with expulsion the carrying on of any occupation which was not honourable.

[4] H. H. L. Bellot, *The Inner and Middle Temple* (1902), p. 235. E. Williams (*Early Holborn*, 973) suggested even less plausibly that Clifford's Inn was Thackeray's model.

[5] Thomas Gregory, Qq. 811–14, 865–6. Lincoln's Inn Fields, it seemed, could provide more attractive accommodation (*ibid.*, Appendix). The Inner Temple Treasurer (Qq. 258–9) attributed the many vacant chambers to the railways which were now carrying professional gentlemen out of town.

[6] A shilling in 1694 (5 Will. & Mar. c. 21) (see p. 266 n. below), it rose to £4 in 1797 (37 Geo. III. c. 90. s. 1), keeping pace with the admission duty at Inns of Court. It shot up to £20 in 1804 (44 Geo. III. c. 48), dropping to £3 four years later (48 Geo. III. c. 149). An Inland Revenue inspector periodically inspected the Admission Books.

to Clement's, as to Furnival's, Inn. A petition from the latter to Lincoln's Inn in 1807 declared that there had been no further admission since the £20 tax was imposed.[1] Fewer than a hundred members joined Clement's Inn in the years from 1800 to 1842; after 1842 there is no admission for ten years; from 1852 to the final entry in 1883 there are only thirty-one new names.[2] In 1854 the membership consisted of nine Ancients and only six "Commoners" or Companions.

In face of this fall in numbers and the failure to attract the legal profession to the Inn we might not have expected to discover, from contemporary directories and law lists, that almost everyone who was admitted from 1800 until the end was an attorney or solicitor. The few exceptions include two barristers and a Cornish surgeon.[3] Gradually, we are given to understand, Clement's Inn became a solicitors' dining club—an assumption which might help to explain the restricted entry. A missing cellar-book[4] would apparently have informed us of the state of the cellar in 1809, the wine consumed between 1800 and 1814, and the obligation upon every new member to contribute two bottles of port. This lost document is said to have recorded also some of the convivial wagers which leavened the legal conversation at table.[5] Be that as it may, the entertainment lacked extravagance in 1854. To economise expense, the steward told the Royal Commission, the Society had reduced its dinners from six per term (the sixth being a "Grand Dinner") to a single meal served up by the porter's wife who was paid 8*s.* 6*d.* for cooking it.[6] We know from other sources that the Ancients got their dinner and their wine free; but they contributed some £25 a year to the Society.[7]

---

[1] *Black Books of Lincoln's Inn*, iv, 105.

[2] There were only thirty-nine admissions at Barnard's Inn between 1800 and the end in 1893; the last was in 1869.

[3] See the footnotes to the admissions in 1814, 1856 and 1866.

[4] The book, a copy of *Farley's Cellar-Book or the Butler's Assistant*, containing manuscript entries of these matters, was advertised for sale in 1932 in a London bookseller's catalogue. It has not been traced since.

[5] The advertisement cited a single example: "3 Feb. 1807 Mr A. W. Strong bets Mr Harvey that Giles tumbles over or breaks the bell-rope before the company leaves the table; a bottle of champagne; lost by A. W. S."

[6] Royal Commission of 1854, Qq. 847–53, 859.

[7] *Ibid.*, Qq. 823, 852–3. And see the Order of 1767, p. 246 below.

XIV. END OF THE INNS OF CHANCERY

FORTESCUE counted ten Inns of Chancery; Denton, Bacon and Cary spoke of nine in 1540. Coke mentioned eight, Strand Inn having disappeared in 1549.[1] More than two centuries later, Thavies, Davies or Davy's Inn was the next to go, unable to meet the requirements of Lincoln's Inn, its landlords. The latter advertised it for sale in 1769, and Mr. Thomas Middleton of Lincoln's Inn was declared the best bidder at £4100. The vendors at first thought they might have to petition Parliament for a Bill to assure him of a good title; later they deemed this unnecessary. Indeed the steward of Lincoln's Inn, giving evidence in another connection before a House of Commons Committee in 1774, said he apprehended that his Society had the same power of alienating its other Inn of Chancery (Furnival's Inn) and even Lincoln's Inn itself.[2]

In 1863 Lyon's Inn, where in 1800 a visitor had discovered a brood of chickens on the benches and tables of the Hall,[3] was demolished under a scheme, never carried out, for building a large hotel.[4] By this time, as we have seen, the Inns of Chancery made little pretence of serving their original purpose of legal education. The Incorporated Law Society, founded in 1825 and honoured with a royal charter in 1831,[5] had taken over their task; it stood ready to extend its operations as further funds were available. There was a plan to amalgamate the Inns of Chancery into a legal university for the would-be solicitor; their "misapplied wealth" was to finance it. Each Inn of Chancery, it was argued, had a noble Hall in fine condition, as well able now as in Fortescue's time to accommodate a hundred students and to provide places for study. Suppose that, on an average, 380 clerks were in the fifth year of their articles; suppose that they were distributed as students equally among four Inns of Chancery incorporated to form the proposed university; suppose that each clerk paid £10. Each Inn would then have an income of £950, and, making the sum up to £1200 from its own resources, would be able to find £400 a year for three Readers, one for each of the three branches of legal science. Were the Inns so far gone in obsolescence and decay as to be unfit for such

---

[1] See note to p. xxv above, and Co. Rep. 3, xxxvi.

[2] *Black Books of Lincoln's Inn*, iii, 397, 399, 401–2, 406, 476.

[3] Ireland, *Picturesque Views with an Historical Account of the Inns of Court* (1800), p. 81.

[4] A Strand Hotel Company, incorporated in 1802 to build and carry on a hotel, was to acquire from Francis Hayman Fowler the site between Wych Street and Holywell Street (see the plan reproduced in our frontispiece) with entrance on Newcastle Street; Fowler was to remove all existing buildings. Only about half the authorised capital was subscribed; the Company was struck off the register as defunct in 1882.

[5] See E. B. V. Christian, *Short History of Solicitors* (1896), cap. vii.

responsibilities? No, it was not yet too late to reform them. The Royal Commission, which was set up in 1854 to examine these and other proposals, dismissed the Inns of Chancery almost without comment. It found no means of making their funds available for promoting legal study; they had "in many instances become private property and in others are heavily indebted"; the Commission had not detected any such appropriation of funds as would fix upon them a liability to contribute to any general purpose.[1] Presently the Law Society approached the Principals of the Inns of Chancery, but without success.[2]

The Age of Reform threatened many ancient foundations with dissolution. In 1857 the Court of Probate Act sanctioned the sale of Doctors' Commons, despite the spirited efforts of Dr. John Lee to save the property and especially to preserve the fine library in trust for the study of the Roman civil law.[3] In 1873 the Judicature Act ended the system under which the degree of Serjeant at Law had been a stepping-stone to judicial appointment.[4] Faced with the extinction of their historic order, the existing Serjeants decided by a majority to dispose of their Serjeants' Inn site in Chancery Lane[5] and to divide the proceeds. The premises were knocked down to Serjeant Cox for £57,100,[6] the shares amounting to about £900 apiece.[7] Unlike the Inns of Court and of Chancery, Serjeants' Inn had not been founded for any 'charitable' purpose of legal education. Some time afterwards, when this precedent came under heavy fire, Lord Bramwell answered that the Society of Serjeants had been a private Society for the convenience of its members; it had no duties, no powers; no one was bound to be a member; no one had a right to be; the members were proposed for election and, when elected, had to pay £450 and their commons. The Serjeants had put up the money to buy their freehold in 1834. His own share of the sale, he said, did no more than return his principal and interest.[8]

---

[1] Report of the Royal Commission of 1854, p. 5. The plan outlined above was submitted to the Commission by C. M. Clode: see *ibid.*, pp. 297–9.

[2] *Annual Report of the Law Society, 1858*, p. 13.

[3] See 20 & 21 Vict. c. 77. s. 116, *London Topographical Survey*, xv (1931), pp. 84–6, and Parl. Papers, 1859, Sess. I (16), vol. xxii, p. 19.

[4] 36 & 37 Vict. c. 66. s. 8. One more Serjeant (Huddleston, also "the last of the barons") was nevertheless appointed in 1875.

[5] For their Fleet Street site see H. C. King, *Records and Documents concerning Serjeants' Inn, Fleet Street* (1922).

[6] *Solicitors' Journal*, 1877, p. 314.

[7] Mr. Justice Denman, reluctant to accept his share, handed over this sum to University College Hospital: Sir William Erle gave his share to charity: Sir Montagu Smith gave £500 to the Truro Cathedral Building Fund. See *Solicitors' Journal*, 1877, p. 314: 1878, pp. 365, 374, 386, 542.

[8] Lord Bramwell's letter, accompanied by one from Serjt. Pulling (*The Times*, Nov. 11, 1886), followed an article on the sale of Staple Inn, published on Nov. 3. Further correspondence attacked Bramwell's view.

Cox was accused of cynically saying that his sole regret was that his share had not been larger.

Whether the lines were parallel or not, the example of Serjeants' Inn was followed. In 1884 the Ancients of Staple Inn sold their property for £80,000[1] to Messrs. Trollope, who resold Nos. 11, 12 and 13 to H.M. Commissioners of Works and Buildings for an extension of the Patent Office: the remainder was bought (for £68,000) by the Prudential Assurance Company,[2] as much to preserve the ancient buildings as to exploit a commercial opportunity; the same company also bought Furnival's Inn in 1888.[3]

Clement's Inn had disposed of part of its area in 1868,[4] had let its statue of the Black Boy go for twenty guineas and had sold "at similarly low prices"[5] its odd collection of portraits.[6] After the 1868 sale Mr. Fairfoot, a senior member of the Inn[7] and partner in a legal firm which had occupied chambers there for nearly fifty years, declared that the status of the Inn would remain unaffected; its members, he added, entertained a confident hope that a new and appropriate building would be erected on their important site and that their Society would flourish for many generations.[8] This assurance was falsified in 1884 when Clement's Inn was sold to one of its members for £65,000,[9] or, according to another version, to two of their number for £63,000.[10] Though the details received little publicity, there was no doubt about the sale. The Law Society, anxious to salvage some part of the purchase price for a scheme of legal education, took the opinion of counsel, who advised that the sale was a breach of trust. The opinion was communicated to the Attorney General (Sir Henry James)[11] and to the Inns of Court. Mr. Attorney passed it to the Charity

[1] See E. Williams, *Staple Inn* (1906), cap. 23, and *The Times*, Dec. 9, 1886, where it is stated that each member got about £8000. For the ownership of the Inn and the power to sell (on which T. C. Worsfold expressed doubt, *Staple Inn and its Story*, 3rd edn., 1913, p. 45) see Williams, *Staple Inn*, pp. 136–43.

[2] See *The Times* of Dec. 9, 1884, and Nov. 6 and 27, 1886. The property, when sold to Trollopes, was already mortgaged for £69,000; H.M. Commissioners paid £32,000 to the mortgagees.

[3] See E. Williams, *Early Holborn*, 492. Furnival's Inn in 1817 had only six Ancients and some sixteen juniors: see *Black Books of Lincoln's Inn*, iv, 147.

[4] Diprose, *Some account of the Parish of St. Clement Danes* (1868), p. 198.

[5] *Notes and Queries*, 1884, Mar. 22. A writer to *The Times* (Dec. 10, 1884) suggested, probably too late, that the pictures be given—as were those of Serjeants' Inn—to the National Portrait Gallery. Barnard's Inn offered its portraits to the N.P.G.

[6] For Blackwell's picture and Halsted's curiously assorted set see pp. 104, 126 below. Mr. Justice Powell, we know from Swift, was a jolly figure, but who would have wanted Scroggs?

[7] Admitted in 1857: see p. 308 below.

[8] See Diprose, *ubi sup.*, p. 314.

[9] See letter of L. J. V. Amos to *The Times*, Dec. 20, 1884.

[10] See *The Times*, 1884, Feb. 23, quoting *The Citizen*.

[11] Questioned in the House of Commons in February, the A.G. had said his attention had not then been called to the sale: *Parl. Deb.* (1884) 284, c. 1333–4.

Commissioners who after some delay—they said they were waiting to study the report of the Royal Commission on the City Companies— announced that the property was not subject to any charitable trust. Thus no action resulted, except that a modest sum was set aside for an annual "Clement's Inn Prize". The Law Society had intervened too late; the proceeds of sale could not be followed. A letter in *The Times* referred to the opinion of counsel, "one of our best black-letter lawyers",[1] and complained that the Council of the Law Society and the Council of Legal Education of the four Inns of Court had taken no notice of it: the money provided by the sale of Clement's Inn and Barnard's Inn would have helped to establish the proposed university in London for teaching law. Another correspondent reminded readers that the Royal Commission had declared that the Inns of Chancery were private property and were heavily indebted, and that in *Brown* v. *Dale*[2] Jessel, M.R., had instanced the disposal of Serjeant's Inn and Lyon's Inn, when deciding that voluntary societies or unincorporated gilds of a similar kind could dispose of their property in any way they liked.[3]

Towards the end of 1884 *The Times* stated that the recent sales of Clement's Inn and Staple Inn were engaging the attention of the Local Government Board. Next day a leading article commented on the substantial profits of members; the value of tenements in Clement's Inn had been enhanced by the proximity of the new Law Courts; no help was likely to come from judicial proceedings; "all the common-law judges, many of whom survive, were members of Serjeants' Inn which set a flagrant example of analogous spoliation". The fate of Barnard's Inn can be told more fully from the day-to-day material in its Pension Books. Like some other Inns it paid a low rent; but its landlords, the Dean and Chapter of Lincoln, exacted a substantial fine whenever the lease fell due for renewal. In 1793 the fine was £600, in 1807 and 1835 £1450. Searching for possible economies, the Inn decided in 1841 not to increase the number of its Ancients, and in 1851 to elect no more; the fee to Ancients for attending Pensions was suspended. Meanwhile the liability for repair of ruinous buildings grew more and more heavy. An attempt was made to enfranchise the leasehold, but the landlords refused to sell. In 1877, however, by which time the Dean and Chapter had been replaced by the Ecclesiastical Commissioners, the Inn managed to buy the freehold for

---

[1] Mr. C. I. Elton, M.P.

[2] See *The Times*, Mar. 25, 1878 (the case of the Fullers and Dyers of Newcastle upon Tyne).

[3] See the account in *Annual Reports of the Law Society*, July 1884, p. 19, and July 1885, p. 16, and *Handbook of the Law Society*, 1938, p. 19. See also *The Times*, 1884, Feb. 23 (the sale) and Dec. 22 and 26 (the comment and rejoinder).

£23,000, raising £24,000 on mortgage at 4 per cent to finance the purchase. It then instructed an agent to sell for not less than £50,000. The Principal was made a trustee for sale; he formally declared that he held the fee simple on trust, when directed by the Ancients, to sell and divide the net proceeds between the seven Ancients and the four Companions, two shares to each Ancient and one to each Companion, with all necessary provisions as Counsel should advise. In 1883 it was resolved "that the Society as a Society for social meetings be discontinued and the affairs thereof wound up"; its real property was to be "put in course of management . . . until it could be advantageously converted into money". The plate and pictures were disposed of and the secretaryship abolished. In 1885 it was decided "That the nominal titles of Principal, Ancients and Companions be discontinued as having now for some time ceased to be appropriate to the present position and the persons interested in the trust property". Tweedie, the last Principal, was to manage the Inn's affairs and have his professional charges. The subsequent meetings are recorded as meetings of the trustees and no longer as "Pentions" of the "Grand Company". The Ancients, as *The Times* remarked, were no longer an Honourable Society with perpetual succession; they were share-holders in a tontine.[1]

Purchasers being shy, Barnard's Inn was put up for auction in August 1888, with a reserve price of £45,000. There were no genuine bidders. A Mr. Percy A. Vidler questioned the title. He had tried to focus public opinion by forming an Inns of Chancery Defence Fund, holding meetings and inviting subscriptions. An article in *The Times* on Barnard's Inn and its history had criticised the inactivity of the Charity Commissioners; if they failed to act, the Attorney General should move; if he failed, then the Home Secretary.[2] The trustees took the opinion of Mr. Wolstenholme who advised them to press Vidler for a statement of claim and then move to strike it out, perhaps also proceeding against him for slander. The advice was successfully taken. Vidler's defence was struck out with costs and negotiations for a sale continued. The Prudential Assurance would offer no more than £30,000. The Ancients were willing to let Tweedie, their chairman, take the property for 40,000 guineas, but in 1892 the Mercers' Company bought it for £43,000. The mortgage of £24,000 was paid off with £700 interest; the balance, reduced by sundry charges, allowed a distribution of £2097 15*s.* 5*d.* (two-sevenths) to each of the seven Ancients and of £1048 17*s.* 9*d.* (one-seventh) to each of the three surviving Companions. And at that point Barnard's Inn and its final Pension Book came to an end.

---

[1] *The Times*, Dec. 8, 1884.
[2] *Ibid.*, June 20, 1888.

New Inn and Clifford's Inn remained. The London County Council acquired the former under its Kingsway Improvement project,[1] the sum of £157,500 being fixed in 1901 as compensation. New Inn held its premises under a lease from the Middle Temple which had nearly 150 years still to run. Though there was no direct proof of a charitable trust, the cause of legal education was taken up by the Law Society and it scored a victory. The Attorney General brought an action against G. J. Coldham, Principal of New Inn, and two Ancients, claiming that the Inn's share of the compensation was a charitable or public fund applicable for the purposes of legal education; he asked the judge to settle a scheme. The parties came to terms. Under Mr. Justice Farwell's order the Attorney General got £55,500 for legal education and the Middle Temple £45,500; the Ancients received £26,000 for their interest in their chambers, for which they had paid only a nominal sum. The surviving members of New Inn divided the rest, less the costs of the action.[2]

And now out of Fortescue's ten Inns of Chancery only Clifford's Inn was left. It had slightly modernised its constitution in 1885. Previously the Society had consisted of a Principal, a body of members sometimes called the Principal's Council but more often called the Rules (the Upper Table) and a lower order called Junior Fellows or Kentish Men (the Lower Table). Thenceforth the distinction between the two tables was abolished and the Kentish Men ceased to exist. No new entrant had been admitted after 1877,[3] and in 1899 some members were minded to sell the Society's assets and divide the spoil. There were then sixteen survivors; five were plaintiffs in a Chancery action, asking the Court to say what their rights were and whether the property was affected by any charitable trust. The Court was told that Clifford's Inn was, and always had been, a voluntary Society, making its own rules and regulations about the election or admission of members, their rights and privileges and the management of the Inn's affairs, including the disposition of its property; cases were cited in which the Courts had refused to interfere with a legal Inn's internal government.[4] The defendants were the other eleven members and the Attorney General who argued successfully that the property was held in trust.[5] Later the Inner Temple, claiming that Clifford's Inn was its

---

[1] See 62 & 63 Vict. c. cclxvi. s. 53. See also 60 & 61 Vict. c. ccxl, and the monograph published by the L.C.C. on "The Opening of Kingsway and Aldwych by H.M. the Queen on Wednesday, 18th Oct. 1905",

[2] See the report in *The Times* of July 23, 1902, p. 3; *Solicitors' Journal*, July 1902, p. 661; *Law Journal*, July 1902, p. 383; *Annual Report of the Law Society Council*, July 1903.

[3] Hay-Edwards, *History of Clifford's Inn*, p. 158.

[4] *R.* v. *Gray's Inn* (1780), 1 Doug. 353; *R.* v. *Lincoln's Inn* (1825), 28 R. R. 482; *R.* v. *Barnard's Inn* (1836), 5 Ad. & E. 17.

[5] *Smith* v. *Kerr*, [1900] 2 Ch. 51.

dependency and had for centuries been under its control in all educational matters, applied for leave to intervene and to be represented at all proceedings for settling a scheme for a trust fund arising out of the sale. The Court held that, on the evidence, the Inner Temple had no paramount right to be regarded as in the position of trustees of the fund. It had sent Readers to Clifford's Inn to give lectures and hold moots, a recognised form of legal education down to the beginning of the 19th century; but, since the middle of the century, there had been no attempt at legal education in the Inn.[1] Judicial dicta conceded that some vague authority was vested in the Inn of Court and the judges for control of the Inn of Chancery.[2] What mattered most was that the feoffment of Clifford's Inn by Lord Clifford in 1618 had not only recited its long use as an Inn of Chancery for furthering the study and practice of the common law of England, but had also assured it so to continue.[3] The decision, founded on the facts of the particular case, was in line with public opinion. When Clifford's Inn was sold in 1903 for £100,000 to Willett,[4] some £77,000 was appropriated for legal education.

The Inns of Chancery had established their final emancipation by dissolving themselves without the leave of their Inns of Court; but equity and conscience had intervened to negative the notion of an exclusively private ownership. Medieval disciplines were dead and buried; but something of the medieval heritage had been preserved for germinal fulfilment.

[1] *Smith* v. *Kerr* (No. 2), [1902] 1 Ch. 774.
[2] For example, *per* Littledale, J., in *R.* v. *Allen* (1834), 5 B. & Ad. 989.
[3] See *Law Quarterly Review*, (1901), xvii p. 7, and *Smith* v. *Kerr*, [1900] 2 Ch., at p. 512.
[4] See *Annual Report of the Law Society Council, 1903*, p. 15.

24. NOV: 1714[1]

Clements Inne in the ⎱ Att a pencon held att Clements Inne aforesaid upon
County of Middlesex ⎰ the 24th Day of November 1714 present Mr Joshua
Blackwell principall, Mr Lake, Mr Gregg, Mr
Dovey, Mr Fowler, Mr. Goodman, Mr Gibbons.

For takeing downe the old Hall & pencon Chamber &c and building a New Hall—WHEREAS the Hall pencon Chamber and the Buildings adjoyning to the said Hall and Severall other Chambers & Buildings belonging to this Inne are very old ruinous & decayed & not fitt to be Repaired and there is a necessity to Rebuild the same AND WHEREAS upon a View of the Ground belonging to this Inne Itt is thought convenient with regard to the Scheme of the new intended Buildings to pull the old Hall quite downe & to Build a new Hall in another more convenient place than where itt now stands AND WHEREAS the Ground in the third Court of this Inne whereon the Buildings No. 15. and No. 16. now stand is thought the most convenient & proper place for a new Hall to be built thereon And the said Buildings No. 15 and No. 16. being also very old & much decayed insomuch as that most of the Chambers therein have for some time last past been empty & unoccupied AND WHEREAS Severall of the Gentlemen of this Society & others have lately agreed to advance & lend to this Society the Summe of twelve hundred pounds for the Building of a New Hall & pencon Chamber and to supply other the Occacions of this House IT IS ORDERED by the principall & Antients of this Society That the said old Hall & pencon Chamber and the Chambers & Buildings over the said pencon Chamber And the whole Buildings in the said third Court called No. 15. and No. 16 be forthwith pulled down And that a new hall and pencon Chamber & other Conveniencyes be built where the said Buildings No. 15. and No. 16. now stand. And the principall for the time being with such others of this Society as he shall from time to time call to his Assistance are hereby desired Authorized & Impowered to see the same performed accordingly.

Josh: Blackwell: Pr:
F Gregg
Wm Fowler
Ever^d Goodman
John Gibbons
John Dovey

[1] Paragraphing, spelling, capital letters and (if any) punctuation have been left unaltered in editing the text. The use of italic type indicates that the words so printed appeared in the margin of the manuscript. Square brackets are occasionally used to mark the abbreviation of a familiar formula.

1 DECEMBER 1714

Clements Inn in the ⎰ At a pention held at Clements Inn aforesaid upon
County of Middlesex ⎱ the first day of December one Thousand seaven
hundred and fourteen present Mr Joshua Blackwell
Principal Mr Lake Mr Gregg Mr Dovey Mr
Fowler Mr Goodman Mr Gibbons

*Mr Ambrose Eldridge for Chambers late Mr Richard Lowth's in the first
Court number 2*—Mr Ambrose Eldridge one of the Companions of this
Society having agreed with Mr Richard Lowth one other of the Companions
of the same Society for the purchase of his Chambers one pair of staies in
the first Court number 2. next adjoyning or over against the Chambers of
Mr Edward Curtis one other of the Companions of this Society which
said Chambers were some time Since granted to the said Mr Richard
Lowth for the terme of ninety nine yeares if he so long lived by a lease to
him thereof made by the then Principal & Antients of the said Society
dated the nineteenth day of May in the yeare of our Lord one thousand
Six hundred & eighty three And the said Mr Richard Lowth (at the request of the said Mr Ambrose Eldridge) having now surrendered and
delivered up this said lease to this Society And the said Mr Ambrose
Eldridge now desiring to be admitted to the same Chambers And that
a new lease may be thereof to him made for the terme of his life It is
thereupon ordered that on payment of the sum of four pounds by the said
Mr Ambrose Eldridge for the use of this Society He the said Ambrose
Eldridge shall be admitted to the said Chambers late of the said Mr
Richard Lowth And that a lease thereof shall be to him made for the
terme of ninety nine yeares if he so long lives with the usual Covenants and
provisoes and according to the usual forme & method of Leases made by
this Society

*Mr Rd. Lowth for pencions and Commons &c And his bond delivered
up*—Mr Richard Lowth one of the Companions of this Society being in
arreare for pencions & absent Commons [1] & for taxes [2] paid for him by
the said Society for the Chambers late in his possession amounting in all to

---

[1] The pension (the fixed contribution towards the general expenses of the Society)
was two shillings per term; the charge for absent commons was five shillings per term;
see the cases of Sherratt and John Harris, pp. 19–20 below. It was usual to allow abatement of half the charge for absent commons if the member had not been in town during
the term; no abatement of pension was conceded: see the order of Pension in 1682/3,
p. 240 below.

[2] There is mention elsewhere of the King's tax and the land tax: see pp. 177, 241–2
below and also 7 & 8 Will. III. c. 18 (house duty chargeable on occupiers) and 8 & 9
Will. III. c. 6. s. 5 (duty on barristers, attorneys and solicitors).

the Sum of twelve pounds Seaventeen Shillings And desiring to compound
for his absent Commons And that on payment of what shall remaine due
from him he may have his bond given to this Society delivered up in regard
he hath discontinued the practice of the law & now lives altogether in the
Country It is thereupon ordered that fifty Shillings be abated of his absent
Commons and that on payment of Ten pounds Seaven Shillings for the
use of this Society in discharge of the said pentions absent Commons &
taxes his the said Richard Lowths said bond be accordingly delivered up.

*Mr Wm Purcell for his lease of his Chambers Number 16. in the third
Court purchased of him by this Society*—WHEREAS Mr William Purcell one
of the Companions of this Society some time since contracted for a lease
of his Chambers up one pair of Staires in the Corner Stair case in the third
Court of this Inn Number 16. and paid to Mr Henry Gregson the former
owner thereof & for the exchange of his own life for the said Mr Gregsons
life the sum of one & thirty pounds and accordingly had a lease made by
this Society dated the fifth day of July in the yeare of our Lord one
Thousand Seaven hundred and Eight unto him the said William Purcell
for the terme of ninety nine yeares if he should so long live And the said
Mr William Purcell having (as he affirms) laid out & expended about Nine
pounds ten shillings in the repaires and alterations of the said Chambers
but is willing to accept of the sum of Thirty two pounds five shillings for
his right & Interest in the same Chambers as & for the consideration for
the surrendring and delivering up of his said lease to this Society in order
to a new intended building on the Ground where the said Chambers with
other Chambers are now Standing and being in the said Inn It is therefore
ordered that the principal do pay to the said Mr William Purcell the said
Sum of Thirty two pounds five Shillings. And that on payment thereof
the said Mr William Purcell do and shall accordingly surrender & deliver
up his said Lease of the said Chambers to this Society in order to the said
new intended building And in testimony of this Agreement the said
Mr William Purcell hath signed this order.

Wm Purcell

Clements Inn in the ⎱ At a pention held at Clements Inn aforesaid upon
County of Middlesex ⎰ the sixth day of December one Thousand Seaven
hundred and fourteen present Mr Joshua Blackwell
Principall Mr Gregg Mr Dovey Mr Fowler Mr
Gibbons Mr Fuller Mr Goodman Mr Bagshaw
Mr Knight Mr Denshire

*Security for £1200 at Interest for building a new Hall pention Chamber
&c.*—WHEREAS at a pention held at this Inn the four and twentieth day of

November last past [1] It was ordered by the principall & Antients then present (amongst other things) that the old hall belonging to this Society & the pention Chamber & the Chambers and Buildings over the said pention Chamber and the whole Building in the Court called the third Court of this Inn marked with the numbers or figures 15 & 16 should be forthwith pulled down & that a New Hall & pention Chamber and other Conveniences should be built where the said building number fifteen & Sixteen now Stands And the principall for the time being with such others of this Society as he shall from time to time call to his assistance are thereby desired & authorized and impowered to see the same performed accordingly AND WHEREAS the now Principall and the major part of the Antients of this Society have agreed to borrow & take up at Interest the Sum of one Thousand two hundred pounds to be applyed for the taking down the said old Buildings & for the buildings of a new Hall & pention Chamber & to supply other the occasions of this House in such manner as the present principall or any other principall of the Society for the time being with such others of this Society as such principall shall from time to time call to his assistance shall think fitt & convenient pursuant & according to the said former order of the said four & twentieth day of November last past the repayment of which said Sum of one Thousand two hundred pounds with lawfull Interest for the same iss agreed shall be Secured by a grant or Mortgage of this Inn or Hostell AND WHEREAS the Fee Simple and Inheritance of this Inn or Hostell by Indentures of Lease & release the lease bearing date the ninth and the release the tenth days of June one Thousand Seaven hundred & Eight was by the direction and appointment of the then principall & Antients of this Society granted and conveyed unto the Right Honorable Sir Thomas Parker Knight (now Lord Chiefe Justice of the Court of Kings Bench by the name of Sir Thomas Parker Knight one of her then Majesties Serjeants at Law [2]) and unto Charles Cox Giles Clarke [3] Henry Barwell (since deceased) and Richard Price Esquires and unto W^m. Dixon Gent (therein named) their Heires & assignes In Trust for this Society & the principall and Antients thereof their Successors & Assignes And to be from time to time disposed of in such manner & sort as they the said principall & Antients and their Successors or the major part of them successively should from time to time direct & appoint

---

[1] See p. 1 above.

[2] Parker, called to the Bench at the Inner Temple in 1705, was appointed Lord Chief Justice in 1710 and created Baron Macclesfield in 1716. Lord Chancellor in 1718 and Earl of Macclesfield in 1721, he resigned the seals in 1725; after his impeachment he took no further part in public affairs.

[3] Possibly the Gyles Clark who in 1715 paid the rent of Lyon's Inn and two adjoining tenements, was in arrear for his commons in the Inner Temple in 1717 and died in 1721: see *Inner Temple Records*, IV, 12, 29, 74.

IT IS THEREFORE NOW ORDERED that the said former order of the said four & twentieth day of November last past shall Stand ratifyed & confirmed And the same is hereby ratifyed & confirmed accordingly And for the Securing the repayment of the said one Thousand two hundred pounds with lawfull Interest as aforesaid We the said principall and Antients here present (being the Major part of the Antients of this Society) according to the Direction & Appointment of the said Indenture of Release hereby desire authorize & impower the said Lord Cheife Justice Parker Charles Cox Giles Clarke Richard Price & Wm. Dixon (who are the surviving trustees named in the said Indenture of Lease & release) to make & execute a Mortgage of the said Inn or Hostell and the Chambers buildings & all other appurtenances thereunto belonging unto Lawrence Carter of Lincolns Inn in the County of Middlesex Esquire [1] Edward Horsman of Lincolns Inn aforesaid Esquire [2] & Wm. Fitzherbert of the Inner Temple London Esquire [3] who have agreed to advance & lend the said one Thousand two hundred pounds for the purposes aforesaid redeemable nevertheless upon the repayment of the said one thousand two hundred pounds And the lawfull Interest thereof And for their so doeing this shall be to them a Sufficient warrant & authority And it is further ordered that such Mortgage shall be made & executed in such manner & forme as Counsell shall advise And in further testimony of this our order we have hereunto subscribed our names.

John Dovey	Josh: Blackwell: Pr:
John Knight	F Gregg
Geo. Denshire	Wm Fowler
	Ever^{d} Goodman
	John Gibbons
	Geo. Fuller
	Charles Bagshaw

Mr George Denshire for Absent Commons—Mr George Denshire one of the Antients of this Society being ten shillings in arrear for Absent Commons in two former Terms when he did not come to Town & desiring to Compound for the same It is ordered that on payment of Five shillings for the use of the said Society he be discharged of the said Absent Commons.[4]

[1] Lawrence Carter (1672–1745) was appointed Recorder of Leicester in 1697; M.P. for Leicester, he became King's Serjeant in 1724 and puisne baron of the Court of Exchequer in 1726. His father, Lawrence Carter, was admitted to Clement's Inn in 1668.

[2] Called to the Bar at Lincoln's Inn in 1700: see *Black Books of L.I.*, III, 205.

[3] Proposed for reader to Clement's Inn in 1726: called to the Inner Temple Bench in 1728: see *I.T.R.*, IV, 139, 175.

[4] An entry in 1743 (p. 205 below) states that by immemorial custom Ancients were excused payment of absent commons; Denshire's arrears must have been incurred before he was called up to the Ancients' Table.

Mr Tilden for Pentions & absent Commons—Mr Tilden One of the Companions of this Society being sixteen pounds fifteen shillings in arrear for Pentions & absent Commons ending this last Michaelmas Term And desireing to compound for the absent Commons in Regard he is a housekeeper in Towne & hath not made the least use of his Chambers in this Inn for above nine yeares last past In Consideration whereof It is ordered that he be abated Four pounds twelve shillings six pence of his absent Commons And that on his payment of the remaining twelve pounds two shillings six pence for the use of this Society he be discharged of the said arrears of Pentions & absent Commons.

Clements Inn in the } At a pention held at Clements Inn aforesaid on the
County of Middlesex } tenth day of December one Thousand Seaven hundred and fourteen present Mr Joshua Blackwell principall Mr Dovey Mr Fowler Mr Goodman Mr Gibbons Mr Fuller Mr Knight

Mr Carrow for pencions & absent Commons—Mr Carrow one of the Companions of this Society being Eight pounds ten Shillings in arreare for pencions & absent Commons ending this last Michaelmas Terme and desireing to compound for his absent Commons in regard he seldom or never comes to town above once in a yeare In consideration whereof it is ordered that he be abated fifty Shillings of his absent Commons And that on his payment of the remaining Six pounds for the use of this Society he be discharged of the said arreares of pentions & absent Commons.

Mr John Gibbons for an Assignement for a Life after his own life now in being of his Chambers number 23. in Kelletts Buildings—Mr John Gibbons one of the Antients of this Society having a lease of his Chambers up one pair of Staires in the Buildings called Kelletts Buildings in the Garden Court number 23: already granted to him by this Society for the terme of ninety nine yeares if he shall so long live And desiring to purchase an Assignement thereof for one life after the expiration of his own life now in being It is ordered that on his payment of the Sum of Thirty pounds for the use of this Society an Assignement be accordingly made of the said Chambers to him the said Mr John Gibbons his Executors Administrators and Assignes for one life after his own life now in being with the usuall Covenants and provisoes and according to the usuall forme & method of making & granting of Assignements by this Society.

Mr John Knight for an assignement for a life after his own life now in being of his Chambers Number 20. in the third Court—Mr John Knight one of the Antients of this Society having a lease of the Chambers up one pair

of Staires in the third Court number Twenty already granted to him by this
Society for the terme of Ninety nine yeares if he Shall so long live And
desireing to purchase an Assignement thereof for one life after the Expiration of his own life now in being It is ordered that on his payment of the
sum of Eight & twenty pounds for the use of this Society an Assignement
be accordingly made of the said Chambers to him the said Mr John Knight
his Executors Administrators and Assignes for one life after his own life
now in being with the usuall Covenants and provisoes & according to the
usuall forme & method of making and granting of Assignements by this
Society.

*The Accounts of Mr Brewster late principall from Hillary terme 1712 to
Hillary terme 1713 allowed*—Whereas by an order of pention made the
thirtieth day of November one Thousand seaven hundred & thirteen
Mr Everard Goodman & Mr John Gibbons two of the Antients of this
Society & Mr Richard Purcell & Mr Mathew Evans two of the Companions of the same Society were appointed Auditors of the Accounts of
Mr Samuel Brewster (late principall of this Society and now deceased) And
they having accordingly perused examined & audited the said Accounts
beginning in Hillary terme one Thousand Seaven hundred & twelve untill
Hillary terme one Thousand Seaven hundred & thirteen & certifyed the
same under their hands It appeares thereby that the Severall Sums of
money received by the said Mr Brewster amount in all unto the Sum of
one hundred Seaventy seaven pounds four Shillings & his payments &
disbursements to the Sum of one hundred fifty seaven pounds twelve
Shillings & four pence so that there remaines in the hands of the said
Mr Brewster or in the hands of his Executors or Administrators the Sum of
nineteen pounds Eleven Shillings & Eight pence due to this Society to
ballance the said accounts It is thereupon ordered that the said Accounts
of the said Mr Samuel Brewster so perused examined & audited as aforesaid be allowed & approved of And the same Accounts are hereby
accordingly allowed & approved of as just & true accounts And on payment of the said Nineteen pounds Eleaven Shillings & Eight pence (the
ballance due as aforesaid) to and for the use & benefit of this Society by
the Executors or Administrators of the said Mr Samuel Brewster they the
said Executors or Administrators are hereby acquitted & discharged of &
from the said Accounts.

Josh: Blackwell: Pr:
John Dovey
Ever^d Goodman
John Gibbons
Geo. Fuller
John Knight

Clements Inn in the ⎰ At a pention held at Clements Inn aforesaid the
County of Middlesex ⎱ Seaventeenth day of December one Thousand
Seaven hundred & fourteen present Mr Joshua
Blackwell principall Mr Gregg Mr Dovey Mr
Goodman Mr Gibbon Mr Bagshaw Mr Fuller
Mr Knight

Francis Mundy Esq[e]. & Mr Edward Mundy for the Chambers late Mr Michael Wrightson in the third Court number 17—Mr Michael Wrightson late one of the Antients of this Society [1] having some time since contracted for a Lease of the Chambers up one pair of Staires in the Stair Case marked with the figure or number 17. in the third Court of this Inn with the Cellar belonging to the same for the terme of ninety nine yeares if he so long lived with power for him & his Executors to nominate two other lives after the decease of him the said Michael Wrightson or his leaving this Society as by the Articles or lease thereof made by the then principall & Antients of the said Society bearing date the Eighteenth day of July one Thousand Six hundred eighty five appeares And the said Michael Wrightson having nominated Francis Mundy Esquire & Edward Mundy (being at this time two of the Companions of this Society) to be the lives after his decease to be put into the lease of the said Chambers & Cellar And the said Francis Mundy & Edward Mundy desireing that such lease may be to them made pursuant to the direccion & nomination of the said Michael Wrightson in & by his last will & testament It is thereupon ordered that they the said Francis Mundy & Edward Mundy shall be admitted to the said Chambers & Cellar & that a lease shall be thereof to them made for the terme of ninety nine yeares if they or either of them shall so long live (according to the Agreement in the said Articles or lease to the said Michael Wrightson & according to his nomination & appointment in & by his said last will) with the usuall Covenants & provisoes & according to the usuall forme of leases made by this Society

Mr Henry Dottin Jun[r]. for the lease of his Chambers N[o]. 15 in the 3[d] Court purchased of him by this Society—Whereas Mr Henry Dottin Jun[r]. one of the Companions of this Society some time since contracted for a lease of his Chambers in the First Stair Case in the third Court on the Right hand in the said Staire case number fifteen a ground Chamber formerly in the occupation of George Yeal Gent for the Sum of Six and twenty pounds & accordingly had a lease thereof made by this Society dated the eight & twentieth day of May one thousand six hundred & ninety one unto him the said Mr Dottin for the terme of ninety nine yeares

---

[1] Wrightson, admitted to the Inn in 1657, became Principal on January 23, 34 Car. II (1682/3): see p. 260 below.

if he should so long live since which time the said Mr Dottin affirms that
he hath at severall times laid out & expended Several sums of money in
the repairs & alterations of the said Chambers & insists on the sum of Six
and twenty pounds for his right & Interest in the same Chambers as & for
the consideration for his surrendring and delivering up of his said lease to
this Society in order to a new intended building on the ground whereas the
said Chambers (with other Chambers) are now standing & being in the
said Inn It is thereupon ordered that the principall do pay to the said
Mr Henry Dottin the said Sum of Six & twenty pounds And that on
payment thereof the said Mr Henry Dottin do and shall accordingly surrender and deliver up his said lease of his said Chambers to this Society
in order to the said new intended building And in testimony of this
Agreement the said Mr Henry Dottin hath signed this order.

Hen. Dottin Jun.ʳ

Clements Inn in the   At a pention held at Clements Inn aforesaid on
County of Middlesex   the fourteenth day of February in the year of our
Lord One Thousand Seaven hundred & fourteen[1]
present Mr Joshua Blackwell principall Mr Dovey
Mr Goodman Mr Gibbons Mr Knight Mr Denshire

*Mr George Denshire for his Lease of his Chambers number 14: purchased
of him by this Society*—Whereas Mr George Denshire one of the Antients
of this Society some time since agreed with the said Society for a Lease of
his Chambers in the Back Buildings in the Middle Court of this Inn
up one pair of Staires Number 14: & paid to the then principall for the use
of this Society the sum of three and twenty pounds and accordingly had
A Lease thereof to him made by this Society dated the twentieth day of
February in the yeare of our Lord One thousand seaven hundred and two
for the term of Ninety nine years if the said Mr George Denshire should so
long live And whereas it also appeares that the said Mr Denshire hath
laid out and expended above the sum of sixteen pounds more than the
said three and twenty pounds in the wainscotting repairing and making
other alteracions in the said Chambers Yet nevertheless for the Encouragement of the New intended Building on the ground where the said Chambers
with other Chambers are or lately were standing and being in the said Inn
is willing to accept of the said Sum of three and twenty pounds for his
Right and Interest in the same Chambers as and for the Consideration for
his surrendring & delivering up of his said Lease to this Society in order
to the said New intended Building It is thereupon ordered that the

---

[1] Until 1752, when it began on January 1st, the English year began on March 25 (the
Feast of the Annunciation): see the Calendar (New Style) Act, 1751 (24 Geo. II. c. 23).

c*

principall do pay to the said Mr Denshire the said sum of three & twenty pounds And that on payment thereof the said Mr George Denshire do & shall accordingly surrender & deliver up his said Lease of the said Chamber to this Society in Order to the said New intended Building And in Testimoney of this Agreement the said Mr George Denshire hath signed this Order

Geo. Denshire

Mr John Woldish for pencions & Commons & Commons & his Bond delivered up—v. fo. 15.[1]*—*Mr John Woldish one of the Companions of this Society being in Arrear for pencions & absent Commons the sum of Eight pounds seaventeen shillings ending this last Hillary Term & desiring to have his Bond given to this Society delivered up in regard he hath discontinued the practice of the Law & now lives altogether in the Country It is thereupon Ordered that on his payment of the said sum of Eight pounds seaventeen shillings for the use of this society in discharge of the pencions and Absent Commons his said Bond be delivered up.

*Mr Tho Clerk for pencions absent Commons and Taxes—*Mr Tho Clerk One of the Companions of this Society being in Arrear for pencions and Absent Commons Ending this last Hillary Term and for taxes paid for him by the said Society for the Chambers in his possession in all amounting to the sum of fifteen pounds fifteen shillings which together with ten pounds seaventeen shillings and tenpence paid by this Society for the Charges of Suit against him on his Bond given to the said Society amounts to the Sum of Six and twenty pounds twelve Shillings & tenpence Whereof it Appeares that there hath been paid to Mr Brewster the late principall the sum of twenty pounds So that there remains due from the said Mr Clerk the sum of Six pounds twelve Shillings and tenpence And he desiring to Compound for his Absent Commons in regard he hath of late very seldom Come to Town in Consideracion whereof it is ordered that the sum of four pounds ten shillings & tenpence be abated him of his Absent Commons & that on payment of the remaining forty two shillings for the use of this Society he be discharged of the said Arrears of pencions & absent Commons & Taxes.

*Mr Gravenor Dyson for pencions & Commons & his Bond delivered up—*Mr Gravenor Dyson one of the Companions of this Society being in Arrear for pentions & absent Commons ending this last Hillary Term the sum of fourteen shillings And desireing to have his Bond given to this Society delivered up In regard he hath discontinued the practice of the Law And now lives altogether in the Countrey It is thereupon ordered that on his payment of the said fourteen shillings for the use of this Society

---

[1] The record to which reference is made here (and at p. 16 below) has not been traced.

in discharge of the said pencions & absent Commons his **Bond** be delivered up.

Clements Inn in the ⎱ At a Pention held at Clements Inn aforesaid on
County of Middlesex ⎰ the one and Twentyeth Day of February in the Yeare of our Lord one Thousand Seaven hundred and Fourteen present **Mr Joshua Blackwell Principall** Mr Dovey Mr Fowler Mr Goodman Mr Gibbons Mr Knight Mr Denshire.

The Gate next New Inn—To take down the wall to open the gate— WHEREAS by an order made at a pention held on Monday the thirtyeth Day of November one Thousand seaven hundred and Thirteen [1] thereby Setting forth that the Principall and Antients of New Inn had Some time then past Sett up a Doore in the Fence Wall Between Clements Inn and New Inn Gardens and Did make use of the Same as A Common high Way in all occasions into and through Clements Inn aforesaid And pretended to keep the Said Doore locked and to open the Same at theire Wills and Pleasures without leave or licence from the principall and Antients of Clements Inn for theire so doeing by which means in process of time the Society of New Inn might Clayme a Right to the Same as a Common highway Therefore to prevent the like for the future It was ordered that in Case the said principall and Antients of New Inn should refuse or Neglect to deliver A Key of the said Doore to the principall and Antients of Clements Inn on or before the first Day of January then next So as that the said Doore might be at the Command and use of the Society of Clements Inn as well as the said Society of New Inn And that in Case the said principall and Antients of New Inn should refuse or Neglect to signe a proper writeing under their hands Signifying that the said Doore and the way used as aforesaid was only by the leave and Sufferance of the Society of Clements Inn In Default of either it was ordered that A Wall or some other sufficient Fence as the principall of Clements Inn should direct should be made and sett up for the hindrance and Stopping of the said Way or Passage And the Principall or Treasurer and Antients of New Inn refusing or neglecting to Comply with what was Insisted on by the said order The principall of this Society did take care to have a fence & wall sett up to hinder the said Way or passage which still continues And Whereas the Treasurer and Antients of New Inn being desireous to have the said Way or passage open have lately Complyed with the said order and by Writeing Dated the Eighteenth Day of this Instant February Signed by Mr Phillip Hodges (Treasurer of the said Inn) for himselfe and the rest of

---

[1] See p. 244 below.

the Antients these have Acknowledged and declared that the passage out of New Inn into Clements Inn is not of right but by permission of the Society of Clements Inn being as is Conceived for the Conveniency of both Societys And have agreed that this Society shall have a Key to the gate between the said houses And have also agreed that the boards lately Erected against some of the Windowes of this Inn shall be taken Downe and that the said Windowes shall not for the future be darkened by the Society of New Inn so long as the said Passage shall continue open and Free And have accordingly Delivered a Key of the said Gate for the Use and Service of this Society And the Principall and Antients of this Society by a Writeing Dated the Nineteenth Day of this Instant February signed by the Principall for himselfe and the said Antients have allso acknowledged and Declared that the Passage out of Clements Inn Into New Inn is not of right but by permission of the Society of New Inn being as is Conceived for the Conveniency of both Societys IT IS THEREFORE ORDERED that the said Fence and Wall so sett up to hinder the said way or passage be taken downe and carryed away To the end the said gateway and passage may be free and open for the Conveniency of both Societys according to the agreements and acknowledgments aforesaid.

Mr George Denshire for a Lease of one of the Chambers Number five Built by Mr Laws—Mr George Denshire one of the Antients of this Society haveing agreed with Mr John Lawes for the Chambers up one paire of Staires on the right hand in the Staire Case number five in the first Court in this Inn with the End Cellar fronting the said Court (being part of the building lately Erected by the said Mr Lawes) for the Terme of yeares and Interrest of the said Mr Lawes in the said Chambers and Cellar for the Sum of one hundred and twenty pounds Chargeable with the yearly payment of Twenty Shillings Ground rent to this Society being part of the ground rent of Six pounds per Annum reserved and payable out of and for the said whole building according to the Articles made and entered into by the said Mr Lawes with this Society And the said Mr Lawes desireing that the said Mr Denshire may accordingly have a Lease made to him of the said Chambers and Celler for the Terme of Sixty yeares from the Twenty Fifth Day of March next being the terme of yeares which the said Mr Lawes then hath in the same by the said Articles It is ordered that in pursuance to and in part of performance of the said Articles a Lease be accordingly thereof made to the said Mr Denshire by this Society with proper Covenants and with the usual covenants and provisoes according to the usuall forme and method of Leases granted by this Society.

Mr Francis Jackson for a Lease of one other of the Chambers Number five built by Mr Lawes—Mr Francis Jackson one of the Companions of this Society having also agreed with the said Mr Lawes for the ground

Chambers on the Right Hand in the same Staire Case Number five with the end Cellar under the said Ground Chambers fronting the same first Court for the sum of one hundred and Twelve pounds Ten Shillings and Chargeable with the like yearly payment of Twenty Shillings ground rent to this Society being further part of the said ground rent of six pounds per Annum and the said Mr Lawes allso desireing the said Mr Jackson may have a Lease made to him of the same Ground Chambers and Celler for the like terme of sixty yeares It is ordered that in further part of performance of the said Articles a Lease be accordingly thereof made to the said Mr Jackson with the same Covenants and provisoes and according to the same forme and method with the lease to be made to Mr Denshire.

Mr Degory King for A Lease of one other of the Chambers Number five built by Mr Lawes—Mr Degory King one of the Companions of this Society having allso agreed with the said Mr Lawes for the Chambers up one paire of Stairs on the left hand in the same Staire Case Number five with the Celler thereto belonging for the sum of one hundred and Twenty pounds and Chargeable with the like yearly payment of Twenty Shillings ground rent to the Society being further part of the said Ground rent of six pounds per Annum and the said Mr Lawes allso desireing the said Mr King may have a Lease made to him of the same Chambers and Celler for the like Terme of sixty yeares It is ordered that in further part of performance of the said Articles a Lease be accordingly thereof made to the said Mr King with the same Covenant and provisoes and according to the same forme and method with the Lease to be made to Mr Denshire.

Mr Joseph Dudbridge for one of the Chambers Number foure built by Mr Lawes—Mr Joseph Dudbridge one of the Companions of this Society having agreed with the said Mr Lawes for the Chambers up two paires of Stairs in the Staire Case Number foure in the first Court in this Inn with the Celler belonging to the same (being other part of the building lately erected by the said Mr Lawes) for the sum of fifty pounds for the like terme of sixty yeares at a pepper Corne rent And the said Mr Lawes desireing that the said Mr Dudbridge may have a Lease made to him of the same Chambers and Celler for the said Terme of sixty yeares It is ordered that in further part of performance of the said Articles a Lease be accordingly thereof made to the said Mr Dudbridge with the same Covenants and provisoes and according to the same forme and method with the Lease to be made to Mr Denshire except as to the yearly rent reserved.

Mr Humphrey Pelham for the Chambers late Mr Thomas Clerke Number Twelve—Mr Humphrey Pelham one of the Companions of this Society haveing agreed with Mr Thomas Clarke one other of the Companions of the same Society for the purchase of his Chambers up one paire of Staires in the Corner Staire Case Number Twelve in the Brick building there which Chambers were sometime since granted to the said Mr Clarke for ninety nine yeares if he should so long live by a Lease to him thereof made by the then Principall and Antients of this Society and the said Mr. Clarke at the Request of Mr. Pelham haveing now Surrendered and delivered up his said Lease to this Society And Mr Pelham Desireing to be Admitted to the said Chambers It is thereupon ordered that on payment of the Sum of Six pounds Nine shillings by the said Mr Pelham for the use of this Society he the said Mr Humphrey Pelham shall be admitted to the said Chambers and that a Lease thereof shall be to him made for the Terme of Ninety Nine Yeares if he so long live with the usuall Covenants and provisoes and according to the usuall forme and method of Leases made by this Society.

Clements Inn pews. The Seats in St Clements Church to be kept free from Strangers &c.—Whereas Complaint is made that the Seats or Pews belonging to this house in the Church of Saint Clements Danes are very often so Crowded with others not being admitted of this Society that the Antients and Companions of this house are frequently disappointed of roome in the said Seats or pews. To prevent the like for the future It is ordered that such Servant or Servants of this house as shall from time to time Keep the Doores of the said Seates or pews shall the first Sunday in Every Terme untill and for the third Sunday after Every Term take care that no person whatsoever be lett into the front Seate or pew but the Principall Antients and Companions of this House and such other one or more Gentleman as the Principall and such one other Gentleman (only and no more) as any Antient or Companion of this house shall bring with him into the said Seat or pew and that none be lett into the Seat or pew next behind the said fronting seate or pew but the Companions of this House and the Clerks of the said principall Antients and Companions And at all other times Such Care shall be taken that the principall Antients and Companions of this house shall not be dissappoynted of Roome in the said Seats or pews.

Clements Inn in the ⎱ At a pention held at Clements Inn aforesaid on
County of Middlesex ⎰ Friday the five & twentieth day of February in the
year of Our Lord One thousand seaven hundred & fourteen present Mr Joshua Blackwell principall Mr Lake Mr Pryor Mr Dovey Mr Goodman Mr Fuller Mr Bagshaw Mr Knight Mr Denshire

Mr Richard Purcell abated ten shillings of Rent—Mr Richard Purcell one of the Companions of this House owing fifty shillings for A year's Rent for the Late Ground Chamber Number 16: Late in his tenure due to this Society this last Hillary Term & craving some Abatement in Consideracion of the Disturbance he has had in the said Chamber by the Workmen being at work near the said Chamber It is ordered that ten shillings be abated out of the said years Rent & that on payment of forty shillings for the Use of this Society he be discharged therefrom.

Auditors for the principall's Accounts beginning in Hillary Term 1713 until Hillary Term 1714—It is ordered that Mr John Dovey & Mr John Knight two of the Antients of this Society & Mr John Penny & Mr William Purcell two of the Companions of this Society shall Examine State & Audit the Accounts of the principall of this Society beginning in Hillary Term One thousand Seaven hundred & thirteen untill Hillary term One thousand seaven hundred & fourteen And that they make their Certificate or Report of the said Accounts the first pention after Easter Term next.

Clements Inn in the ⎱ At a pention held at Clement's Inn aforesaid on
County of Middlesex ⎰ Wednesday the third Day of March in the Year of Our Lord One thousand Seaven hundred & fourteen present Mr Joshua Blackwell principall Mr Lake Mr Dovey Mr Goodman Mr Fuller Mr Pryor Mr Bagshaw Mr Knight

Bonds to be abstracted into the severall Counties and enquired into—Ordered that the Severall Bonds on which their remains any Arrears due to this Society be Abstracted into Several Abstracts each County by itself in order to be examined into by such of the Antients or Companions of this Society who live in or near each Respective County And that such Antients & Companions be desired to take Care therein and to Certify and make their Report as soon as Conveniently may be of the Circumstances of the principall persons bound and of the Sureties in Each Bond in order to the Recovery of the said Arrears.

Mr Lewis Allen for A Lease of one other of the Chambers Number 5 built by Mr Lawes—Mr Lewis Allen One of the Companions of this Society having agreed with Mr John Lawes for the Chambers up two pair of Stairs on the Right hand in the Stair Case Number 5 in the first Court in this Inn with the End Cellar under the Backrooms for the Sum of One hundred & twelve pounds ten Shillings and Chargeable with the yearly payment of twenty Shillings Ground Rent to this Society being further part of the Ground Rent of Six pounds per Annum & the said Mr Lawes desiring the said Mr Allen may have A Lease made to him of the same Chambers & Cellar for the term of Sixty years from the five and twentieth of March next being the Term of years which the said Mr Lawes then hath in the same by his Articles with this Society It is Ordered that in further part of performance of the said Articles A Lease be Accordingly thereof made to the said Mr Allen with the same Covenants and provisoes and according to the same form and Method with the Lease made to Mr Denshire.

Clements Inn in the } At a pencion held at Clement's Inn aforesaid on
County of Middlesex } Monday the thirtieth day of May in the year of Our Lord One thousand Seaven hundred & Fifteen present Mr Joshua Blackwell principall Mr Dovey Mr Goodman Mr Gibbons Mr Bagshaw Mr Fuller Mr Knight Mr Fowler.

Pencions for Easter Term 1715 not to be collected nor any Companion Cast into Commons or Trin. Term following—Forasmuch as the Old Hall where the principall Antients & Companions of this Society used to meet in Commons is now become useless & the new Intended Hall is not yet built & finished so that no Commons could be kept or held this present Easter Term nor can any Commons be held or kept in or for Trinity term next It is therefore Ordered that no Pencion Roll shall be made out or collected for the present Easter term Nor shall any Companion of this Society be Cast into Commons either in this Term or in Trinity Term next.[1]

Mr John Woldish for pencions & Commons & Bond delivered up—v. *fo. 8.*[2]—Mr John Woldish one of the Companions of this Society being in Arrear for pentions and absent Commons Ending in Hillary Term Last the sum of Eight pounds Seaventeen Shillings And desiring to have the Bond by him & his Surety made to this Society delivered up In Regard he hath discontinued the practice of the law and now lives altogether in the Countrey It is thereupon Ordered that on his payment of the said Sum of Eight pounds Seaventeen Shillings for the use of this Society in discharge of the said pencions & absent Commons his Bond be accordingly delivered up to him to be cancelled.

Clement's Inn in the } At a pention held at Clement's Inn aforesaid on
County of Middlesex } Wednesday the first day of June in the yeare of our Lord One thousand Seaven hundred & Fifteen present Mr Blackwell principall Mr Fowler Mr Dovey Mr Goodman Mr Gibbons Mr Fuller.

Bills demanded by the House Carpenter & Bricklayer to be examined & reported next Term—Ordered that the Bills demanded by Mr Dixon Carpenter & Mr Gery Bricklayer to be due from this Society be examined

---

[1] The period was extended in February 1715/16 and July 1716: see pp. 23, 27 below.
[2] See note to p. 10 above.

by Mr Gibbons & Mr Fuller that they Call to their Assistance such other persons as they shall think Convenient in Order to have what Satisfaccion can be had of the severall particulars in the said Bills contained And that Mr Gibbons & Mr Fuller do settle and adjust the said Bills & examine what hath been paid in part of either of the said Bills And what now remains due to the said Mr Dixon and Mr Gery And that Mr Gibbon & Mr Fuller do Certifie and make their Report hereof at the First pencion in or after Trinity Term next in Order to have the said Bills fully discharged and paid.

Mr Callowe's Bill referred to be examined and Adjusted—Ordered that the Bill of Law Charges &c by Mr Thomas Callowe demanded to be due from this Society be referred to Mr Lake & Mr Dovey to be by them examined & adjusted And that they do certify & make their Report what appears to them to be due on the said Bill at the First Pention in or after Trinity term next in Order to have the said Bill fully discharged and paid.

Clements Inn in the ⎫ At a pention held at Clements Inn aforesaid on
County of Middlesex ⎬ Fryday the Eighth day of July in the year of our
Lord one Thousand seaven hundred and fifteen present Mr Joshua Blackwell principal Mr Dovey Mr Fowler Mr Goodman Mr Gibbons Mr Fuller Mr Knight Mr Denshire

Mr Carr Brackenbury for the Chambers late of Mr Power & Mr Taylor Number 24 in Kelletts Buildings—Mr Carr Brackenbury one of the Companions of this Society desiring to purchase a lease for his life of the Chambers in Kelletts Buildings in the Second Stair case N.º 24. up one pair of Stairs next to New Inn late in possession of Mr Power deceased then one of the Antients of this Society & afterwards in possession of Mr Taylor deceased then one of the Companions of the same Society as also to purchase an Assignement thereof for one other life after the Expiration of his own life It is ordered that on his payment of the sum of one hundred and thirty pounds to the principall for the use of this Society a lease and an assignement be accordingly made & granted of the said Chambers to him the said Mr Carr Brackenbury his Executors Administrators & Assignes with the usual Covenants & provisoes & according to the usual form & method of making & granting leases & assignements by this Society.

Mr Lamplugh to have the pailes lately taken away from his Chambers in the first Court—Mr Lamplugh one of the Companions of this Society making Complaint that the pailes sometime since sett up for the preservation of his Chambers being ground Chambers in the first Court N.º 3.

were taken away on account of the new Building thereto next adjoyning And that the same was a prejudice to his said Chambers it is ordered that for a recompense for the said prejudice the said Mr Lamplugh shall & may have & take to his own use the said pailes with the posts thereto belonging & sell & dispose of them without any account to be thereof given to this Society.

Mr Foster Rector of St Clements & Mr Bell & Mr Rogers Lecturers there—Upon examination of what hath formerly been given to the Rector & Lecturers of St Clements Church as a voluntary & free gift from this Society nothing of legal right being due to them It is ordered that the principal do now give to Mr Foster the present Rector as a voluntary and free gift as aforesaid five Guineas & to Mr Bell & to Mr Rogers what he shall think fitt not exceeding two guineas in any one year.

Mr John Haynes for pencions & absent Commons & his Bond delivered up—Mr John Haynes deceased late one of the Companions of this Society being charged to be considerably in arrear for pencions & absent Commons but it appearing that he dyed in Trinity term one Thousand seaven hundred and tenn at which time there were no more than four pounds fourteen shillings due from him And it being prayed on behalfe of his Executors that some abatement be made for the absent Commons It is ordered that on payment of four & twenty shillings for pencions & two pounds fifteen shillings for absent Commons in all being three pounds nineteen shillings for the use of this Society the said arrears be discharged & that the bond from Mr Haynes be delivered up to his Executors.

Mr Fletcher for pencions & absent Commons and his Bond delivered up— Mr Fletcher one of the Companions of this Society being in arreare for pencions & absent Commons ending in Hillary term last the Sum of Eight pounds Seaventeen Shillings & desiring to have the bond by him given to this Society delivered up in regard he hath discontinued the practice of the law & now lives altogether in the Country It is therefore ordered that on his payment of the said sum of Eight pounds Seaventeen Shillings for the use of this Society in discharge of the said pencions & absent Commons his bond be delivered up.

Mr Cooper for absent Commons & his bond delivered up—Mr Nicholas Cooper deceased late one of the Companions of this Society being ten Shillings in arrear for absent Commons ending in Hillary term one thousand seaven hundred & twelve & his Executors desiring to compound for the same & to have his bond delivered up It is ordered that on the payment of Seaven shillings & six pence for the use of this Society he be discharged of the said arreare & that the bond be accordingly delivered up.

Mr Innys Sen! for absent Commons—Mr Innys Sen! one of the Companions of this Society being five & thirty shillings in arrear for absent

Commons ending in Michaelmas term last & desiring to compound for the same & in regard he was not in town in any of the terms he is charged for absent Commons It is ordered that on his payment of twenty Shillings for the use of this Society he be discharged of the said arreare of absent Commons.

Clements Inn in the County of Middlesex { At a pention held at Clements Inn aforesaid on Fryday the fifteenth day of July in the year of Our Lord one Thousand Seaven hundred & fifteen present Mr Blackwell principal Mr Pryor Mr Dovey Mr Fowler Mr Goodman Mr Gibbons Mr Fuller Mr Knight

Mr John White for pencions and absent Commons—Mr John White one of the Companions of this Society being in arrear twelve Shillings for pencions and forty Shillings for absent Commons ending in Hillary term last & desiring to compound for the absent Commons in regard he was not in town in some of the terms he is charged with It is ordered that he be abated fifteen shillings of his absent Commons And that on payment of thirty seaven Shillings for the use of this Society he be discharged of the said arrear of pencions & absent Commons.

Mr Slack for pencions & Rent of his Chambers & his bond delivered up— Mr Slack now deceased late one of the Companions of this Society owing two Shillings for a pencion & eleaven pounds for rent of his Chambers for two yeares & three quarters ending at Michaelmas one Thousand six hundred Ninety six And it being alledged on behalf of his Executors that he dyed leaving little or no assetts & therefore his Executors desired an abatement of the said demands being willing to pay some part of the said arrears & to have his bond delivered up rather than to have any Contest at law with the Society It is ordered that on payment of the two shillings for the pencion & five pounds ten Shillings for rent for the use of the Society his Executors be discharged of the said arrears & that his bond be delivered up

Mr Sherratt for pencions & taxes paid for him by the Society & his bond delivered up—Mr Sherratt now deceased one of the Companions of this Society owing two shillings for a pencion and being charged with Sixteen Shillings for the tax of his Chambers for the yeare one Thousand seaven hundred and ten paid for him by this Society And it appearing that he dyed in November one Thousand Seaven hundred and ten It is ordered that four Shillings of the taxes be abated and that on payment of the two shillings for the pencion & twelve Shillings for the taxes his Executors be discharged therefrom & that his bond be delivered up to his Executors.

Mr John Harris Senr for absent Commons—Mr John Harris Senr one of the Companions of this Society being charged five Shillings for absent Commons in Hillary term one Thousand Seaven hundred and thirteen And it appearing he was not in town in that terme It is ordered that on payment of two Shillings & six pence for the use of this Society he be discharged of the said absent Commons.

Clements Inn in the County of Middlesex ⎱ At a pencion held at Clements Inn aforesaid on Fryday the two and twentieth day of July in the yeare of our Lord one Thousand seaven hundred & fifteen present Mr Blackwell principal Mr Dovey Mr Fowler Mr Goodman Mr Gibbons Mr Fuller Mr Knight

Mr Holden for pencions & absent Commons & his bond delivered up— Mr Holden one of the Companions of this Society being three pounds in arrear for pencions and nine pounds five Shillings for absent Commons ending in Hillary terme last & desiring to compound for the same & to have his bond delivered up in regard he has for some time discontinued the practice of the law & is reduced to mean circumstances It is therefore ordered that on his payment of five pounds for the use of this Society he be discharged of the said arrears of pencions & absent Commons and that his bond be thereupon delivered up.

Mr John Jeffery for pencions & absent Commons & his bond to be delivered up—Mr John Jefferys one of the Companions of this Society being Eight pounds Six Shillings in arrear for pencions & Seven & twenty pounds five Shillings for absent Commons ending in Trinity terme one Thousand seaven hundred and fourteen And it appearing that he has for many yeares been an officer in the Customes & altogether left off the practice of the law And that for some yeares past there hath not any demand been made of any arreares due to this Society nor was he apprehensive that any duties would become due from him from the time he left off his practice of the law And desiring that the premisses may be taken into consideration It is therefore ordered that the principal do compound with the said Mr Jefferys for the said pencions & absent Commons for such sum of money as he shall think fitt and that on payment thereof for the use of this Society the said Mr Jefferys be discharged of all arrears of pencions and absent Commons & his bond be therefore delivered up.

Mr Thomas Fowke for the Chambers late Mr Wm Dixon—Mr Thomas Fowke one of the Companions of this Society having agreed with Mr William Dixon one other of the Companions of the same Society for the purchase of his two Chambers up two pair of Stairs in the Stair case N? 17. in the brick Buildings in the third Court with the Garrett forwards up three pair of Stairs in the same Stair Case over one of the said two Chambers which said two Chambers and garrett the said Mr Dixon held to him & his Assignes by two several leases from this Society for two several terms of Ninety nine years determinable on the death of the said Mr Dixon who at the request of Mr Fowke hath now surrendered and delivered up the said leases to this Society And Mr Fowke desiring to be admitted to the said Chambers and Garrett It is ordered that on payment of the sum of Eight pounds for the use of this Society he the said Mr Fowke be admitted to the said Chambers and Garrett & that a lease thereof shall be to him made for ninety nine years if he shall so long live with the usual Covenants and provisoes and according to the form of leases made by this Society.

Mr Bransby & Mr Townrow for their Chambers late number 14 purchased of them by this Society—Whereas Mr Charles Bransby & Mr Samuel Townrow two of the Companions of this Society on the Sixteenth day of February one Thousand Seaven hundred and eight did agree with the said Society each of them for a lease of the moyety or halfe part of the Chamber & one whole Study with the appurtenances in the brick buildings in the Middle Court of Clements Inn aforesaid up two pair of Stairs at the end of the then entry and then marked with the figure or number 14. over the Chamber there of George Denshire gent & each of them then paid to the then principal for the use of this Society the sums of twelve pounds ten Shillings & twelve pounds ten Shillings in all amounting to five & twenty pounds & accordingly each of them had a lease to them thereof at that time respectively made by this Society for ninety nine years determinable on their respective deaths Since which time the said Mr Bransby & Mr Townrow affirm that they have laid our several sums of money in the repaires and alterations of the said Chamber & Studys and insist on the sum of Thirty two pounds five shillings for their respective rights & Interests in the same Chamber & Studys with the appurtenances as and for the consideration for their surrendring & delivering up of their said several & respective Leases to this Society in order to the Building on the Ground in the said Inn whereon the said Chamber & Studys (with other Chambers) did formerly stand It is thereupon ordered that the principall do pay to each of them the said Mr Bransby & Mr Townrow the Several sums of Sixteen pounds two Shillings and Six pence and Sixteen pounds two Shillings and Sixpence amounting in the whole to the said Sum of Thirty two pounds five Shillings And that on payment thereof the said Mr Bransby & Mr Townrow do and shall accordingly surrender & deliver up their said two several & respective bases of the said Chamber & Studys with the appurtenances to this Society in order to the said new intended building & in testimony of this Agreement the said Mr Bransby & Mr Townrow have signed this order

Charles Bransby   Sam. Townrow

Pavement in the Garden Court & the next Court thro' the passage beyond the new Hall—It is ordered that the way or passage in the Garden Court from Clare Markett Gate to the passage under the principalls Chambers shall be forthwith paved & that two yards wide in the middle shall be paved with broade flaggs the same with the said passage under the principals Chambers & the rest of it with pebble Stones & that the rest of the pavement in the Court where the Hall is building shall alsoe be finished from the place where the pavers left off quite through the new passage into the next Court & that the said passage be paved with broad flaggs in the same manner with the passage under the principals Chambers & in like manner that the Court from the said new passage to the foregate be paved with flaggs of a Convenient breadth and the rest of it with pebble Stones so far as Mr Lawe's building extends.

Clements Inn in the ⎱ At a pention held at Clements Inn aforesaid on
County of Middlesex ⎰ Fryday the nine & twentieth day of July one Thousand seaven hundred and fifteen present Mr Blackwell Principal Mr Dovey Mr Goodman Mr Gibbons Mr Fuller Mr Knight.

Mr Remfry Gartrell for pentions & absent Commons & his bond delivered up—Mr Remfry Gartrell now deceased late one of the Companions of this Society owing nine and forty Shillings for pencions and Eight pounds ten shillings for absent Commons ending in Trinity term one Thousand Six hundred Eighty eight soon after which time he dyed (as is affirmed) insolvent & it being desired by his Sureties that a moderate Composition may be made for the said pencions and absent Commons in regard it must be paid by the Sureties of whom no demand was made till of late It is therefore ordered that on payment of five pounds the same shall be in full of the said pencions & Commons and that thereupon the said Mr Gartrell's bond be delivered up.

Mr Dixon for pentions and absent Commons and his bond delivered up— Mr Dixon one of the Companions of this Society being in arrear twenty Shillings for pentions and three pounds five Shillings for absent Commons & desiring to Compound for the same and that his bond may be delivered up in regard he hath for some time been admitted of the Society of Lincolns Inn and hath now disposed of his Chambers in this House to Mr Fowke one other of the Companions of this Society It is thereupon ordered that on Mr Dixon's payment of twenty Shillings for pencions & two & twenty Shillings & six pence for absent Commons the same be in full discharge thereof And that thereupon his bond be delivered up.

Clements Inn in the ⎱ At a Pention held at Clements Inn aforesaid on
County of Middlesex ⎰ Wednesday the fifteenth day of February in the year of our Lord one Thousand Seaven hundred & fifteen present Mr Blackwell Principal Mr Gregg Mr Dovey Mr Fowler Mr Goodman Mr Gibbons Mr Knight Mr Denshire

Pentions & Commons for Michaelmas & Hillary Terms 1715 remitted &c—Forasmuch as the Hall lately built and intended for the use and Service of the Principall Antients and Companions of this Society to meet in Commons is not yet finished and compleated so as to keep Commons therein It is therefore ordered that no pentions Roll or Rolls shall be made out or collected for Michaelmas and Hillary terms last nor shall any Companion of this Society be cast into Commons in or for both or either of the said terms.[1]

Clements Inn in the ⎱ At a pention held at Clements Inn aforesaid on
County of Middlesex ⎰ Fryday the four & twentieth day of February in the year of our Lord one Thousand Seaven hundred & fifteen present Mr Blackwell principal Mr Dovey Mr Fowler Mr Goodman Mr Gibbons Mr Fuller Mr Knight Mr Denshire

Mr Thomas Humphreys for a Lease of the Chambers number 3. for 6 years—Mr Thomas Humphreys one of the Companions of this Society desiring a lease of the Chambers Number 3. up one pair of Stairs late Mr Traytons for Six years from Ladyday next at such rent as shall be thought reasonable & that the Chambers may be put into repair & made fit for use at the Costs & Charges of the house It is ordered accordingly & that he shall pay twelve pounds per Annum rent for the same payable quarterly.

Mr Sturgeon Fisk & Mr Reeve his surety for pencions & absent Commons & bond to be delivered up—Mr Sturgeon Fisk deceased formerly one of the Companions of this Society being Six pounds nineteen Shillings in arrear for pencions & absent Commons ending in Easter term one thousand Six

---

[1] For a further extension see p. 27 below.

hundred and ninety one & Mr Reeve his Surety being alsoe deceased It is ordered in consideration thereof & in regard the said arrear hath been so long due that it be referred to Mr Denshire one of the Antients of this Society to make such agreement & Composicion for the Same as he shall think fitt with the Executors or Administrators of the said Mr Fisk or Mr Reeve & that upon payment of such Composicion for the use of this Society the bond be delivered up.

*Mr Pennell for pencions & absent Commons & bond to be delivered up—*Mr. William Pennell some time since deceased & one of the Companions of this Society being charged to be more in arrear for pencions & absent Commons than the penalty of his bond which bears date in one thousand six hundred sixty one & was made in ten pounds penalty [1] And there having been a long neglect in demanding of his Executors or Administrators the duties of the House It is ordered that it be referred to Mr Dovey one of the Antients of this Society to make such agreement & composicion for the same as he shall think fit with the Executors or Administrators of the said Mr Pennell & that on payment of such Composicion for the use of this Society the bond be delivered up.

*Mr John Dovey for the Garretts up four pair of Stairs Number 23. in Kelletts Buildings—*Mr John Dovey one of the Antients of this Society desiring to purchase a lease for his life of the rooms or Garretts in Kelletts buildings up four pair of Stairs Number 23. over the East part of the said Mr Dovey's Chambers 3. pair of Stairs in the same Stair case as alsoe to purchase an assignement thereof for one other life after the Expiration of his own life It is ordered that on his payment of the sum of twelve pounds to the principal for the use of this Society A lease & an assignement be accordingly made & granted of the said rooms or Garretts to him the said Mr Dovey with the usual Covenants & provisoes & according to the usual form & method of making & granting leases & Assignements by this Society.

*Mr Goodman for the Garretts up four pair of Stairs Number 24 in Kelletts Buildings—*Whereas Mr Everard Goodman one of the Antients of this Society hath agreed for the purchase of the Garretts up four pair of Stairs N⁰ 24. over the Chambers of him the said Everard Goodman as the said Garretts are now fitted up for the Sum of four pounds Six shillings and hath now paid the said four pounds Six Shillings to the principal for the use of this Society In consideration thereof It is ordered that the said Everard Goodman have a lease made to him of the said Garretts accordingly for life as usual whenever he shall require the same he paying the usual fees for such lease.

---

[1] The penalty was raised to £20 in 1684: see p. 240 below.

Clements Inn in the ⎱ At a pention held at Clements Inn aforesaid on
County of Middlesex ⎰ Monday the Eighteenth day of June in the year of
Our Lord One thousand Seaven hundred & Sixteen
present Mr Joshua Blackwell principall Mr Dovey
Mr Goodman Mr Knight & Mr Denshire.

Mr Halsted for A Lease of the Ground Chamber Number 5 built by Mr Lawes—Mr Edward Halsted One of the Companions of this Society having agreed with Mr John Lawes for the Ground Chambers on the Left hand in the Stair Case Number 5 in the First Court in this Inn with the Cellar next adjoyning to Mr Denshire's Cellar for the Sum of One hundred & One pounds and Chargeable with the yearly payment of Twenty Shillings ground Rent being further part of the ground Rent of Six pounds per Annum And the said Mr Lawes desiring the said Mr Halsted may have A Lease made to him of the said Chambers & Cellar for the Term of fifty nine years from the five & twentieth of March last being the remaining Term of Years which the said Mr Lawes now hath in the Same by his Articles with this Society It is ordered that in full performance of the said Articles A Lease be accordingly thereof made to the said Mr Halsted with the Same Covenants & provisoes & according to the Same form & method with the Lease already made of other Chambers in the Same Building.

Mr Halsted for A Lease of the Chamber up Two pair of Stairs number 5 built by Mr Lawes—The said Mr Halsted having also agreed with the said Mr Lawes for the Chambers up two pair of Stairs on the Left hand in the Stair Case Number 5 in the first Court in this Inn with the Cellar next adjoyning to Mr Jackson's Cellar for the Sum of one Hundred & Nine pounds Ten Shillings and Chargeable with the Yearly payment of Twenty Shillings ground Rent being the remaining part of the Ground Rent of Six pounds per Annum and Mr Lawes desiring that the said Mr Halsted may also have a Lease made to him of the same Chambers & Cellar for the Term of Fifty nine years from the five & twentieth of March last being the remaining Term of years which the said Mr Lawes now hath in the same by his Articles with this Society It is Ordered that in full performance of the said Articles A Lease be accordingly thereof made to the said Mr Halsted with the same Covenants & provisoes & according to the same Form & method with the leases already made of other Chambers in the Same Building.

Mr Halsted for A Lease of the Ground Chamber & the other Chamber up 1 pair of Stairs Number 4 built by Mr Lawes—The said Mr Halsted having also Agreed with the said Mr Lawes for the Ground Chamber &c the other Chamber up One pair of Stairs in the Stair Case number 4: in the First Court with the Two Cellars under the Fore part of the Building for the Sum of One Hundred and fifteen pounds & Mr Halsted desiring also to have the Cellar intended for A Dust Hole & to pay a Yearly Rent for the same to this Society And Mr Lawes desiring the said Mr Halsted may have a Lease made to him of the same two Chambers & Cellars for the Term of Fifty nine years from the Twenty Fifth of March Last being the remaining Term of years which the said Mr Lawes now hath in the same by his Articles with this Society It is Ordered that in full performance of the said Articles A Lease be accordingly thereof made to the said Mr Halsted & that in the Same Lease be inserted and Contained the Cellar reserved for A Dust Hole as before mentioned for the like Term of Fifty Nine Years at the Reserved Yearly Rent of Ten Shillings which Lease is to contain the like Covenants & provisoes & to be according to the same Form & method with the Leases already made of other Chambers in the Same Building.

Mr Vaux for pencions & Absent Commons—Mr Vaux one of the Companions of this Society being in Arrear Three pounds for pencions & Ten pounds for Absent Commons Ending in Hillary Term One Thousand Seaventeen hundred & Fourteen & desiring to Compound for his Absent Commons in regard he hath not been in Town in several of the Terms for which he is charged It is therefore Ordered that he be abated Three pounds of his Absent Commons & that on payment of the remaining Seaven pounds as also Three pounds for pencions to Mr Callow for the use of this Society the said Mr Vaux be discharged of All Arrears of pencions & Absent Commons to & for Hillary Term One Thousand Seaventeen hundred & Fourteen.

Mr Curtiss for pencions & Absent Commons—Mr Edward Curtiss one of the Companions of this Society being in Arrear Ten Shillings for pencions & Five pounds for Absent Commons Ending in Hillary Term One thousand Seaven hundred and Fourteen & desiring to Compound for his Absent Commons in Regard he hath not been in Town in any of the Terms he is Charged for It is therefore Ordered that he be Abated Fifty Shillings of his Absent Commons & that on payment of the remaining Fifty Shillings as also Ten Shillings for pencions to Mr Thomas Callow for the Use of this Society the said Mr Curtiss be discharged of & from All Arrears of pencions & Absent Commons to and for Hillary Term One thousand seaventeen hundred and Fourteen.

Mr Elly for pencions & Absent Commons—Mr Elly one of the Companions of this Society being in Arrear Twenty Shillings for pencions & Six pounds Five Shillings for Absent Commons Ending in Hillary Term One thousand Seaven hundred & Fourteen And desiring to Compound for his Absent Commons for that he hath not been in Town above One Term in A Year for Some years past It is therefore Ordered that he be abated Forty Seaven Shillings & Six pence of his Absent Commons And that on the payment of the remaining Three pounds Seaventeen Shillings & six pence as also the Twenty Shillings for pencions to Mr Thomas Callow for the use of this Society The said Mr Elly be discharged of & from All Arrears of pencions and Absent Commons to & for Hillary Term aforesaid.

Mr Atkinson for pencions and Absent Commons—Mr William Atkinson one of the Companions of this Society being in Arrear Thirty Shillings for pencions & Three pounds for Absent Commons Ending in Hillary Term One thousand Seaven hundred & Fourteen And desiring to Compound for his Absent Commons in Consideration he hath not being in Town Nine of the Terms he is Charged with It is therefore Ordered that he be Abated Two & Twenty Shillings & Six pence of his Absent Commons and that on payment of the remaining Thirty Seaven Shillings & Six pence as also the said Thirty Shillings for pencions to Mr Callow for the Use of this Society he the said Mr Atkinson be discharged of & from All Arrears of pencions & Absent Commons to & for Hillary Term aforesaid.

Clements Inn in the } At A pencion held at Clements Inn aforesaid on
County of Middlesex } Friday the sixth Day of July in the year of Our
Lord One thousand Seaven hundred and Sixteen
Present Mr Joshua Blackwell principal Mr Dovey
Mr Goodman Mr Gibbons Mr Fuller Mr Knight

Mr Chaplin about Judgement obtained against him—Mr Thomas Chaplin One of the Companions of this house being in Arrear for pencions Absent Commons & other payments due to this Society Ending in Hillary Term One Thousand Seaven Hundred & Fourteen the sum of Seaventeen pounds & Fourteen Shillings his Bond hath been put in Suit against him and thereupon Judgement hath been obtained and he desiring to have an Abatement of his Absent Commons in regard to his not being in Town in Several of the Terms he is charged for the Same It is Ordered that Three pounds be abated of his Absent Commons And that on payment of Fourteen pounds Fourteen Shillings (together with the Charges of Suit due to Mr Dovey) within One Month from this Day he be discharged of all Arrears of pencions Absent Commons & other payments to & for Hillary Term aforesaid But in default of payment by the Time aforesaid It is Ordered that Execution be taken out on the Judgement.

Pencions & Commons for Easter Term 1716 & Commons for Trin. Term 1716 remitted—In Consideracion that the Hall lately built & intended for the Use and Service of the Principal Antients & Companions of this Society to meet in Commons is not yet perfectly finished & completed so as to Keep Commons therein It is Ordered that no pencion Roll shall be made Out or Collected for Easter Term last nor shall any Companion of this Society be Cast into Commons in or for Easter or Trinity Terms last or Either of them.

Mr Innys Jun[r]. *for pencions & Absent Commons*—Mr Innys Jun[r]. One of the Companions of this Society being in Arrear two and Forty Shillings for pencions & Four pounds Five Shillings for Absent Commons Ending in Hillary Term 1714 & Desiring to Compound for his Absent Commons for that he hath been in Town but Three Terms of the Seaventeen he is Cast into Commons It is therefore Ordered that he be abated Five and Thirty Shillings of the Absent Commons and that on payment of the remaining Fifty Shillings & the Forty two Shillings for pencions to Mr Callow for the Use of this Society the said Mr Innys be discharged of & from all Arrears of pencions & absent Commons to & for Hillary Term aforesaid.

Mr Richd Wyche for pencions & Absent Commons—Mr Richard Wyche one of the Companions of this Society Owing Four Shillings for pencions & Ten Shillings for Two Terms Absent Commons Ending in Hillary Term 1714 and it appearing that he was not in Town in Either of the Terms It is Ordered that he pay the Four Shillings for the pencions and Five Shillings for the Absent Commons in full discharge for that time

Clements Inn in the County of Middlesex } Att a pencion held att Clements Inne aforesaid on Wednesday the eighteenth Day of July in the yeare of our Lord 1716 present Mr Joshua Blackwell principal Mr Dovey Mr Goodman Mr Gibbons Mr Fuller Mr Knight

Mr Christopher Brewster for the Chamber late Mr Richd Mence's N[o]. *24*—Mr Christopher Brewster one of the Companions of this Society having agreed with Mr Richard Mence one other of the Companions of the same Society for the purchase of his Chambers up two pairs of Staires in the second Stair Case in Mr Kelletts new Building at the upper End of the Garden next adjoyning to New Inne which Chambers were sometime since granted to the same Richard Mence for ninety nine yeares if he should so long live by a Lease to him thereof made by the then principall & Antients of this Society And the said Mr Mence at the request of Mr Brewster having now Surrendred & delivered up his said Lease to this Society And Mr Brewster desiring to be admitted to the said Chambers It is thereupon Ordered that on payment of the Summe of eight pounds by the said Mr Brewster for the Use of this Society he the said Mr Brewster shall be admitted to the said Chambers and that a Lease thereof shall be to him made for the Terme of ninety nine yeares if he so long live with the usuall

Covenants & provisoes and according to the usuall Forme and Method of Leases made by this Society

Clements Inne—Att a pencion held att Clements Inne aforesaid on Fryday the 30th day of Nov.' 1716 present Mr John Dovey Deputy Principall Mr Prior Mr Gregg Mr Fowler Mr Goodman Mr Fuller Mr Denshire

Mr Henry Dottin—damage done his Chamber by the house to be repaired—In consideracion of the damage done to the Chamber of Mr Henry Dottin one of the Companions of this house up 2 pr of Staires adjoyning to or near the hall by pulling downe of the old hall pencion Roome & Chambers over the Same It is ordered that the Wainscott in the said Chambers of the said Mr Dottin be repaired & made good att the Charge of the Society.[1]

Clements Inn—At a pencion held att Clements Inn aforesaid Fryday 7.º December 1716, present Mr Dovey Deputy principal Mr Prior Mr Fowler Mr Goodman Mr Gibbons Mr Fuller Mr Knight Mr Denshire

For Insureing the new Hall—Itt is ordered that the New Hall belonging to this Society be forthwith Insured from Fire in the Hand in Hand Fire Office [2] at the Charge of the Society and that as much money be insured thereon as can be got insured in the name of Mr Dovey Deputy principall.

Clements Inn in the ⎱ At a pention held at Clements Inn aforesaid on
County of Middlesex ⎰ Friday the 8th day of February in the year of our Lord 1716 present Mr Joshua Blackwell principal Mr Gregg Mr Dovey Mr Goodman Mr Fuller Mr Knight Mr Denshire

Mr John Dovey for the Garretts late Mr Lake's up 4 pair of Staires Number 23 in Kelletts Buildings—Mr John Dovey One of the Antients of this Society desireing to purchase a Lease for his Life of the Rooms or Garretts late Mr Lake deceased in Kelletts Buildings up 4 pair of Stairs

---

[1] A further claim by Henry Dottin was considered at a Pension on February 21, 1717/18: see p. 59 below. His chambers were at No. 14: see p. 60 below.

[2] The "Hand in Hand Fire Office", so called from its fire-mark of two clasped hands, was a popular name for the "Contribution for Insuring Houses Chambers or Rooms from Loss by Fire by Amicable Contributionship", founded in 1696. This long title was abbreviated to the "Amicable Contributionship for Insuring from Loss by Fire" (see also p. 108 below) or, yet shorter, the "Amicable Contributionship". See Walford, *Insurance Cyclopaedia*, V, 634. For the renewal of the insurance on the hall seven and fourteen years later see pp. 109, 158 below.

Number 23 over the west part of the said Mr Dovey's Chambers 3 pair of Stairs in the same Stair Case as also to purchase an Assignement thereof for One other Life after the Expiracion of his own Life It is Ordered that on his payment of the sum of Fifteen pounds to the principal for the Use of this Society A Lease and an Assignement be accordingly made and granted of the said Rooms or Garretts to him the said Mr Dovey with the usual Covenants and provisoes and according to the usual Form and method of makeing and granting Leases and Assignements by this Society.

Clements Inn in the) At a pencion held at Clements Inn aforesaid on
County of Middlesex) Wednesday the 13th day of February in the year of our Lord 1716 present Mr Joshua Blackwell principall Mr Pryor Mr Dovey Mr Goodman Mr Fuller Mr Gibbons Mr Knight Mr Denshire Mr Powlett Mr Penny.

Mr Robert Drury for the Chambers late Mr Lakes up two pair of Stairs Number 23 in Kelletts buildings—Mr Robert Drury One of the Companions of this Society desiring to purchase A Lease for his Life of the Chambers late of Mr. Lake deceased late one of the Antients of this Society in Kelletts buildings in the first Stair Case Number 23 up Two pair of Stairs on the left hand of the Stair Case being the End Chamber Eastward of the said Building is ordered that on his payment of the Sum of Seaventy one pounds and Ten Shillings to the principall for the Use of this Society A Lease be accordingly made and granted of the said Chambers to him the said Mr Robert Drury for the Term of Ninety nine years if he shall so long Live with the usual Covenants and provisoes and according to the usual Form and method of making and granting Leases by this Society.

Mr Thomas Pryor for the Chambers up 2 pair of Stairs Number 3 in the first Court with the Garretts over them—Mr Thomas Pryor now One of the Antients of this Society having Some Years Since purchased of Mr Joseph Duckett and Mr George Dalby Two of the Companions of this Society their respective Moietyes of the Chambers Up Two pair of Stairs Number 3 in the first Court now in the possession of the said Mr Pryor and had Assignements to him Accordingly made and Executed by Mr Duckett and Mr Dalby of their respective Interests therein for their Lives and the said Mr Pryor having surrendred and delivered up the said Leases and Assignments to this Society And desiring to have A Lease of the said Chambers as also of the Two garratts over the said Chambers and over the Chamber next adjoyning for his Life and having according to former Orders of pention paid into the Hands of the principall for the use of this Society the Sum of Thirty Two pounds and Six Shillings It is therefore

Ordered that A Lease be accordingly made and granted of the said Chambers and Garretts to him the said Mr Pryor for the Term of Ninety nine years if he shall so long live with the usual Covenants and privisoes and according to the usual Form of making and granting a Lease by this Society.

Clements Inn in the ⎧ At a pencion held at Clements Inn aforesaid on
County of Middlesex ⎩ Monday the Eighteenth day of February in the Year of Our Lord 1716 present Mr Joshua Blackwell principal Mr Pryor Mr Dovey Mr Goodman Mr Gibbons Mr Denshire Mr Powlett Mr Penny.

Separate pentions Commons & other Dutyes to be paid for Every Chamber &c—Whereas it may be A Detriment to and may also lessen the Number of the Companions of this Society by Letting more than One Chamber to any One Member thereof Wherefore to prevent the Same for the time to come It is Ordered that no One Antient or Companion of this Society shall at any time hereafter have or take any Lease or Assignment of more than One Chamber unless such Antient or Companion be obliged by Covenant in such Lease of Assignment to pay Separate Commons pentions and all other Dutyes to the House for Every Chamber he shall have or take more than One Chamber as before mencioned.[1]

Mr John Penny for an Assignment for a life after his own Life now in being of his Chambers Nᵒ 24 in Kelletts Buildings—Mr John Penny One of the Antients of this Society having A Lease of his Ground Chambers in the building called Kelletts Buildings in the Garden Court Number 24 (being the Chambers next adjoyning to New Inn) And Desiring to purchase an Assignement thereof for one Life after the Expiracion of his own Life Now in being It is Ordered That on his payment of the Sum of Twenty Five pounds to the Principall for the Use of this Society an Assignment be accordingly made and granted to him the said Mr John Penny his Executors Administrators and Assignes for one Life after his own Life now in being with the Usual Covenants and privosoes and according to the usual form and method of making and granting of Assignments by this Society.

Mr Richard Bewley for the Chamber up Two pair of Stairs late Mr Traytons Number 3 in the first Court—Mr Richard Bewley one of the Companions of this Society Desiring to purchase A Lease for his Life of the Chambers up Two pair of Staires on the Left Hand of the Stair Case Number 3 in the first Court late of Mr Trayton deceased Late one of the Antients of this Society As also to purchase an Assignement thereof for

---

[1] For the revocation of this order (found inconvenient and impracticable) see p. 180 below.

One other Life after the Expiration of his Own Life It is Ordered that on his payment of the Sum of Fifty pounds to the Principall for the Use of this Society A Lease and an Assignement be accordingly made and granted of the said Chambers to him the said Mr Bewley to commence and begin on the Five and Twentieth Day of March next with a Covenant therein to be Contained on the part of the said Richard Bewley that he his Executors Administrators and Assignes shall within One year from the said Five and Twentieth day of March next lay out and Expend at least the Sum of Ten pounds in placing and setting up Three Sash Windows on that side of the said Chambers looking into the said First Court and in such other Alterations and Additions to the said Chambers as shall be thought fitt and with the usual Covenants and provisoes and according to the Usual Form and method of making and granting Leases and Assignements by this Society

Mr William Walcott for the Ground Chambers in the New Building adjoyning to the Hall—Mr William Walcott One of the Companions of this Society Desiring to purchase a Lease for his Life of the Ground Chambers in the New Building in the first Court adjoyning to the Hall with the Corner Cellar fronting the said Court Northward and Eastward and under part of the Said Chambers As also to purchase an Assignement thereof for One other Life after the Expiration of his own Life And proposing to pay One hundred and Fifty pounds for the Same The said Chambers being first Wainscotted and painted and Stone Chimney peices and Hearths with Coveings [1] of Stone or painted Tiles also sett up and fixed at the Three Chimneys or fireplaces in the said Chambers according to the present Design And as the said Chambers are now Sett out and Divided Which is to be done at the Charge of this Society on or before the first Day of Easter Term next It is thereupon Ordered That on the said Mr Walcotts payment of the said Sum of One hundred and fifty pounds to the Principall for the Use of this Society on or before the said first Day of Easter Term A Lease and an Assignement be accordingly made and granted to him the said Mr. Walcott with the usual Covenants and provisoes and according to the usual form and method of making and granting Leases and Assignements by this Society And in Testimony of the said Mr Walcott's Agreement hereunto he hath subscribed his name to this Order.

Wm Walcot

Mr Tilden for pentions & Absent Commons and his Bond to be delivered up—Mr George Tilden One of the Companions of this Society being in Arrear for pencions and Absent Commons Ending in Hillary Term 1714 Seaven Shillings and for Rent for his Chambers Six Years and an half

---

[1] "The inclined or curved sides of a fireplace, approaching each other towards the back": *N.E.D.*, s.v. "Coving", 2.

at Michaelmas 1715 Three pounds and Five Shillings in all being Three pounds Twelve Shillings out of which is to be allowed him Eleaven Shillings and Six pence for Taxes and it is agreed to abate him Two Shillings and Sixpence of his Absent Commons in regard he had before then parted with his Chambers and Desired that his Bond given by him to this Society might be delivered up he being a Housekeeper [1] within the Libertyes of the City of Westminster It is therefore Ordered that on the said Mr Tilden's payment of the remaining Fifty Eight Shillings he be discharged of the said arrear of pentions Absent Commons and Rent and that for the Reasons aforesaid his said Bond be delivered up to him to be Cancelled.

Mr Richard Bewley for pencions and Absent Commons—Mr Richard Bewley one of the Companions of this Society being Thirty two Shillings in Arrear for pentions and Four pounds and Ten Shillings for Absent Commons ending in Hillary Term 1714 and desiring to Compound for his Absent Commons in regard he hath not been in Town above Two Terms in any One Year for the time he is Cast into Commons It is therefore Ordered That Two and Twenty Shillings and Six pence be abated him of his Absent Commons and that on his the said Mr Bewley's payment of Four pounds Nineteen Shillings and Six pence for the Use of this Society he be discharged of and from the said Arrears of pentions and Absent Commons.

Mr Carvile for Absent Commons—Mr Carvile One of the Companions of this Society being by Mr Callow returned to be in Arrear about Twenty Shillings for Absent Commons in & for Some of the Terms before Hillary Term 1714 And he affirming that he is not indebted the said Arrear nor any part thereof but hath regularly been in Commons And it appearing that he hath paid his pentions and other Dutyes of the house It is thereupon ordered that the said Mr Carvile be discharged of the said Arrear of Absent Commons.

Mr Cosyns and Absent Commons—Mr Cosyns One of the Companions of this Society being Six Shillings in Arrear for pentions and Twenty Shillings for Absent Commons ending in Hillary Term 1714 And desiring to Compound for his Absent Commons being always present in Commons when in Town It is Ordered that Ten Shillings be abated of the said Absent Commons and that on payment of Sixteen Shillings for the Use of this Society he the said Mr Cosyns be discharged of and from the said Arrears of Pentions & Commons.

Mr Edison for pentions and Absent Commons—Mr Edison One of the Companions of this Society being Five and Forty Shillings in arrear for pentions and Absent Commons ending in Hillary Term 1714 And it

---

[1] *I.e.* householder. Cf. Entick, *London*, IV, 128 (1766): "a handsome street inhabited . . . by private housekeepers".

D

appearing that he hath not been in Town Eight of the Terms for which he is Cast in Commons and desiring to Compound for the Same It is thereupon Ordered that Twenty Shillings be abated him of his Absent Commons and that on his payment of Five and Twenty Shillings for the Use of this Society he the said Mr Edison be discharged of and from the said Arrears.

Mr Stubbs and Mr Keeling for pentions and Absent Commons— Mr Stubbs and Mr Keeling Two of the Companions of this Society being each of them Four Shillings in arrear for pentions and Fifteen Shillings for Absent Commons Ending in Hillary Term 1714 and Desiring to Compound for their Absent Commons in regard that neither of them have been in Town in any of the Terms for which they are charged It is therefore Ordered that on their payment each of them of Eleaven Shillings and Six pence for the Use of this Society they the said Mr Stubbs and Mr Keeling be discharged of and from the said Arrears of pentions and Commons.

Clements Inn in the County of Middlesex } At a pention held at Clements Inn aforesaid on Friday the Two and Twentieth day of February in the year of Our Lord 1716 present Mr Joshua Blackwell Principal Mr Pryor Mr Dovey Mr Fowler Mr Goodman Mr Fuller Mr Knight Mr Denshire Mr Powlett Mr Penny

*Auditors of the Principall's Accounts for 3 years beginning in Hillary Term 1713 until Hillary Term 1716—*Whereas at a pention held the Five and Twentieth day of February 1714: It was Ordered That Mr John Dovey and Mr John Knight (Two of the Antients of this Society) and Mr John Penny and Mr William Purcell (Two of the Companions of the Same Society) Should Examine State and Audit the Accounts of the Principal of this Society beginning in Hillary Term 1713 until Hillary Term 1714 And that they should make their Certificate or Report of the said Accounts at the first Pention after Easter Term then next But there being the New Hall then intended to be built and Several Considerable repairs due to be done in and about the house It was afterwards thought more Convenient not to have any Accounts made up by the Principall to be Audited till the Expiration of the Three Years for which he was chosen Principal of this Society And the said Principalls Accounts for the said 3 years beginning with Hillary Term 1713 until this present Hillary Term being now Drawn up It is Ordered That Mr John Gibbons & Mr John Penny (Two of the Antients of this Society) & Mr Edmond Giles Hooper and Mr William Purcell (Two of the Companions of the Same Society) shall and do Examine State and Audit the said Accounts of the Principall for the Three Years beforementioned And that they the said John Gibbons

John Penny Edmond Giles Hooper and William Purcell or any Three of them shall and do make their Certificate or Report of the said Accounts at the first pention in or after Easter Term next or so soon after as the same can or may Conveniently be don.

Mr Benett to be discharged of 5s: demanded of him for Absent Commons—Mr Edward Benett one of the Companions of this Society being charged 5s: for absent Commons in Hillary Term 1714 and it appearing he was admitted of the Society since Hillary Term and should not have been Cast into Commons till after the Expiration of a year from the time of his admission It is therefore ordered that he be discharged of the said Five Shillings for Absent Commons as aforesaid.

Mr Humphreys to be allowed 40s: out of his Rent towards the Charge of painting his Chambers—Mr Thomas Humphreys One of the Companions of this Society having taken a Lease of the Chambers Number 3 up One pair of Stairs which were by Agreement to be repaired and painted at the Charge of the Society and the said Mr Humphreys having painted them at his own Expense and Desiring an Allowance towards the Same out of the Rent for the said Chambers Due from him It is therefore Ordered that the said Mr Humphreys be allowed Fifty Shillings in full payment for painting and all other repairs at the said Chambers to be done by this Society according to their said Agreement.

Mr Powlett & Mr Penny to Examine and State the Accounts of Rents received by Mr Callow & what in Arrear—It is Ordered that Mr Robt Powlett & Mr John Penny Two of the Antients of this Society Do Examine and State the Account of what Rents have been received by Mr Callow And What Rents are in Arrear to this Society That they do make their Certificate or report thereof at the next pention or so soon after as Conveniently they can.

Clements Inn in the ⎰ At a pention held at Clements Inn aforesaid on
County of Middlesex ⎱ Wednesday the 27th Day of February in the year
　　　　　　　　　　of Our Lord 1716 present Mr Joshua Blackwell
　　　　　　　　　　Principal Mr Dovey Mr Fowler Mr Goodman
　　　　　　　　　　Mr Knight Mr Denshire Mr Powlett Mr Penny

Mr Hunt Senr for pencions & Absent Commons—Mr Hunt Senior One of the Companions of this Society being Ten Shillings in Arrear for pentions and Thirty Shillings for Absent Commons Ending in Hillary Term 1714 and having sometime since desired to compound for his Absent Commons It was therefore Agreed he should be abated fifteen Shillings in regard of his being Severall of the Terms out of Town and he having accordingly in July last paid Five and Twenty Shillings for the Use of this Society It is therefore Ordered that the said Mr Hunt be discharged of the said Arrears of Pencions and Absent Commons.

Mr Feilder's Bills to be Examined and adjusted—It is ordered that Mr Goodman Mr Fuller and Mr Gibbons or any two of them do Examine the Bills demanded by Mr Feilder to be due to him from this Society for Smithwork and Severall Goods had of him in the way of his Trade and that they do settle and adjust what remains due to him and make their Certificate or report thereof at the next pention or as soon after as conveniently they can.

Mr Robt. Powlett for An Assignment after his own Life in his Chamber N° 20:—Mr Robert Powlett One of the Antients of this Society having A Lease for his own Life of his Chambers in the Stair Case Number 20: up Two and Three pairs of Stairs with the Garretts over them and desiring to purchase an Assignment of the Same Chambers and Garretts for Another Life after the Expiracion of his own Life now in being It is Ordered that on his payment of Thirty Six pounds to the Principal for the Use of this Society an Assignment be accordingly made and granted to him the said Mr Powlett his Executors Administrators and Assignes for One Life after his Own Life now in being with the usual Covenants & provisoes and according to the usual form and method of making and granting Assignments by this Society.

Mr Tyson's Demands to be adjusted for what he expended in fitting up the Chambers in part of the Old Building where the Hall stands—Mr Tyson One of the Companions of this Society alledging that he was Tenant to this Society from year to year for a Chamber up 2 pair of Stairs in part of the Old Building where the Hall is now built and that Mr Brewster the former Principal gave him Encouragement to fitt up the said Chamber and that he accordingly expended above £25: therein and was soon after removed therefrom It is thereupon Ordered That it be referred to Mr Mathew Evans one other of the Companions of this Society to Examine Settle and Adjust what shall be reasonable to be allowed by this Society to the said Mr Tyson for what he so expended as aforesaid And that Mr Evans do make his Certificate and report thereof at the next pention or as soon after as conveniently he can.

Clements Inn in the } At a pencion held at Clements Inne aforesaid upon
County of Middlesex } Friday the 8th Day of March in the yeare of our
       Lord 1716 present Mr Joshua Blackwell principall
       Mr Prior Mr Dovey Mr Goodman Mr Fuller
       Mr Knight Mr Powlett Mr Penny Mr Gibbons

Mr John Knight for the Chambers 2 pr of Staires in the New Buildings adjoyning to the Hall—Mr John Knight one of the Antients of this Society desireing to be the purchaser of a Lease for his Life of the Chambers up two pair of Staires in the first Court in the New Buildings adjoyning to the Hall with the back Cellar in the same Buildings fronting the passage next the Hall northwards as also to be the purchaser of an Assignment thereof for one other Life after the Expiracion of his owne Life And proposing to pay One hundred & thirty pounds for the same & forthwith to Lay out & expend the Summe of fifty pounds in wainscotting & painting & in Stone Chimney peices & hearths & otherwise fitting up the said Chambers for the best Improvement of them And also proposing that Mr Trott Mr Haynes & Mr Shepherd (whome he designs to have in the said Chambers) shall be admitted of this Society & give Bonds as usuall on or before the End of Trinity Terme next It is thereupon Ordered that on the said Mr Knights payment of the said Summe of £130 to the principall for the use of this Society on or before the Last day of Trinity Terme next and on his haveing the said Mr Trott Mr Haynes & Mr Shepherd admitted as before mencioned & forthwith laying out & expending the said Summe of £50 in fitting up the said Chambers as aforesaid A Lease & an Assignment be accordingly made & granted to him the said Mr Knight or to them the said Mr Trott Mr Haynes & Mr Shepherd (when admitted) or to any one or more of them with the usuall Covenants & provisoes & according to the usuall Forme & Methods of makeing & granting Leases & Assignments by this Society And in Testimony of the said Mr Knight's Agreement hereunto he hath subscribed his name to this order.

John Knight

Mr Steggall for a Life & an Assignment in the Ground Chambers in Kelletts Buildings Nº 23. Late Mr Watsons—Mr Thomas Steggall one of the Companions of this Society desiring to purchase a Lease for his Life of the double ground Chamber on the left hand of the Stair case No. 23. in Kelletts Buildings in the Garden Court late the Chamber of Mr Henry Watson deceased late one of the Companions of this Society as also to purchase an Assignment thereof for one other life after the Expiracion of his owne Life Itt is Ordered that on his payment of the Summe of eighty pounds to the principall for the use of this Society a Lease & an Assignment be accordingly made & granted of the said Chambers with the appurtenances to him the said Mr Steggall with the usuall Covenants & provisoes & according to the usuall Forme & method of makeing & granting of Leases & Assignments by this Society.

Mr Edward Halsted for a Life & an Assignment in the Chambers 1 pr of Staires in the New Building adjoyning to the Hall—Mr Edward Halsted one of the Companions of this Society desireing to purchase a Lease for his Life in the Chambers up one pair of Staires in the first Court in the New

Building adjoyning to the Hall with the Cellar where the Chimney is called the Kitchen Cellar & the back Cellar adjoyning to it in the Same Building as also to purchase an Assignment thereof for one life after the Expiracion of his owne Life and proposing to pay One hundred & Eighty pounds for the same and to lay out & expend at least the Summe of fifty pounds within 12 months from the date hereof in wainscotting & painting & in Stone Chimney peices & hearths & otherwise fitting up the said Chambers to the best Improvement of them Itt is Ordered and Agreed that on the said Mr Halsteds immediate payment of one hundred pounds to the principall for the Use of this Society & also on payment of the remaining eighty pounds on or before the last day of Trinity Term next to the principall for the use likewise of this Society A Lease & an Assignment be accordingly made & granted to him the said Mr Edward Halsted of the said Chambers & Cellars subject to the payment of Separate Commons pencions & other dutyes to the house according to a late Order of pencion made for that purpose [1] & with the usuall Covenants & provisoes & according to the usuall Forme & Method of makeing & granting of Leases & Assignments by this Society And with a Covenant also on the part of the said Mr Halsted to lay out & expend the said Summe of £50 in wainscotting & fitting up the said Chambers within the time before mencioned And in Testimony of the said Mr Halsteds Agreement hereunto he hath subscribed his name to this Order.

Edwd Halsted

Clements Inn in the } At a Pention held at Clements Inn aforesaid on
County of Middlesex } Tuesday the six and Twentieth day of March in the year of our Lord 1717 Present Mr Joshua Blackwell Principall Mr Dovey Mr Goodman Mr Fuller Mr Knight Mr Penny Mr Gibbons

Mr Mathew Evans for the old & new Chambers & for his overlookeing the New Buildings & repairs lately done &c.—Whereas at a Pention held the 10th day of February 1713 in Consideracion that Mr Mathew Evans one of the Companions of this Society had then Surrendred and delivered up his Lease of his Moietys of the Severall Chambers therein mencioned (on part of the Ground since built upon by Mr John Lawes) It was Ordered that the said Mr Evans should have the use of other Chambers therein also mencioned without payment of rent or other allowances for them (except taxes) and that when he should be removed from them or should think fitt himself to leave them the Principall should pay him Thirty pounds as and for the Consideracion for his Surrendring and delivering up of his said

[1] See p. 31 above.

Lease And Whereas the said Mr Evans was soon after obliged to remove from the said last mencioned Chambers (being on part of the Ground where the Hall is now built) to the Chambers in the buildings called Kelletts Buildings in the Garden Court in the Stair Case Number 24 up two and three pair of Staires in the Same Stair Case and hath repaired and fitted them up with the Garrett over them and is now in possession of the said Chambers and Garretts And Whereas the said Mr Evans did give his attendances and assistances in Settleing and perfecting the Articles with the said Mr Lawes for the Ground whereon he built and in overlooking and taking Care that the building was done and performed by Mr Lawes according to his Articles And the said Mr Evans did likewise give his attendances and assistances in Contriving building and finishing the Hall and Chambers thereto adjoyning and in repairing and fitting up Severall old Chambers and in and about Severall other repairs and works belonging to the House and did make Contracts and Agreements with the Severall Workmen for the Same and accordingly hath taken Care of and Surveyed and overlooked the said works and kept the Accounts thereof And Whereas there are yet Severall other works & repaires to be done in and about Clemments Inn aforesaid the particulars whereof are mentioned and Contained in a paper writeing Signed by the said Mr Evans which he is willing and doth hereby promise and agree to take care of and overlooke in the best way and manner that he can for the benefit and advantage of the Society And in Consideracion of the premisses desires to have a Lease for his Life and also an Assignment after the expiracion of his life of the said Chambers two and three pair of Staires Number 24 with the Garretts over them which he agrees and is willing to accept and take in full payment satisfaction and discharge of and for all and every the Matters things and premisses hereinbefore mencioned And doth hereby accordingly acknowledge and declare the Same to be in full payment satisfaction and discharge thereof and of all other demands on any account whatever due to him from the Society as also for his takeing Care of and overlooking the said Severall other works and repaires yet to be done and in the said paper writeing by him signed particularly mencioned It is therefore ordered for the Consideration aforesaid that a Lease and an Assignement of the said last mencioned Chambers & Garrett be accordingly made and granted to him the said Mr Mathew Evans with the usuall Covenants and provisoes and according to the usuall form and method of making and granting Leases and Assignements by this Society And in Testimony of the Consent and Agreement of the said Mr Mathew Evans to all and every the matters and things in this Order mencioned and Contained he hath Subscribed his Name hereunto.

Matt. Evans

Mr Thomas Hinder for a Lease for Seven yeares from Michaelmas 1717 of the Cellers and vaults under Kelletts buildings—Thomas Hinder Vintner desireing to take a Lease of the Cellars and vaults under Kelletts Buildings for Seven yeares from Michaelmas next and proposing to have Twenty pounds laid out and expended by the Society in the repairing and improvement of them and to give Twenty pounds per Annum rent for the Same It is Ordered that a Lease be accordingly thereof made and granted to the said Thomas Hinder with usuall Covenants Provisoes and Agreements therein to be contained.

Mr Aldey & Mr Steggall for dividing a fence to part their yards & liberty for repairing &c—Mr Roger Aldey and Mr Thomas Steggall two of the Companions of this Society making a Complaint that the Pailes or fence which divides the yards belonging to their respective Chambers in Kelletts buildings is very much out of repair And desireing that the same may be repaired and made a good and sufficient fence at the Charge of the Society And altho' it doth not appear that it of right belongs to the Society to repair the Same yet in Compliance to the desire of the said Mr Aldey & Mr Steggall It is ordered that the said fence be forthwith made good and sufficient at the Charge of the Society and Sett up and fixed in the same manner it now is And in consideracion thereof the said Mr Roger Aldey & Mr Thomas Steggall do hereby severally and respectively Consent and agree for their respective parts to keep the said fence in good and sufficient repair and that the Principall and Antients of this Society for the time being with his and their Workmen and Materialls shall and may have full and free leave liberty Lycence and authority to enter and come into and upon their respective parts of the said yard when divided for the doing and performing all such outward repairs belonging to the house as shall be wanting when and as often as occasion Shall be and require the said Principall and Antients clearing the said yard and making good such damage as shall from time to time at the doing or performing of such repaires be done to the said Roger Aldey & Thomas Steggall respectively In Testimony whereof the said Roger Aldey & Thomas Steggall have hereunto subscribed their names

Ro^r Aldey
Tho: Steggall

Clements Inn in the\
County of Middlesex } At a pencion held at Clements Inn aforesaid on Wednesday the first day of May in the year of our Lord 1717 Present Mr John Dovey Deputy Principall Mr Goodman Mr Gibbons Mr Knight Mr Powlett Mr Penny

Mr Edwd Stanton to be discharged out of Exec.ⁿ & Bond delivered up—
It is ordered that Edwd Stanton a Companion of this Society (in respect

of his poverty & the miserable condition of his wife being big with Child) be discharged out of Execution on the payment of Mr Callow's Bill of charges the Sherriffs poundage & Bayliffes Fees And that on payment of the said Costs & Fees (the said Mr Stanton's security being dead insolvent) the bond to this Society from the said Stanton be delivered up.

Clements Inn in the ⎱ Att a pencion held at Clements Inn aforesaid the
County of Middlesex ⎰ 18th day of May 1717 present Mr John Dovey
Deputy Principall Mr Prior Mr Fowler Mr Goodman Mr Gibbons Mr Knight Mr Poweltt Mr Penny

Mr Darell Shorts Bond delivered up on payment of the full demand & 10s. to Servts; £9 11s 0d to Mr Dovey—Mr Darell Short one of the Companions of this Society having a desire to take up his Bond given to this Society he being entred in the Middle Temple as it appeared to us & there being due to the said Society from him for Commons & Pencions £9 11s. It is therefore ordered that on the payment of the said £9 11s. to Mr Dovey for the use of this Society & 10s. to the Servants of this Society that the said Bond be delivered up.

Richmonds Bond delivered to Mr Masterman on his payment of £10: to the House &c & 10s. to Servts. & to be discharged out of Custody—Upon Mr Masterman (who is bound for Mr Richmond one of the Companions of this Society) paying to the House £10. and discharging Mr Callows bill Sherriffes & Bailiffes fees and paying to the Servts. 10s. It is ordered that Mr Masterman shall have the bond delivered up to him & that Mr Richmond shall be discharged out of Custody when Mr Masterman Shall require the same.

Clements Inn in the ⎱ At a pencion held at Clements Inn aforesaid on
County of Middlesex ⎰ Friday the 24th day of May Anno Domini 1717
present Mr Dovey Deputy Principall Mr Pryor Mr Fowler Mr Fuller Mr Gibbons Mr Powlett Mr Penny

Mr Goldwires bond delivered up £10. 9s. paid to Mr Dovey—Mr Thomas Nuttall as surety for Mr Christopher Goldwire one of the Companions of this House attending & giving Satisfaccion that the said Mr Goldwire has left of his practice It is Ordered that on the payment of £10. 9s. (being the full Commons & pencions now due) to Mr Dovey for the use of this Society & 10s. to the Servts. that the said bond be delivered to the said Mr Nuttall.

Edw.ᵈ Walker bond delivered up—*£20 pencions received by Mr Callow*—Mr Edw.ᵈ Walker one of the Antients of this Society haveing paid to

D*

Mr Thomas Callow £20 in full for pencions to this time & having left of business desired his bond to this Society may be delivered up which is ordered & the bond delivered up accordingly.

W^m. Walker Commons compounded & paid to Mr Callow for pencions & Commons £4. 8s. 6d.—Mr William Walker one of the Companions of this Society haveing paid his pencions to Mr Callowe being £3. 6s. & Mr Callowe desireing to compound for his Commons which are £2. 5s. the said William Walker not haveing been in Towne It is ordered that the said Commons be compounded at £1. 2s. 6d. which the said Mr Callow charges himself with for the use of this Society.

Principalls accounts audited & confirmed—Whereas Mr John Gibbons & Mr John Penny two of the Antients of this Society and Edmund Giles Hooper & Mr William Purcell two of the Companions of the same Society being by Order of Pencion made the 22d of February last appointed Auditors of the accounts of Mr Joshua Blackwell (now principall of Clements Inn) have perused and examined the said principalls accounts of Receipts & Disbursements in Clements Inn from the beginning of Hillary Terme 1713 untill the beginning of Hillary Term 1716 and have found the totall of the said principalls receipts in those 3 yeares to be £1900. 7s. 6d. & the totall of his disbursements to be £2074. 4s. 9d. so that there remained due to him on this account £173. 17s. 3d from this Society as appeares by their report dated the 10th day of this instant May Now it is hereby ordered that the said account so audited as aforesaid be allowed & the same are hereby accordingly allowed & approved of as just & true accounts & the said Mr Joshua Blackwell is hereby discharged therefrom and it is also ordered that the said Mr Blackwell be paid the said £173 17s. 3d. being the ballance due to him on the said account out of the first money that shall be received for the use of the said Society.

Tho. Pryor
John Dovey Dep. Pr.
W^m. Fowler
Geo. Fuller
Tho. Powlett
John Penny

Clements Inn in the ⎱ At a pencion held at Clements Inn aforesaid on
County of Middlesex ⎰ Friday the 31st day of May Anno Domini 1717
Present Mr Dovey Dep. Pr. Mr Pryor Mr Fowler
Mr Fuller Mr Gibbons Mr Powlett Mr Penny

Mr Falkner £5. 2s. for pencions paid to Mr Dovey—Mr Falkner One of the Companions of this Society being in arrear £5. 2s. for pencions and

£16 for absent Commons ending this Terme & desiring to Compound for his absent Commons in regard he has not been in Town severall Termes for which he is Charged It is therefore ordered that on his payment of the £5. 2s. for pencions & £9. 15s. for Commons for the use of this Society He the said Mr Falkner be discharged of & from the said arreares of pencions & Commons.

Clements Inn in the At a pencion held at Clements Inn aforesaid on
County of Middlesex Friday the 7th day of June Anno Domini 1717 present Mr Dovey Dep. Pr. Mr Pryor Mr Fowler Mr Gibbons Mr Knight Mr. Powlett Mr Penny

Mr Sturgis bond delivered up £6. 19s. paid to Mr Dovey—Mr Sturgis being Antient & haveing left of business Mr Cox desired to have up his bond It is ordered on payment of £1. 14s. for pencions & £5. 5s. for Commons being the full Demand due to the Society & 10s. to the Servants that the bond be delivered up.

Clements Inn in the At a pention held at Clement's Inn aforesaid on
County of Middlesex Friday the Fifth day of July in the year of Our Lord One thousand Seaven hundred and Seaventeen present Mr Blackwell principal Mr Pryor Mr Dovey Mr Fowler Mr Goodman Mr Gibbons Mr Fuller Mr Denshire Mr Powlett Mr Penny.

Servants Rolls to be compounded for and paid as well as Absent Commons —It is Ordered that no Companion of this Society shall be admitted to compound for Absent Commons unless such Companion Do at the Same time Compound for and pay six pence to the Servants Rolls for each Term for which he shall so compound for Absent Commons as aforesaid.

Mr Jollands Executors for pencions taxes & Absent Commons and his Bond to be delivered up—Mr Jollands deceased late one of the Companions of this Society being in arrear eight shillings for pencions eight shillings for Taxes and Thirty five shillings for Absent Commons ending in Hillary Term one thousand Seaven Hundred and Eleaven and his Executors desiring to Compound for his Absent Commons the said Mr Jolland not having been in Town for several Terms before his Death and to have his bond delivered up It is Ordered that on payment of sixteen shillings for pencions and Taxes and Seaventeen shillings and six pence for Absent Commons to the Principal for the use of this Society in all being Three and thirty shillings and six pence the same be accepted in full discharge And that the said Mr Jollands bond be delivered up to be cancelled.

Mr Moor for pencions Taxes and Absent Commons—Mr Robert Moor One of the Companions of this Society being in arrear Twenty five shillings for pencions six shillings for Taxes and Three pounds Ten shillings for Absent Commons ending the present Trinity Term and desiring to compound for his absent Commons not having been in Town for some years It is Ordered that on his paying of One and Thirty shillings for pencions and Taxes & Thirty Five shillings for Absent Commons (in all being Three pounds six shillings) to the principal for the use of this Society the same be in full discharge of the said arrear.

Clements Inn in the County of Middlesex ⎱ At a pencion held at Clements Inn aforesaid on Friday the Twelfth day of July in the year of our Lord one thousand Seaven hundred and seaventeen present Mr Blackwell principal Mr Pryor Mr Dovey Mr Fowler Mr Goodman Mr Gibbons Mr Knight Mr Denshire Mr Powlett Mr Penny.

Mr Millward for pencions and Absent Commons and his Bond delivered up—Mr Millward one of the Companions of this Society being in arrear Twenty eight pounds Eighteen shillings for pencions and Absent Commons ending in Hillary Term One thousand Seaven Hundred and Fourteen and Mr Haynes (his Surety in the Bond given to this Society) desiring to compound for the same and to have the Bond delivered up For that the said Mr Millward hath for many years been gone into parts beyond the seas and hath not been heard of whether living or Dead for above Fifteen years past It is ordered that on payment by Mr Haynes of Five pounds Seaven shillings and six pence to Mr Thomas Callowe for the use of this Society and the like Composition to the Servants Rolls the same be in full discharge of the said Arrears and that thereupon the said Bond be delivered up.

Mr Wickham Junr *for pencions & Absent Commons & his bond to be delivered up*—Mr Wickham Junr now deceased And late one of the Companions of this Society being in Arrear forty two shillings for pencions and Seaven pounds Five shillings for absent Commons ending in Hillary Term one thousand Seaven hundred and Fourteen And Mr Jolland late deceased being his Surety in the bond given to this Society and the Executors of the said Mr Jolland desiring to compound for the Absent Commons in regard that the said Mr Wickham was not in Town above two Terms in a year and also to have the Bond delivered up It is thereupon Ordered that Thirty Six Shillings be abated of the Absent Commons and that on payment of the remaining Five pounds Nine Shillings for Absent Commons and the Forty Two Shillings for pencions (in all being Seaven pounds Eleaven Shillings) to the principall for the Use of this Society and the like Composition to the Servants Rolls the same be in full Discharge of the said Arrear and that thereupon the said Bond be delivered up.

Clements Inn in the \
County of Middlesex } At A pencion held at Clements Inn aforesaid on Wednesday the Seaventeenth day of July In the year of our Lord one thousand Seaven hundred and Seaventeen present Mr Blackwell Principal Mr Johnson Mr Dovey Mr Fowler Mr Goodman Mr Gibbons Mr Fuller Mr Knight Mr Denshire Mr Penny.

Sir John Statham for the Lease of the Chambers Nº 9: purchased of him by this Society—Whereas Sir John Statham Knight one of the Companions of this Society on the sixteenth day of February in the year of our Lord one thousand Seaven hundred and one had a Lease made and granted by this Society to him the said Sir John Statham (By the name of John Statham gent) of All that Double Chamber together with Two Little Lofts over the same with the Appurtenances being Two pair of Stairs and then in the Second Court of Clements Inn aforesaid and marked with the Number or figure 9: to hold to him and his Assignes for the Term of Ninety nine yeares if he should so long live And hath agreed with this Society for the Sum of Nineteen pounds Ten Shillings for the right and Interest of him the said Sir John Statham and all other persons claiming under him in the same chambers and premisses with the Appurtenances as and for the Consideration of and for the surrendring and delivering up the said Lease to this Society in order to the New intended building on the ground whereon the said Chambers (with other Chambers) are now standing and being in the said Inn It is therefore ordered that the principal do pay to the said Sir John Statham or to whom else he shall Direct & appoint to receive the same the said Sum of Nineteen pounds Ten Shillings and that on payment thereof the said Sir John Statham and All persons claiming under him Do and Shall accordingly Surrender and Deliver up the said Lease of the said chambers and premisses to this Society in Order to the said New intended building And in Testimony of this Agreement the said Sir John Statham hath signed this order [1]

Mr Johnson for his Lease of his Chambers Number 11: purchased by him by this Society—Whereas Mr Maurice Johnson (Now one of the Antients of this Society) on the 10th day of February In the year of Our Lord one thousand six hundred eighty Seaven for the Consideration of the Sum of Twenty Nine pounds by him then paid to the then principal for the

---

[1] No signature follows. For Statham see p. 267 n. below.

use of the said Society had a Lease made and granted unto him by the then principal and Antients of all those Two Chambers with the Appurtenances then in the Middle Court of Clements Inn aforesaid one of them up one pair of Stairs and the other of them over the same Chamber and up two pair of Stairs and marked with the Number or figure (11) to hold to him the said Mr Johnson and his Assignes for 99 years if he should so long live and be and continue a Member or Companion of the said Society And the said Mr Johnson now demanding the like sum of Twenty nine pounds for his right and Interest in the said Chambers with the Appurtenances as and for the Consideration of and for his surrendring and delivering up of the said Lease to this Society in order to the New intended building on the ground whereon the said Chambers (with other Chambers) are now standing and being in the said Inn It is thereupon Ordered that Mr Blackwell the present principal Do pay unto the said Mr Johnson the said Sum of Twenty Nine pounds and that on payment thereof the Said Mr Johnson Do and Shall accordingly Surrender and Deliver up to this Society his said Lease of the said Chambers with the Appurtenances and all his Interest and Term therein in order to the said New intended building And in Testimony of this Agreement the said Mr Johnson hath signed this order.

Maur. Johnson

Mr Squire for the Leases of the Chambers N°. 12: purchased of him by this Society—Whereas on the Five and Twentieth Day of February in the year of our Lord One thousand six Hundred Eighty three A Lease was made and granted by this Society to Mr Arthur Squire one of the Companions of this House of all those Two Chambers with the Appurtenances situate & being in the West Corner of the Court then called the Second Court in Clements Inn aforesaid in the Timber building up One pair of Stairs and one other Chamber up Two pair of Stairs over one of the said Two Chambers and next adjoyning to the Chamber then of Francis Johnson gent Which said Three Chambers then were in the possession of him the said Arthur Squire and are in the Stair Case now marked with the figure or Number 12: To hold the said Three Chambers with the Appurtenances to him the said Arthur Squire and his Assignes for the Term of Ninety nine years if he should so long live and be and continue a Member or Companion of the said Society And Whereas also on the Twenty fifth day of April in the year of our Lord one Thousand Seaven hundred and Ten one other Lease was made & granted by this Society to the said Arthur Squire of all that chamber and Study in the Corner of the same Court and then called the Middle Court in Clements Inn aforesaid in the same Stair Case marked with the figures or Number 12: up Two pair of

Stairs & then also in the possession of him the said Arthur Squire To hold the said Chamber with the Appurtenances to him the said Arthur Squire and his Assignes for the like Term of Ninety Nine years if he should so long live and be and continue a Member or Companion of the said Society And Whereas the said Arthur Squire hath agreed with this Society for the Sum of Thirty Nine pounds for the right Title and Interest of him the said Arthur Squire and All other persons claiming under him of in and to the said Four Chambers with the Appurtenances As and for the Consideration of and for the surrendring and delivering up the said Two Several Leases to this Society in order to the New intended building on the ground whereon the said Chambers (with other Chambers) are now standing and being In the said Inn IT IS THEREFORE ORDERED that Mr Blackwell the present principal Do pay to the said Arthur Squire or to whom else he shall Direct and appoint to receive the same the said Sum of Thirty Nine pounds And that on payment thereof the said Arthur Squire and all persons claiming under him Do and Shall accordingly surrender & deliver up to this Society the said Two Several Leases of the said Four Chambers with the Appurtenances in Order to the said New intended building and in Testimony of this Agreement the said Mr Arthur Squire hath signed this Order.

A.^r Squier

Mr Trott Mr Haynes and Mr Sheppard for a Lease of the Chambers 2 pair of Staires in the New building adjoyning to the Hall—WHEREAS at a pention held the Eighth day of March last past Mr John Knight one of the Antients of this Society desired to be the purchaser of A Lease for his Life of the Chamber up Two pair of Stairs in the first Court in Clements Inn aforesaid in the New buildings adjoyning to the Hall with the back Cellar in the same building fronting the passage next the Hall Northwards as also to be the purchaser of An Assignment thereof for One other Life after the Expiration of his own Life and proposed to pay One hundred and Thirty pounds for the same And forthwith to lay out and expend the Sum of Fifty pounds in Wainscotting and painting and in Stone Chimney peices & hearths and otherwise fitting up the said Chambers for the best improvement of them and also proposed that Mr Trott Mr Haynes and Mr Shepherd (whom he designed to have in the said Chambers) should be admitted of this Society and give Bonds as usual on or before the end of Trinity Term there next IT WAS THEREUPON ORDERED that on the said Mr Knights payment of the said Sum of one hundred and Thirty pounds to the Principal for the use of this Society on or before the Last Day of the same Trinity Term and on his having the said Mr Trott Mr Haynes & Mr Shepherd admitted as before mencioned and forthwith laying out and expending the said sum of Fifty pounds in fitting up the said Chambers as aforesaid A Lease & an Assignment should be accordingly made and granted to him the said Mr Knight or to them the said Mr Trott Mr Haynes and Mr Shepherd (when admitted) or to any one or more of them with the usual Covenants and provisoes and according to the usual form & method of making and granting Leases and Assignments by this Society AND WHEREAS the Agreement so made by the said Mr Knight was by the Order and Direction and in Trust for the said Mr Trott Mr Haynes & Mr Shepherd who are accordingly admitted & now are Companions of this Society and have laid out and Expended the said Sum of Fifty pounds in Wainscotting painting and otherwise fitting up the said Chambers And have also paid to the principal for the use of this Society the said Sum of One hundred and Thirty pounds But desire that Instead of having a Lease for the Life of the said Mr Knight and an Assignment granted to them of the said Chambers and Cellar the same may be made and granted for the Lives of them the said Mr Trott Mr Haynes and Mr Shepherd or of the Survivors or Survivor of them IT IS THEREUPON ORDERED that A Lease be accordingly made and granted of the said Chambers and Cellar to the said Mr Trott Mr Haynes & Mr Shepherd to hold for Ninety Nine years if they or any of them shall so long live and be and continue Members or Companions of this Society with the usual Covenants and provisoes and according to the Usual form and method of making and granting Leases by this Society And in Testimony that the said Mr Knight Mr Trott Mr Haynes and Mr Shepherd have agreed hereunto they have signed this order.

John Knight	Bap: Trott
	Jos: Haynes
	Richard Shepperd

Interest of the £1200. for Two years to be paid—It is ordered that the principal Do pay to the Several Gentlemen that have advanced and Lent the Twelve hundred pounds on Security of this house the Two years Interest which was due to them for their respective Shares & parts thereof on the eighteenth day of December last past in All amounting to the Sum of one hundred and Twenty pounds.

Mr Aldwinckle deceased for pencions & Absent Commons & his Bond to be delivered up—Mr Aldwinckle deceased late one of the Companions of this Society being in Arrear Twelve Shillings for pencions and Forty Five Shillings for Absent Commons ending at the time of his Death & his widow & Executrix desiring to Compound for the Absent Commons for that the said Mr Aldwinckle was not in Town in Four of the Terms for which he is charged for Absent Commons It is thereupon ordered that Ten Shillings be abated of the Absent Commons and that on payment of Twelve Shillings for pencions and Thirty Five Shillings for Absent Commons (in all being Forty Seaven Shillings) to Mr Thomas Callow for the use of this Society and the like Composition for the Servants Rolls the same be in full Discharge of the said arrears And that thereupon the said Bond be delivered up.

Mr Bell for pencions and Absent Commons—Mr Posthumus Bell one of the Companions of this Society being in arrear Twenty Eight Shillings for pencions and four pounds Ten Shillings for Absent Commons ending in Trin. Term now last past & Mr Bridges on his behalf desiring to compound for the Absent Commons in regard the said Mr Bell hath not been in Town above one Term in A year during the time he is charged with Absent Commons It is ordered that Thirty Five Shillings be abated of the Absent Commons and that on payment of the Twenty Eight Shillings for pencions and Fifty five Shillings for Absent Commons to Mr Callow for the use of this Society and the like Composition to the Servants Rolls the same be in full Discharge of the said Arrear.

Mr Heathcoate for pencions and Absent Commons—Mr Heathcoate One of the Companions of this Society owing Two Shillings for one pencion and Three pounds Five shillings for Absent Commons ending in Hillary Term One thousand Seaven hundred and Fourteen And Mr Heathcoate his son (on his fathers behalf) Desiring to Compound for the Absent Commons in regard his Father hath not been in Town in any of the Terms he is charged therewith It is thereupon ordered that on payment of the Two shillings for the pencion & Two and Thirty Shillings and six pence for the Absent Commons to Mr Callow for the use of this Society and the like Composition to the Servants Rolls The Same be in full Discharge of the said pencion & Absent Commons.

Clements Inn in the ⎱ At a Pencion held at Clements Inn aforesaid on
County of Middlesex ⎰ Friday the Eighth Day of November in the year of our Lord one Thousand Seven Hundred & Seventeene Present Mr John Dovey Deputy Principall Mr Pryor Mr Fowler Mr Goodman Mr Fuller Mr Gibbons Mr Powlett & Mr Penny

Nath: Smith for Pencions & Commons & Bond delivered up—Mr Nathaniell Smith one of the Companions of this Society being indebted for Commons & Pencions in Trinity Terme last in the Summe of Eleven pounds Seventeene Shillings And whereas he hath been & is infirme & not able to follow businesse or come to Town It is agreed that on his payment of Seven pounds five shillings to Mr Dovey for the use of this Society his bond be delivered up.

Clements Inn in the } At a pencion held at Clements Inn aforesaid on
County of Middlesex } Friday the 15th Nov.ʳ 1717 present Mr Dovey
Deputy Principall Mr Pryor Mr Fowler Mr Good-
man Mr Fuller Mr Penny

Mr Nettleton for pencions—Mr John Nettleton being indebted to the
Society to Trinity Terme Past inclusive for pencions one pound twelve
Shillings & Commons five pounds in all six pounds twelve shillings & he
having beene but one Terme in Towne It is ordered that he payes one
pound twelve shillings for pencions & two pounds twelve shillings and
six pence for absent Commons in full till the end of last Terme He paying
twelve Shillings as a Composicion for the Servants

Clements Inn in the } At a pencion held at Clements Inn aforesaid on
County of Middlesex } Friday the 22.ᵈ Nov.ʳ in the yeare of our Lord 1717
present Mr Dovey Dep. Pr. Mr Pryor Mr Fowler
Mr Goodman Mr Fuller Mr Gibbons Mr Knight
Mr Denshire Mr Powlett and Mr Penny

*Sir John Stathams Lease delivered up by Mr Eccles & Cons.ⁿ Money
paid*—Whereas at a pencion held the 17th of July last It was ordered that
on Sir John Stathams Surrender of his Lease of his Chamber in the said
order mencioned that nineteen pounds ten Shillings should be paid to the
said Sir John Statham or to whom else he should direct by the principall
of this Society And it now appearing that the said Sir John Statham had
assigned over his Interest in the said Lease and Chambers to Mr Sam.ˡ
Eccles a Companion of this Society And that the said Sam.ˡ Eccles now
attending & offering to accept of the said Nineteen pounds ten Shillings
for his Interest in the said Chambers & Lease & to deliver up the said
Lease to the Society It is therefore ordered that Mr Blackwell the present
Principall do pay to the said Samuell Eccles the said Summe of Nineteen
pounds ten Shillings on his surrender and delivering up the said Lease of
the said Chambers and premisses to be cancelled.

Fire Plugg & water laid in to the Inn—It is ordered that Mr Evans doe
forthwith order the Fire Plugg to be laid in to this Society & also the New
River Water to be laid into the Kitchin.

Clements Inn in the } At a pencion held at Clements Inn aforesaid on
County of Middlesex } Friday the 6th of December in the year of our Lord
1717 present Mr Dovey Dep. Pr. Mr Fowler
Mr Goodman Mr Fuller Mr Gibbons Mr Powlett
Mr Penny.

Mr Lamplughs Bond delivered up—John Lamplugh one of the Companions of this Society being indebted for pencions and Commons five

pounds Seven Shillings and having paid the full and parted with the Interest in his Chambers in this Society and being entred and paying Commons in Grayes Inn It is ordered that his bond be delivered up.

Tho. Beachs Lease delivered up to the Society and his bond to him—Mr Harman King Son-in-Law to Mr Thomas Beach one of the Companions of this Society appearing by the order of the said Mr Beach and desiring to Surrender the Lease and Interest in the Moity of his Chamber N? 9 In Consideration of the delivery up of Mr Beaches bond to this Society and remitting fourteen pounds One Shilling due from him to this Society It is ordered that on the delivering up the said Lease for the use of this Society to be Cancelled That the said bond be delivered up to the said Mr King and the said fourteen pounds one Shilling be remitted.

Mr Robt Powlett for the Chambers No. 3 late Mr Lamplughs—Mr Rob! Powlett One of the Antients of this Society having agreed with Mr Lamplugh one of the Companions of the Same Society for the purchase of his Interest in the Ground Chambers in the Stair Case No. 3 in the first Court And the said Mr Lamplugh at the request of the said Mr Powlett haveing now Surrendred & delivered up his said Lease to this Society And the said Mr Powlett haveing now paid Eight pounds for a fine for the use of this Society and desireing to be admitted to the said Chambers It is thereupon ordered That the Said Mr Powlett or such other person as he shall nominate before the end of next Hillary Terme shall be admitted to the Said Chambers & a Coale Hole under the Staires in the said Stair Case held with the said Chambers and that a Lease thereof shall be made to him or such other person as he shall Nominate as aforesaid (He the said Mr Powlett being in perfect Health at the making thereof) for the Terme of Ninety nine years If he or such person so by him to be named as aforesaid shall so long live with the usuall Covenants & Provisoes and according to the usuall forme & Method of Leases made by this Society

Clements Inn in the   At a pencion held at Clements Inn aforesaid on
County of Middlesex   Friday the Thirteenth day of December in the year
                      of our Lord One Thousand Seven hundred and
                      seventeen present Mr Dovey Deputy Pr. Mr Good-
                      man Mr Gibbons Mr Knight Mr Powlett &
                      Mr Penny

Mr Hillier for pencions and Commons—Mr John Hillier one of the Companions of this Society being indebted £1. 4s. for Pencions & £4 for Absent Commons He not haveing been in Town It is ordered that on payment of his pencions & £2. for Commons in all £3. 4s. in full for

Commons & pencions to this Time And has paid to Servants by Composicion for 3 yeares 6s.

<table>
<tr><td>Clements Inn in the
County of Middlesex</td><td>At a Pention held at Clements Inn aforesaid on Friday the seaventh day of February, in the year of our Lord one Thousand Seaven hundred and Seaventeen Present Joshua Blackwell Principall Mr Greg Mr Dovey Mr Fowler Mr Goodman Mr Knight Mr Denshire Mr Penny</td></tr>
</table>

William Cock Esq^e for A Lease for his Life of the Chambers late Mr Chris Brewsters—William Cock Esquire one of the Companions of this Society haveing agreed with Mr Christopher Brewster one other of the Companions of the same Society for the purchase of his double Chamber up two pair of Stairs in the Second Stair Case in Kelletts buildings at the upper end of the Garden in Clements Inn aforesaid on the Left hand of the said Stair Case Next adjoyning to New Inn with the appurtenances which the said Mr Brewster held to him and his Assignes by a Lease or Articles from the Society for the Terme of ninety nine years determinable on the death of him the said Mr Brewster who at the request of the said William Cock hath now surrendred & delivered up the said Lease or Articles to this Society And the said William Cock desireing to be admitted thereunto It is ordered that on payment of the summe of fifteen pounds to the Principall for the Use of this He the said William Cock be admitted to the said double chamber with the appurtenances and that a Lease thereof shall be to him made and granted for ninety nine years if he shall so long Live with the Usuall Covenants & Provisoes and according to the Usuall forme and method of Leases made by this Society—

Mr Christopher Brewster for a Lease for his life of the Chamber Garrett and Cellar late Mr Charles Bagshawes—Mr Christopher Brewster one of the Companions of this Society desireing to purchase a Lease for his Life of the Chambers up two pair of Stairs and the Chamber over it up three pair of Stairs with the Garrett over the same and the Cellar to the said Chambers belonging in the Hall Court in the Stair Case marked with the number or figure 20: over the Arch Leading into the Garden in Clements Inn aforesaid with the appurtenances late of Mr Charles Bagshaw deceased late one of the Antients of this Society It is ordered that on payment of one hundred twenty one pounds ten shillings to the Principall for the Use of this Society A Lease be accordingly made and Granted of the said Chambers Garrett and Cellar with the appurtenances to him the said Mr Christopher Brewster for ninety nine years if he shall so Long Live with the Usuall Covenants and Provisoes and according to the Usuall form and Method of makeing and Granting Leases by this Society.

Clements Inn in the } At a pention held at Clements Inn aforesaid on
County of Middlesex } Friday the fourteenth day of February in the year
of Our Lord one Thousand Seaven hundred and
Seaventeen present Joshua Blackwell Principall
Mr Gregg Mr Dovey Mr Fowler Mr Gibbons
Mr Powlett Mr Penny.

Mr Mense for Pencions and absent Commons—Mr Mence one of the
Companions of this Society being in arrear two and Twenty shillings for
Pencions and four pounds Ten Shillings for absent Commons ending in
Hillary Terme now Last past and desireing to Compound for his absent
Commons not haveing been in Towne thirteen of the Termes he is Charged
therewith It is Ordered that he be abated two and Thirty Shillings and Six
pence of his absent Commons and that on his payment of the said two and
Twenty shillings for pencions & Seaven and fifty Shillings and Six pence
for absent Commons to Mr Callow for the Use of this Society and the like
Composition for the Servants Roll the same be in full discharge of the said
arrears of pencion and absent Commons.

*Mr Blakemore deceased for pencions & absent Commons and his Bond
delivered up £7. 10s.*—Mr Blakemore deceased late one of the Companions
of this Society being in arrear two and fifty shillings for pencions & Eight
pounds Ten shillings for absent Commons at the time of his decease &
Catherine Blakemore his widow & Executrix desireing to Compound for
the absent Commons for that the said Mr Blakemore was not in Towne in
Severall of the Termes for which he is Charged for absent Commons and
also desireing that the said Bond may be delivered up It is ordered that
three pounds Twelve shillings be abated of the absent Commons and that
on payment of the said Two and fifty shillings for arrears of Pencions &
four four pounds eighteen shillings for absent Commons to Mr Callow
for the Use of this Society As also Ten shillings to the Servants for their
Rolls The same be in full discharge of the said arrears and that thereupon
the said Bond be delivered up—

Mr Curtis for Pencions & absent Commons—Mr Curtis one of the
Companions of this Society being in arrear Ten Shillings for Pencions and
and five and Twenty shillings for absent Commons ending in Michaelmas
Terme last past and desireing to Compound for his absent Commons in
regard he was not in Town in any of the Termes for which he is Charged
with the same It is Ordered that he be abated Twelve shillings and Sixpence
of his absent Commons and that on his payment of the said Ten shillings
for pencions and Twelve shillings and Six pence for absent Commons to
Mr Callow for the Use of this Society and the like Composicion for the
Servants Roll the same be in full discharge of the said Arrears of Pencions
and absent Commons—

Mr Brackenbury for Pencions & absent Commons—Mr Brackenbury one of the Companions of this Society being in arrear ten shillings for Pencions and Thirty shillings for absent Commons ending in Hillary Terme now last past and desireing to Compound for his absent Commons in regard he was not in Town in three of the Termes Charged on him It is therefore Ordered that he be abated Seaven shillings and Six pence of his absent Commons and that on his payment of the said Ten shillings for Pencions and two and twenty shillings six pence for absent Commons for the Use of this Society and the like Composicion for the Servants Rolls the same be in full discharge of the said arrears of Pencions and absent Commons—

Mr Robert Peart for Pencion & absent Commons—Mr Robert Peart one of the Companions of this Society being in arrear Six shillings for Pencions and Twenty shillings for absent Commons ending in Michaelmas Terme last but not being in Town three of the Termes Charged on him for absent Commons desires an abatement for those three Terms It is ordered that he be accordingly abated Seaven shillings and Six pence of his absent Commons and that on his payment of the six shillings for Pencions and Seaventeen shillings and six pence for absent Commons (the Servants Rolls being by him paid) the same be in full discharge of the said arrear of Pencions and absent Commons.

Mr John Blackwell for pencion & absent Commons—Mr John Blackwell one of the Companions of this Society being in arrear Twelve shillings for Pencions and five and Twenty shillings for absent Commons ending in Hillary Terme now last past and not being in Town three of the Termes for which he is Charged desires an abatement for them It is therefore ordered that he be abated seaven shillings and Six pence for the three terms and that on his payment of the Twelve Shillings for pencions and Seaventeen shillings and Six pence for absent Commons he shall be discharged of the said arrears he haveing fully paid the Servants Rolls—

Clements Inn in the } At a Pention held at Clements Inn aforesaid on
County of Middlesex } Friday the one & Twentieth day of February In the year of our Lord one Thousand Seaven hundred and Seaventeen present Joshua Blackwell Principall Mr Pryor Mr Dovey Mr Fowler Mr Goodman Mr Gibbons Mr Fuller Mr Knight Mr Denshire Mr Powlett Mr Penny.

Mr Carters twenty pounds & Interest to be paid due from the Society—
Lawrence Carter Esquire deceased late one of the Antients of this Society haveing in November one Thousand Seaven hundred and two lent to this Society the Summe of Twenty pounds according to an order of Pencion

made the Sixth of July one Thousand Seaven hundred and two which was to be paid him with Interest at Six pounds per Cent whereof three pounds twelve shillings for three years Interest hath been paid in part thereof so that there remains due to the Executors of the said Lawrence Carter for Principall and Interest the summe of thirty four pounds fourteen shillings and Mr Tho: Carter one of the Companions of this Society requiring payment thereof by the Order and for the Use of the said Executors It is Ordered that the Principall do pay to the said Executors or to the said Mr Thomas Carter by the order and for the use of the said Executors the said Summe of Thirty four pounds fourteen shillings in full discharge of the said Debt & Interest.

Auditors of the principall's Accounts for one year beginning in Hill. Term one Thousand seaven hundred and Sixteen until Hill. Terme one thousand seaven hundred and Seaventeen—It is ordered that Mr George Fuller and Mr John Knight two of the Antients of this Society and Mr Edward Halsted & Mr Humphry Pelham two of the Companions of the same Society shall and do Examine State and audite the accounts of the Principall of This Society for one whole year beginning in Hillary Terme one Thousand Seaven hundred and Sixteen untill Hillary Terme one Thousand seaven hundred and Seaventeen and that they the said George Fuller John Knight Edward Halsted and Humphry Pelham or any three of them shall and do make their Certificate or report of the said Accounts as soon as the same Can or may Conveniently be done.

Mr Francis Jackson for Pencions & absent Commons—Mr Francis Jackson one of the Companions of this Society being in arrear Twenty shillings for absent Commons ending Hillary Terme now past & desireing to Compound In regard he was not in Towne in three of the Termes Charged on him It is ordered he be abated seaven shillings and Six pence and that on payment of twelve shillings and Six pence to Mr Callow for the Use of the Society the same be in full discharge thereof the Servants Rolls being paid—

Mr Guest for Pencions & absent Commons and his bond delivered up—Mr Guest one of the Companions of this Society haveing by Mr Penny one of the Antients of this Society paid to the Principall the summe of Eleaven pounds two shillings in full of all Pencions and absent Commons due from him to the Society and desireing to have his bond delivered up in regard he hath Left off and discontinued the practice of the Law It is Ordered that the said Mr Guests Bond be accordingly delivered up to him to be Cancelled.

Mr Turner for Pencions & absent Commons—Mr Turner one of the Companions of this Society being in arrear six shillings for Pencions & five and Fifty shillings for absent Commons ending in Hillary Terme now past and desireing to Compound for his absent Commons not being in Town five of the Terms he is Charged for Commons It is ordered that twelve shillings and six pence be abated of the absent Commons and that on payment of the said six shillings for pencions and forty two shillings six pence for absent Commons to Mr Callow for the Use of this Society the same be in full discharge of the said arrears of pencions and Commons he having paid the Servants Rolls.

EASTER TERME ANNO DOMINI 1717

Contributors names to the Clock Gowne & Staffe

A Particular Account of the Gentlemen Companions of the Society of Clements Inn who were Contributors towards the Clock or hand Dyall in the Hall of the same Inne as also for the Silver head and ornaments of the Staff and Cloth Tufted Gowne for the Porter[1] of the back Gate of the said Inne and which are all Now in Use and are to Continue for the benefit of all the said Society in Generall are as follows & is herein Entred at their request.

	s		*s*		*s*
Mr Evans	10	Mr Eldridge	10	Mr Cousins	10
Mr C: Lake	10	Mr John Harris Sen.r	10	Mr Carter	10
Mr Cromwell	10	Mr Ballett	10	Mr Atkinson	10
Mr Bowles	10	Mr Druery	10	Mr Carvile	10
Mr Humphreys	10	Mr Wakeling	10	Mr Hyde	10
Mr Piggott	10	Mr Nelthorpe	10	Mr Blackwell Jun.r	10
Mr Adams	10	Mr G. Peart	10	Mr Brightwell Smith	10
Mr Tufton	10	Mr Allen	10	Mr Robert Peart	10
Mr Hope	10	Mr Bennett	10	Mr Walcott	10
Mr Tyson	10	Mr Aldey	10	Mr Dudbridge	05
Mr. Pelham	10	Mr Jackson	10	Mr Morris	05
Mr Fowke	10	Mr Truesdale	10	Mr Davenport	05
				Mr Halsted	
		28th February 1717		Collector of these Contrib.s	10

£17. 15.

This is a True Account as
Witness my hand
Edw.d Halsted

---

[1] Cf. the similar provision in the Inner Temple, *I.T.R.*, III, 212, 272 (silver-headed staff and gown for the porter), 263 (a dial for the clock in the hall).

Clements Inn in the ⎞ At a Pention held at Clements Inne aforesaid on
County of Middlesex ⎠ Friday the Eight and Twentieth day of February
In the year of our Lord one thousand Seaven hundred and Seaventeen present Joshua Blackwell Principall Mr Pryor Mr Gregg Mr Dovey Mr Fowler Mr Goodman Mr Gibbons Mr Fuller Mr Knight Mr Denshire Mr Powlett Mr Penny

No Assignments to be Granted of any Chambers after Trin. Terme—Upon full Consideracion of the State and Condition of this Society it is ordered that from and after the last day of Trinity Terme next no Assignment or Assignments of any one or more Chamber or Chambers in this Society shall be made granted or agreed for to or with any person or persons whatsoever.[1]

Mr George Fuller for an Assignment for a life after his own Life in his two Chambers No. 12 & 14—Mr George Fuller one of the Antients of this Society haveing a Lease for Ninety nine years if he so Long Live of his Chambers in the Brick building now in the first Court of this House up one pair of Stairs in the Entry Leading into the Hall Court formerly marked with the Number or Figure 14: now in his possession as also another Lease for Ninety nine years if he so long Live of his other Chambers up one pair of Stairs in the same building in the Corner Stair Case marked with the Number or Figure 12 now also in his possession and desireing to purchase an Assignment of these two Chambers with the appurtenances for one other Life after the Expiracion of his own Life now in being in them and proposeing for such Assignment to release and discharge the Society of and from all damages and demands whatsoever don to these two Chambers or either of them for or by reason or on account of the Late new building and also to pay the Summe of two and thirty pounds to the Principall for the Use of the said Society It is ordered that in Consideracion of the premises an Assignment be accordingly made and Granted of the said two Chambers with the appurtenances to him the said Mr George Fuller his Executors Administrators and Assignes for one Life after his own Life now in being with the Usuall Covenants and Provisoes and according to the Usual form & method of makeing and Granting assignments by this Society

Mr Robert Powlett for an Assignment for a Life after his own life in his Chambers Number 3: late Mr Lamplugh's—Mr Robert Powlett one of the Antients of this Society haveing a Lease lately Granted him for the terme of Ninety nine yeares if he shall so Long Live of his Ground Chambers in the first Court of this House in the Stair Case marked with the Number or

---

[1] For relaxations of the ban on assignments see pp. 144, 160 below.

Figure 3 late in the possession of Mr John Lamplugh with the Cole hole under the Stairs & thereunto belonging & desireing to purchase an Assignment thereof for one other Life after the Expiracion of his own Life now in being It is ordered that on his payment of the Summe of Eight & Twenty pounds to the principall for the Use of this Society an Assignment be accordingly made & Granted to him the said Mr Robert Powlett his Executors Administrators and Assignes of the said two Chambers & Cole hole with the appurtenances for one Life after his own Life now in being with the Usuall Covenants and provisoes and according to the usuall forme and method of making and Granting Assignments by this Society.

Mr Callowe Senr. for his Lease of his Chambers Number 7 purchased of him by this Society & for a Lease granted to him for his life of the ground Chambers Number 17—Whereas Mr Thomas Callowe the Elder one of the Companions of this Society by Articles bearing Date the third day of December in the year of our Lord one thousand six hundred Ninety two for the Consideracions therein mencioned had a Lease made and Granted to him by the Then Principall & Antients of this Society of All that Chamber with the appurtenances at the North East End of the then dineing Hall near the then Kitchen in Clements Inn up one pair of Stairs marked with the Number or Figure 7 then in the possession of him the said Tho: Callow To hold to him the said Tho: Callowe and his Assignes for ninety nine yeares if Tho: Callow (son of John Callow late Citizen and Skinner of London then deceased) should so Long Live & be and continue a member or Companion of this Society and the said Tho: Callowe Senr. haveing for many years held and enjoyed the Ground Chamber now standing and being next the New late erected Hall in Clements Inn aforesaid in the Stair Case marked with the Number of Figure 17 without payment of Rent or other Satisfaccion for the same to this Society and the said Thomas Callow the son of the said John Callow being in arrear for Pencions & absent Commons due to the Society and the said Chambers with the appurtenances Number 7 being and standing with other Chambers on part of the Ground whereon a New building is intended to be Erected & built for which purpose the right and Interest of the said Tho: Callowe Senr. of and in the same Chambers Number 7 is to be purchased of the said Tho: Callowe Senr. and for which the principall and Antients of this Society are Content and have Consented and agreed not onely to release the said Tho: Callowe Senr. of all demands for the time he has been in possession of the said Chambers Number 17 as aforesaid and to release the said Tho: Callow the son of the said John Callow of all the said arrears of pencions and absent Commons but also to Give and Grant unto him the said Tho: Callow Senr. a Lease of the said Chambers Number 17: for Ninety nine years if he shall so Long Live under the Usuall Covenants

Provisoes and Agreements to which the said Tho: Callow Senr hath readily agreed It is therefore ordered that for the Consideracions aforesaid he the said Tho: Callowe Senr do and shall surrender and deliver up to this Society or Assigne or release the said Articles or Lease of the said Chambers Number 7 & all his Interest and Terme therein unto this Society in order to the said New intended building and that a Lease be made and Granted to the said Tho: Callow Senr of the said Chambers Number 17: for the Terme of Ninety nine yeares if he shall so Long Live with Usuall Covenants and provisoes and according to the Form and Method of makeing and Granting Leases by this Society And in Testimony that the said Tho: Callow Senr hath agreed to the premisses as aforesaid he hath Signed this order.

Tho Callowe

Mr Henry Dottin about Damage done to his Chambers by the New building—Whereas at a Pention held the thirtieth day of November one thousand Seaven hundred & Sixteen [1] It was ordered that in Consideracion of the damage done to the Chambers of Mr Henry Dottin one of the Companions of this Society up two pair of Staires adjoyning to or Near the Hall by pulling down of the Old Hall Pencion Room & Chambers over the same It was ordered that the Wainscott in the said Mr Dottins Chambers should be repaired and made Good at the Charge of this Society & accordingly some money hath been Laid out & Expended in and about the same and the said Mr Dottin hath Lately brought in some further bills relateing thereto It is therefore ordered that it be referred to Mr Gibbons Mr Powlett & Mr Penny antients of this Society or any two of them to Examine Settle and adjust with the said Mr Dottin what part of the said Bills shall be paid by this Society in order to a Final determinacion and agreement with the said Mr Dottin for the said Damage and that they or any two of them do make their Certificate and report thereof at the next Pencion or as soon after as Conveniently may be done—

St Clements Inn in the ⎱ At a Pention held at Clements Inn aforesaid on
County of Middlesex ⎰ Friday the Seaventh day of March in the Year of Our Lord one thousand Seaven hundred and Seaventeen present Joshua Blackwell Principall Mr Dovey Mr Fowler Mr Goodman Mr Gibbons Mr Fuller Mr Knight Mr Powlett & Mr Penney

Principalls Accounts Audited & Confirmed—Whereas Mr George Fuller & Mr John Knight two of the Antients of this Society & Mr Edward

---

[1] See p. 29 above.

Halsted and Mr Humphrey Pelham two of the Companions of the same Society by order of Pencion made the one & twentieth day of February last past were appointed Auditors of the Accounts of Mr Joshua Blackwell principall of this Society and have accordingly Examined Stated and audited the said Principalls Account of receipts and disbursements from the beginning of Hillary Terme One Thousand Seaven hundred and Sixteen until Hillary Terme now last past being for one whole year and have found the summe Totall of the said principalls receipts in that year to be one thousand forty eight pounds Eight Shillings and two pence and the summe Totall of the disbursements to be one thousand one hundred ninety three pounds Six Shillings and three pence so that there remains due from this Society to the principall on the said Account the summe of one hundred forty four pounds Eighteen Shillings and one penny as appears by their Certificate or report thereof dated the eight and twentieth day of February now also last past It is therefore ordered that the said Account so Examined Stated audited and Certified as aforesaid be allowed and approved of and the same is hereby accordingly allowed and approved of as a Just and true account And the said Mr Joshua Blackwell is hereby discharged therefrom And it is also ordered that the said Mr Blackwell be paid the said Summe of one hundred forty four pounds Eighteen shillings and one penny (being the ballance of the said Account) out of the first money that shall be received for the Use of the Society

R^d Powlett	John Gibbons	John Dovey
John Penny	Geo: Fuller	Wm Fowler
	John Knight	Ever^d Goodman

Mr Henry Dottin for an assignement for a Life after his own Life in his Chamber Number 14—Mr Henry Dottin one of the Companions of this Society having a Lease granted him for ninety nine years If he shall soe long live of his Chambers in the Brick buildings now in the first Court of this House up two paire of Stairs in the Entry leading into the Hall Court formerly marked with the number or figure 14 now in his possession and desiring to purchase an Assignement of the said Chamber with the appurtenances for one other Life after the Expiracion of his own Life now in being in them And the said Mr Dottin proposing as & for the Consideracion for such Assignement to release and discharge the Society of and from all demands whatsoever due to him from the Society for or on account of all or any the damages done to his said Chamber by or by reason or on account of the late New Buildings in Clements Inn as aforesaid and also to pay the Summe of Sixteen pounds to the Principall for the Use of this Society It is thereupon ordered that in Consideracion of the premisses an Assignement be accordingly made & granted of the said

Chamber with appurtenances to him the said Mr Dottin his Executors Administrators & assignes for one Life after his owne Life now in being with the usuall Covenants & provisoes and according to the usuall forme & Method of making & granting Assignements by this Society And in Testimony of the said Mr Dottin's consent & agreement to the premisses herein before mencioned he hath subscribed his name to this Order.

Hen Dottin

Clements Inn in the ⎱ At a Pention held at Clements Inn aforesaid on
County of Middlesex ⎰ Fryday the Seaven and Twentieth day of June in the year of Our Lord One Thousand Seaven hundred & Eighteen Present Joshua Blackwell principall Mr Pryor Mr Dovey Mr Fowler Mr Goodman Mr Gibbons Mr Penny.

Bill bookes to be examined & abstracted—It is ordered that Mr William Fowler Mr George Fuller & Mr George Denshire (three of the Antients of this Society) shall and do Examine the bill books belonging to the said Society and Settle and adjust the Severall Summs of Money due from Each respective Member thereof or from the Executors or Administrators of Such of them as are dead & make an Extract of the said Severall Sums of money so due and where it appears that any Member has discharged what appears due in the said books or either of them by Composition or otherwise or are become insolvent so that the same Cannot be recovered that an Entry or Memorandum thereof be made & entred in the said Books accordingly And the said Mr Fowler Mr Fuller & Mr Denshire are to Certify what they have done pursuant to this order so soon as Conveniently they Can.

Clements Inn in the ⎱ At a pention held at Clements Inn aforesaid on
County of Middlesex ⎰ Wednesday the ninth day of July in the yeare of Our Lord one Thousand Seaven hundred and Eighteen Present Mr Blackwell principall Mr Dovey Mr Fowler Mr Goodman Mr Gibbons Mr Knight Mr Denshire Mr Powlett Mr Penny.

Mr Mence to have his Bond delivered up—Mr Richard Mence one of the Companions of this Society oweing two shillings for a pencion and ten shillings for absent Commons ending in Trinity Terme now past and desireing to have his bond given on his admission to this Society delivered up he being admitted into the Society of the Inner Temple as by a Certificate thereof now by him produced appeares It is ordered that on his payment of the said Twelve Shillings to the Principall for the Use of this Society with what is due to the Servants Rolls his Bond be accordingly delivered up.

Mr Zachary Allnutt deceased his Bond delivered up—Mr Zachary Allnutt deceased late one of the Companions of this Society oweing two shillings for a pencion and ten shillings for absent Commons ending in Trinity Terme now past & Mr Carvile desireing (on the behalf of Mr Allnutts Executors) to have the Bond given by Mr Allnut on his admission into this Society delivered up It is ordered that on payment of the said Twelve Shillings to the Principall for the Use of this Society with what is due to the Servants Rolls the said Bond be accordingly delivered up.

Mr Purcell Jun.ʳ twenty shillings for a quarters rent due at Michaelmas 1716 in dispute remitted—Mr William Purcell one of the Companions of this Society being by Mr Callow returned Twenty shillings in arrear for a Quarters rent due at Michaelmas one thousand seaven hundred and Sixteen and produceing Mr Callows Acquittance for the same & affirming that he has paid to Mr Callowe all rent due before that time It is ordered that the Quarters rent due at Michaelmas one thousand seaven hundred and Sixteen be discharged in the house Rentall & that the same be remitted.

Clements Inn in the } At a pention held at Clements Inn aforesaid on *County of Middlesex* } Wednesday the Thirtieth day of July in the year of our Lord one Thousand Seaven hundred and Eighteen Present Mr Blackwell Principall Mr Gregg Mr Dovey Mr Fowler Mr Goodman Mr Gibbons Mr Fuller Mr Knight Mr Powlett Mr Penny.

Mr Tho: Tufton to be Steward or Clerke of the Society in the room & place of Mr Tho. Callow deceased—Mr Thomas Tufton one of the Companions of this Society haveing made his application and desireing to be admitted in the office or place of Steward or Clerke of the Society in the room and place of Mr Thomas Callowe deceased It is ordered that he the said Mr Tufton be accordingly admitted into the said Office or place but to continue therein onely during the Good Will and pleasure of the principall and Antients and their Successors and no Longer And the said Mr Tufton is also to Give a bond with two other sufficient persons to be bound with him in the penalty or Summe of two hundred pounds for the due performance of his said Office or place dureing such time as he shall be Continued therein—

Mr Wᵐ Forster Rector of St Clements to have Six Guineas Given him as a gratuity—Ordered that the principall do Give to the Reverend Mr William Forster Rector of Saint Clements Danes six Guineas as a free & Voluntary Gift of this Society Nothing of right being due to him from this Society.

Clements Inne in the⎱ Att a pencon held at Clements Inne aforesaid on
County of Middlesex⎰ Fryday the 28th day of November in the yeare of
Our Lord 1718 Present Mr Goodman Deputy
Principall Mr Greg Mr Dovey Mr Fowler Mr Fuller
Mr Knight Mr Powlett Mr Gibbons Mr Penny.

Mr Blackwell the principall to have Interest for the moneys due to him from the Society—Whereas the Society stands indebted to Mr Joshua Blackwell Principall upon the ballance of the account allowed the seventh day of March 1717 the Summe of one hundred and forty four pounds eighteen shillings and one penny And whereas the said Mr Blackwell upon the 2.^{d} day of October last past did advance and lend to the Society the Summe of Sixty three pounds three shillings four pence which hath been layd out towards carrying up the New building at the Upper End of the first Court next to the Talbott Alehouse and upon the necessary repaires of this Inn And whereas the said Mr Blackwell upon the twenty second day of November instant did advance & lend to this Society the further Summe of fifty pounds for the carrying on the said New building and whereas It will require yet a further Summe of money to carry up & cover in the said New building It is ordered that the said Mr Blackwell be paid Interest after the rate of five pounds per Cent per Annum for the said one hundred and forty four pounds eighteene shillings one penny the ballance of the said account from the said seventh day of March last and the like Interest for the said Severall Summes of sixty three pounds three shillings four pence and fifty pounds from the days they were respectively advanced & lent as aforesaid And that the said Mr Blackwell be paid the like Interest for all such further Summes of money which he shall advance for the carrying up and covering in the said New building & and other Uses of this Society from the times of lending thereof untill the same shall be repaid And it is further Ordered that the said Severall Summes of one hundred forty four pounds eighteen shillings one penny and Sixty three pounds three Shillings four pence and fifty pounds together with such other moneys as the said Mr Blackwell shall advance for the purposes aforesaid together with Interest for the same after the rate aforesaid be paid to the said Mr Blackwell out of the first moneys that shall be received for the Use of this Society.

Ever.^{d} Goodman Dep. Pr.
F. Gregg
John Dovey
Wm. Fowler
Geo. Fuller
John Gibbons
John Knight
John Penny
R.^{d} Powlett

Clements Inne in the ⎫ Att a pencion held att Clements Inn on Thursday
County of Middlesex ⎭ the 18ᵗʰ day of December 1718 present Mr Good-
man Depᵗʸ principall Mr Gregg Mr Dovey
Mr Gibbons Mr Fuller Mr Powlett.

Mr Gregory for a Lease of the Chambers late Mr Allnutts—Mr Henry
Gregory one of the Companions of this Society haveing agreed with
Martha Allnutt widow & Executrix of Zachary Allnutt deceased late one
of the Companions of this Society for the purchase of her Interest under
certaine Articles made between this Society and the said Zachary Allnutt
bearing date the 19th of June 1713 purporting to be a Lease with an
Assignment of All That Chamber then or late in the possession of Mathew
Carvile gen. being a ground Chamber in the building looking into the
garden in the Stair Case marked with the Figures or Number (22) and one
part of the Cellar under the said Chamber then or late also in the possession
of the said Mathew Carvile with the appurtenances And the said Martha
Allnutt haveing surrendered into the hands of the Principall and Antients
of this Society the said recited Articles & the Estate Interest & Terme of
yeares thereby granted of in & to the said premisses To the Intent that the
now Principall & Antients should admitt the said Henry Gregory to the
said Chamber & part of the Cellar with the appurtenances for the terme
of 99 yeares if he shall so long live persueant to the Agreement on the part
of the said Principall & Antients in the said in part recited Articles Itt is
ordered That a Lease be made to the said Henry Gregory of the said
Chamber & part of the Cellar with the appurtenances for the Terme of
99 yeares if he shall so long live with the usuall Covenants & provisoes &
according to the usuall forme & Method of makeing & granting Leases
by this Society.

Clements Inn in the ⎫ At a pention held at Clements Inn aforesaid on
County of Middlesex ⎭ Monday the Twenty third day of February One
Thousand Seaven hundred & Eighteen Present
Mr Blackwell principall Mr Dovey Mr Fowler
Mr Goodman Mr Fuller Mr Denshire Mr Penny

Mr Wyche for pencions & absent Commons—Mr Richard Wyche one of
the Companions of this Society being three pounds four shillings in arrear
for Pencions & absent Commons ending in Hillary Terme now Last past and
desireing to Compound for the same It is ordered that in regard he was not
in Town in nine of the terms for which he is charged for absent Commons
that he be abated two and twenty Shillings and Six pence and that on his
payment of forty one Shillings and Six pence to Mr Tufton for the Use of his
Society the same be in full discharge thereof the Servants Rolls being paid.

Mr Eccles for pencions & absent Commons—Mr Samuel Eccles one of the Companions of this Society being four pounds eighteen Shillings in arreare for taxes for his late Chambers & for pencions and absent Commons ending in Hillary Term Last & desireing to Compound for the absent Commons for that he was not in Town in nine of the terms he is Charged therewith It is thereupon ordered that two & twenty shillings and Six pence be abated him for absent Commons and that on his payment of three pounds fifteen Shillings & Six pence to Mr Tufton for the Use of this Society the same be in full discharge thereof he haveing paid the Servants Rolls.

Auditors of the Principalls Accounts for one year beginning in Hillary Term 1717 untill Hillary Term 1718—It is ordered that Mr John Dovey & Mr Everard Goodman two of the Antients of this Society and Mr Roger Aldey & Mr John Hope two of the Companions of the same Society shall and do Examine State and audite the Accounts of the Principall of this Society for one whole year beginning in Hillary Term One thousand Seaven hundred and Seaventeen untill Hillary Terme One thousand Seaven hundred and eighteen now Last past And that they the said John Dovey Everard Goodman Roger Aldey and John Hope or any three of them shall & do make their Certificate and Report of the said Accounts so soon as the same Can or may conveniently be done.

The Agreement with Sarah Smith widow about the buildings & other matters in the Lamb Inn Yard to be Settled and adjusted—It is ordered that the Principall of this Society or his Deputy for the time being together with Mr George Fuller & Mr Robert Powlett two of the Antients of this Society and Mr Edward Halstead one of the Companions of the same Society shall and do treat & Agree with Sarah Smith widow or any others Concerned for her touching & Concerning the Buildings Windows Gutters and water pipes and all other matters in the Lamb Inn Yarde now in Controversy between this Society and the said Sarah Smith and that They the said principall or his Deputy & the said George Fuller Robert Powlett and Edward Halstead or any two of them shall and do Settle and adjust the Articles of Agreement relating thereto so soon as Conveniently the same Can or may be done and make their Certificate or report thereof at Some pention hereafter to be held by this Society.

Clements Inn in the⎫ At a Pention held at Clements Inn aforesaid on
County of Middlesex⎭ Wednesday the Eighteenth day of March In the
                    yeare of Our Lord One thousand Seaven hundred and
                    eighteen present Mr Blackwell Principall Mr Gregg
                    Mr Dovey Mr Goodman Mr Gibbons Mr Knight
                    Mr Penny Mr Fowler Mr Fuller Mr Denshire

Security to Mr Dovey & others for the Severall Sums of money by them advanced with Interest for the same—WHEREAS it is adjudged that it will be

E

more for the benefitt and advantage of this Society to build and Erect Chambers on the Ground in the first Court of this house where the Chambers of Mr Maurice Johnson & Mr Arthur Squire lately stood than to Lett out the said Ground on a Building Lease and accordingly the said Building is Set about & now in hand AND WHEREAS to Supply the want of a present summe of money to Carry on and perfect the said Building & for other Necessary works and repairs to be done in and about the house The Severall Gentlemen hereafter named (being Antients of this Society) have agreed to advance and Lend the Severall and respective Sums of money hereinafter mencioned viz.ᵗ Mr John Dovey the summe of one hundred pounds Mr Everard Goodman the summe of Fifty pounds Mr John Gibbons the summe of Fifty pounds Mr John Knight the summe of Fifty pounds and Mr John Penny the sum of one hundred pounds in all amounting to three hundred and fifty pounds IT IS THEREFORE ORDERED that the said John Dovey Everard Goodman John Gibbons John Knight and John Penny shall Severally and respectively be paid the said Severall and respective Sums of money so by them agreed to be advanced & Lent as aforesaid together with Interest for the same (after the rate of five pounds per Cent per annum) from the Severall and respective times the said Severall and respective sums of money shall be by them the said John Dovey Everard Goodman John Gibbons John Knight & John Penny advanced and paid into the hands of the said Principall for the Use of this Society And that the said Severall and respective summs of money with Interest as aforesaid shall be Secured and paid unto the said John Dovey Everard Goodman John Gibbons John Knight & John Penny by and out of the Stock and other rents and profitts of this Society as the same Can or may from time to time be raised and received

	Josh: Blackwell
	F: Gregg
The above Named Mr John Gibbons did not advance & Lent the Fifty pounds above mencioned Therefore is not Charged Received in my Accounts Josh: Blackwell; Pr:	John Dovey
	Everard Goodman
	John Gibbons
	John Knight
	John Penny
	Wᵐ Fowler
Geo. Denshire	Geo. Fuller

Mr Wᵐ Seabrooke undertaker for the new intended building—Whereas Mr William Seabrooke Bricklayer hath for some time been in Treaty with this Society for a new intended building in the first Court on the East Side thereof between the building called Lawes building and the new building lately erected by the Society And Articles of agreement for that purpose are now perfected and agreed upon It is ordered that the said articles be engrossed and Entered in the booke wherein other articles & leases made by this Society are usually Entered and that both parts thereof be signed by the principall and antients of this Society or a sufficient number of them as also by the said Mr Seabrooke according to the method & custom of this house in Such cases.

Clements Inn in the \
County of Middlesex } At a Pention held at Clements Inn aforesaid on Wednesday the Sixth day of May 1719 present Mr Penny Deputy Principall Mr Dovey Mr Fowler Mr Goodman Mr Gibbons Mr Fuller

Mr Bernard Evans for a Lease of his Chambers &c as Nominee of Matthew Evans deceased—WHEREAS Matthew Evans Gent (Late one of the Companions of this Society) was in his life time possessed of all those Chambers and Garretts in the building called Kelletts building in Garden Court in the Staircase marked with the figure or Nº (24) up two three and four pair of Stairs on the left hand of the said stair case for the term of 99 years (if he so long livd & continued a Companion of this Society) With a power for him his Executors or Administrators at any time within two terms after the death or putting extra [1] of the said Matt. Evans to nominate & appoint any one other companion admitted of the said house To hold the said Chamber and Garretts with the Appurtenances Which said person so nominated was to be admitted by the Principall & Antients of this Society to the said Chambers for Ninety Nine years (if the said nominee should so long live and continue a member of the said Society) AND WHEREAS the said Matthew Evans in or about January last departed this life a member of the said Society having first duly made his will in writing & thereby given all his estate right title and interest of in & to the said Chamber & Garretts unto his son Bernard Evans Gen. And Whereas Ann Evans the daughter and only acting Executrix of the said Matthew Evans deceased hath (within two terms after the death of the said Matthew Evans) at the instance & request of the said Bernard Evans surrendred into the hands of the said Principall & Antients of the Society the said recited Articles and the estate interest & terme of years thereby granted of in and to the said Chamber & Garretts with the Appurtenances To the intent that the said Principall and Antients should admitt the said Bernard Evans to the same according to the true intent & meaning of his said fathers

---

[1] *I.e.* leaving the Society (cf. the Mundy and Wrightson entry, p. 8 above). The Latinised formula (*posuit se extra*) occurs in interlineations in the Admission Book, *e.g.* under William Scrimshire, p. 250 below.

Articles & Will AND WHEREAS the said Bernard Evans is admitted a Companion of this Society and being under age himselfe hath procured two sufficient persons to enter into a Bond to the Principall & some of the Antients on his behalfe for his performance of the orders & constitutions of the said Society & for payment of all dues & payments as usuall IT IS ORDERED that a Lease be made to the said Bernard Evans of the said Chambers & Garretts with the Appurtenances for the term of Ninety Nine years (if he shall so long live & continue a member of the said Society) with the usuall covenants & provisoes and according to the usuall form & method of making & granting leases by this Society.

Clements Inn in the At a Pention held at Clements Inn aforesaid on
County of Middlesex Wednesday the Thirteenth day of May one Thousand seven Hundred and Nineteen present Mr Penny Deputy Principall Mr Pryor Mr Dovey Mr Fowler Mr Goodman and Mr Fuller

Principalls Accounts audited confirmed—Whereas Mr John Dovey and Mr Everard Goodman (Two of the Antients of this Society) and Mr Roger Aldey and Mr John Hope (Two of the Companions of the same Society) by order of Pention made the Twenty third day of February last past were appointed Auditors of the Account of Mr Joshua Blackwell Principall of this Society and have accordingly examined stated and audited the said Principalls Account of receipts and disbursements for one whole year beginning from the beginning of Hillary term One Thousand Seven Hundred and Seventeen untill Hillary term One Thousand Seven Hundred and Eighteen and have found the sum totall of the said Principalls receipts in that year to be Four Hundred ninety one pound one Shilling and the sum totall of his disbursements to be Five Hundred Fifty Nine pound Twelve shillings one penny halfpenny So that there remaines due from this Society to the Principall on the said Account the sum of Sixty Eight pound eleven shillings one penny halfpenny as appears by their certificate or report thereof dated the Eighth day of this instant month of May It is therefore ordered that the said Account so examined stated audited and certified as aforesaid be allowed and approved off And the same is hereby accordingly allowed and approved off as a just and true account And the said Mr Joshua Blackwell is hereby discharged therefrom And it is also ordered that the said Mr Blackwell be paid the said sum of Sixty Six [1] pounds Eleven shillings and one penny halfpenny being the ballance of the

---

[1] Slips of the pen are often made good (sometimes in a different script), but here the error (of "six" for "eight") was overlooked.

said Account out of the first money that shall be received for the use of this Society

John Penny Dep^{ty} Pr.　　Tho Pryor
Ever^d Goodman　　　John Dovey
Geo. Fuller　　　　　Wm Fowler

Mr Dymock composicion and bond delivered up—Mr Thomas Dymock deceased (late one of the Companions of this Society) being in arrear at his death for Taxes Pentions and absent Commons Thirteen pound three shillings and Mr Goodman (one of the Antients of this Society) desiring on the behalfe of Mr Dymock's Executrix to compound for his absent Commons (he being severall terms out of town and his Chambers rendred useless by the pulling down of other Chambers in the said Inn) It is thereupon ordered that Three pounds Three shillings be abated for absent Commons and that on payment of Ten pound to the Principall for the use of this Society the bond given by Mr Dymock on his admission into this Society be delivered up The Servts. rolls being paid

Clements Inn in the ⎱ At a pention held at Clements Inn aforesaid on
County of Middlesex ⎰ Fryday the Nineteenth day of June in the yeare of
　　　　　　　　　　Our Lord one thousand Seaven hundred and
　　　　　　　　　　Nineteen present Mr Blackwell principall Mr Dovey
　　　　　　　　　　Mr Fowler Mr Goodman Mr Gibbons Mr Fuller
　　　　　　　　　　Mr Knight Mr Powlett Mr Penny

Mr Hillier for pencions and absent Commons and his bond delivered up—Mr John Hillier one of the Companions of this Society haveing Compounded for absent Commons the thirteenth of December one thousand Seaven hundred and Seaventeen and Mr Adrian Moore now appearing on his behalf and desireing that his bond may be delivered up in regard that the said Mr Hillier hath Left off and discontinued the practice of the Law It is ordered that on payment of Fifty two Shillings for two yeares pencions and Commons from the time of his Last Composicion to Mr Tufton for the Use of this Society and paying to the servants eight Shillings for their Rolls the said Mr Hilliers Bond be accordingly delivered up to be Cancelled.

Mr Thomas Callowe for a Lease for his Life of the Ground Chambers Number 17:—Mr Thomas Callowe one of the Companions of this Society desiring to purchase a Lease for his Life of the Ground Chambers now in his possession next adjoyning to the Hall in the Stair Case marked with the Number or Figure (17) in the building formerly Called Maydwells building in Clements Inn aforesaid with the Cole hole on the Left hand of the passage Leading to the said Chambers as also the Yard or backside lying on the South Side of part of the said Chambers It is ordered that on his payment of forty five pound to the Principall for the Use of this Society A Lease be accordingly made & Granted of the said Chambers Cole hole and Yard to him the said Thomas Callowe for Ninety nine yeares if he shall so Long Live with the Usuall Covenants & provisoes & according to the form & Method of making and granting Leases by this Society

Mr William Pacey for a Lease for his Life of the Chambers Late Mr Henry Paceys his father—Mr William Pacey one of the Companions of this Society haveing agreed with his father Mr Henry Pacey one other of the Companions of the same Society for the purchase of his Chambers up two pair of Stairs in the Stair Case marked with the Number or Figures (12) in the first Court of Clements Inn aforesaid which the said Henry Pacey held to him and his assignes by a Lease or Articles from this Society for the term of Ninety nine yeares determinable on the death of him the said Henry Pacey who at the request of the said William Pacey hath now Surrendred and delivered up the said Lease or Articles to this Society and the said William Pacey desiring to be admitted to the said Chambers It is ordered that on his payment of five pounds to the Principall for the Use of this Society a Lease be made and granted of the said Chambers to him the said William Pacey for ninety nine yeares if he shall so Long live with the Usuall Covenants and provisoes and according to the forme & Method of Leases Made by this Society.

Mr Henry Pacey for Pencions & absent Commons & his Bond delivered up—Mr Henry Pacey one of the Companions of this Society having paid to Mr Tufton for the Use of the said Society five pounds six Shillings in full for Taxes Pencions and absent Commons ending in Trinity Terme now Last past and desireing to have his bond delivered up In regard he hath Left off and discontinued the practice of the Law It is ordered that the said Mr Henry Pacey's Bond be accordingly delivered up to be cancelled he haveing paid the Servants Rolls

Clements Inn in the ⎱ At a pention held at Clements Inn aforesaid on
County of Middlesex ⎰ Fryday the Six and Twentieth day of June In the
yeare of Our Lord One thousand Seaven hundred and Nineteen present Mr Blackwell Principall Mr Dovey Mr Fowler Mr Goodman Mr Gibbons Mr Fuller Mr Denshire Mr Penny

Mr Owen for pencions and absent Commons & his Bond delivered up—Mr Edward Owen one of the Companions of this Society being in arreare for pencions and absent Commons Something more than the penalty of his bond given on his admission into this Society (which was twenty pound) and insisting that he was under age when he entred into the said Bond yet

Nevertheless Offering to pay Eighteen pound on his Bond being delivered up And it appearing that he was not of full age when he entred into the said Bond & that Mr William Stratford his bondsman hath been Long since dead and it is not known whether he Left assetts Sufficient to the Value of the said bond or any part thereof It is therefore ordered that on Mr Owen's payment of eighteen pounds to Mr Tufton for the Use of this Society his Bond be delivered up to him to be Cancelled he haveing paid half a Guinea to the Servants for their Rolls

Mr Parke for pencions & absent Commons—Mr Richard Parke one of the Companions of this Society oweing three pounds Eighteen shillings for pencions and absent Commons ending in Trinity Terme now Last past and desiring to Compound for his absent Commons not being in Town four of the Termes for which he is Charged It is ordered that ten shillings be abated of the absent Commons and that on payment of Three pounds eight shillings to Mr Tufton for the Use of this Society and the Rolls to the Servants the same be in full discharge of the said pencions and absent Commons

Clements Inn in the ⎱ At a Pention held at Clements Inn aforesaid on
County of Middlesex ⎰ Friday the third day of July in the yeare of Our
Lord One thousand Seaven hundred and Nineteen present Mr Blackwell principall Mr Fowler Mr Goodman Mr Gibbons Mr Fuller Mr Knight Mr Penny

Mr Turner for pencions & absent Commons—Mr William Turner one of the Companions of this Society oweing six and twenty shillings for pencions and absent Commons ending in Easter terme last & not being in Town in any of the four termes for which he is Charged with absent Commons and therefore desireing to Compound for the same as Usuall It is ordered that ten shillings be abated of the absent Commons and that on his payment of Sixteen shillings to Mr Tufton for the Use of this Society the same be in full discharge of the said pencions & absent Commons the Servants Rolls being paid

Mr Curtis for pencions & absent Commons—Mr Edward Curtis one of the Companions of this Society oweing Six and twenty shillings for pencions & absent Commons ending in Easter terme Last & not being in towne in any of the four terms for which he is Charged with absent Commons & therefore desireing to Compound for the same as Usuall It is ordered that ten shillings be abated of the absent Commons and that on his payment of Sixteen shillings to Mr Tufton for the Use of this

Society the same be in full discharge of the said Pencions & absent Commons the Servants Rolls being paid

Mr Hodgkis for pencions & absent Commons—Mr John Hodgkis one of the Companions of this Society being in arrear for Pencions & absent Commons ending in Trinity terme now Last past the summe of Seaven pounds Seaventeen shillings & desireing to Compound for his absent Commons not being in town Sixteen of the Termes he is Charged for absent Commons It is therefore ordered that he be abated forty shillings of the said absent Commons and that on his payment of five pound Seaventeen shillings to Mr Tufton for the Use of this Society the same be in full discharge of the said pencions & absent Commons the Servants Rolls being paid

Mr Truesdale for pencions and absent Commons—Mr Thomas Truesdale one of the Companions of this Society being in arreare for Pencions and absent Commons ending in Trinity Terme now last past & not being in Towne ten of the termes he is Charged with absent Commons and therefore desiring to Compound for the same as Usuall It is ordered that he be abated five and twenty shillings of the absent Commons and that on his payment of five pounds Seaventeen shillings to Mr Tufton for the Use of this Society the same be in full Discharge of the said pencions & absent Commons the Servants Rolls being paid

Mr Heckfords Bond delivered up—Mr Samuel Heckford in Hillary terme last desireing his bond given on his admission into this Society might be delivered up in regard he was Leaveing his Chambers & was to be a house keeper in the parish of Saint Clements Danes It was then agreed that on his payment of the rent of his Chambers to this Society to and for Midsummer one thousand Seaven hundred & Nineteen his Bond should be delivered up and he having accordingly paid the said rent & all other duties to the house except twelve shillings for a pencion & absent Commons in Easter & Trinity terms Last which is in time since the said agreement was made with him and in both which terms he was a house keeper It is therefore at his request ordered that the said twelve shillings be remitted and discharged and that his bond be delivered up according to the agreement before mencioned

Mr Benson for pencions & absent Commons and his Bond delivered up—Mr James Benson oweing six and twenty shillings for pencions and absent Commons ending in Hillary Terme last before which time he left his Chambers in this Society and went to travell in parts beyond the Seas & intends there to Continue for a Considerable time and it being therefore desired by his father that his bond Given on his admission into this Society may be delivered up It is ordered that on payment of the said Six

and twenty shillings to Mr Tufton for the Use of this Society the said
Bond be accordingly delivered up the Servants Rolls being paid

Clements Inn in the
County of Middlesex } At a pencion held at Clements Inn aforesaid on Friday the Seven and Twentieth day of November in the year of our Lord 1719 Present Mr John Dovey Deputy Principall Mr Pryor Mr Fowler Mr Goodman Mr Fuller Mr Knight Mr Penny Mr Powlett

Mr Pavey for a Lease of Chambers late Mr Priors—Thomas Pryor Gent
one of the Antients of this Society having agreed with Mr William Pavey
one of the Companions of the same Society for the Purchase of the
Chamber two pair of Stairs and two Garretts in the Stair case marked
N.º (3) in the First Court of Clements Inne aforesaid with the Appurten-
ances which the said Mr Pryor held to him & his Assignes by a Lease or
Articles from this Society for the Terme of Ninety Nine years determinable
on the Death of him the said Thomas Pryor who at the request of the said
William Pavey hath now delivered up the same Lease or Articles to this
Society And the said William Pavey desiring to be admitted thereunto
It is Ordered That on Payment of the Summe of Ten pounds to the
Principall for the Use of this Society He the said William Pavey be admitted
to the said Chamber and Garretts with the Appurtenances and that a
Lease thereof shall be made to him and granted for Ninety Nine years if
he shall so long live with the usuall Covenants and Provisoes and according
to the usuall forme and Method of Leases made by this Society.

Clements Inne in the
County of Middlesex } At a pencion held at Clements Inne aforesaid on Wednesday the Sixteenth day of December in the year of our Lord One Thousand Seven hundred and Nineteen Present Mr John Dovey Deputy Principall Mr Pryor Mr Goodman Mr Gibbons Mr Fuller Mr Knight Mr Penny.

*Sir John Statham for pencions and Absent Commons and Bond delivered
up*—Sir John Statham one of the Companions of this Society being in
Arrear for Pencions and absent Commons the Summe of Nine pounds and
Six Shillings and having left off the Practice of the Law and having paid
the said Nine pounds and Six Shillings to Mr Tufton for the use of this
Society It is therefore ordered his Bond be delivered up to him to be
cancelled.

E*

Clements Inn in the At a pention held at Clements Inn aforesaid on
County of Middlesex the tenth day of February One thousand Seaven
hundred and Nineteen present Mr Blackwell
Principall Mr Pryor Mr Dovey Mr Fowler Mr
Goodman Mr Fuller Mr Penny.

*Auditors of the Principalls Accounts for one year beginning in Hill.
Terme 1718 untill Hillary Terme 1719*—It is ordered that Mr William Fowler
& Mr John Gibbons two of the Antients of this Society & Mr Edward
Bennet & Mr Robert Drury two of the Companions of the said Society
shall and do examine State & audite the Accounts of the Principall of this
Society for one whole year beginning in Hillary Terme one thousand
Seaven hundred & eighteen untill this present Hillary Terme one thousand
Seaven hundred and Nineteen And that they the said William Fowler
John Gibbons Edward Benett & Robert Drury or any three of them shall
and do make their Certificate & Report of the said Accounts so soon as
the same can or may Conveniently be done.

Clements Inn in the At a Pention held at Clements Inn aforesaid on
County of Middlesex Wednesday the ninth day of March One thousand
Seaven hundred and Nineteen present Mr Blackwell
Principall Mr Prior Mr Dovey Mr Fowler Mr
Goodman Mr Gibbons Mr Knight Mr Fowler
Mr Penny

The Principalls audited Accounts Confirmed—WHEREAS Mr William
Fowler & Mr John Gibbons (two of the Antients of this Society & Mr
Edw.d Benett & Mr Robert Drury (two of the Companions of the same
Society) by order of pencion made the tenth day of February Last past
were appointed Auditors of the Accounts of Mr Joshua Blackwell
Principall of this Society and have accordingly examined stated & audited
the said Principalls Accounts of Receipts and Disbursements for one whole
year beginning in Hillary Terme one thousand seaven hundred & eighteen
until Hillary Terme now Last past & have found the Summe totall of the
said Principalls Receipts in that year to be five hundred fifty three pounds
seaven pence halfpenny and the summe totall of his Disbursements to be
Six hundred ninety nine pounds four shillings ten pence halfpenny so that
there remains due from this Society to the said Principall on Ballance of
the said Accounts the summe of one hundred forty six pounds four shillings
three pence as appeares by their Certificate or Report thereof dated the
seaventh day of this Instant March IT IS THEREFORE ordered that the said
Accounts so examined stated audited and Certified as aforesaid be allowed
& approved of and the same are hereby accordingly allowed & approved

of to be Just and true and the said Joshua Blackwell is hereby discharged therefrom And it is also ordered that he be paid the said Ballance of one hundred forty six pounds four shillings & three pence out of such money as shall be Received for the Use of this Society

John Gibbons   Tho Pryor
Geo. Fuller   John Dovey
John Knight   Wm Fowler
John Penny   Ever.^d Goodman

Mr Joseph Barras to be Steward or Clerke of the Society in the Room & place of Mr Thomas Tufton—Mr Joseph Barras one of the Companions of this Society haveing made his application and desireing to be admitted into the Office or place of Steward or Clerke of this Society in the Room and place of Mr Thomas Tufton It is ordered that he the said Mr Barras be accordingly admitted into the said Office or place but to Continue therein onely during the Good Will and pleasure of the principall and Antients & their Successors & no Longer and the said Mr Barras is also to Give a Bond with two other sufficient persons to be bound with him in the penalty or summe of two hundred pounds for the due performance of his said Office or place dureing such time as he shall be Continued therein.

Mr Nathaniel Edison for pencions & absent Commons—Mr Edison being two pounds Sixteen shillings in arreare for pencions and absent Commons ending in Trinity Terme one thousand seaven hundred & Nineteen & desiring to Compound for His absent Commons in regard he was not in Towne in nine of the Termes he is Charged therewith It is ordered that he be abated two & twenty shillings & six pence & that on his payment of three & thirty shillings & six pence to Mr Tufton for the Use of this Society & also paying the Servants Rolls the same be in full discharge of the said Arrear

Mr Samuel Eccles for absent Commons—Mr Eccles oweing seaven shillings for a pencion and absent Commons in Easter Terme one thousand seaven hundred and nineteen and desiring an abatement for the Commons not being in Towne that terme It is ordered that he be abated two shillings & six pence & that on payment of four shillings & sixpence to Mr Tufton for the Use of this Society the same be in full discharge thereof he having paid the Servants Rolls

Mr Carr Brackenbury for Pencions & absent Commons—Mr Brackenbury being six and twenty shillings in arreare for pencions & absent Commons ending in Trinity Terme one thousand seaven hundred and nineteen & desiring on Abatement for three Termes he is Charged for Commons not being in Town in any of those termes It is ordered that he be abated seaven shillings & six pence & that on his payment of eighteen shillings & six pence to Mr Tufton for the Use of this Society the same be in full discharge of the said arreare he having paid the Servants Rolls

Mr Stephen Bramston for pencions & absent Commons—Mr Bramston oweing five & forty shillings for pencions & absent commons [ending in Trinity term 1719: not in town two of the terms charged: abated 5s.: to pay 40s. and Servants Rolls].

Mr Richard Sheppard for pencions & absent Commons—Mr Sheppard being Nineteen shillings in arreare [not in town three of the terms charged: abated 7s. 6d.: to pay 11s. 6d. and Servants Rolls]

Mr Baptist Trott for pencions & absent Commons—Mr Trott oweing fourteen shillings for pensions and absent Commons [for Michaelmas 1718 and Easter 1719: not in town in either term: abated 5s.: to pay 9s. and Servants Rolls]

Mr William Walcott for pencions & absent Commons—Mr Walcot oweing two shillings for a pencion & ten shillings for absent Commons [for Michaelmas 1718 and Easter 1719: not in town either term: abated 5s.: to pay 7s. and Servants Rolls]

Mr William Hardwick for pencions & absent Commons—Mr Hardwick being five and forty shillings in arreare for pensions & absent Commons [ending in Trinity term 1719: not in town five terms: abated 12s.: to pay 32s. 6d. and Servants Rolls]

Mr Joseph Hayne for pencions & absent Commons—Mr Hayne oweing fourteen shillings for pencions & absent Commons [ending in Easter term 1719: not in town either term: abated 5s.: to pay 9s. and Servants Rolls]

Mr Robert Peart for pencions & absent Commons—Mr Robert Peart owing seaventeen shillings [for period ending Easter term 1719: not in town for three terms charged: abated 7s. 6d.: to pay 9s. 6d. and Servants Rolls]

Mr Ignatius Hussey for pencions & Commons & Bond delivered up—Mr Hussey one of the Companions of this Society oweing nineteen shillings for pencions and absent Commons ending in Hillary Terme Last past and desiring to have his Bond given on his admission into this Society delivered up in Regard he is now admitted of Grays Inn as by Certificate appeares It is ordered that on his payment of the said nineteen shillings to Mr Tufton for the Use of this Society & also paying the Servants Rolls his Bond be accordingly delivered up.

Mr W. Stubbs for pencions & absent Commons—Mr Walter Stubbs being three pounds & two Shillings in arrear [for period ending Trinity term 1719: not in town eight of the terms charged: abated 20s.: to pay 42s. and Servants Rolls]

Mr R. Keeling for pencions & Absent Commons—Mr Richd Keeling being fifty four Shillings in arrear [for period ending Trinity term 1719: not in town six terms: abated 15s.: to pay 39s. and Servants Rolls]

Clements Inn in the ⎱ At a pencion held There on Wednesday the first
County of Middlesex ⎰ day of June Anno Domini 1720 present Mr John
Dovey Deputy Principall Mr Fowler Mr Goodman
Mr Gibbons Mr Knight and Mr Penny

Mr Nath. Lye for pencions & absent Commons and Bond d^d. up— Mr Nathaniel Lye one of the Companions of this Society being in arrear for pencions and Commons and desireing to have his Bond delivered up in regard he hath left off & discontinued the practice of the Law It is ordered that on payment of Eight pounds to Mr Barras for the use of this Society and ten Shillings to the Servants his Bond be Delivered up to be cancelled.

Mr John Wintle. the like—Mr Nathaniel Lye being Security for Mr John Wintle late one of the Companions of this Society and Desireing to have the said Mr Wintles Bond delivered up by payment of his arrears and alledging that he dyed in June 1714 at which time twenty Six Shillings were due from the Said Mr Wintle for pencions & absent Commons It is ordered on payment thereof the said Bond be delivered up to the said Mr Lye to be Cancelled.

Mr William Walker for pencions & absent Commons—Mr Wm Walker being four pounds & five Shillings in arrear for pencions & absent Commons ending Easter Term last desires an Abatement of his said Commons in regard he was not in town in any of the Terms charged It is ordered that he be Abated thirty two Shillings & Six pence for twelve Terms in which he was not in Town And that on payment of fifty two shillings & Six pence for the Use of this Society the same be in full discharge thereof. The Servants Rolls being also paid.

Mr Brightwell Smith an abatement of Rent—Mr Brightwell Smith desireing an allowance of a quarters rent of his late Chamber No. 19 now Mr Netlhorps due at Christmas last for that when the said Building was repairing his said Chamber was laid open & rendered thereby unfitt for use And it appearing that the said Mr Smith was Interrupted in his possession on that account & could not make use of his Said Chamber during the greatest part of that quarter It is ordered that thirty five Shillings for the said quarters rent be allowed and remitted unto the said Mr Smith & he is hereby discharged thereof accordingly.

Clements Inne in the ⎫ At a pencion held there on Monday the fourth day
County of Middlesex ⎭ of July Anno Domini 1720. Present Mr Blackwell
        Principall Mr Dovey Mr Fowler Mr Goodman
        Mr Gibbons Mr Knight.

Mr John Harris for a Lease of his Chamber No. 22.—WHEREAS a Lease of the Chamber up 2 pair of Stairs N⁰ 22 with the Garret Turret Cellar and Appurtenances thereunto belonging were by the then Principall & Antients of this Society by Articles bearing date the 14th of February 1689 granted unto Wᵐ Walker gent one of the Companyons of the Said Society for 99 years if he Should So long Live And John Harris gent one of the Companyons of the Said House now alledging that the Said premisses were granted to the said Mr Walker in trust only and that the said Articles are lost or mislaid But the Said trust and equitable Interest in the Said premisses became afterwards vested in Thomas Chaplin gent Since deceased and late one of the members of this Society And that after the said Mr Chaplin's death Administration of all his goods Chattells rights and Creditts was granted to James Tooth Esqᵉ Since which the said William Walker by the direction & appointment of the Said James Tooth hath assigned all his Estate and Interest in the premisses to the said Mr Harris And therefore the said Mr Harris now desires a Lease may be granted to him of the Said premisses for his own life IT IS ORDERED that on the Said Mr Harris's Surrendring all his said Interest and Estate to the said Chamber and premisses and delivering up the Said assignement executed by the said Mr Walker and Mr Tooth as aforesaid and on his payment of ten pounds to the now principall of Clements Inne for the use of the said Society A New Lease be granted unto the Said Mr Harris of the Said premisses for his own life in Such forme and with the usual Covenants & agreements as leases are wont to be granted by the Said principall & Antients of this Society the said Mr Chaplin's arrears being first also discharged

Mr Chaplin's Bond delivered up—Mr Thomas Chaplin deceased late one of the members of this Society being forty shillings in arrear for pencions & absent Commons and Mr John Harris desireing to have his Bond delivered up on payment thereof It is ordered that on payment of the same the said Mr Chaplin's bond be delivered up to the said Mr Harris to be Cancelled he also paying the Servants Rolls.

Mr James Hardwick for pencions & absent Commons—Mr James Hardwick being in arrear twenty eight Shillings for pencions & four pounds five shillings for absent Commons ending Easter Term last [desires abatement for fifteen terms not in town: abated 37s. 6d.: to pay £3. 15s. 6d. and Servants Rolls]

Mr Turner the like—Mr William Turner being in arrear fifteen shillings for 3 Terms Absent Commons Ending in Easter Term desires an abatement of the same in regard he was not in Town any of the said Terms [abated 7s. 6d.: to pay 7s. 6d.]

<table>
<tr><td>*Clements Inn in the*
County of Middlesex</td><td>At a pention held at Clements Inn aforesaid on Wednesday the thirteenth day of July in the year of Our Lord one thousand Seaven hundred and twenty present Mr Blackwell Principall Mr Pryor Mr Dovey Mr Fowler Mr Gibbons Mr Fuller Mr Knight Mr Denshire Mr Penny</td></tr>
</table>

John Cheals to be Butler & porter of the foregate in the Room & place of Arthur Moseley—John Cheals by his Peticon praying to be admitted into the Severall Offices or places of Butler and Porter of the Foregate in this Society in the Room and place of Arthur Mosely who is discharged and displaced therefrom It is ordered that the said John Cheals be accordingly admitted into the said Severall Offices or places but to Continue therein onely during the Good Will and pleasure of the Principall and Antients and their Successors for the time being or the Major part of them and no Longer And the said John Cheals is to enter into Bond with one or More Sufficient person or persons to be bound with him in the penalty or Summe of Fifty pounds for the due performance of the said Severall Offices or places during such time as he shall be continued therein

Mr George Batemans bond delivered up—Mr George Bateman one of the Companions of this Society being Greatly in arreare for pencions and absent Commons his bond given on his admission into the said Society in the penalty of twenty pounds was some time since ordered to be put in Suit and thereupon the said twenty pound hath been Recovered against him and is now paid to the Principall by Mr John Penny one of the Antients of this Society It is therefore ordered (at the desire and Request of the said Mr Bateman) that the said Bond be delivered up to be Cancelled

<table>
<tr><td>*Clements Inn in the*
County of Middlesex</td><td>Att a pencion held at Clements Inn aforesaid on Fryday the fourth day of November in the year of our Lord 1720. Present Mr Penny Dep. Pr. Mr Dovey Mr Fowler Mr Knight Mr Fuller Mr Gibbon</td></tr>
</table>

Mr Matt: Carvile for pencions & abs: commons & bond to be deliv^d *up*— Mr Matthew Carvile one of the Companions of this Society being in arrear for pencions & absent commons the Summe of one pound eleaven shillings and having Left off the practice of the law & paid the said Summe of one pound eleaven to Mr Barras for the use of this Society It is therefore ordered that his bond be delivered up to him to be cancelled

Mr Wotton for a lease N°. 23 late Carviles—Mr William Wotton one of the Companions of this Society having agreed with Mr Matt: Carvile one other of the Companions of the same Society for the purchase of his Chamber up two pair of stairs in the staircase marked with the number or figures (23) in the building commonly called Kelletts building in Clements Inn garden Which the said Matt: Carvile held to him & his Assignes by a lease or articles from this Society for a term of ninety nine years determinable upon the death of him the said Matt: Carvile And the said Matt: Carvile at the request of the said William Wotton hath surrendred & delivered up his said lease or articles unto this Society in order to be cancelled & to have a lease made of the said Chambers unto the said William Wotton and the said William Wotton appearing and desiring to be admitted to the said Chambers It is ordered that on payment of fifteen pounds to the Principall or his Deputy for the use of this Society a new lease be made & granted of the said Chambers to him the said William Wotton for ninety nine years if he shall so long live & continue a member of this Society with the usuall covenants & according to the form & method of making & granting leases by this Society.

Mr John Stretehays bond up—Mr John Stretehay one of the Companions of this Society being greatly in arrear for pencions & absent commons and having paid Mr Barras for the use of the said Society ten pounds being the full penalty of his bond he having left off practice It is ordered at his request that his bond be delivered up to be cancelled. And in regard it is a very Stale debt he not having been resident in the Inn or had any demand made of him for the money for 30 or 40 years It is ordered all cost of suit be remitted

Mr Gregson's bond up—Ordered Mr Gregsons bond be delivered up on payment of ii: 9: 0

Clements Inn in the ⎱ At a pencion held at Clements Inn aforesaid on
County of Middlesex ⎰ Fryday the 27th day of January 1720 Present Mr
                       Penny Deputy Principall Mr Dovey Mr Fowler
                       Mr Gibbon Mr Knight Mr Fuller.

Mr Edwd. Halstead for a Lease for his Life and an assignment of the Chambers one pair of Stairs N° 7 and the vault under them—Mr Edward Halstead (one of the Companions of this Society) desiring to purchase a Lease for his life with an assignment for one other life after the Expiration of his owne life in the Chambers up one pair of Stairs in the New building at the end of the First Court in a Stair Case designed to be marked or

Numbered with the Figure of 7. and fronting the First Court and Clements Inn Gate South and the Talbott Yard north Together with a Vault at the Bottome of the Cellar Stairs in the same Stair Case and Extending itself Under the Pavement of the First Court and proposeing to pay One Hundred & Ten Pounds for the same and to Wainscott & paint the said Chambers and to fitt them Up in a decent handsome manner with Marble Chimney peices hearths & Slabbs It is ordered & agreed that on the said Mr Halstead's Immediate Payment of the said One Hundred & Ten pounds to the Principall or his Deputy for the Use of this Society a Lease & Assignment be accordingly made & granted to him the said Mr Halstead of the said Chambers and Vault Subject to the Payment of Seperate Commons Pencions & other duties to this House according to a late Order of Pencion made for that purpose and with and Under the Usuall Covenants & Provisoes and according to the Usuall forme and Method of making & granting of Leases & assignments by this Society And with a Covenant from Mr Halstead to Wainscott & Paint the said Chambers and to fit them Up in a Decent handsome manner with Marble Chimney peices hearths & Slab. In Testimony of which said agreement the said Mr Halstead hath Subscribed his Name to this Order.

Edwd Halsted

Clements Inn in the ⎰ At a pencion held at Clements Inn aforesaid on
County of Middlesex ⎱ Friday the Tenth day of February in the year of our
Lord 1720. Present Mr Blackwell Pr Mr Pryor Mr Dovey Mr Fowler Mr Gibbons Mr Knight Mr Fuller Mr Penny.

Mr Halsted for a life & an assignment in the Chambers 2 pr. of Stairs N° 7. with the Garretts over them and 3 cellars under the Ground Chamber in the Same Building—Mr Edward Halsted (one of the Companyons of this Society) desireing to purchase a Lease for his life with an Assignment for one other life after the expiracion of his own life in the Chamber up two pair of Stairs in the New Building at the upper End of the First Court in the Stair Case designed to be marked or Numbred with the figure 7 and fronting the first Court & Clements Inne Gate South and the Talbot yard North together with the Garretts over the said Chambers and the 3 Cellars under the ground Chamber in the Same Building and proposeing to pay £160 for the Same and to Wainscot and paint the said Chambers and to fitt them up in a Decent & Handsome manner with marble Chimney peices Hearths & Slabbs as also to fitt up the Said Garretts & Cellars conveniently and fit for use and Service It is ordered and agreed that on Mr Halsted's present payment of £60 to the Principall for the use of this

Society and also on payment of the remaining £100 on or before the twenty fourth day of June next to the Principall for the use of this Society A Lease and an Assignement be accordingly made and granted to him the Said Mr Halsted of the Said Chambers Garretts and Cellars Subject to the payment of Separate Commons pencions and other Dutyes to the House according to the order of pencion for that purpose And with and under the usual Covenants and Provisoes and according to the usual form & method of makeing and Granting of Leases and Assignments by this Society and with a Covenant from Mr Halsted to wainscot and paint the Said Chambers and to fit them up in a decent and handsome manner with marble Chimney peices Hearths & Slabbs as also to fitt up the Said Garretts and Cellars conveniently and fit for use and service In Testimony of which said agreement the Said Mr Halsted hath Subscribed his name to this order.

Edwd Halsted

Auditors of the Principalls accounts for one year beginning Hillary Term 1719 to Hillary Term 1720—It is ordered that Mr Thomas Pryor and Mr John Penny two of the Ancients of this Society and Mr Richard Cromwell & Mr Brightwell Smith two of the Companyons of the Same Society Shall and do examine and Audit the Principalls Accounts of this Society for one whole year beginning in Hillary Term one Thousand Seaven hundred and Nineteen untill this present Hillary Term one Thousand Seaven hundred and twenty and that they the said Thomas Pryor John Penny Richard Cromwell & Brightwell Smith or any three of them Shall and do make their Certificate & Report of the Said accounts as soon as the Same can or may Conveniently be done.

Clements Inn in the ⎱ At a Pention held at Clements Inn aforesaid on
County of Middlesex ⎰ Fryday the Seaventeenth of February one thousand
　　　　　　　　　Seaven hundred & twenty
　　　　　　　　　　present Mr Blackwell Principall Mr Dovey Mr
　　　　　　　　　　Fowler Mr Knight Mr Fuller Mr Denshire &
　　　　　　　　　　Mr Penny

The Principall's Audited Accounts Confirmed—Whereas [Pryor, Penny, Cromwell and Smith were appointed auditors of the Principal's accounts for the year as above] and have found the Summe totall of the said Principalls Receipts in that yeare to be three hundred and twenty pounds ten shillings and Seaven pence and the Sum totall of his Disbursements to be Six hundred Sixty eight pounds Nine shillings and three pence so that there Remains due from this Society to the said Principall on ballance of the said Accounts the Summe of three hundred forty Seaven pounds eighteen shillings and eight pence as appeares by their Certificate or Report thereof dated the Fifteenth day of the same present month of February IT IS THEREFORE ORDERED that the said Accounts so examined Stated audited & Certified as aforesaid be allowed and approved of and the same are hereby accordingly allowed and approved of to be Just & true and the said Joshua Blackwell is hereby discharged therefrom And it is also ordered that he be paid the said Ballance of three hundred forty Seven. pounds. eighteen shillings & eight pence out of such money as shall be Received for the Use of this Society.

Tho Pryor
John Dovey
Wm Fowler
John Knight
Geo. Fuller
Geo. Denshire
John Penny

Mr Carrow for pencions & absent Commons—Mr Robert Carrow being in arrear for pencions twenty eight Shillings and four pounds & ten Shillings for Absent Commons ending Michaelmas Term 1720 and Mr Edwd Halsted on his behalf desireing an Abatement of the Said Commons alledging that Mr Carrow was not in Town fourteen of the Terms charged to his account It is ordered that he be Abated thirty five Shillings for those fourteen Terms And on payment of Four pounds & three Shillings the same be in full discharge thereof The Servants Rolls being first discharged.

Clements Inn in the **)** At a Pencion held at Clements Inn aforesaid on
County of Middlesex **)** Friday the third day of March in the year of Our
Lord 1720 present Mr Blackwell principall Mr Dovey Mr Fowler Mr Gibbons Mr Fuller Mr Knight Mr Penny.

Mr Wm Seabrooks accounts & vouchers to be examined & Certified—It is ordered that Mr John Gibbons Mr George Fuller & Mr John Knight (Antients of this Society). or any two of them Shall & do examine and Audit the Accounts of Mr Wm Seabrooke with the vouchers thereunto Since the time of the last Account And make their Certificate & Report thereof as soon as the Same can or may conveniently be done.

Mr Dobson for a Lease of one of the Chambers N° 6 built by Mr Wm Seabrook—Mr John James Dobson one of the Companyons of this Society having agreed with Mr Wm Seabrooke for the Chamber up one pair of Stairs on the Left hand in the Stair Case marked or Intended to be marked with the figure or Number (6) in the first Court in this Inn with the Garret over the front part of the Said Chamber & next but one adjoyning to the Building called Lawes's Building as also for the Vault under the Stepps leading to the Said Chamber out of the Said first Court together with use of the yard in Common with other Occupyers of the rest of the Chambers there (being part of the Building lately erected by the Said Mr Seabrooke) for the Interest and Term of years of the Said Mr Seabrook in the said Chamber Garret & Vault for the Summe of three hundred & fifteen pounds chargeable with the yearly payment of forty shillings ground rent to this Society being part of the ground rent of twelve pounds per annum reserved and payable out of & for the Said whole Building according to the Articles made & Entred into by the said Mr Seabrook with this Society And the Said Mr Seabrooke desireing that the Said Mr Dobson may accordingly have a Lease made to him of the Said Chamber Garret & Vault with the use of the Yard as aforesaid for the Term of sixty yeares from the Feast of St Michael the Archangell now last past being the Term of years which the Said Mr Seabrook hath therein by the Said Articles It is Ordered that pursuant to & in part of performance of the Said Articles a Lease be accordingly thereof made to the Said Mr Dobson by this Society with proper Covenants and with the usual Covenants and provisoes and according to the usual forme & method of Leases granted by this Society And in regard the said Mr Dobson hath not attained his full age of 21 years he is to procure a Sufficient person to be a party in the Said Lease who is to Covenant for the due performance of all the Articles Covenants Provisoes payments Condicions & agreements therein to be Contained

Mr Michael Wrightson's Executors £146. 10s. 6d. principle money with Interest due to be paid—Mr Michael Wrightson deceased late one of the Antients of this Society haveing in his life time advanced and lent to this Society at Several times the Severall & respective Summes of one hundred pounds twenty Six pounds ten Shillings & Six pence & twenty pounds principal money as appears by Severall orders of pencion formerly made And it appearing that on the Nineteenth day of May in the year of our Lord 1711 Mr Samuel Brewster (then Principall of this Society and since deceased) ordered payment to be made by Mr Thomas Callowe (Since also deceased) unto Mr Jonathan Freeman one of the Executors of the Last will of the Said Mr Michael Wrightson of the Severall Summes following viz.ᵗ twelve pounds for two years Interest of the one hundred pounds due on the 18th of February 1710 three pounds three shillings for two years Interest of the twenty Six pounds ten Shillings & Six pence due on the 20th of March 1710 and twenty four Shillings for two years Interest of twenty pounds due on the 18th of July 1710 which was accordingly paid But no Interest hath at any time Since been paid for the Said three Severall

principall Sums of money or any of them And the said Mr Jonathan
Freeman requiring payment of all the Said three Several principal Summes
of money together with the Interest for the Same Which Interest amounts
to Eighty Six pounds and upwards It is ordered that Mr Joshua Blackwell
Principal of this Society Shall & doe pay to the Said Mr Jonathan Freeman
the Said Interest money And that he also pay the Said three Several
principal Summes of one hundred pounds twenty Six pounds ten Shillings
& Six pence and twenty pounds By and out of the rents & profitts of the
House as the Same Shall come to the hands of the Said Principal Notwithstanding any former order of pencion made for applying the said rents
& profitts to other payments.

Clements Inn in the ⎱ At a pencion held there on Wednesday the 8th day
County of Middlesex ⎰ of March in the year of our Lord 1720 present
Mr Blackwell Principall Mr Dovey Mr Gibbons
Mr Fuller Mr Knight Mr Penny.

Mr Seabrook to have a Lease of his new Erected Building N°. 6.—
Whereas Mr W^m. Seabrook by Articles bearing Date the 18th day of
March 1718 agreed with the then Principall and Antients of this Society
within one year and an halfe then next at his own charges to erect & Build
on a peice of ground on the East Side of the first Court in Clements Inn
aforesaid in length from the Building forming the Stair Case then called
Number (12) unto a Building called Lawes's Building from North to South
46 foot of assize A New Building of the length & Depth as in the Said
Articles is mencioned three storys above ground with Garrets above &
Cellars under the Same according to the Dimensions & Scantlings [1]; and
to finish & perfect the Same with the pavements & other appurtenances
thereto belonging in Such manner & form as in the Same Articles are
contained And the Principal & Antients of this Society were within one
month after the Said Building was So Erected & Built to make unto the
said W^m. Seabrook his Executors Administrators & Assignes a good
Lease with usual & proper Covenants & according to the Custome of the
Said House free from all Incumbrances from any persons Lawfully claiming title to the Said premisses of the Said Building Ground & premisses
(Except as therein excepted) for the Term of 61 years from Michaelmas
then next at the rent of a pepper corne for the first year & under the yearly
rent of £12 for the residue of the said Term payable half yearly without any
deduction whatsoever with & under Several provisoes Condicions &
agreements in the Said Articles comprized And which Said New Building
& premisses the Said Mr Seabrook was & is to keep in good repair During

---

[1] Prescribed measurements.

the Said Term and So to leave the Same at the Determinacion thereof And which Said Building the Said Mr Seabrooke hath erected & finished according to the Said Articles AND WHEREAS the said Mr Seabrooke hath agreed with Mr John James Dobson one of the Companyons of this Society for the Chamber or floor up one pair of Stairs in the Said New Building & the Garret over the front part of the Same and next but one adjoyning to the Said Lawes's Building and also the Vault under the Steps leading to the Said Chambers with the use of the Yard in Common with the rest of the occupyers of the Said New Building (being part of the Said new erected Building) during the Term or Interest of the Said Mr Seabrooke And accordingly the Said Principall & Antients by Articles dated this day at the request & with the Consent of the Said Mr Seabrooke and in part of performance of the Said Articles entred into with and by him Have Leased unto the Said John James Dobson the Said Chambers Garret Vault & use of the yard as aforesaid for the Term of 60 years from Michaelmas last past under the yearly rent of 40s. being part of the above mencioned rent of £12 And the Said Mr Seabrooke now desireing to have a Lease made to him of the residue of the said Building and Chambers therein contained with the Appurtenances thereto belonging according to the said first mencioned Articles alledging and averring that he hath done & performed all and every thing on his part to be done according to the Same Articles IT IS THEREFORE ORDERED that in pursuance & full performance of the Said first mencioned Articles a Lease be made to him the Said W^m. Seabrooke of the Said New Erected Building And the Chambers therein contained with the Appurtenances except such Part thereof as is already Leased as aforesaid To HOLD to him the Said W^m. Seabrook his Executors Administrators and Assignes for the Term of 60 years from the Feast of St Michael the Archangell now last past at and under the yearly rent of £10 being the residue of the Said reserved rent of £12 per annum with proper Covenants provisoes and Condicions therein to be Contained And according to the Covenants provisoes and Condicions therein to be Contained And according to the form and Method of Leases made by this Society

William Seabrooke

Mr Edw. Halsted for a life & an Assignment in the ground Chamber N°. 7 & the Cellar under the Stairs—Mr Edwd Halsted (one of the Companyons of this Society) Desireing to purchase a Lease for his life with an Assignement for another life after the expiracion of his own in the ground Chamber in the New Building at the upper End of the first Court fronting Clements Inne Gate South and the Talbot Yard North together with the Cellar under the Stair Case of the Said Building and adjoyning thereto and proposeing to pay £75 for the Same And to wainscot & paint the Said Chambers and to fit them up in a decent & handsome manner with marble Chimney peices Hearths and Slabbs as also to fit up the Said Cellar conveniently and fit for use & Service It is Ordered and agreed that on Mr Halsteds present payment of £25 to the Principal for the use of this Society and on payment of the remaining £50 on or before the 29th day of September next to the Principall for the use of this Society A Lease & an Assignement be accordingly made & granted to the Said Mr Halsted of the Said Chamber & Cellar Subject to the payment of Separate pencions Commons and other Dutyes to the House according to the order of pencion for that purpose [and with the usual covenants &c., in the usual form and with a covenant from Halsted to wainscot, paint and fit up &c. as above]   In Testimony of which agreement the said Mr Halsted hath Subscribed his name to this Order.

Edw.d Halsted

Clements Inn in the } The names of the Principall Antients and Com-
County of Middlesex } panyons of the Said Society who have contributed towards the Repairs of the Church & Steeple of the parish of St Clements Danes in the Said County of Middlesex with the Severall Summes of money by each of them given as hereinafter Set down

	£ s d		£ s d		£ s d
Mr Blackwell		Mr Atwood	. . .	Mr Carter	0.10.6
principall	1. 1.0	Mr Adams	0.10.6	Mr Curtis	0.10.6
Mr T. Bagshaw	. . .			Mr Carrow	. . .
Mr Johnson	. . .	Mr E Bagshaw	. . .	Mr Cosyn	0.10.6
Mr Pryor	1. 1.0	Mr Bramston	. . .	Mr Cromwell	0.10.6
Mr Gregg	1. 1.0	Mr Bell	. . .	Mr Catchpoole	. . .
Mr Dovey	1. 1.0	Mr Barnes	. . .	Mr Child	0.10.6
Mr Fowler	1. 1.0	Mr Bewley	0.10.6	Mr Colley	. . .
Mr Goodman	1. 1.0	Mr Ballett	. . .	Mr Cock	0.10.6
Mr Gibbons	1. 1.0	Mr Backwell		Mr Cotton	. . .
Mr Fuller	1. 1.0	Jun.r	0.10.6		
Mr Knight	1. 1.0	Mr Benet	0.10.6	Mr Dottin	1. 1.0
Mr Denshire	1. 1.0	Mr Bracken-		Mr Davenport	0. .
Mr Powlett	. . .	bury	0.10.6	Mr Dudbridge	0.10.6
Mr Penny	1. 1.0	Mr Bowles	. . .	Mr Drury	0.10.6
		Mr Brewster	0.10.6	Mr Dewes	0.10.6
T. Lake Esqe	1. 1.0	Mr Barras	0.10.6	Mr Eldridge	0.10.6
		Mr Ballan	0.10.6	Mr Edison	0.10.6
Companyons		Mr Bridges	. . .	Mr Elly	. . .
Mr. Abney	. . .			Mr Eccles	. . .
Mr Aldey	0.10.6	Mr Cookes	. . .	Mr Evans	. . .
Mr Allen	. . .	Mr Callowe	. . .	Mr Falkener	. . .

	£ s d		£ s d		£ s d
Mr Fowke	0.10.6	Mr Keelinge R	0.10.6	Mr Steggall	0.10.6
Mr Fish	. . .	Mr Kelying T	0.10.6	Mr Shepperd	0.10.6
Mr Grayhurst	. . .	Mr Love	. . .	Mr Smith B	0.10.6
Mr Gwynne	. . .	Mr Lake C	. . .	Mr Smith T	0.10.6
Mr Gregory	0.10.6	Mr Lyte	. . .	Mr T Swift	. . .
Mr Heathcoate	0. . .	Mr Moore	. . .	Mr R Swift	. . .
Mr Harris Sen.r	0.10.6	Mr Mundy E	. . .		
Mr Halsted	1. 1.0	Mr Morris	. . .	Mr Till Adam	. . .
Mr Hunt	. . .	Mr Noyes	. . .	Mr Townrow	. . .
Mr Harris N	0.10.6	Mr Nettleton	. . .	Mr Tyson	. . .
Mr Hooper	1. 1.0	Mr Nelthorpe	. . .	Mr Truesdale	. . .
Mr Hodgkis	. . .	Mr Oldershaw	. . .	Mr Turner	. . .
Mr Hardwick J	. . .			Mr Tufton	
Mr Harris B	0. 5.0	Mr Purcell Sen.r	. . .	Collector	. . .
Mr Humphreys	0.10.6	Mr R.Peart	0.10.6	Mr Trott	0.10.6
Mr Hardwick W	0.10.6	Mr Purcell Jun.r	. . .	Mr Twyne	0.10.6
Mr Hope	0.10.6	Mr Parke	. . .	Mr Vaux	. . .
Mr Hayne	0.10.6	Mr Pelham	0.10.6	Mr Walker	. . .
Mr Hyde	0.10.6	Mr Peart J.	0.10.6	Mr Wyche	. . .
Mr Hurst	. . .	Mr Pigott	. . .	Mr Wallet	. . .
Mr Hester	. . .	Mr W. Powlett	. . .	Mr White	. . .
		Mr Pacey	0.10.6	Mr Walcot	0.10.6
		Mr Pavey	. . .	Mr Wakelin	0 . .
Mr Innys Sen.r	. . .	Mr Squier	. . .	Mr Wynde	. . .
Mr Innys Jun.r	. . .	Mr Stubbs	0.10.6	Mr Wotton	. . .
Mr Jackson	0.10.6	Mr Shuckforth	0.10.6	Mr Yates	0.10.6

40. 3

Clements Inn in the } At a pencion held there on Wednesday the 24th
County of Middlesex } day of May in the year of our Lord 1721 present
Mr Dovey Dep. pr. Mr Pryor Mr Fowler Mr
Goodman Mr Fuller Mr Knight Mr Penny

Mr Till Adam for pencions & absent Commons—Mr John Till Adam
being in arrear for pencions thirty eight Shillings & for absent Commons
Six pounds Ending Easter Term 1721 And desireing an Abatement of the
Said Commons [not in town 19 of the terms charged: abated 48s.: to pay
£3. 12s. [1] in full discharge of the commons] The Servants Rolls being also
first discharged

---

[1] At this point the clerk has the habit of adding up in the margin the items to be
paid. Thus his figures here show that Mr. Till Adam has to pay £5 10s. (£1 18s. 0d. +
£3 12s. 0d.). As stated above (p. 2 n.), the abatements relate only to absent commons;
the pension arrears remain payable in full.

Clements Inn in the ⎱ At a pencion held there on Monday the 3d day of
County of Middlesex ⎰ July in the year of our Lord 1721. present Mr
Blackwell pr. Mr Dovey Mr Fowler Mr Gibbons
Mr Knight Mr Denshire Mr Penny.

Mr Moore pencions and absent Commons &c.—Mr Robert Moore being in arrear for pencions twenty four Shillings and for absent Commons three pounds & fifteen shillings Ending Easter Term 1721. And desireing by Mr Richd Calton an abatement of the absent Commons in regard he was not in Town in any of the Terms charged to his account It is ordered that he be abated thirty Seven Shillings & Sixpence for The Said Terms And on payment of thirty Seven Shillings & Six pence for Commons the Said twenty four Shillings for pencions and thirty Nine Shillings for the Kings Tax paid by this Society for his Chamber for the years 1716. 1717. 1718 & 1719. The Same be in full discharge of all arrears to the End of Easter Term 1721. The Servants Rolls being also discharged.

Mr White for pencions & absent Commons—Mr John White being in arrear for pencions thirty Shillings and for absent Commons Ending Easter Term 1721 four pounds & fifteen Shillings And desireing an abatement of the Said Commons in regard he was not in Town ten of the Terms charged to his Account It is ordered that he be abated twenty five shillings for Those ten Terms And on payment of three pounds & ten Shillings the Same be in full discharge of the Said Commons. The Servants Rolls being first discharged.

Mr Elly for pencions & Absent Commons—Mr James Elly being in arrear for pencions Thirty Shillings, and for Absent Commons four pounds & fifteen Shillings Ending in Easter Term 1721. And by Mr Richard Elly his Son desireing an Abatement of the Said Commons in regard he was not in Town any of the Terms (except one) Charged to his account And not able to come to Town by reason of his age & great Infirmities It is ordered that he be abated forty five Shillings of the Said Commons And on payment of fifty Shillings the Same be in full Discharge of the Said Commons. The Servants Rolls being also paid.

Mr Bewley for pencions & absent Commons—Mr Richard Bewley haveing paid his pencions & absent Commons to the End of Trinity Term 1719 as appears by Mr Tho. Tuftons Receipt for the Same Dated 22th February 1719 And being now in arrear for pencions twelve Shillings and for absent Commons Thirty five Shillings Ending Easter Term 1721 And desireing an Abatement of the Said Commons [not in town 4 of the terms charged: abated 10s. for those terms: to pay 25s. in full discharge of the commons] The Servants Rolls being also discharged.

Mr Atkinson for pencions & absent Commons & Bond d.d up—Mr W.m Atkinson Deceased late one of the Companyons of this Society being at the time of his death in arrear for pencions Six Shillings and forty five Shillings for Absent Commons ending Trinity Term 1719 and Mrs Sarah Atkinson his widow & Executrix by Mr Maurice Johnson Jun.r desireing an Abatement of the Said Commons in regard the Said Mr Atkinson was not in town any of the Termes charged to his Account It is ordered that she be abated twenty two Shillings & Six pence of the Said Commons And on payment of twenty two Shillings & Six pence the Same be in full Discharge of the Said Commons and that his Bond be Delivered up to the Said Sarah Atkinson. The Servants Rolls being first Discharged.

Mr Joseph Hunt Jun.r for pensions & absent Commons—Mr Hunt Jun.r being in arrear for pencions three pounds & eight Shillings and Seven pounds & ten Shillings for absent Commons Ending Michaelmas Term 1720 And Desireing an abatement of the Said Commons [not in town 15 of the terms charged: abated 37s. 6d. for those terms: to pay £5. 12s. 6d. in full discharge of the commons] the Servants Rolls being also discharged

Mr Hunt Sen.r for the like & Bond d.d up—Mr Joseph Hunt deceased late one of the Companyons of this Society being at the time of his death in arrear Six Shillings for pencions and fifty five Shillings for absent Commons ending Easter Terme 1720 And Mr Joseph Hunt Raleigh Knight & John Letherland Executors of his last will desireing an abatement of the Said Commons in regard the Deceased was not in Town Eight of the Terms charged to his Account It is Ordered that twenty Shillings be Abated for those Terms and on payment of 35s. & the Said 6s. the Same be in full of all arrears and the Said Deceaseds Bond be delivered up to the Said Executors to be cancelled.

Mr Bulstrode the like—Mr Edward Bulstrode deceased late one of the Companyons of this Society being in arrear at the time of his death for pencions forty Shillings and for absent Commons Seven pounes & five Shillings Ending Trinity Term 1718 and dying Insolvent Mr Hunt Mr Knight & Mr Letherland Executors of the last Will of Mr Joseph Hunt deceased who was Surety to the Society for the Said Edward Bulstrode Desire an Abatement of the Said Commons for that the Said Mr Bulstrode was not in Town any of the Terms Charged to his account untill he became a prisoner in the Fleet prison in the year 1710 And so continued till his death which happened before Michaelmas 1718 as they aver It is therefore ordered that three pounds twelve Shillings & Six pence be abated and on payment of three pounds twelve Shillings & Six pence with the Said forty Shillings the Same be in full discharge of all arrears from the Said Mr Bulstrode and his Bond be delivered up to the Said Executors.

Clements Inn in the ⎫ At a Pencion held there on Monday the 17th day
County of Middlesex ⎭ of July in the year of our Lord 1721 present Mr
　　　　　　　　　　　Blackwell Pr. Mr Dovey Mr Fowler Mr Gibbons
　　　　　　　　　　　Mr Fuller Mr Penny

Mr Halsted for a Life & an Assignment in the Chambers up 1 & 2 pair of Stairs & the Garretts over them with the Vault & Cellar in the Building Nº 7 & next to Mr Seabrooks Building—Mr Edw.ᵈ Halsted (one of the Companions of this Society) Desireing to purchase a Lease for his life with an Assignment for another life after the Expiracion of his own in the Severall Chambers up one & two pair of Stairs & the Garratts over the Same in the New Building at the Upper End of the first Court on the left hand in the Stair Case Mark'd with the figure or Number (7) Abutting on St Clements Lane North East & next adjoyning to Mr Seabrooks Building Westward in Clements Inn aforesaid together with the Vault (under that part of the Said Building & Chambers now used for the Dust Hole &) lying next to the Talbot Alehouse & the little Cellar on the Right hand within the Said Vault & adjoyning to the pavement leading to the Said Stair Case out of which little Cellar there is a Window into the Said Court and allsoe two little Clossetts Cupboards or holes one being on the Top of the Cellar Stairs on the right hand goeing down & the other on the first landing place goeing up one pair of Stairs on the left hand in the Said Staircase & proposeing to pay £350 for the Same And to Wainscott & paint the Severall Said Chambers & to fit them up in a Decent & handsome manner with Marble Chimney peices Hearths & Slabbs for three Chimneys in each of the Said Chambers as also to fit up the Said Garretts Vault & Celler Conveniently & fit for use & Service It is ordered & agreed that on the said Mr Halsteds payment of the Said £350 on or before the 25th day of March next to the Principall for the use of this Society a Lease & an Assignment be accordingly made & granted to the Said Mr Halsted of the Said Severall Chambers Garretts Vault Celler & Clossetts Subject to the payment of Separate pencions Commons & other Dutys to the House for each of the Said Chambers or Floors respectively According to the order of pencion made for that purpose [with the usual covenants &c. and in the usual form and with a covenant from Halsted to wainscot, paint and fit up, &c.] In Testimony of which Agreement the Said Mr Halsted hath Subscribed his Name to this Order

　　　　　　　　　　　　　　　　　　　　　Edw.ᵈ Halsted

Mr Edw.ᵈ Cotton & Marriot for his arrears & Bond d.ᵈ up—Mr Edward Cotton late a Member of this Society now deceased being at the time of his Death Indebted for pencions & absent Commons in a Considerable Summ to this Society But dyeing insolvent & being in a mean Condition for

Severall years before his Death Mr Wm Marriot who was Security for the Said Mr Cotton desires to have the Said Bond Delivered up to him to be cancelled it is ordered for the reasons aforesaid that on payment of ten pounds for the use of this Society by the said Mr Marriot with such Costs of Suit as Mr John Dovey shall accept from him in full discharge The Said Bond be delivered up accordingly to the Said Mr Marriot.

Clements Inn in the ⎱ At a pencion held there on Friday the first day of
County of Middlesex ⎰ December in the year of our Lord 1721 present
Mr Penny Dep. Pr. Mr Dovey Mr Fowler Mr Gibbons Mr Fuller Mr Knight

Mr Tho. Swift for a Lease of the Chambers & Cellar N.º 17 late Mr Mundy & the back Garrett over them late Mr Dixons—Mr Thomas Swift one of the Companyons of this Society haveing agreed with Mr Edward Mundy one other of the Companyons of the Said Society for the purchase of his Chambers up one pair of Stairs in the Stair Case marked with the figures or number (17) formerly in the possession of Michael Wrightson gent deceased together with the Cellar under the Same and under the Chamber of Mr Thomas Callowe lately granted to Francis Mundy Esq.^e (then one of the Companyons of the Said House Since Deceased) and the Said Edward Mundy and their Assignes by a Lease or Articles from this Society for 99 years if they or either of them Should So long Live And the Said Edward Mundy at the request of the Said Mr Swift hath Surrendred & delivered up the Said Articles unto this Society in order to be cancelled And a new Lease of the said Chambers and Cellar to be made to the Said Thomas Swift And the Said Thomas Swift now appearing & desireing to be admitted to the Same And desireing also to purchase a Lease for his own life in the back Garrett in the Said Stair Case next adjoyning to the Angell Inn late in the possession of Wm Dixon gent and now in the possession of the Said Mr Swift And there being Some outside window Shutters Sett up to the windows on the walls of the Said Chambers without leave from this Society and to the prejudice of the Said walls which ought not to have been done the Said Mr Swift agrees that the Said window Shutters Shall be forthwith taken down It is therefore Ordered that on payment of £20 to the Principall or Mr Barras the Steward for the use of this Society A New Lease be made & granted of the Said Chambers Cellar & Garrett to him the Said Thomas Swift for 99 years if he Shall So long Live and be & continue a Member of this Society with usual Covenants & provisoes and according to the form & Method of making & granting Leases by this Society And also with a Covenant from Mr Swift to take down the Said Shutters And that no outside window Shutters Shall at any time hereafter be Sett up or continued there And also that the Society Shall & may be at Liberty at any time hereafter to Stop up or Build against the North lights or windows of the Said Chambers & Cellar by any New Building hereafter to be Erected on the Ground lying Northward of the Said Chambers without any allowance or other recompence or Satisfaction to be made or given to the Said Mr Swift for the Same And in testimony of this agreement the Said Mr Swift hath Subscribed his name to this Order

Tho: Swift

Mr Arth. Squiers & his Bond to be d^d up—Mr Arthur Squier being in arrear for pencions & absent Commons Ending Trinity Term last nine pounds & ten Shillings & his Bond haveing been put in Suit and Judgment obtained thereon and Mr Wm Benson now appearing on his behalfe and affirms that the Said Mr Squier is reduced into mean Circumstances and not able to pay all his Debts Desires to Compound for the Said Debt due to this Society and proposeing to pay £6 for the use of this Society & 50s. for the Costs of Suit on his Said Bond It is ordered that on payment of the Said £6 for the use of this Society & 50s. to Mr Barras for the Said Costs The Same shall be in full of all Demands from this Society And the Said Mr Squiers Bond to be delivered up to be Cancelled.

Clements Inn in the County of Middlesex } At a pencion held there on Wednesday the fourteenth day of February in the year of our Lord 1721 present Mr Blackwell Pr. Mr Gregg Mr Dovey Mr Fowler Mr Gibbons Mr Fuller Mr Knight Mr Denshire Mr Penny Mr Carter Mr Halsted Mr Hooper.

Mr Sam. Townrow for pencions & absent Commons—Mr Townrow being in arrear for pencions forty four Shillings and Seven pounds for absent Commons Ending Hillary Term 1721 [desires abatement of his commons: not in town more than two of the terms charged: abated £3. 5s. of his commons: to pay £3 15s. and be discharged of the commons]

Mr Oldershaws Bond delivered up—Mr John Oldershaw being greatly in arrear for pencions & absent Commons and haveing left off practice It is ordered that on payment of ten pounds being the penalty of his Bond the Said Bond be delivered up

Mr Hopes Bond d^d up—Mr John Hope produceing a Certificate of his being admitted a member of the Society of Lincolns Inn the 5th of Decr. Last [1] It is ordered that on payment of his arrears being fifty Shillings the Said Bond be delivered up to be Cancelled

---

[1] Hope's death is recorded in 1761: *Black Books of L.I.*, iii, 372.

Mr Barnes to be Sued—Mr Wm Barnes being greatly in arrear for pencions & absent Commons and a prosecution haveing been Some time Since begun against him And he not paying what is due to the Society according to his Severall promises It is ordered that he be forthwith prosecuted on his Bond for the Said arrears with effect.

Mr Gwynes Chambers to be padlockt—Mr Morgan Gwyne being greatly in arrear for pencions absent Commons & Rent and haveing been often requested to Pay the Same which he has neglected to do It is ordered that his Chamber be forthwith padlockt up

Mr Monger to be padlockt out unless admitted—Mr Monger haveing been for Some time past & Still continues resident in Mr Henry Gregorys Chamber without being admitted a member of this Society Contrary to the Orders of the Same And haveing been often requested to be admitted & hitherto has neglected the Same It is ordered that unles that he Cause himselfe to be admitted of the Said Society within one week next comeing [1] The Said Chambers be padlockt up

Auditors of the Principalls Accounts from Hillary Term 1720 to Hillary Term 1721—It is ordered that Mr George Denshire and Mr Edward Halsted two of the Antients of this Society and Mr John Dewes and Mr Charles Bowles two of the Companyons of the Same Society Shall and do Examine and audit the Principalls Accounts of this Society for one whole year beginning in Hillary Term one thousand Seven hundred and twenty untill Hillary Term then next following And that the said George Denshire Edward Halsted John Dewes and Charles Bowles or any three of them Shall and do make their Certificate and Report of the Said Accounts as Soon as the Same can or may Conveniently be done.

Mr Love for pencions & absent Commons—Mr Andrew Love being in arrear 15s. & 6d. on his old Composicion made in 1713 and Since that for pencions 36s. and for absent Commons Ending Michaelmas Term last £6 & 15s. and desireing an abatement of the Said Commons in regard he was not in Town 24 of the Terms charged to his Account [abated £3 for those terms: to pay £3 15s. with the 15s. 6d. and 36s. and be discharged of all arrears] The Servants Rolls being discharged

Security to Mr Dovey & others for £250 by them Lent with Interest for the Same—WHEREAS It is become necessary to pull down the Buildings at the Fore Gate of this Society and the Porters Lodge there in order to Erect a new Gate Stead [2] & Gate according to the plott or plan thereof made and agreed on AND WHEREAS to Supply the want of a present Summe of money to carry on & perfect the Same & other necessary workes

---

[1] Monger, of the Six Clerks' Office, was admitted on February 26, 1721/2; for his exit six years later see p. 133 below.

[2] Supporting framework: cf. bedstead.

& repairs to be done in & about the House The Severall Gentlemen here-
after named (being Antients of this Society) Have agreed to advance &
Lend the Severall Summes of money hereinafter respectively mencioned
viz. Mr John Dovey the Summe of Fifty pounds Mr John Penny the
Summe of Fifty pounds Mr Thomas Carter the Summe of Fifty pounds
Mr Edward Halsted the Summe of Fifty pounds and Mr Edmund Giles
Hooper the Summe of Fifty pounds in all amounting to two Hundred &
fifty pounds It is ordered Therefore That the Said John Dovey John
Penny Thomas Carter Edward Halsted and Edmund Giles Hooper Shall
be Severally & respectively paid the Said Severall Summes of money So
by them agreed to be advanced & Lent as aforesaid together with Interest
for the Same (after the rate of five pounds per cent per annum) from the
twenty fifth day of March next ensueing the Same being by them Severally
& respectively to be paid into the hands of the Principall for the use of
this Society on or before the next Pencion And it is Ordered that the
Said Severall Summes of money with Interest as aforesaid shall be respectively Secured and paid unto the Said John Dovey John Penny
Thomas Carter Edward Halsted and Edmund Giles Hooper and each of
them by and out of the Stock and other Rents and profitts of this Society
as the Same can or may from time to time be raised & received

	Josh: Blackwell: Pr:
	John Dovey
F. Gregg	Wm Fowler
Tho: Carter	Geo. Fuller
Edwd Halsted	John Knight
John Gibbons	John Penny
Geo. Denshire	Edm Giles Hooper

The above named Mr Edm. Giles Hooper
did not advance and Lend the Summ of
Fifty pounds above mencioned and Therefore is not charged received in my account

Josh: Blackwell: Pr:

Mr Hayne for pencions & absent Commons—Mr Joseph Hayne being
in arrear for absent Commons thirty Shillings [desires abatement (not in
town 4 of the terms charged): abated 10s.: to pay 20s. in full discharge]

Mr Shepperd for the like—Mr Richard Shepperd being in arrear for
absent Commons ending Michaelmas Term thirty five Shillings [desires
abatement (not in town any of the terms charged): abated one half of the
commons: to pay 17s. 6d. in full discharge]

Mr Trott for the like—Mr Baptist Trott being in arrear 25s. for absent
Commons Ending Michaelmas Term last [desires abatement (not in town

4 of the terms charged): abated 10s. for those terms: to pay 15s. in full discharge]

Clements Inn in the } At a pencion held there on Wednesday the 21ˢᵗ day
County of Middlesex } of February in the year of our Lord 1721 present
        Mr Blackwell Principall Mr Dovey Mr Fowler
        Mr Gibbons Mr Fuller Mr Penny Mr Carter
        Mr Halsted

The Principall's audited Accounts Confirmed—WHEREAS Mr George Denshire & Mr Edward Halsted two of the Antients of this Society and Mr Charles Bowles and Mr John Dewes two of the Companyons of the Same Society by order of pencion made the fourteenth day of this Instant February were appointed Auditors of the Accounts of Mr Joshua Blackwell Principall of this Society and have accordingly Examined Stated and audited the Said Principall's Accounts of Receipts & Disbursements for one whole year beginning in Hillary Term one Thousand Seven hundred & twenty Untill Hillary Term Now last past And have found the Summ Totall of the Said Principalls Receipts in that year to be Six hundred & twenty pounds Eighteen Shillings and two pence And the Summ Totall of his Discharges to be Nine hundred twenty Six pounds Eleven Shillings and ten pence So that there remains due from this Society to the Said Principall on Ballance of the Said Accounts the Sum of three hundred and five pounds thirteen Shillings and eight pence as appears by their Certificate or report thereof dated the Sixteenth day of the Said month of February IT IS THEREFORE ORDERED that the Said Accounts So Examined Stated and audited and Certified as aforesaid be allowed and approved off And the Same are hereby accordingly allowed & approved of to be Just and true And the said Joshua Blackwell is hereby discharged therefrom And it is also ordered that he be paid the Said Ballance of three hundred and five pounds thirteen Shillings and eight pence out of Such money as Shall be received for the use of this Society.

      John Dovey Edwᵈ Halsted
      Wᵐ Fowler
      Geo. Fuller
      John Gibbons
      John Penny
      Tho: Carter

Mr Hunt for the Surrender of his old Chambers over the fore gate & purchase of Chambers up 2 pair of Stairs Nº 1. in possession of Mr Chr. Lake—WHEREAS by Articles bearing date the fifth of December 1704 the then Principall and Antients of Clements Inn aforesaid Did Lease to Joseph Hunt the Elder for the Consideracions therein mencioned one Moyety or halfe part of the two Chambers being one over the other & two Garretts over them in Clements Inn aforesaid Over the Porters Lodge & Gate belonging to the Said Inn for ninety & nine years If Joseph Hunt the younger Should So long Live AND WHEREAS the Said Joseph Hunt the Elder in his life time did Assigne over the Said Lease and all his Interest & Estate in the Said Chambers & Garretts to the Said Joseph Hunt the younger his Son & afterwards dyed AND WHEREAS it is become necessary to pull the Said Chambers & Building down in order to Erect a new Gate Stead Gate & other Conveniencyes there And the Said Joseph Hunt the Son Haveing come to an agreement with the Principall & Antients of the Said House to Surrender up the Lease and all the Estate & Interest thereby granted to him in the Said Chambers & Garretts and in lieu thereof desireing to purchase a Lease for his own Life of the Chambers up two pair of Stairs with the Garretts over them in the Said Stair Case marked with the figure or Number (3) in the possession of Mr Christopher Lake as Tenant to this Society And haveing agreed to pay to the use of this Society ten pounds for the Same in Exchange IT IS THEREFORE ORDERED That on the Said Joseph Hunt the Son his Surrendring & delivering up the Said Lease & Interest in the first mencioned Chambers & Garretts and his giveing up & releasing the possession of them on or before the 25th day of March next and on his paying ten pounds for the use of this Society A new Lease of the Said last Mencioned Chambers & Garretts be made & granted to the Said Mr Hunt for his own life to Commence from Lady Day next according to the method & form of makeing & granting Leases by this Society And in Testimony of this Agreement the Said Joseph Hunt the Son hath signed this Order.

Jos. Hunt

Mr Pavey for absent Commons—Mr Wm Pavey being in arrear 25s. for absent Commons ending in Michaelmas Term last [desires abatement: not in town 4 of the terms charged: abated 10s.: to pay 15s. in full discharge]

Mr Hinder to be allowed 20s. for mending his windows & repairs &c— Mr Tho Hinder Tenant of the Cellar at the Back Gate affirming that he laid out thirteen Shillings about Some repaires in the Said Cellar by order of the late Mr Evans deceased and also Seven Shillings in mending the windows of the Said Cellar broken by the workmen & others during the time the Building over the Same Cellar was repairing It is ordered that he be allowed & abated the Said 20s. out of the next Rent he shall pay to Mr Barras for the use of this Society and the Said Mr Barras is hereby directed to allow the Same.

F

Clements Inn in the⎱ At a pencion held there on Friday the Second day
County of Middlesex⎰ of March in the year of our Lord 1721 present
Mr Blackwell pr. Mr Dovey Mr Fowler MrGibbons
Mr Fuller Mr Knight Mr Halsted Mr Hooper

*Mr Anth. Cocke for a Lease for his life in the Chambers 1 pr of Stairs
N.º 3 Late Mr Humphreys*—Mr Anthony Cocke one of the Companyons
of this Society Desireing to purchase a Lease for his life of the Chambers
formerly containing two Severall Chambers or Apartments up one pair of
Stairs in the Stair Case marked with the figure or Number (3) in the first
Court in Clements Inn aforesaid lately Leased to & in the possession of
Mr Thomas Humphreys as Tenant to this Society with the appurtenances
It is ordered that on payment of the Summ of Eighty Six pounds to the
Principall for the use of this Society a Lease be made & granted of the
Said Chambers with the Appurtenances to him the Said Anthony Cocke
for ninety & nine years if he so long Live to Commence from Lady day
with the usual Covenants and provisoes and according to the usual forme
& method of makeing & granting Leases by this Society In Testimony of
which agreement the Said Anthony Cocke hath Signed this order

A Cocke

*The Old Gate & Buildings there to be taken down & a new Gate & Shop
to be erected*—Whereas the Buildings at & over the Fore Gate of this
Society and over the Porters Lodge there and the Said Gate Lodge &
Shop adjoyning are become So old & ruinous that it is necessary to pull
down the Same And it being Judged more for the Improvement & benefitt
of the Said Society to Erect a New Gate of Iron & a Flat rooft Shopp only
without any Chambers over the Same instead of the Said Old Buildings &
Gate according to the plans or draughts thereof made & produced It is
Therefore ordered that the Said Old Building & Gate be with all Convenient Speed taken down And a new Iron Gate and Shop according to
the Severall Plans or Draughts aforesaid be Sett up & erected And the
Principall and Deputy Principall for the time being with Such others as he
shall Call to his assistance are hereby desired authorized & Impowered to
See the Same performed accordingly.

Clements Inne—   At a Pencion held there on Friday the 11th day of
May Anno Domini 1722—present Mr Penny
Dep.ʸ Pr: Mr Dovey Mr Fowler Mr Fuller Mr
Knight Mr Halsted Mr Gibbons

*Lease to Mr Wilkins of the New Shop and the Fore part of the Cellar
under it at the Fore Gate*—Ordered that A Lease of the New Shop at the

Fore Gate of this Inn & the Fore part of the Cellar under the Same be made from this Society according to the usual Method of makeing Leases from the Said Society & with usual Covenants unto Thomas Wilkins Stationer for the Terme of Eleven years from Midsommer next under the yearly rent of Sixteen pounds payable quarterly And in Testimony of the Said Mr Wilkins' agreement to this order he hath Signed the Same

Tho:ˢ Wilkins

Mr Swifts Bond d.ᵈ up—Mr Richard Swift being in arrear for pencions & absent Commons three pounds & one Shilling and desireing to have his Bond delivered up And it appeareing that he doth not now nor hath at any time within three years past practized the Law in any respect It is ordered That on payment of the Said Arrears & Clearing the Servants Rolls his Bond be delivered up to be Cancelled.

Mr Allen the like—Mr Lewis Allen produceing a Certificate of his being admitted a member of the Society of the Middle Temple And desireing to have his Bond given to this Society delivered up It is ordered on payment of his arrears being four pounds that his Said be delivered up to him to be Cancelled

Mr T Swift for pencions & absent Commons—Mr Thomas Swift being in arrear Six Shillings for pencions & twenty Shillings for absent Commons Ending this present Easter Term desireing an Abatement for one of the Terms Charged to his account in regard he was not in Town It is ordered that he be abated two Shillings & Six pence for that Term and on payment of Seventeen Shillings & Six pence the Same be in full of the Said Commons

Clements Inn in the ⎰ At a pencion there held on Friday the Fifteenth day
County of Middlesex ⎱ of June Anno Domini one thousand Seven hundred
twenty & two present Mr Blackwell Principall
Mr Dovey Mr Fuller Mr Fowler Mr Knight Mr
Penny Mr Halsted Mr Gibbons Mr Carter

Mr Hen: Nelthorpes Bond d.ᵈ up—Mr Henry Nelthorpe being in arrear thirty Eight Shillings for pencions & absent Commons and desireing to have his Bond delivered up on payment thereof And it appearing that he doth not now nor hath at any time in three years past practised the Law in any respect It is ordered that on his payment of the Said arrears & clearing the Servants Rolls his Bond be delivered up to be cancelled.

Mr Humphreys to be Sued—Mr Thomas Humphreys being greatly in arrear to the Society for rent & other Dutyes And haveing been often requested to pay the Same It is ordered That unless he do pay the Said arrears within ten days after notice of this order the Said Mr Humphreys & his Surety be Sued for the Same

Mr Halsted for the Rooms & Dust hole at the upper End of the first Court—Mr Edwd Halsted (one of the Antients of this Society) desireing to purchase a Lease for his life with an Assignment for another life after the expiracion of his own life in the ground roome at the upper End of the first Court in Clements Inn aforesaid lying between the Building lately erected by Mr Seabrooke on the East Side & the Room or place Intended for & Sometime used as a Dust hole on the West Side thereof with the Cellar under the Same rooms and also the Said room or Dust hole being next to the Talbot Ale house the whole fronting Clements Lane North and the Said first Court South as the Same are now made & divided together with the Doors particions & window Shutters thereto belonging and also the deal Boards & other things & Stuff now being on the Said premisses in the Said Dust hole not used And proposeing to pay £95 for the same on or before the Last day of Trinity Term 1723 and to Floor, wainscott & paint the Said rooms or Such part thereof as wants So to be done & to fitt up the Same in a decent & handsome manner with Chimney peices Hearths & Slabbs & also fitt up the Said Cellar conveniently & fit for use & Service It is ordered & agreed that Mr Halsted may Enter & take possession of the premisses at any time when he shall think fitt & that on payment of the Said Sum of ninety five pounds within the time aforesaid to the Principall then being for the use of this Society A Lease & Assignement be accordingly made & granted to the Said Mr Halsted of the Said Rooms Cellar & premisses with the appurtenances Subject to the payment of Separate pencions Commons & other Dutyes to the House According to the order of pencion made for that purpose & with & under the usual Covenants Provisoes & agreements and according to the usual form & method of makeing Leases by the Said Society And with a Covenant from Mr Halsted to floor wainscott & paint the Said rooms as aforesaid & fitt them up in a decent & handsome manner with Chimney peices Hearths & Slabbs & also to fitt up the Said Cellar conveniently & fit for use & Service In Testimony of which agreement the Said Mr Halsted hath Subscribed his name to this order

Edwd Halsted

Acknowledgment for the lower window from N°. 9 into the Lamb Inn and of a Shed sufferred in the Said Inn—Whereas Mr Samuel Roach Tenant of the Lamb Inn Situate near & adjacent to Some part of the ground belonging to this Society had a Stable erected for the Standing of Horses at the upper End of his yard in the North west Corner thereof & adjoyning & contiguous to Some part of the Walls of the Old Hall belonging to the Said Society on the East Side thereof in the which part of the Said Old Hall there was of right Antients windows or Lights over the Said Stable looking

Eastward into the Said yard And Whereas for the greater Improvement of the Said Society The Said Hall was taken down And a New Building now marked with the figure or Number (9) in this Inn for Chambers was erected on part of the ground whereon the Said Old Hall Stood And the Society haveing a right to make lights or windows in the upper part of the Same Building for the benefitt of the Chambers up one & two pair of Stairs there looking Eastward into the Said yard on that Side & part of the Same where the Said Stable Stood above the Same and it being Convenient for the ground Chamber in the Said Building to have the like Window or Light which could not be effected without removeing & takeing away the Said Stable And in regard that for that purpose the Said Mr Roach did remove and take away the Said Stable And agreed not to Sett up or Suffer any other Edifice Erection or other thing whatsoever to be Sett up or placed there to Stop up hinder or obstruct the Said Window or Light It was agreed on the part of this Society that the Summ of Five pounds Seven Shillings & Six pence should be paid to the Said Mr Roach And also that he should be permitted to continue a Shed or place Erected for the Standing of a Coach or Chaise in his Said yard adjoyning to the lower part of the wall of the Building on the South Side in the first Court of this Inn marked with the figure or Number (2) which he hath done accordingly It is now ordered in performance of the Said agreement that the Said five pounds Seven Shillings & Six pence be forthwith paid to the Said Mr Roach And he the Said Mr Roach Doth hereby promise & agree Not to do or Suffer anything to be done whereby or by means whereof the Said Window or Light Looking Eastwards into his Said yard in the Said New Building may be any ways Stopped up hindred or obstructed And the Said Mr Roach doth hereby acknowledge that the Said Shed adjoyning to the Building marked Number (2) as aforesaid was Sett up & is continued not of right But by permission & Sufferance from this Society only In Testimony whereof he the Said Mr Roach hath Sett his hand to this order

Witness Joseph Barras   Sam.ll Roch

Lease to John Hale of the Fruit Shop at the Back Gate—Ordered that a Lease of the fruit Shop in the Passage at the back Gate be made from this Society to John Hale the now Tenant thereof according to the usual Method of makeing Leases by this Society and with usual Covenants & agreements for the Term of Seven years from Midsomer next under the yearly rent of Seven pounds payable quarterly of which Said Lease the Said John Hale agrees to accept accordingly And in Testimony of his agreement to this Said order he hath Signed the Same

                                                    John Hale

Clements Inn in the ⎱ At a pencion held there on Friday the twenty
County of Middleszx ⎰ Second day of June in the year of our Lord one
Thousand Seven hundred & twenty two present
Mr Blackwell Pr. Mr Dovey Mr Fowler Mr Gibbons
Mr Fuller Mr Penny Mr Halsted Mr Carter

Mr Heathcoates Bond d.^d up—Mr Samuel Heathcoate being in arrear for pencions & absent Commons Ending in Hillary Term Six pounds & Eighteen Shillings and desireing his Bond given on his Admission into this Society may be delivered up in regard that he is now become Antient & Infirm & hath left off the practice of the Law It is ordered that on payment of the Summ of £6 18s. & discharging the Servants Rolls his Said Bond be Delivered up to be cancelled and that the pencion & Commons for Easter Term last be remitted

Mr Curtis for absent Commons—Mr Curtis being in arrear for pencions 12s. and 43s. for absent Commons Ending Easter Term last And Desireing an Abatement of the Said absent Commons in regard he was not in Town any of the Terms charged to his account It is ordered that he be abated twenty two Shillings & Six pence of the Said Commons and on payment of twenty two Shillings and Six pence the Same be in full discharge of the Said Commons

Mr W. Vaux for pencions & absent Commons—Mr Wm Vaux being in arrear 36s. for pencions & £6 for absent Commons Ending Trinity Term last past [desires abatement (not in town in Easter term last): abated 2s. 6d. for that term: to pay £5. 17. 6 in full discharge of his Commons].

Clements Inn in the ⎱ At a Pencion held there on Friday the thirtieth day
County of Middlesex ⎰ of November Anno Domini 1722 present Mr Dovey
Dep. Pr. Mr Fowler Mr Fuller Mr Knight Mr
Penny Mr Halsted

Mr Humphreys to be Sued—Mr Thomas Humphreys being greatly in arrear to this Society for rent pencions & other Dutyes & neglecting to pay the Same though often requested It is ordered that his Bond be forthwith put in Suit against himselfe & his Surety.

Mr Chr. Lake—The like order is made concerning Mr Christopher Lake

Mr Gwyns Chamber to be lockt up—Mr Morgan Gwyne being greatly in arrear for Rent & other Dutyes to this Society and haveing been very often desired to discharge the Same which he has neglected to do It is ordered that the Chambers wherein he now resides be forthwith padlockt up and he be removed thereout forthwith

Mr Bramston for absent Commons—Mr Stephen Bramston being in arrear 50s. for absent Commons Ending this last Michaelmas Terme and desireing an Abatement [not in town 4 of the terms charged: abated 10s.: to pay 40s. in full discharge of the commons]

Clements Inn in the ⎱ At a pencion there held on Friday the twenty first
County of Middlesex ⎰ day of December 1722 present Mr Dovey Dep.ᵞ Pr.
Mr Fuller Mr Gibbons Mr Knight Mr Penny Mr Halsted Mr Hooper

Mr John Dewes for a Lease of the Chamber & Garretts late Mr Paveys—Mr John Dewes one of the Companyons of this Society haveing agreed with Mr Wm Pavey one other of the Companyons of the Same Society for the purchase of his Chamber & Garretts up 2 & 3 pair of Stairs in the Stair Case No. (3) which Mr Pavey Held by Lease or Articles from this Society for 99 years determinable with his life And the Said Wᵐ. Pavey at the request of the Said John Dewes hath Surrendred up his Said Articles unto this Society in order to have a Lease made of the Said Chamber & Garretts unto the Said John Dewes And the said John Dewes appearing and desireing to be admitted to the Said Chamber & Garretts It is ordered that on payment of Eleven pounds for the use of this Society a New Lease be made & granted of the Said Chamber & Garretts to the Said John Dewes if he Shall So long Live and be & continue a member of the Said Society with the usual Covenants & provisoes and according to the form & Method of making & Granting Leases by this Society

Mr Paveys Bond up—Mr Wᵐ. Pavey produceing a Certificate of his being admitted a Member of the Society of the Middle Temple And desireing to have his Bond given to this Society Delivered up It is ordered that on payment of his arrears being 24s. his Said Bond be delivered up to him to be Cancelled.

Mr Cock for absent Commons—Wᵐ. Cock Esqᵉ being in arrear 22s. for pencions and for absent Commons £3. 15s. ending Trinity Terme 1722 and desireing an Abatement [not in town 6 of the terms charged: abated 15s.: to pay £3 in full discharge of the commons]

Mr Stubbs for pencions & absent Commons—Mr Walter Stubbs being in arrear 20s. for pencions & £3 5s. 0d. for absent Commons ending Michaelmas Term 1722 and desiring an Abatement [not in town 10 of the terms charged: abated 25s.: to pay 40s. in full discharge of the Commons]

Mr R. Keeling Dᵒ.—The Same order for him.

CONTRIBUTORS to the Drawing Mr Blackwells the Principalls Picture of Clements Inn a whole length to be Sett up in the Hall of the Same Inn in a gold frame (viz.̣)

		£	s	d
Mr Dovey	.	5:	5:	0
Mr Gregg	.	3:	3:	0
Mr Fowler	.	5:	5:	0
Mr Goodman	.	5:	5:	0
Mr Gibbons	.	3:	3:	0
Mr Fuller	.	3:	3:	0
Mr Knight	.	3:	3:	0
Mr Denshire	.	3:	3:	0
Mr Penny	.	5:	5:	0
Mr Carter	.	5:	5:	0
Mr Halsted	.	5:	5:	0
Mr Hooper	.	3:	3:	0

Collected by Mr Halsted   50: 8: 0

	£	s	d
paid Mr Gouge[1] painting the said picture as by Agreement Forty Guineas	42:	0:	0
paid Mr Garry for the Gold Frame	10:	10:	0
paid the Smith for the Iron Work to hang up the said Picture & Small Expenses amongst the Workmen att that time	00:	10:	6

Disbursed   53: 0: 6

Mr John Dovey Principall

Clements Inn in the } At a pencion held there on Friday the fifteenth day
County of Middlesex } of February Anno Domini 1722 present Mr Dovey Principall Mr Fowler Mr Fuller Mr Penny Mr Carter Mr Halsted

Back Gate—It is ordered the back Gate belonging to this Society opening towards Clare Market Shall not be opened or Suffered to be Open by the Porter or Other person there watching after twelve of the Clock in the night time on any account or pretence whatsoever But

[1] An artist named Gouge, living in 1726 in Covent Garden Piazza, is mentioned in the note-books of George Vertue (1685–1756), published by the Walpole Society (1933–4), vol. III, pp. 35, 51. He was one of the experts consulted in the dispute over Sir Richard Thornhill's decorative work at Moor Park in 1728. This portrait of Blackwell has not been traced. There is no record of one at the National Portrait Gallery. See, further, p. 126 n. below.

Immediately after 12 a Clock the Said Porter or other person there watching Shall Carry down & leave with the Porter of the Fore Gate the Key belonging to the Said Back Gate [1] and the person acting Contrary to this order Shall be forthwith turned out of his office & displaced.

Mr Humphreys & Mr Lake to be Sued—Ordered that Mr Tho. Humphreys and Mr Chr: Lake and the persons bound with them be forthwith prosecuted with effect.

Mr Bridges for absent Commons—Mr James Bridges being in arrear 12s. for pencions & for absent Commons Ending this present Hillary Term 40s. and desireing an Abatement of the Said Commons for Six Terms charged to his account in which he was not in Town It is ordered that he be abated 15s. for those 6 Terms And that on payment of 25s. the Same be in full discharge of the Said Commons.

Mr M. Innys for Absent Commons—Mr Martin Innys being in arrear 40s. for Pensions and absent Commons £6. 10s. Ending Hillary Term 1722 and desireing an abatement of the Said Commons in regard he was not in Town 20 of the Terms Charged to his Account It is ordered that he be abated fifty Shillings for those Terms And that on payment of four pounds the Same be in full discharge of the Said Commons. The Servants Rolls being first paid.

Mr Gregory for absent Commons—Mr Hen Gregory being in arrear 14s. for pencions and 35s. for absent Commons for 7 Terms Ending Michaelmas 1722 [desires abatement (not in town any of those terms): abated 17s. 6d.: to pay 17s. 6d. in full discharge of the commons] the Servants Rolls being also paid

Clements Inn in the⎱ At a Pencion there held on Wednesday the 29th
County of Middlesex⎰ day of May Anno Domini 1723 present Mr Dovey
        principall Mr Fowler Mr Gibbons Mr Knight
        Mr Penny Mr Halsted

Mr P. Smiths Bond d^d up—Mr Philip Smith being retired into the Country and not a practizer of the Law and desireing to have his Bond given to this Society to be delivered up It is ordered that on payment of what is due from him to the Society & Clearing the Servants Rolls the Said Bond be delivered up to be cancelled

Mr Tyson to be Sued—Mr Wm Tyson being considerably in arrear for pencions & absent Commons and haveing neglected to pay the Same though often Requested it is ordered that his Bond be put in Suit for Recovery thereof

---

[1] For the variation of this order in 1729 see p. 143 below.

F*

Clements Inn in the ⎞ At a pension there held on Wednesday The 19th
County of Middlesex ⎠ day of June Anno Domini 1723 present Mr Dovey
Principall Mr Blackwell Mr Fowler Mr Gibbons
Mr Fuller Mr Knight Mr Penny Mr Halsted

Auditors of the late Principalls Accounts from Hillary Term 1721 to Hill. 1722—It is ordered that Mr George Fuller & Mr John Penny two of the Antients of this Society and Mr Thomas Fowke & Mr Wm. Wotton two of the Companyons of the Same Society Shall and do examine and audit the accounts of Mr Blackwell late Principall of this Society for one whole year beginning in Hillary Term one Thousand Seven hundred twenty one untill Hillary Term then next following And that the Said George Fuller John Penny Thomas Fowke & Wm. Wotton or any three of them Shall and do make their Certificate & Report of the Said accounts assoon as the Same can or may conveniently be done

Mr Eccles for absent Commons—Mr Samuell Eccles being in arrear 14s. for pencions and 40s. for absent Commons ending in Easter Term last [desires abatement (not in town any of the terms charged): abated 20s.: to pay 20s. in full discharge of the commons]

Mr Turner for absent Commons—Mr Wm. Turner being in arrear 18s. for pencions & 50s. for absent Commons ending in Easter Term last [desires abatement (not in town any of the terms charged): abated 25s.: to pay 25s. in full discharge of the commons]

Mr James Hardwicke for absent Commons—Mr James Hardwicke being in arrear for absent Commons 35s. ending in Easter Term last [desires abatement (not in town any of the terms charged): abated 17s. 6d.: to pay 17s. 6d. in full discharge]

Clements Inn in the ⎞ At a Pencion there held on Friday the tenth day of
County of Middlesex ⎠ July Anno Domini 1723 present Mr Dovey
principall Mr Blackwell Mr Fuller Mr Fowler
Mr Denshire Mr Penny Mr Halsted

The late Principalls audited accounts Confirmed—Whereas Mr George Fuller and Mr John Penny two of the Antients of this Society and Mr Thomas Fowke and Mr Wm. Wotton two of the Companyons of the Same Society by order of pencion made the nineteenth day of June now last past were appointed Auditors of the accounts of Mr Joshua Blackwell late Principall of this Society And have accordingly examined Stated and audited the Said late Principalls accounts of Receipts & Disbursements for one whole year beginning in Hillary Term one thousand seven hundred & twenty one untill Hillary Term now last past And have found the Summe Totall of the Said late Principalls Receipts in that year to be nine hundred fifty three pounds three Shillings and two pence And the Summe Totall of his Discharges to be Eleven hundred Eighty three pounds Six Shillings and ten pence So that there remains due from this Society to the Said late Principall on the ballance of the Said accounts the Summe of two hundred Thirty pounds three Shillings & eight pence as appears by their Certificate or Report thereof Dated the twenty ninth day of the Said month of June IT IS THEREFORE ORDERED That the Said Accounts So examined Stated and Audited and Certified as aforesaid be allowed & approved off And the Same are hereby accordingly Allowed and approved of to be just and true And the Said Joshua Blackwell is hereby discharged therefrom AND IT IS ALSO ORDERED that he be paid the Said Ballance of two hundred thirty pounds three Shillings and ten[1] pence out of Such money as Shall be Received for the use of this Society

> John Dovey
> Geo: Fuller
> Wm Fowler
> Geo. Denshire
> John Penny
> Edwd Halsted

To Mr Blackwell Rector of St Clem. Danes 10 guineas—Ordered that the Principall do give to the Rev^d Mr Thomas Blackwell Rector of St Clements Danes ten guineas as a free gift from this Society Nothing of right being due to him from the Said Society

Mr Curtis for absent Commons—Mr Curtis being in arrear 15s. for absent Commons ending Easter Term 1723 and having not been in town any of the Terms It is ordered that he be abated 7s. 6d. for the Said Commons

Clements Inn in the County of Middlesex } At a Pencion there held on Thursday the Eighteenth day of July Anno Domini 1723 present Mr Dovey principall Mr Blackwell Mr Fowler Mr Fuller Mr Gibbons Mr Knight Mr Denshire Mr Penny Mr Halsted

Mr Seabrooke for a Lease of the Area & vaults N° 6.—WHEREAS Mr Wm Seabrooke has made a demand of this Society of one hundred twenty nine pounds five Shillings & four pence for Severall Draughts plans & Estimates of Buildings within the Said Society and for treating with Workmen and receiving and paying Severall Summs of money and Surveying the Repairs of the Said Society for Severall years AND WHEREAS the Said Society has also a demand on the Said Mr Seabrooke for an area before his Building Number (6) and the Vaults under the Court before the Said Building

---

[1] A clerical error; "ten" should be "eight."

And Whereas it is agreed that one Demand Shall be Sett off against and in discharge of the other respectively And in pursuance of Such Agreement the Said Mr Seabrooke hath agreed to discharge the Said Society of his Said Demand It is now Ordered that the Said William Seabrooke Shall have a Lease made unto him of the Said Area and vaults for the Remainder of the Term of years which he hath in the Said Building N° (6) with all other appurtenances to the Said Building belonging or used therewith by him or in his possession And accordingly the Said Wm Seabrooke Doth hereby release and discharge the Said Society of & from the Said demand & Summ of one hundred twenty nine pounds five Shillings & four pence and of & from all other Demands due from the Said Society to this Day [1] And in Testimony hereof the Said Wm Seabrooke hath hereunto Subscribed his name

William Seabrooke

Declaracion of the Policy for the Building N° (7)—Whereas by a Policy of Insurance granted by the Amicable Contributionship for the Insurance of Houses &c from fire [2] Number 39095 and dated the 31th day of July 1722 Mr Edward Halsted one of the Antients of this Society hath insured the Brick house or Building Situate on the East & West Sides of the Stair Case at the North East Corner of the first Court in Clements Inn aforesaid at one Thousand pounds value The Said Edward Halsted Doth hereby declare that five hundred pounds part of the Said £1000 is in trust and for the use & benefit of the Said Society And that the other £500 is for his own use & benefit Which Said Policy is left amongst the writeings Books & papers belonging to the Said Society In Testimony whereof the Said Edward Halsted hath hereunto Subscribed his name

Edwd Halsted

Clements Inn in the⎱ At a Pencion there held on Friday the Eighth Day
County of Middlesex⎰ of November in the year of our Lord 1723 present
Mr Dovey Principall Mr Blackwell Mr Fowler
Mr Fuller Mr Knight Mr Penny Mr Halsted

Mr Barnes's Bond d^d up to Mr Smith his Surety on paymant of £15 4s. 0d.—Mr Wm Barnes being in arrear to this Society for Pencions & absent Commons Ending in Trinity Term last £15. 4s. and his Bond haveing been put in Suit for recovery thereof Mr James Smith who is Surety by Bond for him Now Desires the Said Bond may be delivered up to him It is ordered that on payment of the Said Summ of £15. 4s. for the use of this Society

---

[1] It is significant that Seabrooke was admitted to membership of the Inn (Joshua Blackwell being his surety) on July 20, 1723: see p. 273 below.

[2] See footnote, p. 29 above.

ten Shillings for the Servants Rolls and the Charges at Law the Said Bond be Delivered up to the said Mr Smith

Mr Trevors Bond d^d up—Mr Thomas Trevor being in arrear 31s. for pencions & absent Commons Ending in Trinity Term last And haveing not practised the Law and now liveing in the Country desires to have his Bond delivered up It is ordered that payment of the Said Sum of 31s. his Said Bond be accordingly delivered up to him.

Nich. Hollis Porter of the Back Gate—Ordered that Nicholas Hollis be admitted Porter at the Back Gate of this Society next to Clare Market in the room & place of John North deceased late Porter there But to continue therein only during the good will & pleasure of the Principall & Antients & their Successors for the time being or the major part of them and no longer

Porter of the Fore Gate not to carry back the key of the back gate after 12.—Ordered that the Porter or person watching at the Fore Gate of this Society for the time being Do not on any pretence whatever after the Key of the Back Gate Shall be brought down to him by the Porter there, Carry the Said Key or open the Said Back Gate for any person whatever after twelve a Clock at Night on pain of being displact [1]

Mr Tyson for absent Commons—Mr Wm Tyson being in arrear for pencions 36s. & for absent Commons £6 due & ending in Easter Term last [desires abatement (not in town 8 of the terms charged): abated 20s.: to pay £5 in full discharge of the commons]

Clements Inn in the ⎱ At a pencion there held on Wednesday the fourth
County of Middlesex ⎰ day of December in the year of our Lord 1723
present Mr Dovey principall Mr Blackwell Mr
Fowler Mr Gibbons Mr Penny Mr Halsted

Hall to be insured de novo—Ordered that the Hall belonging to this Society be forthwith new Insured at the Expence of this Society for Seven years in the name of Mr Dovey the now principall.[2]

Lecturers to Mids. 1723—Ordered that the Principall Do pay to the Lecturers of St Clements Danes 15s. for halfe a year Ending at Midsomer last as a free gift from this Society.

The Interest of Mr Brewsters £100 to be paid to 18 December instant—WHEREAS Mr Chr. Brewster one of the Companyons of this Society did heretofore advance & Lend the Summ of £100 towards rebuilding the New Hall & Supplying the other occasions of this Society The repayment whereof with other money was Secured by a Mortgage made of this Inne or Hostell to Lawrence Carter Esq^e & others Trustees named for that purpose AND WHEREAS the Said Mr Brewster hath Since assigned the

---

[1] For the change in 1729 see p. 143 below.
[2] For the previous insurance seven years earlier see p. 29 above.

Said £100 & all Interest thereon Due and also all his Estate & right to the Same Unto Henry Rogers of London Goldsmith And the Said Mr Rogers haveing required payment thereof AND WHEREAS Mr John Dovey now principall hath agreed to advance & pay off the said £100 principall money out of his own proper moneys on the Said Security IT IS NOW ORDERED that the Said Principall do out of the Stock & profitts of this Society pay all such Interest as now is or Shall be due for the Said £100 on the 18th day of this Instant December.

Mr W^m. *Powlett for the Chambers N*^o. *3 late Mr Rob. Powletts—* Whereas Mr Robt Powlet lately deceased held by Lease from this Society the ground Chamber N°. 3 for 99 years determinable with his Life with power for him or his Executors to name another member to be admitted to the Same for the like Term of 99 years determinable with the Life of Such person And Alice Powlet Sole Executrix of the last will of the Said Robt Powlett haveing nominated Wm Powlett gent to be admitted thereunto who is admitted a member of this Society and desires to be admitted to the Said Chambers And the Said Alice Powlett haveing to that Intent Surrendred the Said Lease & the Estate & Interest thereby Granted It is Ordered that a new Lease of the Said Chambers be made to the Said Wm Powlett for 99 years If he Shall So Long Live according to the usual method & forme of Granting Leases by this Society.

Mr Tho: Powlett for the Chambers N^o. *20 late Mr Rob*^t. *Powletts—* Whereas the above named Robt Powlett held in manner aforesaid All those Chambers up two & three pair of Stairs & the Garretts over them being over the Chambers of Mr John Knight in the Stair Case marked N°. 20 with the Cellar therewith enjoyed to which the Said Alice Powlett hath nominated Tho: Powlett gent who is to be forthwith admitted a member of this Society to be admitted and for that purpose She hath Surrendered the Lease thereof and all the Estate & Interest thereby Granted It is Ordered that a new Lease of the Said Chambers Garrett & Cellar be made to the Said Tho Powlett for 99 years if he Shall So long Live According to the method & forme of Granting Leases used by this Society.

Clements Inn in the ⎱ At a Pencion there held on Friday the Fourteenth
County of Middlesex ⎰ day of February 1723 present Mr Dovey Principall
                                 Mr Fowler Mr Knight Mr Denshire Mr Penny
                                 Mr Halsted

Mr John Grayhursts Bond up—Mr Grayhurst being advanced in years and haveing left off his practice of the Law desires to have his Bond delivered up It is ordered accordingly on payment £7 16s. for his arrears due to the Society and Discharging the Servants Rolls

Mr Hyde D°.—Mr Humphrey Hyde having not practized the Law and going to the Country for his health desires to have his Bond delivered up which is ordered accordingly on payment of what is Due to the Society Being 10s.

Mr W™ Walcot D°.—Mr W™ Walcot late a member of this Society being Dead his Executrix haveing paid All his arrears desires to have his Bond delivered up which is ordered accordingly

Auditors of the Principalls Accounts from Hillary 1722 to Michaelmas Term 1723—It is ordered that Mr John Knight & Mr John Penny two of the Antients of this Society and Mr John Green & Mr John James Dobson two of the Companyons of the Said Society Shall & doe examine and audit the accounts of Mr John Dovey principall of this Society for one whole year beginning in Hillary Term One Thousand Seven hundred & twenty two Untill Hillary Terme then next following And that the Said Mr Knight Mr Penny Mr Green & Mr Dobson or any three of them Shall & doe make their Certificate & Report thereof Assoone as the Same can or may Conveniently be done.

Mr Wyche for absent Commons—Mr Richard Wyche being in arrear fourteen Shillings for Pencions and three pounds ten Shillings for absent Commons Ending Michaelmas Term last [desires abatement (not in town 11 of the terms charged): abated 27s. 6d.: to pay 42s. 6d. in full discharge of his commons]

Mr Hayne for absent Commons—Mr Joseph Hayne being in arrear 10s. for pencions due Hill 1723 and for absent Commons Ending Michalemas Term 1723 30s. [desires abatement (not in town 5 of the terms charged): abated 12s. 6d.: to pay 17s. 6d. in full discharge of his commons]

Mr Shepperd D°.—Mr Richard Shepperd being in arrear 10s. for pencions due Hillary 1723 and 35s. for absent Commons ending Michaelmas Term 1723 [desires abatement (not in town any of the terms charged): abated 17s. 6d.: to pay 17s. 6d. in full discharge of his commons]

Mr Trott D°.—Mr Baptist Trott being in arrear 10s. for pencions due Hillary 1723 & 25s. for absent Commons [desires abatement (not in town 4 of the terms charged): abated 10s. for those terms: to pay 15s. in full discharge of his commons]

Clements Inn in the } At a Pencion there held on Friday the thirteenth
County of Middlesex } day of March 1723 present Mr Dovey principal
                Mr Gibbons Mr Knight Mr Penny Mr Halsted
                Mr Hooper Mr Goodman

Principalls audited accounts Confirmed—Whereas Mr John Knight & Mr John Penny two of the Antients of this Society and Mr John Green and

Mr John James Dobson two of the Companyons of the Same Society by Order of pencion made the 14th day of February now last past were appointed Auditors of the accounts of Mr John Dovey now principall of this Society And have accordingly audited Stated & Examined the Said Principalls accounts of receipts & Disbursements for one whole year beginning in Hillary Term 1722 Untill and Ending Hillary Term now last past And have found the Summ Totall of the Said Principalls Receipts in that year to be two hundred Ninety Eight pounds & four Shillings And the Summ Totall of his Disbursements to be two hundred Eighteen pounds Nineteen Shillings and Nine pence So that there remains due from the Said principall to this Society on the ballance of the Said Accounts the Summ of Seventy nine pounds four Shillings & three pence as Appears by their Certificate or report thereof Dated the Seventh day of March Instant IT IS THEREFORE ORDERED That the Said Accounts So Examined Stated & audited and Certified as aforesaid be allowed & approved off And the Same are hereby accordingly allowed & approved of to be just and true And the Said John Dovey is hereby Discharged from the Said Sum of £218. 19s. 9d. So Disbursed as aforesaid

John Gibbons
John Knight
Edwd Halsted
Edm.^d Giles Hooper
John Penny
Ever.^d Goodman

Mr Jackson for absent Commons—Mr Fran: Jackson being Indebted to this Society 4s. for two pencions due Michaelmas & Hill 1722 and Fifty five Shillings for Absent Commons Ending Michaelmas 1722 [desires abatement (not in town 2 terms): abated 5s.: to pay £2. 10s. in full discharge of the commons]

Mr Halsted for a Lease of the Chambers late Mr Fullers N.^o (12) now N.º 8—Mr Edward Halsted one of the Antients of this Society haveing agreed with Mrs Mary Fuller Sole Executrix of Mr George Fuller deceased for the purchase of her Interest under certain Articles made between the Society & the Said Mr Fuller bearing Date the Seventh day of March 1717 purporting to be a Lease with an assignement of all that Chamber with the appurtenances up one pair of Stairs in the Brick Building in the Second Court in the Corner Stair Case then marked with the figures or number (12) then in his possession And the Said Mary Fuller having Surrenderd into the hands of the now Principall & Antients the Said Articles And the Estate Interest & term of years thereby granted of in & to the premisses To the Intent the Said Mr Halsted should be admitted thereunto pursuant to the agreement in the Said Articles contained It is ordered that a Least be made to the Said Edward Halsted of the Said Chambers with the appurtenances for 99 years if he Shall So long Live with the usual Covenants & provisoes & according to the usual form & method of making & granting Leases by this Society.

Mr John Dovey Junr. for a Lease of the Chamber late Mr Fullers (N°. 14) now N°. 9—Mr John Dovey Junr. one of the Companyons of this Society haveing agreed with Mrs Mary Fuller Executrix of the last will of Mr George Fuller deceased late one of the Antients of this Society for the purchase of her Interest under certain Articles made between this Society & the Said Mr Fuller bearing Date the 7th day of March 1717 purporting to be a Lease and Assignment of all that Chamber with the appurtenances in the Brick Building in the Court formerly called the Middle Court up one pair of Stairs in the Stair Case formerly marked with the figures or Number (14) then in his possession   And the Said Mary Fuller haveing surrendred into the hands of the now principall & Antients the Said Articles and all the Estate Interest & Term of years thereby granted of in & to the said premisses to the Intent that he the Said Mr Dovey should be admitted thereunto pursuant to the agreement in the Said Articles contained It is ordered that a Lease be made to the Said Mr Dovey of the Said Chamber with appurtenances for the Term of 99 years if he Shall So long Live with the usual Covenants & provisoes and according to the method & form of making & granting Leases by this Society.

Clements Inn in the ⎱ At a Pencion there held on Thursday the 21th day
County of Middlesex ⎰ of May 1724 present Mr Dovey Principall Mr
                        Fowler Mr Gibbons Mr Knight Mr Penny Mr
                        Halsted

Mr Edw. Curtis for a Lease of the Chambers late Mr Walcots—Whereas Mr W^m. Walcot late one of the Companyons of this Society was possessed in his life time under certain Articles made Between this Society & the Said Mr Walcot bearing Date the 17th day of July 1717 of all that ground Chamber with the appurtenances in the new Building in the first Court adjoyning to the Hall in Clements Inn with the Corner Cellar fronting the Said Court Northwards & Eastward with a power for him his Executors Administrators or Assignes to nominate another to enjoy the Same for another Term of 99 years from the Death or putting Extra of the Said Mr Walcot if the Said Nominee Should So long Live And Whereas the Said Mr Walcot in his life time agreed with Mr Humphrey Hyde gent then one of the Companyons of this House that in case he Should Survive the Said Mr Walcot He the Said Mr Hyde should appoint such person to be nominated as aforesaid to be admitted to the Said premisses And Whereas Mr Edward Curtis one of the Companyons of this Society hath agreed with the Said Mr Hyde & Mrs Elizabeth Walcot Sole Executrix of the last will of the Said Mr Walcot for the purchase of their Interest in the Said Chamber & Cellar with the appurtenances who thereupon by Indenture bearing Date the first day of February 1720 Did assigne the Same to Mr Noah Curtis one of the Companyons of this Society in trust for the Said Edward Curtis And Whereas the said Noah Curtis hath Surrendred into the hands of the now principall & Antients the Said Articles & Indenture of Assignment & all the Estate Interest & Term of years thereby granted & assigned to the Intent that the Said Edward Curtis should be admitted thereunto pursuant to the agreement in the Said Articles contained And the Said Edward Curtis desireing to have a Lease thereof made to him for the Term of 99 years if the Said Noah Curtis Shall So long Live & continue a member of the Said Society It is Ordered that a Lease be made to the Said Edward Curtis of the Said Chamber with the appurtenances for the Term of 99 years If the Said Noah Curtis Shall So long Live & continue a member of the Said Society with the usual Covenants & provisoes and according to the usual form & method of makeing & granting Leases by this Society

Clements Inn in the ⎱ At a Pencion there held on Friday the twenty Sixth
County of Middlesex ⎰ day of June Anno Domini one Thousand Seven hundred twenty four present Mr Dovey Pr. Mr Blackwell Mr Fowler Mr Halsted Mr Harris Mr Carter Mr Noyes Mr Eldridge

Mr Pennys release of £37. 10s. for Int. of £100 lent by Mr Denshire & assigned to him—Whereas the Society of Clements Inn was the Eighteenth day of this Instant June 1724 Indebted unto Mr George Stevens in Trust for Mr George Denshire in the Summ of one hundred pounds principle and thirty Seven pounds ten Shillings Interest on Mortgage made by the Trustees of the Said Society And Whereas the Said George Stevens and George Denshire in Consideracion only of one hundred pounds have assigned their right title & Interest in the Said one hundred thirty Seven pounds & ten Shillings to Mr John Penny Now the Said John Penny Doth hereby freely release and forgive the Said Society and their Trustees the Said thirty Seven pounds & ten Shillings Interest already due And Doth declare it is his Intencion not to make any advantage of the said Assignment but only to Secure the Said one hundred pounds paid by him and the Interest thereof from the Said Eighteenth day of June

John Penny

Mr Edw. Twine & Mr Tho. Yates to be Sued—Mr Edwd Twine & Mr Thomas Yates being in arrear to this Society for pencions & absent Commons and haveing neglected to pay the Same after Several requests It is ordered that their Bonds be put in Suit respectively Unless they pay their Said arrears in a weeks time after Notice of this order.

Mr Curtis for absent Commons—Mr Edwd Curtis being in arrear ten Shillings for absent Commons of Michaelmas & Hillary Terms last and Not haveing been in Town either of those Terms desires an Abatement for the Same It is ordered that he be abated 5s. for those Terms & that on payment of 5s. the Same be in full discharge of the Said Commons

Mr Vaux D.º—Mr Wm Vaux being in arrear 12s. for pensions & 40s. for absent Commons Ending this present Trinity Term [desires abatement (not in town 2 of the terms charged): abated 5s.: to pay 35s. in full discharge of the commons]

Mr John Blackwell D.º—Mr John Blackwell being in arrear 36s. for pencions & £4. 15s. for absent Commons Ending Easter Term last [desires abatement (not in town 17 of the terms charged): abated £2. 2s. 6d. for those terms: to pay £2. 12s. 6d. in full discharge of the commons]

Mr M. Innys D.º—Mr Martin Innys being in arrear 8s. for pencions and 30s. for absent Commons Ending Trinity Term last [desires abatement (not in town four of the terms charged): abated 10s. for those terms: to pay 20s. in full discharge of the commons]

Clements Inn in the } At a pencion there held on Wednesday the twenty
County of Middlesex } Second day of July Anno Domini 1724 present
Mr Dovey principal Mr Blackwell Mr Gibbons Mr Knight Mr Penny Mr Halsted

Mr Blackwells release of Interest—Whereas on the ballance of the account of Mr Joshua Blackwell late Principall of this Society audited & Settled the 28th day of February 1717 and allowed the Seventh of March then next there was due to the Said Mr Blackwell from the Said Society the Summ of one hundred forty four pounds Eighteen Shillings & one penny And Whereas on the Second day of October 1718 the Said Mr Blackwell did advance and Lend to the Said Society the Summ of Sixty three pounds three Shillings & four pence and also on the twenty Second of November then next the further Summ of Fifty pounds which were laid out towards carrying on the new Building at the upper End of the first Court & in the necessary repairs of the Said Inn And Whereas by order of pencion made the Twenty Eighth day of November 1718 It was Ordered that the Said Mr Blackwell Should be paid Interest after the rate of five pounds per cent per annum for the Said £144. 18*s*. 1*d*. from the Said

Seventh day of March and the like Interest for the Said Severall Summs of £63. 3s. 4d. and £50 from the days they were respectively advanced & Lent as aforesaid And also that he Should be paid the like Interest for all Such further Summs of money as he Should advance for the use of the Said Society from the times of Lending thereof untill the Same Should be repaid And Whereas there was due to the Said Mr Blackwell from this Society on the ballance of his Account Ending Michaelmas Term 1718 the Summ of Sixty Eight pounds Eleven Shillings & three half pence and also on the ballance of his account Ending Michaelmas Term 1719 the Summ of one hundred forty Six pounds four Shillings & three pence and likewise on the ballance of his account Ending Michaelmas Term 1720 the Summ of three hundred forty Seven pounds Eighteen Shillings and Eight pence And also on the ballance of his account Ending Michaelmas Term 1721 the Summ of three hundred & five pounds thirteen Shillings & Eight pence and on the ballance of his Account Ending Michaelmas Term 1722 the Summ of two hundred thirty pounds three Shillings Eight pence And Whereas the Said Severall Summs of money have been paid to him the Said Mr Blackwell But he hath never received or been allowed any Interest on the Same or any part thereof Now the Said Mr Blackwell doth hereby freely forgive acquit and release the Said Society of and from all Interest of and for all every or any of the Severall Summs abovemencioned and of and from every part & parcell thereof by virtue of the Said order of pencion ordered to be paid or allowed him as aforesaid And in Testimony hereof the Said Joshua Blackwell hath hereunto Subscribed his name

Josh. Blackwell

Clements Inn in the } At a Pencion there held on Wednesday the Second
County of Middlesex } day of December 1724 present Mr Dovey Principall
Mr Fowler Mr Gibbons Mr Knight Mr Penny
Mr Halsted Mr Hooper Mr Noyes Mr Eldridge

Mr Halsted for a Lease of the Chambers N.º 8 late Mr Pelhams—Mr Edw.ᵈ Halsted one of the Antients of this Society desireing to purchase a Lease for his Life of the Chambers in the brick Building in the Corner in the now first Court of this Inn up one pair of Stairs in the Stair Case now marked with the figure or Number (8) formerly in the possession of Thomas Clerke gent deceased and late in the tenure of Humphrey Pelham gent also deceased with the appurtenances It is ordered that on payment of Sixty five pounds to the principall for the use of this Society A Lease be accordingly made and granted to him of the Said Chamber with the appurtenances for Ninety & Nine years if he Shall So long Live with the usual Covenants & agreements and according to the usual form & method of makeing & granting Leases by this Society

Mr Goodman for a Lease of the Chamber N? 24 late Mr Evans's— Mr Everard Goodman one of the Antients of this Society desireing to purchase a Lease for his life of the Severall Chambers & Garretts in the Building called Kelletts Building in the Garden Court in the Stair Case marked with the figures or Number (24) up two three & four pair of Stairs on the left hand in the Said Stair Case lately belonging to Mr Bernard Evans deceased It is Ordered that on payment of one hundred Sixty two pounds & ten Shillings to the Principall for the use of this Society A Lease be made & granted of the Said Severall Chambers & Garretts with the appurtenances to the Said Mr Goodman for Ninety Nine years If he Shall so long Live with the usual Covenants & provisoes and according to the usual form & method of makeing & granting Leases by this Society

*And for a Lease of the Chambers N? 24 late Mr W. Cocks—*The Said Mr Goodman desireing to purchase a Lease for his life of the Double Chamber up two pair of Stairs in the Second Stair Case marked with the figures or Number (24) in the Building called Kelletts Building at the upper End of the Garden in this Inn on the Side of the Stair Case next adjoyning to New Inn with the Appurtenances formerly in tenure of Richard Mence gent & late in the possession of Wm Cock Esq^e deceased It is Ordered that on payment of one hundred and four pounds to the Principall for the use of this Society A Lease be made & granted of the Said Chamber with the appurtenances to the Said Mr Goodman for Ninety & Nine years If he Shall So long Live with the usual Covenants & provisoes And according to the usual form & method of makeing & granting Leases by this Society.

Mr Goodman to be paid £50 & Interest & also £40 for 8 years Interest of £100 by him lent.—It is ordered that a Summ of fifty pounds advanced & lent by the Said Mr Goodman in pursuance of an agreement & order of pencion made the 18th day of March 1718 to the Society together with all Interest Due for the Same to this Day be paid & allowed to the Said Mr Goodman by the Principall out of his purchase money above mencioned And it is also Ordered that the Principall Do pay or allow to the Said Mr Goodman out of the Said purchase money the Summ of Forty pounds which will be due to him on the 18th day of this Instant December for Eight years Interest of one hundred pounds advanced & Lent to this Society by the Said Mr Goodman in pursuance of the agreement & order of pencion made the Sixth day of December 1714.

*Mr Evans's Executors to be paid £100 & Interest—*Whereas Mr Matthew Evans deceased did in his life time in pursuance of an agreement or order of pencion made the Sixth of December 1714 advance & lend to this Society one hundred pounds It is ordered that the Principall Do pay to the Executors or Administrators of the Said Mr Evans the said Summ of £100 and all Interest due for the Same or to be due on the 18th Instant.

Mr Greggs Executors to be paid all Interest of £100 to 18 Dec. *1724*—Whereas Mr Francis Gregg gent late one of the Antients of this House deceased did in his life time in pursuance of the Said order of pencion made the 6th of December 1714 lend to this Society one hundred pounds It is ordered that the Principall Do pay to the Executors or Administrators of the Said Mr Gregg all Such Interest for the Same as now is or will be due on the Eighteenth day of this Instant December

Interest of £1200 for 2 years ending 18 Dec. *1718 to be paid.*—It is ordered that the Principall do pay to the Severall Gentlemen to whom Interest is due who have advanced & Lent the twelve hundred pounds on Security of this House two years Interest which was due to them for their respective Shares and parts thereof on the Eighteenth day December 1718 Such persons as have already received Satisfaccion thereof excepted.

Mr Gregory for absent Commons—Mr Hen: Gregory being in arrear 12s. for pencions & 40s. for absent Commons Ending Michaelmas Term last [desires abatement (not in town): abated: to pay 30s. in full discharge of the Commons]

Mr Madgwicks Bond d^d *up*—Mr Tho Madgewicke produceing a Certificate of his being Entred a Member of the Society of Bernards Inne & Desireing his Bond given to this Society may be delivered up to him It is ordered that on payment of what is due from him his Said Bond be delivered up accordingly

Clements Inn in the ⎱ At a Pencion there held on Wednesday the Seven-
County of Middlesex ⎰ teenth day of February Anno Domini 1724 Present Mr Dovey Principall Mr Fowler Mr Gibbons Mr Knight Mr Penny Mr Halsted Mr Hooper Mr Noyes Mr Eldridge

Mr Brewster for absent Commons—Mr Christopher Brewer[1] being in arrear forty eight Shillings for pencions and Eight pounds for absent Commons Ending the last Hillary Term [desires abatement (not in town 16 of the terms charged): abated 40s. for those terms: to pay £6 in full discharge of the commons]

Mr Hooper for the Chambers late Mr Childs—Mr Hooper one of the Antients of this Society desireing to purchase the Chambers late Mr Childs up one pair of Stairs N°. 19. And proposeing to quit & deliver up the possession of the ground rooms under the Same Chambers which he now holds to the Said Society It is Ordered that the Said Mr Hooper delivering up the possession of the Said Ground rooms & paying the arrears of rent due for the Same to the Principall for the use of this Society Sometime

---

[1] Another clerical error.

before Lady Day next He Shall and May hold & Enjoy the Said Chambers up one pair of Stairs as Tenant to this Society for Such time and Term as he Shall nominate from Lady Day aforesaid at and under & paying for the Same the yearly rent of Six pounds and Ten Shillings quarterly But in Case the Said Mr Hooper shall not pay the Said arrears and deliver up possession of the Said ground Rooms before Lady Day next as aforesaid The Society then will dispose of the Said Chambers up one pair of Stairs as they Shall think fitt.

Mr Hinder for the Cellar—Mr Thomas Hinder desireing to take a new Lease of the Cellar belonging to this Society at the Back Gate now in his possession It is ordered that a New Lease be made to him for Fourteen Yeares from Lady Day under the yearly rent of twenty pounds and the like Covenants provisoes & agreements as in his former Lease.

Mr Halsted for a Lease of the Garretts N.º 9—Mr Edward Halsted one of the Antients of this Society desireing to purchase a Lease for his Life in the Garretts over Mr Dottins Chambers in the Stair Case marked with the figure or Number 9 now in the Said Mr Dottins occupacion and over the arch near the Hall in Clements Inn It is ordered that on payment of Thirty nine pounds to the Principall for the use of this Society A Lease be accordingly made & granted to him of the Said Garretts with the appurtenances for Ninety & nine years If he Shall So long live with the usual Covenants & agreements and according to the usual form and method of makeing and granting Leases by this Society.

Clements Inne in the ⎱ At a pencion there held on Friday the Twenty
County of Middlesex ⎰ Sixth day of February Anno Domini 1724 present
　　　　　　　　　　　Mr Dovey Principall Mr Fowler Mr Gibbons
　　　　　　　　　　　Mr Penny Mr Halsted Mr Carter

Auditors of the Principalls Accounts from Hillary Terme 1723 to Michaelmas 1724—It is ordered that Mr Gibbons and Mr Edward Halsted two of the Antients of this Society and Mr Henry Jones and Mr Charles Baldwyn two of the Companyons of the Said Society Shall and doe examine and audit the accounts of Mr John Dovey principall of this Society for one whole year beginning in Hillary Term one Thousand Seven hundred twenty three untill Hillary Term then next following And that the Said Mr Gibbons Mr Halsted Mr Jones and Mr Baldwyn or any three of them Shall and Doe make their Certificate and report thereof assoon as the Same can or may conveniently be done

Mr Brackenbury for absent Commons—Mr Brackenbury being in arrear 18s. for pencions & £3 for absent Commons & desireing an abatement of the Said Commons for 11 terms wherein he was not in Town It is ordered that he be abated 27s. 6d. for those Terms.

Clements Inn in the ⎱ At a pencion there held on Wednesday the twelfth
County of Middlesex ⎰ day of May Anno Domini 1725 present Mr Dovey principall Mr Fowler Mr Gibbons Mr Halsted Mr Noyes Mr Eldridge & Mr Curtis.

Principalls audited accounts Confirmed—Whereas Mr John Gibbons & Mr Edward Halsted two of the Antients of this Society And Mr Henry Jones & Mr Charles Baldwyn two of the Companyons of the Same Society by order of pencion made the twenty Sixth day of February last were appointed Auditors of the accounts of Mr John Dovey now principall of this Society And have accordingly audited Stated and examined the Said principalls accounts of receipts & Disbursements for one whole year beginning in Hillary Term Anno Domini 1723 Untill and Ending Hillary Terme now last past And have found the Summ Totall of the Said principalls Receipts for that year to be Six hundred twenty four pounds thirteen Shillings and one penny And the Summ Totall of his Disbursements to be Six hundred ninety five pounds Six Shillings and nine pence So that there remains due on that account from the Said Society to the Said principall the Summ of Seventy pounds thirteen Shillings and Eight pence As appears by their Certificate or Report thereof Dated the Seventh day of this Instant May It is therefore Ordered that the Said accounts So examined Stated audited & Certified as aforesaid be allowed and approved off And the Same are hereby accordingly allowed and approved of to be just and true And the Said John Dovey is hereby Discharged from the Said Summ of Six hundred twenty four pounds thirteen Shillings and one penny So received as aforesaid And it is also ordered that he be paid the Said Ballance of Seventy pounds Thirteen Shillings and eight pence out of Such money as Shall be received for the use of this Society

Wm Fowler
John Gibbons
Edwd Halsted
W. Noyes
Ambrose Eldridge
Edw: Curtis

Mr Henry Dottin for absent Commons—Mr Dottin being in arrear 30s. for pencions And for absent Commons Ending in Easter Term last £5. 15s. [desires abatement (not in town 2 terms): abated 5s.: to pay £5. 10s. in full discharge of the commons]

Clements Inne in the ⎱ At a pencion there held on Friday the 25th day of
County of Middlesex ⎰ June Anno Domini 1725 present Mr Dovey pr.
Mr Fowler Mr Gibbons Mr Denshire Mr Halsted
Mr Noyes

Mr Adams Bond delivered up—Mr Wm Adams being a housekeeper and
no practizer desireing to have his Bond given to this Society to be Delivered
up to him It is ordered that the said Bond be delivered up to him on
payment of his arrears to be cancelled

Mr Taubman the like—Mr Thomas Taubman being a Housekeeper
within the Liberty of Westminster Desires likewise to have his Bond
delivered up It is accordingly ordered that on payment of what is due from
him the Said Bond be delivered up to him.

Mr Millers Goods to be distrained—Mr Humphrey Miller being Dead
& five pounds ten Shillings for half a years rent of his Chamber Ending
at Midsomer last being due to the Society It is ordered that a Distress on
his Goods & Chattells in the Said Chambers be made forthwith by
Mr Barras for Secureing the Said Rent

Mr Pollen for a Lease of the Chambers late Mr Wottons—Mr Edward
Pollen one of the Companyons of this Society haveing agreed with Mr W.^m
Wotton one other of the Companyons of the Said Society for the purchase
of his Chambers up two pair of Stairs in the Stair Case marked with the
figures or Number (23) in the Building called Kelletts Building in Clements
Inn Garden which the Said Mr Wm Wotton held to him & his assignes by
a Lease or Articles from this Society for a Term of Ninety Nine years
determinable on the Death of the Said Mr Wm Wotton And the Said
Wm Wotton haveing at the request of the Said Edwd Pollen Surrendred
up his Said Lease or Articles to the principall of this Society to the Intent
a New Lease may be granted of the Said Chamber to the Said Edwd Pollen
And the Said Edwd Pollen desireing to be admitted to the Same It is
ordered that on payment of Fourteen pounds to the principall for the use
of this Society A New Lease be made & granted of the Said Chamber to
the Said Edwd Pollen for Ninety nine years if he Shall So long Live &
continue a member of this Society with the usual Covenants & provisoes
& according to the usual Method & form of makeing & granting Leases
by this Society.

Edwd Pollen

Mr Wm Turner for absent Commons—Mr Turner being in arrear 8s.
for pencions & for absent Commons Ending Easter Term last 30s.
[desires abatement (not in town any of the 6 terms charged): abated 15s.
for those terms: to pay 15s. in full discharge of the commons]

Mr Richard Wyche for absent Commons—Mr Wyche being in arrear fifteen Shillings for absent Commons Ending in Easter Term last & ten Shillings for pencions [desires abatement (not in town any of the 3 terms charged): abated 7s. 6d. for those terms: to pay 7s. 6d. in full discharge of the commons]

Clements Inn in the } At a pencion there held on Wednesday the Tenth
County of Middlesex } day of November Anno Domini 1725 present Mr Dovey principall Mr Fowler Mr Gibbons Mr Penny Mr Halsted Mr Eldridge.

Mr Wm Wottons Bond d^d up—Mr Wotton haveing taken a house within the Liberty of Westminster desires to have his Bond given on his admission to be a member of this Society delivered up It is ordered that on payment of what is due from him the Same be delivered up to be Cancelled

Mr Sheldon for a Lease of the Chamber late Mr Paceys & the Garrett over the Same—Mr Hugh Sheldon desireing to purchase a Lease for his Life of the Chamber in the Brick Building in the North West Corner of the First Court of this House up two pair of Stairs on the Left hand in the Stair Case marked with the figure or Number (8) lately leased to Mr Wm Pacey deceased & formerly in the tenure of Joshua Blackwell gent and also the Garrett over the Same late in the possession of Mr Tho Shuckforth & now in the occupacion of Mr Anth Cocke as Tenant to this Society It is ordered that on payment of Fifty two pounds to the principall for the use of this Society A Lease be accordingly made him of the Said Chamber & Garrett with the appurtenances for Ninety & nine years If he Shall So long Life with the usual Covenants & agreements & according to the usual Form & method of makeing & granting Leases by this Society The Said Mr Sheldon first admitting himselfe a Member of this Society in the usual Manner.

Clements Inn in the } At a pencion there held on Friday the Third day of
County of Middlesex } December Anno Domini 1725 present Mr Dovey Principall Mr Fowler Mr Gibbons Mr Knight Mr Penny Mr Halsted Mr Noyes & Mr Eldridge

Eleccion of a new Principall Mr Dovey rechose—Whereas on Friday the twenty Sixth day of November in Michaelmas Term now last past This Society proceeded to the Choice of a new principall for three years next comeing according to the order & usage of this Society Three of the Antients being nominated for Candidates by the principall & Antients then in Commons one whereof vizt Mr John Dovey the present principall was unanimously Elected by the Antients & Companyons then in Commons according to the Order & usage of the Said House It is ordered That the Said Eleccion & proceedings therein be Entred in this Booke and is as follows

Michaelmas Term 1725

Clements Inn
Friday
26 November 1725

Persons nominated by the Antients for the Choice of a new principall for three years next ensueing

Principall	Mr Fowler	Mr Penny
Ro. Aldey		
Saml Heckford		
Robt Drury		
Charles Bowles		
John Harris N		
John Atwood		
John Harris B		
Tho. Fowke		
John Green		
Bri. Smith		
Jos. Goodacre		
Edw. Benet		
Ch. Lake		
John Dewes	We Consent to approve	
A. Cocke	and Confirme this Choice	
John Ja Dobson	Wm Fowler	
Henry Jones	John Penny	
T. Burrell	Edwd Halstead	
John Hogg	Wm Noyes	
Jos. Dudbridge	Ambrose Eldridge	
Chas. Baldwyn		
Tho. Tufton		
Wm Noyes		

Mr Cromwells Bond up—Mr Richd Cromwell being a housekeeper in London & desireing that his Bond given on his Admission to be a member of this Society may be delivered up to him It is ordered that on payment of what is due from him to this Society the Said Bond be delivered up to be Cancelled

Clements Inn in the
County of Middlesex }
At a pencion there held on Wednesday the twenty third day of February Anno Domini 1725 present Mr Dovey principall Mr Fowler Mr Gibbons Mr Halsted Mr Noyes Mr Eldridge

Auditors of the principalls Accounts from Hill. 1724 to Hill. 1725—It is ordered that Mr John Gibbons and Mr Edward Halsted two of the Antients of this Society and Mr Samuel Heckford and Mr Edward Johnson two of the Companyons of the Said Society Shall & Doe examine and audit the accounts of Mr John Dovey Principall of this Society for one whole year beginning in Hillary Term 1724 Untill Hillary Term 1725 And that the Said Mr Gibbons Mr Halsted Mr Heckford & Mr Johnson or any three of them Shall & do make their Certificate & Report thereof as soon as conveniently may be done

Clements Inne in the County of Middlesex } At a pencion there held on Friday the Twenty Seventh day of May Anno Domini 1726 present Mr Dovey Principall Mr Fowler Mr Gibbons Mr Penny Mr Halsted [1]

Clements Inn in the County of Middleszx } At a pencion there held on Monday the fourth day of July Anno Domini 1726 present Mr Dovey Principall Mr Fowler Mr Gibbons Mr Halsted Mr Noyes Mr Curtis Mr Denshire Mr Eldridge

Mr Fullers £100 & Int paid to be allowed to the Principall—Whereas Mr George Fuller did in his lifetime advance & Lend for the use of this Society the Summ of one hundred pounds in the name of Shadrack Blundell Esq. And whereas there was due for Interest thirty Seven pounds three Shillings & ten pence for the Same on the Eleventh day of June last past and Mrs Mary Fuller Executrix of the last will of the Said George Fuller haveing been very desireous & pressing to be paid the said money due as aforesaid and Mr John Dovey the present principal having paid the Same to her on the account of this Society being in the whole the Summ of one hundred thirty Seven pounds three Shillings & ten pence for principle & Interest It is now Ordered that the Same be allowed unto the Said Principall in his accounts out of the money by him received or to be received for the use of this Society.

Mr Keeling R for absent Commons—Mr Rich. Keeling being in arrear 20s. for pencions & £3. 5s. for absent Commons Ending Easter Term last [desires abatement (not in town 9 of the Terms charged): abated £1. 2s. 6d. for those terms: to pay £2. 2s. 6d. in full discharge of the commons]

Mr Stubbs D.—Mr Walter Stubbs being in arrear 22s. for pencions and £3 10s. for absent Commons Ending in Easter Term last [desires abatement not in town 9 of the terms charged): abated £1. 2s. 6d.: to lay £2. 7s. 6d.: in full discharge of the commons]

---

[1] Half a page is left blank beneath this entry, no business being recorded.

Mr Carrow D?—Mr Robert Carrow being in arrear £1. 14s. for pencions and £5. 15s. for absent Commons Ending in Trinity Term last [desires abatement (not in town 21 of the Terms charged): abated £2. 12s. 6d. for those terms: to pay £3. 2s. 6d. in full discharge of the commons]

Mr Hodgkis D?—Mr John Hodgkis being at the time of his Indebted to this Society 30s. for absent Commons his widow now desires an Abatement of the Said Commons for 5 Terms in regard he was not in Town by reason of his Illness It is ordered that he be abated 12s. 6d. and on payment of 17s. 6d. the Same be in full discharge of the Said Commons and that his Bond be delivered up to the Said Mrs Hodgkis his widow & Administratrix

Mr Taubman excused for his Admittance fee—Mr Tho Taubman haveing been very lately admitted and Immediately afterwards had his Said Bond delivered up in regard he was a housekeeper in Westminster and being now willing to become a Member of this Society But desires his Admittance may be remitted to him It is Ordered accordingly

Mr Blackwell Jun. *for absent Commons*—Mr John Blackwell being in arrear 12s. for pencions & 30s. for absent Commons ending Trinity Term last [desires abatement (not in town 5 terms): abated 12s. 6d.: to pay 17s. 6d. in full discharge of the commons]

Mr Turner for absent Commons—Mr W^m. Turner being in arrear 6s. for pencions and fifteen Shillings for absent Commons Ending Easter Term last [desires abatement (not in town any of the terms charged)] It is ordered that he be abated one moiety thereof & that on payment of 7s. 6d. the Same be in full of said Commons

Mr Bramston D?—Mr Stephen Bramston being in arrear £1. 2s. for pencions & £3. 5s. for absent Commons Ending in Easter Term last [desires abatement (not in town 7 terms charged): abated 17s. 6d.: to pay 17s. 6d. in full discharge of the commons]

Clements Inn in the } At a Pencion there held on Friday the Second day
County of Middlesex } of December Anno Domini 1726 present Mr Dovey
                principall Mr Fowler Mr Gibbons Mr Penny Mr
                Halsted Mr Hooper Mr Noyes Mr Eldridge

Persons refuseing to pay arrears to be Sued.—Ordered that Mr Barras Doe Call on Mr Lake Mr Sandys Mr Tufton & Mr Burton the Taylor for the arrears due from them respectively to this Society And that on refuseing or neglecting to pay the Same on or before the Tenth day of January next Such person neglecting to be Sued for the Said arrears

The Following pictures in Frames Mr Halsted of Clements Inn made a present to that Society and are now Sett upp in the pencion Roome [1] (viz.)

1. The Lr.d C Justice Cooke a ½ length in a Gilt Frame
2. The Lr.d C Justice Hales a ½ length in a Gilt Frame
3. The Lr.d C Justice Crew a ½ length in a Gilt Frame
4. The Lr.d C Justice Scroggs a ½ length in a Gilt Frame
5. The Lr.d C Justice Richardson in a 3 quarter Frame
6. The Lr.d Coventry in a Frame
7. Judge Powell in an ovell Frame

Edw.d Halsted

Clements Inn in the
County of Middlesex   At a pencion there held on Friday the fourth day of May Anno Domini 1727 present Mr Dovey principal Mr Fowler Mr Gibbons Mr Knight Mr Halsted Mr Hooper Mr Noyes

Auditors of principalls accounts from Hill. 1725 to Hill. 1726—It is ordered that Mr John Penny & Mr William Fowler two of the Antients of this Society and Mr Brightwell Smith & Mr Thomas Burrell two of the Companyons of the Said Society Shall & do examine & audit the Accounts of Mr John Dovey of this Society for one whole year beginning in Hillary Term 1725 Untill Hillary Term 1726 And that the Said Mr Penny Mr Halsted Mr Smith & Mr Burrell or any three of them Shall & do make their Certificate & Report thereof assoon as conveniently may be done

Mr Pigotts Bond up.—Mr Ralph Pigot being a House Keeper in Towne desires to have his Bond given to this Society on his Admittance Delivered up. It is ordered that on payment of all arrears from him the Said Bond be Delivered up to be Cancelled

---

[1] Herbert, in 1804, stated that the Clement's Inn hall contained "a good portrait of Sir Matthew Hale and five other pictures of no importance": *Inns of Court*, p. 278. Earlier, Ireland, after noting that Blackwell's portrait (see p. 104 above) "hangs at the upper end of the hall and is a respectable painted picture", continues with some seeming inaccuracy: "There are five other portraits in this room, viz. Sir Matthew Hale and Sir Edward Coke, painted in 1613, both by the same hand, and, if originals, are but indifferently executed: a three-quarter portrait painted in 1631 of Sir Thomas Rich [*sic*] and I should think original: a Lord Coventry dated 1525 and a Lord Keeper Coventry which hangs near it are, however, well painted and have the appearance of being genuine": *Picturesque Views*, pp. 69, 70.

The Inner Temple purchased four of these pictures at a sale in 1894. Of these the Coke and Coventry were destroyed by enemy action in 1940–1: the Hale, also then badly damaged, was restored and presented to the Royal Courts of Justice, where it hangs near the Bar Library: the portrait of Sir Randolph Crewe is still in the Inner Temple. One of Sir Thomas Richardson, now in Lincoln's Inn, is possibly the one given by Halsted to Clement's Inn.

Mr Jas Child D°.—Mr James Child haveing been a Considerable time past troubled with the Gout in Such manner as hath rendered him Incapable of Doeing Business It is desired on his Behalfe that the Bond given by him on his Admittance may be delivered up which is hereby ordered Shall be done accordingly on payment of his arrears

Mr Edw. Austen for the Chambers late Mr Drury—Mr Robt Drury one of the Companyons of this Society haveing agreed with Mr Edwd Austen one other Companyon of the Said Society for the purchase of his Chamber up two pair of Stairs in the Stair Case marked N°. (23) which the Said Mr Drury held by Articles for 99 years determinable on his Death And he having Surrendred the Said Articles & the Term thereby granted And the Said Edwd Austen desireing to be admitted to the Same & to the Cellar at the Bottom of the Said Stairs It is ordered that on payment of £15 to the Principall for the use of the Society A new Lease be granted thereof to the Said Edward Austen for ninety & nine years Determinable on his Death according to the usual method & forme of granting Leases by this Society.

Mr Chas Baldwyn for the Chambers late Mr Hoopers—Mr Edwd Giles Hooper one of the Antients of this Society haveing agreed with Mr Charles Baldwyn one of the Companyons of the Said Society for the purchase of his Chambers being ground rooms & cellar in the Stair Case marked Number 20 which the Said Mr Hooper held by Articles for 99 years Determinable on his Death with a power of nominating another member to be admitted thereunto for the like Terme And he haveing Surrenderd the Said Articles & Interest thereby granted And the Said Charles Baldwyn desireing to be admitted to the Same It is ordered that on payment of £18 to the Principall for the use of this Society A new Lease be granted thereof to the Said Charles Baldwyn for Ninety & nine Determinable on his Death with a power to nominate another member to be admitted therunto afterwards for another like Terme of 99 years Determinable in manner aforesaid according to the Custome & Method of granting Leases by this Society.

Clements Inn in the } At a Pencion there held on Wednesday the 17th
County of Middlesex } day of May Anno Domini 1727 present Mr Dovey
Principall Mr Fowler Mr Penny Mr Halsted
Mr Noyes Mr Eldridge

Principalls Accounts audited Confirmed—Whereas Mr John Gibbons and Mr Edward Halsted two of the Antients of this Society and Mr Saml Heckford & Mr Edwd Johnson two of the Companyons of the Same Society by order of pencion made the Twenty Third day of February 1725 were appointed Auditors of the accounts of Mr John Dovey now principall of this Society And haveing accordingly audited Stated and examined the Said Mr Doveys Accounts of Receipts and Disbursements for one whole year beginning in Hillary Term 1724 untill the beginning of Hillary Terme 1725 And have found the Summ Totall of the Said Principalls Receipts for that year to be £354 11s. 6d. and the Summ Totall of his Disbursements to be £208. 12s. 4d. So that there remains due on that account from the Said principall to this Society one hundred Forty five pounds Nineteen Shillings & two pence as appears by their Certificate or report thereof Dated the 24th day of May 1726 It is therefore Ordered that the Said accounts So audited Stated examined and Certified as aforesaid be allowed & approved off and the Same are hereby accordingly allowed and approved of to be just and true And the Said John Dovey is hereby Discharged of and from the Said Summ of £208. 12s. 4d. So by him Disbursed as aforesaid.

Wm Fowler
John Penny
Edwd Halsted
W. Noyes
Ambrose Eldridge

Mr Hum: Pelhams Bond d.^d up—Mr Humphry Pelham late a member of this Society being dead at the request of Mr John Pelham his Father It is ordered that his Bond given at his Admission be delivered up on payment of his arrears

Mr Gregory for Absent Commons—Mr Henry Gregory being in arrear 14s. for pencions and 45s. for absent Commons ending in Hillary Term last [desires abatement (not in town 4 of the terms charged): abated 10s.: to pay £1. 15s. in full discharge of the commons]

Mr Sandys & others to be Sued—Mr John Sandys Mr Wm Jackson Mr Christopher Lake Mr Leigh Langley & Mr Thomas Tufton being Severally in arrear to this Society It is ordered that unles they respectively pay what Shall be Due from them Severally to this Society unto the Principall or Mr Barras for the use of this Society on or before Monday the 29th Instant their respective Bonds be put in Suit & vigorously prosecuted by Mr Barras for the Recovery of the moneys due & oweing respectively from the Severall persons abovenamed

Mr Edm.^d Webb for the Chambers late Mr Bewleys—Mr Richd Bewley one of the Companyons of this Society haveing agreed with Mr Edm.^d Webb one of the Companyons of this Society for the purchase of his Chambers being up two pair of Stairs in the Stair Case marked with the figure or number 2 on the left hand formerly in the tenure of Nathl

Trayton Gent which the Said Mr Bewley held by Lease or Articles for 99 years determinable with his Life with a power of nominating another member to be admitted thereunto for the like Terme And he haveing Surrendred the Said Articles & Interest thereby granted And the Said Edmund Webb desireing to be admitted to the Same It is ordered that on payment of Seven pounds to the Principall for the use of this Society A New Lease be granted thereof to the Said Edm.d Webb for 99 years determinable on his death with a power to nominate another member to be admitted thereunto for another like Term of 99 years afterwards determinable in manner aforesaid According to the Custome & method of Granting Leases used by this Society

Clements Inn in the ⎱ At a Pencion there held on Friday the 23d day of
County of Middlesex ⎰ June Anno Domini 1727 present Mr Dovey
principall Mr Fowler Mr Knight Mr Denshire Mr Noyes Mr Eldridge

Principalls Audited Accounts Confirmed—WHEREAS Mr Wm Fowler & Mr John Penny two of the Antients of this Society & Mr Brightwell Smith and Mr Thos: Burrell two of the Companyons of the Said Society by vertue of an order of pencion made the Fourth day of May last past were appointed Auditors of the Accounts of Mr John Dovey now Principall of this Society And haveing accordingly audited Stated and examined the Said Mr Doveys accounts of Receipts and Disbursements for one whole year beginning in Hillary Terme 1725 and ending the beginning of Hillary Term 1726 And have found the Summ Totall of the Said Principalls Receipts for that year to be (including the Summ of £145. 19s. 2d. being the ballance of the Last years account in the hands of the Said Principall) to be £295. 13s. 11d. and the Totall of his Disbursements to be £287. 15s. 11d. So that there remains due on that account to the Society from the Said Principall Seven pounds and Eighteen Shillings as appears by their report or Certificate Thereof Dated the 17th day of May last IT IS THEREFORE ORDERED that the Said Accounts So Stated audited examined and Certified as aforesaid be allowed and approved and the Same are hereby allowed and approved off to be just and true and the Said Mr John Dovey is hereby discharged of and from the Said Sum of £287. 15s. 11d. So by him Disbursed as aforesaid.

John Knight
Geo. Denshire
John Gibbons
W. Noyes
Ambrose Eldridge

G

Mr Wyche for absent Commons—Mr Richd Wyche being in arreare 12s. for pencions and £1. 15s. for absent Commons ending Easter Term last [desires abatement (not in town 5 of the terms charged): abated 12s. 6d.: to pay £1. 2s. 6d. in full discharge of the commons]

Mr Jackson for absent Commons—Mr Francis Jackson being in arrear 18s. for pencion & £2. 5s. 0d. for Absent Commons ending Easter Term last [desires abatement (not in town in Easter term last): abated 2s. 6d.: to pay £2. 2s. 6d. in full discharge of the commons]

Mr John Vaux for the Chambers late Mr Wm Vaux's—Mr Wm Vaux one of the Companyons of this Society haveing agreed with Mr John Vaux for the purchase of his Chambers being up one pair of Stairs in the Building called Wrights Building in the first Court formerly in possession of Jonas Geary gent which the said Mr Wm Vaux held by Articles for 99 years determinable with his Life And he haveing Surrendred the Said Articles & the Interest thereby granted And the Said John Vaux desireing to be admitted to the Same It is ordered that on payment of four pounds he being admitted a member of the Said Society to the Principall for the use of this Society A New Lease be granted thereof to the said John Vaux for 99 years determinable on his Death according to the usual Method & forme of granting Leases By this Society

Pews new lined by contribucions—The names of such of the Antients of Clements Inn who contributed to the New lining the Church pews.

Mr Dovy Pr.	1 . 1 . 0	Mr Eldridge	1 . 1 . 0
Mr Fowler	1 . 1 . 0	Mr Curtis	1 . 1 . 0
Mr Goodman	1 . 1 . 0	Mr Hardwick	1 . 1 . 0
Mr Penny	1 . 1 . 0	Mr Aldey	1 . 1 . 0
Mr Carter	1 . 1 . 0	Mr Blackwell	1 . 1 . 0
Mr Halstead	1 . 1 . 0	Mr Bennett	1 . 1 . 0
Mr Noys	1 . 1 . 0		
			13.13. 0

Collected by Mr Penny who paid	Upholsterer	6. 6.
	Joiner	1. 1.
	Hassocks	. 8. 6
	Mr Dovy as Pr. towards new painting the garden pales	5.17. 6
		13.13.

Clements Inn in the ⎱ At a pention there held on Wednesday the 29th
County of Middlesex ⎰ day of November 1727 present Mr Dovey principall
Mr Fowler Mr Penny Mr Halsted Mr Noyes Mr
Eldridge

Mr Walletts Bond up & Compos: by Adm^r.—Mr John Wallett late one
of the companyons of this Society being in arrear for pencions £2. 16s.
and for absent Commons £9. 5s. ending in Michaelmas Term 1726 and he
dying in December following in very mean Circumstances and haveing
not been in Town in any of the Terms charged to his Account and an
abatement being desired by Mr Richd Russell his Administrator in regard
of the premisses It is ordered that £4. 12s. 6d. of the Said Commons be
abated And that on payment of the Said £2. 16s. and of £4. 12s. 6d. the
Same be in full and the Said Mr Walletts Bond be delivered up to his Said
Administrator the Servants Rolls being discharged

Mr Geo: Ward Comp. for absent Commons—Mr George Ward being
in arrear 18s. for pencions and £3 for Absent Commons ending the last
Term [desires abatement (not in town 2 of the terms charged): abated 5s.:
to pay £2. 15s. in full discharge of the Commons]

Mr John Grove for the Chambers late Mr Gibbons's—WHEREAS John
Gibbons Gent late one of the Antients of this Society held by Articles
All That Double Chamber in Mr Kelletts Building in the Stair Case marked
(23) over the passage leading into Clare Market up one pair of Stairs for
99 years determinable on his death with a power to nominate another
Companyon of this Society to be admitted to the Same for the like Term
of 99 years determinable with the life of such person And the Said Mr
Gibbons haveing by his last will devised the Said Chambers & his Interest
therein to John Grove Gent who is now admitted a member of this Society
And Anne Trimnell widow Sole Executrix of the last will of the said John
Gibbons who is lately deceased haveing Surrendred the Articles or Lease
granted by the Principall & Antients to the Said Mr Gibbons of the Said
Chambers and all the Estate & interest thereby granted To the Intent the
Said John Grove Should be admitted to the Said Chambers And the Said
John Grove desireing to be admitted thereunto who being Under the age
of 21 years hath procured Edwd Austen Gent one of the Said Companions
of this Society to Enter into Articles on his behalfe IT IS ORDERED that in
performance of the Said Articles Enterd into by the Principall & Antients
with the Said Mr Gibbons & in pursuance of his Said Will A new Lease of
the Said Chambers be made & granted to the Said John Grove for 99 years
If he Shall So long Live with the usual Covenants & provisoes and according to the usual method & forme of Granting Leases by this Society.

Mr Michael Hattons Bond delivered up—Mr Michael Hatton being an
Housekeeper in Town and no practiser and Desiring to have his Bond

given to this Society on his Admittance delivered up It is Ordered that on payment of all Arrears due from him his said Bond be delivered up to be Cancelled

    Mr Ralph Pigott's Bond d.ᵈ up—[Mr Pigott the like.]

    Mr James Bridges Comp.ⁿ for absent Commons—Mr James Bridges [in arrear £1 8s. for pensions and £4 15s. for absent commons, desires abatement (not in town 16 of the terms charged): abated £2 for those terms: to pay £2. 15s. in full discharge of the commons]

    Interest paid to December 1724—It is ordered that the Principall Do pay to the severall persons hereafter named the severall Summes hereafter mencioned for Interest to them respectively due & owing from this Society to the respective Dayes & times hereafter particularly mencioned

		£	s	d
Knight	To Mrs Sarah Knight Executrix of Mr John Knight deceased thirty pounds for Six yeares Interest due on Mortgage for one hundred pounds (In the name of Wᵐ. Leach In Trust for the said John Knight) the 18th of December 1724	30	00	00
	And also to the said Sarah Knight fifteen pounds for Six Years Interest due the 21ˢᵗ Day of March 1724 for fifty pounds lent this Society by the said Jno Knight by an Order of pencion dated the Eighteenth Day of March 1718 . . .	15	00	00
Halsted	To Mr Edward Halsted Six pounds Seventeen Shillings & Six pence for the Interest of fifty pounds (lent by him to this Society by an order of pencion made the 14th February 1721) due the 25th Day of December 1724 being two yeares & 3 Quarters Comencing from Lady Day 1722 .	6	17	6
Carter	To Mr Tho.ˢ Carter Six pounds seventeen Shillings & Six pence for the Interest of fifty pounds (lent by him to this Society by an order of pencion made the 14th February 1721) for two Yeares & three Quarters Comencing from Lady Day then next & ending the 25th December 1724 . . .	6	17	6

Clements Inne in the County of Middlesex   At a Pencion there held on Friday the 16th day of February 1727 Present Mr Dovey Principall Mr Fowler Mr Denshire Mr Halsted Mr Noyes Mr Eldridge Mr Hardwick

    Mr Brightwell Smith to be Steward or Clerk of the Society in the room & place of Mr Joseph Barras deceased—Mr Brightwell Smith one of the

Companions of this Society having made his Application and desiring to be admitted into the Office or place of Steward or Clerk of this Society in the Room & place of Mr Joseph Barras deceased Itt is Ordered that the said Mr Smith be accordingly admitted into the said Office or place Butt to Continue therein only during the good Will and pleasure of the Principall & Antients and their Successors & no longer And the said Mr Smith is also to give a Bond with two other sufficient persons to be bound with him in the penalty or Summe of Two hundred pounds for the due performance of his said Office or place during such time as he shall be continued therein

Mr Peter Monger's Bond D^d *up*—Mr Peter Monger one of the Companions of this Society being in Arrear for pencions and Absent Commons Two pounds fourteen Shillings and being in very mean Circumstances and Mr Nathaniel Trayton who is his Surety having desired that the said Mr Monger's Bond given to this Society may be delivered up Itt is ordered that upon payment of Two pounds fourteen Shillings by the said Mr Trayton the said Bond be delivered up to him the said Mr Trayton to be cancelled The Servants Rolls being Discharged.

Mr Blackwell Rector of St Clements Danes—Ordered that the principall of this Society Do give to the Reverend Mr Thomas Blackwell Rector of St Clements Danes nine Guineas as a free Gift from this Society nothing of Right being due to him from the said Society

Mr Jno. Blackwell Comp^d *for absent Commons*—Mr Jno. Blackwell being in Arrear ten shillings for pencions and One pound for absent Commons ending the last Michaelmas Term [desires abatement (not in town 3 of the terms charged): abated 7s. 6d. for those terms: to pay 12s. 6d. in full discharge of the commons]

Mr Posthumous Bell Comp^d *for absent Commons*—Mr Posthumous Bell being in Arrear three pounds two shillings for pencions And ten pounds & five Shillings for absent Commons ending the last Michaelmas Term and desiring an abatement of the said Commons in regard he was not in Town any one of the Termes Charged to his Account Itt is ordered that he be abated five pounds two Shillings & Six pence for those Termes which together with three pounds Six Shillings formerly paid by the said Mr Bell in part of the said Commons reduces his said Commons to one pound Sixteen Shillings & Six pence And on payment of the said £1. 16s. 6d. the Same be in full Discharge of the said Commons to the end of last Michaelmas Term And Itt is further Ordered that upon payment of the Summe of Three pounds into the hands of the principall for the Use of this Society the said Posthumous Bell's Bond be delivered up to him to be Cancelled

Clements Inn in the ⎱ Att a pencion there held on Friday the 23d Day of
County of Middlesex ⎰ February 1727 present Mr John Dovey principall
Mr Fowler Mr Penny Mr Denshire Mr Halsted
Mr Eldridge Mr Blackwell Mr Hardwick Mr Aldey
& Mr Bennett,

Mr Nath! Trayton for the Chambers late Mr Knight's—Whereas John
Knight Gent late one of the Antients of this Society Held by Articles All
that Chamber with the Appurtenances up one pair of Stairs in the Brick
Building adjoyning to the Building called Dobbs' Building in the third
Court in the Stair Case marked with the Figures or Number (20) formerly
in the Occupation of Jno. Tichborne Gent & then late in the possession of
Edward Walker Gent And also the Cellar in his the said Edward Walker's
possession for 99 years determinable upon his Death with a power to
nominate another Companion of this Society to be admitted to the same
for the like Term of 99 years determinable with the Life of such person
And the said Mr Knight having made his last Will and Testament in
Writing and appointed Sarah Knight his Widdow sole Executrix of his
said Will who hath Surrendred the Articles or Lease granted by the
Principall & Antients to the said Mr John Knight of the said Chamber
and all the State & Interest thereby granted To the Intent that Nathaniel
Trayton one of the Companions of the said Society should be admitted to
the said Chambers & Cellar And the said Nathaniel Trayton desiring to be
admitted thereto Itt is ordered that in performance of the said Articles
entred into by the Principall & Antients with the said Mr John Knight
A new Lease of the said Chambers & Cellar be made and granted to the
said Nathaniel Trayton for ninety nine years If the said Sarah Knight
shall so long live with the usuall Covenants & provisoes and according to
the usuall Method & form of granting Leases by this Society

Mr Jno. Blackwell for the Chambers late Mr Joshua Blackwell's—
Whereas Joshua Blackwell Gent late one of the Antients of this Society
Held by Articles All that Chamber with the Appurtenances up one pair of
Stairs over the passage or Entry into the Building adjoyning to the
Building called Dobb's Building in the third Court in the Stair Case
marked with the Figures or Number (20) then in the possession of the said
Joshua Blackwell and also the Cellar in his the said Joshua Blackwell's
possession for 99 Years determinable upon his Death with a power to
nominate another Companion of this Society to be Admitted to the same
for the like Term of 99 Yeares determinable with the Life of such Person
And the said Joshua Blackwell being lately dead And Mr John Blackwell
the only acting Executor of the last Will of the said Joshua Blackwell
having Surrendred the Articles or Lease granted by the Principall &

Antients to the said Mr Joshua Blackwell of the said Chamber and all the Estate & Interest thereby granted To the Intent that the said John Blackwell one of the Antients of this Society should be Admitted thereto And the said Jno. Blackwell Desiring to be Admitted thereto ITT IS ORDERED That in Performance of the said Articles entred into by the said Principall and Antients with the said Mr Joshua Blackwell a new Lease of the said Chambers & Cellar be made & granted to the said Mr Jno. Blackwell for 99 years If the said Jno. Blackwell shall so long live with the usuall Covenants & provisoes and according to the usuall Method & form of granting Leases by this Society.

Auditors of the principall's Accounts from Hillary Term 1726 to Hillary Term 1727—Itt is ordered that Mr Edward Halsted and Mr Roger Aldey two of the Antients of this Society & Mr John Green and Mr Joseph Goodacre two of the Companions of this Society shall & do examine & auditt the Accounts of Mr John Dovey Principall of this Society for one whole Year beginning in Hillary Term 1726 untill Hillary Term 1727 And that the said Mr Halsted Mr Aldey Mr Green & Mr Goodacre or any three of them shall & do make their Certificate & Report thereof as soon as conveniently may be done

Mr Jno Peart Companion [1] *for absent Commons*—Mr John Peart being in Arrear Two pounds eighteen shillings for pencion and eight pounds for absent Commons ending in Michaelmas Term last [desires abatement (not in town 28 of the terms charged): abated £3. 10s. for those terms: to pay £4. 10s. in full discharge of the commons]

Mr Robert Peart Comp. *for absent Commons*—Mr Robert Peart being in Arrear one pound fourteen Shillings for pencion and four pounds fifteen Shillings for absent Commons ending in Michaelmas Term last [desires abatement (not in town 17 of the terms charged): abated £2. 2s. 6d. for those terms: to pay £2. 12s. 6d. in full discharge of the commons]

Itt is ordered that the Principall Do pay to the severall persons hereafter named the severall Summes hereafter mencioned for Interest to them respectively due & owing from this Society to the respective Dayes & times hereafter particularly mencioned as followeth (Viz.)

Interest paid to December 1724

Trimnell Executrix Gibbons To Mrs Anne Trimnell Executrix of Mr John Gibbons deceased thirty pounds for Six years Interest due on Mortgage for one hundred pounds (in the name of Edward Jackson Esq. In Trust for the said Jno. Gibbons deceased) to the 18th December 1724 .   . — £ s d — 30 : 0 : 0 :

---

[1] Presumably a clerical error for "Composition".

		£	s	d
Penny To Mr John Penny twenty eight pounds fifteen shillings for five years & three Quarters Interest of one hundred pounds due the 20th December 1724 lent to the Society by order of pencion made 28th March 1718		28	15	0 :
And also to the said John Penny Six pounds Seventeen Shillings & Six pence for two Years & three quarters Interest due the 25th December 1724 lent to this Society by order of pencion made the 14th February 1721 the Interest to commence from Lady Day then next . . .		6	17	6 :

Clements Inn in the County of Middlesex Att a pencion there held on Friday the 16th Day of July 1728 present Mr Jno. Dovey principall Mr Fowler Mr Penny Mr Halsted Mr Blackwell Mr Aldey & Mr Bennett.

Mr Thos Hurst Comp.ⁿ for absent Commons—Mr Thos Hurst being in Arrear Two pounds eighteen Shillings for pencions and Eight pounds for absent Commons ending in the last Trinity Term [desires abatement (not in town 27 of the terms charged) abated: £3. 7s. 6d. for those terms: to pay £4. 12s. 6d. in full discharge of the commons]

Principall's Audited Accounts Confirmed—WHEREAS Mr Edward Halsted & Mr Roger Aldey two of the Antients of this Society and Mr Joseph Goodacre & Mr Jno. Green two of the Companions of the said Society by Vertue of an Order of pencion made the twenty third day of February last were appointed Auditors of the Accounts of Mr John Dovey now Principall of this Society And having accordingly Audited stated & Examined the said Mr Dovey's Accounts of Receipts & Disbursements for one whole Year beginning in Hillary Term 1726 and ending the beginning of Hillary Term 1727 And have found the Summe Totall of the principall's Receipts for that Year (including the Summe of Seven pounds eighteen Shillings being the Ballance of the last Year's Account in the hands of the said principall) to be £268 : 2s : 9d : and the Totall of his Disbursemens to be £77 : 6s : so that there remains due on that Account to the Society from the said Principall One hundred and ninety pounds sixteen Shillings & nine pence As appears by their Report or Certificate thereof Dated the 20th Day of March last ITT IS THEREFORE ORDERED that the said Accounts so Stated Audited Examined & Certified as aforesaid be allowed and approved And the same are hereby allowed and approved of to be just & true And the said Mr John Dovey is hereby discharged of & from the said Summe of £77 : 6s. so by him disbursed as aforesaid

Wm Fowler
John Penny
Edwd Halsted
Rog.^r Aldey

Clements Inn in the ⎱ Att a pencion there held on Friday the twenty ninth
County of Middlesex ⎰ day of November Anno Domini 1728 present Mr
Dovey Principall Mr Penny Mr Halsted Mr
Eldridge Mr Noyes Mr Aldey Mr Benett

Eleccion of a new Principall—Mr Penny chosen—Whereas on Thursday
the twenty first Day of November in Michaelmas Term now last past This
Society proceeded to the Choice of a New Principall for three Years next
Coming according to the Orders & Usage of this Society Three of the
Antients being nominated for Candidates by the Principall & Antients
then in Commons One whereof Viz^t Mr John Penny was unanimously
elected by the Antients & Companions then in Commons according to the
Order and Usage of the said House Itt is ordered that the said Eleccion &
proceedings therein be entred in this Book and is as followes

MICHAELMAS TERM 1728

Clements Inne   ⎱
Thursday 21 Novr. 1728 ⎰ Persons Nominated by the Antients for the
Choice of a new Principall for three Years next ensuing

Principall	Mr Penny	Mr Aldey
Mr Dovey	Wm Purcell	
	Henry Jones	
	Nathaniel Trayton	
	John Dovey Junr.	
	David Thomas	
We whose Names are	Edward Cosyn	
Underwritten being all	John Dewes	
the Antients in Commons	John Ja. Dobson	
approve this Choice	T Burrell	
John Dovey Pr.	John Green	
Roger Aldey	James Peters	
	Sam! Coote	
	Bri: Smith	
	Jno. Mackay	
	Chas Baldwyn	

Mr Noyes Junr. Bond up—Mr W^m. Noyes Junr. being retired into the
Country and having left of practising the Law and Desiring that his Bond
given to this Society may be delivered up It is ordered that upon Payment
of what is due from him to the Society & Discharging the Servants Rolls
the said Bond be delivered up to be Cancelled

Mr Brewster's bond d^d up to Mr Goodman his Surety on payment of 4.10.
—Mr Christopher Brewster being in Arrear to this Society for pencions &
absent Commons ending in Trinity Term last £4. 10s. . . . And Mr Everard

G*

Goodman one of the Antients of this Society (who is Surety for the said Christopher Brewster to the said Society) having paid the said £4 : 10s. for the Use of the said Society Now Desires the said Bond may be delivered up to him [Ordered accordingly: Mr Goodman to discharge the Servants Rolls:] And Itt is further ordered that the pencion & Commons for Michaelmas Term last be Remitted

Hr Hen: Dottin Composition for absent Commons—Mr Henry Dottin being in Arrear one pound for pencions and three pounds ten Shillings for absent Commons due to this Society att the End of Michaelmas Term last [desires abatement (not in town 4 of the terms charged): abated 10s. for those terms: to pay £3 in full discharge of the commons]

Mr Sam.! Wynde Bond D.ᵈ up—Mr Samuel Wynde having left of practising the Law Itt is Desired on his behalf that the bond given by him on his Admittance may be delivered up Which is hereby ordered to be done accordingly upon his paying his Arrears due to this Society and Discharging the Servants' Rolls.

Clements Inn in the ⎱ Att a Pencion there held on Friday the fourteenth
County of Middlesex ⎰ Day of February 1728 present **Mr Penny Principall**
Mr Fowler Mr Halsted Mr Noyes Mr Eldridge
Mr Hardwicke Mr Benett.

Commons one week in a Term only—WHEREAS it is found not only an Inconveniency but also an expence to the Society to have the Commons of the House continued for two weeks in the Issuable Terms [1] Itt is ordered that for the future the Commons shall continue but one week in each Issuable Term as they now doe in the other Terms which are not issuable.

Jno. Beeding his Bond up—Mr John Beeding being indebted to this Society in Twelve pounds OR bond and being poor and offering to pay down Nine pounds tenn shillings and to give his note for two pounds tenn shillings payable in Six Months [2] on his having up his bond Itt is ordered that the same be accepted and his bond delivered up.

Mr Edward Benett Composition—Mr Edward Benett (one of the Antients of this Society) being One term in Arrears for Commons which Term he was out of Town and desiring to Compound for the Same itt is ordered that on his paying Two Shillings and Six pence to Mr Smith he be discharged from his said absent Commons having paid the Servants Rolls.

---

[1] "Hilary or Trinity terms, which, from the marking up of the issues therein, are usually called issuable terms"—Blackstone, *Comm.* (1768), III, 353.

[2] A marginal entry (in what looks like Penny's handwriting) states "pd. in Mich: foll."

Mr James Hardwick Composition—Mr James Hardwicke (One of the Antients of this Society) being Three pounds In Arrears for absent Commons and desiring to Compound for the Same for that he was not in town those terms Itt is ordered that on his paying thirty Shillings to Mr Smith he be discharged from the said absent Commons having paid the Servants rolls.

Mr Jos. Hunt Composition—Mr Jos: Hunt (One of the Companions of this Society) being two pounds ten shillings in Arrears for pencions and eight pounds five shillings for absent Commons and desiring to Compound for his Commons he being in town but two terms in a year Itt is ordered that upon his payment of two pounds tenn shillings for the pencions and Six pounds three Shillings and Six pence for absent Commons to Mr Smith he be discharged from the said pencions and Commons (he paying the Servants Rolls).

Mr Edm.^d Giles Hooper Bond up—Mr Edmund Giles Hooper (late one of the Antients of this Society) being indebted two pounds five shillings and he being deceased his Executrix applying to have his bond up Itt is ordered on her paying two pounds five shillings to Mr Smith and the Servants Rolls his bond be delivered up

Mr Jno. Stafford Abatement of rent—Mr John Stafford (One of the Companions of this Society) Complaining that by the pulling down the front of the buildings (N.º 19) he lost the Use of his Chamber and wanting an Abatement of rent It is ordered that the Quarter's rent from Michaelmas to Christmas last be abated

Mr Edwd Johnson his Bond D.^d up—Mr Edward Johnson (one of the Companions of this Society) being now an Housekeeper in London And desiring upon payment of his Arrears to have his Bond up Itt is ordered upon his payment of four pounds twelve Shillings to Mr Smith and the Servants' Rolls his bond be delivered up

Mr Carr Brackenbury Composition—Mr Carr Brackenbury (one of the Companions of this Society) being three pounds tenn Shillings in Arrears for absent Commons and desiring to Compound for the same for that he was not in town & of those Terms Charged to his Account Itt is therefore ordered that on his paying two pounds ten shillings to Mr Smith & the Servants Rolls he be discharged from those Commons

Mr Robt Powlett Bond up—Mr Robt Powlett (late one of the Antients of this Society) being indebted Six Shillings for pencions to this Society and be being dead & his Executor Applying to have his bond up Itt is ordered on his paying Six Shillings to Mr Smith and the Servants Rolls his Bond be Delivered up

Mr John Gibbons Bond up—Mr John Gibbons (late one of the Antients of this Society) being indebted eight Shillings for pencions to this Society and he being dead and his Executrix applying to have his Bond up Itt is ordered on her paying eight Shillings to Mr Smith & Discharging the Servants Rolls the said Bond be delivered up

Mr Christopher Lake's Bond d^d up—Mr Lake being gone beyond Seas and being in mean Circumstances Itt is ordered upon the Application of Mr Richard Brereton his Security that his Bond be Delivered up to the said Mr Brereton upon his paying twelve pounds fifteen Shillings & Eight pence due from the said Mr Lake for Arrears to the Society

SUBSCRIPTIONS by Severall Gentlemen of the Society of Clements Inn for 59 fire Bucketts 2 Leather Capps 2 prong poles or Fire Hooks 2 Shovels and 2 pick Axes & 2 Staffes to take them off the pinns [1] and collected by Mr Halsted together with a Lamp at the Foregate are as Followes (vizt)

	£		
Mr Dovey Pr.	1 : 1 : 0	Mr Johnson	0 : 10 : 6
Mr Fowler	0 : 10 : 6	Mr Aldey	0 : 10 : 6
Mr Goodman	0 : 10 : 6	Mr Trayton	0 : 10 : 6
Mr Penny	0 : 10 : 6	Mr Webb	0 : 10 : 6
Mr Curtis	0 : 10 : 6	Mr Jones	0 : 10 : 6
Mr Noyes	0 : 10 : 6	Mr Dewes	0 : 10 : 6
Mr Eldridge	0 : 10 : 6	Mr Austin	0 : 10 : 6
Mr Halsted	0 : 10 : 6	Mr Lethbridge	0 : 10 : 6
		Mr Trott	0 : 10 : 6
Mr Nicholls	0 : 10 : 6	Mr Ja: Hardwicke	0 : 10 : 6
Mr Dobson	0 : 10 : 6	Mr Bennett	0 : 10 : 6
Mr Heckford	0 : 10 : 6	Mr T: Powlett	0 : 10 : 6
Mr Limbrey	0 : 10 : 6	Mr Honnor	0 : 10 : 6
Mr Coote	0 : 10 : 6	Mr Blackwell	0 : 10 : 6
Mr R: Pert	0 : 10 : 6	Mr Waldron	0 : 10 : 6
Mr Baldwyn	0 : 10 : 6	Mr Bond	0 : 10 : 6
		Mr Brayfield	0 : 5 : 0

Collected Summe Tot^l £ 17 : 1 : 0

Paid Mr Davis for the 59 Bucketts att 4^{s.} a piece	11 : 16 : 0
and for the Capps and fire Hookes	1 : 2 : 0
paid Mr Powell for the Shovells and Pick Axes	0 : 13 : 0
paid Mr Cock the Joyner making the pinns and hanging the Bucketts &c.	2 : 7 : 0
paid Mr Duxon for the said Lamp and Iron	1 : 2 : 6
Expences on the Workmen	0 : 2 : 0

Disbursed £17 : 2 : 6

---

[1] For the further provision of a fire engine in 1730 see p. 153 below.

Clements Inn in the } Att a pencion there held on Wednesday the
County of Middlesex } Nineteenth day of February 1728 present Mr Penny
Pr. Mr Fowler Mr Halsted Mr Noyes Mr Eldridge
Mr Hardwicke.

Mr Simon Stanton's Chamber to be padlockt—Mr Simon Stanton
having for a long time been in Mr Hunt's Chambers N⁰ (1) up 2 pair of
Stairs without being admitted a Member of the Society (tho often Summoned) ordered that a padlock be putt upon his Chamber door for his
Contempt. Which was accordingly done butt on his Admission & giving
bond with Security itt was taken off again.

Writings to be entred in the Lease book—Ordered that the Abstract
of the Deeds & writings relating to Clements Inn's title be entred into the
book of Leases.

Mrs Barras ordered to deliver a bill—Ordered that Mrs Barras doth
deliver in a bill of her Demands upon the Society which bill is referred to
Mr Dovey Mr Halsted & Mr Aldey to Settle who are also to consider what
is due from her late husband to the Society for rent and money received
for the houses Use and that Mr Smith the Steward do give her Notice
thereof

Mr Mill's Goods distrained for rent to be sold—Ordered that the Goods
of Mr Mills[1] (formerly a Companion of this House) which were distrained
by Mr Barras for £5: 10s: rent be Sold to pay the rent and Charges (if not
already done by Mr Barras)

Mr Downton's bond d.ᵈ up—Mr Downton being poor and gone abroad
so that his Security is obliged to pay his Arrears ordered that on Mr
Lethbridges paying nine pounds two Shillings & Servants Rolls the bond
be delivered up

Mr Berry's bond d.ᵈ up—Mr Berry being poor & his Security coming to
pay his Arrears & desiring to have up his bond the said Mr Berry being no
Practiser ordered that on paying £8: 15s. & Servants Rolls his bond be
delivered up

Auditors of the late principall's Accounts—Ordered that Mr John Penny
the present principall & Mr Edward Halsted One of the Antients of this
Society & Mr Samuell Heckford & Mr James Peters two of the Companions of this Society shall & do examine & Audit the Accounts of
Mr John Dovey late principall of this Society for one whole year beginning
in Hillary term 1727 Untill Hillary Term 1728 And that the said Mr
principall Mr Halsted Mr Heckford & Mr Peter or any three of them shall
and do make their Certificate & report thereof as soon as conveniently
can be done.

[1] ? Miller: see p. 121 above.

Mr Philip Smith Composition—Mr Philip Smith one of the Companions of his Society being three pounds five shillings in Arreare for absent Commons [desires abatement (not in town 2 of the terms charged): to pay £3 and the servants rolls]

Mr Jos. Goodacre Composition—Mr Joseph Goodacre being forty shillings in arrear for absent Commons [desires abatement (not in town one of the terms charged): to pay 37s. 6d. and the servants rolls]

Mr Geo. Bond Composition—Mr George Bond being fifteen Shillings in Arrear for absent Commons [desires abatement (not in town any of the terms charged): to pay 7s. 6d. and the servants rolls]

Clements Inn in the } Att a pencion there held on Monday the 12th Day
County of Middlesex } of May 1729 present Mr Penny Principall, Mr Dovey, Mr Fowler, Mr Halsted, Mr Eldridge, Mr Aldey, Mr Benett,

Mr Dovey the late Principall's Accounts audited confirmed—WHEREAS Mr Penny the present principall Mr Edward Halsted one of the Antients of this Society & Mr Samuel Heckford & Mr James Peters two of the Companions of the Said Society by Vertue of an Order of pencion made the nineteenth Day of February last were Appointed Auditors of the Accounts of Mr John Dovey late principall of this Society And having accordingly audited stated and examined the said Mr Dovey's Accounts of Receipts & Disbursements for one whole year beginning in Hillary Term 1727 and ending the beginning of Hillary Terme 1728 And have found the Summe tottall of the Principall's Receipts for that year (including the Summe of One hundred and ninety pounds sixteen Shillings & nine pence being the Ballance of the last Years Accounts in the hands of the said late principall) to be four hundred forty five pounds two Shillings & Six pence and the totall of his Disbursements to be two hundred ninety four pounds nine Shillings & ten pence halfpenny so that there remains due on this Account from the said late principall to this Society one hundred and fifty pounds twelve Shillings and sevenpence halfpenny As appears by their Report or Certificate thereof Dated the twenty eighth Day of March last ITT IS THEREFORE ORDERED that the said Accounts so stated audited examined & certified as aforesaid be allowed and approved and the same are hereby allowed and approved of to be just & true And the said Mr John Dovey is hereby discharged off & from the said Summe of two hundred ninety four pounds nine shillings & ten pence so by him disbursed as aforesaid AND ITT IS FURTHER ORDERED that the said Mr John Dovey Do pay over the said Summe of one hundred and fifty pounds twelve

Shillings & seven pence halfpenny unto the said Mr Penny the present principall for the Use of this Society

> John Penny Pr.
> Wm Fowler
> Edwd Halsted
> Ambrose Eldridge
> Ro. Aldey
> Edw. Benet.

Samuel Law porter of the back gate—Ordered that Samuel Law be admitted Porter at the Backgate of this Society next to Claremarkett in the Room and Place of Nicholas Holles deceased late porter there But to continue therein only during the good Will and pleasure of the Principall and Antients and their Successors for the time being or the Major part of them & no longer

All persons to be Cast into Commons the next Term after Admission—Ordered that for the future whosoever shall be admitted a Companion of this Society shall be Cast into Commons the next Term after he is admitted if admitted in Vacation And the Same Term if admitted before going into Commons.

All Interest to be paid to Christmas last—Ordered that the Principall Do pay all such Interest as is due from this Society to Christmas last out of the first Moneys that shall Come to his hands

Mr William Hardwicke Composition—Mr Wm Hardwick one of the Companions of this Society being in Arrear three pounds for Pencions and nine pounds fifteen Shillings for absent Commons including this present Term [desires to compound (not in town 30 of the terms charged): on paying £6 and the servants rolls to be discharged from the commons]

Clements Inn in the } Att a pention there held on Thursday the 22nd Day *County of Middlesex* } of May 1729 present Mr Penny Principall, Mr Dovey, Mr Fowler, Mr Halsted, Mr Eldridge, Mr Noyes, Mr Benett & Mr Aldey.

Samuel Law to have the Use of the ground room N° 8 during pleasure—WHEREAS the Porter's Lodge att the Backgate is so close and dark that itt is not fitt for him to lay in itt ITT IS THEREFORE ORDERED that he may lay in the ground room N° 8 (which the Joyner now uses) during the pleasure of the Principall & Antients and untill another order is made to the contrary And also that when he goes from the Gate att 12 a Clock att night he Carry the Key with him to his own Lodging & not leave itt att the foregate as lately ordered.[1]

----

[1] See the order about the back gate in 1722/3, p. 105 above.

The Pr. & Antients to grant Assignments after the 1st Day of Trinity Term next untill 25th December 1730 and for pulling down N? 18 & building a New Stair Case in the room thereof—Whereas the Stair Case or Building (N? 18) in the Middle Court of the said Inn is become very old ruinous & decayed so as to be thought not fitt to be repaired but necessary to be quite pulled down & new built Itt is therefore ordered that the said Stair Case or Building with all the Chambers therein contained and the appurtenances thereunto belonging be taken down and that a new Stair Case with Chambers and other Conveniencyes for the same be new erected & built in the room thereof att the Charge of the said Society And in order to raise a fund to defray the Charge & expence thereof without running into further Debt or borrowing money att Interest to build withall Itt is ordered that (notwithstanding the Order made the 28th of February 1717 against Assignments[1]) the principall & Antients from & after the first Day of Trinity Term next untill the 25th of December 1730 & no longer may grant Assignments of any Chamber or Chambers (after one life) as they formerly used to do (before the said last mencioned order was made) at the usual rates of four years purchase for an Assignment alone and ten years purchase for a life & Assignment when taken together

> John Penny Pr.
> John Dovey
> Wm Fowler
> Edwd Halsted
> W. Noyes
> Ambrose Eldridge
> Edw. Benet
> Ro: Aldey

The Pr. to pay Matt. Green one Guinea for officiating as Porter of the Back gate—Ordered that the Principall pay to Matt: Green for officiating as Porter of the Backgate from the death of Nich: Hollis to the Eleccion of Sam: Law One Guinea

Clements Inn in the } At a pention there held on Wednesday the Eleventh
County of Middlesex } Day of June 1729 present Mr Penny Principall Mr Dovey Mr Fowler Mr Halsted Mr Eldridge Mr Aldey Mr Blackwell

*Mr Goodman for Assignment of all his Chambers & Garretts N? 24—*WHEREAS Mr Everard Goodman (one of the Antients of this Society) the

---

[1] See p. 57 above, and, for another relaxation of the ban on assignments, p. 160 below.

4th day of Aprill 1713 had a Lease of a Chamber up 3 pair of Staires in the Building called Kelletts' Building in the Garden Court Numbered (24) formerly Mr Edward Bearcrofts, granted unto him by the Society for the term of 99 Yeares' (if he should so long live) AND WHEREAS by an order of pencion dated 24th February 1715 in Consideration of £4: 6s. then paid by the said Everard Goodman for the Use of the said Society Itt was ordered that he should upon request have a lease made to him of the Garretts over his said Chambers for life as usuall AND WHEREAS the 2^d of December 1724 a Lease of a Chamber up two pair of Staires in the said building Numbered (24) being under the said other Chambers and late in the possession of Willm Cocke deceased was granted unto him by the said Society for 99 years (if he should so long live) AND WHEREAS on the same Date another Lease of the Chambers up two & three pair of Staires & Garretts over the same in the said Building Numberd (24) late in the possession of Matt Evans deceased was granted unto him by the said Society for 99 Years (if he should so long live) And the said Everard Goodman now desiring to have a Lease made to him of the said Garretts pursuant to the said Order of pencion and desiring also to purchase an Assignment as well of the said last mencioned Garretts as of all the said severall Chambers & Garretts granted to him by the said 3 severall Leases for one Life after the Expiration of his own Life now in being and having now paid to the Principall for the Use of this Society the Summe of ONE HUNDRED NINETY THREE POUNDS ITT IS ORDERED in Consideration thereof [that a lease and assignment be made to him accordingly, with the usual covenants &c. and in the usual form, &c.]

Mr Truesdales bond d^d up—Mr Thomas Truesdale one of the Companions of this Society being in Arrear one pound Six Shillings for pencions and four pounds five Shillings for absent Commons And being since dead Itt is ordered that on Mr John Blackwell Executor of Mr Joshua Blackwell Security for the said Mr Truesdale paying three pounds eight Shillings & Sixpence as a Composition for the said Commons & in full for the pencions In regard that the said Mr Truesdale was not in Town any one of the Terms charged to his Account, the bond given by the said Mr Truesdale upon his Admission to this Society be delivered up to the said Mr John Blackwell

Mr Parke's bond d^d up—Mr Richard Parke one of the Companions of this Society being dead & in Arrear two pounds nineteen Shillings to the said Society for pencions & absent Commons Itt is ordered that on payment of the said two pounds nineteen Shillings by Mr John Blackwell Security for the said Richard Parke the bond given to the said Society upon the said Richard Parke's Admission be delivered up to the said Mr John Blackwell

Mr Tho. *Swift's Composition*—Mr Thomas Swift being in Arrear forty shillings for pencions due Hillary Term last and five pounds fifteen shillings for absent Commons ending in Hillary Term last [desires abatement (not in town 11 of the terms charged): to pay £4 7s. 6d. in full discharge of the commons]

Mr P: Smith for a Lease of Mr Turner's Chamber N.º 2—Ordered that on Mr Philip Smith's paying five pounds for the Use of this Society a new Lease be made to him of Mr W.ᵐ Turner's ground Chamber N.º 2 instead of Mr Turner's Lease now Surrendred for that purpose

Clements Inn in the ⎫ Att a Pention there held on Wednesday the
County of Middlesex ⎭ Eighteenth Day of June 1729 present Mr Penny Principall Mr Dovey, Mr Fowler, Mr Halsted, Mr Eldridge, Mr Aldey, Mr Blackwell

Mr W.ᵐ Turner's Bond d.ᵈ up—Mr William Turner (one of the Companions of this Society) being admitted a Member of the Inner Temple [1] And desiring upon payment of his Arrears to have his Bond delivered up Itt is ordered upon payment of his Arrears & the Servants Rolls that his Bond be Delivered up

Mr Stubbs Composition—Mr Walter Stubbs being in Arrear Eighteen Shillings for pencions and three pounds for absent Commons due to this Society at the End of Easter Term last [desires abatement (not in town 7 of the terms charged): abated 17s. 6d. for those terms: to pay £2. 5s. 6d. in full discharge of the commons]

Mr R: Keeling Composition—Mr Rich.ᵈ Keeling being in Arrear Eighteen Shillings for pencions & three pounds for absent Commons due at the End of Easter Term last [desires abatement (not in town 9 of the terms charged: abated £1. 2s. 6d. for those terms: to pay £1. 17s. 6d. in full discharge of the commons]

Clements Inn in the ⎫ Att a Pention there held on Wednesday the twenty
County of Middlesex ⎭ fifth Day of June 1729 present Mr Penny Principall Mr Dovey Mr Fowler Mr Halsted Mr Curtis Mr Noyes Mr Aldey Mr Benett

Mr Gregory's Composition—Mr Henry Gregory being in Arrear fourteen Shillings for pencions due att the End of Easter Term last and two pounds five Shillings for Commons Ending this Term [desires abatement (not in

---

[1] The only William Turner shown as admitted to the Inner Temple during this half-century was admitted in 1736/7: see *I.T.R.*, IV, 359.

town 3 of the terms charged): abated 7s. 6d. for those terms: to pay £2. 2s. 6d] in full discharge of those Commons and also for the Commons due for this present Trinity Term

Mr Wyche's Composition—Mr Richard Wyche being in Arrear twelve Shillings for pencions & forty five Shillings for absent Commons ending this present Term [desires abatement (not in town any one of the terms charged): abated 22s. 6d. for those terms: to pay 22s. 6d. in full discharge of the commons]

Mr Limbrey's bond d.ᵈ up—Mr Limbrey one of the Companions of this Society being an Housekeeper in Town and desiring to have his bond delivered up Itt is Ordered that upon payment of his Arrears and the Servants Rolls his Bond be delivered up.

Clements Inn in the⎰ Att a Pention there held on Wednesday the second
County of Middlesex⎱ Day of July 1729 present Mr Penny Principall
       Mr Fowler, Mr Noyes, Mr Halsted, Mr Eldridge,
       Mr Hardwick, Mr Benett,

Mr Eldridge for an Ass.ᵗ of his Chamber N.º 2—Whereas Mr Ambrose Eldridge (one of the Antients of this Society) the first day of December 1714 had a Lease of a Chamber up one pair of Staires in the Building called Wright's Building in the 1st Court (numbered 2) formerly Mr Rich.ᵈ Lowth's granted unto him by the Society for the Term of 99 years (if he should so long live) And the said Ambrose Eldridge now desiring to purchase an Assignment of the said Chamber granted to him by the said Lease for one Life after the Expiration of his own Life now in being & having now paid to the Principall for the Use of this Society the Summe of Twenty four pounds Itt is ordered in Consideration thereof that an Assignment be made to him the said Ambrose Eldridge his Executors Administrators & Assigns for one Life after his own Life now in being of the said Chamber already granted to him the said Ambrose Eldridge by the said Lease with the usuall Covenants & provisoes and according to the usuall form & Method of making and granting Assignments by this Society

Mr Henry Gregory for an Assignment of his Chamber N.º 22—Whereas Mr Henry Gregory (one of the Companions of this Society) the 18th Day of December 1718 had a Lease of a Chamber being a Ground Chamber in the Building or Stair case Marked with the figures (22) formerly in the possession of Matthew Carvile granted unto him by the Society for the Term of 99 Yeares (if he should so long live) And the said Henry Gregory now desiring to purchase an Assignment of the said Chamber [for one life after the expiration of his own and having paid £40 to the Principal,—

ordered that an assignment be made to him &c. accordingly, with the usual covenants &c. and in the usual form &c. (as in the use of Eldridge above)]

Mr John Harris of North. for an Assignment of his Chamber N.º 22 two pr. of Staires—Whereas Mr John Harris of Eyston in the County of Northampton Gentleman one of the Companions of this Society the 4th Day of July 1720 had a Lease of a Chamber up 2 pair of Staires & one Garrett over the same & two small rooms or Studys & a Turrett over the Staires leading to the said Chamber And one part of the Cellar under the said Chamber In the brick building on the South East part of the Garden in Clements Inn aforesaid formerly in the Possession of Mr W.ᵐ Walker Granted unto him by the Society for the Term of 99 Yeares (if he should so long live) And the said John Harris now desiring to purchase an Assignment of the said Chamber & premisses [for one life after the expiration of his own and having paid the Principal £40—ordered that an assignment be made to him &c. accordingly, with the usual covenants &c. and in the usual form &c. (as in the two preceding entries)].

Mr John Harris of Bucks. for an Ass.ᵗ of Mr Noyes's Chamber N.º 22 1 pr. of Staires—Whereas Mr Henry Harris deceased late one of the Companions of this Society on the 15th Day of February 1693 had a Lease of a Chamber up one pair of Staires in the brick building adjoyning the Chamber formerly in the Possession of Mr Bowler Gentleman together with that part of the Cellar belonging to the said Chamber then in the Tenure of the said Henry Harris Granted unto him by the Society for 99 Yeares (if W.ᵐ Noyes then one of the Companions & now one of the Antients of this Society should so long live) And the said John Harris now desiring to purchase an Assignment of the said Chamber [for one life after the expiration of the life of Mr Noyes and having paid the principal £40—ordered that an assignment be made to him &c. accordingly, with the usual covenants &c. and in the usual form &c. (as in the preceding entries)]

Mr Tho.ˢ Fowke for an Assignment of his Chamber & Garretts N.º 17 2 pr of Stairs & 3 pr of Stairs—Whereas Thomas Fowke Gent one of the Companions of this Society the 22nd Day of July 1715 had a Lease of A Chamber with the Appurtenances Up two pair of Stairs forwards and also of a Chamber up two pair of Staires Backwards in the Stair Case Numbred (17) in the Building formerly built by Godfrey Maydwell And also of a Garrett forwards up three pair of Staires in the same Stair Case Granted unto him by the Society for the Terme of 99 Yeares (if he should so long live) And the said Thomas Fowke desiring to purchase an Assignment of the said Chambers & Garrett [for one life after the expiration of his own and having paid the Principal £50—ordered that an assignment be made to him &c. accordingly, with the usual covenants &c. and in the usual form &c. (as in the preceding entries)]

Mr Carrow's Composition—Mr Robert Carrow being in Arrear three pounds for absent Commons and desiring to Compound for the same [(not in town 9 of the Terms charged): abated 22s. 6d.: to pay £1. 17s. 6d. and the servants' rolls]

Mr Noah Curtis Composition—Mr Noah Curtis being in Arrear four pounds fifteen shillings for absent Commons and desiring to Compound for the same [(not in town 10 of the terms charged): abated 25s.: to pay £3. 10s. and the servants' rolls]

Mr Wm Hester's bond to be d^d up—Mr Wm Hester (one of the Companions of this Society being now an Housekeeper in London And desiring to have his Bond Delivered up Itt is ordered that upon payment of his Arrears and the Servants Roll his bond be Delivered up to him.

Mr Bernard Evans's bond d^d up—Itt appearing that Mr Bernard Evans having formerly paid One pound Six Shillings for pencions & absent Commons for Michaelmas & Hillary Terms 1723 and Easter & Trinity Terms 1724 And one pound three Shillings being still in Arrear and the said Bernard Evans being dead Itt is Ordered that upon payment of the said One pound three Shillings his bond be delivered up.

Mr Richd Tidmarsh Composition & bond D^d up—Mr Richard Tidmarsh being dead & in Arrear two pounds four shillings for pencions and Seven pounds five Shillings for absent Commons And an Abatement being desired by Mrs Tidmarsh his Administratrix In regard that he was out of Town Twelve of the Terms Charged to his Account Itt is Ordered that One pound ten Shillings of the said Absent Commons be abated And that on payment of the said £2. 4s. for the pencions And five pounds fifteen Shillings for the said absent Commons the same be in full And that the said Mr Tidmarsh's Bond be delivered up to the said Mrs Tidmarsh his Administratrix The Servants Rolls being first Discharged

Clements Inn in the ⎱ County of Middlesex ⎰ Att a pention there held on Friday the twenty eighth day of November 1729 present Mr Penny Principall Mr Fowler Mr Halsted Mr Noyes Mr Eldridge Mr Aldey Mr Benett

Mr Wm Purcell for a Lease of his Chambers N° 19 2 pair of stairs—Whereas Mr William Purcell one of the Companions of this Society desiring to take a Lease of the Chamber now in his possession up two pair of Stairs N° 19 & also of the Chamber thereto adjoyning in the same Stair Case formerly in the possession of Morgan Gwyne and since in the possession of Joseph Barras (both which Chambers are to be laid together and made one Chamber) And the said Mr Purcell having been already at great Charges in fitting up the said other Chamber now in his possession and will be at further Expences in fitting up the said other Chamber & laying them both into one Chamber Itt is therefore Ordered that the said Wm Purcell have a Lease made to him of the said Chambers for the Terme of seven years (if he so long live) to commence from Christmas next Att the rent of Eight pounds per Annum payable quarterly with usuall Covenants whenever he shall require the same he paying the usuall fees for such Lease

Mr Edwd Cozyn's Composition—Mr Edward Cosyn being in Arrear £0: 18s. : 0d. for pencions and £2 : 15s. : 0d. for absent Commons ending in Trinity Term last [desires abatement (not in town 3 of the terms charged): to pay £2. 7s. 6d. (in full dishcarge of the commons) and the servants rolls]

Mr James Child Composition—Mr James Child being dead and in Arrear forty shillings for pencions & Eight pounds fifteen shillings for absent Commons And Mr Joseph Child his Executor desiring an abatement of the said absent Commons In Regard the said James Child was not in town twenty eight of those Terms charged to his Account Itt is therefore Ordered that upon the said Joseph Child's paying the said pencions And also five pounds five shillings for the said absent Commons and discharging the Servants Rolls the said James Child's Bond be delivered up to the said Joseph Child and that an Abatement of three pounds ten shillings be made of the said absent Commons

Mr Robt Abney Composition—Mr Robert Abney being in arrear three pounds eight shillings for pencions due in Easter Term 1729 and Eleven pounds ten shillings for absent Commons ending Trinity Term 1729 And praying an Abatement [of the absent commons (not in town any of the terms charged): abated £5. 15s. for those terms: to pay £5. 15s. (in full discharge of the Commons) and the servants rolls]

Mr Stephen Bramston Composition—Mr Stephen Bramston being in Arrear Eighteen shillings for pencions due in Easter Term last And three pounds five shillings for absent Commons ending in Trinity Term last And desiring an abatement of twenty shillings of those absent Commons In Regard he was not in town Eight of the Terms charged to his Account [abated 20s.: to pay £2. 5s. (in full discharge of the commons) and the servants' rolls]

Mr Andrew Love Composition—Mr Andrew Love [in arrear £2. 8s. for pensions and £8 for absent Commons, desires abatement of £4 of the absent commons (not in town any of the terms charged): abated £4: to pay £4 (in full discharge of the commons) and the servants' rolls]

Mr John White Composition—Mr John White [in arrear £2. 8s. for pensions and £8. 5s. for absent commons to the end of Trinity term last, desires abatement of £3 (not in town 24 of the terms charged): abated £3: to pay £5. 5s. (in full discharge of the commons) and the servants' rolls]

Mr Thos*. Shuckforth Bond d*^d *up*—Mr Thomas Shuckforth being no practiser and having retired into the Country and desiring to have his Bond delivered up Itt is therefore Ordered that upon payment of two pounds twelve Shillings for his Arrears to the End of this present Term And discharging the Servants Rolls his bond be delivered up accordingly

Mr Jno. Peirce's Bond delivered up—Mr John Peirce being in Arrear Seven pounds two Shillings for pencions & absent Commons And his Security John Gould having been sued for the same and desiring upon payment of the said Arreares to have the said Mr Peirce's Bond delivered up to him And the said Mr Peirce being no practiser and having retired into the Country Itt is therefore Ordered that upon the said Mr Gould's paying the Summe of Seven pounds two Shillings in full of the said Mr Peirce's Arreares & discharging the Servants Rolls the said Bond be delivered up to him

Clements Inn in the⎫ Att a pencion there held on Friday the Sixth day of
County of Middlesex⎭ February 1729 present Mr Penny Pr. Mr Dovey
Mr Fowler Mr Noyes Mr Halsted & Mr Aldey

Auditors of the Principall's Accounts—Ordered that Mr James Hardwick & Mr Edward Benett two of the Antients of this Society & Mr John Dewes & Mr Henry Jones two of the Companions of this Society shall & do examine & audit the accounts of Mr John Penny the present principall of this Society for one whole year beginning in Hillary Term 1728 untill Hillary Term 1729 And that the said Mr Hardwick Mr Benett Mr Dewes & Mr Jones or any three of them shall & do make their Certificate & Report thereof as soon as conveniently can be done

Mr Tho: Fowke for the Chambers & Garrett late Mr Tho: Fowke's his Father N^o*. 17 2 p*^r *of Staires*—Whereas Thomas Fowke late one of the Companions of this Society held by Articles All that Chamber with the Appurtenances up two pair of Stairs forwards in the Stair Case marked with the figures or Number (17) in the Building in the 3rd Court formerly built by & leased to Godfrey Maydwell Gent And also All that Chamber with the Appurtenances up two pair of Staires Backwards in the same Stair Case And also All that Garrett forwards with the Appurtenances up three pair of Staires in the same Stair Case being over the said first mencioned Chamber (All which Chambers & Garrett were then in the possession of the said Thos Fowke) for 99 Yeares determinable upon the Death of the said Thos Fowke with a power to Nominate another Companion of this

Society to be admitted to the same for the like Term of 99 Yeares determinable with the Life of such person And the said Mr Fowke having made his last Will in Writing And appointed Thomas Sells & Anne Fowke his Widdow and also his Brother in Law Henry Whitaker Executors thereof Which said Thos Sells & Anne Fowke have since proved the said Will And the said Henry Whitaker hath never acted in the said Executorship And Whereas the said Thos Sells & Anne Fowke have Surrendred the Articles or Lease granted by the said Principall & Antients to the said Thomas Fowke of the said Chambers & Garrett And all the Estate & Interest thereby granted To the Intent That Thos Fowke Son of the said Anne Fowke and one of the Companions of this Society should be admitted to the said Chambers & Garrett And the said Thos Fowke desiring to be admitted thereto Itt is Ordered that In Performance of the said Articles entred into by the Principall & Antients with the said Thos Fowke in his lifetime, A new Lease of the said Chambers & Garrett be made & granted to the said Thomas Fowke the Son for 99 Years If he shall so long live with the usuall Covenants & provisoes and according to the usuall Method & form of granting Leases by this Society

Mr Edward Manby for the Chamber late Mr Steggall's N.º 23.— Whereas Thomas Steggall late one of the Companions of this Society held by Articles All that Double ground Chamber with the Appurtenances situate lying & being in the Garden Court in the first stair Case marked with the figures or Number (23) in Mr Kelletts Building att the Upper End of the Garden in Clements Inn formerly in the Tenure of Henry Watson Gentleman deceased for 99 years determinable upon the Death of the said Thos Steggall with a power to Nominate another Companion of this Society to be admitted to the same for the like Term of 99 Years determinable with the Life of such person And the said Mr Stegall having made his last Will in Writing And appointed Joseph Johnson Executor thereof who hath Surrendred the Articles or Lease granted by the Principall & Antients to the said Thos Steggall of the said Chamber & all the Estate & Interest thereby granted To the Intent that Edward Manby one of the Companions of this Society should be admitted to the said Chambers And the said Edward Manby desiring to be admitted thereto Itt is Ordered that In Performance of the said Articles entred into by the Principall & Antients with the said Thos Steggall A new Lease of the said Chamber be made & granted to the said Edward Manby for 99 Yeares If he shall so long live with the Usuall Covenants and provisoes and according to the usuall Method & form of granting Leases by this Society

*Mr Seabrook appointed Surveyor of the new building N.º 18—*Ordered that Mr Seabrook be appointed Surveyor for the new intended Buildings in the 2nd Court N.º 18 And that he be allowed thirty Guineas for his pairs & trouble in making Draughts, contriving the Buildings, contracting with the workmen and seeing the Work done as it should be.

Clements Inn in the ⎱ Att a pention there held on Friday the thirteenth
County of Middlesex ⎰ day of February 1729 present Mr Penny Pr. Mr
Dovey Mr Fowler Mr Noyes Mr Hardwick Mr
Eldridge Mr Aldey & Mr Benett

Mr Barras's bonds delivered up—Mr Joseph Barras (late Steward of this Society) being dead And his Executrix having answered and paid all Demands and Debts due from him to the said Society Itt is ordered that as well the Bond given by him (when entred as a Companion) as also that given by him when made Steward be delivered up to his Executrix to be Cancelled

A Fire Engine to be provided and a building to be erected to sett itt in— Whereas the Society are provided with Bucketts & other necessaryes to be used in Case of Fire [1] Butt as yett have no fire Engine nor any convenient place to keep itt in dry Itt is therefore ordered that itt be left to the principall to provide such a fire Engine And erect such a Building for itt to stand in as he shall think fitt att the Charge of the said Society

Mr Bewley's Composition—Mr Bewley one of the Companions of this Society [in arrear £2. 12s. for pensions ending last Hilary term and £8. 15s. for absent commons also so ending, desires abatement (not in town 19 of the terms charged): abated £2. 7s. 6d. for those terms: to pay £6. 7s. 6d. (in full discharge of the Commons) and the servants' rolls]

Mr Brackenbury's Composition—Mr Brackenbury one of the Companions of this Society [in arrear 10s. for absent commons for Easter and Michaelmas terms last, desires abatement (not in town either term): abated 5s.: to pay 5s. and the servants' rolls]

Mr Wm Vaux's bond delivered up—Mr Wm Vaux, one of the Companions of this Society having left of practise and desiring that his Bond given upon his Admittance into this Society may be delivered up Itt is Ordered that upon payment of £6: 17s. for his Arrears due to this Society his said bond be delivered up to him to be Cancelled He paying his Arrears due to the Servants

Mr Blackwell Rector of St Clement Danes—Ordered that the principall of this Society do give to the Reverend Mr Thomas Blackwell Rector of St. Clement Danes four pounds as a free Gift from this Society nothing of Right being due to him from the said Society

[1] See p. 140 above.

Clements Inn in the ⎫ Att a pencion there held on Friday the twentieth
County of Middlesex ⎭ day of February 1729 present Mr Penny Pr. Mr
Dovey Mr Halsted Mr Hardwick Mr Aldey Mr
Blackwell & Mr Benett Mr Fowler & Mr Eldridge

Principalls Accounts Confirmed—Whereas Mr James Hardwick &
Mr Edward Benett two of the Antients of this Society and Mr John Dewes
and Mr Henry Jones two of the Companions of the said Society By
Vertue of an Order of pention made the 6th day of February 1729 were
appointed Auditors of the Accounts of Mr John Penny now principall of
this Society And having accordingly audited stated & examined the said
Mr Penny's Accounts of Receipts & Disbursements for one whole Year
beginning in Hillary Term 1728 and ending the beginning of Hillary Term
1729 Have found the Summe Totall of the said Principall's Receipts for
that year to be One Thousand forty six pounds thirteen shillings & eleven
pence halfpenny And the totall of his Disbursements to be £529: 01s.: 08d.
so that there remaines due on that Account to the Society from the said
Principall £517: 12s.: 3½d. As appeares by their Report or Certificate
thereof Dated the 16th Day of this instant February Itt is therefore
Ordered that the said Accounts so stated audited examined & certified as
aforesaid be allowed and approved And the same are hereby allowed and
approved of to be just & true And the said Mr Penny is hereby discharged
of & from the said Summe of £529: 01s.: 08d. so by him discharged as
aforesaid.

> John Dovey
> Edwd Halsted
> Ambrose Eldridge
> James Hardwick
> Jno Blackwell
> Ro. Aldey
> Edw: Benet.
> W^m. Fowler

Mr Francis Jackson's Composition—Mr Francis Jackson [Companion,
in arrear 4s. for pensions due last Michaelmas term and £2. 5s. for absent
commons to the end of last Michaelmas term, desires abatement of the
commons (not in town 2 of the terms charged): abated 5s.: to pay £2 in
full discharge of the commons, also discharging the servants rolls]

Mr Philip Smith's Composition—Mr Philip Smith [Companion, in
arrear 6s. for pensions due last Hillary term and 20s. for absent commons
to the end of that term, desires abatement (not in town one of the terms
charged: abated 2s. 6d.: to pay 17s. 6d. in full discharge of the commons,
also discharging the servants rolls]

Clements Inn in the ⎱ Att a Pencion there held on Wednesday the fourth
County of Middlesex ⎰ day of March 1729 present Mr Penny Pr., Mr
Dovey, Mr Fowler, Mr Halsted, Mr Eldridge,
Mr Aldey & Mr Benett,

Mr Charles Eyres for the Chamber late Mr Pollen's—Whereas Edward
Pollen one of the Companions of this Society holds by Articles All that
Double Chamber with the Appurtenances in Mr Kellett's Building att the
Upper End of the Garden in the Stair Case next to the passage leading
through the said Building into Clare markett up two pair of Staires over
the Chambers of Mr John Dovey now one of the Antients of this House
for the Term of 99 Yeares determinable upon the Death of the said Edward
Pollen And he having contracted with Charles Eyres (who is admitted a
Companion of this Society) for the purchase of the said Chamber and
having Surrendred the said Articles & all the Term & Interest thereby
granted into the Hands of the now principall & Antients of the said Society
To the Intent that a new Lease be made thereof unto the said Charles Eyres
And the said Charles Eyres desiring to be admitted to the same and have a
new Lease thereof Itt is Ordered that on payment of the Summe of
twenty pounds to the Principal for the Use of this Society, A new Lease be
granted of the said Chamber unto the said Charles Eyres for 99 yeares
determinable on his Death, according to the usuall Method & form of
granting Leases by this Society

  Clements Inn   29 Apr. 1730

This day James Jenyns Esq.[1] came in the Room of Tho[s] Jones
of Chester Esq. and bringing a case upon the Stat. 8 H. 6
upon amendments [2] Hee read upon the Same in the presence of
Mr Jos. Ward & Mr Tho: Bayley two Students of the Inner
Temple [3] and the Gentlemen of Clements Inn.

            John Penny Pr.

---

[1] Jenyns, called to the Bar in 1708 (at the same time as Thomas Jones, for whom he here is deputy), was proposed for reader at Clifford's Inn in February 1728/9 when Jones was proposed for reader at Clement's Inn; in May 1730 the two were discharged for their readings at Clifford's and Clement's Inn respectively: *I.T.R.*, IV, 193, 220.

[2] 8 Hen. 6. cc. 12 and 15, both repealed by the Statute Law Revision and Civil Procedure Act, 1883.

[3] Ward and Bayley were both called to the Bar in June 1730: Bayley died in 1740/1; Ward, who came as substitute reader to Clement's Inn in 1732 (see p. 173 below), was proposed as reader to Clifford's Inn in 1746: *I.T.R.*, IV. 223–4, 426, 503. For the duty of barristers and other members of the Inner Temple to accompany the reader to an Inn of Chancery, see *ibid.*, I, 143 (order of 1546), and III, 361 (order of 1701).

Clements Inn in the ⎱ Att a Pention there held on Friday the twelfth day
County of Middlesex ⎰ of June 1730 present Mr Penny Pr. Mr Dovey Mr
Blackwell Mr Aldey Mr Eldridge and Mr Fowler

Mr Brayfield Bond D.ᵈ up—Mr Brayfield one of the Companions of this Society being an Housekeeper in London & praying that his Bond given upon his Admittance may be delivered up Itt is Ordered that upon payment of his Arrears his Bond be delivered up to him to be Cancelled He also discharging the Servants Rolls

Mr Edward Pollen Bond D.ᵈ up—Mr Pollen having retired into the Country and being no Practiser and Desiring his Bond to be delivered up Itt is Ordered that upon payment of his Arrears & discharging the Servants Rolls his Bond be delivered up accordingly.

Mr Wyatt for a Lease of the Chamber & Garrett N.º 17 for the Life of Mrs Whitaker—Mr Edward Wyatt one of the Companions of this Society desiring to purchase a Lease for the Life of Mrs Alice Whitaker of the Chambers two pair of Stairs & the Garretts to them belonging in the Stair Case Marked N.º 17 lately belonging to Mr Tho.ˢ Fowke deceased in the Middle Court in Clements Inn And also the Cellar in the passage on the Ground floor in the same Stair Case Itt is Ordered that on payment of One hundred & five pounds to the Principall for the Use of the Society a Lease be accordingly made to him of the said Chambers Garrett & Cellar with the Appurtenances for ninety nine Yeares If the said Alice Whitaker shall so long live With the usuall Covenants & Agreements & according to the usuall form & method of making & granting Leases by this Society

Mr Trotts Composicion—Mr Baptist Trott [in arrears £1. 6s. for pensions and £4. 15s. for absent commons, desires abatement (not in town 14 of the terms charged): abated £1. 15s.: to pay £3 in full discharge of the commons] he discharging the Servants Rolls.

Mr Eccles's Composicion—Mr Samuel Eccles [in arrear £3. 15s. for absent commons, desires abatement (not in town any of the terms charged): abated £1. 17s. 6d. for those terms: to pay £1. 17s. 6d. in full discharge of the commons] He discharging the servants' rolls

Clements Inn in the ⎱ Att a pencion there held on Wednesday the 24th
County of Middlesex ⎰ day of June 1730 present Mr Penny Pr. Mr Dovey
Mr Fowler Mr Halsted Mr Noyes Mr Eldridge
Mr Hardwick and Mr Bennett

Mr Tho.ˢ Tufton for the Lease of his Chamber N.º 21—Mr Thomas Tufton one of the Companions of this Society desiring to purchase a Lease of the Ground Chamber N.º 21 in the Building formerly built by

William Wheatley and Leased to Mr Jno. Bowler situate in the Garden Court in Clements Inn and the Cellar thereto belonging now or late in the possession of the said Thomas Tufton for his own Life and an Assignment for one Life after the Expiracion of his own Life And having paid to the Principall for the Use of this Society Seventy pounds Itt is Ordered In Consideracion thereof that a Lease be made to him the said Thomas Tufton for his own Life and an Assignment for one Life after his own Life now in being of the said Chamber and Cellar with the usuall Covenants & provisoes and according to the usuall form and Method of making and granting Leases & Assignments by this Society

Mr John Dewes for the Lease of his Chamber N.º 22—Mr John Dewes one of the Companions of this Society desiring to purchase a Lease of the Chamber up one pair of Staires in the Building formerly built by William Wheatley and leased to Mr John Bowler in the Garden Court in Clements Inn and also the Cellar thereto belonging now in the possession of the said John Dewes for his own Life And an Assignment for one Life after the Expiracion of his own Life And having paid to the Principall for the Use of this Society Eighty pounds [ordered that John Dewes have a lease and assignment accordingly with the usual covenants &c. and in the usual form &c. (as in the preceding entry)]

Mr Geo: Petre for the Lease of his Chamber N.º 22—Mr George Petre one of the Companions of this Society desiring to purchase a Lease of the Chamber up two pairs in the Building formerly built by William Wheatley and leased to Mr John Bowler In the Garden Court in Clements Inn & the Cellar thereto belonging now in the possession of the said George Petre for his own Life And an Assignment for one Life after the Expiracion of his own Life And having paid to the Principall for the Use of this Society Eighty pounds [ordered that George Petre have a lease and assignment accordingly with the usual covenants and in the usual form (as in the two preceding entries)]

Mr Till Adam Bond D.ᵈ up—Mr John Till Adam one of the Companions of this Society being dead And his representative Mr Thomas Till Adam praying to have his Bond delivered up Itt is Ordered that the same be delivered up to be Cancelled upon his paying one Guinea for the Arrears due from the said John Till Adam to the Society

Clements Inn in the ⎱ At a pencion there held on Monday the twenty
County of Middlesex ⎰ ninth day of June 1730 present Mr Penny Pr., Mr
Dovey, Mr Fowler, Mr Halsted, Mr Hardwick
Mr Aldey & Mr Benett.

The old Garden Railes to be taken down and Iron Railes to be erected—
The Garden Railes being ruinous and decayed so as not to be worth

repairing Itt is ordered that itt be left to the Principall to cause the same to be taken down and in the Room thereof to erect Iron Railes in such Manner as he shall think fitt.

> John Penny Pr.
> John Dovey
> Wm Fowler
> Edwd Halsted
> Ro. Aldey
> Edw: Benet.
> James Hardwicke

Clements Inn in the ⎱ Att a Pention there held on Friday the 20th Day of
County of Middlesex ⎰ November 1730 present Mr Penny Pr., Mr Fowler, Mr Halsted, Mr Aldey, Mr Benett, Mr Dovey

Hall to be Insured—Whereas the policy for Insuring the Hall belonging to Clements Inn from Fire in the Hand in Hand Fire Office is near expired [1] Itt is Ordered that the same be forthwith renewed for 7 Yeares att the Charge of the said Society in the name of Mr John Penny the present Principall

Mr Madgewick's Bond to be d.^d up—Mr Thos Madgewick being an Housekeeper in Town and desiring to have his Admittance Bond delivered up Itt is Ordered that upon his paying all his Arrears and discharging the Servants' rolls his Bond be delivered up to him to be Cancelled

Mr Nicoll's Bond to be d.^d up—Mr Joseph Nicoll being admitted a Member of the Society of Grays Inn desiring to have his Admittance bond delivered up Itt is Ordered that upon his paying all his Arrears due to this Society and discharging the Servants Rolls His said Bond be delivered up to him to be cancelled

Mr Noah Curtis's absent Commons Compounded—Mr Noah Curtis [in arrear 4s. for pensions and £1. 5s. for absent Commons including this present Michaelmas term, desires abatement (out of town one of the terms charged): abated 2s. 6d.: to pay £1. 2s. 6d. in full discharge of the commons] he also paying the Servants Rolls.

Mr Sheppard's bond ordered to be d.^d up—Mr Richard Sheppard being dead and Mr Wakelyn having applyed on the Behalf of his Representative to have his Admittance Bond delivered up Itt is Ordered that on payment of the said Mr Sheppard's Arrears due to this Society his bond be delivered up to be Cancelled

---

[1] See pp. 29, 109 above.

Clements Inn in the ⎱ Att a Pention there held on Friday the fourth Day
County of Middlesex ⎰ of December 1730 present Mr Penny Pr., Mr
Dovey, Mr Fowler, Mr Halsted, Mr Noyes, Mr
Eldridge, and Mr Benett.

Mr Rob.! Paltock [1] *for the Chambers late Mr Hugh Sheldon's*—Whereas Mr Hugh Sheldon one of the Companions of this Society holds by Articles All that Chamber with the Appurtenances up two pair of Staires in the building marked with the Figure or Number (8) in the first Court of this Inn and also the Garrett being three pair of Staires in the same building & directly over the said Chamber (which Chamber and Garrett are on the Left hand side of the said Building) For the Term of 99 Yeares determinable on the Death of the said Hugh Sheldon, And he having Contracted with Mr Robert Paltock one of the Companions of this Society for the Purchase of the said Chamber & Garrett and having Surrendred the said Articles and all the Term and Interest thereby granted into the Hands of the now Principall & Antients of the said Society To the Intent that a new Lease be made thereof unto the said Rob.! Paltock And the said Robert Paltock desiring to be admitted to the same and to have a new Lease thereof Itt is Ordered that on payment of the Summe of twelve pounds to the Principall for the Use of this Society A new Lease be granted of the said Chamber & Garrett unto the said Robert Paltock for 99 Yeares Determinable on his Death according to the usuall Method & Form of granting Leases by this Society.

Mr Sheldon's absent Commons Compounded—Mr Hugh Sheldon [in arrear £1. 6s. for pensions and £3. 15s. for absent commons to the end of last Michaelmas term, desires abatement (not in town 12 of the terms charged): abated 30s. for those terms: to pay £2. 5s. in full discharge of the commons] he paying also The Servants Rolls

Mr Bond's absent Commons Compounded—Mr George Bond [in arrear 20s., desires abatement (not in town any of the terms charged): abated 10s.: to pay 10s. and the servants' rolls]

Mr Gregory's absent Commons Compounded—Mr Henry Gregory [in arrear 25s., desires abatement (out of town one of the terms charged): abated 2s. 6d.: to pay 22s. 6d. and the servants' rolls]

Mr Nathaniel Trayton for an Assignment of his Chambers N.º 20— Whereas Mr Nathaniel Trayton one of the Companions of this Society the 29th Day of March 1728 had a Lease of a Chamber with the Appurtenances up one pair of Stairs in the Brick Building numbred (20) in the Court formerly called the third Court now the Middle Court in Clements Inn late Mr John Knights together with the Cellar belonging to & enjoyed with the said Chamber granted unto him by the Society for the Term of 99

---

[1] See pp. lviii above and 273 below.

Years (If Sarah Knight should so long live) And the said Nathaniel Trayton now desiring to purchase an Assignment of the said Chamber & Cellar granted to him by the said Lease for one Life after the expiration of the Life of the said Sarah Knight now in being & having now paid to the principal for the Use of this Society the Summe of £80 Itt is ordered in consideration thereof that an Assignment be made to him the said Nathaniel Trayton his Executors Administrators and Assignes for one Life after the Life of the said Sarah Knight now in being of the said Chamber & Cellar already granted to him the said Nathaniel Trayton by the said Lease with the Usuall Covenants & provisoes & according to the Usuall Form and Method of making and Granting Assignments by this Society

Assignments to be granted of the new Building in the Middle Court Nº 12 only.—WHEREAS by an Order of Pention made the Twenty second day of May 1729 Itt was ordered that (notwithstanding the order made the 28th day of February 1717 against assignments) the Principall & Antients from & after the first day of Trinity Term then next untill the 25th of December 1730 & no longer might Grant Assignments of any Chamber or Chambers after one life (as they formerly had used to do) [1] AND WHEREAS a new Stair Case or Building hath been lately new erected and built in the Room of the old Stair Case or Building Nº 18 in the Middle Court of this Inn ITT IS ORDERED that (notwithstanding the said Order of the 28th of February 1717 & the said Order of the 22nd of May 1729 or either of them) The Principall & Antients from & after the 25th of December 1730 untill the Twenty fourth Day of June 1731 & no longer may Grant Assignments of any Chamber or Chambers in the said new Stair Case or Building & no other (after one Life) as they formerly Used to do (before the said Order of the said 28th of February 1717 was made) at the Usuall rates of four years purchase for an Assignment alone and ten years for a Life & an Assignment when taken together

All Intᵗ. to be paid to Chr. next—Ordered that the Principall do pay all such Interest as is due from this Society att Christmas next and out of the Money arising by Sale of the new Buildings in the Middle Court (after he has paid himself what he has expended on Account of the Society) that he pay off so much of the Principall & Interest then remaining as he shall think fitt

Clements Inn   10th February 1730

This Day Philip Ward Esqᵉ [2] came and bringing a Case relating to Tithes He read upon the same in the presence of Mr Thomas

---

[1] See pp. 57, 144 above.

[2] Ward, proposed for reader to Clement's Inn in May 1730 and discharged from that duty a year later, was invited to the Bench of the Inner Temple in February 1742/3: see *I.T.R.*, IV, 221, 241, 456.

Vaughan And Mr Gerard Dutton two Students of the Inner Temple [1] and the Gentlemen of Clements Inn.

John Penny. Pr.

Clements Inn in the ⎱ Att a pention there held on Friday the twelfth Day
County of Middlesex ⎰ of February 1730 present Mr Penny Pr. Mr Fowler
Mr Noyes Mr Eldridge Mr Aldey and Mr Bennett

Mr Rich.ᵈ Cave for a Chamber & Cellars late Mr Edw.ᵈ Halsted's N.º 9—Whereas Edward Halsted Gent late one of the Antients of this Society held by Articles All that Chamber up one pair of Staires in the first Court in the new Building adjoyning to the Hall in this Inn with the Cellar where the Chimney is (called the Kitchen Cellar) and the back Cellar adjoyning to itt in the same Building with the Appurtenances sometime since in the possession of him the said Edward Halsted for 99 Yeares determinable upon his Death with a power to nominate another Companion of this Society to be admitted to the same for the like Term of 99 Yeares determinable with the Life of such Person And the said Mr Edward Halsted having made his last Will & Testament in Writing And appointed Frances Cave Wife of Richard Cave his sole Executrix thereof And the said Richard Cave and Frances his Wife have Surrendred the said Articles granted by the Principall & Antients to the said Edward Halsted of the said Chamber & Cellar & all the Estate & Interest thereby granted To the Intent that the said Richard Cave (who is admitted & become a Companion of this Society) may be admitted to the said Chamber & Cellar And the said Richard Cave desiring to be admitted thereto Itt is Ordered that In Performance of the said Articles A New Lease of the said Chamber & Cellars be made and granted to the said Richard Cave for 99 Yeares (If the said Richard Cave shall so long live) with the usuall Covenants & provisoes and according to the usuall Method and Form of granting Leases by this Society.

Mr Rich.ᵈ Cave for the Chamber 2 pair of Stairs N.º 7 fronting the Gate & Garretts & Cellars—Whereas Edward Halsted Gent late one of the Antients of this Society held by Articles All those Chambers up two pair of Staires in the new Building att the Upper End of the first Court fronting the Gateway of Clements Inn aforesaid South and the Talbot Yard North marked with the Figure or Number (7) together with the Garretts over the said Chambers and the Cellars under the Ground Chambers in the said Building for 99 Yeares determinable upon his Death with a power to nominate another Companion of this Society [to be admitted thereto for a like term of 99 years determinable with such persons's life, and Halsted

---

[1] Vaughan, called to the Bar at the Inner Temple in 1732, was proposed for reader to Clement's Inn in 1748: see *I.T.R.*, IV, 260, 531.

H

by his will appointed Frances Cave his executrix, and Richard and Frances Cave have surrendered the articles (as in the preceding entry)] To the Intent that the said Richard Cave may be admitted to the said Chambers Garretts & Cellars for the life of John Bearblock Jun.ʳ of West Smithfield in the Parish of St. Bartholomew the less Woollendraper [and Richard Cave desiring to be so admitted—ordered that a lease be granted to Richard Cave accordingly for 99 years if Bearblock shall so long live, with the usual covenants &c. and in the usual form &c.]

Mr Rich.ᵈ Cave for the Chamber one pair of Staires N.º 7 fronting the Gate & a Cellar—Whereas Edward Halsted Gent late one of the Antients of this Society held by Articles All those Chambers up one pair of Stairs in the new Building at the upper end of the first Court fronting the Gateway of Clements Inn aforesaid South and the Talbot Yard North marked with the figure or Number (7) together with the Cellar or Vault at the bottom of the Stairs in the same Stair Case extending itself under the pavement of the said first Court leading to the Stair Case of the said Building for 99 years determinable upon his Death with a power to nominate another Companion of this Society [to be admitted thereto for a like term of 99 years determinable with such person's life, and Halsted by his will appointed Frances Cave his executrix, and Richard and Frances Cave have surrendered the articles (as in the two preceding entries)] To the Intent that the said Richard Cave may be admitted to the said Chambers and Cellar or Vault for the life of Darby Rhodes of West Smithfield in the Parish of St. Sepulchre London Whipmaker [and Richard Cave desiring to be so admitted—ordered that a lease be granted to Richard Cave accordingly for 99 years if Rhodes shall so long live, with the usual covenants &c. and in the usual form &c.]

Auditors of the Principalls Accounts—Ordered that Mr John Dovey and Mr Jno. Blackwell two of the Antients of this Society and Mr W.ᵐ Purcell & Mr Nath. Trayton two of the Companions of this Society Shall & do examine and Audit the Accounts of Mr John Penny the present Principall of this Society for one whole year beginning in Hillary Term 1729 until Hillary Term 1730 and that the said Mr Dovey Mr Blackwell Mr Purcell and Mr Trayton or any three of them shall and so make their Certificate & Report thereof as soon as conveniently can be done

Gorham the Bricklayer to be paid—Ordered that the Principall do pay to Tho.ˢ Gorham forty shillings for Bricklayer's Work done in the Year 1725 in Clements Inn

Mr Sandys's bond delivered up—Mr John Sandys one of the Companions of this House haveing left of Practise and retired into the Country and praying to have his Bond delivered up Itt is Ordered that upon paying his Arreares & discharging the Servants Rolls his Bond be delivered up

Clements Inn in the ⎫ Att a Pencion there held on Friday the nineteenth
County of Middlesex ⎬ day of February 1730 present Mr Penny Pr. Mr
  Dovey Mr Fowler Mr Aldey Mr Eldridge and
  Mr Benett

Mr Richard Cave for a Lease of the Grd. Chambers N°. 7 fronting the Gate—Whereas Edward Halsted Gentleman late one of the Antients of this Society held by Articles All those Ground Chambers in the new building at the upper End of the first Court in this Inn fronting the Gate South & the Talbot Yard North & marked with the Figure or N°. 7 together with the Cellar under & adjoyning to the Stair Case of the said Building for 99 Yeares determinable upon his Death with a power to nominate another Companion of this Society [to be admitted thereto for a like term of 99 years determinable with such person's life, and Halsted by his will appointed Frances Cave his executrix and Richard and Frances Cave have surrendered the articles (as in the other entries relating to Cave at the previous pension) to the intent that Richard Cave be admitted to the premises] for the life of John Walton of West Smithfield in the parish of St Bartholomew the less Linendraper [and Richard Cave desiring to be so admitted—ordered that a lease be granted him accordingly for 99 years if John Walton shall so long live, with the usual covenants &c. and in the usual form &c.]

Mr Richard Cave for a Lease of the ground rooms N°. 7 formerly the Dust hole—Whereas Edward Halsted Gent late one of the Antients of this Society held by Articles All those Ground Roomes att the Upper End of the first Court in Clements Inn aforesaid lying between the Building lately erected by Mr W^m. Seabrook towards the South And the Talbot Alehouse towards the North part thereof being formerly intended and sometimes used as a Dust hole with the Cellar under the same rooms the whole fronting Clements Lane East & the said first Court West together with the Appurtenances being on the East side of the Stair Case marked with the Figure or Number (7) in the first Court of Clements Inn aforesaid for 99 Yeares determinable upon his Death [with power to nominate (as in the preceding entry), and Halsted has appointed Frances Cave his executrix, and Richard and Frances Cave have surrendered the articles to the intent that Richard Cave be admitted to the premises] for the life of George Peach of West Smithfield in the parish of St Sepulchre London Whipmaker [and Cave desiring to be so admitted—ordered that a lease be granted him accordingly for 99 years if George Peach shall so long live, with the usual covenants &c., and in the usual form &c.]

Mr Richard Cave for a Lease of the Chambers 1 & 2 pair of Staires N°. 7 & the Garretts over them—Whereas Edward Halsted Gentleman late one of the Antients of this Society held by Articles All those Severall Chambers up one & two pair of Stairs and the Garretts over them at the Upper End of the first Court on the left hand in the Stair Case marked with the Figure or Number (7) abutting on St. Clements Lane East and adjoyning to Mr Seabrooke's Building towards the South & to the Talbot Alehouse towards the North and fronting the said first Court West together with the Vault lying under part of the Ground Rooms of the Same Building next to the Talbot Alehouse aforesaid and the little Cellar on the right hand within the said Vault and adjoyning to the pavement leading to the said Stair Case out of which little Cellar there is a Window into the first Court And also the two little Clossetts Cupboards or Holes one being on the Top of the Cellar Stairs on the right hand going down and the other on the first landing place going up one pair of Stairs on the left hand in the said Stair Case for 99 years determinable upon his Death [with power to nominate (as in the previous entries relating to Cave), and Halsted has appointed Frances Cave his executrix, and Richard and Frances Cave have surrendered the articles to the intent that Richard Cave be admitted to the premises] for the Life of George Foster of Snow Hill in the parish of St. Sepulchre London Soapboiler [and Cave desiring to be so admitted—ordered that a lease be granted him accordingly for 99 years if George Foster shall so long live, with the usual covenants &c., and in the usual form &c.]

Mr W^m. Hardwick's bond d^d up—Mr William Hardwick being no Practiser and desiring to have his Bond delivered up Itt is Ordered that on paying his Arreares & all Dutyes of the House untill the End of next Easter Term and discharging the Servants Rolls his Bond be delivered up to be cancelled

Mr Henry Dottin's absent Commons Compounded—Mr Henry Dottin [in arrear 14s. for pensions and 45s. for absent commons to the end of last Hillary Term, desires abatement (out of town 2 of the terms charged): abated 5s. for those terms: to pay £2 in full discharge of the commons] he paying the Servants Rolls

Clements Inn in the ⎱ Att a Pencion there held on Friday the twenty
County of Middlesex ⎰ sixth day of February 1730 present Mr Penny Pr.
                     Mr Dovey Mr Fowler Mr Aldey Mr Blackwell
                     and Mr Benett.

Mr Hen: Masterman for the Chamber 2 pair of Staires N° 8 late Mr Innys's Chamber—Whereas Andrew Innys Gent late one of the Companions of this Society held by Articles All that Chamber with the Appurtenances in the Brick Building in the Corner of the Middle Court (now the first Court) of the said House up two pair of Stairs then marked with the Figures or Number (12) & now marked with the Figure or Number (8) now in the possession of Wᵐ Morphy Gent for 99 Yeares determinable upon the Death of Martin Innys one other of the Companions of this Society And the said Andrew Innys being dead having first made his last Will & Testament in Writing & appointed the said Martin Innys sole Executor thereof And the said Martin Innys having Surrendred the said Articles and all the Estate & Interest thereby granted To the Intent that the said Wᵐ Morphy or such other person as the said Wᵐ Morphy should nominate & appoint might be admitted to the same Chamber with the Appurtenances And the said Wᵐ Morphy having nominated & appointed Henry Masterman Gent one other of the Companions of this Society to be admitted thereto And the said Henry Masterman desiring to be admitted thereto Itt is Ordered that on payment of the Summe of Eight pounds unto the Principall for the Use of this Society A new Lease be granted of the said Chamber with the Appurtenances unto the said Henry Masterman for 99 Years determinable on his Death according to the usuall Method & form of granting Leases by this Society.

Principall's audited Accounts confirmed—Whereas Mr John Dovey & Mr Jno. Blackwell two of the Antients of this Society and Mr William Purcell and Mr Nathaniel Trayton two of the Companions of the said Society By Vertue of an Order of Pention made the twelfth day of February 1730 were appointed Auditors of the Accounts of Mr John Penny now principall of this Society And having accordingly audited stated and examined the said Mr Penny's Accounts of Receipts and Disbursements for one whole Year beginning in Hillary Term 1729 and ending the beginning of Hillary Term 1730 have found the Summe Totall of the said Principall's Receipts for that Year to be Eleven hundred seventy four pounds four shillings one penny halfpenny and the totall of his Disbursements to be Sixteen hundred seventy nine pounds one shilling and eleven pence so that there remaines due on that Account to the said Principall from this Society the Summe of five hundred and four pounds seventeen shillings nine pence halfpenny As Appeares by their Report or Certificate thereof Dated the twenty fifth day of February instant Itt is therefore Ordered that the said Accounts so stated audited examined and certifyed as aforesaid be allowed and approved And the same are hereby allowed and approved of to be Just & true And the said Mr Penny is hereby discharged of & from the said Accounts And itt is also ordered that he be paid the said Ballance of five hundred and four pounds seventeen shillings nine pence halfpenny out of such money as shall be received for the Use of this Society

> John Dovey
> W^m. Fowler
> Ro. Aldey
> Jno. Blackwell
> Edw: Benet.

Mr Morphy's Bond delivered up—Mr W^m. Morphy one of the Companions of this Society, being no practiser and desiring to have his Admittance Bond delivered up, Itt is Ordered that on payment of his Arrears due to this Society and discharging the Servants Rolls his Bond be delivered up to him to be Cancelled

Mr Stukeley's Composition for absent Commons—Mr Adlard Squire Stukeley one of the Companions of this Society [in arrear 15s. for absent commons, desires abatement (not in town any of the terms charged): abated 17s. 6d.: to pay 7s. 6d. and the servants' rolls]

Mr Philip Smith Composition for absent Commons—Mr Phillip Smith one of the Companions of this Society [in arrear 15s. for absent commons, desires abatement (out of town one of the terms charged): abated 2s. 6d.: to pay 12s. 6d. and the servants' rolls]

Mr Lancaster for the Chamber one pair of Stairs in the New building in Middle Court for a Life & an Assignment—Mr Matthew Lancaster one of the Companions of this Society desiring to purchase a Lease of the Chamber up one pair of Stairs in the new brick building in the Middle Court now not markt but intended to be markt with the number (12) together with the Garrett forwards over the said Chamber next the Hall and the Clossett next the Window in the Entry or passage up three pair of Stairs going into the said Garrett and also the Kitchen or Cellar with a Chimney in it forwards next the Court with the Vault under the Court before the said Kitchen and also the Clossett next the door in the Entry or passage below where the Kitchen is with the free Use (in common with other Tenants of the same Buildings) of the House of Office or necessary House and the passages or Entries leading to the Same and to the Kitchen Vault Garrett & Closetts aforesaid for his own Life & an Assignment for one Life after the expiration of his own Life And having paid to the principal for the Use of this Society Three hundred thirty Six pounds and agreed to lay out & expend the Summe of fourteen pounds within Six Months from the Date hereof in Chimney peices Locks Keys & other Things needfull & convenient for the Improvement of the said Chamber & premisses It is ordered in consideration thereof that a Lease be made to the said Matthew

Lancaster for his own Life & an Assignment for one Life after his own Life now in being of the said Chamber & premisses with the Usuall Covenants & provisoes & according to the usuall form & Method of making & granting Leases & Assignments by this Society And with a Covenant also on the part of the said Mr Lancaster to lay out & expend the said Summe of fourteen pounds in the Manner & within the time before mentioned

Mr Budgett for a Lease of the Chamber two pair of Staires in the same Building for a Life & an Assignment—Mr John Budgett one of the Companions of this Society desiring to purchase a Lease of the Chamber up two pair of stairs in the new brick Building in the Middle Court now not markt but intended to be markt with the number (12) together with the Garrett backwards over the said Chamber looking towards the Angell Inn & the Closett next to the Door in the Entry or passage up three pair of Stairs going into the said Garrett and also the Cellar forwards in the said Building without a Chimney lying next to the Building now numbred (19) but intended to be numbred (13) in the said Inn together with the Hole under the Stairs leading to the said Cellar with the free Use (in Common with the other Tenants of the Same Buildings) of the house of Office or necessary House and of the passages or Entrys leading to the Same and to the Garrett Closett & Cellar aforesaid for his own Life and an Assignment for one Life after the expiration of his own Life and having paid to the Principal for the Use of this Society Two hundred and forty pounds and agreed to lay out & expend the Summe of Ten pounds within Six months from the Date hereof in Chimney peices Locks Keys & other Things needful & convenient for the Improvement of the said Chamber and premisses Itt is ordered in consideration thereof [that a lease and assignment be made accordingly to John Budgett with the usual covenants &c. and in the usual form &c. (as in the preceding entry) and a covenant by Budgett to spend £10 as previously stated]

Mr Lethieullier for a Lease of the ground Chamber in the same Building for a Life & an Assignment—Mr Wm. Lethieullier one of the Companions of this Society desiring to purchase a Lease of the Chambers or Rooms on the Ground Floor in the new Brick building in the Middle Court in Clements Inn now not markt but intended to be markt with the Number (12) together with the Garrett forwards next to the Stair Case now numbered (19) but intended to be markt with the number (13) having a large Closett within the same and also the Kitchen or Cellar (with a chimney in it) backwards looking towards the Angell Inn & the Closett next the Window in the Entry or passage going into the said Kitchen with the double Vault under the Court in the Airy next the House of Office or necessary House with the free Use (in common with other Tenants of the same Building) of the House of Office or necessary house & of the passages or Entries leading to the same & to the Kitchen Vaults & Garrett aforesaid for his own Life & an Assignment for one Life after the Expiration of his own Life & having paid to the principall for the Use of this Society Two hundred and Eighty eight pounds [and agreed (as in the preceding entry) to spend £12 within 6 months on Chimney pieces, Locks, Keys &c.—ordered that a lease and assignment be made to him with the usual covenants &c. and in the usual form &c. and with a covenant by him to spend £12 in 6 months as previously stated]

Mr Mander for a Lease of the ground Chamber N°. 11 formerly N°. 17 for his Life—Mr Thomas Mander One of the Companions of this Society desiring to purchase a Lease of the Chamber or Ground Room in the Stair Case next adjoyning to the Hall in the Middle Court of Clements Inn now markt with the Number (17) but intended to be markt with the Number (11) together with the Yard or Backside lying on the South side of part of the said Chamber for his own Life And having paid to the Principal for the Use of this Society Seventy eight pounds Itt is ordered in consideration thereof that a Lease be accordingly made to him of the said Chamber and premises with the Appurtenances for Ninety nine Years if He shall so long live with the Usual Covenants and agreements and according to the Usual form and Method of making and granting Leases by this Society

New Numbring the Staircases—Whereas by the Alterations in the Buildings in Clements Inn there are now no Numbers on Chambers or Stair Cases between the Numbers 10 & 17 and from 17 the Stair Cases are numbred up to 24 tho' there are not above 18 in the whole Inn Itt is therefore ordered that the Stair Case now markt 17 be marked 11 The new Buildings in the Second Court be marked 12 the Building now marked 19 be marked 13 the Building now marked 20 be marked 14 the Buildings now marked 21 & 22 be marked 15 & 16 the Building now marked 23 be marked 17 And the Building now marked 24 be marked 18

Clem^{ts.} Inn—16 Nov: 1731.

This day Wm. Newlands Esq^{e.} [1] came from the Inner Temple to read on the Stat. 3 & 4 QA on promissory notes [2]

John Penny Pr.

---

[1] William Newland, eldest son of George Newland of London, scrivener, was admitted to the Inner Temple in March, 1702/3.
[2] 3 & 4 Ann., c. 8, repealed by the Bills of Exchange Act, 1882 (45 & 46 Vict. c. 61).

Clem^{ts} Inn
Thursday. 25. Nov. 1731.

Mich. Term 1731

Persons nominated by the antients (who are in Commons) for the choice of a new principall for three years from the first day of Hillary Term next ensueing.

Mr Penny the present principall   Mr Fowler   Mr Noyes

Wm Purcell
Nathaniel Trayton
John Dovey Junr.
I. Honnor
Da: Thomas
Henry Jones
Cha: Eyre
John Dewes.
Chas. Baldwyn
Geo. Petre.

Wee the antients under written confirm this choice.
John Dovey
Wm Noyes
Ambrose Eldridge
Ro. Aldey

Clements Inn in the } Att a pension there held on Friday the 11th day of
County of Middlesex } February 1731 present Mr Penny Princ. Mr Fowler
Mr Noyes Mr Eldridge Mr Aldey Mr Bennett.

Auditors of the principall's accts. for the year 1731—Ordered that Mr W^m. Fowler & Mr Ambrose Eldridge Two of the antients of this Society and Mr John Dovey & Mr Geo. Petre Two of the Companions of this Society shall & do examine & audite the accounts of Mr John Penny the present principall of this Society for one whole Year beginning Hill. 1730 untill Hillary Term 1731 and that the said Mr Fowler Mr Eldridge Mr Dovy & Mr Petre or any three of them shall & do make their certificate & report thereof as soon as conveniently can be done

Clements Inn in the } Att a pencion there held on Wednesday the 26th
County of Middlesex } of February 1731 present Mr Penny Pr. Mr Fowler
Mr Noyes Mr Eldridge Mr Aldey Mr Bennett

Principalls accts. confirmed—Whereas Mr W^m. Fowler Mr Ambrose Eldridge Mr John Dovey Junr. & Mr Geo: Petre by virtue of an order of pencion made the 11th day of this Instant February were appointed Auditors of the accounts of Mr John Penny now principall of this Society.

H*

and having accordingly audited stated & examined the said Mr Penny's accounts of Receipts and Disbursements for one whole year beginning Hillary Term 1730 and ending the beginning of Hillary Term 1731 have found the summe totall of the said principall's Receipts to bee Eleaven hundred ninety two pounds seventeen shillings eight pence and the totall of his disbursements to be one thousand ninety three pounds nineteen shillings fourpence halfpenny So that there remaines due on this account from the said principall unto the said Society ninety eight pounds eighteen shillings threepence halfpenny as appears by their report or certificate thereof dated this day It is therefore ordered that the said accounts so stated audited examined & certified as aforesaid bee allowed & approved and the same are hereby allowed & approved to be Just & true and the said John Penny is hereby discharged from the said Summe of one thousand ninety five pounds nine shillings and fourpence halfpenny so by him discharged as aforesaid

Wm Fowler
Wm Noyes
Ambrose Eldridge
Ro. Aldey
Edw. Benet

Mr Edm.^d Webbs Composition[1]—Mr Edmund Webb one of the Companions of this Society being in Arrear twelve Shillings for Pencions and two pounds for Absent Commons to the End of Hillary Term last and desireing an Abatement of the said Absent Commons In Regard he was not in Town one of the Termes charged to his Account It is therefore Ordered that he be abated two Shillings and Six pence And that on payment of two pounds and nine Shillings and Sixpence the Same being in full Discharge of the said Absent Commons he paying the Servants Rolls.

Mr Edward Cosyns Composicion—Mr Edward Cosyns one of the Companions of this Society being in Arrear for Pencions & Absent Commons to the End of Hillary Term last and desireing an Abatement for the same being out of Town part of the said time It is ordered that he be abated five Shillings and that on payment of fifteen Shillings the same be in full discharge of the said Pencions or absent Commons he paying the Servants Rolls.

Mr Carr Brackenburys Composicion—Mr Carr Brackenbury one of the Companions of this Society being in Arrear for Pencions or Absent Commons to the End of Hillary Term last and desireing an Abatement

---

[1] At this point the record of arrears &c. is less careful and exact: Edmund Webb's entry, for example, is duplicated on the next page. Cf. p. 176 below (R. Peart).

for the same being out of Town part of the said time It is ordered that he be abated tenn Shillings and that on payment of one pound and nine shillings the same be in full discharge of the said Pencions or absent Commons he paying the Servants Rolls.

Mr James Bridge's Composicion—Mr James Bridges one of the Companions of this Society being in arrear for pencions or absent Commons to the End of Hillary Term last and desireing an Abatement for the same being out of Town part of the said Time It is ordered that he be abated One pound Seventeen Shillings and Six pence and that on payment of three pounds thirteen Shillings and Six pence the same be in full discharge of the said Pencions or absent Commons he paying the Servants Rolls.

Mr Henry Gregory's Composicion—Mr Henry Gregory one of the Companions of this Society being in Arrear for Pencions or absent Commons to the End of Hillary Term last [desires abatement (not in town part of the time): ordered that he be abated 2s. 6d.] and that on payment of one pound tenn Shillings and Six pence the same be in full discharge of the said Pencions or absent Commons he paying the Servants Rolls.

Joseph Haines Composition—Mr Joseph Haines one of the Companions of this Society being in arrear for Pencions or Absent Commons to the End of Hillary Term last and desireing an abatement for the same being out of town It is Ordered that he be abated three pound five shilling and that on payment of five pounds seventeen shillings the same be in full Discharge of the said Pencions or absent Commons he paying the Servants Rolls.

Mr Baptist Trott's Composicion—Mr Baptist Trott one of the Companions of this Society [in arrear for pensions or absent commons to the end of Hilary term last, desires abatement (out of town for part of the time): abated 12s. 6d.: to pay £1. 13s. 6d.] in full discharge of the said Pencions or absent commons he paying the Servants Rolls.[1]

Edmund Webb's Composition[2]—Mr Edmund Webb one of the Companions of this Society being in arrear for Pencions or Absent Commons to the End of Hillary Term last and desireing Abatement for the same being out of Town part of the said time It is Ordered that he be abated two Shillings and Six pence and on payment of two pounds nine Shillings and Six pence the same be in full Discharge of the said Pencions or absent Commons he paying the Servants Rolls.

---

[1] For Trott's death see next page (entry as to John Smith).

[2] A duplicate *per incuriam* of the entry on the previous page.

Francis Jackson's Composition—Mr Francis Jackson one of the Companions of this Society being in arrear for Pencions or Absent Commons to the end of Hillary Term last [desires abatement (out of town part of the time): abated 10s.: to pay £2. 9s. in full discharge of the pensions or absent commons] he paying the Servants Rolls.

Joseph Hunt's Composition—Mr Joseph Hunt one of the Companions of this Society being in arrear for Pencions or absent Commons to the end of Hillary Term last [desires abatement (out of town part of the time): abated 17s. 6d.: to pay £2. 19s. 6d. in full discharge of the pensions or absent commons] he paying the Servants Rolls.

Mr Harry Butler Pacey's bond delivered up—Mr Harry Butler Pacey haveing paid all his Arrears and haveing left the Inn and become a housekeeper and desireing to have his bond given to this Society on his Admittance delivered up Itt is Ordered that his said Bond be delivered up to be Cancelled.

Mr John Smith for a Chamber late Mr Haines—Whereas Joseph Haynes one of the Companions of this Society holds by Articles All that Chamber up two pair of Stairs in the first Court in the new Building adjoining to the Hall in Clements Inn now marked with the figure or number (9) together with the back cellar in the same building fronting the passage next to the said Hall northward with the Appurtenances for the term of 99 years determinable upon the death of Baptist Trott the said Joseph Haines & Richard Sheppard of whom the said Baptist Trott and Richard Sheppard are already dead and the said Joseph Haines having contracted with John Smith who is admitted a Companion of this Society for the purchase of the said Chamber and having Surrendred the said articles and all the term & interest thereby granted into the hands of the now principall & Antients of the said Society To the intent that a new lease be made thereof unto the said John Smith and the said John Smith desiring to be admitted to the same and have a new lease thereof It is ordered that as payment of the summe of eighteen pounds to the principall for the use of this Society a new lease be granted of the said Chamber to the said John Smith for 99 years determinable on his death according to the usuall method & form of granting Leases by this Society.

Mr St. Brampston Composition—Mr Stephen Brampston one of the Companions of this Society being in arrears for pencions & abs: Commons to the end of Hill. term last & desiring an abatement for the time he was out of town It is ordered that he be abated twelve shillings & Six pence.

Mr Gofton Steward—Mr Smith the Steward having resigned It is ordered that Mr Gofton be steward during the pleasure of the principall & antients on giving Security as Mr Smith did. but not to begin till he has paid his arrears.

Clements Inn   24. Nov: 1732.

This day Joseph Ward Esq[e] [1] came in the Room of Stephen Holmes Esq[e] [2] from the Inner Temple with a case to read on

John Penny Pr.

Clements Inn in the ⎞ Att a pencion there holden on Fryday the 24th day
County of Middlesex ⎠ of November 1732 present Mr Penny Pr. Mr Fowler
Mr Noyes Mr Eldridge Mr Aldey Mr Bennett

Mr Obrians Chamber padlockt—Mr W[m] Obrian having been for a long time in Mr W[m] Powletts Chambers being a ground floor N[o] 3 in Clements Inn without being admitted a member of the Society (tho' often called upon) It is ordered that a padlock be put upon his Chamber door for his contempt unless he procures himself to be admitted a member of the said Society within a week after notice of this order.[3]

Mr Limbreys. D[o]—The like order for Mr Charles Limbrey in Mr Tho[s]. Powletts chambers up 3 pr of stairs N[o] 14.[4]

Mr Peltiers bond up—Mr Philip Elias Peltier being no practiser & having paid all arrears desiring to have his bond up It is ordered the same be delivered up accordingly.

Mr Stubbs Composition—Mr Walter Stubbs being in arrear £4. 10s. for pencions & absent Commons due to this Society at the end of Michaelmas Term last and desiring an abatement of his Commons in regard he was not in Town Seven of the Terms charged to his account It is ordered that he be abated 17. 6 for those terms and that on payment of 3. 12. 6 the same be in full discharge he paying the porters rolls

Mr R. Keeling—Mr Richard Keeling being in arrear 4. 10. for pensions & absent Commons due to the Society at the end of Michaelmas term last and desiring an abatement of his Commons in regard he was not in Town 14 of the said terms charged to his account It is ordered that he be abated 1. 15. for those terms and that on payment of 2. 15. the same be in full discharge he paying the porters rolls.

Clements Inn in the ⎞ Att a pencion there held on Fryday the 8th day of
County of Middlesex ⎠ February 1732 present Mr Penny Pr. Mr Fowler
Mr Noyes Mr Eldridge Mr Aldey.

Auditors of the principals accounts—Ordered that Mr Noyes & Mr Roger Aldey two of the antients of this Society and Mr Brightwell Smith and Mr Nash Mason two of the Companions of this Society shall & do

---

[1] Ward had attended a Clement's Inn reading as a student in 1730: see p. 155 above.

[2] Stephen Holme or Holmes paid all his duties at the Inner Temple and had his bond delivered up in June 1733: *I.T.R.*, IV, 276.

[3] There is no record of his admission.

[4] Limbrey was admitted in 1733: see p. 275 below.

examine & audit the accounts of Mr John Penny the present principall of this Society for one whole year beginning in Hillary Term 1731 untill Hillary Term 1732 and that the said Mr Noyes Mr Aldey Mr Smith & Mason or any three of them shall & do make their certificate & report thereof as soon as conveniently can be done

Mr Doyleys bond up—Mr Shirley Doyley desiring to have his bond up being going beyond Sea and leaving off practice It is ordered that on paying his arrears & Servants Rolls his bond be delivered up.

Mr Pearts admᵗ. to have further time to name a life—Whereas Mr Robᵗ Peart (late a Companion of this Society) was possessed of a Chamber up one pair of stairs Nᵒ 18 (formerly 24) for 99 years if he so long lived with power for his Executors or administrators to nominate another life within two Terms after his death and whereas the time for nomination is near out but by reason of disputes at law about administracion no one can as yet take out letters of administracion and Mr Humberston appearing on the behalf of Mr Peart's Son desiring longer time to name a life It is ordered that if any administrator to Mr Peart shall come before Midsummer next & name a new life a new lease as usuall be made to such nominee on paying as well the arrears due in Mr Pearts life as all such pencions & commons for the severall terms since his death to the time of such new lease

Mr Jos. Brian for the chamber late Mr John Harris—Whereas John Harris of Eydon in the County of Northampton Gent late one of the Companions of this Society held by articles all that chamber up 2 pair of stairs in the brick building in the South East part of the Garden in Clements Inn & one garret over the said Chamber with two small roomes or studies & a Turrett over the stairs leading to the said chambers with all other appurtenances to the said Chamber belonging and also one part of the Cellar under the said Chambers formerly in the possession of Wᵐ Walker and the use of the passage to the said Cellar & other the Cellars in Common with those who had Chambers & Cellars in the said building for 99 years determinable upon the death of the said John Harris with a power for his executors or administrators to nominate another Companion of the said Society to be admitted to the same for the like term of 99 years determinable with the life of such person and whereas the said John Harris made his will in writing & appointed Ann Stevens wife of Matthew Stevens executrix who having proved the said will hath with her husband delivered up the said articles granted to the said John Harris To the intent that Joseph Brian of London gen. may be admitted to the said Chambers & premisses with the appurtenances for 99 years if he the said Joseph Brian should so long live and the said Joseph Brian being admitted a Companion of the said Society & desiring to be admitted to the said Chambers

It is ordered that in performance of the said articles a new lease be made of the said Chambers garret Cellars & appurtenances to the said Jos. Brian for 99 years if he shall so long live [with the usual covenants, &c. and in the usual form &c.]

Mr John Mason composition—Mr John Mason being in arrear 1. 6. & desiring an abatement of commons for two terms he was absent It is ordered he be allowed 5s. out of the said 1. 6.

Clements Inn in the ⎱ Att a pencion there holden on Monday the
County of Middlesex ⎰ Seaventh day of May 1733 present Mr Penny Pr.
                Mr Fowler Mr Noyes Mr Eldridge Mr Aldey Mr
                Bennet

Principalls accts. confirmed—Whereas Mr Noyes Mr Roger Aldey Mr Brightwell Smith & Mr Nash Mason by virtue of an order of pencion made the 8th day of February last were appointed auditors of the accounts of Mr John Penny now principall of this Society and having accordingly audited stated & examined the said Mr Penny's accounts of receipts & disbursements for one whole year from the beginning of Hillary Term 1731 to the beginning of Hillary Term 1732 have found the Summe Totall of the said principalls receipts to be Three hundred seventy Six pounds seven shillings ten pence halfpenny and the Totall of his disbursements to be three hundred forty eight pounds seventeen shillings Eightpence halfpenny So that there remains due on this account from the said principall unto the said Society Twenty Seven pounds ten shillings two pence as appears by their report or certificate thereof dated the 13th day of February 1732 It is therefore ordered that the said accounts so stated audited examined & certified as aforesaid be allowed & approved and the Same are hereby allowed & approved to be just & true and the said John Penny is hereby discharged from the said Summe of three hundred forty eight pounds Seventeen Shillings eight pence halfpenny so by him disbursed as aforesaid

                Wm Fowler
                W. Noyes
                Ambrose Eldridge
                Ro. Aldey
                Edw. Benet

Clements Inn in the ⎱ Att a pencion there holden on Wednesday the 28th
County of Middlesex ⎰ day of June 1733 present Mr Penny Pr. Mr Fowler
                Mr Eldridge Mr Hardwick Mr Aldey Mr Bennett

Mr Wm Gofton chosen Steward in the room of Mr Smith—Mr Wm Gofton one of the Companions of this Society having made his application

& desiring to be admitted into the office or place of steward or clerk of this Society in the room or place of Mr Smith who has resigned and having paid his arrears & given Security It is ordered that the said Mr Gofton be admitted into the said office But to continue therein only during the pleasure of the principall & antients & their Successors & no longer

Mr Joshua Peart for his father's Ch: N?. 18—WHEREAS Robert Peart (late one of the Companions of this Society) held by Articles All that double Chamber with the Appurtenances up one pair of Stairs in the Second Staircase in Mr Kellet's Buildings then marked with the Figures or Number (24) and since Number (18) at the upper end of the Garden in Clements Inn aforesaid formerly in the possession of Samuel Aldridge & since of Thomas Smith for Ninety nine Years determinable upon the Death of the said Robert Peart with a Power for his Executors or Administrators to nominate another Companion of the said Society to be admitted to the same for the like Term of Ninety nine Years determinable upon the Life of such Nominee AND WHEREAS the said Robert is deceased Intestate and Administration is granted to John Peart Brother of the said Robert Peart who has surrenderd up the said Articles granted to the said Robert Peart To the Intent that Joshua Peart Son of the said Robert Peart and one of the Companions of the said Society should be admitted to the said Chambers IT IS ORDERED that in Performance of the said Articles [and in consideration of the surrender a new lease be made of the chambers to Joshua Peart for 99 years if he shall so long live with the usual covenants &c. and according to the usual form &c.] But in regard the said Joshua Peart is under the Age of one & twenty years It is Ordered that the said John Peart shall Covenant for the said Joshua Peart.

Mr Stukely's Composition—Mr Stukely being in arrear for absent Commons one pound fifteen shillings [desires abatement (out of town 4 terms): abated 10s.: for those terms: to pay £1. 5s. in discharge]

Mr R. Peart's Composition & bond up—Mr Rob! Peart being in arrear for pencions Commons &c. and his Executors desiring an abatement for 13 terms being out of town It is ordered that he be abated one pound twelve Shillings & Six pence & that on payment of six pounds five shillings & six pence & Servants Rolls his bond be delivered up

Mr Elisha's Composition—Mr Samuell Elisha being in arrears for pencions & commons five pounds four shillings [desires abatement (not in town any of the terms): abated £2: to pay £3. 4s. in discharge of the pensions and commons] paying The Servants rolls

Mr R. Peart's Composition [1]—Mr Rob! Peart being in arrear for pencions & commons six pounds seventeen shillings & desiring an abatement in regard he was not in town 13 Terms It is ordered he be abated

---

[1] In part a duplicate of the penultimate entry.

one pound twelve shillings Six pence & that on payment of five pounds four Shillings & Six pence he be discharged of the said pencions & commons paying the servants rolls

Clements Inn in the } Att a pencion there held on Fryday the 15th day of
County of Middlesex } February 1733 present Mr Penny pr. Mr Fowler
Mr Noyes Mr Eldridge Mr Aldey Mr Bennett.

Mr Roger Aldey for a Chamber late Mr Manbys—Whereas Edward Manby Gent one of the Companions of this Society holds by articles All that double Ground Chamber with the appurtenances scituate lying and being in the Garden Court in the first staircase formerly marked with the figures or numbers (23) but now (17) in Mr Kelletts building at the upper end of the Garden in Clements Inn aforesaid heretofore in the tenure of Henry Watson Gent. deceased for the term of 99 years determinable upon the Death of the said Edward Manby and the said Edward Manby having contracted with Roger Aldey Gent. one of the Antients of the said Society for the purchase of the said Chambers and having delivered up the said articles & the term & Interest therein unto the hands of the now principall & antients of the said Society to the intent that a new lease be granted to Roger Aldey for 99 years if Richard Aldey his son shall so long live [and Roger Aldey applying to be admitted and to have a new lease, a new lease to be granted to Roger Aldey accordingly, on payment of £10, in the usual form &c.]

Mr Manby's bond—Mr Edward one of the Companions of this house being no practicer & having sold his Chambers & paid his arrears It is ordered that his bond be delivered up.

Mr Gofton removed from being Steward—Mr Wm Gofton Steward of this Society having spent a considerable Summe of the house's Money as well as money received by him for the land tax It is ordered that he be removed from being Steward & that his bonds be sued against him & his Security for his arrears and to prevent the Society's being prosecuted for the King's tax It is ordered that the Principall be desired to lay down & pay the King's tax for the year 1732 & that the same be allowed him in his accounts.

Mr John Dewes for a Chamber late Mr Petre—WHEREAS George Petre Gent. one of the Companions of this Society held by articles all that chamber with the appurtenances up two pair of stairs in the building formerly built by Wm Wheatley and leased to Mr John Bowler scituate in the Garden Court in Clements Inn and also the Cellar to the said Chamber belonging and therewith usually held & enjoyed which said Chamber or Sellar now are or late were in the tenure of the said George

Petre for the term of 99 years determinable upon his death with a power of nominating another Member to be admitted thereunto for the like term and the said Geo: Petre having contracted with Mr John Dewes another Companion of the said Society for the purchase of the said Chambers [and having delivered up the articles to the intent that a new lease be made to John Dewes who desires to be admitted to the same for his own life with power to nominate for another life after his own,—ordered that on payment of £8 a new lease be granted accordingly to John Dewes, with power to nominate &c.] AND WHEREAS the Chamber which Mr Dewes already hath (being under Mr Petre's Chamber) is too little for his convenience alone as well as Mr Petre's Chamber he therefore proposes to lengthen both into one which will be some expence to him, in consideration whereof & for that Mr Dewes at first took his life & assignment at the request of the said principall & Antients in order to raise mony to supply their wants IT IS ORDERED that during such time as the said Mr Dewes occupies the said Chamber himself only he shall not be obliged to pay double Commons pencions & duties to the house according to an order of pencion made 18th day of February 1716 But in case he lets the same or takes in a Chamberfellow or assigns grants or devises the same to any other all such persons so claiming shall be liable to the said order of the 18 February 1716.[1]

Mr Petre's bond up—Mr Petre having parted with his chamber & paid his arrears & being an housekeeper in Town ordered his bond be given up.

Mr Drury's bond up—Mr Drury being very poor & his Security having paid all his arrears ordered his bond be delivered up.

Mr Henry Saxby's bond up—Mr Saxby having left the Society & paid his arrears and being no practicer It is ordered his bond be delivered up.

Mr P Smith Composition—Mr P Smith being in arrears three pounds eighteen shillings & desiring an abatement for four Terms that he was out of Town It is ordered that he be abated ten shillings

Mr Rich bond up—Mr Rich being poor and Mr Brownsword his Security having paid all his arrears It is ordered that Mr Rich's bond be delivered up to Mr Brownsword.

Mr Love bond up—Mr Andrew Love being in arrear Six pounds three Shillings and applying to have his bond up he being infirm & uncapable of following busyness It is ordered that on payment of his arrears & Servants rolls his bond be delivered up.

---

[1] The words from "But in case" to the end of the paragraph are underlined and against them in the margin the words "Repealed by an order of the 29 Novr 1734" are inserted. See p. 180 below for the repealing order which revoked the original order of February 18, 1716/17 (p. 31 above).

Mr White bond up—Mr White having paid all dues & being lame & infirm so as to be incapable to practice It is ordered that his bond be delivered up.

Mr John Vaux Composition—Mr John Vaux being in arrear Seven pounds Eighteen shillings and desiring an abatement for 20 terms he was out of Town It is ordered he be abated fifty Shillings.

Mr Josh: Peart Composition—Mr Josh: Peart being in arrear [23s. and desiring abatement for 3 terms, abated 7s. 6d.: to pay 15s. 6d.]

Mr Honnor—Mr Isaac Honnor being in arrears one pound three shillings and desiring upon payment thereof to have his bond up he being entred of the Temple & having left the Society It is ordered his bond be delivered up he paying his said arrears

> Clements Inn 20th Nov. 1734. This day Geo. Wheate Esq[1] came as Reader from the Inner Temple to Clements Inn bringing a Case upon the Statute of Distributions 22 & 23 Car. 2.[2]
>
> W[m] Fowler Deputy Pr.

Michaelmas Term 1734

Thursday 28. Nov: 1734.

Persons nominated by the antients (who are in Commons) for the choice of a new principall for three years from the first day of Hillary Term next ensueing

Mr Penny present principall	Mr Eldridge	Mr Aldey

W[m] Purcell
Tho. Hunt
Henry Jones
Nathaniel Trayton
John Dovey Jun[r]
John Dewes
Gilbert Burton
Chas. Baldwyn

We whose names are underwritten do confirm this choice wee being all the antients in Commons

Ambrose Eldridge
Roger Aldey
Edw[d] Benett

---

[1] George (afterwards Sir George) Wheate or Wheat was called to the Bar in 1715 and invited to the bench of the Inner Temple in 1744: *I.T.R.*, IV, 8, 478, 497: but see p. 492.

[2] 22 & 23 Car. II. c. 10, repealed by the Administration of Estates Act, 1925 (15 & 16 Geo. 5. c. 23).

Clements Inn in the ⎱ Att a pension there held on Fryday the 29th day of
County of Middlesex ⎰ November 1734 present Mr Penny princ. Mr Fowler
Mr Goodman Mr Eldridge Mr Aldey Mr Benet.

The order 18 Feb. 1716 for double duties set aside—Whereas the order
of pencion made 18 Feb. 1716 to oblige every Antient or Companion who
should take leases of more than one Sett of Chambers to enter into a
Covenant to pay separate Commons & duties [1] has never been regularly
put in practice and it has been found inconvenient & impracticable to
carry the same to Execution It is ordered that the said order be Set aside
& made void As also so much of the order of the 15th Feb. 1733 relating
to Mr Dewes lease which obliges his lessee assignee or Devisee to pay such
Double duties.

Antients to be chosen—The principall acquainting the pension that
there wanted a call of Antients, there scarce being enow to make up a
pencion to transact the affairs of the house, and having proposed Mr
Brackenbury Mr Hurst Mr Dewes Mr Wm Powlett & Mr Green as proper
persons to be chosen antients It is ordered that next Term the said five
Gentlemen be called up to the Antients table.

Mr John Dovey Junr life & ass. to all his father's Chambers—Mr John
Dovey Senr (one of the antients of this Society) being desirous to part with
his Severall Leases & assignments of his Severall Chambers garrets &
rooms up one pair three pair & four pair of Stairs up the staircase formerly
numbred 23 & now 17 in Mr Kellets buildings in Clements Inn gardens
unto his Son John Dovey Jun. (one of the Companions of the said Society)
and the said John Dovey Junr desiring his own life may be put in the place
of his fathers and that he may have a new lease & assignment made to
himself It is ordered that upon the surrendring up the old leases &
assignments & payment of £38 to the principall for the use of this Society
a new lease be granted thereof to the said John Dovy Jun. for 99 years
determinable on his death or putting extra with power for him his Executors
Administrators or Assigns to nominate another member to be admitted
thereto after his death for another term of 99 years determinable upon the
death of such nominee according to the custome & method of granting
leases & assignments of this Society.

Mr Stubbs composition—Mr Stubbs being in arrear 2. 12. for pencions
& absent commons due to this Society this Term and desiring an abatement of commons for four Terms absence It is ordered that he be abated
10s. for those Terms and that upon payment of two guineas he be discharged (paying the porters rolls).

Mr R. Keeling D^o.—Mr Richard Keeling being in arrears for pencions

---

[1] See p. 31 above.

& absent commons due this term to the Society and desiring an abatement of commons for five terms absence It is ordered that he be abated 12. 6 for those terms and that upon payment of 1. 19. 6 he be discharged (he paying the porters rolls)

Mr Hurst—Mr Hurst being in arrears [£4. 15s. for pensions and absent commons, desires abatement for 9 terms' absence: abated £1. 2s. 6d.: on paying £3. 12s. 6d. to be discharged] he paying the Servants rolls

Mr Gregory D?—Mr Gregory being in arrear [£3. 3s. for pensions and absent commons, desires abatement for 3 terms' absence: abated 7s. 6d.: on paying £2. 15s. 6d. to be discharged] he paying Servants rolls

Persons left out of the Roll being insolvent & not paying arrears—Whereas the severall persons following viz! Tho: Colly Leonard Cotton Morgan Gwyn Lewis Jones Tho: Hayley W™ Jackson Thos. Lyte Tho: Smyth James Scott Joseph Stratton Sam: Townrow Jos: Wakelyn Joseph Walker & John Mordant Wilkins are greatly in arrears to this Society and their Debts lookt upon as Desperate It is ordered that their names be struck out of the Rolls and they not to be cast into Commons any longer.

Mr John Wood bond up—Mr John Wood having left the Inn and practise as an attorney being gone to be clerk to a Councill & desiring to have up his bond It is ordered that on paying of his arrears & Servants rolls he may have up his bond.

Mr W™ Room bond up—Mr Room having left the Inn and being no lawyer nor practicer of it and desiring to have his bond up upon paying his arrears & Servants rolls It is ordered accordingly.

Mr Simon Stanton bond up—Mr Stanton being in arrears 8. 10. for pencions & Commons & his Security being obliged to pay It is ordered Mr Eyre the Security may have up his bond.

11 FEBR. 1734

Clements Inn—Antients called up & sworne—Whereas the principall having acquainted the antients in a pention held the 29th of November last that there wanted a new Call of Antients (there often not being enough in Town to make a pention to transact the affairs of the House) And having nominated Mr Carr Brackenbury Mr Thos. Hurst Mr John Dewes Mr W™ Powlet & Mr John Green (Companions of the said Society) as proper persons to be chosen It was ordered that the said Gentlemen should be called up this Term to be antients In pursuance of which nomination and order they were this day called up and after their taking the Oaths of Allegiance and Supremacy to His Majesty King George the Second in the publick hall before the principall & Antients in Commons the said Mr Brackenbury Mr Hurst Mr Dewes Mr Powlett & Mr Green were admitted Antients of the said Society of Clements Inn.

John Penny Pr.
Wm Fowler
Ro: Aldey

Mackay bond up—Ordered upon Mr Mackay paying his arrears he may have his bond up he being a housekeeper [1]

Clements Inn in the County of Middlesex } Att a pension there held on Fryday the 14th day of February 1734 present Mr Penny princ. Mr Fowler Mr Eldridge Mr Hardwick Mr Aldey Mr Brackenbury Mr Hunt Mr Dewes Mr Powlett

Mr Brackenbury's Composition—Mr Blackenbury[2] [in arrear 30s. for absent commons, out of town for the terms charged: to be discharged on paying 15s.]

Mr Winder D^o—Mr Winder [in arrear £4. 5s. for pensions and absent commons] and being beyond Sea eight of the Terms he stands charged It is ordered on payment of three pounds five Shillings he be discharged.

Mr J. Mason D^o—Mr Mason [in arrear £2. 12s. for pensions and absent commons, desiring abatement for 4 terms out of town, abated 10s.: to be discharged on paying £2. 2s.]

Mr Noah Curtis D^o—Mr Noah Curtis [in arrear £4. 15s. for pensions and absent commons, desiring abatement for 9 terms out of town: abated £1. 2s. 6d. for those terms]

Mr Harding D^o—Mr Harding being in arrears for ten years pencion and absent commons & desiring to compound for the same he not having been in Town It is ordered he be abated four pounds ten shillings for those ten years.

Clements Inn in the County of Middlesex } Att a pencion there held on Wednesday the 19th day of Febr. 1734 present Mr Penny princ. Mr Fowler Mr Goodman Mr Eldridge Mr Hardwick Mr Aldey Mr Hurst Mr Dewes Mr Powlett Mr Green

Mr John Attwood bond up—Mr Attwood having paid all arrears & being a housekeeper in town & thro' infirmities having left off his busyness & desireing his bond up It is ordered accordingly.

Mr Tho: Keeling D^o—Mr Keeling having paid his arrears & left the Town & busyness desiring his bond up It is ordered accordingly

---

[1] See further p. 189 below.   [2] So written in the MS.

Clements Inn in the ⎱ Att a pencion there held on Fryday the 26th day of
County of Middlesex ⎰ May 1735 present Mr Penny princ. Mr Fowler
Mr Eldridge Mr Bennett Mr Brackenbury Mr Hurst
Mr Dewes

Mr Bramston Composition—Mr Brampston [in arrear £3. 18s. for
pensions and absent commons desires abatement for 4 terms out of town:]
It is ordered that he be abated 10s,
Mr Rob![.] Abney's Composition—Mr Rob![.] Abney [in arrear £7. 11s. for
pensions and absent commons, desires abatement (not in town 18 terms):]
It is ordered he be abated 2 : 5.
Mr Bond his bond upp—Mr Geo: Bond having left the Society &
become a housekeeper in the liberty of Westminster desiring to have up his
bond It is ordered on payment of his arrears to the house & Servants
rolls his bond be delivered up.
Mr Aldey—Mr Richard Aldey the like order being a housekeeper in
London.

Clements Inn 20th Nov. 1735 This day Thomas Parker Esq![e] [1]
came in the Room of Sir Henry Edwards Barr![t] as Reader from
the Inner Temple to Clements Inn bringing a Case to read on

John Penny Pr.

Clements Inn in the ⎱ Att a pencion there held on Monday the 24th day
County of Middlesex ⎰ of November 1735 present Mr Penny principall
Mr Fowler Mr Goodman Mr Eldridge Mr Aldey
Mr Bennett Mr Dewes Mr Green Mr Powlett

*Mr Cave for a new lease of ground rooms 1. 2 & 3 pr Stairs N![o] 7 next
Mr Seabrooks*—Whereas Mr Richd. Cave one of the Companions of this
Society lately held by articles All those ground rooms att the upper end of
the first Court in Clements Inn aforesaid lying between the building lately
erected by Mr W![m] Seabrook towards the South and the Talbot alehouse
towards the north part thereof being formerly intended & sometime used
as a dust hole with the cellar under the same rooms The whole fronting
Clements Lane East and the said first Court west as the same was then
divided Together with the appurtenances being on the East side of the
staircase marked with the figure or number (7) in the first Court of Clements Inn aforesaid for the term of 99 years determinable upon the death of

---

[1] Thomas Parker, called to the Bar in 1724, was called to the Bench of the Inner
Temple in 1736 on appointment as Serjeant-at-law: see *I.T.R.*, IV, 109, 317, 319, and
see p. 186 below.

George Peach who is since dead And Whereas the said Richard Cave does now hold by articles All those Severall Chambers up one and two pair of stairs and the garrets over them in the same staircase being all over the said ground rooms before mencioned together with the vault lying under part of the ground rooms of the same buildings next to the Talbot alehouse aforesaid and the little Cellar on the right hand within the said vault and adjoining to the pavement leading to the said staircase out of which little Cellar there is a window into the first Court and also the two little clossets cupboards or holes one being on top of the Cellar stairs on the right hand going down and the other on the first landing place going up one pair of stairs on the left hand in the said staircase for the term of 99 years determinable upon the death of George Foster who is now living And Whereas the said Richard Cave is willing to give 84. 10. for the repurchase of the said ground rooms for his own life But it being found to be inconvenient to the Society to have the ground rooms upon a different life from the 1. 2 & 3 pair of stairs by reason of the dividing the Cellars & vaults Therefore the principall & antients (in Case the said Richard Cave will surrender up his old lease made for 99 years determinable upon the death of George Foster as aforesaid as well as pay the said Summe of 84. 10—) have agreed to grant a new lease not only of the said ground rooms but the rooms & garrets up 1. 2 & 3 pair of stairs over the said ground rooms Togeather with the vaults & Cellars under the same & clossets on the staircase as before in these presents are particularly described for 99 years determinable upon the death of the said Richard Cave and the said Richard having agreed to comply with the said proposall It is ordered for the considerations aforesaid that a lease be made to the said Richard Cave of the said ground rooms and the Chambers & garret 1. 2 & 3 pair of stairs with the appurtenances before described for 99 years if the said Richard Cave shall so long live under the usual covenants & provisoes & according to the usual method & form of granting leases by this Society.

*Tho: Miller Esq*ᵉ *bond up*—Mr Miller being at the Barr & of the Middle Temple and having left Clements Inn & paid his arrears It is ordered that his bond be delivered up to him.

Mr Pollexfens bond up—Mr Pollexfen having left the Society & following no busyness It is ordered on payment of his arrears & Servants rolls his bond be delivered up.

Mr Burrells bond up—Mr Burrell being at the Barr & of the Inner Temple [1] & having left Clements Inn & paid his arrears It is ordered that his bond be delivered up to him

---

[1] Thomas Burrell was admitted to the Inner Temple in 1718/9, called to the Bar in 1732, proposed for reader to Lyon's Inn in 1748, and invited to the Bench in 1762: see *I.T.R.*, IV, 59, 259, 531, and V, 150.

Mr Smith—Mr Smith being in arrears five pounds four shillings & there being a dispute about it It is ordered that on payment of two pounds four shillings he be abated three pounds upon payment of which he being a housekeeper he is to have up his bond

Clements Inn in the ⎫ Att a pencion there holden on Monday the second
County of Middlesex ⎭ day of February 1735 present Mr Penny principall
                        Mr Fowler Mr Goodman Mr Aldey Mr Dewes
                        Mr Green

Auditors of the princ. accounts—Ordered that Mr Goodman & Mr Green two of the Antients of this Society and Mr Brownsword and Mr Burton two of the Companions of the same Society shall & do examine & audite the accounts of Mr John Penny the present principall of this Society from the beginning of Hillary term 1732 untill the beginning of this present Hillary Term 1735 and that the said Mr Goodman Mr Green Mr Brownsword & Mr Burton or any three of them shall & do make their certificate & report thereof as soon as conveniently it can be done.

Mr Carrow bond up—Mr Carrow being grown old & infirm so as not to be able to follow busyness & desiring his bond up on his paying all his arrears It is ordered accordingly.

Mr Francis Jackson Dº—Mr Francis Jackson having left off his busyness to his son & paid all arrears to the Society It is ordered that his bond be delivered up.

Mr Loyds bond up—Mr Tho: Loyd having left the Society & taken an house & paid all arrears It is ordered his bond be delivered up.

Mr J. Mason—Mr John Mason being indebted one pound six shillings for pencions & Commons & being not in Town in Trinity Term last It is ordered he be abated two shillings and six pence.

Clements Inn in the ⎫ Att a pencion there holden on Wednesday the 26th
County of Middlesex ⎭ day of May 1736 present Mr Penny principall
                        Mr Fowler Mr Goodman Mr Aldey Mr Bennett
                        Mr Dewes & Mr Green

Principalls accounts confirmed—Whereas Mr Everard Goodman Mr John Green Mr Roger Brownsword and Mr Gilbert Burton by virtue of an order of pencion made the second day of February 1735 were appointed auditors of the accounts of Mr John Penny now principall of this Society and having accordingly audited stated & examined the said Mr Penny's accounts of receipts and disbursements for three whole years from the beginning of Hillary Term 1732 to the beginning of Hillary Term 1735 have found the Summe Totall of the said Principall's receipts to be 969: 4. 6 (including the ballance due from him on his last accounts) and the Totall of his disbursements to be 1005. 7. 10½ So that there remains due on this account from the said Society unto the said principall Thirty six pounds three shillings 4½d. as appears by their report or certificate thereof dated the 21th day of Aprill 1736 It is therefore ordered that the said account so stated audited examined & certified as aforesaid be allowed & approved off as a Just & true account and the said Mr John Penny is hereby discharged therefrom and it is also ordered that the said Mr Penny be paid the said thirty Six pounds three shillings fourpence ½ being the ballance of the said account out of the first mony that shall be received for the use of this Society

Wm Fowler

Ever.^d Goodman   Ro: Aldey

John Green   Edw. Benet

John Dewes

Easter Term 1736—New Call of Serjeants [1]—The King having appointed a Call of Serjeants on the 4th of June (being Crastino Ascentionis) the following Gentlemen appeared in Chancery (Each being presented by two Benchers) where they took the oath of a Serjeant &c. their names follow vizt

Thomas Parker Esq.^e (Kings Serjeant)

Thomas Hussey
Abraham Gapper
Robert Price
Michaell Foster
Thos. Burnett
Wm Wynn
John Agar   } Esq.^s
Richard Draper
Robt Johnston Kettleby
Wm Hayward
Samuell Prime
Tho: Barnardiston
Edwd Bootle

The Motto of the Rings was Libertas nunquam Gratior
9 June the procession was to Westminster vizt
The principall antients & Companions of Clements Inn mett in their own Hall about 8—from thence they walked to the Inner Temple Hall

---

[1] See p. xxvi above and the Inner Temple account, *I.T.R.*, iv, 325.

(being the Society they belong to) The Butler & Two porters walked before the principall bare headed. In the Inner Temple Hall they were treated with Wine & Bisketts.

from the Inner Temple Hall Clements Inn & Lyons Inn went Togeather to the Middle Temple Hall (being the Hall where the Chief Justice was of) Clements Inn taking the right hand this time; the next time Lyons Inn must have it. After them Cliffords Inn went, being followed by the Students, Barristers, Benchers & new Serjeants of the Inner Temple.

In the Middle Temple Hall all the Judges mett. Where the new Serjeants came & Counted before them, and after a speech made by the Chief Justice. Each Judge putt on a White Coif on a new Serjeant the Serjeant Kneeling while done.

The Judges, Kings old Serjeants & Councill then went in coaches to Westminster—The new Serjeants retired into the Middle Temple parliament Chamber to robe themselves

after which the procession to Westminster was thus

Thavies Inn & Furnivalls Inn (as belonging to Lincolns Inn) walked togeather, being preceeded by their Butlers & porters bareheaded

Then New Inn alone (as belonging to the Middle Temple).

Then Clements Inn & Lyons Inn togeather as before & Cliffords Inn alone (all belonging to the Inner Temple)

Then Lincolns Inn Students Barristers & Benchers

Middle Temple   d.°

Inner Temple   d.°

(NB there being no new Serjeants of Grays Inn that Society & Staple Inn & Bernards Inn belonging to them never attended)

New Serjeants attended by two clerks each one carrying the hoods black caps &c with other their Hatts. Each Serjeant was preceeded by a Barrister who was to deliver out his Rings.

Clements Inn in the ⎫ Att a pension there holden on Fryday the third day
County of Middlesex ⎭ of December 1736 present Mr Penny Principall
Mr Goodman Mr Aldey Mr Benet Mr Hurst
Mr Dewes Mr Green.

Mr Ed: Benet for a lease of his Chamber one pr stairs N.° 2—Mr Edward Benet (one of the antients of this Society) desiring to purchase a lease for his own life of all that Chamber with the appurtenances now in his own possession being up one pair of stairs in the stair case marked with the figure or Number (2) in the first Court in the said Society (lately belonging to Mr Edwd Curtis deceased) together with the Colehole in the passage at

the bottom of the stairs belonging to the said stair case It is ordered that
on payment of thirty nine pounds to the principall for the use of the
Society a lease be accordingly made to him of the said Chambers & Colehole
with the appurtenances for 99 years if the said Edwd Benet shall so long
live under the usual covenants & according to the usual form & method
of making & granting leases by the said Society. And also that on payment of three pounds more as aforesaid he be discharged from all demands
of rent due since the death of the said Mr Edwd Curtis.

Clements Inn 26th Jan: 1736 This day Alexander Forester Esq^e.
came (in the room of Samuell Forster Esq^e) [1] as Reader from
the Inner Temple to Clements Inn to read on the Stat. of
maintenance

John Penny

Clements Inn in the ⎫ Att a pension there holden on Wednesday the 9th
County of Middlesex ⎭ day of February 1736 present Mr Penny princ. Mr
Fowler Mr Aldey Mr Bennett Mr Brackenbury &
Mr Dewes

Mr Roger Aldey for exchange of a life—Whereas Roger Aldey Gent one
of the antients of this Society holds by articles All that double Ground
Chamber with the appurtenances Scituate lying & being in the garden
Court in the first staircase formerly marked with the figures or number 23
but now 17 in Mr Kelletts building at the upper end of the garden in
Clements Inn aforesaid herebefore in the tenure of Edward Manby & now
in the possession of the said Roger Aldey for the term of 99 years determinable upon the death of Richard Aldey son of the said Roger Aldey and
whereas the said Roger Aldey is desirous to change the life of the said
Richard Aldey and to putt in the life of Philadelphia Aldey his wife in the
room of Richard Aldey his son and having delivered up the said articles &
the term & Interest therein into the hands of the now principall & Antients of
the said Society To the Intent that a new lease be made thereof unto the said
Roger Aldey for 99 years if Philadelphia Aldey his wife shall so long live It is
ordered that on payment of £10 to the principall for the use of this Society

[1] Alexander Forester, called to the Bar in 1731, was proposed as reader to Clement's
Inn in 1747 but was excused (for ill health): he was invited to the Bench in 1762; his
executors were given leave to place a memorial of him in the Temple Church in 1788:
I.T.R., IV, 244, 516, 528; V, 150, 501. Samuel Forster, called in 1719, was invited to the
Bench in 1745/6: the Principal of Clement's Inn was ordered in May 1737 to certify
whether Forster had read, by himself or by his deputy, at the appointed time: *I.T.R.*,
IV, 54, 319, 348, 350, 501.

a new lease be granted of the said Chambers to the said Roger Aldey for 99 years determinable upon the death of the said Philadelphia Aldey according to the usuall method & form of granting leases by this Society

Mr B. Smith bond upp—Ordered that on Mr Brightwell Smiths paying fifty three pounds nineteen shillings in full of all rents & Commons due at Christmas he be discharged of his lease & being an housekeeper he may have his bond up

Mr J Smith Composition—Ordered Mr John Smith be abated forty five shillings for absent Commons being out of Town 18 Terms

Mr P. Smith composition—Ordered Mr P. Smith be abated ten shillings being out of Town four terms

Mr Mackay bond up—Mr Mackay having paid all arrears & being an housekeeper ordered his bond delivered up.

Clements Inn in the ⎱ Att a pension there holden on Monday the three
County of Middlesex ⎰ and twentieth day of May 1737 present Mr Penny pr. Mr Fowler Mr Aldey Mr Eldridge Mr Bennett Mr Hurst Mr Dewes

Mr Roper & Mr Marshall to bee entred—Whereas Mr Roper & Mr Marshall have had Chambers in Clements Inn for a considerable time without being entred as members of the said Society and tho' severall times summoned have refused or neglected to be entred or to show cause why they are not It is ordered that unless the said Mr Roper & Mr Marshall shall procure themselves to be entred as Members of the said Society before the first day of next Trinity Term [1] their Chambers be padlockt up and themselves expelled the Society & never be permitted to be Entred afterwards

Barras Executrix a bill to be paid—Mr Brightwell Smith in behalf of his wife who was executrix of Mr Barras deceased appearing and demanding a debt due to Mr Barras for busyness done for the Society and mony paid by him for taxes for the Inn [2] and it appearing to be a Just debt It is ordered that the principall pay the said Mr Smith and his wife the said bill amounting to

Mr Steukly composition—Mr Steukly being indebted to the Society two pounds nineteen shillings & desiring an abatement for Eight Terms being out of Town It is ordered he be abated 20s.

[1] See below, p. 276 (Roper) and 202 (Marshall).
[2] See p. 141 above.

Mr Jos. Peart—Mr Peart being indebted to the Society three pounds nine shillings & desiring an abatement for six terms being out of Town It is ordered he be abated fifteen Shillings

Clements Inn Michaelmas Term 1737

Persons nominated by the principall and antients (who are in Commons) for the choice of a new principall for three years from the first day of Hillary Term next ensuing.

| Mr Penny Pr. | | Mr Eldridge Mr Dewes |

Nathaniel Trayton
Henry Jones
John Dovey
Da Thomas
Thos. Powlett
Gilb.t Burton
Sanders Edwards
　John Green
　John Dewes
　Edward Bennett   Being all the Antients
　Ambrose Eldridge   in Commons confirm
　Roger Aldey   the choice

Clements Inn 19 Nov. 1737. This day Francis Capper Esq.e [1] came as Reader from the Inner Temple to Clements Inn to read on a case whether the Stat. of Limitations 22. Jac. 1 cap. 26 could be pleaded to an action of Debt brought against a Sherriff for suffering one in Execution to escape.

John Penny Pr.

Clements Inn in the ⎱ Att a pention there holden on Wednesday the 30th
County of Middlesex ⎰ day of November 1737 present Mr Penny princ.
　　　　Mr Eldridge Mr Aldey Mr Bennett Mr Dewes

Mr Brampston composition—Mr Stephen Brampston being in arrears three pounds ten shillings & desiring an abatement for 4 terms he was out of town It is ordered be he abated 10s.

Mr Dottin D.o—Mr Dottin being in arrears 4. 13. & desiring an abatement for 6 terms being out of town It is ordered he be abated 15s.

---

[1] Capper, called to the Bar in 1721, obtained a certificate of his standing and call and had his bond delivered up on payment of all duties in 1743: *I.T.R.*, IV, 76, 459.

Mr Gregory—Mr Gregory being in arrears 4. 6. & desiring the same abatement It is ordered he be abated 15s.

Clements Inn in the } *County of Middlesex* } Att a pencion there held on Monday the 13th of February 1737 present Mr Penny Princ. Mr Fowler Mr Eldridge Mr Bennett Mr Brackenbury & Mr Dewes

Auditors of the Princ. accounts—Ordered that Mr Brackenbury & Mr Powlett Two of the antients of this Society and Mr Thomas & Mr Harris two of the Companions of the same Society shall & do examine and audite the accounts of Mr John Penny the present principall of this Society from the beginning of Hillary Term 1735 untill the beginning of Hillary Term 1737 and that the said Mr Brackenbury Mr Powlett Mr Thomas and Mr Harris—or any three of them do make their certificate and report thereof as soon as conveniently it can be done.

Clements Inn in the } *County of Middlesex* } Att a pencion there held on Monday the 20th day of February 1737 present Mr Penny princ. Mr Fowler Mr Goodman Mr Dewes Mr Green Mr Bennett Mr Aldey

Principalls accounts confirmed—[Whereas the two ancients and two companions were appointed auditors as in the preceding entry] and having accordingly Audited stated and examined the said Mr Penny's accounts of receipts & disbursements for two whole years from the beginning of Hillary Term 1735 to the beginning of Hillary Term 1737 have found the summe Totall of the said principalls receipts to be 597 . 12 . 7½ and the Totall of his disbursements to be 573 . 16 . 6 (including the ballance due to him on last acccunt) So that there remains due on this account unto the said Society from the said principall 23 . 16 . 1½ as appears by their report or certificate thereof dated the 17th day of February 1737 It is therefore ordered that the said account so stated audited Examined & certified as aforesaid be allowed and approved off as a Just & true account and the said Mr Penny is hereby discharged therefrom on payment of the said Ballance due

Wm Fowler
John Dewes
Edw. Benet
John Green
Ever^d Goodman
Ro: Aldey

Clements Inn in the ⎱ Att a pension there held on Wednesday the 10th
County of Middlesex ⎰ day of May 1738 present Mr Penny Princ. Mr
Goodman Mr Aldey Mr Blackwell Mr Hurst
Mr Dewes Mr Green

Antients to be chosen—The principall acquainting the pension that there
wanted a Call of Antients there often being Scarce enough to make a
pension to transact the affairs of the house and having proposed Mr
Gregory Mr Jones Mr Trayton Mr Goodacre & Mr Dovy as proper persons
to be chosen It is ordered that the said five Gentlemen be called up to the
Antients Table when the Principall thinks fitt. So as they keep their
Seniority as above named.

 Mr Fowlers bond—Mr W.ᵐ Fowler one of the antients of this Society
having left off practice and quitted London and desiring his bond up
having paid all his dues. It is ordered that his bond be Delivered up
accordingly.

12. MAY. 1738.

Antients called up—Whereas the principall having acquainted the
pension the 10th of this instant that there wanted a Call of Antients there
often being scarce enough to make a pension to transact the affairs of the
house and having nominated Mr Gregory Mr Jones Mr Trayton Mr
Goodacre & Mr Dovy as proper persons to be chosen It was ordered that
the said five Gentlemen be called up to the antients table when the principall should think fit so as they keep their seniority as abovenamed in
pursuance of which nomination and order they were this day called up and
the four last appearing & taking the oaths of allegiance Supremacy &
abjuration in the publick hall before the principall & antients in Commons
they were admitted antients of the said Society of Clements Inn

14 JULY 1738

Mr Gregory appearing this day & taking the oaths of allegiance &
Supremacy and the abjuration oath as before he was admitted an antient
of Clements Inn taking his place according to the order of 10th May 1738

Clements Inn in the ⎱ Att a pention there holden on Wednesday the 22nd
County of Middlesex ⎰ day of June 1738 present Mr Penny princ. Mr
Goodman Mr Bennett Mr Aldey Mr Brackenbury
Mr Dawes Mr Gregory Mr Green Mr Trayton
Mr Goodacre Mr Dovy.

Mr Cave for a Ch: up one pr of stairs N.º 7—Whereas Mr Richard Cave
one of the Companions of this Society lately held by articles All those

Chambers up one pair of stairs in the new building at the upper end of the first Court fronting the Gateway of Clements Inn aforesaid South & the Talbott Yard North marked with the figure or Number (7) Togeather with the Cellar or Vault at the bottom of the stairs in the same staircase extending itself under the pavement of the said first Court leading to the staircase of the same building for the Term of 99 years determinable upon the death of Darby Rhodes who is since dead And Whereas the said Richard Cave is desirous to repurchase the said Chamber for his own life and offers to give £104 for the same Itt is ordered that on payment of £104 to the principall for the use of the Society a new lease be made & granted of the said Chambers Cellar & appurtenances to the said Mr Cave for 99 years from the 25th of March last If he the said Mr Cave shall so long live [under the usual covenants &c. and in the usual form &c.]

> *Clements Inn*   9th Feb. 1738
>
> This day Wm Brown Esq^{e1} came as Reader from the Inner Temple to Clements Inn bringing a Case to read upon Stat. of Costs 3 H. 7. Cap. 10.
>
> Ambrose Eldridge
> Deputy Principall

Clements Inn in the⎱ At a pention there held the first Day of June 1739
County of Middlesex⎰ present Mr Aldey, Deputy principall, Mr Eldridge, Mr Bennet, Mr Dewes, Mr Green, Mr Gregory, Mr Jones, Mr Trayton, Mr Goodacre, & Mr Dovey.

Auditors of the principall's accounts—Ordered that Mr Jones & Mr Trayton two of the Antients of this Society and Mr Browne & Mr Saunders Edwards two of the Companions of the same Society shall & Do Examine and Audit the Accounts of Mr John Penny the present principal of this Society from the beginning of Hillary Term 1737 to the beginning of Hillary Term 1739 And that the said Mr Jones Mr Trayton Mr Browne & Mr Edwards or any three of them do make their Certificate and report thereof as soon as conveniently it can be Done.

Mr Richd Keeling for absent Commons bond up—Mr Richd Keeling (one of the Companions of this House) being indebted to the Society 5.11 ... for pencions and abs: Commons and Mr John Dovy (one of the Antients of the said House) desiring to have his bond up upon payment of the said debt (he having left of practice) It is ordered that upon payment

---

[1] William Brown, called to the Bar in 1722, had been in danger of having his chambers padlocked up and his security prosecuted for the arrears he had incurred, but was invited to the Bench in 1751: *I.T.R.*, IV, 84, 121, 123, 126–7, 140; V, 12.

I

of 5.11 ... to the Principall for the use of the Society together with what is due to the Servants Rolls his bond will be delivered up

Mr Walter Stubbs for abs: Commons and bond up—The like order for Mr Walter Stubbs on payment of the like Summe and Servants Rolls.

Mr Richard Bewley for abs: Commons and bond up—The like order for Mr Richd Bewley on payment of 11.14 ... and Servants Rolls.

Elisha &c—The like order for Mr Elisha on payment of 7: 16: & Servants Rolls.

Mr John Peart for abs: Com: & bond up—Mr John Peart (late one of the Companions of this House) being indebted to the Society 7.16 ... for pencions and abs: Commons Mr John Blackwell (one of the Antients of the said House) being Security for him desiring an abatement for the Terms he was out of Town It is ordered that upon payment of 5.6 ... and Servants Rolls the bond be delivered up to Mr John Blackwell

Clements Inn in the ⎱ At a Pention there held the 11 day of July 1739
County of Middlesex ⎰ present Mr Penny Principall Mr Aldey Mr Bennett
Mr Dewes Mr Trayton Mr Goodacre Mr Dovy.

Leverland Bond up—Mr W^m. Leverland (one of the Companions of this House) being indebted to this Society 7.16 ... for pencions and absent Commons and 18s for Porters Rolls in all 8.14 ... and having met with misfortunes so as to apply for an abatement It is ordered that he be abated 4.13 ... and that upon payment of Three pounds Three Shillings to the Principall for the use of the Society and 18s. to him for the Servants Rolls his Bond shall be delivered up.

Mr Gilbert Burtons Bond up—Mr Gilbert Burton (one of the companions of this House) being Removed and Entred of Grays Inn and desiring to have his Bond up upon paying his Arrears to the principall and discharging the Porters Rolls It is ordered accordingly.

Clements Inn in the ⎱
County of Middlesex ⎰

15th November 1739

This day John Knowler Esq^e [1] came as Reader from the Inner Temple to Clements Inn bringing a Case to read upon the Stat. Westminster 2nd de Donis conditionalibus

Roger Aldey Deputy Principle

[1] Knowler, who came to the Inner from the Middle Temple, was called to the Bar in 1722, and was invited to the Bench in 1751: *I.T.R.*, IV, 84, 87; V, 12.

Mr Ropers bond up—Mr Roper having paid all dues to the Inn & left the Inn It is ordered his bond be delivered up

Mr Brian D?. The like order for Mr Bryan & Hodgson

Mr Quaile—The like order for Quaile

Clements Inn Miclaelmas Term 1739

Thursday 22ⁿᵈ Nov. 1739

Persons nominated by the principall and Antients (who are in Commons) for the Choice of a new principall (in the room of Mr Penny who desires to resign upon account of his ill State of health) for Three years from the first day of Hillary Term next Ensuing

Mr Benet	Mr Green	Mr Dovey
John Dovey	Edwᵈ Benet	
		Da Thomas
		Wᵐ Atwood
		S. Edwards
		J. Brown
		Theo : Darley
		J. Yorke
		J. Bambridge
		Roger Aldey
		John Dewes
		John Green
		H: Gregory
		Henry Jones

Clements Inn in the At a Pencion there held the first day of February
County of Middlesex 1739 Present Mr Dovy Principall Carr Brackenbury
Mr John Dewes Mr Aldey Mr Henry Jones Mr Nathaniel Trayton Mr Joseph Goodacre

Principalls Accounts Confirmed—Whereas Mr Jones & Mr Trayton (Two of the Antients of this Society and Mr Brown and Mr Edwards (Two of the Companions of the Same Society) By Virtue of an order of Pencion made the first day of June last were appointed Auditors of the Accounts of Mr John Penny (the Principal of the said Society) And having accordingly Audited Stated & Examined the said Mr Penny's Accounts of Receipts & disbursements for Two whole years from the beginning of Hillary Term 1737 to the beginning of Hillary Term 1739 Have found the Summe Total of his receipts to be 687 . 2 . 11 (Including the Ballance due from him on his last Account) And the Totall of his disbursements to be 308 . 11 . 5½ So that there remains due on this Account unto the said Society from the said Mr Penny to the said Society 378 . 11 . 5½ as appears by their Report or Certificate thereof dated the first day of February 1739 It is therefore Ordered that the said Account So Stated Audited Examined & Certified as aforesaid be allowed & approved off as a Just and true Account And that the said Mr John Penny is hereby discharged therefrom on payment of the said 378 . 11 . 5½ unto Mr John Dovy the present Principall for the use of the Society .

John Dovey Pr.
Carr Brackenbury
John Dewes
Henry Jones
Nathaniel Trayton
Jos Goodacre

Clements Inn in the } At a pention there held the twenty eighth Day of
County of Middlesex } July 1740 present John Dovey principal Mr Bennet
Mr Dewes Mr Trayton Mr Goodacre and Mr Penny

ORDERED that the Back Gate of this Inn from and after the twenty ninth Day of September 1740 unto the 25th Day of March then next be Shut at Nine of the Clock in the Evening and opened at Six of the Clock in the Morning and from the said 25th Day of March unto the 29th Day of September 1741 the Said Gate Shall be Shut at ten of the Clock in the Evening and opened at Five of the Clock in the Morning and So Continued for the Future And after the Said Gate is Shut as above No person Shall be Admitted to pass thro the Same AND IT IS FURTHER ORDERED that no person or persons shall be suffered to pass thro the Said Inn with Burthens

John Dovey Pr.
John Penny
Edw. Benet
John Dewes
Nathaniel Trayton
Jos Goodacre

Clements Inn   17th Nov. 1740

This Day Beverley Butler Esq^e [1] came as Reader from the Inner Temple to this Society bringing a Case to read upon

John Dovey Pr.

Mr Roomes Bond up—Mr William Room having paid all Dues to this Inn & left the Society It is ordered his bond be delivered up which was accordingly Done

---

[1] Butler, called to the Bar in 1723, was invited to the Bench in 1754, but declined because of ill health: *I.T.R.*, IV, 96; V, 44, 47.

Clements Inn in the ⎱ At a pention there held the Seventeenth Day of
County of Middlesex ⎰ July 1741 present John Dovey principal Mr Benet
           Mr Dewes Mr Green Mr Jones Mr Trayton &
           Mr Goodacre

ORDERED that a Watchman be forthwith appointed by Mr Principal [1]
with Such Sallary as he Shall think fit and proper to Allow him for Such
his Service and that a Watchhouse & Every thing Necessary for the Greater
Security of the Members of this Society be provided as Mr Principall shall
think proper.

                                   John Dovey Pr
                                   Edw. Benet
                                   John Dewes
                                   John Green
                                   Nathaniel Trayton
                                   Jos Goodacre

Mr Robert Abney's Bond up—Mr Rob.t Abney having paid all Dues to
the Inn & left the Society It is ordered his bond be Delivered up which
which was accordingly Done

14 Aug.t 1741—Agreed with Thomas Pratt and Thomas Leeke to be
Watchmen of this Society at fifteen pounds a Year Each to Commence
from this Day Pursuant to the above order.

Hillary Terme 1741

Clements Inn   8 Feb: 1741

       This Day Thomas Stephens Esq.e [2] Came as Reader from the
       Inner Temple to this Society bringing a Case upon the Statute
       of 11 Geo 2nd for the more effectual Secureing the payment of
       Rents and preventing frauds by Tenants [3] to read upon

Trinity Term 1742

Mr John Mason—Mr John Mason paid all Dues to the Inn and left
the Society. It is Ordered his bond be delivered up. Which was Done
accordingly

---

[1] John Penny, a former Principal, had been murdered in his chambers on June 17:
see p. 267 n. below. The watchmen's duties are detailed at p. 202 below.

[2] Stephens had been called to the Bar in 1722; he was in trouble for arrears in
1725/6: *I.T.R.*, IV, 84, 140.

[3] 11 Geo. II. c. 19.

Clements Inn in the ⎱ At a pention there held the twenty Fourth Day of
County of Middlesex ⎰ November 1742 present John Dovey principal Mr
Dewes Mr Jones Mr Green Mr Trayton & Mr
Goodacre

ORDERED that Mr Green & Mr Goodacre two of the Antients of this
Society and Mr William Gason & Mr Thomas Perkins two of the Companions of the same Society Shall & Do Examine and Audit the Accounts
of Mr Dovey the present principal of this Society from the beginning of
Hillary Term 1739 to the beginning of Hillary Terme 1742 And that the
said Mr Green Mr Goodacre Mr Gason & Mr Perkins or any three of
them do make their Certificate & Report thereof as soon as conveniently
it can be Done

Michaelmas Term 1742

Clements Inn   Thursday 25th November 1742

Persons Nominated by the Principall and Antients (who are in
Commons) for the Choice of a New Principall for three Years from
the first Day of Hillary Terme next ensueing

Mr Dovey P^r	Mr Green	Mr Goodacre

Da: Thomas	Theo Darley
Jno Browne	Richard Fleming
Antony Ryan	Tho: Perkins
John Price	F Green
John Dews	John Caldecott
Joseph Good-	Charles Pryce
acre	John Dovey

Saturday 27 November 1742

Mr John Green came into the Hall and paid his Fine (being Forty
Shillings) for refuseing to Serve the office of Principall [1] Whereupon the
Antients then in Commons Sent Down three of the Antients [2] That one
might be Elected to Serve the Office of Principall vizt Mr Gregory Mr Jones
& Mr Trayton (none of them being then in Commons) when Mr Trayton
was Elected.

---

[1] See Orders 54 and 62 at pp. 228, 231 below.
[2] As required by Order 62: see p. 231 below.

Saturday 27 Novr. 1742

Clements Inn. Persons Nominated by the Principall and Antients (who are in Commons) for the Choice of a New Principall for three years from the First Day of Hillary Terme next Ensuing

Mr Gregory	Mr Jones	Mr Trayton
		Da: Thomas
		Jno Browne
		Theo Darley
		J. Yorke
		Anto: Ryan
		Richard Fleminge
		John Price
		Thos. Perkins
		Fra: Green
		Charles Pryce
		John Dewes

Clements Inn   26 Novr 1742

This Day   Came in the Room of Richard Dashwood Esq[e] [1] as Reader from the Inner Temple to this Society bringing a Case to Read on

John Dovey Pr.

Michaelmas Term 1742

Clements Inn in the \
County of Middlesex \
At a pention there held on the Eighth Day of December 1742 present John Dovey Principal Mr John D'Ewes Mr John Green Mr Henry Gregory Mr Henry Jones Mr Nathaniel Trayton & Mr Joseph Goodacre

ORDERED that one of the Companions of this Society be appointed to Execute the Office of Steward or Clerk of this Society for the Future (Subject to the Antient Rules and Orders of this Society and that such Steward so to be appointed shall receive from the said Society the yearly Summe of ten pounds for his Salary & reward for Executeing the Said Office of Steward over and above the Antient Fees & perquisites belonging to the said office of Steward

John Dovey Pr. \
John Dewes \
John Green \
H: Gregory \
Henry Jones \
Nathaniel Trayton \
Jos Goodacre

---

[1] Dashwood was called in 1726: *I.T.R.*, IV, 146. The Principal failed to record the name of his deputy.

Michaelmas Term 1742

At a pention there held on the Eighth Day of December 1742 present Mr John Dovey principal Mr John D'Ewes Mr John Green Mr Henry Gregory Mr Henry Jones Mr Nathaniel Trayton & Mr Joseph Goodacre

MR THOMAS PERKINS One of the the Companions of this Society haveing made his Application and desiring to be admitted into the Office or place of Steward or Clerk of this Society It is ORDERED that the said Mr Perkins be accordingly admitted into the said Office or place but to Continue therein only during the good will and pleasure of the Principal and Antients & their Successors & no longer And the said Mr Perkins is to give a Bond with two other Sufficient persons to be bound with Him in the penalty or Summe of two Hundred pounds for the due performance of his said Office or place dureing such time as he shall be Continued therein The Sallary of ten pounds a year to Commence from the first Day of Hillary term next

> John Dovey Pr.
> John Dewes
> John Green
> H: Gregory
> Henry Jones
> Nathaniel Trayton
> Jos Goodacre

Hillary Term 1742

Clements Inn in the
County of Middlesex } At a Pention there held the ninth day of February 1742 Present Joseph Goodacre Principall Mr Roger Aldey Mr John Dewes Mr John Green Mr Nathaniel Trayton & Mr Henry Jones

Clements Inn—Mr Trayton having declined accepting the Office of Principal & paid the usual Fine and thereby excused The persons following are nominated by the Antients in the Commons for the Choice of a new Principal for three years from the first day of this Term

Mr Gregory	Mr Jones	Mr Goodacre
		Da: Thomas
		E Wyatt
		A Cocke
		Nash Mason
		Theo: Darley
		Anthony Ryan
		J Price.
		Tho Perkins
		F Green
		D Henriques

Principalls Accounts Confirmed—Whereas Mr Green & Mr Goodacre (two of the antients of this Society) and Mr Gason & Mr Perkins (two of the Companions of the same Society) By vertue of an order of Pention made the twenty fourth day of November last were appointed Auditors of the Accounts of Mr John Dovey (then Principal of the said Society) and having accordingly Audited Stated & examined the said Mr Doveys accounts of Receipts & Disbursements for three whole years from the beginning of Hillary Term 1739 to the beginning of Hillary Term 1742 Have found the Summe Totall of his Receipts to be £807. 17s. 6½d. and the Totall of his Disbursements to be £548. 1s. 10¾d. so that there remains due on this account unto the said Society from the said Mr Dovey £259. 15s. 7¾d. as appears by their Report or Certificate thereof Dated the first day of February 1742 It is therefore Ordered that the said Account so stated audited examined & Certified as aforesaid be allowed and approved of as a just and true account And the said Mr John Dovey is hereby Discharged therefrom on payment of the said £259. 15s. 7¾d. unto Mr Joseph Goodacre the present Principal for the use of this Society.

> Jos Goodacre Pr.
> Roger Aldey
> John Dewes
> John Green
> Nathaniel Trayton
> Henry Jones

Antients to be Chosen—The Principall acquainting the Pension that there wanted a Call of Antients there often being Scarce enough to Make a Pention to transact the Affairs of the house and having proposed Mr Antony Cocke Mr Edward Wyatt Mr Nash Mason and Mr David Thomas as Proper Persons to be Chosen It is Ordered that the Said Four Gentlemen be Called Up to the Antients Table when the Principall thinks fitt So as they Keep their Seniority as above Named

Clements Inn in the ⎫ At a Pention there held on Friday the 18th day of
County of Middlesex ⎭ February 1742 Present Mr Goodacre Principal
Mr Dovey Mr Dewes Mr Wyatt Mr Mason and Mr Thomas

Antients called up—Whereas the Principall having acquainted the Pention the 9th of this instant that there wanted a Call of Antients (there often being scarce enough to make a Pention to transact the affairs of the House) and having nominated Mr Anthony Cocke Mr Edward Wyatt Mr Nash Mason and Mr David Thomas as proper persons to be chosen

I*

It was ordered that the said four Gentlemen be called up to the Antients'
Table when the Principal should think fitt so as they Keep their Seniority
above named In pursuance of which nomination and Order they were
that day called up and all of them appearing and taking the Oaths of
Allegiance Supremacy and abjuration in the Publick Hall before the
Principall and Antients in Commons they were admitted Antients of the
said Society of Clements Inn.

Clements Inn in the County of Middlesex—Mr Marshall having intruded
himself into this Society and having been often summoned to be enterd as a
Member thereof but having hitherto refused to be so enterd and still
refusing It is ordered that unless the said Mr Marshall Do enter himself a
Member of the said Society within a week from the date hereof [1] that the
Chambers wherein he now resides be Padlocked up and he be refused
entrance into the said Inn Dated this eighteenth day of February 1742.

The like order was made at the same time upon Mr Longfellow [1]

Clements Inn in the County of Middlesex—Whereas John Cheeles Porter
of the fore Gate having hitherto payed six pounds per Annum for the
Ground Chambers on the left hand N.º 2 in this Inn which being thought
too much It is ordered that the said Rent be reduced to twenty shillings
per annum from Christmas last and so to continue till further Order.

Clements Inn in the County of Middlesex—Orders to be observed by the
Porters & Watchmen & their Successors

THAT the Watchmen or one of them shall come upon the Watch with
Candle & Lanthorn and his Staff In the Months of November December &
January at 5 in the evening and go off at 7 in the Morning And in the
Months of October and February at 6 in the Evening & go off at 6 in the
Morning And in the Months of September & March at 7 in the Evening
and go off at 5 in the Morning And in the Months of Aprill & August
at 8 in the Evening and go off at 5 in the Morning And in the Months of
May June & July at 9 in the Evening and go off at 5 in the Morning And
that he shall go up every Stair case in the Inn and into the Boghouse
thereto belonging each Night immediately after the Gates of the Inn are
shut and once afterwards every Night to see that the Doors Lamps and
everything else be safe And that he shall begin to cry the Hour every
Night at 11 and shall cry that and every Hour after in each of the three
Courts till he goes off the Watch and shall not go into the Lodge of the
said Inn during the time of their Watch And it is further Ordered that the
Porter whose turn it is to set up at the Gate of the said Inn shall not go

---

[1] Neither Marshall nor Longfellow became members of the Inn within the time-
limit or, apparently, thereafter.

from the said Gate till such time in the Morning as the Watchmen are hereinbefore directed to go off their said Watch And it is further Ordered that the Porter of the foregate do Keep the first Court clean and that the Porter of the Back Gate do keep the Garden Court clean and that Thomas Pratt one of the Watchmen belonging to this Inn do keep the middle Court clean And that Thomas Leak the other Watchman belonging to the said Inn do keep the Boghouse clean and that both the said Porters & Watchmen do take care to remove all Beggers and other disorderly persons out of the said Inn And if either of the Porters or Watchmen shall refuse or neglect to observe & perform the directions hereinbefore given they shall be dismissed from their respective Service or forfeit & lose such part of their Wages as the Principall & Antients in Pention shall think reasonable and order.

Clements Inn in the At a Pention held at Clements Inn aforesaid on
County of Middlesex Thursday the 21st day of April in the year of our
Lord 1743 present Mr Goodacre Principal Mr Dovey Mr Trayton Mr Cocke Mr Wyatt & Mr Mason Mr Jones & Mr Thomas

Samuel Law to be Butler & Porter of the Fore Gate in the Room & place of John Cheals—Samuel Law having applyed to be admitted into the severall offices or places of Butler & Porter of the fore Gate in this Society in the Room and place of John Cheals deceased It is ordered that the said Samuel Law be accordingly admitted into the said several Offices or places but to continue therein only during the good will & pleasure of the Principal and Antients and their Successors for the time being or the major part of them and no longer And the said Samuel Law is to enter into Bond with one or more sufficient person or persons to be bound with him in the penalty or summe of fifty pounds for the due performance of the said severall Offices or places during such time as he shall be continued therein.

Thomas Pratt Porter of the back Gate—Ordered that Thomas Pratt be admitted Porter of the back Gate of this Society next to Clare Markett in the room & place of Samuel Law who is removed to the Offices or places of Butler & Porter of the fore Gate But to continue therein only during the good will & pleasure of the Principal and Antients and their Successors for the time being or the Major part of them & no longer.

John Hadley Under Watchman of this Society—Ordered that John Hadley be admitted Under Watchman of this Society

Upon the Petition of Ruth Cheals the Widow & relict of John Cheales late Butler and Porter of this Society seting forth her having been an old

Servant in the Society and being left in bad Circumstances and praying some Relief and Assistance from the said Society It is ordered that the said Ruth Cheales be paid the summe of twenty pounds out of the publick Stock of the said Society

Jos Goodacre Pr
John Dovey
Nathaniel Trayton
Henry Jones
A. Cocke
Edw. Wyatt
Nash Mason
Da Thomas

Clements Inn in the At a Pention held on Monday the 20th day of June
County of Middlesex in the year of our Lord 1743 present Mr Goodacre Principal Mr Dovey Mr Dewes Mr Trayton Mr Jones and Mr Thomas.

Mr Nash Mason for the Chambers & Garretts N? *18 late Mr Everard Goodmans*—WHEREAS Mr Everard Goodman lately deceased held by Lease from the Society the Chambers & Garretts up two three & four pair of Stairs on both sides the Stair Case at N.° 18 for ninety nine years determinable with his life with power for him or his Executors to nominate another Member to be admitted to the same for the like term of ninety nine years determinable upon the life of such person and Nash Mason the only acting Executor of the said Everard Goodman having nominated himself to be admitted thereunto who is admitted a Member and is an Antient of this Society and desires to be admitted to the said Chambers & Garretts And the said Nash Mason having to that intent Surrendred the said Lease and the Estate & Interest thereby granted It is ORDERED that a new Lease of the said Chambers & Garretts be made to the said Nash Mason for ninety nine years if he shall so long live according to the usual method & form of Granting Leases by this Society.

Mr Jorden's Bond delivered up—Mr Humphrey Jorden having paid all dues to the Inn & left the Society It is ordered his Bond be delivered up which was accordingly done.

Jos Goodacre Pr.
John Dovey
John Dewes
Henry Jones
Nathaniel Trayton
Da Thomas

Clements Inn in the } At a pention held on Friday the second day of
County of Middlesex } December in the year of our Lord 1743 present
Mr Goodacre Pr. Mr Dovey Mr Dewes Mr Jones
Mr Wyatt Mr Mason and Mr Thomas.

Mr Goodmans Bond delivered up—Mr Nash Mason (Executor of Mr Everard Goodman deceased) having paid all dues due from the said Mr Goodman to the time of his death It is ordered that the said Mr Goodmans Bond be delivered up which was accordingly done

Mr Osgoods Bond delivered up—Mr John Osgood haveing paid all dues to the Inn and left the Society It is ordered that his Bond be delivered up which was accordingly done

Clements Inn in the County of Middlesex—WHEREAS it has been a Custom time immemorial that the Antients of this Society should be excused the payments of absent Commons but such Custom being found inconvenient in some respects & prejudicial to the said Society IT IS THEREFORE ORDERED that from & after the first day of Hillary Term next every Antient of the said Society who shall be resident in the Society during the time of Commons there or the greatest part thereof and shall absent himself from Commons shall be lyable to pay and shall pay for absent Commons the like Summe & in like manner as any other Member or Companion of the said Society is now lyable to pay any former Custom or usage to the Contrary thereof in anywise notwithstanding [1]

Jos Goodacre Pr.
John Dovey
John Dewes
Henry Jones
Edw. Wyatt
Nash Mason
Da Thomas

Clements Inn 10th Febry 1743 Thursday Henry Hall Esquire [2] came in the room of Awnsham Churchill Esquire [3] as Reader from the Inner Temple to Clements Inn bringing a case to read upon.

[1] For the repeal of this order, see p. 245 below.

[2] Hall, if correctly identified, was called to the Bar in 1739/40: a man of that name was proposed for reader to Lyon's Inn in 1754; invited to the Inner Temple Bench in 1775, elected Reader of his Inn in 1784, and died in that year: *I.T.R.*, IV, 411; V, 48, 310, 444, 450.

[3] Churchill, called to the Bar in 1727, was invited to the Bench in 1760: *I.T.R.*, IV, 160; V, 125.

Clements Inn in the } At a Pention there held the 14th day of February
County of Middlesex } 1743 Present Mr Goodacre Pr. Mr Dovey Mr
              Hurst Mr Dewes Mr Trayton Mr Wyatt Mr Jones
              Mr Mason Mr Thomas

Ordered that Mr Jones & Mr Wyatt two of the Antients of this Society & Mr Ryan & Mr Ellers two of the Companions of the said Society shall & do examine & audit the accounts of Mr Goodacre the present Principall of this Society from the beginning of Hillary Term 1742 to the beginning of Hillary Term 1743 and that the said Mr Jones Mr Wyatt Mr Ryan & Mr Ellers or any three of them do make their Certificate & report thereof as soon as conveniently it can be done.

Clements Inn in the } At a Pention held on Friday the 11th day of May
County of Middlesex } 1744 present Mr Goodacre Pr. Mr Dovey Mr
              Jones Mr Aldey Mr Mason Mr Thomas

It is ordered that the following notice be given to each of the proprietors of Chambers in the building N.º 14—

> *Clements Inn in the County of Middlesex*—At a Pention held on Friday the 11th day of May 1744—The building N.º 14 wherein you have Chambers being in a Ruinous Condition and there being a necessity to have something done thereto You are to take notice that a Pention will be held on Friday the 15th day of June next at 7 in the Evening at the Publick Hall of the said Inn to treat with you concerning the said Building and your property therein and to receive any proposals you shall think proper to make concerning the same and in default of your then Attendance the Society will proceed to act therein as they shall think proper.
>
>   Jos Goodacre Pr.
>   John Dovey
>   Roger Aldey
>   Henry Jones
>   Da Thomas
>   Nash Mason

Clements Inn   Monday 11th February 1744

> Samuel Bonner Esq.ᵉ came in the room of Bartholomew Tate Esq.ᵉ as Reader from the Inner Temple to this Society bringing a Case to read on.[1]

---

[1] Bonner had been called in 1731 as an utter barrister; he was sued for non-payment of duties in 1748; Tate had been called in 1728: *I.T.R.*, IV, 179, 247, 531.

Mr Grews Bond delivered up—Mr George Grew having paid all dues to the Inn & left the Society it is ordered his Bond be delivered up which was accordingly done.

Easter Term 1745

Clements Inn   Thursday 23rd May

The Office of Principal being vacant by the death of Mr Goodacre the persons following are nominated by the Antients in Commons for the Choice of a new Principal for the Remainder of the late Principals time being to Hilary Term next

Mr Dewes   Mr Gregory   Mr Jones

John Crawford
Jno Brown
J. Yorke
Anthony Ryan
Tho. Perkins
Fra: Green
D. Henriques
G Elers
John Dovey
Tho. Hurst
Nash Mason

Clements Inn in the County of Middlesex At a Pention held on Friday the 28th day of June 1745 present Mr Dewes Principal Mr Dovey Mr Mason Mr Jones Mr Wyatt & Mr Thomas

Ordered that Mr Dovey & Mr Mason two of the Antients of this Society and Mr Price & Mr Francis Green two of the Companions of the said Society shall & do examine & audit the Accounts of Mr Goodacre late Principal of the Society from the beginning of Hilary Term 1743 to the beginning of Easter Term 1745 And that the said Mr Dovey Mr Mason Mr Price and Mr Green or any three of them do make their Certificate & Report thereof as soon as conveniently it can be done.

Watchman Fined for neglect of duty—John Hadley one of the Watchmen of this Society having misbehaved himself in his said Office and neglected his duty as Watchman It is Ordered that twenty shillings as a fine by way of punishment for such his said misbehaviour and neglect be stoped and deducted out of his quarters wages due to him from the said Society on the 14th of May 1745

Mr Bridges's Bond delivered up—Mr James Bridges late one of the Companions of this House being lately dead and at his death indebted to this Society in £12. 1s. 0d. for Pentions & absent Commons and Mr Adderley one of the Companions of the said Society having applyed on behalf of the Widow & Executrix of the said Mr Bridges for an abatement alledging she is left with a large Family of Children in low circumstances and not well able to pay the whole In Consideration of the premisses It is ordered that there be an abatement of £4. 12s. 6d. out of the said dues and that upon payment of £7. 18s. 6d. to the Principal or to the Steward of the said Society for the use of the said Society and what is due to the Porters of the said Society the said Mr Bridges's Bond be delivered up.

Clements Inn in the ⎱ At a Pention held on Saturday the 3rd day of
County of Middlesex ⎰ August 1745 present Mr Dewes Pr. Mr Dovey
Mr Green Mr Wyatt Mr Mason Mr Thomas

Whereas the Building N.º 14 in this Inn is in a ruinous Condition and in danger of falling and it being necessary that the same should be taken down & rebuilt It is ordered that the same be taken down and rebuilt as soon as conveniently it can be done and that the underwritten Notice be given to each Proprietor of Chambers in the said Building

It is ordered that unless Mr Parke Mr Thos. Heckford & Mr Samuel Worth are entred of this Society before the first day of Nov.ᵗ next their Chambers be padlocked and they be refused entrance into the said Inn they having been severally summoned for that purpose & neglecting so to do or giving any reason to the contrary And that they have notice of this order [1]

John Dewes Pr.	Nash Mason
John Dovey	Da Thomas
Edw.ᵈ Wyatt	John Green

Clements Inn in the County of Middlesex—Whereas this Society has not been able to agree for the absolute purchase of the Estate & Interest of the severall proprietors of Chambers in the building N.º 14 in this Inn and the said Building being now in a ruinous Condition and in danger of falling it is become necessary to take it down & rebuild it as soon as conveniently it can be done Therefore the said Society have resolved and hereby signify their intention to begin to take down the said Building on the 29th day of November next and do hereby give you notice to remove & take away all the furniture & inside work which belongs to you as Lessee in your

---

[1] Parke and Heckford were admitted in 1746: see p. 278 below.

Chambers in the said Building on or before the last day of Michaelmas Term next

Dated the 3d day of August 1745.

Michaelmas Term 1745

Thursday 21st Nov.ᵣ 1745

In Commons

Clements Inn Persons nominated by the Antients in the absence
of the Principal for the choice of a new Principal for three years
from the first day of Hilary Term next ensuing

Mr Dewes	Mr Gregory	Mr Jones

John Crawford
John Brown
Theo: Darley
Anthony Ryan
J. Price
Tho. Perkins
D. Henriques
G. Elers
John Dovey
Nash Mason
Da Thomas

Clements Inn—At a Pension held on Thursday the 20th day of March
1745 Present Mr Dewes Pr. Mr Dovey Mr Green Mr Jones Mr Trayton
Mr Wyatt Mr Mason & Mr Thomas

We whose Names are hereunder written do agree to advance & lend
the Sum of one hundred pounds each towards erecting a new Building in
the said Inn in the Room of a Building now marked or numberd (14) in
the said Inn And we do agree to cause a proper Security by way of
Mortgage of this Society to be made for securing the repayment thereof
with Interest for the same after the Rate of five pounds by the hundred
by the year from the several times the before mentioned Sums or any of
them shall be advanced

John Dewes Pr.
John Dovey
John Green
H: Gregory
Nathaniel Trayton
Nash Mason
Da Thomas
Henry Jones

Clements Inn in the } At a Pention held on Friday the twentieth day of
County of Middlesex } June in the year of our Lord one thousand seven
hundred and forty six Present Mr Dewes Principal
Mr Dovey Mr Green Mr Jones Mr Mason and
Mr Thomas.

WHEREAS at a Pention here held the third day of August last It was
Ordered by the Principal and Antients then present that the Building
Nº 14 in this Inn should be taken down and rebuilt as soon as conveniently
it could be done AND WHEREAS at another Pention held in this Inn the
twentieth day of March last the severall persons following viz.ᵗ Mr John
Dewes Principal Mr John Dovey Mr Thomas Hurst Mr John Green Mr
Henry Gregory Mr Henry Jones Mr Nathaniel Trayton Mr Nash Mason
and Mr David Thomas Antients of the same Society Did agree to advance
and lend the summe of one hundred pounds each towards erecting the
said Building AND WHEREAS the said Building has been accordingly pulled
down and the same being now Rebuilding To supply the want of a present
Summe of money towards carrying on and perfecting the same the severall
persons following viz.ᵗ the said John Dewes John Dovey Thomas Hurst
John Green Henry Gregory Henry Jones Nathaniel Trayton Nash Mason
and David Thomas have advanced and this day paid towards the charge of
erecting the said Building the Summe of fifty pounds apiece making together the summe of four hundred and fifty pounds in part of the said one
hundred pounds which each of the said Gentlemen so as aforesaid agreed
to advance IT IS THEREFORE ORDERED that the said severall summes of
fifty pounds so by them the said John Dewes John Dovey Thomas Hurst
John Green Henry Greogry Henry Jones Nathaniel Trayton Nash Mason
and David Thomas respectively advanced and paid as aforesaid together
with Interest for the same after the rate of five pounds per Cent per Annum
from the date hereof shall be secured and paid to them severally and
respectively and to their severall and respective Executors Administrators
and Assigns by and out of the Stock and other Rents and profits of this
Society.

John Dewes Pr.
John Dovey
Henry Jones
Nash Mason
Da Thomas
John Green

We whose names are underwritten Doe hereby severally acknowledge
to have this 9th day of March 1746 had and received of & from the Society
of Clements Inn aforesaid the severall & respective Summs of fifty pounds

apiece in the above order mentioned to be advanced by us for the use of the said Society together with all the Interest due thereon

John Dewes Pr.
John Dovey
Henry Jones
John Green
Nash Mason
Da Thomas
Nathaniel Trayton

February 11th 1746 This Day George Nares Esq^e^ came in the Room of William Selby Esq^e^ as Reader from the Inner Temple to this Society bringing a Case to read upon.[1]

Clements Inn in the County of Middlesex } At a Pension held on Thursday the twelfth day of February in the year of our Lord one thousand seven hundred and forty six present John Dewes Pr. Mr John Dovey, Mr John Green, Mr Henry Jones, Mr Nathaniel Trayton, Mr Edward Wyatt Mr Nash Mason and Mr David Thomas

WHEREAS at a Pension held in this Inn on Saturday the third day of August 1745 It was Ordered by the Principal & Antients then present that the Building No. 14 in this Inn should be taken down and Rebuilt as soon as conveniently it could be done AND WHEREAS the said Building has been accordingly pulled down and Rebuilt and in Order as well to defray the expence thereof as to supply other the occasions of this House It has been found necessary and the now Principal and Antients whose names are under written being the major part of the Antients of this Society have agreed and do hereby agree to borrow and take up at Interest the summe of One Thousand One Hundred pounds The repayment of which said One Thousand One Hundred pounds with lawfull Interest for the same is likewise hereby agreed and Ordered to be secured by a Grant or Mortgage of this Inn or Hostell with the appurtenances AND WHEREAS the Fee Simple & Inheritance of this Inn or Hostell by Indentures of Lease and Release bearing date the fifteenth and sixteenth days of June in the year of our Lord 1733 was by the direction and appointment of the then Principal and the major part of the Antients of this Society Granted &

[1] Nares, called in 1741 and proposed for reader at Lyon's Inn in 1755, was invited to the Bench on becoming Serjeant-at-law in 1755: he was thanked by the Inner Temple for presenting his portrait (as the Hon. Mr. Justice Nares) in 1785; William Selby of the Mont, Kent, called in 1730, was invited to the Bench in 1761: *I.T.R.*, IV, 223–4, 430–1, 503; V, 62, 104, 113, 468.

Conveyed unto Edward Jackson Esq.^e William Noel Esq.^e William Chetwynd Esq.^e since deceased Pelsant Reeves Esq.^e John James Dobson Esq.^e Walter Dovey Esq.^e William Dixon Junr Esq.^e (since deceased) and Samuel Clarke Gent. their Heirs & Assigns In Trust for this Society and the Principal and Antients thereof their Successors and Assigns and to be from time to time disposed of in such manner & sort as they the said Principal & Antients & their Successors or the major part of them successively should from time to time direct and appoint Now for securing the repayment of the said One Thousand One Hundred pounds with lawfull Interest as aforesaid We the Principal and Antients aforesaid being the major part of the Antients of this Society Doe hereby Desire authorize and impower the said Edwd Jackson William Noel Pelsant Reeves John James Dobson Walter Dovey and Samuel Clarke (who are the Surviving Trustees named in the said Indentures of Lease and Release) to make & execute a Mortgage of the said Inn or Hostell and the Chambers Buildings and all other appurtenances thereunto belonging unto John Ford of the Middle Temple London Esq.^e and Peter Holford of Lincolns Inn in the County of Middlesex Esq.^e who have agreed to advance & lend the said summe of One Thousand One Hundred pounds for the purposes aforesaid Redeemable nevertheless upon the Repayment of the said one thousand one hundred pounds and the lawfull Interest thereof and for their so doing this shall be to them a sufficient Warrant and Authority AND IT IS FURTHER ORDERED that such Mortgage shall be made and executed in such manner & form as Councell shall direct and advise and IN TESTIMONY of this our Order we have hereunto subscribed our names.

	John Dewes Pr.
Da Thomas	John Dovey
John Green	Nash Mason
Henry Jones	Nathaniel Trayton
Edwd Wyatt	

Clements Inn in the } At a Pention held on Friday the 20th day of March
County of Middlesex } 1746 by & before Mr Dewes Principal Mr Dovey
Mr Green Mr Jones Mr Wyatt and Mr Mason

Whereas Mr Biddulph Mr Provost Mr Watts and Mr Goodwin have been summoned severall times to show Cause why they have not been admitted of this Society and have severally refused or neglected to show any Cause It is hereby Ordered that unless the said Mr Biddulph Mr Provost Mr Watts and Mr Goodwin do procure themselves to be admitted of the said Society before the 15th day of May next [1] their respective Chambers be padlocked and they refused entrance into the said Inn.

Clements Inn in the ⎱ At a Pention held on Tuesday the seventh day of
County of Middlesex ⎰ July 1747 Present Mr Dewes Principal Mr Dovey
Mr Mason Mr Trayton Mr Thomas and Mr Green

It is Ordered that Mr Dovey and Mr Mason two of the Antients of this Society and Mr Carmalt and Mr Fraine two of the Companions of the said Society Do and shall Examine and audit the Accounts of Mr John Dewes Principal of this Society from the beginning of Easter Term 1745 to the beginning of Trinity Term 1747 and that the said Mr Dovey Mr Mason Mr Carmalt and Mr Fraine or any three of them do make their Certificate and Report thereof as soon as conveniently it can be done.

> John Dewes Pr.
> John Dovey
> Nash Mason
> Nathaniel Trayton
> Da Thomas
> John Green

Clements Inn in the ⎱ At a Pension held on Wednesday the 15th day of
County of Middlesex ⎰ July 1747 Present Mr Dewes Pr.

Whereas Mr John Dovey Mr Nash Mason Mr John Carmalt and Mr John Fraine were by Order of pension made the seventh day of this instant July appointed Auditors of the Accounts of Mr John Dewes now Principal of this Society and they having accordingly audited stated & examined the said Mr John Dewes's accounts of Receipts & disbursements from the beginning of Easter Term 1745 to the beginning of Trinity Term 1747 have found the totall of the said Principals Receipts to be two thousand one hundred & nine pounds one shilling and sixpence farthing and the totall of his disbursements to be two thousand & one pounds eight shillings & one halfpenny so that there remained due on that account from the said Principal unto the said Society one hundred & seven pounds thirteen shillings & five pence three farthings as appears by their Report or Certificate thereof dated the 14th instant It is therefore Ordered that the said Accounts so stated audited examined & Certifyed as aforesaid be allowed and approved and the same are hereby allowed & approved to be just & true and the said John Dewes is hereby discharged from the said

---

[1] Edward Biddulph was admitted on February 22, 1748/9, Peter Prevost (who was chosen principal in 1770) on July 16, 1747, and Thomas Goodwin on May 16, 1747.

summe of two thousand & one pounds eight shillings & one halfpenny so by him disbursed as aforesaid.

John Dewes Pr.
John Dovey
Edw.ᵈ Wyatt
Nash Mason
Da Thomas
Nathaniel Trayton

15th July 1747

Clements Inn in the County of Middlesex—Whereas the Principal having acquainted the Antients in a Pension held this day that there wanted a new call of Antients (there seldom being enough in Town to make a Pension to transact the affairs of the House) And having nominated Mr James Lawson Mr John Yorke Mr John Crawford Mr John Brown & Mr Anthony Ryan (Companions of the said Society) as proper persons to be chosen It is Ordered that the said five Gentlemen be called up to the Antients Table when the Principal shall think fit so as they keep their Seniority as above named.

12th February 1747

Antients called up—Whereas the Principal having acquainted the Pension the 15th of July last that there wanted a call of Antients (there seldom being enough in Town to make a Pension to transact the affairs of the House) and having nominated Mr James Lawson Mr John Yorke Mr John Crawford Mr John Brown and Mr Anthony Ryan as proper persons to be chosen It was then Ordered that the said five Gentlemen should be called to the Antients Table when the Principal should think fit so as they kept their Seniority as above named In pursuance of which nomination and Order they were this day called up and all of them appearing and taking the Oaths of Allegiance & Supremacy & Abjuration in the Publick Hall before Mr Nash Mason Deputy Principal and the Antients in Commons they were admitted Antients of the Society of Clements Inn.

Clements Inn in the County of London At a Pension held at Clements Inn Hall on Thursday the 30th day of June 1748 present Mr Dewes Principal Mr Trayton Mr Wyatt Mr Thomas and Mr Ryan & Mr Lawson

Ordered that Mr Trayton & Mr Lawson two of the Antients of this Society and Mr Clifton & Mr Cooke two of the Companions of the said

Society shall & do examine & audit the accounts of Mr John Dewes Principal of this Society from the beginning of Trinity Term 1747 to the end of Trinity Term 1748 and that the said Mr Trayton Mr Lawson Mr Clifton & Mr Cooke or any three of them do make their Certificate & Report thereof as soon as conveniently it can be done

> John Dewes Pr.
> Nathaniel Trayton
> Edw. Wyatt
> Da Thomas
> Ja. Lawson
> A: Ryan

Clements Inn in the County of Middlesex At a Pension held at Clements Inn Hall on Friday the 15th day of July 1748 present Mr Dewes Principal Mr Dovey Mr Trayton Mr Lawson Mr Brown Mr Ryan

Whereas Mr Nathaniel Trayton Mr Lawson Mr Clifton and Mr Cooke were by Order of pension made the 30th day of June 1748 appointed Auditors of the Accounts of Mr John Dewes now Principal of this Society and they having accordingly Audited Stated & examined the said Mr John Dewes's Accounts of Receipts & Disbursements from the beginning of Trinity Term 1747 to the 14th of this instant July have found the total of his Receipts to be Three hundred twenty nine pounds three shillings and seven pence three Farthings and the total of his Disbursements to be Three Hundred twenty pounds thirteen shillings & three pence halfpenny so that there remained due on that account from the said Principal unto the said Society Eight pounds ten shillings & four pence farthing as appears by their Report or Certificate thereof dated the said 14th of July instant It is therefore Ordered that the said Accounts so stated Audited examined & Certifyed as aforesaid be allowed & approved and the same are hereby allowed and approved to be just and true and the said Mr John Dewes is hereby discharged from the said summe of Three hundred twenty pounds thirteen shillings & three pence half penny so by him disbursed as aforesaid.

> John Dewes Pr.
> John Dovey
> Nathaniel Trayton
> Ja. Lawson
> Jno. Brown
> A: Ryan

Michaelmas Term 1748

Thursday 24th November.

Clements Inn—Persons nominated by the Antients in Commons (in the absence of the Principal) for the Choice of a new Principal for three years from the first day of Hilary Term next ensuing

Mr Dewes Pr.	Mr Jones	Mr Mason

Richd Fleming
Tho Perkins
Willm Clifton
G Elers
Fountaine Cook
J. Fraine
W. H. Ashhurst
Nathaniel Trayton
Henry Jones
Jas. Lawson
A Ryan

Clements Inn   Tuesday the 7th of February 1748

George Perrott Esq.^e [1] came as Reader to this Society

Clements Inn in the County of Middlesex \} At a Pension held at Clements Inn Hall on Wednesday the 29th Day of November 1749 Present Mr Nash Mason Deputy Principal Mr Gregory Mr Jones Mr Thomas Mr Yorke Mr Brown Mr Crawford

Whereas Mr Carter late a Member of this Society is Dead & left his Chambers not fitted up agreeable to his Covenant contained in his Lease Granted by this Society and Mr Francis Green another member of this Society has laid out some money towards fitting them up and there is due from the said Mr Carter for Dues to this Society besides Porters Rolls Eight pounds six shillings and Mr Hood having proposed on behalf of the Executors of Mr Carter to reimburse the money laid out by Mr Green and to pay Twenty Guineas to the Society as a satisfaction as well of the said Dues as of the said Covenant We do hereby agree to accept the said proposalls Provided the said Mr Green be reimbursed and the said summe of Twenty Guineas be paid to the Steward of this Society for the use of the said Society within three weeks from the Date hereof And we do order

---

[1] George Perrott, called in 1732, was invited to the Bench in 1757 on producing his patent as one of H.M. Council learned in the law; he received his £10 gratuity as Serjeant and was appointed a Baron of the Exchequer in 1763: *I.T.R.*, IV, 260; V, 83, 147, 152, 162.

that the said Steward Do pay out of the said Twenty Guineas when received what is due to the porters of this House on account of the said Mr Carter

Nash Mason Deputy to Mr
John Dewes Principal

J. Yorke	H: Gregory
John Crawford	Henry Jones
	Da Thomas

Mr Elers Bond up—Mr Elers Haveing paid all arrears & being enterd of the Temple [1] & desireing to have his Bond Delivered up It is Ordered accordingly

Clements Inn in the County of Middlesex } At a Pension held at Clements Inn Hall on Wednesday the fourteenth Day of March 1749 present Mr Dewes Principal Mr Trayton Mr Mason Mr Thomas Mr Crawford & Mr Wyatt

Ordered that Mr Yorke & Mr Brown two of the Antients of this Society and Mr Clowdesly and Mr George Green two of the Companions of the said Society shall & do examine & audit the Accounts of Mr John Dewes Principal of this Society from the end of Trinity Term 1748 to the end of Hilary Term 1749 and that the said Mr Yorke Mr Brown Mr Clowdesly and Mr George Green or any three of them do make their Certificate & Report thereof as soon as conveniently it can be done.

John Dewes Pr.
Nathaniel Trayton
Nash Mason
Da Thomas
John Crawford
Edwd Wyatt

---

[1] George Elers, son and heir of Peter Elers of Chelsea, was admitted to the Middle Temple on November 10, 1738.

THE CONSTITUTIONS AND ORDERS
of
CLEMENT'S INN

Preliminary Note.—For the three known versions or instalments of the Constitutions and Orders see pp. li–lii above.

The following text begins with the title-page from the fly-leaf of the first version[1] and continues with Orders 1–62 which that version comprises. Where these Orders are in French (or in the case of Order 61, in Latin), the translation available in the third version is substituted; the substitution is indicated by the use of square brackets.

For Orders 63–84 and the subsequent unnumbered extracts from Pension Books the text is that of the third version.

LE LIVER DES CONSTITUCIONS & ORDERS
DEL HOSPIC. DE CLEMENTS INNE

Tho Holbeche prin[s] Anno Domini 1635

Hoc Hospicium fuit Hospicium hominum Cur. leg. temporal.
Nec non hominum Consiliariorum ejusdem legis[2]

Mich. 19 E. 4.

Livre dentries fo. 107a

No. 1. [That every Companion at the Time of his Admittance shall be bound with one other in the Sum of £10 for his good Behaviour and for the Payment of his Debts and Duties Due to the House.][3]

No. 2. [Also that every Companion being generally admitted shall pay for his Admittance Eight Shillings and four pence and every one specially admitted shall pay Sixteen Shillings and eight Pence.]

No. 3. [Also that every Companion admitted shall pay for the Christmas after his Admission Six Shillings and Eight pence for a Royal Noble

---

[1] Inside the cover there is written 'Richardus Edwardes xiiii Februarii xxxviii', followed by "This booke was shewed unto Francis Gerrarde & Edward Gerrard gent. at the tyme of their Severall Examinacions taken in Chancery on the part of Thomas Sturmy gen. & others Compl[ts] ag[t] Francis Kellett gen. def[t]—R. Peyton." Richard Edwards retired from the principalship in 1620: see Order 53 below.

For the Kellett litigation see p. xlvii above.

[2] Clement's Inn naturally cherished this evidence from the Book of Entries of its existence as a legal Inn in 1480—*et diu antea*. See p. xvii above.

[3] Increased in 1684 to £20: see p. 240 below.

and the third Christmas after his Admission Three Shillings and four pence for a Marshall mark [1] except that a Grand Christmas be held.]

No. 4. [Also that every Companion who is generally admitted not being in Commons all the two next Vacations after his Admittance shall pay for each of them that he is not in Commons Six Shillings and Eight pence.]

No. 5. [Also that every Companion who shall be chosen Steward and refuses it shall for every Refusal pay Twelve pence in the Name of an Essoyne And that no one shall be Steward but who hath been one Year of the said House and that every Steward shall find two Pledges for his duly accounting.]

No. 6. [Also that the Office of Steward [2] shall begin at the Fountain Chamber and go on through the whole House unto the Chamber next the Church [3] and shall always begin where it leaves off and the youngest in every Chamber shall be first chosen.]

No. 7. [Also that the Steward shall show his Roll of Commoners to the Principal or his Deputy on Demand on payment of Twelve pence and that every Steward shall finish his Account within ten days after the End of the Week on pain of Twenty Shillings and never to be Steward more.]

No. 8. [Also that every Steward for non-Attendance at Eating Times or Times of Learning or not doing his Duty and also for his superfluous Expence during his Week shall be amerced at the Discretion of the Principal or his Deputy and that every Steward shall answer to the House for the Profit he shall make of the Provision of the House during his week on pain of loosing Ten Shillings for the Use of the House.]

No. 9. [Also that every Companion who shall not pay his Commons to the Steward every Week before the New one Enters shall pay one penny And for every day after before the End of the Week another penny And every one who shall not pay his Commons every Week before the Accounts are made up shall be amerced Six pence.]

No. 10. [Also the Youngest of the First Mess of every Table at Meals shall every Working day put a Law Case [4] to the Steward or his Servitors

---

[1] The royal noble or ryal was valued at 10s., the noble (down to the middle of the fifteenth century) at 6s. 8d., and the mark at 13s. 4d.; a 'marshall mark' at 3s. 4d. is apparently unknown. See further, p. liii n. above.

[2] The early arrangements in this group of orders for the office of steward, which was apparently allotted by rotation for a week at a time to some junior member, are not easily reconciled with the continuous appointment of a responsible Companion during the period of our Pension Book: see p. xxxix above.

[3] The "faire fountain called Clement's Well", after which Stow suggests that Clement's Inn was named, had apparently been situated some 200 feet north of St. Clement Danes Church and some 90 feet east of the final position of the Hall of the Inn: see A. S. Foord, *Springs, Streams and Spas of London* (1910), pp. 61, 65.

[4] For case-putting see p. xxviii above.

which Case they shall put to that and every other Table on pain of forfeiting for every Default Four Pence.]

No. 11. [Also that the Lectures and Moots in the Two Vacations shall commence at the Chamber next the Church and proceed in order through the Chambers but at other times shall begin where they left off and the Youngest in every Chamber shall be first taken to the Moots and Readings.]

No. 12. [Also that it shall be lawful for the Principal to call to the Barr [1] to Moot such of the Companions that shall appear to him in his Discretion to be able to do it and every Companion that refuses to moot at the Outer Barr shall forfeit Twenty pence for every Refusal or otherwise to be put out of Commons at the Election and Discretion of the Principal or his Deputy.]

No. 13. [Also that if any Moot shall cease or be quashed in Default of the Outer Barristers each outer Barrister shall forfeit Six Shillings and eight Pence and if in Default of the Inner Barristers each Inner Barrister shall forfeit three shillings and four Pence [2] and if any outer Barrister take the Moot upon him and quash it through his own default he alone shall loose Six Shillings and eight Pence and if any Inner Barrister take upon him the Moot and quash it by his own default [3] he alone shall loose Three Shillings and four Pence And every Outer Barrister who refuseth to report shall forfeit Six Pence and if any one take it upon him and quash it he also shall forfeit Twelve Pence And everyone that shall moot or report shall do it perfectly without Book on pain of forfeiting for every Report Six pence or otherwise be put out of Commons at the election and Discretion of the Principal].

No. 14. [Also that the Principal or his Deputy Every working Day shall read a Writt in Natura Brevium as well in the Term as in the Vacation and every Companion being absent from thence and lying in the House not being of two years Standing shall forfeit for every Time one Penny.]

No. 15. [Also that no Companion generally or specially admitted shall be absent at the Moot or reading upon pain of forfeiting for every reading Two pence and for every Moot four pence (Attorneys and Clerks Attendants in the Offices of Law excepted) but that only in Term time and except all those of Twelve Years Standing.]

---

[1] See p. xix above. The report of Denton, Bacon and Cary to Henry VIII on the state of legal education, printed by Waterhous, *Fortescutus Illustratus*, when explaining 'utter barristers' at Inns of Court, states that at moots "they sit uttermost on the formes which they call the Barr" (*ib.*, p. 544).

[2] Outer barristers: see previous note. "Their degree is the chiefest degree for learners in the house, next the benchers, for of these be chosen and made the readers of all the Inns of Chancery. . . . All the residue of the learners are called inner barristers which are the youngest men that for lack of learning and countenance are not able to argue or reason in motes"—Waterhous, *ibid.*

[3] See p. xxvii above.

No. 16. [Also that the Principal ought ex Officio to admit any of the Companions to any Chamber at their Request without taking any thing But if they are once admitted to one Chamber and would be admitted to another they shall pay to the Use of the House for every Admission after the first Six Shillings and Eight pence And that no Companion being Attendant as Clerk or Servitor with any Person or shall be Clerk in any Office of the Law shall be admitted into any Chamber but if he be such Admittance to be ipso facto void And that it shall be lawful for any other in the Chamber to enter and keep him out.]

No. 17. [Also that none of the Companions shall enter the Buttery to eat without Licence of the Steward And that the Steward shall answer for the Misdemeanors there and then done if he does not give Notice to the Principal thereof Nor shall any enter into the Kitchen to disturb the Cook on pain of forfeiting Twelve pence.]

No. 18. [Also that none of the Companions shall use any Words to occasion the Displeasure of any of the Companions on pain of forfeiting Twenty Pence for every Offence Nor shall any of them beat another on pain of forfeiting Three Shillings and four pence Nor shall any of Them thrust any Weapon against another on pain of forfeiting Six Shillings and Eight Pence and be put out of the Inn until he hath more Grace.]

No. 19. [Also that none of the Companions shall use or go to any manner of unlawfull Games [1] within the House or Parish of St Clements nor use or go to any publick house within the same Parish but to eat or drink or for such like honest and necessary Business on pain of forfeiting for every Time three Shillings and four pence Nor shall lye with any Woman within the House or Parish on pain of forfeiting Twenty Shillings for the first Time and to be expelled for the Second.]

No. 20. [Also that no Companion shall disturb or disquiet any of the Companions at any Time within the House on pain of forfeiting three Shillings and four Pence for every Offence.]

No. 21. [Also that no Companion shall beat the Butler [2] nor the Cook nor any other officer of the House nor shall take upon him to displace any of them or put them out of their Office on pain of forfeiting Six Shillings and Eight pence but they shall be corrected or ordered by the Principal or his Deputy.]

No. 22. [Also that none of the Companions shall break any Table Tressell form Door or Window or pull up extirpate or destroy any Herb Plant fruit or Tree in the Garden on pain of Twenty pence for each Offence.]

[1] The corresponding regulations (Nos. 23–4) at Clifford's Inn specifically forbade tennis, dice, tables, cards, quoits and 'newefaire'. The *Early Records of Furnival's Inn*, edited by D. S. Bland (1957), pp. 34, 41, show amercements for playing in hall tennis, pennybrick and dice.

[2] For a case of butler-beating in 1686 see p. 240 below.

No. 23. [Also that no Companion who is not a noble Pensioner shall lye within the House not being in Commons (whatsoever is the Cause of his being out) On pain of forfeiting twelve pence per Week or Six pence for a half Week And that none of the Companions being out of Commons and out of Town for one Week shall keep his Chamber or Study Shut till he has been of the House Seven Years but that any other being in Commons and admitted to the said Chamber may enter into it and keep it until his Return And every Companion being in Town at the Time of reading in the Grand Vacations not being in Commons shall pay Twelve pence for every Week and Six pence for a half Week (those who shall have their Masters and Wives in Town only excepted).]

No. 24. [Also that every Companion seen in the Town [1] any Week within which any of the feasts shall be that are held principally and solely in the House and not in Commons shall pay Twelve Pence per Week nomine penae (those who have their Wives in Town only excepted) And every one being in Commons the Week of Nomine Poenae [2] and not being in Church at the Time of Service in the day of the Feast of Nomine Poenae shall pay Twelve Pence Per Diem and being absent from Church every other Saints Day shall pay Six Pence.]

No. 25. [Also that every Companion being a noble Pentioner shall be in Commons every Term one Week if the Term so long endures upon pain of forfeiting their Privilege.]

No. 26. [Also that no Companion shall convey any Vessell or other thing out of the Kitchen Without the Delivery of the Cook nor any Battell Pott [3] without the Delivery of the Butler upon pain of forfeiting every Time four Pence And if he doth and doth not deliver it back again before the next Meal he shall forfeit for every Meale that he does not deliver it Four pence.]

No. 27. [Also that none of the Companions at any Time or Place in Commons or out shall contradict the Principal or his Deputy [4] nor use any opprobrious Words or other unseemly Behaviour towards him on pain of forfeiting Forty Shillings.]

No. 28. [Also that every Companion shall behave himself Duly and lawfully at the Time of solemn Revels and at Times of Eating and Drinking and at the Time of Learning and other like Times without Disturbance or Loud Speaking And that none shall enter the Hall without his Gown and shall have his Head uncovered after his Entry into the Hall until he is

---

[1] The phrase *visus in villa* is familiar in the records of the legal Inns.

[2] Du Cange, *Glossarium Mediae et Infimae Latinitatis*, s.v. *Poena*, explains *Hebdomada poenalis* as Holy Week.

[3] The vessel in which the ration of beer or wine was drawn.

[4] Clifford's Inn had a statute (No. 37) specifically penalising a companion who challenged the principal's construction of the rules.

placed and when he goes out his Head shall be uncovered until he is out of the Hall nor shall any one use his Hatt in the Hall at any one of the above said Times on pain of forfeiting for every several Offence Twelve pence a Time and every one being in Commons that Shall not accompany the Principal or his Deputy at the Time of solemn Revels shall forfeit Four pence.]

No. 29. [Also that every Companion being in Commons in Term Time shall pay his Pension due the same Term before the End thereof upon pain of forfeiting Twelve Pence And every one that is in Arrear for the Payment of his Pensions for the Space of three years be he in Commons or not shall loose his Chamber And every Companion who shall be out of Commons being anyways indebted to the House shall pay it all when he comes into Commons within four Days after Demand or Notice on pain of Forfeiting Six Shillings and Eight Pence.]

No. 30. [Also if any of the Companions being out of Commons shall behave himself so as to disturb another Companion being in Commons or shall do any thing within the House or Parish that shall be to the Infamy or Dishonour of the House he shall be as well and in the same Manner reformed as if he had been in Commons at the Time of doing the Fact And if during the Time there is no Commons any Companion behave himself after any dishonest or disorderly Manner he shall be as well corrected at the Next Entring into Commons and By such Order as if Commons had been kept at the Time the Fact was Committed.]

No. 31. [Also that the Butler shall shutt the Doors every Night in Winter at Nine and at Ten in Summer [1] And before he shuts the Door next to the Street he shall knock a good While to give Warning on Pain of forfeiting Twelve pence for every Default and none shall enter after the Gates are Shutt without paying Six Pence And whoever comes in after the Gates have been shutt an hour shall pay twelve Pence And that no one shall scale the Walls on pain of forfeiting Three Shillings and four Pence And that no one shall piss within the Gates but at the Places made for that Purpose on pain of forfeiting two pence a Time.]

No. 32. [Also that no Companion being admitted and in Commons in any Inns of Court shall be in this House above Twenty days but that then the next in the Chamber may enter and keep him out.]

No. 33. [Also that the Principal with the Grand Council or Six of them at least shall establish and ordain good Statutes and Ordinances at their Discretions from Time to Time for the Maintenance and good Government of the House And that as well the Principal as the Grand Council shall be bound by them and that the Principal shall have Authority at any Time to Correct and reform at his Discretion any thing that shall be

---

[1] See Order 57 below (doors to be locked at 11 p.m.).

committed by any of the Companions against the Furtherance of Learning or the Advantage Reputation and Quiet of the House or any of the Companions therein tho' there be no express Statute or Ordinance provided for the Reforming thereof.]

No. 34. [Also that every one of the Grand Councill summoned to meet for any thing or Matter concerning the House and doth not come at the Time appointed shall pay Four pence.]

No. 35. [Also that the Principal shall be ready to give up his Accounts every year before the Auditors assigned of the said House on pain of forfeiting Forty Shillings And that the said Auditors at the next Grand Councill assembled shall declare the State of the Accounts.]

No. 36. [Also that the Principal shall read the Statutes in being twice every year viz: Easter and Michaelmas Terms openly in the Hall of the said House on pain of Forfeiting Forty Shillings.]

No. 37. [Also that no Companion of the House unless one of the Grand Council or such a Companion who hath been of the House Sixteen Years shall have his Servant in Commons without the Cook in the same House on Pain for every Week that he shall so have to forfeit to the Use of the same House Three Shillings and four pence.]

No. 38. [Also that every Companion being in Commons (unless one of the Grand Council) shall moot when he comes to his Chambers or find a Companion of the same House to moot for Him or pay to the Use of the House Twelve Pence And After they have all mooted in their Turn through their Chambers or have paid for the same Moot as before said then they shall moot who have no Chambers according to the Discretion of the Principal or his Deputy and if any of them shall refuse to moot he shall pay likewise Twelve pence.]

No. 39. [Also that every Companion being in Commons in the Grand Vacation shall be attending in the Hall at the Time of mooting for the Space of an hour and if he shall be absent from the Moot shall pay twelve Pence.]

No. 40. [Also that no Companion that shall hereafter be Steward shall cheat the House or seek his own Profit in his Office of Steward on Pain of Expulsion.]

No. 41. [Also that the Principal shall not demand any Allowance in his Accounts of any Debts of such who shall hereafter be admitted (of whom a Bond shall be taken) at any Time after it shall be due And of those heretofore admitted he shall demand no Allowance of any Debts if they are in Commons at any Time for the Space of one Month without reasonable Cause to be shewn to his Auditors.

No. 42. It is ordered by the Principall and Aunceints that every Companion that lyeth in the House or kepeth his Chamber and Studye or hath recourse into the same & not in Commons so that his pewnes [1] admitted into the same Chamber by his lyinge in the sayd Chamber or Kepinge the Kayes & resortinge thither cannot enjoye the same they & every of them that soe keepe their said Chamber shall by the Stewarde at the next beginning of the weeke or halfe weeke be put in Commons & soe kept in soe longe as he lyeth in any Chamber or soe resorteth to the same those of the Grand Companye & sutche others as have their wyves in Towne onely excepted and none other unlesse uppon some resonable & speciall cause by the said partye shewed to the Principall & allowed by hym & the Aunients that then shalbe in Commons.

No. 43. Forasmuch as uppon view of the State of the House by the Books Rolls and Accompts of the same it appereth that the said House runneth contynyally in arrerage and dett and of late Tyme hath had no stock to defraye the reparations and other necessaries which daylie increase more and more whereby the Companyons of the House are drawen to extraordinary and unaccustomed chardge For redresse whereof it is ordered that from henceforth and from tyme to tyme all the rolls shalbe made indented and a duplycat of the booke by the Principal whereof one part to remayn with the Principall and the other part with the Senior auncient for the tyme being or suche other auncient as they shall thinke mete And that all admittances and receits shalbe entred into the saide Duplicates in the middle or before the end of every tearme and so offred to the aunciens or the moste Part of them and when the greatest nomber of them shalbe in Commons and frome hensforth none to be admitted into this House before he have entred into a bonde as heretofore hathe been used.

No. 44. Item that hereafter the Principall shall receive of no Companyon being dettor to the house any Lesse some or sommes of money then that which shalbe due by hym or them so indetted without the assent of the aunciens or the most part of them when the moste nomber of them be in Commons.

No. 45. Item yt ys orderyd that no companyon of this house shalbe admytted into the chamber of any of the auntyents of the same house without the consent of the sayd auncyente.

No. 46. Item forasmuche as by secrett compact without the assent or knowledge of the aunciens the office of the principall hathe bene heretofore many tymes boughte and solde to the great detryment of the house for reformacion whereof it is orderyd that the principall and aunciens or the more part of them so that the nomber be not under sixe yf so many be lyvinge shall frome hensforthe by their dyscrecions make eleccion of three

---

[1] Puisnes, *i.e.* juniors: cf. 'puisne' judges and (*I.T.R.*, III, 92) "the third, fourth and puisne butlers".

K

names of the most meatest persons for that place and rome and by lyke assent one of them to be freely elected and chosen to be principall [1] And also that frome hensforth the Auncients shalbe elected and chosen in the lyke sorte Provided that the nomber maye be as many or fewe as the Graund Company shall thinke needful any order or statute heretofore made to the contrarye notwithstandying.

No. 47. [Also that those who have Chambers appointed for Students shall be in Commons all the Time of readings in the Grand Vacation (except those who have been admitted to them Sixteen Years before the publishing of this Order which was Michaelmas Term 19 of our late King) otherwise their Admittance to be void unless for reasonable Cause shown to the Principal and by him allowed he shall have Leave to be absent.]

No. 48. [Also that every one that is admitted or hereafter shall be admitted to Students Chambers shall perform their Exercises of Learning in the Time of Reading whenever required by the Principal or his Deputy as well to be present all the Time as to moot in Person on pain of Forfeiting of Six Shillings and Eight Pence for every outer Barrister and three Shillings and four pence every Inner Barrister.

The Chambers appointed for Students are these The 1st, 8, 13, 15, 17, 19, 22, 23, 24, 25, 27, 28, 29, 33, 35.] [2]

No. 49. [Also that the Principall shall admitt any Companion being a Student or intending to study to any Students Chamber at his Request without taking any thing And that he shall also admitt any other Companion at his Request to any other Chamber and when he who is so admitted comes into Possession of it he shall pay the Sums following (viz!) for every upper Chamber Forty Shillings to the Use of the House and to the Use of the Principal Six Shillings and Eight Pence and for every lower Chamber Twenty Shillings to the House and five Shillings to the Principal and if he refuses to pay it he shall be put out and another shall be admitted to it paying such Sums (the leased and other priviledged Chambers excepted).]

No. 50. [Also that the Ordinary Elections and disposing and placing of Officers shall be made by the most Voices of the Principal and five Antients at least being in Commons Where the Principal shall have two Voices.]

No. 51. [Also that every Companion not being of the Grand Company or being a noble Pensioner having Possession of any Chambers in the

---

[1] See also Order 62 below. In a case from Clifford's Inn (where a similar provision was in force) it was ruled that no one outside the three nominees must be chosen: *I.T.R.*, III, 115–8.

[2] An order of the Lord Chancellor and judges in 1664 directed each Inn of Court to survey its Inns of Chancery so that there might be a competent number of chambers for students: *I.T.R.*, III, 30.

House either leasehold or not shall be put in Commons every Michaelmas Term for two Weeks at least and every other Term one Week at least [1] and shall pay for his Commons though he does not come to take them.]

No. 52. [Also that every Companion of the House being of the Grand Company or other being in Town at the Time of reading in the Grand Vacation being thereunto required by the Principal or his Deputy shall be in Commons for the whole time of the said Readings in the said Grand Vacation on pain of forfeiting for every Default Five Shillings.]

No. 53. Clements Inne viii vo Julii 18 Jac. Reg. 1620. Whereas Richard Edwards gent the nowe principalle of Clements Inne having bestowed many yeares in that place and in respect of his age and other imployment is well pleased to withdrawe himselfe and to resigne the office to such person being of the graund company of that Society as he and the same graund company or the greater part of them ordinarily keeping commons in Clements Inne aforesaid shall nomynate & preferre therunto To take upon hym & to exercise the office of principall of the same Inne by the space of one whole yeare And after the first yeare shalbe ended then the same graund Company or greater parte of them keeping in commons usually there shall from yeare to yeare forever henceforward make choyce of one other of the same Company to exercise & use the principalls place office & authorytie for one whole yeare or ells if such graund company in their wysdomes shall approve and allowe of the carriage government & disposinge of the affayres & businesses of the same howse by any person soe elected to be principall within the same his yeare That then they or the greater part of them as aforesaid shall and may in their discretions appoynt allowe and continewe the same man in that office by the space of one or twoe yeares afterwards at their pleasures and as they upon due consideracion shall fynde just occasion Soe that noe one man at any tyme henceforward shall upon any pretence allegacion or other excuse be suffered to be and remayne principall above three yeares but then at the farthest to proceede to a newe eleccion And this shalbe a standing order in Clements Inn for ever to continue [2] for the eleccion of their principall from tyme to tyme as often as any eleccion shalbe requirable And that noe principall of this house at any tyme hereafter shall remove or displace any servant or officer of the house of his owne authorytie without the pryvitie assent &

---

[1] See Orders 56 and 60 below.

[2] See also Order 62 below. Both Joshua Blackwell and John Penny held the principalship of Clement's Inn for more than twice the maximum period here prescribed. At Clifford's Inn it was decided in 1668 that the office should be held in future for three years instead of for life, but principals were often re-elected: only 21 men served as principal there between 1668 and the final year of 1890—Hay-Edwards, *History of Clifford's Inn* (1912), p. 141. From 1691 the Treasurer of the Inner Temple held office for one year only—*I.T.R.*, III, 274.

consent of the Graund company for the tyme being or of the greater part of them Keeping in commons in Clements Inn at their being in town

> Signed Nicholas Edwards John Nye William Browne Otho Gayer John Chadwicke John Richards Antho: Langston Nicholas Yonge Tho: Holbeche Hnery Michell

No. 54. Memorandum the xxiiii day of March 1623 It is alsoe ordered that whosoever of the grand Company that shalbe elected to be principall accordinge to the former order & shall refuse to take upon him the place shall forfeit for such his refusall to the use of the house forty shillings [1] And that noe man from and after the end of this Terme shalbe freed of his pencions but during the tyme of his being principall.

> Signed Anth: Langston Princ. Otho Gayer William Browne Nicholas Yonge Tho: Holbeche John Tirer Thomas Style Godfrey Maydwell

No. 55. Clements Inn xvii May 1628 It is agreed & declared by the Principall and Auncients that the buildings in the Garden late Mr Dilkes [2] shalbe Lett at the rates hereafter following viz:

> the two lower Chambers at xxxs a peece
> the two middle Chambers at ls a peece
> the two upper Chambers at xxxiiis. iiiid. a peece

And that there shalbe two in everye Chamber & the fine to the House to be dispensed withall but the dutyes to the principall to remayne & be payd upon every admittance & upon theise rents every one is hereafter to be admitted to the chambers & not otherwise.

No. 56. Item it is ordered that everye companion of the house haveing a Chamber in the howse or lyeing in the howse shalbe in Commons for three weeks in Michaelmas Terme & two weeks in everye other terme or ells shalbe cast in Commons & pay his Commons for the said weekes any former order notwithstanding.[3]

No. 57. Item it is ordered that the streete gate shalbe lockt everye night at eleaven of the Clocke [4] & if any Companyon of the howse or clarke to any Companyon of this howse shall come in after that tyme he shall pay xiid & the master shall pay for his clarke And if the gate be found unlocked after eleaven of the clock the Keeper of the Gate shall pay for every tyme xiid to be deducted out of his wages & he shall every Saterday give notice at the accompts of the week of this order in the precedent weeke

---

[1] See also Order 62 below. For the successive refusals by John Green and Nathaniel Trayton see pp. 198, 200 above. [2] See p. xlvii above.
[3] See Order 51 above and Order 60 below. [4] See Order 31 above.

No. 58. Item it is ordered that the butler shall attend in the buttery in Easter Terme & Trinity Terme betweene six & seaven of the Clocke in the forenoone & betweene eight & nyne in the afternoone & in Michaelmas Terme & Hillary Terme betweene seven & eight in the forenoone & betweene eight & nyne in the afternoone And that if any Companion of this howse call for any beere at any tyme except the Cloathes be layd in the hall he shall battle the same [1]

> Signed Thomas Style princ. Otho Gayer Anth: Langston Tho: Holbeche Rowland Fryth John Tyrer Emor Bylclyffe Lewis Atterbury Chr Naylor William Fryth Martin Yaldon Richard Keylway William Clove

No. 59. Clements Inne 3 Junii 1634 Item that every Companyon of this house being in Towne that shall neglect or not come to receave the blessed Sacrament in St Clements Church once everye yere in Trinity terme uppon publique notice given of the certaine daye in Clements Inne hall shall forfeit for every severall default to the use of the house the sum of vis viiid.

No. 60. Item Whereas the xviith of May 1628 [2] an order was made that every Companyon of this House haveing a Chamber in the house or lying in the house shalbe in Commons 3 weeks in Michaelmas terme & 2 weeks in every other terme or ells shalbe cast in commons for the said week any former order notwithstanding. Which Order hath bene fownd to be very beneficiall to the said house but forasmuch as it is conceaved that no Companyon lying in the house or haveing a chamber in the house ought to be out of commons at any tyme during terme tyme which thing is the only support of the Society It is therefore further ordered that every Companyon whatsoever having a Chamber in the house or lying in the house shall not only be in commons the said 3 weeks in every Michaelmas terme & 2 weeks in every other terme according to the said former order of the xviith of May 1628 but shall also be in commons every other weeke during the contynuance of every terme if he be in towne or ells be cast in Commons for soe many weeks more as he shalbe in town in terme tyme any former order to the contrary notwithstanding

> Signed Rowland Frith princ. Tho: Holbeche Thomas Style Godfrey Maydwell Emor Bilcliffe Chr. Nailor Geo. Widoson Richard Keylway

---

[1] *Semble*, he will pay for it on his battery account: cf. Roger North, *Lives of the Norths*, I, p. 300, "He kept a table there and his family were allowed to battle in the butteries".

[2] See Order 56 above.

No. 61. [*Writt of Nusance for Clements Inn against Ford*—Charles &c. to the Sheriff of Middlesex Greeting WHEREAS we lately caused it to be publicly proclaimed (amongst other Things) that no person should erect any Walls whatsoever or build any Sheds thereupon within our City of London or Suburbs thereof or within the Distance of three Miles from any Gate of the same City or from the Palace of Westminster Licence not being first had of our Commissioners assigned for additional Buildings in those Parts [1] Nevertheless one Thomas Ford late of the Parish of St Andrew in Holbourn in your County Yeoman lightly regarding our Royal Publick Command not having obtained a Licence of our said Commissioners in a Certain Field in the parish of St Clement Danes without the Barrs of the New Temple London on the North part of a certain Antient Inn called Clements Inn long since appointed for the Residence of Men applying themselves to the Study of our Laws hath begun to erect a Certain Wall to which any Shedds may be added with Bricks Morter and Sand and to inclose part of the said Field into a Court and Common Place to play at with Bowls and hath already put upon the Foundation of the said Wall Bricks Lime and Sand in order to make a further Proceeding on the said Wall as it is said And if the said Place should be so inclosed it will happen That the Members of the said Inn undertaking the Study of our Laws will be disturbed by the Noise and Clamour of those resorting to the said Place insomuch that they will be unable to follow their Study WE being willing that our Commands should be observed and to preserve the Tranquility and Quiet of the said Students that they may not be diverted from their Studies COMMAND you that you do not omitt by Reason of any Liberty within your County But that on our Behalf you Cause the said Thomas to be Commanded that he altogether desist from any further erecting of a Wall in the Place aforesaid And the Wall begun and Foundations of the Wall by him laid in the Place aforesaid he cause to be demolished under pain of our Displeasure WITNESS ourself at Westminster the 19th day of November in the 9th year of our Reign

Cartwright

By the Lord Keeper of the Great Seal of England Return thereof

By Virtue of the Writt to me directed I have Caused to be Commanded the within named Thomas that he desist from any further erecting the Wall within written in the place within written and that he cause the Wall begun and the Foundations of the same Wall to be demolished as I am within Commanded

The Answer of Hugh Perry   ⎫
         and   ⎬   Sheriffs
Henry Andrews   ⎭

---

[1] See Patent Rolls 6 Car. I, pars 11 (C 66/2543).

Delivered of Record in Michaelmas Term 8th year aforesaid Wrote in Roll 1667

Moyle]

No. 62. Clements Inne. Whereas the Principall of Clements Inne hath heretofore by Order of the grand Company of the said Society or the greater number of them being in Commons bene elected and chosen Principall of the said Society for one two or three yeares as they or the greater part of them Keeping in Commons should in their discretions appoint and allow of As by an order of the said grand Company appeareth [1] Now for that the said place or office of a Principall is a place of Trust and doth generally concerne the good and welfare of the whole house and every Companion of the said Society is equally concerned therein and may challendge to have a vote in the eleccion of such person of the grand Company as shalbe nominated and proposed by the said grand Company or the greatest number of them Keeping in Commons to be in the place or office of a Principall as aforesaid Therefore the said grand Company for the reasons aforesaid doe think fitt and order that from tyme to tyme as often as any eleccion of a principal shall be requirable or thought requisitt by the said grand company or the greater number of them keeping in commons that the names of three of the grand company shalbe nominated and proposed by the said grand company unto the rest of the Companions of the said house then alsoe being in Commons and that out of those three persons soe nominated and proposed as aforesaid by the said grand company the said grand Company together with the said Companions or the Major part of them Keepinge in Commons as aforesaid shall out of those three persons soe nominated and proposed as aforesaid make their eleccion and such of the said three persons as shall have most voices in the said eleccion shall thereuppon be preferred to stand and be in the place office & authority of a Principall of the said Society for one two or three yeares as the said grand Company or the greater number of them Keeping in Commons shall in their discretions think fitt & requisite any former order to the contrary notwithstanding [2] And it is further ordered that if any person or persons soe elected as aforesaid shall refuse to accept of the said place or office of a principall he shall for such his refusall forthwith pay the somme of Fourty shillings to the use of the said Society [3] and thereuppon a new eleccion to be had accordinge to the Order

James Prescott principal Godfr: Maydwell Ric: Keylway Henrie Bailie J. Grene Ambrose Holbeche E: Gerard:

---

[1] See Order 53, p. 227 above.   [2] See Orders 46 and 53 above.
[3] See also Order 54 above.

Note the last Order was signed by the Persons own Hands who are thereunder named

Here Ends the Book of Orders entered on the Velom Leafs.[1]

Clements Inn. The Book of Orders 1650. Bound in a Book with a Parchment Cover beginning No. 63

No. 63. 20th May 1650. It is ordered by the Principal and Antients of this House that every Companion of the House shall pay unto the Now Principal his Pensions and all other Duties in Arrear before the End of this present Easter Term in the Common Dining Hall of the said House at such Days and Times and upon such Notice as shall be appointed and given by the said Principal and that All Pensions and Duties that for the future shall grow due and payable by any Companion of the said Society shall be paid unto the Principal for the Time being at such Days and Times and upon such like Notice as aforesaid And in Case any Companion of this House shall refuse or neglect to do the same his Chamber is thereupon to be forfeited and seized to the Use of the said House and he himself to be expelled the said House.

No. 64. It is Ordered by the Principal and Antients aforesaid that if any Companions of this House shall permitt or suffer Any one whatsoever to lie in his Chamber unless he be first admitted a Companion of the said House or a Servant to a Companion of the House he shall forfeit his Chamber and the Same shall be seized to the Use of the said House and he himself to be expelled the said House

> James Prescott Princ. — Godfrey Maidwell —
> Richd Keylway — Edw. Alleyn — R Williams
> — Jo Rattenbury — Edwd Pegg — Jo Alywyn
> — Geo. Merrifield — Henry Bailey — J Green
> — A Holbech — E Gerard

Clements Inn   5th July 1650

No. 65. Whereas the Kitchen of this House is in Great Decay and ready to fall down for Want of due Reparations It is ordered by the Principal and Antients of the House that the Roof of the said Kitchen be taken down and the said Roof and Walls of the said Kitchen be new built and repaired

---

[1] This book (the 'first version' mentioned at p. li above) is more fully described by the compiler of the third version as "a Book bound in Calves skin with Clasps and marked thus M $\frac{C}{I}$ H It has Velom Leaves and goes no further than No. 62".

The fly-leaf of the third version bears the title "Translation of Clements Inn Old Orders". It translates the citation from the Book of Entries (see p. xvii above)—"This Inn was a Society of men of the Temporal Law-Courts and of Councellors of the same Law". Its text, from this point until the end of Order 84 (see p. 239 below), presumably follows the missing 'second version', the "Book of Orders 1650", described above as "with a Parchment Cover beginning No. 63".

And towards the Building and Repairs thereof that the Principal and Antients shall every of them pay the Sum of Ten Shillings apiece And every other Companion of the said House shall pay five Shillings which Monies is forthwith to be paid and that Mr Godfrey Maidwell and Mr A Holbech Sen.r are hereby appointed Collectors thereof

> James Prescott Princ. — Godfr. Maidwell — Richd Keylway — Edw Alleyn — Jo Aylwyn — Geo: Merrifield — Henry Baillie — J. Green — A Holbeech . Clements Inn 28th November 1650

No. 66. Whereas by an Order of the fifth of July last past the great Decay of the Kitchen of the said House was ordered to be new built and repaired And Whereas by the Fall of some Chambers the last long Vacation a great Part of the Hall and Entries were beaten down whereby the New Building and repairing of the said Kitchen Hall Entries and Chambers Thereunto adjoyning doth amount unto the Sum of £132 19s. 8d. as by the several Bills thereof appeareth And whereas the particular Charges of the New Building and repairing of the said Kitchen Hall and Entries amount to the Sum of £71 15. 0 as by the Workmens Estimate appeareth And Whereas the Sum collected on the former Rate by the said Order of the 5th of July last amounteth but unto the Sum of thirty pounds four Shillings and six pence It is therefore ordered by the President and Antients that they the said Principal and Antients shall every of Them pay the Sum of ten Shillings apiece and every other Companion of the said House shall pay five Shillings apiece towards the further Satisfaction of the said £71. 15s. 0d. which Monies are forthwith to be paid And that Mr John Green and Mr Gerard are hereby appointed Collectors thereof

> James Prescott Pr. — Godfr. Maidwell — Richd Keylway — Jo Aylwyn — Geo Merifield — Hen: Bailie — A Holbeach

> Clements Inn   29th April 1651

No. 67. Whereas the House of Office belonging to the same Society was very Ruinous and in Decay and Dangerous for the Companions of the Society to make Use thereof And Whereas the Companions of the same Society did earnestly desire that the same should be new built which accordingly hath been done the Last Lent Vacation the Charge whereof amounting to the Sum of £43. 18s. 4d. as appeareth by the particular Bills under the Workmens Hands It is therefore ordered by the Principal and Antients of the same Society that every Companion of the said House shall forthwith pay the Sum of 5s. apiece for and towards the satisfying the said Charges

> James Prescott Principal and 8 Antients

K*

Clements Inn   14th June 1651

No. 68. Whereas by an Order of the 29th day of April last past It was ordered by the Principal and Antients of the same Society that every Companion of the Same should pay the Sum of Five Shillings apiece for and towards the New Building the House of Office belonging to the Same Society But finding that Proportion to fall very Short of the Sum expended as appears by the particulars hereunder written It is therefore hereby ordered by the said Principal and Antients that every Companion of the same Society shall forthwith pay for satisfying the several Charges disbursed in and about the same Building the Sum of Four Shillings and six pence Witness our Hands James Prescott Pr. and Eight Antients

Disbursements

To the Bricklayer	22 . 9 . 11		Rec^d 23 . 0 . 0
Carpenter	18 . 7 . 7		
Smith	1 . 18 . 9	43 . 18 . 4	
Painter	0 . 17 . 1		
Laborers	0 . 5 . 0		Rec^d 20 . 8 . 4

Clements Inn   July 6th 1652

No. 69. Whereas Thomas Coverly Bricklayer hath repaired the Roof of four Chambers in Clements Inn which are held by Lease of the same Society by several Companions thereof for several years yet to come and unexpired for repairing of which Roof the said Coverly hath produced and attested under his Hand that the Repairing of the said Roof doth amount unto the Sum of Thirty nine Shillings and four pence It is therefore ordered by the Principal and Antients of the same Society that the several Lessees of the said four Chambers or their Assigns shall immediately upon Notice hereof pay the said Thirty Nine Shillings and four pence by four equal Shares or proportions for the said Work done by the said Coverly And in Default thereof the several Chambers shall stand seized to the Use of the said Society until the Defaulters of Payment shall pay the Particular Proportions of the said Charge and of Repairs

Geo Merifield Princ. and Six Antients

No. 70. An Order for admitting John Luss to John Woods Chambers

No. 71. An Order for lowering Sam: Holbeech's Rent on paying a Fine

No. 72. May 10th 1655 Clements Inn in the County of Middlesex. It is ordered by the Principal and Antients of the same Society that John Tidy be from henceforth displaced from any further Service of or to the same

Society and likewise he is hereby discharged from being Gardiner to the same Society or any other Employment whatsoever and that he forthwith remove his Habitation and Dwelling from thence.

Geo Merifeild Princ. — H. Bailie — A Holbeech — E Gerard

No. 73. July 4th 1655. Whereas Mr Gosnold and Mr Fyfield and other Companions of the same Society are Suddenly to repair the Building in their Possession being the Cross Building next the Garden in Clements Inn It is ordered by the Principal and Antients of the same Society that the Passage or Arch under the same Building be not straitned or made narrower than now the Same is by the Repairing the Same

Signed by Principal and five Antients

Clements Inn   October 16th 1655

No. 74. Whereas several Principals of the Same Society have heretofore granted Divers Chambers in Revertion to the great Impoverishing the said Society For the Prevention of which Inconvenience for the future It is by the now Principal and Antients hereby ordered that all Grants in Reversion from henceforth to be granted be null and void to every Chamber or any Part of any Chamber now built or hereafter to be Built within the same Society But all Chambers hereafter to be granted to any Companion of the same Society shall be granted by the Principal and the Major Part of the Antients in Commons within one Week before the End of every Term And that no Chambers be henceforth granted by the Principal and Major Part of the Antients but upon such Fine or Yearly Rent or Both as they shall think most fitt for the Necessary Occasion of the same Society [1]

Geo Merifeild Princ. & five Antients

No. 75. October 16th 1655

Whereas Several Buildings at the Present are in the Possession of Particular Companions of this Society (who were Builders thereof) or their Assigns And Whereas they have granted particular Interests or Terms to Companions of this Society who do permitt and suffer Strangers who are not admitted to Lodge in and make use of several Chambers Granted as aforesaid It is therefore ordered by the Principal and Antients that the several Builders or their Assigns do forthwith bring in a Note of their Several Grants or Contracts by them made to or with any Person Whatsoever and for what Term whereby the Principal and Antients may take Notice who are the Possessors of any Chambers against any former Orders of the same Society

Geo Merifield Princ. and 5 Antients

---

[1] For the repeal of this order in 1697 see p. 242 below.

No. 76. Whereas Several young Clerks Servants to such who are Companions of this Society have of late taken upon them so much Rudeness as to Committ several Offences against the Antient Orders of this Society they not being liable to the Penalties Contained in the same Orders in Respect they are not admitted of the same Society The Principal and Antients being by several Complaints made sensible of the Inconveniences thereby arising They do therefore hereby order for the future that all the Companions of this Society whose Clerks or Servants that shall either lodge in or have Recourse to their Masters Chambers shall be liable to all such Orders as are heretofore made concerning the Civil Government of this Society and that All such Mulcts of Money as are forfeited by the Breach of any Orders shall be imposed on and paid by the Masters of such Servants who shall committ any such Offence as if his said Master had committed the Same.

Geo Merifield and five Antients

No. 77. Clements Inn   6th February 1656

Whereas Divers Abuses have been occasioned by Casting of Water and Emptying of Chamber Potts out of Windows and Doors of the same Society Whereupon Several Complaints have been made to the Principall And Antients of the same Society It is therefore ordered by the Principall and Antients of the same Society That if any Water or Chamber Potts be cast forth or emptied out of any Windows or Door of any Chamber of the same Society by any Person whatsoever the Inhabitant or Inhabitants of the Same Chambers being a Companion of the same Society shall forfeit to the Use of the House for every such Offence the Sum of Six pence [1]

Geo Merifield and 7 Antients

No. 78. August 24th 1659 Clements Inn in the County of Middlesex concerning Mr Jo. Allen's Chambers Whereas the Principal and Antients have ordered a padlock to be sett and afixed upon this Chamber Door It is therefore ordered by the said Principal and Antients that no Companion of this Society presume to strike off the said Padlock upon pain to be expelled this Society

J. Grene Princ. and four Antients

No. 79. Clements Inn 9th March 1660 Whereas the Principal and Antients have entered into and seized to the use of the said House a Chamber in the Middle Court up one pair of Stairs late in the Possession of Mr Pegg and Mr Jackson which is a House Chamber & now belonging

---

[1] This nuisance periodically required disciplinary action in the legal Inns: see, for example, *I.T.R.*, II, 319 (1656/7), III, 150 (1679), 383 (1704), 430 (1711).

to the Principal and Antients to dispose of for the Benefit of the said House But is now possessed by Mr Henry Kniveton and Mr Thomas Bolwell two Companions of the said House It is therefore ordered by the said Principal and Antients that a Padlock be sett and afixed upon the said Chamber Door and that No Companion of this House or any of their Servants presume to strike of the same upon Pain of being expelled the same Society

J. Green Princ. and 4 Antients

No. 80. Clements Inn   2d December 1676
Whereas Mr John Ekins late Principal of the same Society hath accounted according to the Orders of the said House by which account there remains due to the Society from the said Mr Ekins for the whole three years he was Principal the sum of £139. 15s. 7d. whereof there is already paid by the Order and Consent of the Antients of the Same Society to Mr Thomas Sturmy the present Principal the Sum of £50 Now we the Antients whose Names are hereunder written do consent agree and order that the said Mr Ekins shall pay over unto the said Mr Sturmy the present Principal The Sum of £89. 15s. 7d. being the Residue of the said Sum of £139. 15s. 7d. remaining in the Hands of the said Mr Ekins and for his so doing this Order shall be his sufficient Discharge

Ralph Edge   Ric. Bourne   A Holbech   J. Coates

No. 81. Clement's Inn 5th July 1682 Whereas Several Gentlemen of this Society are in Arrears for Pensions and other Duties It is therefore ordered by the Principal and Antients that the respective Bonds of all such Persons who are in Arrears shall be put in Suit the next Michaelmas Term unless they in the Mean Time do pay and discharge the same

A Holbech

No. 82. Clements Inn in the County of Middlesex 15th February Anno Domini 1683 Whereas the Several Persons hereafter named did upon the Account of the Society of Clements Inn on the 27th day of February 1682 lend and advance the several Sums of Money hereafter mentioned (vizt)

Mr M Wrightson the Present Principal	75.	8.	6
Mr Edwd Gerrard	200		
Mr A Holbeech	200		
Mr W Callow	150	and	
Mr Thos Bagshaw	200		

and for Security thereof an Assignment was made Dated 27th February 1682 unto Mathew Johnson Esq^e Nich: Bagshaw and Mathew Hall gen.

(amongst other things) of Divers buildings in Clements Inn for the Terms
and upon such Trusts as are therein mentioned as thereby may more fully
appear [1] And Whereas Mr Wm Gibson did afterwards pay unto the said
A Holbeech £100 part of the said £200 Now it is ordered and agreed that
the several sums of Money aforesaid so lent and advanced by the Several
persons aforesaid together with what other Monies shall at any Time or
Times hereafter be Lent or advanced by any other of the Members of the
said Society for and towards the Payment and Discharge of any other of
the Monies mencioned in the said Assignment which are to be paid by or
out of the said Assignment on the Trust thereof shall be satisfyed and paid
by and out of the Buildings in Clements Inn and the Rents and Revenues
thereof with Interest for the same after the Rate of £6. 0. 0 Per Cent per
Annum from the respective Times of the Several Payments or Advance-
ments thereof respectively Provided always that this Order shall not any
ways impeach or impair the Security of the said Assignment of any other
the lands Tenements or Hereditaments therein mentioned

> M. Wrightson Prin. E Gerard W Hutchinson Fr
> Scampton W Byrd A Richards Philip Style A Holbeach
> Wm Callow W Gibson

No. 83. Clements Inn Com. Midd.   26 November 1684

Whereas Mr M Wrightson now Principal and Mr E Gerard one of the
Antients of this Society have paid £812 more than they formerly laid down
towards Satisfaction of the Monies secured to Mrs Rogers and Mrs
Brawne on the Security of Mr Kelletts Building and Dobbs Building in
this House and other things viz.[t] £412 by Mr Principal and £400 by
Mr Gerard as by Acquittances under the Hands and Seals of the said
Mrs Rogers and Mrs Brawne doth appear [2] It is ordered and agreed that
the said £800 and Interest for the same from the Time of Payment thereof
shall be repaid to Mr Principal and Mr Gerard respectively out of the
Revenues and Profits of this Society together with the other Monies by
them formerly paid and laid down on the same Account

No. 84. Clements Inn Com. Midd.   18 February 1686

Whereas the Several Persons hereafter named Did upon the Account of the
Society of Clements Inn on the 27th day of February 1682 lend and advance
the several sums of Money hereafter mentioned viz.[t] Mr M Wrightson then
present Principal the sum of £75. 8s. 6d. Mr E Gerard £200 Mr A Holbeach £200 Mr W Callow £150 and Mr Tho: Bagshaw £200 And for

---

[1] The transactions recorded in Orders 82–4 were stages in the clearing up of the
difficulty with Francis Kellett, for which see pp. xlvii–xlix above.

[2] See the previous note. As stated at p. xlix above, Kellett obtained on mortgage £1600
from James Rogers: Mrs. Anne Rogers and Mrs. Anne Brawne were the widow and
daughter of James Rogers; Frances Rogers was an unmarried daughter of James Rogers.

Security thereof an Assignment was made bearing Date the said 27th Day of February 1682 unto Math Johnson Esq.[e] Nich Bagshaw and Math Hall gentlemen (amongst other Things) of Divers Buildings in Clements Inn for the Terms and upon such Trusts as are therein mentioned as thereby may more fully appear And Whereas Mr William Gibson did afterwards pay to the said A Holbeach £100 part of the said £200 And Whereas the said E Gerard and M Wrightson did on the 3rd day of March 1683 pay unto Ann Brawn in the Assignment named £110 10s. and to Fra. Rogers £710 10s. in all £812 whereof £400 was paid by the said E Gerard which with the £200 before mentioned is still due to him with some Interest for the same And the said Mr Wrightson did pay £412 Residue and Remainder of the said £812 in Discharge of so much due to the said Ann Brawn and Franc Rogers on the Security of the said Assignment And Whereas the said Mr Wrightson Did on the 9th day of March 1685 pay unto Charles Brawn Esq.[e] the Sum of £200 for the Use of Elizabeth and Ann Brawn Infants and to Ann Brawn their Mother £9. 6s. 8d. Secured by the said Assignment and in Discharge thereof in Pursuance of an Order of the Court of Exchequer as by several Acquittances and Receipts may appear All the Said Sum so paid by the said Mr Wrightson amounting to £696 15s. 2d. and a great Part thereof with Interest is still due and unpaid to the said Mr Wrightson And Whereas Mr William Hutchinson a member of the said Society of Clements Inn hath this day paid and advanced to the said Mr. Wrightson the sum of £100 in part of the Monies so by him the said Mr Wrightson laid down and advanced as aforesaid Now it is ordered and agreed that the said William Hutchinson His Executors and administrators shall be satisfyed and paid the said £100 so by him This day paid and advanced to the said Mr Wrightson with Interest for the same after the Rate of £6 per Cent per Annum by and out of the Buildings in Clements Inn and the Rents and Revenues thereof

Here Ends the Books of Orders[1] All Since are in the Pension Books

Note
In the purchase deed 1677 from Lord Clare[2] there is this Exception
Except and always reserved out of the said grant and release a free foot passage or way for all persons whatsoever to pass or go through the said Inn (without burthens) to and from Clare Market and Clare Market Place at all times in the Day particularly from 5 in the morning till 10 at night from Lady Day to Michaelmas and

[1] *I.e.*, the 'first version' (the book 'with velom leaves') and the missing 'second version' (the book 'with a parchment cover'): see pp. li–lii, 218 above.
[2] The deed by which Francis Kellett bought the Inn premises for £350: see pp. xlvii, xlix above.

from 6 in the morning till 9 at night from Michaelmas to Lady Day other than Sundays in Church Time.

At a pension Hill. 34 & 35th Cha. 2d   9th February 1682 Principal & Antients [not named]

Rates for a Composition for Commons—Memorandum It was unanimously agreed that the Composicion for all Arrears of Duties to this Inne shall be after this manner vizt That all Pencions Essoignes Hearth Money and Rent shall be entirely paid without abatement & those persons that live in Town & have Chambers in the House shall pay their full Castings into Commons And those who have Chambers and live in the Country shall pay one Moiety of their Castings into Commons And those who live in the Country and have no Chambers shall pay one third part of their Castings into Commons PROVIDED THAT those that have Chambers in the House pay their Duty as aforesaid before the end of Easter term next and the rest before the end of Trinity term next but in the mean time no Proceedings at Law to be stayed And from henceforth no Abatement to be made of the Castings into Commons or other Duties as aforesaid But if any person or persons from henceforth that shall not be in town & shall pay his or their Pensions termly and shall give notice to the Principal for the time being of such his or their Absence that then he or they giving such notice shall not be cast into Commons

Pension 14th November 1684

Penalty of Bonds—That all Penaltys in Admittance Bonds be £20 from henceforward [1]

Chief Justices Warrant against those who Knockt off Padlocks—That inasmuch as the Principal did Padlock Mr Rouses Mr Bartons & Mr Turtons Chambers & Mr F. Rouse & Mr Gullock who hath intruded & not admitted did Knock off Mr Rouses Padlock Mr Cam a Person not admitted being an Attorney of Common Pleas Knockt off Capt Bartons & Mr R Middlemore Knockt off Mr Turtons It is agreed that Warrants be procured from the Chief Justice against them

New Padlocks Ordered—That Mr Oldshaws & Fields Chambers be Padlockt as also Mr Rouses Turtons & Bartons de novo.

Pension 11th February 1686 Principal & 6 Antients

Assaulting the Butler—It is Ordered that unless Mr Middlemore do on Fryday night next attend the Principal & Antients or acknowledge his wrong done in striking & abusing Mr Leigh the Butler of this Society & give satisfaction & assurance of his good behaviour for the time to come

---

[1] Previously £10: see Order 1, p. 218 above.

That he is expelled the Society & that the Chamber he now holds & for which he has paid no Rent these five years the Commons whereof amount unto £20 shall be Padlockt & he kept out of the said Chamber And inasmuch as the said Mr Leigh conceives himself in continual Danger of Bodily harm by the said Mr Middlemore It is further Ordered that the said Mr Leigh may if he think good apply by himself to the Lord Chief Justice of England for his Lordships Warrant against the said Mr Middlemore for the abuses already done him & his future Security

Pension 26th November 1688 Principal & 5 Antients

Commons excused for the Troubles—Ordered that all Castings into Commons of this Term shall be Spared by reason of the present Comotions.[1]

Pension 24th November 1690 Principal & 4 Antients

Auditors Choze—The Principal & Antients having agreed that Mr Prior & Mr Holbech shall take their [? audit of] Mr Wrightsons Account during the time he was Principal & has not yet accounted for the gentlemen of the Society have on their part Elected & nominated Mr Edwd Fienes & Mr Giles Hooper for that purpose

Pension 27th February 1696

Choosing Assessors—This pension was appointed pursuant to the Precept directed to the Principal of this Society from Wm Petyt John Holloway and John Trenchard Esq[es] Commissioners (amongst others) for putting in Execution within the Society of the Inner Temple and Inns of Chancery thereunto belonging An Act of Parliament made in the 8th year of His Majesty that now is over England &c and entituled An Act for granting to His Majesty an Aid as well by a Land Tax as by several Subsidies & other Duties payable for One Year[2] requiring them to return in writing to them and the rest of the Commissioners acting for the said Society in the Inner Temple Library on Tuesday the 2nd day of March as is therein specified the names of three or more able and Knowing Persons to be Assessors & Collectors for this Society of the said Tax & Rates by the said Act And we have accordingly proceeded & nominated Mr Thos Callow Mr Arthur Squire & Mr Arthur Lake members of this Society for

---

[1] London was in a ferment: William of Orange had landed at Torbay: King James had set out to join his army at Salisbury and then come back: eminent leaders had left him.

In November 1689 the Inner Temple summoned the Principal and Ancients to show cause why Clement's Inn was not in Commons, but the matter was apparently dismissed: see *I.T.R.*, III, 267–8.

[2] 8 & 9 Will. III. c. 6.

to attend for the purposes aforesaid Ordered the Principal accordingly to make his Return

Pension 28th June 1697

Order in 1655 agst Grants in Reversion Repealed—Forasmuch as the 16th of October 1655[1] It was Ordered that all Grants in Reversion of any Chamber or parts of Chambers in this Inn should from thenceforth be null & void And that such Grants should be from time to time made within one week before the end of every Term Which Order may prevent the making the best benefit of the Chambers in the House & may be too narrow a Confinement to the Principal and Antients to make Leases and Contracts relating to them as occasion may happen likewise to the disadvantage of the Society In Consideration whereof It is Ordered that the said Order before mentioned be Repealed Vacated and sett aside and that for the future the Principal & Antients shall be at Liberty to Let the Chambers in Reversion or otherwise & at such times & meetings as they shall agree to be most for the Improvement of the Incumb of the Society

Pension 29 June 1699

About New Inn stopping of Lights in the Garden—Mr Carvile on behalf of himself and the rest of the Gentlemen concerned in the building where his Chamber is Informed that the Butler of New Inn had lately given notice from that Society that they had Ordered the shutting up the Lights that look out of the said Building into their Garden which would be of great Prejudice to the respective Owners Ordered that Mr Callow do from this Table attend Mr Principal & the Antients of New Inn to know the occasion of this Message and that he may Friendly Confer with them about the inoffensiveness of the said Lights that no difference be promoted between the Societies

Pension 4th December 1701

Admitted as a Repaster[2] to choose a Principal—Mr Hawford a Question being started whether he might come in for a Repast to the Election of a Principal or be at Commons half a Week Agreed that (without Precedent) he be as a Repaster and discharged in the Commons Roll.

Pension 7th May 1703

Shop Rate by the Parish to Land Tax—Mr Garfoot appears with Mr Stacey and informs the Society of an action pending by Mr Stacey against Falconer late Collector of the Land Tax for the Parish of St Clement Danes in Trover and Conversion for a Watch which was Distrained by the said

---

[1] See Order 74, p. 235 above.
[2] One who eats in Hall when not in commons that week.

Collector in the Shop at the Foregate as the goods of the said Mr Garfoot for the said Tax Ordered & Agreed that this Society will prosecute the said Suit to Tryal at the charges of the Society in order to make appear that the said Shop being part of this Inn is to be Assessed as part thereof and not in the said parish at large the said Mr Stacey promising that in Case a Verdict shall pass for the Plaintiff this Society shall be reimbursed their Expenses out of the Costs recovered thereupon And in Case the Plaintiff shall be Non Suit or a Verdict pass for the Defendant this Society will bear Mr Stacey harmless from the Costs.

Pension 18th June 1703

Nuisance by a Horse Pond in the Lamb Inn—The Horse Pond in the Lamb Inn and the Dunghill there are great nuisances to the Chambers adjoining to the said Horsepond and to the common Dining Hall near the said Dunghill Ordered that Notice be given to Mr Cloton the Innkeeper that the Principal & Antients desire to speak with him at the next Pension.

Writings of the Society to be Abstracted into Book of Leases—It is the Opinion of this Pension that the Writings & Evidences relating to the Title of this House should be Abstracted into the Book of Leases[1] And that the Person or Persons who have the same in his or their Custody do subscribe such Abstract to the end that in case of Mortality the Society may know where to have recourse to them.

Pension 25th June 1703

Horsepond at the Lamb Inn Nuisance Redressed—Mr Cloton Innkeeper of the Lamb Inn now appearing is admonished of the Nuisance for the Horsepond and a Dunghill mentioned at last Pension & promising it shall be amended and that the door made in the Stable opening into the Yard adjoining to Mr Purcells Chamber shall forthwith be shut & fastened up.

Pension 16th February 1704

Ordered that Five Guineas be paid to the Churchwardens of St Clements Church towards the Charge of Beautifying the said Church & amending of the Organ.

Pension 1st December 1707

Whereas there has been Dispute about the granting of the Leases to Mr Michael Wrightson formerly Principal & late one of the Antients of this Society tis unanimously agreed that the Lease formerly granted to him the said Michael Wrightson by this Society be confirmed & tis hereby Ordered that the Principal & Antients of this Society have power to Grant

---

[1] An 'Abstract of the Deeds and Writings relating to Clement's Inn, taken the 8th April, 1713' is written on the blank pages following the 'third version' (see p. lii above) of the Constitutions and Orders of the Inn.

& Lease any Chamber of the said Society for the Term or Terms of one Life & two Assignments according to the Usage & Custom of the Society of the Inner Temple.[1]

Pension 30th November 1713

Whereas the Principal & Antients of New Inn have some time since set up a Door in the Fence Wall between Clements Inn & New Inn Gardens & do make use of the same as a Common Highway on all occasions into & thro' Clements Inn aforesaid and pretend to keep the said Door Lockt & to open the same at their Wills & Pleasures without any Leave or Licence from the Principal & Antients of Clements Inn for their so doing by which means in process of time the Society of New Inn may claim a Right to the same as a Common Highway Therefore to prevent the like for the future It is Ordered that in Case the said Principal & Antients of New Inn shall refuse or neglect to deliver a Key of the said Door to the Principal & Antients of Clements Inn on or before the 1st day of January next so as that the said Door may be at the Command & Use of the Society of Clements Inn as well as the said Society of New Inn And in case the Principal & Antients of New Inn shall refuse or neglect to sign a proper writing under their hands signifying that the said Door and the way used as aforesaid is only by the leave & sufferance of the Society of Clements Inn in default of either a Wall or some other sufficient Fence as the Principal of Clements Inn shall direct shall be made and set up for the hinderance & stopping of the said way or passage.[2]

[The extracts listed below, being copies of entries in the Pension Book of 1714–50, have already appeared in the text of the present volume at the pages indicated in brackets:—

1714/5, Feb. 21: the gate next New Inn (p. 11).
   ,,   ,,   seats in St Clements Church to be kept free from strangers (p. 14).
1716, July 18: separate pensions &c. for every chamber (p. 31)— "Repealed by Order of 29th November, 1734",
1717/18, Easter term: contribution (£17. 15s.) for clock or dial (p. 56).
1721: contributions (£40. 3s. 0d.) for repair of St Clement Danes steeple (p. 87).
1722, June 15: ancient lights and shed in Lamb Inn yard (p. 100).
1722/3: contribution (£50. 8s. 0d.) for principal Blackwell's picture (p. 104).

---

[1] Later, in 1771, the Inner Temple decided to grant no more assignments except in very special circumstances; it also adopted a table of rates for fines on exchange of lives.—*I.T.R.*, V, 260–1. See pp. 57, 144, 160 above for Clement's Inn's decisions on assignments.

[2] For the subsequent adjustment of this dispute with New Inn see p. 11 above.

1726: pictures presented by Halsted (p. 126).
1727: contribution (£13. 13s. 0d.) for lining the church pews (p. 130).
1728, November 21: election of new principal (p. 137).
1728/9: subscription (£17. 1s. 0d.) for fire buckets &c. (p. 140).
1729, May 22: assignments to pay for pulling down and rebuilding
   No. 18 (p. 144).
1730, April 25: reading by James Jenyns Esq. (p. 155).
1734, November 28: insolvents left out of the rolls (p. 181).
1736, Easter term: new call of Serjeants (p. 186).
1743, December 2: Ancients liable to commons (p. 205).]

Pension, 19th June, 1752. [Repeal of the last listed order]
 Whereas at a pension held the 2d day of December 1743 it was ordered [as at p. 205 above] And Whereas it has been found by Experience that the said Order has only affected one or Two of the Antients thereof and has not Answered the general good purpose thereby intended It is therefore Ordered that the said Order of Pension be Repealed And the same is hereby Repealed accordingly.

Pension, 10th May, 1760, *Lessee for another Person to pay Double Commons &c.*—Ordered that every Antient or Companion of this Society who shall hereafter be nominated as Lessee of Chambers for any other Person not admitted of the same do pay such Pensions & Commons as are now usually paid for himself as also Pensions & Commons for the Owner of such Chamber.

Mr Whitfield Acknowledgment as to Light &c.—Whereas I have lately opened a Window or Light in a Shed erected on part of Ground of Premisses occupied by me situate in Clements Lane & East of Clements Inn in the County of Middlesex which Window or Light looketh into the Garden of the said Inn Now I do hereby declare that the same Window or Light is suffered to remain without any Erection made upon the same by the Permission of the Principal & Antients of the same Inn the said Window or Light & all other Windows or Lights made out of my Shed Built on the Premisses so held by me which look into the said Inn being new opened and such as the said Principal & Antients have right to build against And I do declare that the Boards now hanging over or on part of the Wall belonging to the said Inn is an encroachment on the ground and Premisses thereof and that I will at the request of the Principal of the said Inn remove the same or that the said Principal or his Steward or Agents shall at their Will and Pleasure take the same down Witness my hand the 9th day of July 1763

Tho Whitfield

Pension 26th June 1767

Commons &c. of the Principals Table to be paid out of the Society's Stock—It is Ordered that the Commons & Exceedings of the Principal & Antients in Commons be hereafter sustained out of the Stock of the Society as is accustomed in other Societies.

Pension 17th July 1775

No Signs &c. to be hung out—Ordered that no Person holding Chambers in this Society do hang out or fix up any Board Sign or Paper signifying any Trade Occupation or profession they Follow.

Pension 8th March 1775

Mr Devon restored to his standing—Mr Wm Devons Letter directed to the Steward of this Society being Read requesting to be restored to his Precedence as a Commoner of this Society Ordered that on Payment of his Arrears from the time of his taking up his first Bond and Executing a Second he be intitled to his Precedence & Standing in this Society from the time of his first admission the same being agreable to the Usage of the Society of the Inner Temple as this day Reported to the Pension by the Steward who had made the necessary Enquiry relative to the said Readmission

Thursday 25th May 1775

Order as to the Gate leading to Horseshoe Court—This being Ascension Day by Order of the Principal of the Society The Gate of this Inn opening into Horseshoe Court[1] was (from 12 o Clock at noon for the Remainder of this Day) Locked up and no Person or Persons suffered to pass or repass thro' the same being the property of this Society and no thoroughfare.

Pension 1st July 1776

Servants Wages increased—Ordered that the Head Porters Salary be increased to Twenty Pounds a Year as Porter and Four Pounds a Year as Butler And that the under Porters Salary be increased to Twelve Guineas a Year and an Additional Stipend of Three Guineas per Annum as Gardener to commence on the 15th January last.

Pension 1st July 1779

Order for Covenants in Leases—Ordered that a Covenant be incerted in all future Leases from the Society Restraining the Tenant from Breaking the Walls of any Chambers to be Let in order to make Drains, Doorways,

---

[1] Horseshoe Court, "a pretty handsome Place with a Freestone Pavement having a Prospect into St Clement's Inn Garden" (Stow, *Survey*, Strype's edn. (1720), I, 118), gave entry to the Garden Court from the direction of Clement's Lane. See p. xliv above.

New Lights affixing Window Shutters or for any other purpose whatsoever without Leave first obtained from this Society.

Pension 14th April 1780

Covenant in Leases—Took into consideration the Covenants of the present Leases—Resolved & Ordered That in all future Leases and Agreements made for Chambers in this Society a Covenant or Agreement be incerted That no Lessee or Occupier of Chambers shall either Let Set or Assign the same or any part thereof for all or any part of the Term therein to any Person or Persons or permit or suffer any Person or Persons whatsoever to Inhabit hold use occupy or enjoy the same or any part thereof for all or any part of the Term the said Lessee or Occupier may have therein but such Person who shall be first approved and admitted a Member & Companion of this Society.

Pension 11th May 1780

Incroachment by Mr Fossick & Mr Coupland—Ordered that the Steward apply to Mr Fossick & Mr Coupland & acquaint them that unless they do within two Months totally shut up their Lights looking into this Inn a Wall will be carried up against them.

Pension 29th June 1780

Incroachment by Fossick & Coupland—The Steward Reported that he had given Notice to Mr Fossick & Mr Coupland pursuant to the Order of Pension dated 11th day of May last and they severally Attending and alledging that they had begun to stop up the Lights agreable to the said Order & that they would comply therewith Resolved that the said Order be compleatly carried into Execution.

Same day

Incroachments by the Owner or Occupier of the Angel Inn—It appearing upon a View that the Owner or Occupier of the Angel Inn behind St Clements (the boundary whereof runs in a line behind the Chambers No. 12 in this Inn and bounds upon the said Yard or Area) hath also opened a New Light upon & into the same Ordered that an Application be made to the Owner or Occupier of the said Inn & that he or they be informed that unless such Incroachment be removed & the Lights totally shut up He or they will be Prosecuted.

Pension 1st December 1780

Incroachments by Coupland's Executrix—Ordered that the Executrix of the late George Coupland be called upon by the Steward in order to compleatly stop up the Light in the Building looking into this Inn pursuant to the Order of Pension of the 11th May last.

Pension 31st January 1781

Incroachment by Couplands Executrix abated—The Steward Reported that the Executrix of the late George Coupland had complyed with the Order of the last Pension and compleatly shut up the Light complained of.

Pension 24th May 1781

As to the Encroachment Angel Inn—Took into consideration the Encroachment made by the Owner or Occupier of the Angel Inn by having opened a New Light from a New Erected Building which looks into the Area or back Yard of this Society belonging to No. 12 in this Inn And the Principal with several of the Antients having viewed the same in Company with the Carpenter & Bricklayer of the Society And it having been signified to the Pension that Mr Grantham the present Owner of the Angel Inn was willing to sign an Acknowledgment to the said Society that such Light hath been thrown out upon Sufferance Resolved that such Acknowledgment be accepted.

The Owner & Tenant's acknowledgment of a Light from the Angel Inn— Mr John Grantham Owner of the Angel Inn situate in the Parish of Saint Clement Danes in the County of Middlesex and Richard Watson Tenant of the said Premises do hereby severally acknowledge that the Light from the New Building which looks into the Area or Back Yard of the Society of Clements Inn behind the Chambers No. 12 in the said Inn is a new made Light which is continued by Permission of the Principal & Antients of the said Society Witness our hands 4th July 1781

John Grantham
Richard Watson

APPENDIX

LIST OF ADMISSIONS TO CLEMENT'S INN
1656–1883

NOTE—*This list of members of Clement's Inn, with their sureties, has been compiled from the two Admission Books presented by R. S. Taylor to the Public Record Office (see pp. vii, xi, above). The formula of the record is shown at p. liv above.*

These two books set out the entries term by term—Hilary, Easter, Trinity, or Michaelmas, as the case may be. To save space the list omits the term and the day of the month of the admission; the names have been grouped by the calendar year, and, for simplification, the year is taken as beginning on January 1st and not (as in the Old-Style calendar before 1752) on March 25th. The name of the admittee is followed in the same line by that of his surety or pledge (see p. lv above). The original spelling of the place-names is retained (e.g. "Chiltenham"); the county is omitted where mention seemed unnecessary. The recurrent description "gent", "gen" or "gentleman" has been abbreviated to "g."

Some personal particulars, gratefully collected from the catholic pages of the Dictionary of National Biography *or from the courteous and competent replies of county and city archivists,[1] have been inserted in footnotes. Admittedly the information is of uneven value and relevance, but it seemed a pity to withhold such biographical details as came to hand about A or B merely because the same were not available for X or Y. The customary repetition of the same baptismal name in family pedigrees has naturally increased the speculative element in identifications.[2]*

The clerk who entered the admissions has sometimes interpolated a note of such facts as the beginning of a new principalship, the remission of the new member's fees and so on. These remarks have been reproduced (in italics) in the following list as they occur.

---

[1] Abbreviated to "C.A." in the footnotes to the following pages.

[2] Where identical names are repeated in the Admission Books, they are presumably those of separate persons—often father and son. But the contingency of a member having been re-entered, perhaps after withdrawal or expulsion for some default, cannot be ruled out. Thus the name of Foster Powell is entered in 1761 and again in 1765; if the later entry be not a duplication, which of the two is the pedestrian celebrated in the *Dictionary of National Biography*? The entries of Francis Grose in 1771 and 1783 raise a like problem. Other possible instances of double entry (involving liability, in later years substantial, for a second payment of stamp duty) are the cases of Thomas Watkins (twice in 1664), Thomas Taubman (1725 and 1726), Joseph Settree (1762 and 1770) and Hesketh Davis (1791 and 1793). Earlier, *temp.* Edw. IV, anyone admitted to Furnival's Inn, if he "happen to discontynue for a season", was not received into commons or accepted as a member until his readmission with fresh mainpernors—*Early Records of F.I.* (ed. Bland, 1957), p. 32. See also pp. 273 n. (Madgwick) and 304 n (Rudhall) below.

1656

Bernard Kendall, Lanlivery, Cornwall, g.—Mr Sloper.
Thomas Taylor, Bradley, Hants., g.—Mr Hodges.
Ferdinando Meighen, Gloucester, g.—Mr Sloper.
William Gibson, Stratford upon Avon, g.—Mr Copley.
Samuell Brewster,[1] Gloucester, g.—Mr J. Brewster.
Thomas Younge, Keynton,[2] Salop, g.—Mr Coates.
Thomas Sloper,[3] Chiltenham, Glos., g.—Mr W. Sloper.
Thomas Dobbes,[4] Clements Danes, Middx., g.—Mr Kellett.
John Serjeant,[5] Milmeese, Staffs., g.—Mr Kellett.
John Muston, Coventry, g.—Mr Gibson.
Christopher Bradgate, Wibdofte,[6] Warw., g.—Mr Muston.
William Camplyn, Winchester, g.—Dennett.

1657

Edward Jones, Llanvaire, Montgom., g.—Callowe.
Michaell Wrightson,[7] Cragg, Yorks., g.—Hutchinson.
William Garnett, St Andrews, Holborn, g.—Dand.
Edward Palmer the Younger, Leicester, g.—E. Palmer Senior.
John Milwarde, Chesterfield, g.—J. Allen.
John Hayne,[8] Ashborne, Derby, g.—Degge.
Richard White, Stoughton, Sussex, g.—Attweeke.
Isaac Foxcroft, St Giles, Cripplegate, g.—R. Gregg.
Francis Read, Henley, Salop, g.—Sloper.
Urian Baldwyn, Munslowe, Salop, g.—Stedman.
William Raffyn, Isle of Wight, g.—Kecke.[9]
William Scrimshire, Cotgrave, Notts., g.—Jo. Scrimshire.
    25 to Januarii 1680 posuit se extra solvit omnia debita per composicienem et obligatio deliberata fuit.

[1] Mentioned as of Clement's Inn in a disentailing deed in 1681 relating to the King and Ayland families (C.A., Glos.). For another of that name see 1665 below.

[2] Caynton, a parish two miles north-east of Edgmond, on the river Mees.

[3] Died 1703: his surviving children included Charles Sloper, chancellor of Bristol, and William Sloper (died 1715), one of the attorneys of the Common Pleas at Westminster—*Glos. Notes and Queries*, I, 231; III, 171 (C.A., Glos.).

[4] A Thomas Dobbes undertook in 1626 to build chambers in the Inn: see p. xlvi above. The Thomas Dobbes above was presumably the father-in-law of Francis Kellett: see pp. xlvii, xlix above.

[5] His will, proved Jan. 1673/4, shows that he held property at Slindon, Millmeece, Darleston and Stone, all close to his home at Eccleshall (C.A., Staffs.).

[6] Wibtoft, a parish on Watling Street some ten miles north-east of Coventry.

[7] Principal of the Inn in 1683: see also pp. 8, 237–8, 243, above.

[8] Coroner, Derbyshire, 1683–1713. A writ *de coronatore exonerando* was served on the sheriff to remove him from his coronership as "too sick and infirm to exercise the said office"—County Record Office, Derbs. See also the admissions (below) in 1682 (John Hayne junior) and 1717 (Joseph Hayne).

[9] His original bond, among the Taylor papers (item 11, p. xi above), shows that Samuel Kecke of Oxfordshire was admitted in 1655, Walter Sloper being his surety and George Merifield the then principal.

John Pacy, St Clement Danes, g.—Callow.
Roger Fowler, Eggleton, Rutland, g.—Lister.

1658

Tymothie Shelley,[1] Sullington, Sussex, g.—Mr Callowe.
Francis Gramer,[2] Badgley Ensor, Warw., g.—[No surety named.]
James Lane the younger, East Retford, Notts., g.—Mr Hobson.
    pardonatus quia filius Antiqui.
Arthur Hatton, Newark upon Trent, g.—his father, William Hatton.
Francis Levinge, Great Sheepie, Lincs., g.—Thomas Levinge.[3]
Theophilus Greene, Marston, Northumb., g.—T. Greene.
John Ball, Newport, Isle of Wight, g.—Mr Oglander.
John Hough the younger, Nottingham, g.—Mr Hough.
Thomas Cripps, Lewes, Sussex, g.—Mr Callow.
Thomas Sturmy, Hampton upon Thames, g.—Mr Sturmy, his father.
James Partridge, St Andrews, Holborn, g.—J. Allen.
Richard Knighton,[4] Irtlingborowe, Northants., g.—Mr Ekyns.
John Hansard, St Clement Danes, g.—T. Dobbes junior.
Edward Archer,[5] Portsmouth, g.—Coperthwaite.
    16 to Maii 1681 solvit omnia debita et posuit se extra.
Luke Cropley, Midhurst, Sussex, g.—B. White.
    at the request of Mr Shelton late Redor pardoned.
John Powell, Wells, Somerset, g.—Mr Coates.

1659

John Grene Principall beginneth the 20th day of January 1658.

John Hunt, Thorpe, Rutland, g.—Mr William Hutchinson.
George Etheredge, Beconsfield, Bucks., g.—Mr F. Harris.
Richard Middlemore, Haselwell, King's Norton, Worcs., g.—Mr Ekyns
Francis Johnson,[6] Spaldinge, Lincs., g.—John Giles.
    pardonatus ad requisitionem principalis.
John Giles, Stone, Glos., g.—Francis Johnson.
    pardonatus ad requisitionem principalis.
Thomas Beach, West Ashton, Wilts., g.—Mr Robert Beach.
    pardonatus filius Antiqui.
Thomas [? Chislet [7]], Bristol, g.—Mr. Walter Sloper.

[1] Clerk of the peace 1661–8: one of the same name was his deputy 1669–71—C.A., Sussex.

[2] Gramer's first wife was a daughter of Thomas Levinge of Great Sheepie, Lincs., surety for Francis Levinge, who was also admitted in 1658.

[3] Several of this surname, however spelt, were admitted at the Inner Temple—a Richard in 1633, 1648, 1671 and 1742, a Samuel in 1689, a Thomas in 1618 and 1633, and a Timothy in 1597. See also the preceding note.

[4] His will was proved in 1672 (C.A., Northants.).

[5] Town clerk of Portsmouth 1666–88 (C.A., Hants.).

[6] For the Johnson family of Spalding see note to 1684 admissions below.

[7] The surname is scarcely legible; the first three letters seem to be CHI. A Chislet was attorney at Bristol in a later generation, and a Robert Chislet was admitted a freeman there in 1655/6—C.A., Bristol.

Edward Cholmeley,[1] Medborne, Leics., g.—Mr John Dand.[2]

1660

James Lane the younger, East Retford, Notts., g.—Mr John Coates.
> *14 May 1684 solvit omnia onerata per composicionem et posuit se extra et obligatio deliberata fuit Mr Whitmore.*

John Kidgell,[3] Northall Greene, Bucks., g.—Mr Edmund Gosnold.
Harry Fryth, Wolverhampton, Staffs., g.—Edward Fryth.
John Yardley, Warwick., g.—Mr Robert Harvey.
John Stansby, St Dunstan in the West, London, g.—Mr Ralph Gregg.
Stephen Bull, Coleshill, Warw., g.—Mr William Bonell.
William Bonell, Sheldon, Warw., g.—Mr. Stephen Bull.
Humfry Walker, Salt, Staffs., g.—Mr John Giles.
> *pardonatus ad requisicionem principalis.*

Francis Ives,[4] Wellingborough, Northants., g.—Mr John Wyther.
Thomas Wood, Newcastle under Lyme, Staffs., g.—Mr Humfry Walker.
Richard Pococke,[5] Newbury, Berks., g.—Mr John Munday.
James Earle,[6] Winchester, g.—Mr Richard Dennett.

1661

Charles Blunt, London, g.—Mr John Blunt.
William Markwicke, Bosam, Sussex, g.—Mr. John Bold.
Joseph Garrard,[7] Newberry, Berks., g.—Mr Richard Bourne.
Laurence Athorpe,[8] Nottingham, g.—Mr John Coates.
William Richards, Walsall, g.—Mr Ralph Gregge.
Francis Garrarde, East Garston, Bucks., g.—Mr Joseph Garrard.
William Pennell, Cleobury Mortimer, Salop, g.—Mr Thomas Brumstead.
George Fox, Fulwood, Yorks., g.—Mr Henry Balgay.
John Rawlins, Litchfield, Staffs., g.—Mr John Dand.
Christopher Pegge, Ashborne, Derby, g.—Mr Edward Pegge.
> *pardonatus filius Antiqui.*

Henry Wilson, Eckington, Worcs., g.—Mr John Coates.
Richard Handley, London, g.—Mr Charles Blount.

---

[1] His will, proved 1667, stated "Item 1 give unto Mr Edward Browne of Leicester all my books in Clements Inn"—C.A., Leics.

[2] On Nov. 10, 1667, John Dand of Clement's Inn petitioned for a lease of the small fines of the Court of Common Pleas (value £18 to £20 a year) with power to levy—*Ent. Book*, 13, p. 363.

[3] A John Kidgell bought in 1657 the manor of Butlers in the parish of Edlesborough, in which Northall Green is situated. He died in 1690, leaving it to his son John, who sold it in 1696—C.A., Bucks.

[4] Buried at Wellingborough March 1686/7 (C.A., Northants.).

[5] Mayor of Newbury 1673, town clerk (presumably thereafter) till 1676, subsequently appointed Senior Attorney of the Borough Court of Record (C.A., Berks.).

[6] Auditor of the Twenty Four at Winchester 1683–4, mayor 1686–7; buried in the cathedral 1696 (C.A., Hants.).

[7] Mayor of Newbury 1675, town clerk 1676–87 (then, with others, displaced from office) and 1688–95 (C.A., Berks.).

[8] Town clerk of Nottingham 1692–1701 (C.A., Nottingham).

James Rowse, Wokingham, Berks., g.—Mr Thomas Dobbs.
William Seard, Kington, Herefords., g.—Mr Charles Blount.
William Lane, Witton, Ashton near Birmingham, g.—Mr Stephen Bull.
pardonatus ad instanciam Lectoris.

1662

Thomas Aram, Newnham, Glos., g.—Mr Samuell Astry.
Thomas Barnwell, Aylesbury, Bucks., g.—Mr Thomas Phillips.
Morgan Bolwell, Derby, g.—Mr Francis Johnson.
Anthony Blake, Sheviocke, Cornwall, g.—Mr Thomas Beach.
Benjamyn Okeshott,[1] Portsmouth, g.—Mr John Hurst.
Edward Harfeild,[2] Winchester, g.—Mr Richard Dennett.[3]
Thomas Bagshaw, Rowley, Derby, g.—Mr William Nicholson.
John Tyrer the younger, Elmley Lovell, Worcs., g.—Mr Thomas Tyrer.
Samuell Phillips, Carmarthen, g.—Mr John Stedman.
John Stedman, Llangammarch, Brecon, g.—Mr Samuell Phillips.
William Howe, Abbots Langley, Herts., g.—Mr Thomas Howe.
Thomas Ervington, New Windsor, Berks., g.—Mr William Callowe.
Robert Thornton, Horncastle, Lincs., g.—Mr John Thornton.[4]
Richard Wakeman,[5] Bath, Somerset, g.—Mr William Hutchinson.
Henry Dottin, Sherford, Devon, g.—Humfry Walker.
Humfry Wirley the younger, St Clements Danes, g.—Humfrey Wirley senior, his
    father.

1663

Edwardus Gerrard principalis Hospicii predicti incepit 24 Jan. 1662.
Tobias Eden, Clements Inn, g.—Charles Blount.
Thomas Stone, Clements Inn, g.—Robert Morse.
Walter Walker, London, g.—George Lynn.
Hugh North, Hertford, g.—James Lane.
Thomas Meakyns, St Brides, London, g.—Richard Lowth.
Samuell Rawlyns,[6] Marston Sicca, Glos., g.—John Knight.
Josiah Geary, Clements Inn, g.—Francis Harris.
Mathew Heath, Clements Inn, g.—Thomas Stone.
Thomas Cope, Clements Inn, g.—John Lowe.
Thomas Colnett, Clements Inn, g.—Hugh North.
Edwyn Baldwyn junior, Clements Inn, g.—Edwyn Baldwyn senior.
Andrew Hull, Clements Inn, g.—Michael Wrightson.
Nicholas Covert, Clements Inn, g.—Josiah Geary.

[1] Fined for erecting a messuage and two water towers on the town waste at Portsmouth
C.A., Hants.).
[2] Buried in Winchester cathedral 1693 (C.A., Hants.).
[3] Auditor of the Twenty Four at Winchester 1650–1, 1657–8; buried in the cathedral
1667 (C.A., Hants.).
[4] Clerk of the peace, Lindsey 1665–79 (C.A., Lincs.).
[5] ? son of Theodore Wakeman, town clerk of Bath 1654 (Collinson, *History of
Somerset*, i, B71).
[6] A younger brother of Serjeant Rawlins of Stratford-on-Avon (C.A., Glos.).

John Bargett, Cirencester, Glos., g.—Robert Morse.[1]
John Savage, Clements Inn, g.—Hugh North.

1664

Thomas Nicholls alias Nix, Banbury, g.—Will. Gibson.
Mathew Dodsworth, London, g.—Thomas Aram.
Edward Noell, London, g.—Thomas Brumpstead.
 13 Maii 1681 posuit se extra et solvit omnia debita per composicionem.
Richard Bewly, Markett Rasyn, Lincs., g.—John Dand.
Gilbert Yarde, Clements Inn, g.—Thomas Stone.
John Butlyn, Eyston, Northants., g.—John Dand.
Henry Jones, London, g.—Henry Dottyn.
Samuel Gregge, Clements Inn, g.—Ralph Gregge.
John Gregge, Clements Inn, g.—Ralph Gregge.
Ezekiel Yarde,[2] Ottery St Mary, Devon, g.—Gilbert Yarde.
 20 Febr. 1682 posuit se extra et solvit omnia debita per composicionem.
Thomas Watkins, London, g.—Samuel Holmes.
Robert Leeke, Hallam, Notts., g.—Walter Sloper.
John Watson, Boston, Lincs., g.—John Coates.
John Grace, Kilbourne, Derby, g.—Ralph Edge.
William Wakeman, Barnstaple, g.—Richard Wakeman.
Marcus Ashley, Chesterfield, g.—Thomas Bolwell.
Thomas Shawe, Newcastle upon Lyme, Staffs., g.—Richard Middlemore.
Edmund Eede, Clements Inn, g.—Francis Eede.
Michael Turston, Wolverhampton, g.—William Richards.
 15 Febr. 1683 solvit debita per compositionem et posuit se extra.
John Browne, Bottesford, Leics., g.—Thomas Buck.
John Mudd, Horncastle, Lincs., g.—John Greene.
Thomas Watkins, Grosmend, Mon., g.—William Callowe.
Huan Duffeild, Sherborne, Yorks., g.—Ralph Gregge.
Charles Ballett, St Clement Danes, g.—John Polkett.

1665

William Godwyn, Cardington, Beds., g.—William Richards.
John Hannam, Chew Magna, Somerset, g.—John Millington.
Timothy Harrison, Ellell, Lancs., g.—John Coates.
Henry Baldwyn, Worcester, g.—John Hannam.
William Turner, Derby, g.—John Coates.
George Rasen, Doncaster, g.—Samuell Gregge.
Samuel Brewster,[3] Gloucester, g.—Samuel Brewster.
John Garlike, Northampton, g.—Joseph Parker.

[1] The Morse family lived at Stone, Glos., where a memorial in the church describes John Morse (died 1728, *aet.* 67) as "an eminent solicitor in Chancery" "... the clergy in particular resorted to him as their only advocate" (C.A., Glos.).
 [2] Gilbert and Ezekiel Yarde died at Ottery St Mary in 1679 and 1684 respectively. Several members of the family were barristers (Inner Temple) or attorneys. Phillippe Yarde, attorney, was sheriff of Exeter in 1586; Robert Yarde was a Master in Chancery in 1728.
 [3] See note to admission of another Samuel Brewster in 1656, p. 250 above.

James Baskervill, Bristol, g.—William Callowe.
Richard Rayson, Leicester, g.—George Rayson.[1]
Daniel Sulley, Nottingham, g.—Laurence Athorpe.
George Worden, Derby, g.—Edward Browne.
Samuel Robinson, Nuneaton, g.—Thomas Barton.
John Goodwyn, Henley on Thames, g.—Thomas Wolley.
    pardonatus ad instantiam Lectoris.

1666

Thomas Richardson,[2] Langdon Hills, Essex, g.—Robert Leake.
Michael Saward, Chelmsford, g.—[No surety named.]
Joseph Gormey, Walsall, g.—William Richards.
Thomas Peckham, Arundel, Sussex, g.—George Merifield.
Joseph Yate,[3] Badminton, Glos., g.—John Giles.
    5 to Julii 1682 posuit se extra et solvit onerata debita per compositionem.
Philip Downey, Bristol, g.—James Baskerville.
John Langford, Alverdiscott, Devon, g.—Henry Langford.
John Gale, Clements Inn, g.—John Swansby.
John Roland, St Giles extra Cripplegate, g.—John Coates.
Patrick Shore,[4] Methringham, Lincs., g.—Bartholomew Tothill.
Thomas Charnells,[5] Leicester, g.—Edward Palmer.
    15 May 1683 posuit se extra persolvit omnia debita per compositionem.
George Greene, Marston Trussell, Northants., g.—Theophilus Greene.
    pardonatus quia filius Antiqui.

1667

Richard Ball,[6] Kingham, Oxon., g.—Samuel Kecke.
William Rogers,[7] Hasleton, Glos., g.—Thomas Stone.
Thomas Stokes, St Clement Danes, g.—Henry Baldwyn.
Edward Ferrar, Clements Inn, g.—John Greene junior.
Edward Fisher,[8] Chawton, Hants., g.—John Harfell.[9]
John Brooke, Newcastle upon Lyme, Staffs.—Thomas Parker.
Barnabas Tonstall, St Andrew, Holborn—Henry Dottin.

   [1] Clerk of the peace for Leicestershire 1665–6 (C.A., Leics.).
   [2] A Richardson acted as surveyor of highways of the parish of Langdon Hills (some eight miles north of Tilbury) in 1648 (C.A., Essex).
   [3] The Yates were lords of the manor of Arlingham until the 18th century: a Joseph Yate married May Ayland in 1679 (C.A., Glos.). See also note to 1656 admission (above) of Samuel Brewster.
   [4] Under-sheriff 1684 (C.A., Lincs.).
   [5] A Thomas Charnell was sheriff of Leicestershire 1702; for the family pedigree see J. Nichols, *History of Leicestershire* (C.A., Leics.).
   [6] The bond signed by Ball and Kecke and witnessed by John Milward (bond in Latin, conditions in English) is among the Taylor papers (item 11, p. xi above).
   [7] Died 1734, *aet.* 76: memorial in Dowdeswell church "Magistrorum Curiae Cancellariae nuper primus". A justice of the peace for Gloucestershire 1727 (C.A., Glos.).
   [8] Deputy steward in the hundred and manor of Alton 1674–1711 (C.A., Hants.).
   [9] Lay vicar and (1660) chapter clerk, Winchester: buried in the cathedral 1680 (C.A., Hants.).

Thomas Oldfield, Bristol, g.—Joseph Yate.
Antony Collingwood, Newark on Trent, g.—Patrick Shore.
Nicholas Parker, Tamworth, Warw., g.—Richard Middlemore.
John Arthur,[1] Doncaster, g.—William Crashaw.
Edward Secker, Grantham, Lincs., g.—John Thornton.
William Edge, Nottingham, g.—Ralph Edge.[2]
John Vivian, Clements Inn, g.—Richard Knighton.

1668

Benjamin Walker, St Martins in the Fields, g.—Walter Sloper.
Laurence Carter,[3] Leicester, g.—George Rayson.
William Flamsteed, Hallam Parva, Derby, g.—Will Turner.
    Trin. 1684 solvit onerata per compositionem et posuit se extra.
Richard Peachey, Chichester, g.—Nicholas Covert.
Thomas Winford, Astely, Worcs., g.—John Greene junior.
    25 Feb. 1683 solvit onerata in fine Mr Squier et obligatio deditur ei et posuit se extra.
John Bowler, Newport, Isle of Wight, g.—Barnabas Tonstall.
Joseph Coling, Coventry, g.—Joseph Yate.
William Norton, Cobham, Surrey, g.—William Hutchinson.
Samuel Aldridge, Stanes, Midd., g.—James Rous.
Samuel Cryer, St Clement Danes, g.—Samuel Taylor.
John Stockton, Portsmouth, g.—Edward Archer.
Stephen Baldwyn, Evesham, Worcs., g.—Henry Dottin.
Ralph Milbourne, St Clement Danes, g.—Edward Ferrar.
Thomas Knype, St Clement Danes, g.—Samuel Aldridge.

1669

William Parker, St Clement Danes, g.—Francis Stampton.
John Langston, Middle Aston, Oxon., g.—Peter Langston.
John Coates, Newberry, Berks., g.—Richard Pococke.
Robert Lawrence,[4] Gloucester, g.—Walter Sloper.
John Clarke, St Andrews, Holborn, g.—Edward Noell.
Robert Williamson, Clements Inn, g.—[No surety named.]
Gabriel Armiger, Clements Inn, g.—Tobias Eden.
Andrew Harrison, St Giles outside Cripplegate, g.—Richard Middlemore.
William Hall, Chobham, Surrey, g.—Mathew Dodsworth.
Richard Hitchcock, Aylesbury, Bucks., g.—John Stansby.

---

[1] Town clerk of Doncaster, died 1715, *aet.* 69. A son, John Arthur (died 1740, *aet.* 59), was mayor of Doncaster; a grandson, John Arthur (died 1773, *aet.* 63), was a member of the Middle Temple.

[2] Ralph Edge (1622–84), attorney at law, was town clerk of Nottingham from 1658 till his death: mayor 1664–5, 1671–2 and 1678–9 (C.A., Nottingham).

[3] Afterwards an Ancient. His executors retrieved in 1717/8 a loan he had made to the Inn: see p. 54 above. For his son, Laurence Carter of Lincoln's Inn, see p. 5 n. above and *D.N.B.*

[4] Died 1670, *aet.* 20: his mother was a daughter of John Rogers of Hazleton—see 1667 admissions (William Rogers) above (C.A., Glos.).

John Hawford, London, g.—Samuel Taylor.
Edward Chambers, Studley, Warw., g.—Thomas Winford.
John Sturmy, St Clement Danes, g.—Thomas Sturmy.
    pardonatus quia filius Antiqui.
Edward Walker, Clements Inn, g.—William Byrd.
Henry Jones, Monmouth, g.—William Callowe.
Simon Urlin,[1] Ampthill, Beds., g.—Thomas Winford.
William Church,[2] Tunstall, Salop, g.—John Weston.
Thomas Callowe,[3] Clements Inn, g.—William Callowe.
    pardonatus ad instantiam Principalis et Antiquorum.
Ralph Gregge junior, Hammersmith, Midd., g.—Ralph Gregge senior.
    pardonatus ad requisitionem Principalis.

1670

George Gosnold principalis hospicii predicti incepit 23 die Jan. 1669.

John Swindell, Ashby de la Zouch, Leics., g.—Thomas Dudley.
Robert Constable, St Clement Danes, g.—Thomas Knype.
Thomas Smith,[4] Beconsfield, Bucks., g.—Edward Gosnold.[5]
Thomas Palmer, Leicester, g.—Edward Palmer.
Antony Kerchivalli, Southall, Notts., g.—Robert Leeke.
Thomas Wood junior, Newcastle upon Lyme, Staffs., g.—Thomas Wood.

1671

Joseph Hunt, Stratford upon Avon, g.—William Gibson.
Richard Lannyng, East Orchard, Iwerne Minster, Dorset, g.—Joseph Hunt.
Halmer Lunn, Evesham, Worcs., g.—Edward Walker.
Henry Champante, St Clement Danes, g.—John Hawford.
George Wooddeson, New Windsor, Berks., g.—Thomas Stone.
Robert Egleton, Clements Inn, g.—Francis Kellett.

1672

William Goldan, Brill, Bucks., g.—Richard Hitchcock.
Samuel Grant, St Clement Danes, g.—Mathew Dodsworth.
William Hawkins, Clements Inn, g.—Francis Harris.

[1] Admitted an attorney of the Bedford Court of Pleas 1667: practised in the Common Pleas 1678. A son, Sir Simon Urling, was serjeant at law 1729, deputy recorder of the City of London 1731 and recorder 1742: he was knighted 1744 and died 1746 (C.A., Beds.).

[2] William Church of Tunstall (one mile north-east of Market Drayton) was sheriff in 1715 (C.A., Salop).

[3] For other Thomas Callowes see admissions of 1686 and 1692 below. And see pp. 58, 62 above.

[4] Clerk of the peace for Bucks. 1689–1702, appointed by Lord Wharton when *custos rotulorum*, displaced when Wharton was dismissed from his posts by Queen Anne (C.A., Bucks.).

[5] Sworn a burgess of Chepping Wycombe Jan. 1672/3 (C.A., Bucks.).

Samuel Player, Clements Inn, g.—Simon Urlyn.
  7 die Julii 1682 solvit onerata debita per compositionem et posuit se extra.
John Titchborne, Woking, Surrey, g.—William Hall.
John Cheble, Evesham, Worcs., g.—William Bird.
Henry Harris, St Clement Danes, g.—Francis Harris.
Richard Gosnold, Beconsfield, Bucks., g.—Thomas Smith.
Peter Noyes, St Clement Danes, g.—Robert Egleton.

1673

  Johannes Ekins principalis hospicii predicti incepit 23 Jan. 1672.
Thomas Truesdale, Bourne, Lincs., g.—John Coates, Clements Inn.
John Fifeild, Richmond, Surrey, g.—John Fifeild Antiquus.
  pardonatus quia filius Antiqui.
John Foster, Warkworth, Northumb., g.—John Serle.
John Serle, London, g.—John Foster.
George Jolland junior, Glamford Briggs, Lincs., g.—Henry Harris junior,
    Clements Inn.

1674

Edward Bulstrode,[1] Twyning, Glos., g.—Joseph Hunt.
Henry Watson, Clements Inn, g.—Edward Ferrar.
Thomas Statham,[2] Tiddeswall, Derbs., g.—Walter Ashmore, g.
Samuel Greene, Warwick, g.—Thomas Smyth.
James Sherratt, Tiddeswall, Derbs., g.—John Hayne, g.
Paul Burrard,[3] Lymington, Hants., g.—John Bold, g.
  pardonatus ad instantiam principalis.
Robert Ellyott, Clements Inn, g.—John Emes.
  14 Julii 1685 solvit onerata per compositienem et posuit se extra.
John Emes, Pershore, Worcs., g.—Robert Ellyott.
John Woods, Woodborough, Notts., g.—Ralph Edge.
William Saunders, Breedon, Worcs., g.—Edward Bulstrode.
Charles Holbech, Mereden, Warw., g.—Martin Holbetch.
William Wingfeild, Werkesworth, Derbs., g.—Thomas Statham.
Elkenah Breedon,[4] Wing, Bucks., g.—Henry Harris junior.

[1] Brother of Whitelock Bulstrode of Clifford's Inn; son of Sir Richard Bulstrode (1610–1711), agent for Charles II at Brussels; Sir Richard's father, a justice itinerant in North Wales, had a sister Elizabeth who married Sir James Whitlock, chief justice of Chester (C.A., Glos.).

[2] Died 1702 (C.A., Derbs.): father of Sir John Statham for whom see 1701 admissions below.

[3] Paul Burrard, born 1648, son of Thomas Burrard, was M.P. for Lymington from 1700 till his death in 1706. His only son Paul was also M.P. for Lymington 1706–13 and 1719–27 and for Yarmouth, I. of Wight, 1727 till his death in 1735, receiver-general of the land tax for Hants., commissioner for control of leather duties (1714), D.L. for Hants. (1721) and ranger of the New Forest (1722). A Paul Burrard was mayor of Lymington in several years between 1678 and 1733—C.A., Hants. (and see Burrard, *Annals of Walhampton* (1874)).

[4] One Elkanah Breedon (with Zachariah Allnutt, ? admitted to Clement's Inn in 1677) witnessed the will of Thomas Breedon of Chesham, fellmonger, in 1671 (C.A., Bucks.).

1675

Giles Hooper, Westminster, g.—William Little.
William Little, Clements Inn—Giles Hooper.
Joseph Thicknesse, the Rolls Chappell, Chancery Lane, g.—Giles Hooper.
Nathaniel Couchman, Canterbury, g.—Thomas Callowe.

1676

Thomas Sturmy principalis hospicii predicti incepit 24° die Jan. A.D. 1675.

William Sturmy, son of the principal—John Sturmy.
   pardonatus.
John Oldershaw, Clements Inn, g.—John Hawford.
Joseph Stamford, Clements Inn, g.—John Coates, Peterborough.
Thomas Gregg, Clements Inn, g.—Mathew Dodsworth.
Robert Rowlin, Castleton, Derbs., g.—Thomas Bagshaw, g.
Andrew Hull, Frilsworth, Leics., g.—Francis Stampton, g.
John Stretehay, London, g.—Robert Egleton.
Thomas Vower, St Clement Danes, g.—Robert Elliott.
John Slack,[1] Wyrkesworth, Derbs., g.—John Roland, g.
Thomas Granger, St Martin in the Fields, g.—Giles Hooper, g.

1677

George Osborne, Haselinge, Surrey, g.—Arthur Lake.
Arthur Lake, Pendhurst, Kent, g.—George Osborne.
Robert Quadring,[2] Spilsby, Lincs., g.—John Coates.
William Kinaston, Lee, Salop, g.—William Little, g.
John Sherman, Higham on the Hill, Leics., g.—John Stretehay, g.
William Style, Banbury, g.—Philip Style, g.
Christopher Cook, Helstone, Cornwall, g.—Robert Sloper, g.
Andrew Manwaring, St Clement Danes, g.—Samuel Brewster, g.
Zacharyah Alnutt,[3] Amersham, Bucks., g.—Samuel Floyer, g.
George Wakeford, Blackmoore, Hants., g.—Paul Burrard, g.
Shem Hanwell, Clements Inn, g.—Charles Dymocke, g.

1678

Henry Lane, son of Edward Lane, New Windsor—Thomas Granger.
James Motteram, St Warburdge, Derbs., g.—John Ramsby.
Charles Denton, St Pauls, Covent Garden, g.—James Rous.
Richard Tyler, son of Samuel Tyler, Shattery, Warw., g.—William Gibson.
   Trin. 1684 Mr Gibson solvit onerata per compositionem et posuit eum extra et recepit obligationem.

[1] Described as "now deceased" in 1715: see p. 19 above.

[2] Other members of the Quadring family had been admitted at Gray's Inn—William in 1582, Gabriel in 1618 and William in 1639.

[3] Attorney of the court of record of Chepping Wycombe, now High Wycombe: under-sheriff 1708: elected a burgess of Chepping Wycombe 1713—C.A., Bucks. See also p. 62 above. For another of his name see 1714 admissions below; and see 1674 admissions above for note to Breedon's entry.

George Palmer,[1] Owan End, Solihull, Warw., g.—Thomas Gregg.
John Price, East Barnet, Herts., g.—John Price of East Barnet procuravit premium
    ipsius John Price.
Arthur Squire, Laneast, Cornwall, g.—John Stretehay.

1679

Ambrosius Holbech principalis hospicii predicti incepit xxvii die Maii 1679.

Remfry Gartnell, Phillick, Cornwall, g.—John Cook.

1680

Richard Gage,[2] Oundle, Northants., g.—Paul Burrard.
Henry Lawson,[3] Aysell, Cumb., g.—Samuel Nelson.
Thomas Barton junior, Brigstocke, Northants., g.—Thomas Barton senior.
Andrew Gardiner, St Clement Danes, g.—Thomas Bagshawe.
Joseph Gregge, Clements Inn, g.—T. Gregge.
Edward Bearcroft, Clements Inn, g.—Robert Elliott.

1681

John Stubbs, Bristol, g.—Giles Hooper.
George Carter, Inner Temple, g.—Edward Carter.

1682

Thomas Cookes,[4] Evesham, Worcs., g.—William Byrd.
Philip Nicholas, Manston, Dorset, g.—Edward Atwell.
    26 Nov. 1686 solvit onerata per compositionem et posuit se extra.
Edward Atwell,[5] Shaftesbury, Dorset, g.—Philip Nicholas.
Joseph Duckett,[6] Northampton, g.—George Grene.
Thomas Langston, Middle Aston, Oxon., g.—Reginald Williams.
Richard Davies, Allt Vawe, Montgom., g.—Edward Farrer.
John Hayne junior, Ashborne, Derbs., g.—James Sherratt.

1683

Michaelis Wrightson principalis incepit 23 Jan. 1682.

Mathew Carvile, St Andrew, Holborn, g.—Henry Harris.
Richard Lowth, Uppingham, Rutl., g.—Henry Champante.

[1] A brother of Benjamin Palmer of Olton End, who was admitted at Clement's Inn
in 1686.
[2] Two Richard Gages, one of Raunds, the other of Higham Ferrers, subscribed the
oaths of supremacy and allegiance in 1673. One of that name was deputy steward of the
Duchy of Lancaster hundred and manor courts of Higham Ferrers and district till *c.* 1692,
when he was succeeded by William Whitwell (for whom see the 1683 admissions below)
(C.A., Northants).
[3] Fifth son of Sir Wilfred Lawson, bt., of Isell.
[4] ? connected, or identifiable, with Sir Thomas Cookes of Worcestershire, who died
in 1701, a benefactor of Gloucester Hall, Oxford, for whom see *D.N.B.*
[5] Clerk of the peace for Dorset 1680–1703, town clerk of Shaftesbury 1684, coroner
to 1688, mayor of Shaftesbury 1699: died before 1704.
[6] Clerk of the peace for Northamptonshire 1680–92 (C.A., Northants).

James Rogers, Birch, Heref., g.—Henry Lane.
William Bach,[1] Leominster, Heref., g.—William Rudge.
William Rudge, Treesley, Staffs., g.—William Bach.
George Dalby, North Newton, Oxon., g.—William Style.
Cornelius White, Blakewell, Derbs., g.—John Slacke.
Stephen Morris, Manordivie, Pemb., g.—Edward Hooton.
Edward Hooton, Lincoln, g.—Stephen Morris.
George Cawdron, St Andrew, Holborn, g.—Stephen Morris.
Thomas Holbeche, Fillongley, Warw., g.—Henry Dottin.
Charles Whinyates,[2] Peterborough, g.—Richard Gage.
Thomas Umfrevile,[3] Langham, Essex, g.—William Pulter.
   Trinitate 1684 solvit onerata et posuit se extra et recepit obligationem.
William Pulter, Wisbech, Ely, g.—Thomas Umfrevile.
Paige Robinson, Midhurst, Sussex, g.—Richard Robinson.
Edward Bagshaw, son of Henry Bagshaw, Grays Inn, g.—Thomas
      Bagshawe, g.
William Wright, Great Longson, Derbs., g.—Thomas Bagshawe, g.
Francis Rous, St Giles in the Fields, g.—Thomas Rous, g.
Francis Gregge, London, g.—Joseph Gregge, g.
John Whitmore, St Dunstan in the West, London, g.—Thomas Stone.
William Whitwell,[4] Oundle, Northants., g.—Charles Whinyates, g.

1684

Robert Moore, Winster, Derbs., g.—Thomas Gregge.
Nathaniel Smyth,[5] Boston, Lincs., g.—Thomas Truesdale.
Samuel Barneby, Brockhampton, Heref., g.—Henry Lane.
Robert Cookes, Evesham, Worc., g.—William Byrd.
Humphrey Luke,[6] Cople, Beds., g.—Thomas Shuckforth.
Thomas Shuckforth, Saham, Norf., g.—Humphrey Luke.
Miles Sandys,[7] Cirencester, Glos., g.—Henry Lane.
Nathaniel Trayton,[8] Lewes, Sussex, g.—Miles Sandys.
Thomas Legh, Castleton, Derbs., g.—Andrew Gardiner.
George Ullocke, St Clement Danes, g.—Francis Rous.

[1] Bailiff (mayor) of Leominster, 1696 (County Librarian, Herefordshire).

[2] Clerk of the peace for the Liberty of Peterborough, died March 1714/15 *aet.* 46 (C.A., Northants.).

[3] For the Umbreville family of The Valley House, Langham (a parish some five miles north of Colchester) see L. C. Sier, *Transactions of the Essex Archaeol. Soc.*, X, 325. Thomas, who left the Inn in 1684 (as stated above), and is said to have become a captain in H.M. forces, had an elder half-brother Charles, a lawyer, who was knighted in 1661 (C.A., Essex).

[4] A wealthy attorney of Oundle, steward of many manors (C.A., Northants.). See also note to 1680 admissions above (Gage).

[5] Clerk of Kesteven and Holland 1675–83 (C.A., Lincs.).

[6] Born 1657/8, a grandson of Sir Samuel Luke of Woodend, Cople (C.A., Beds.).

[7] A Miles Sandys was sheriff of Gloucestershire in 1678, and a justice of the peace (C.A., Glos.).

[8] Born 1665, died 1715: purchaser of the manor of Southover (C.A., Sussex). See also the 1722 admissions below.

Maurice Johnson,[1] Spalding, Lincs., g.—Morgan Bolwell.
William Todd, Wath, Yorks., g.—Edward Hooton.
Richard Purtell, Wolverhampton, g.—William Whitwell.

1685

Joshua Blackwell,[2] Stamford, Lincs., g.—William Whitwell.
Richard Gates, Canterbury, g.—Isaac Seward.
Samuel Heathcote, Derby, g.—William Wingfeild.
Isaac Seward, Hereford, g.—Richard Gates.
Thomas Keele, Richmond, Surrey, g.—Samuel Brewster.
John Lane, Dodford, Northants., g.—Thomas Pryor.
Robert Chambers, West Malling, Kent, g.—Thomas Power.
Benjamin Child, Reading, g.—Josiah Geary.
William Maynard,[3] Daventry, Northants., g.—Thomas Pryor.
Jeremiah Barfoote, Atherton, Warw., g.—Benjamin Thorneton.
Sampson Baker, Ashbourne, Derbs., g.—William Wingfeild.
Sturgeon Fiske,[4] Hadley, Suff., g.—William Reeve.
John Jackson, Lincoln, g.—Sturgeon Fiske.
Richard Levis, Derby, g.—John Slacke.
William Reeve, Melton Mowbray, g.—Sturgeon Fiske.
Christopher Staveley, Castleton, Lincs., g.—Thomas Wright.
Benjamin Thornton, Ashby de la Zouch, g.—Jeremiah Barfoote.
Oliver Whiddon, Launceston, Cornwall, g.—Arthur Squier.
George Ward, Loughborow, Leics., g.—Benjamin Thornton.
Thomas Piddock, Ashby de la Zouch, g.—Thomas Statham.
Thomas Wright,[5] Shirland, Derbs., g.—Christopher Staveley.
John Worlidge,[6] Petersfield, Hants., g.—Richard Robinson.
Charles Done, Duddon, Chesh., g.—Jane Done.
James Mowting, Milton alias Middleton, Kent, g.—Thomas Power.
William Hardham, Brighthelmstone, Sussex, g.—Arthur Lake.
Richard Good,[7] Winchester, g.—Paul Burrard.
Thomas Nicholls, Banbury, g.—William Style.
George Lee, Sheffield, g.—Thomas Statham.
Edward Fisher,[8] Alton, Hants., g.—John Roland.

[1] Father of Maurice Johnson (1688–1755), who founded the Spalding Gentlemen's Society and in 1717 was honorary librarian of the Society of Antiquaries; a barrister of the Inner Temple.

[2] Many years principal of Clement's Inn: see p. 134 above for his death. He had been treasurer of South Kesteven before 1714 and clerk of the peace for Kesteven in 1714 (C.A., Lincs.). See also note to 1707 admissions (Peart) below.

[3] One of this name was bailiff (mayor) of Daventry in 1668.

[4] Described as deceased in 1716/16: see p. 22 above. A Zachariah Fiske was rector of Hadleigh 1691–1708 (Ipswich and East Suffolk C.A.).

[5] Justice of the peace for Derbyshire (C.A., Derbs.).

[6] Author of *Systema Agriculturae* (1669, sheep fattening, &c.) and *Vinetum Britannicum* (1676, cider-making)—*Victoria County History of Hampshire*, V, 475, 497.

[7] Deputy clerk of the peace between 1691 and 1709, under-sheriff 1681 and 1687, deputy sheriff 1705, auditor of the Commonalty, Winchester, 1673–4, auditor of the Twenty Four 1692–3 and 1695–6, mayor 1699–1700 (C.A., Hants.).

[8] Deputy steward of the manor and hundred of Alton 1674–1711 (C.A., Hants.).

Robert Harrison, Brumpton super Swaile, Yorks., g.—James Wilkinson.
  pardonatus quia servus et cognatus principalis.
Samuel Welles junior,[1] Cheping Wycombe, Bucks., g.—Mathew Carvile.

1686

Thomas Bagshaw principalis Hospitii predicti incepit 23 Jan. 1685.

George Day, Chichester, g.—Henry Newnham, Samuel Corlet.
James Ellam, Windsor, g.—Shem Hanwell.
Theophilus Buckworth, Gorburton alias Gorsburkirk, Lincs., g.—Maurice
  Johnson.
Peter Baldwin, Glamford Briggs, Lincs., g.—George Jolland.
Thomas Horwell, Launceston, g.—Henry Dottin.
John Jeffery, Grimsby, g.—Laurence Stamford.
Humphrey Yardley, Warwick, g.—Samuel Greene.
Charles Hope, Kedlestone, Derbs., g.—John Hawford.
Samuell Russell, Gloucester, g.—Nathaniel Trayton.
William Stratford, Napton on the Hill, Warw., g.—Nicholas Dunmoll.
Nicholas Dunmoll, Wadhurst, Sussex, g.—William Stratford.
Edward North,[2] Benaker, Suff., g.—Arthur Squier.
Oliver Fullwood, Colsill, Warw., g.—Charles Ballett.
Benjamin Palmer,[3] Olton End, Solihull, Warw., g.—Oliver Fullwood.
Robert Milward, son of Thomas Milward, Eaton, Derbs., g.—John Hayne junior.
Robert Walter, Banbury, g.—William Gibson.
William Sitwell, Sheffeild, g.—Thomas Legh.
John Bucke, Fleet, Lincs., g.—Theophilus Buckworth.
Thomas Harris,[4] Leominster, g.—William Rudge.
John Greaves, Cowley, Derbs., g.—William Wingfield.
Thomas Callowe junior,[5] son of William Callowe A., g.—Thomas Callowe senior.
  pardonatus quia filius Antiqui.
William Cockcroft, Mayroide, Yorks., g.—Samuel Russell.

1687

Edward Jagoe, Filley, Cornwall, g.—Henry Dottin.
John Scott, Walsall, g.—Benjamin Thornton.

[1] A Samuel Welles was mayor of Chepping Wycombe 1668–9: his will (1697, proved 1713) was witnessed by Ambrose Eldridge, for whom see 1701 admissions below. Another was clerk of the peace in 1726 (C.A., Bucks.).

[2] Second son of Henry North of Laxfield, who purchased the manor of Benacre, himself the second son of Sir Henry North of Mildenhall. Edward North's marriages—(1) to a daughter of Edmund Eade, D.D., and (2) to a daughter of John Arthur—suggest a link with the Eede and Arthur admitted to the Inn in 1664 and 1667 above (C.A., Ipswich and East Suffolk).

[3] Brother of George Palmer who had been admitted in 1678. Born 1668/9, died *aet.* 64, buried at Solihull, where a mural tablet states that he practised the law for over 40 years.

[4] A Thomas Harris was bailiff (mayor) of Leominster in 1685 (County Librarian, Herefs.).

[5] For Thomas Callowe (described as "senior"), son of John Callowe, see p. 58 above and admissions of 1692: see also those of 1669.

Will Marriott, Northampton, g.—Edward Cotton.
Edward Cotton, Daventree, Northants., g.—William Marriott.
Francis Woodhouse, Larport, Heref., g.—Henry Dottin.
William Champernowne, son and heir apparent of William Champernowne,
          Chesterfield, Derbs., g.—Robert Milward.
Ralph Baton, Droitwich, Worcs., g.—Henry Lane.
Edward Harris, Chesham, Bucks., g.—Edward Umfrevile esquire.
John Blakemore, Blimehill, Staffs., g.—John Scott.
William Allen, Faversham, Kent, g.—[No surety named.]
Edward Temple, Leicester, g.—John Hawford.
John Harris, Bradford, Worcs., g.—Edward Bearcroft.
Thomas Edwards, St Clement Danes, g.—Edward Bearcroft.
Edward Owen, Evesham, Worcs., g.—William Stratford.

1688

Nathaniel Whitby, Great Addington, Northants., g.—William Stratford, Mathew
          Carvile.
Edward Stephens, Isle of Wight, g.—Henry Dottin.
Thomas Stokes, St Clement Danes, g.—Francis Norborn.
Francis Norborn, idem, g.—Thomas Stokes.
John Cheese, Comberton, Orlton, Heref., g.—William Rudge.
Thomas Peckham, Arundell, Sussex, g.—Richard Robinson.
Robert Powlett, St Clement Danes, g.—Edward Stephens.
John Stubbs, Springehouse, Durham, g.—William Stratford.
Jonathan Lee, Chesterfield, g.—Robert Milward.
Alexander Robinson, Chichester, g.—Richard Robinson.
John Purnell, Stoncombe, Stinchcombe, Glos., g.—Henry Dottin.

1689

George Yeal, St Clement Danes, g.—Edward Stephens.
Benjamin Osborne, St Giles in the Fields, g.—Samuel Emes.
William Walker, Evesham, Worcs., g.—Edward Walker.
James Gilbert, Chambers Court, Longdon, Worcs., g.—Henry Dottin.
John Pleydell, St Clement Danes, g.—Francis Norborne.
Charles Hodgkins, Ampthill, Beds., g.—Simon Urlin.
Edward Jaques, Thulstone, Derbs., g.—Elias Baker.
Elias Baker, Guildford, Surrey, g.—Edward Jaques.
Henry Bagshaw, Clements Inn, g.—Charles Hope.
William Lee, Clements Inn, g.—John Hawford.
Pollard Crosswell, Bethersden, Kent, g.—Arthur Squier.
Henry Willett, Eye, Suff., g.—William Parker.

1690

Thomas Roebucke, Barnsley, Yorks., g.—William Sitwell.
Edward Paston, Burton upon Trent, Staffs., g.—Thomas Statham.
Thomas Paley, Stamford, Lincs., g.—Charles Whinyates, Joshua Blackwell.
Daniel Wickham, Caistor, Lincs., g.—Thomas Power.

Thomas Brackenbury,[1] Spilsby, Lincs., g.—William Whitwell.
Robert Sloper, Clements Inn, g.—Charles Hope.
George Tilden, Brede, Sussex, g.—William Cockcroft.
Richard Pearce, Penzance, g.—Henry Dottin.
William Vaux,[2] Marsh Gibbon, Bucks., g.—John Prince.
John Prince, Chesham, Bucks., g.—William Vaux.

1691

Francis Mallory, Kimbolton, Hunts., g.—Andrew Hull.
John Boley, Sawley, Derbs., g.—James Motteram.
John Browne, Wolverhampton, g.—John Blakemore.
William Fregleton, Claverley, Salop, g.—John Harris.
John Brocklesby, Melton Mowbray, g.—Joshua Blackwell.
Henry Dottin junior, son of Henry Dottin A, g.—Henry Dottin senior.
    pardonatus quia filius Antiqui.
Charles Bagshaw,[3] Bakewell, Derbs., g.—Thomas Statham.
    pardonatus quia filius Principalis.
William Dixon, Rookeby, Yorks., g.—Robert Harrison.
Thomas James, Stanton, Yorks., g.—John Pleydell.
William Lister, St Giles in the Fields, g.—Charles Hope, g.
William Noyes, Reading, g.—Henry Harris, g.
George Rickards, Nottingham, g.—Arthur Rickards, g.
    pardonatus quia filius Antiqui.
Richard Firth, London, g.—John Pleydell, g.

1692

George Gregson, Turnditch, Derbs., g.—William Lee, g.
Samuel Smart, Bromsgrove, Worcs., g.—John Harris, g.
Thomas Callowe,[4] son of John Callowe, late citizen and pelterer of London—
    Samuel Russell, g.
George Halfhide, Ordsall, Notts., g.—John Pleydell, g.
Thomas Goddard, Atherston, Warw., g.—Henry Lane, g.
Charles Ballett junior, St Clement Danes, g.—William Wingfield.
Edward Pain, Oundle, Northants., g.—William Whitwell.
Talbott Lloyd, Six Clerks Office, g.—William Style, g.

1693

John Hall, Greenwich, g.—Thomas Power, g.
Andrew Innys, Bristol, g.—Samuel Brewster, g.

[1] Members of the Brackenbury family were clerks of the peace for Lindsey—Thomas 1760–71, Joseph (admitted to Clement's Inn in 1742 below) 1787–1826 (C.A., Lincs.). See also the admission of Charles (Carr) Brackenbury, 1714 below.

[2] A William Vaux was lord of the manor of Caversfield 1704–35 (C.A., Bucks.).

[3] Son of Thomas Bagshaw, admitted in 1662, Charles Bagshaw's son married the daughter of Sir John Statham (admitted in 1701 below), the son of his surety (admitted in 1674 above). See also the note to the 1710 admission below (Samuel Eccles).

[4] For other Thomas Callowes see the admissions of 1669 and 1686 above, and see pp. 58, 62.

L*

Martin Innys, son of Andrew Innys, Bristol, g.—Andrew Innys, Samuel Brewster.
Nicholas Guest, Handsworth, Staffs., g.—Arthur Squier, g.
James Smith, Worcester, g.—Henry Toy, g.

1694

John Powle,[1] Leominster, g.—William Rudge, g.
George Fuller, Greenwich, g.—Edward Stephens.
Thomas Chaplin,[2] Bedford, g.—George Vaughan.
John Bellinger, St Clement Danes, g.—John Pleydell.
George Ivye, St Clement Danes, g.—John Pleydell.

1695

Thomas Clerke, Aston Rowant, Oxon., g.—John Eyre.
John Dovey,[3] St Clement Danes, g.—William Fowler.
William Fowler, St Clement Danes, g.—John Dovey.
William Wyne, Wellington, Som., g.—John Pleydell.

1696

Charles Willerton, Alford, Lincs., g.—Charles Ballett.

1697

William Lee, Inner Temple, g.—Edward Dummer.
Everard Cater, St Andrew, Holborn, g.—Charles Hope.

1698

Thomas Emes junior, London, g.—John Emes.
Edward Chapman junior, Bowar, Molash, Kent, g.—William Wyne.
George Turkington, Ely, g.—Edward Chapman.
Lyon Falkener, Uppingham, Rutl., g.—Ferdinando Hudleston.

1699

George Leach, St Clement Danes, g.—John Knight.
John Knight, Six Clerks Office, g.—George Leach.
Everard Goodman, Moulso, Bucks., g.—John Gibbons.
John Gibbons, Wolverhampton, g.—Everard Goodman.
George Davenport, Bromhall, Chesh., g.—George Leech.
Thomas Rogers, Stamford, Lincs., g.—Joshua Blackwell.
Thomas Carter, son of Laurence Carter esquire,[4] Leicester, g.—Laurence Carter,
    John Hawford.

[1] Several members of the Powle family were bailiffs (mayors) of Leominster. John
Powle's entry here is the first in the Admission Book to attract stamp duty.
[2] ? son or nephew of Thomas Chaplin, steward and town clerk of Bedford, named
recorder and clerk in the Bedford charter of 1684; after the charter was withdrawn his
appointments were re-granted in 1688 (C.A., Beds.).
[3] Principal of the Inn 1722/3–8: see pp. 104, 122 above.
[4] See note to p. 5 above.

1700

Charles Clements, Fulham, Midd., g.—Thomas Clements.
George Bateman, Derby, g.—George Davenport.
Andrew Symes, Jokford, Bucks., g.—William Vaux.
John Lamplugh,[1] Kibworth, Leics., g.—Thomas Parker esquire.
Charles Dymoke,[2] son of Charles Dymoke of Cranfeild, g.—Charles Dymoke
    senior, Thomas Dymoke.

1701

Ambrose Eldridge,[3] Chepping Wycombe, Bucks., g.—Thomas Clerke.
John Statham,[4] Wigan, Derbs., g.—Charles Bagshaw.
Robert Taylor, West Malling, Kent, g.—Thomas Power.
John Penny,[5] St Clement Danes, g.—Thomas Power.

1702

    Edwardus Walker principalis Hospitii predicti 23° die Jan. 1701.

Edward Halsted, St Giles in the Fields, g.—John White.
    hec obligatio cancellata et nova obligatio sigillata fuit per Ricardum Arnold gen.
    pleg. per ordinatum factum 26 Nov. 1703.
John White, Portsmouth, g.—Edward Halsted.
    termino S. Mich. 1703 posuit se extra et recepit obligationem.
Richard Brereton,[6] Charlton Kings, Glos., g.—Thomas Belsire.
Thomas Belsire, Yate, Glos., g.—Richard Brereton.
George Denshire,[7] Stamford, Lincs., g.—William Whitwell.

1703

Christopher Goldwire, Kingston upon Thames, g.—Thomas Nuthall.
William Holden, Todhall, Haslingden, Lancs., g.—William Wyne.

    [1] Afterwards at Gray's Inn: see pp. 50–1 above.

    [2] A Charles Dymoke or Dimock was steward of the manor of Cranfield (where the family was settled early in the 17th century) in 1666 and 1714, and county coroner in 1662, 1665, 1684 and 1688 (C.A., Beds.).

    [3] Sworn attorney of the borough of Chepping Wycombe in 1702; witness (1697) to the will (proved in 1713) of Samuel Welles (admitted at Clement's Inn in 1685) (C.A., Bucks.).

    [4] Son of Thomas Statham (see 1674 admissions above). Sir John was Surveyor of Lands in the North Parts of the Duchy of Lancaster (in 1706 by assignment and in 1708 by formal appointment) and M.P. for St Michael's (Mitchell, Cornwall) 1713–15: knighted 1714; first gentleman of the Privy Chamber. He surrendered his chambers in Clement's Inn in 1717 and was described in 1719 as having given up legal practice: see pp. 50, 73 above.

    [5] Principal of the Inn 1728–39: see pp. 137, 169, 179, 190, 195 above. Murdered in his chambers in 1741: see Caulfield, *Portraits, Memories and Characters of Remarkable Persons*, III, 261.

    [6] Born in 1680: member of the Middle Temple in 1707: son of Theophilus Brereton of Charlton Kings (C.A., Glos.).

    [7] A George Denshire was treasurer of South Kesteven 1732–43, clerk of the peace Holland 1748 and 1769–77, and clerk of the peace Kesteven 1727–41, 1741–69 and 1769–77 (C.A., Lincs.).

1704

Mathew Evans,[1] Amersham, Bucks., g.—Henry Harris.
Edward Curtis,[2] Stamford, Lincs., g.—Richard Lowth.
Stephen Bramston,[3] Oundle, Northants., g.—Thomas Rogers.
Henry Gregson,[4] Derby, g.—Charles Bagshaw.
John Handley, St Clement Danes, g.—Samuel Aldridge.
Joseph Hunt, son of Joseph Hunt of Stratford on Avon, g., g.—Joseph Hunt
　　　　senior, Edward Bulstrode.
John Harris, Eydon, Northants., g.—George Ivye.

1705

Samuel Brewster principalis hospitii predicti incepit 23 Jan. 1704.

James Judge, Berkhamsted, Herts., g.—Ambrose Eldridge.
Edward Giles Hooper, Clements Inn, g.—John Jaques.
Edward Yonge, St Martin in the Fields, g.—Robert Dent.
John Richmond, St Clement Danes, g.—Henry Masterman.
Henry Masterman, idem, g.—John Richmond.
John Aldwinckle, Cottingham, Northants., g.—John Lamplugh.
Nathaniel Edison, Spilsby, Lincs., g.—Charles Willerton.
Robert Abney, Newton Burgalan, Leics., g.—George Davenport.
Posthumus Bell, Gloucester, g.—Richard Brereton.
Andrew Love,[5] Okeham, Rutl., g.—Thomas Power.
Richard Wyche,[6] Stamford, Lincs., g.—Charles Willerton.
Theodor Wickham, Castor, Lincs., g.—George Jolland.
John Haynes,[7] East Harding Street, St Brides, g.—Robert Haynes.

1706

John Till-Adam, Bristol, g.—Thomas Belsire.
John Hillier, Horsley, Glos., g.—Edward Morse.
John Bulleme, Evesham, Worcs., g.—Edward Walker.
Henry Pacey,[8] Boston, Lincs., g.—Joshua Blackwell.
Benjamin Hyett, Gloucester, g.—Charles Hyett.

1707

John Grayhurst, Cirencester, Glos., g.—William Grayhurst.
Charles Bransby, Great Grimsby, Lincs., g.—Samuel Townrow.

[1] Died ? 1719, father of Bernard Evans, who was admitted in 1719: see p. 67 above.
See also pp. 38–9, 117, 149 above.
[2] Other members of the Curtis family were admitted in 1724 (Nicholas) and 1735
(Robert).
[3] A successful Oundle attorney, who founded a family firm (C.A., Northants.).
[4] County coroner 1718–35.
[5] A Love (christian name not available) was clerk of the peace for the county of
Rutland before 1742 (C.A., Lincs.).
[6] A Richard Wyche was town clerk of Stamford in 1701 (C.A., Lincs.).
[7] Described as deceased in 1715: see p. 18 above.
[8] He quitted the Inn, having given up practice, in 1719: see p. 70 above. A Henry
Pacey was M.P. for Boston from 1722 till his death in 1729, mayor of Boston in 1708 and
1720, and deputy recorder in 1709 (C.A., Lincs.).

Samuel Townrow, Lowth, Lincs., g.—Charles Bransby.
Darell Shorte, Wadhurst, Sussex, g.—John Fletcher.
John Fletcher, Chichester, Sussex, g.—Darell Shorte.
Nathaniel Lye, Gloucester, g.—John Wintle.
John Wintle, Gloucester, g.—Nathaniel Lye.
Robert Carrow, Canterbury, g.—[No surety named.]
Edward Stanton junior, St Martins in the Fields, g.—Edward Stanton senior.
John Woldish, Maidstone, Kent, g.—William Woldish.
Robert Peart,[1] Lincoln, g.—Joshua Blackwell.
William Tyson, Upper Tooting, Surrey, g.—John Pogson.
James Elly, Gloucester, g.—Daniel Watts.

1708

John Wallett, Stamford, Lincs., g.—William Whitwell.
William Purcell, Clements Inn, g.—Richard Purcell.
Francis Mundy, son of Francis Mundy of Marketon, Derbs., esquire—Francis
     Mundy senior.
Edward Mundy, son of the above Francis Mundy esquire—Francis Mundy senior.
Thomas Truesdale, Stamford, Lincs., g.—Joshua Blackwell.
John Hodgkis, Bristol, g.—John Osborne.
Arthur Kynaston, St Andrew, Holborn, g.—Edward Halsted.

1709

William Atkinson, Spalding, Lincs., g.—Maurice Johnson.
William Barnes, Whitborne, Heref., g.—James Smith.
Richard Bewley, Binbrook, Lincs., g.—[No surety named.]
Richard Mence,[2] Rock, Worcs., g.—Arthur Lake.
Walter Stubbs, Beckbury, Salop, g.—John Dovey.[3]
John White, Portsmouth, g.—Edward Halsted.
Richard Keelinge, Sedgley, Staffs., g.—John Dovey.
Nicholas Cooper, Bristol, g.—Andrew Innys.

1710

John Nettleton, Boston, g.—Henry Pacey.
Edward Sparkes,[4] Peterborough, g.—[No surety named.]
Samuel Eccles,[5] Tiddeswall, Derbs., g.—Charles Bagshaw.

[1] Town clerk of Lincoln: he married the daughter of Joshua Blackwell (see note to
1685 admissions above) (C.A., Lincs.). See also p. 176 above.
[2] Admitted (1717/18) "by certificate from Clement's Inn" at the Inner Temple: see
p. 61 above and *I.T.R.*, IV, 47.
[3] Dovey, the surety for Stubbs, was interested in property near Bridgnorth, not far
from Beckbury (C.A., Salop).
[4] A kinsman of Joseph Sparkes, the antiquary (1683–1740), for whom see *D.N.B.*
[5] Eccles married a daughter of Thomas Statham, a half-sister of Sir John Statham
(see note to 1701 admissions above) and was thus connected with Bagshaw, his surety.
See also p. 50 above.

1711

Richard Kettleby, St Mary le Savoy, Midd., g.—Mohun Cesar Warren.

1712

James Hardwicke, Bristol, g.—Samuel Prigg.
Gravener Dyson, St Andrew, Holborn, g.—John Ryley.
Roger Aldey, St Clement Danes, g.—Henry Whiting.

1713

Thomas Shuckforth junior, Saham, Norf., g.—William Ballett.
William Ballett, Enfield, Midd., g.—Thomas Shuckforth.
William Turner junior, Derby, g.—Samuel Eccles.
Thomas Tufton, St Clement Danes, g.—John Hooke.
Edward Cosyn, Westerham, Kent, g.—William Cosyn.
Zachariah Allnutt,[1] Chepping Wycombe, Bucks., g.—Mathew Carvile.

1714

Joshua Blackwell principal beginning 23 Jan. 1713.
John Blackwell, Stamford, Lincs., g.—John Dovey.
   pardonatus.[2]
Edward Benet, Stamford, Lincs., g.—George Denshire.
Christopher Lake, Six Clerks Office, g.—Richard Brereton esquire.
Richard Parke, Lutton, Lincs., g.—John Blackwell.

1715

Lewis Allen,[3] Middle Temple, g.—John White.
Joseph Dudbridge, Woodchester, Glos., g.—Robert Cowne.
Francis Jackson, Duddington, Northants., g.—Edward Benet.
Degory King, Wadebridge, Cornwall, g.—Nathaniel Houlding.
Humphrey Pelham,[4] St Martin in the Fields, g.—John Pelham.
Charles Brackenbury, Spilsby, Lincs., g.—John Crosley.
Thomas Fowke, St Andrew, Holborn, g.—Mathew Evans.
John Harris, Great Missenden, Bucks., g.—Benjamin Rawlins.
Charles Bowles, Six Clerks Office, g.—Benjamin Rawlins.
John Atwood, St Clement Danes, g.—Thomas Callowe.

1716

William Adams, St Clement Danes, g.—Wiseman Clagett.
Thomas Humphreys, St Clement Danes, g.—William Humphreys.
Samuel Heckford, St Clement Danes, g.—Joseph Dudbridge.

---

[1] For an earlier member of this name see the 1677 admissions above.
[2] Excused fees, &c. (*pardonatus*) doubtless because a son of the principal.
[3] Afterwards admitted a member of the Middle Temple: see p. 99 above.
[4] Described as dead in 1727: son of his surety: see p. 128 above.

Christopher Brewster, St Clement Danes, g.—Everard Goodman.
Thomas Yates, St Clement Danes, g.—William Tyson.
John Battersby, Lincolns Inn, g.—John Ford.
Richard Cromwell, Inner Temple, g.—William Cromwell.

1717

John Catchpole, Sudbury, Suff., g.—Laine Smith.
Morgan Gwyne, Munachty, Cardigan, g.—Jenkin Davies.
John Peart,[1] Sleaford, Lincs., g.—John Blackwell.
William Walcot, Oundle, Northants., g.—Thomas Carter.
Robert Drury, St Clement Danes, g.—Thomas Lake, William Pitt.
Jonas Wakelin, New Inn, St Clement Danes, g.—John Seymor.
William Hardwick, Spilsby, Lincs., g.—Charles Brackenbury.
Ralph Pigott, St Clement Danes, g.—John Briquett.
Thomas Steggall, St Clement Danes, g.—Nathaniel Witham.
William Morris, St Giles in the Fields, g.—Humphrey Humphreys.
Humphrey Hyde, Oundle, Northants., g.—William Walcot.
Brightwell Smith, St Clement Danes, g.—Charles Bowles.
Edward Twine, St Clement Danes, g.—Thomas Yates.
James Child, Agmondesham,[2] Bucks., g.—Mathew Evans.
Thomas Colley, St Clement Danes, g.—John Blandew.
William Cock, Leatherhead, Surrey, esquire—Christopher Brewster.
Thomas Hurst, Stamford, Lincs., g.—John Blackwell.
James Benson, St Pauls, Covent Garden, g.—Hezekia Benson.
John Hope, St Clement Danes, g.—William Adams.
Henry Nelthorpe, Six Clerks Office, g.—Charles Bowles.
Richard Shepperd, Derby, g.—Baptist Trott, Joseph Hayne.
Baptist Trott,[3] Mapleton, Derby, esquire—Richard Sheppard, Joseph Hayne.
Joseph Hayne,[4] Derby, g.—Baptist Trott, Richard Shepperd.

1718

Leonard Cotton, St Martin in the Fields, g.—John Harris.
John Dewes,[5] Studley, Warw., g.—John Fortescue.
Ignatius Hussey, Grays Inn, g.—Thomas Humphreys.
William Powlett, St Clement Danes, g.—Henry Gregory.
Henry Gregory, St Clement Danes, g.—William Powlett.

1719

Thomas Smith, Newbery, Berks., g.—Robert Atkins.
Thomas Swift, Bromley, Kent, g.—Richard Swift senior.

[1] Brother of Robert Peart and uncle of Joshua Peart: see p. 176 above. Town clerk of Lincoln (C.A., Lincs.).

[2] *Alias* Amersham. For Child's death see p. 150 above.

[3] A justice of the peace for Derbyshire.

[4] A Joseph Hayne was clerk of the peace for Derbyshire 1710–60 and sworn in as coroner in 1718.

[5] An Ancient of the Society in 1734 and principal in 1745: see pp. 181, 209 above.

Richard Swift junior, Bromley, Kent, g.—Richard Swift senior.
Thomas Kelynge, St Andrew, Holborn, g.—William Buckland.
Thomas Fish, Enfield, Midd., g.—Francis Mills.
Bernard Evans, Crutched Friers, London, g.—John Birch, Richard Salter.
Thomas Lyte, Six Clerks Office, Chancery Lane, g.—George Prowse.
William Pacey,[1] Boston, g.—Richard Pacey.
Joseph Barras,[2] Battley, Yorks., g.—William Pavey junior.
William Pavey junior, Portsmouth, g.—Joseph Barras.
Samuel Wynde, Cheshunt, Herts., g.—Thomas Shuckforth.

1720

Samuel Robert Ballam, St Mary Magdalene, Bermondsey, g.—James Moore.
Thomas Bridges, Keynsham, Som., g.—Samuel Waters.
William Hester, Camberwell, Surrey, g.—Charles Bowles.
William Wotton, St Clement Danes, g.—Thomas Garrard.

1721

John James Dobson,[3] St Clement Danes, g.—Edward Halsted, James Dobson.
Richard Tidmarsh, Chancery Lane, London, g.—John Hook, James Latimer.
John Green, St Clement Danes, g.—Thomas Thompson.
John Downton, St Clement Danes, g.—Thomas Lethbridge.
Thomas Lethbridge, St Clement Danes, g.—John Downton.
Michael Hatton, St Pauls, Covent Garden, g.—Philip Smith, John Hodson, Samuel Hatton.
Philip Smith, St Clement Danes, g.—Michael Hatton, John Hodson, Samuel Hatton.
Lewis Jones, London, esquire—George Fenn.
Thomas Berry, Great Farringdon, Berks., g.—Luke Langdon.
Thomas Brufield, Middle Temple, g.—Jonathan Whishall junior.
Thomas Trevor, St Clement Danes, g.—Edward Halsted.
Joseph Nicoll, Penvose, Cornwall, g.—Richard Turner.
Thomas Hayley, St Giles in the Fields, g.—Lionel Playter.
Henry Jones, Chastleton, Oxon., g.—Edward Johnson.
Richard Sturgeon, Sompting, Sussex, g.—Charles Bowles.

1722

John Sandys, St Clement Danes, g.—William Vaux.
Peter Monger,[4] Six Clerks Office, g.—Nathaniel Trayton.
Anthony Cocke, Redruth, Cornwall, g.—Samuel Harris.
Nathaniel Trayton, Lewes, Sussex, g.—Peter Monger.
James Scott, St Margaret, Westminster, g.—[No surety named.]

[1] Son of Richard Pacey, his surety: see p. 70 above.
[2] Afterwards steward of the Inn: see pp. 75, 141, 153 above.
[3] Under age when admitted: see p. 84 above. A man with these names was admitted at the Inner Temple 1718/19, called to the bar 1726, and proposed for reader to Clifford's Inn 1742: see *I.T.R.*, IV, 59, 145–6, 446.
[4] Admitted under pressure: see p. 94 above. See also p. 133.

Thomas Burrell,[1] Billinghurst, Sussex, g.—Edward Halsted, John Burrell.
Samuel Coote junior, Rotherhithe, Surrey, g.—Samuel Coote senior.
John Hogg, St Clement Danes, g.—Joseph Goodacre.
Joseph Goodacre, St Dunstan in the West, g.—John Hogg.
Samuel Heckford, St Clement Danes, g.—Thomas Bunce.
Joseph Walker, Winchester, g.—William Burrows.
Robert Paltock,[2] Middle Temple, g.—John Paltock.
John Wilkins Mordaunt, Bury Street, St James, Westminster, g.—Francis
    Reynolds.

1723

Johannes Dovey principalis hospicii predicti incepit 23 Jan. 1722.

Edward Wyatt, Ninehead Florey, Som., g.—Thomas Hill.
William Seabrooke,[3] London, g.—Joshua Blackwell.
John Pierce, Coventry Court, St James, Westminster, g.—John Gould.
William Jackson, Silver Court, near Hanover Square, g.—James Bradley.
Thomas Madgwick,[4] Bromley, Kent, g.—William Wigholm.

1724

Thomas Powlett, St Clement Danes, g.—William Powlett.
George Ward, Middle Temple, g.—Charles Bowles.
Nicholas Curtis, Stamford, Lincs., g.—Edward Curtis, Edward Benet.
John Dovey junior,[5] Clements Inn, g.—Thomas Rowley, William Fowler.
Philip Smith, St Paul, Covent Garden, g.—John Hodson.
Charles Baldwin, Inner Temple, g.—Brightwell Smith.
William Noyes junior, Reading, g.—William Noyes senior.
John Harding,[6] Charterhouse Hinton, Som., g.—Stephen Skurray.
Richard Washington, Staple Inn, g.—Ralph Byde.
Edward Johnson, Shrewsbury, g.—Henry Jones.
Richard Limbrey, Oxford, g.—[No surety named.]

1725

James Peters, Bristol, g.—John Hogg.
Thomas Taubman, St Anne, Westminster, g.—Thomas Farr esquire.
John Walrond junior, London, g.—Bartholomew Jeffery.
Edward Pollen, St Paul, Covent Garden, g.—Edward Ennly.
Hugh Sheldon, Monyash, Derbs., g.—William Feeler.

1726

Thomas Taubman, Covent Garden, g.—[No surety named.]
Nash Mason, Maidstone, g.—Everard Goodman, John Mason.

[1] See note to p. 184, above.
[2] Member of a legal family and author of a romance *The Life and Adventures of
Peter Wilkins, a Cornish Man*: see *D.N.B.* and pp. lviii, 159 above.
[3] See p. xlvii above.
[4] See pp. 118, 158 above and the 1727 entry (? a re-admission) below.
[5] Principal of the Inn in 1739: see p. 195 above.
[6] High sheriff of Somerset in 1752.

William Morphy, York Building, Strand, Midd., g.—James Lally.
Joseph Stratton, Hemlock Court, St Clement Danes, g.—William Rawlinson.

1727

Edward Austen, Tenterden, Kent, g.—Robert Ritson.
Edmund Webb, son of Richard Webb, Merton Abbey, Surrey, g.—Richard Webb, Richard Horne.
David Thomas, Colvinston, Glamorgan, g.—George Bond.
George Bond, Redbrooke, Glos., g.—David Thomas.
John Grove, St Clement Danes, g.—John Morris, Henry Edwards.
Isaac Honnor, St Andrew, Holborn, g.—Robert Andrews.
Thomas Madgwick, Barnards Inn, g.—Robert Moxon.
John Mackay junior, St Andrew, Holborn, g.—George Kitchin.

1728

Henry Saxby, St Clement Danes, g.—Thomas Collins.
John Stafford, St Giles, Midd., g.—William Mears, John Peters.
Thomas Miller,[1] Middle Temple, esquire—Thomas Taubman.

1729

Samuel Elisha,[2] Shrewsbury, g.—Francis Gibbons[3] of St Martins in the Fields, esquire.
John Penny principal beginning 23 Jan. 1728.[4]
William Gofton, St Clement Danes, g.—John Theophilus Desaguliers.
John Wood, St Clement Danes, g.—George Parker.
George Petre, St Clement Danes, g.—Thomas Fortescue, vintner.
Adlard Squire Stukeley,[5] Holbeach, Lincs., g.—Thomas Hunt, Stamford, g.
Edward Rich, Canterbury, g.—Roger Brownsword, Clements Inn, g.
John Vaux, Caversfield, Bucks., g.—William Vaux, Caversfield, g.
Simon Stanton,[6] St Clement Danes, g.—Vincent Eyre, Grays Inn, esquire.
William Winder, London, esquire—John Blackwell, Stamford, g.
Roger Brownsword, St Clement Danes, g.—Charles Crumpe, London, g.
William Raymond junior, Thornbury, Glos., g.—James Hardwick, John Jenkins.
Henry Butler Pacy,[7] Boston, Lincs., g.—Joseph Fearon.
Richard Aldey,[8] St Clement Danes, g.—Roger Aldey.

[1] Afterwards at the bar at the Middle Temple: see p. 184 above.
[2] Coroner for Shrewsbury in 1740 (C.A., Salop).
[3] Francis Gibbons "of London, esquire, son of James Gibbons of London esquire", had been admitted a burgess of Shrewsbury in 1725 (C.A., Salop).
[4] For his election see p. 137 above.
[5] A first cousin of William Stukeley, the antiquary.
[6] Admitted under pressure: see p. 141 above (see also p. 181).
[7] He left the Inn soon afterwards: see p. 172 above. One of this name, prothonotary of the Common Pleas, died in 1754; another was deputy recorder of Boston in 1778 (C.A., Lincs.).
[8] Son of Roger Aldey, his surety (who had been admitted in 1712): see p. 188 above.

1730

Edward Manby, Lincolns Inn, g.—Robert Manby, g.
Thomas Fowke, St Clement Danes, g.—Thomas Sells, Anna Fowke.
Arthur Bissell,[1] Portsmouth, g.—John Buckworth.
Charles Eyres,[2] Exchequer Office, Inner Temple, g.—Thomas Eyre.
John Mason, Maidstone, g.—Nash Mason, g.
Thomas Atkinson, London, g.—John Bidduck, g.
John Watkins, St Clement Danes, g.—Richard Croft.
Isaac Goodwin, St Clement Danes, g.—Edward Umfrevile esquire.
Shirley d'Oyly, Clements Inn, esquire—John d'Oyly, Barr.[3]

1731

Richard Cave, St Sepulchre, London, g.—Samuel Sadler.
Thomas Bulcock, Staple Inn, g.—Jonathan Cadwallader.
Henry Masterman, Middle Temple, g.—John Dovey junior.
John Budgett, Chelsea, g.—Thomas William Burman.
Mathew Lancaster, St Paul, Covent Garden, g.—John Budgett, g.
William Lethieullier, St Clement Danes, esquire—John Budgett, g.
William Leverland, St Dunstan in the West, g.—James Myatt.
Thomas Mander, Toddingham, Glos., g.—Thomas Mawer esquire.
Philip Elias Peltier, Clements Inn, g.—Robert Philipps.
Humphrey Jorden, New Court, Chancery Lane, g.—John Dovey junior.
John Pollexfen, Clements Inn, g.—William Newton.
William Atwood, St Clement Danes, g.—John Atwood.

1732

John Smith, Clements Inn, g.—Brit. Smith.
William Smith, Clements Inn, g.—Thomas Nicholl.
Richard Johnson, Clements Inn, g.—Edward Wyatt.
Thomas Lloyd, Clements Inn, g.—Maurice Lewis esquire.

1733

Joseph Bryan, London, g.—Matthew Stevens.
Joshua Peart,[4] Lincoln, g.—John Blackwell, g.
Charles Limbrey, St Clement Danes, g.—Richard Limbrey junior, g.
William Room, St Clement Danes, g.—Charles Sandcroft.
Gilbert Burton,[5] St Clement Danes, g.—George Burton.

[1] A Charles Bissell was town clerk of Portsmouth 1688–1711 and 1713–27 (C.A., Hants.).

[2] If rightly identified with Charles Eyre of the Inner Temple (surety for Pacey in 1759 below), the third son of Thomas Eyre of Burnham, Bucks. He was admitted at the Inner Temple in 1731/2.

[3] An Edward Doyley (or D'Oyley) was admitted at the Inner Temple in 1721/2; a Christopher Doyley was called there in 1744 (*I.T.R.*, IV, 87, 437, 476).

[4] Later town clerk of Lincoln, like his grandfather (C.A., Lincs.). For his relationship to Robert and John Peart, see p. 176 above.

[5] Son and heir of George Burton of Hatton Garden, according to the records of Gray's Inn to which he transferred himself in 1739: see p. 194 above.

1734

Benjamin Teasdale, Fenchurch Street, London—John Chumley.
Philip Parry Hetherington—Jarman Marchant.
John Osgood, Clements Inn—James Lamborn.
John Robinson, St Anne, Westminster, g.—William Brean.
James Norton, Clements Inn, g.—Nathaniel Benton.
James Lawson, Grays Inn, g.—Isaac Honnor, g.
Benjamin Griffin,[1] Clements Inn—John Shuckeburgh, bookseller.

1735

James Quaill, Clements Inn, g.—John Hall.
William Duffy, Clements Inn, g.—Thomas Powlett.
Henry Burdon, Clements Inn, g.—Lancelot Hall.
Ralph Hodgson, Clements Inn, g.—Robert Pollard.
Timothy Mansfield, Clements Inn, g.—Isaac Mansfield.
Robert Curtis, Stamford, Lincs., g.—Edward Benett, g.
John Hanne, St Clement Danes, g.—Andrew Hanne, George Bradshaw.
    dead Mich. 1755.
Robert Rochester, Clements Inn, g.—Richard Marshall, St Pauls, Covent
    Garden, victualler.
John York, Clements Inn, g.—Edward York, St Margarets, Westminster, gold-
    smith.

1736

William Room, St Clement Danes, g.—Charles Sandcroft.
William Bowness junior, St George the Martyr, Midd., g.—William Bowness
    senior, Charles Creed.

1737

Warren Johnson, Clements Inn, g.—Francis Kentish, Lyons Inn.
Saunders Edwards, Bodenham, Heref., g.—John Dovey, g.
John Crawford, Clements Inn, g.—David Thomas, g.
William Ferrour, Clements Inn, g.—Thomas Powlett, g.
Thomas Rowley, Clements Inn, esquire—John Dovey, g.
Theodore Darley, Clements Inn, g.—William Newton.

1738

John Brown, Clements Inn, g.—Francis Walker.
Francis Roper,[2] Clements Inn, g.—James Houghton.
John Southerton, Clements Inn, g.—John Gardner.
William Gason, Clements Inn, g.—John Hinds.

---

[1] ? the actor and dramatist (1682–1740, son of the Rev. Benjamin Griffin), who was
a member of the company with which Christopher Rich's re-built theatre in Lincoln's
Inn Fields was opened: see *D.N.B.*, and see pp. lviii above and 281 n. below.
[2] Admitted under pressure: see p. 189 above.

George Sacvile Turner, Clements Inn, g.—Joseph Worsley, St Clement Danes,
    baker, Anthony Sackfield, St Clement Danes, butcher.
George Green, Clements Inn, g.—John Green, g.
John Chumley, Clements Inn, g.—Joseph Worsley, Anthony Sackfield.
James Bambridge,[1] Clements Inn, g.—Thomas Bambrigg.

1739

John Proutt, Clements Inn, g.—Thomas Powlett, g.
Henry Loyd, Clements Inn, esquire—Charles Wightwick, g.
Charles Wightwick, Clements Inn, g.—Henry Loyd esquire.
            John Dovey principal of the said Inn.[2]
John Elwick, Cheshunt, Herts., esquire—Richard Green.
William Eldridge, Wickam, Bucks., g.—Richard Whitchurch, Anthony Turney.
    son of an ancient.

1740

Anthony Ryan, Clements Inn, g.—Richard Goodlad, Much Haddow, Essex,
    esquire.
William Smyth, Clements Inn, g.—John Turner, Dufour Court, Midd., esquire.
Matthew Unwin junior, St James, Clerkenwell, g.—John Turner, Dufour Court,
    Midd., esquire.

1741

John Price, Exchequer Office, Inner Temple, g.—Richard Fleming, Six Clerks
    Office, Chancery Lane, g.
Thomas Perkins, Clements Inn, g.—Francis Green, Clements Inn, g.
Francis Green, Clements Inn, g.—Thomas Perkins, Clements Inn, g.
John Adderley, Clements Inn, g.—Robert Roch, St Clement Danes, vintner.
John Caldecot, Clements Inn, g.—John Brown, Clements Inn.

1742

David Henriques, Clements Inn, g.—Theodore Darley, Clements Inn, g.
Robert Pardoe,[3] Lincolns Inn, g.—Thomas Lloyd, Lincolns Inn, g.
George Green, Clements Inn, g.—William Smith, Chancery Lane, shoemaker.
Thomas Wotton,[4] London, citizen and stationer—John Davies, St Dunstan in the
    West, bookbinder.

[1] Admitted (1743/4) to the Inner Temple "by certificate from Clement's Inn" (*I.T.R.*,
IV, 480).
[2] For his election see p. 195 above.
[3] Appointed solicitor to act for Lincoln's Inn in an assessment appeal (1772): see
Black Books of L.I., III, 414–15, &c.
[4] Thomas Wotton (son of Matthew Wotton, bookseller, near St Dunstan's church)
was warden (1754) and master (1757) of the Stationers' Company: he compiled the
Baronetage and published Rushworth's *Historical Collections* and editions of Bacon and
Selden: died 1766–see *D.N.B.*

Thomas Brackenbury,[1] Spilsby, Lincs., g.—Charles Brackenbury, Spilsby, Lincs.,
    esquire.
Charles Pryce, Clements Inn, g.—James Carrington, Fetter Lane, esquire.
John Green, Leather Lane, St Andrew, Holborn, brewer—George Hatsell, St
    Andrew, Holborn, brewer.
William Mills, Clements Inn, g.—Robert Roch, St Clement Danes, innholder.

1743

Joseph Goodacre principal of the said Inn 23 Jan. 1742.[2]

Henry Champante, Clements Inn, g.—Francis Werrey, Red Lion Square, g.
George Elers,[3] Clements Inn, g.—Thomas Rowley, Clements Inn, esquire.
Stephen Masterman, Shoe Lane, London, brewer—Simon Stratford, Shoe
    Lane, g.
Henry Gunter, Clements Inn, g.—Charles Pryce, Clements Inn, g.
William Wall, Clements Inn, g.—Solomon Jeddere, St Giles in the Fields, iron-
    monger.

1744

Lewis Richards, Clements Inn, g.—Thomas Mackdowall, St James, Midd., g.

1745

John Ashe, Clements Inn, g.—John Carmalt, Clements Inn, g.
John Carmalt, Clements Inn, g.—John Ashe, Clements Inn, g.
William Vaughan,[4] Inner Temple, g.—Joseph Palmer, White Friars, g.
Thomas Clark, Clements Inn, g.—Nathaniel Ebrall, St Paul, Covent Garden,
    apothecary.
John Dewes esquire Principal 23d May, 1745.[5]

Tomkyns Dew, Lincoln's Inn, g.—Silett Dew, Chelsea, widow.
Michael Hodgson, Clements Inn, g.—Silver Crispin, St Andrew, Holborn,
    confectioner.
John Fraine, Clements Inn, g.—George Westron, St Clement Danes, haberdasher
    and hosier.

1746

James Budgett junior—James Budgett, Bread Street, London, druggist, Thomas
    Merryfield, Lombard Street, London, druggist.
Thomas Heckford, Clements Inn, g.—Samuel Heckford, Clements Inn, g.
James Parke, Clements Inn, g.—John Styth, Lincolns Inn, g.
N.B. Tomkyns Dewe Admitted 16th July 1745 Omitted.
William Clifton, Clements Inn, g.—Thomas Perkins, Clements Inn, g.
Fountain Cooke, Clements Inn, g.—[No surety named.]

[1] Treasurer of Lindsey 1750, clerk of the peace for Lindsey, 1760–71 (C.A., Lincs.).
[2] For his election see p. 200 above.
[3] Afterwards at the Middle Temple: see p. 217 above.
[4] Two William Vaughans were admitted at the Inner Temple in 1721, one the son of
Thomas Vaughan of Lincoln's Inn, the other the son of John Vaughan of Merioneth.
[5] For his election see p. 207 above.

1747

James Cloberry Gascoigne, Clements Inn, g.—George Harvest,[1] Magdalen College, Cambridge.
William Phelps, Hendon, Midd., g.—William Kinsley, New Inn.
Thomas Goodwin, Clements Inn, g.—George Davids, Chelsea, g.
Peter Prevost, Lincolns Inn, g.—Fountaine Cooke, Clements Inn.
Thomas Miller, St James, Westminster, g.—Thomas Roles, Grays Inn, g.
Thomas Devon, Clements Inn, g.—John Fludd, Temple Barr, goldsmith.
Hugh Morgan, St Giles in the Fields, g.—William Cheesebrough, St Austin, London, refiner.

1748

Edward Biddulph, Clements Inn, g.—James Parke, Clements Inn, g.
John Worgan, Clements Inn, g.—Richard Collett, Golden Square, St James, g.
Harry Cloudesley, Clements Inn, g.—John Carmalt, Clements Inn, g.
  W. Ashhurst should have been entered here instead of the other side.
George Green, Clements Inn, g.—John Green, Clements Inn, g.
Joseph Freeman, Pond's End, Midd., periwigmaker—George Dottin, Cheshunt, Herts., g.
William Henry Ashhurst,[2] Clements Inn, g.—Harry Cloudesley, g.
  W. Ashhurst's Admittance should have been entered next after Mr Cloudesley on the other side.

1749

Thomas Leigh, Clements Inn, g.—Charles Bill, Lyons Inn, g.
John Perrott, Clements Inn, g.—William Plaxton, Clements Inn, g.
William Plaxton, Clements Inn, g.—John Perrott, Clements Inn, g.
Charles Masrey, Clements Inn, g.—Fountaine Cooke, Clements Inn, g.
William Titterson, Clements Inn, g.—Peter Prevost, Clements Inn, g.
Robert Hall, Clements Inn, g.—John Firth, New Inn, g.
Lewis Christian Austin Granom, Clements Inn, esquire—Thomas Roome, Fleet Street, undertaker.

1750

John Winder, Clements Inn, esquire—William Winder, Clements Inn, esquire.
Robert Simpson, St Clement Danes, g.—James Morton, St Clement Danes, distiller.
  Mr Simpson should not have been entered till after Mr Ford, twas by mistake.
Thomas Ford, Aldermanbury, g.—Elias Philip Delaport, St Paul, Covent Garden, g.
  Mr Ford should have been entered before Simpson.

[1] Admitted at the Middle Temple 1724: ordained 1741: fellow of Magdalene College 1745: died 1780. Son of William Harvest, brewer, of Thames Ditton (Venn, *Alumni Cantab.*).

[2] The names are those of the King's Bench judge (1725–1807), admitted to the Inner Temple in 1750, who became the target of Jeremy Bentham in *The Truth v. Ashhurst*—see *D.N.B.*

1751

26 Nov. 1751 Mr Gregory made Pr.

Robert Garnett, New Castle Court, St Clement Danes, g.—John Langford, Fisher Street, Red Lyon Square, St George the Martyr, taylor.
James Worgan, Clements Inn, g.—John Worgan, Clements Inn, g.

1752

Winde William Van der Esch,[1] Mint, Tower of London, g.—Abraham Stevens, Fleet Street, hatter.
James Cox, Paternoster Row, g.—Paul Taylor, Chancery Lane, coffeeman.
George Langdale, St Clement Danes, g.—Samuel Roch, St Clement Danes, innholder.
Christian Lau [? Lan], New Inn, g.—William Staveley, St Clement Danes, perukemaker.

1753

John Pitt, London, g.—James Worgan, Clements Inn, g.
Thomas Roles, Clements Inn, g.—Thomas Miller, Cliffords Inn, g.
Robert Kirke junior, Clements Inn, g.—Robert Kirke senior, Dorset Court, Channell Row, Westminster, g.
William Pate, Clements Inn, g.—James Boddicoates, Cornhill, woollendraper.
George Robinson,[2] Gough Square; g.—James Solas Dodd,[3] Gough Square, surgeon.
John Hebden, Clements Inn, g.—John Worgan, Clements Inn, g.
John Chapone,[4] Clements Inn, g.—Robert Kirke, Clements Inn, g.
Richard Rolt,[5] Clements Inn, g.—Walter Baker, Helmet Court, Strand, chymist, John Pritchard, Charing Cross, weaver.

1754

James Madden, Clements Inn, g.—John Worgan, Millman Street, St Andrew, Holborn.

---

[1] One of this name, "son of Henry Van der Esch of Gray's Inn esquire", had been admitted at Gray's Inn in March 1727/8. Henry Van der Esch had been admitted there in the previous month: he was deputy master of the Mint from 1725 to 1762: a William Winde was inspector of prosecutors there during part of that period.

[2] ? the London bookseller (1737–1801) who published Baretti's *Easy Lessons in Italian and English* for which Dr Johnson wrote a preface in 1775—see Boswell, *Life of Johnson, ubi sup.*, I, 22, II, 290, 509 n.

[3] Author of *An Essay towards the National History of the Herring* (London, 1752, dedication dated from Gough Square).

[4] The attorney whose wife Hester Chapone (*née* Mulso) wrote essays for *The Rambler* and corresponded with Dr Johnson—see Boswell, *Life of Johnson, ubi sup.*, IV, 246 n., 247, V, 211, and *D.N.B.*

[5] For Richard Rolt (1725?–70), to whose *Dictionary of Trade and Commerce* Dr Johnson contributed a preface, see Boswell, *ibid.*, I, 21, 358–9, II, 344–5, and *D.N.B.*

1755

7 Febr. 1755 Mr Thomas Elected principal.

Edward Bowman, Chancery Lane, g.—John Bowman, Inner Temple, g.

Thomas Hammond, Clements Inn, g.—John Glover, Theobalds Court, St Martin in the Fields, staymaker.

William Davids, Clements Inn, g.—[No surety named.]

1756

John Osbaldeston, Clements Inn, g.—William Hobbs, Six Clerks Office, Chancery Lane, g.

Thomas Wright, Clements Inn, g.—Joseph Reading, Clare Street, Clare Market, distiller.

Pitt Lethieullier, St James, Westminster, esquire—Christopher Burrow, Crown Office, esquire.

Zachariah Stephens, Staple Inn, g.—Maurice Morgan, New Inn, g.

1757

Matthew Chessell, Clements Inn, g.—Joseph Reeve, St Clement Danes, coal merchant.

Thomas Hopkins, Clements Inn, g.—Joseph Girdler,[1] Gray's Inn, esquire.

John Osgood, Furnivals Inn, g.—John Battam, Warner Street, Cold Bath Fields, carpenter.

William Hart, Clements Inn, g.—George Langdale, Boswell Court, St Clement Danes, Robert Roch, Clements Lane, wine merchant.

1758

Josiah Brown,[2] Clements Inn, g.—Thomas Brown, St Peter, Cornhill, merchant.

Richard Way, Clements Inn, g.—James Mason, Carey Street, St Clement Danes, upholder.

Christopher Mosyer Rich,[3] Clements Inn, g.—John Green, General Post Office, Lombard Street, g.

George Williamson, Clements Inn, g.—James Dolling, Great Russel Street, St George, Bloomsbury, g.

1759

William Stafford, Clements Inn, g.—Thomas Gamall, Pump Court, Middle Temple, g.

John Pacey, Clements Inn, g.—Charles Eyre, Inner Temple, esquire, Henry Butler Pacey.

[1] Son and heir of Joseph Girdler (admitted at the Inner Temple in 1728), Serjeant at law.

[2] Entering the Inner Temple (1764/5), Brown unsuccessfully claimed seniority there as from the date of his admission to Clement's Inn. Called to the bar in 1770, he was proposed for Reader at Clement's Inn in 1773 (*I.T.R.*, V, 184, 239–40, 243, 291).

[3] A brother of John Rich, pantomimist and theatrical manager: their father, Christopher Rich (died 1701), originally an attorney, afterwards controlling the Drury Lane, Dorset Gardens and Haymarket theatres, left to his two sons the new theatre he had begun to erect in Lincoln's Inn Fields—see *D.N.B.*

William Devon, Clements Inn, g.—Francis Colman, New Inn, esquire.
William Lander, Clements Inn, g.—Charles Lander, Great St Helens, Bishopsgate Street, g.
John French, late of St Paul, Covent Garden, now Clements Inn, g.—Zachariah Stephens, Clements Inn, g.
Alexander Bassett, Clements Inn, g.—James Hossack, St Clement Danes, peruke-maker.
John Clementson, Clements Inn, g.—John Humphrey Babb, Abbots Ripton, Hunts., g.
David Thomas junior, St Andrew, Holborn, g.—Hopkin Rees, St Andrew, Holborn, g., William Thomas, St Andrew, Holborn, g.

1760

Redmond Byrne, Clements Inn, g.—David Jennings, Cliffords Inn, g.
Richard Wilsford, Clements Inn, g.—Christian Lau [? Lan], Clements Inn, g.
John L'Archevesque, Clements Inn, g.—Lewis Christian Austin Granom, Clements Inn, esquire.
William Perrott, Northleigh, Oxon., esquire—Thomas Bedwell, Wandsworth, Surrey, g.
John Lambert, St Martin in the Fields, builder—Joseph Brown, St Clement Danes, glazier.
Martin Challis, St John, Hackney, esquire—Henry Folkes, St George, Blooms-bury, esquire.
Thomas Barratt, Old Brentford, Midd., esquire—Zachariah Stephens, Clements Inn, g.
Robert Mason, Clements Inn, g.—William Jones, Stanhope Street, St Clement Danes.
Benjamin Green,[1] Castle Yard, Holborn, g.—Thomas Gibbons, Crowell, Oxon., clerk.

1761

Mr Welch & Mr Powell should be entered before Mr Hyde.
James Hyde, Russell Street, Covent Garden, engraver—Thomas Fletcher, Gutter Lane, Cheapside, plaisterer.
John Welch, Clements Inn, g.—Edward Wood, Middle Temple, g.
Foster Powell,[2] Clements Inn, g.—William Bristowe, Six Clerks Office in the Liberty of the Rolls, g.

Mr George Green principal.
Edward Wood, Clements Inn, g.—John Welch, Clements Inn, g.
Evan James, Clements Inn, g.—Thomas Jones, St James, Westminster, cheese-monger.
William Strong, Clements Inn, g.—John Hannam, Clements Inn.

[1] ? the mezzotint engraver (? 1736–? 1800), for whom see *D.N.B.*
[2] See the identical entry in 1765 below. Powell (1734-93), born in Leeds, came to London as clerk to an attorney in the Temple. He owes his inclusion in *D.N.B.* to his feats of pedestrianism (among the earliest of our athletic records). He died in his rooms in Clement's Inn.

John Hannam, Clements Inn, g.—William Strong, Clements Inn.
Alexander Fortie, Clements Inn, g.—James Stewart, St Leonard, Shoreditch, timber merchant.

1762

Joseph Settree,[1] Clements Inn, g.—Redmond Byrne, Clements Inn.
Thomas Davies, Clements Inn, g.—Robert Clarke, St Martin in the Fields, cabinetmaker.
James Masfen, Clements Inn, g.—Thomas Ford, London, g.
John Asbridge, Clements Inn, g.—Richard Lyster, St Paul, Covent Garden, apothecary.
Charles Walker,[2] Inner Temple, esquire—Thomas Long, Cheapside, g.
Henry Wood Woodward, Clements Inn, g.—Zachary Stephens, Clements Inn, g.
Thomas Zachary, Clements Inn, g.—Samuel Bruchfield, Friday Street, ribbon weaver.
John Parmire, London, merchant—George Arnane, King Street, St Ann, g.
Richard Hinde, Clements Inn, esquire—John Mayer, Grays Inn, g.
   1 April 1763 paid Mr Green in full. M.C.[3]

1763

John Barrow, Clements Inn, g.—Robert Wilson, Cliffords Inn, surgeon.
Charles Edwards Beresford,[4] Clements Inn, g.—The Reverend Thomas Higgins,[5] St Paul's School.
Robert Dobson, York, esquire—Francis Caryll, St Martin in the Fields, man's mercer.
Samuel Gawler, Clements Inn, g.—John Newland,[6] Inner Temple, g.
Edmund Amiss, Clements Inn, g.—Philip Hallier, Fetter Lane, brushmaker.
William Lindeman, St Martin in the Fields, oilman—John Lunel, Doctors Commons, g.
John Smith, Clements Inn, g.—Robert Roch, St Clement Danes, dealer in brandy.
Robert Hanson, Clements Inn, g.—John Harris, Kings Langley, Herts., g.
Alexander Thistlethwayte, Wadham College, Oxford, esquire—William Strong, Clements Inn.

1764

4th June 1764 accounted to Mr Green.
Peter Remen,[7] St Paul, Covent Garden, g.—John Warcup, Carey Street, St Clement Danes, cheesemonger.

   [1] Another Joseph Settree appears among the 1770 admissions below.
   [2] Admitted to the Inner Temple 1751/2, called to the bar 1759: left the Inner Temple in 1762: see *I.T.R.*, V, 24, 90, 94.
   [3] Presumably the clerk or steward (? Matthew Chessall, admitted in 1757) thus records his settlement with the principal.
   [4] Son of William Beresford, White Hart Yard, Drury Lane, tailor: entered St Paul's School 1750: he is described as of the Stamp Office when surety to John West in 1785.
   [5] Son of Thomas Higgins of Paternoster Row: scholar at St Paul's School 1752, captain 1756, and (after graduating at Cambridge) usher from 1763 till he resigned in 1782.
   [6] A John Newland was admitted at the Inner Temple 1739/40, called to the bar 1795, and proposed for reader to Lyon's Inn 1799: see *I.T.R.*, V, 534, 593, 643.
   [7] The St Paul's rate-books spell his surname twice as Remen and twice as Reman.

John Allen, Clements Inn, g.—John Smith, Clements Inn, g.
Samuel Goodman, Inner Temple, g.—Samuel Hendy, New Inn, g., Henry Kiddell, New Inn, g.
George Herne, Clements Inn, g.—Thomas Oldfield, St Luke, Chelsea, brewer.
Joseph Hodges, Clements Inn, g.—Charles Gapper, Furnivals Inn, g.
William Davids, Clements Inn, g.—George Sanderson, Blewetts Buildings, Fetter Lane, g.
William West, Furnivals Inn, g.—William Cullingworth, Little Russell Court, St Martin in the Fields, brewer.

1765

Jegon Wellard, Lincolns Inn, g.—William Thorpe, St Clement Danes, coal merchant.
Thomas Knipe, Clements Inn, g.—Thomas Cresswell, Dyot Street, St Giles in the Fields, victualler.
Joseph Baird, Clements Inn, g.—James King, Queen Street, Golden Square, bucklemaker.
Court Dewes,[1] Clements Inn, esquire—Bernard Dewes,[1] Clements Inn, g.
Thomas Fullwood, St Paul, Covent Garden, g.—Richard Atkinson, Nicholas Lane, Lombard Street, merchant.
John Redhead, Clements Inn, g.—Thomas Morris, Ludgate Street, mercer.
Richard Brocklesby,[2] St Clement Danes, doctor of physick—William Devaynes, Spring Garden, St Martin in the Fields, g.
Foster Powell,[3] Clements Inn, g.—William Bristowe, Six Clerks Office, Liberty of the Rolls, g.

1766

William Campion, Clements Inn, g.—Samuel Pawson, St Clement Danes, esquire.
Philip Scott, Clements Inn, g.—John Welch, Clements Inn, g.
Thomas Martin,[4] New Inn, g.—Charles Collyer, Strand, St Clement Danes, dealer in rum and brandy.
William Williams, Kensington, clerk—George Jones, Lincolns Inn, g.
John Crawley, Clements Inn, g.—William Crawley, York Buildings, g.
Isaac Allix, Cliffords Inn, g.—Samuel Hooper, Strand, bookseller.
James Medlicott Flack, Lincolns Inn, g.—Thomas Heydon, Queen Street, Lincolns Inn Fields, g.

[1] One of this name (for another, see the 1781 admissions below) was called to the bar at the Middle Temple in 1766, admitted to the Inner Temple *ad eundem gradum* in 1770, and proposed for reader to Lyon's Inn in 1771: he died in 1794—*I.T.R.*, V, 244, 263, 577. He was perhaps a kinsman of John Dewes, principal in 1745 (see p. 209 above). A John Dewes (or d'Ewes) of Wellesbourne, Warw. (born 1707, died 1761) was father of Court (born 1742, called to the bar at the Middle Temple 1766, died 1793), Bernard (born 1743, died 1822, who had a son Court) and John (born 1744, died 1826). In 1794 a Bernard Dewes, as executor of a Court Dewes, dealt with the latter's chambers: see *I.T.R.*, V, 577.

[2] Schoolfellow of Burke and friend, correspondent and medical attendant of Dr Johnson: see *D.N.B.* and Boswell's *Life of Johnson* (ed. Hill & Powell, 1934), IV, 176, 264, 338.

[3] See note to identical entry under the year 1761 above.

[4] ? the antiquary (1697–1771) who was clerk to Robert Martin, attorney, his brother—see *D.N.B.*

Henry Knowles, Liberty of the Rolls, cook—Nicholas Maskell, Brook Street, St Andrew, Holborn, bricklayer.

John Atkinson, St James, Westminster, cheesemonger—John Ball, Long Acre, bricklayer.

Thomas Allen, St James, Westminster, plumber—Alexander Wilson, St James, Westminster, carpenter.

Capel Pick, Clements Inn, g.—Thomas Gibbeson, St Clement Danes, g.

William Swainston, Hatton Garden, g.—Richard Swainston, Hatton Garden, g.

Robert Studley Vidal,[1] St Clement Danes, g.—Robert Methuen, g.

John Moody,[2] Clements Inn, g.—Thomas Sturgeon, St Clement Danes, baker.

1767

Edward Stanley, Clements Inn, g.—John Hains, St Clement Danes, g.

Peter Henry Barker, Clements Inn, g.—Thomas Druke, Bread Street, merchant.

John Livett, St Mary le Strand, apothecary—Martha Whincop, Clements Inn, widow.

Caleb Davies, Clements Inn, g.—William Dignam, St Andrew, Holborn, victualler.

Nathaniel Carter, Clements Inn, g.—John Tekell, Clements Inn, g.

Francis Waters, Clements Inn, g.—John Adams, Southampton Buildings, Chancery Lane, g.

John Brown, Carey Street, St Clement Danes, g.—Isaac Brown, Strand, haberdasher.

1768

Thomas Adams, Warwick Court, Holborn, merchant—Roger Simpkinson, Fleet Street, jeweller.

Charles King, Clements Inn, g.—William Bramsford, Lymington, Hants., g.

Robert Hayes, Clements Inn, g.—William John Millen, Dukes Court, Bow Street, cordwainer.

Edward Hoare, Clements Inn, g.—Joseph Cruttenden, London, g.

George Glenny, Grays Inn, g.—Robert James junior, Newgate Street, laceman.

Thomas Hugbon, Clements Inn, g.—Joseph Settree, Clements Inn, g.

Thomas Jeffreys, Gloucester Street, Red Lion Square, g.—Robert Aldus, Bedford Street, Bedford Row, g.

Francis Baronneau, Clements Inn, g.—William Campion, Clements Inn, g.

John Hoole,[3] Clements Inn, g.—Ralph Winter, Birch Anger, Essex, esquire.

1769

Thomas Jackson, Clements Inn, g.—John Jackson junior, St Mary le Bone, g.

John Janney, Clements Inn, g.—Thomas Smith, Piccadilly, musical instrument maker, James Lamb, Great Mary Bone Street, grocer.

---

[1] Probably the London solicitor who died at Exeter in 1796, named as father of Robert Studley Vidal (1770–1811), antiquary, in the account of the latter in *D.N.B.*

[2] For another entry of a John Moody see 1779 admissions below. It is the name of the actor, *né* Cochran (see *D.N.B.*), Boswell's "old acquaintance". See p. lviii above.

[3] Hoole (1727–1803), translator, was a friend and correspondent of Dr Johnson for whom he "collected" a City club: Johnson wrote dedications for two of his translations and bequeathed him a book from his library—see Boswell, *ubi sup.*, IV, 70, 87, 187, 360, 402, 525 and *D.N.B.*

Harry Mynors Long, Clements Inn, g.—Thomas Boid, St Mary Islington, brick-
    layer.
Edward Peach, Clements Inn, g.—Atwood Wigzell, Sandersted, Surrey, esquire.
William Offley, Clements Inn, g.—William Campion, Clements Inn, g.
Thomas Hewitt, St Dunstan in the West, g.—William Steele, Clements Inn, baker.
John Stephens, London, g.—Andrew Allsopp, St Paul, Covent Garden,
    upholsterer.
Robert Gapper, Tooley Street, Southwark, g.—Samuel Sedgwick, Southwark,
    carpenter.
Vaughan Phillips, Custom House, g.—Coan Haverkam, Clements Inn, g.
William Fletcher, Clements Inn, g.—Foster Powell, Clements Inn, g.
Erasmus Phillips, Liberty of the Rolls, esquire—John Wynde, Liberty of the Rolls,
    apothecary.

1770

William Palmer, Clements Inn, g.—John Welch, Clements Inn, g.
Joseph Settree, Clements Inn, g.—James Settree, Clements Inn, g.

John Allen Steward from this Time.

Thomas Mitchell, Grays Inn, g.—John Allen, Clements Inn, g.
John Lindeman,[1] Student of Bennet College, Cambridge—William Lindeman,
    Clements Inn, g.
William Skipper, Drury Lane, g.—Joseph Manlove, St Clement Danes, fishmonger.
George Hill, New Inn, g.—William Strong, g.

Mr Prevost principal.

Joshua Jones Prichard, late of Islington, now of Clements Inn, g.—Edward
    Benskyn, Knightsbridge, g.
William Gapper, Clements Inn, g.—John William Holwell, Newport Street, St
    Martin in the Fields, esquire.
Joseph Hatt Turner, Stoke Newington, g.—William Bartlett, Bishopsgate Street,
    druggist.

1771

John Long, Preshaw,[2] Hants., esquire—Zachariah Stephens, Chancery Lane, g.
Robert Shaw, Clements Inn, musician—John Hurnell, Lincolns Inn, stationer.
Francis Grose,[3] Wandsworth, esquire—Dagge More,[4] Inner Temple, esquire.
Ralph Winter, Clements Inn, esquire—John Hoole, St Clement Danes, g.
Thomas Parker, Strand, g.—John Tompset, Southend, Lewisham, Kent, inn-
    holder.
Henry Jaffray, Strand, undertaker—John Stokes, New Inn, g.

---

[1] Son of William Lindeman, his surety (for whose admission see under 1763 above):
vicar of St Sithney, Cornwall 1789–1819: died 1819, *aet.* 72

[2] A John Long bought Preshaw, a manor in the parish of Corhampton in 1728: it
remained in the family till 1898 (C.A., Hants.).

[3] ? (see another Francis Grose admitted in 1783 below) the antiquary and draftsman
(1731?–91) described in *D.N.B.*, son of a Richmond jeweller.

[4] Dagge More or Moore was called to the bar at the Inner Temple 1772 and proposed
for reader to Clifford's Inn 1771–*I.T.R.*, V, 175, 285, 341.

The Rev. Offspring Pearce,[1] Clements Inn, clerk—Edward Peach, Inner
     Temple, g.
John Smith, New Inn, g.—Abell Jenkins, New Inn, g.

1772

Robert Gallaway, Clements Inn, g.—James Atkins, Clements Inn, g.
Richard Samuel, Clements Inn, g.—John Samuel, Lawrence Poultry Lane,
     merchant.
Richard Weld, Clements Inn, g.—George Glenny, Clements Inn, g.
John Elmslie, Clements Inn, esquire—George Glenny, Clements Inn, g.
Thomas Mortimer,[2] Clements Inn, g.—Charles Smart, Clements Inn, g.
John Thomas, St Clement Danes, g.—George Glenny, Clements Inn, g.
Philip Weldon, St Andrew, Holborn, g.—Benjamin Deacon, St Andrew, Hol-
     born, g.
Charles Smart, Clements Inn, g.—Thomas Mortimer, Clements Inn, g.
Giles Long, Chigwell, Essex—John Charles Long, Chigwell, Essex, merchant.
Thomas Price, Fetter Lane, g.—George Papps, Upper Mary le Bone Street,
     Oxford Road, g.

1773

Daniel Gyles, Water Street, St Clement Danes, watchmaker—Edward Starling,
     Drury Lane, carver.
John Pritchard, York Street, Covent Garden, shoemaker—Hassall Hutchins,
     King Street, Covent Garden.
Arthur Ricard junior, Clements Inn, g.—William Rooks, Grays Inn, esquire.

Robert Kirke esquire principal.

John Welch junior, Clements Inn, g.—John Welch senior, Clements Inn, g.
Joseph Potts, Holborn, g.—William Potts, captain of the King's or 8th Regiment
     of Foot.
Thomas Bland, Tunstall House, near Sittingbourn, Kent, esquire—Joseph Ives,
     Dean Street, Fetter Lane, g.
John Webb, Clements Inn, esquire—Daniel Webb, Gloucester, esquire.
William Devon,[3] Middle Temple, g.—John Pacey,[4] Inner Temple, g.
Robert Thackrey, St Martins Lane, g.—Joseph Marshall, St Clement Danes,
     stationer.
William Roberts, White Hall, Midd., g.—Owen Brown, Maiden Lane, jeweller.
     *a new bond given and James Baird of St Thomas Apostle esquire pledge 20 Dec.
     1773.*

[1] St John's College, Cambridge: curate of St Paul's, Shadwell: afterwards rector of
a parish in South Carolina.
[2] ? the author (1730–1810) who returned to England in 1768 from consular service
abroad and resumed writing on economic and other subjects: see *D.N.B.*
[3] Principal in 1782: see admissions of 1759 (William Devon) and 1810 (Charles
Devon): see also p. 246 above.
[4] ? the John Pacey admitted in 1759 and an Ancient in 1774: see pp. 281 above and
288 below. Entered at the Inner Temple in 1769/70; died 1780—*I.T.R.*, V, 251, 379.

1774

John Samson Tadwell, Clements Inn, g.—John Stone, St Martin in the Fields,
     staymaker.
Andrew Donaldson, Clements Inn, merchant—George Glenny, Norfolk Street,
     wine merchant.
George Snowden, Clements Inn—John Wallace, Bedford Street, Covent Garden.
Thomas Lacey, Clements Inn, g.—Joshua Jones Prichard, Clements Inn, g.
Peter Wallace, Pauls Grave Head Court, St Clement Danes, esquire—John
     Elmslie, Clements Inn, esquire.

Mr Wm Strong Steward from this Time.

Daniel Norcutt, Great Queen Street, Lincolns Inn Fields, g.—Stephen Popham,
     Lincolns Inn Fields, g.
William Cooper, Middle Temple, g.—Samuel Cooper, Quality Court, Chancery
     Lane, g.
William Rigge, St Clement Danes, g.—John Pacey, Ancient, g.
Daniel Webb, Clements Inn, esquire—Humphrey Roberts, Strand, coffeeman.
Nehemiah Winter, Clements Inn, esquire—John Bedford, Portsmouth Common,
     Hants., g.

1775

John Shering, Clements Inn, g.—John Allnutt, Clements Inn.
     upon the 1st day of Jan. last in the year 1774 and then omitted to be entred.
James Edge, Clements Inn, esquire—William Bolton, Old Jury, g.
Thomas Pearson, Clements Inn, g.—George Pearson, Essex Street, g.
Arthur Wilkinson, Clements Inn, esquire—John May, Strand, wine merchant.
John Vaughan, Upper Thames Street, esquire—Casten Rhode, Lemon Street,
     Goodmans Fields, esquire.
George Greives, Navy Office, Crutched Fryers, g.—Daniel Taylor, New London
     Street, grocer.
John Thomas, Clements Inn, esquire—John Elmslie, Surrey Street, Strand,
     esquire.
Samuel Baldwin, Clements Inn, g.—Alexander Bassett, a Companion of this
     Society.
Archibald Duthie, Clements Inn, esquire—George Glenny, a Companion of this
     Society.
John Asbridge, Clements Inn, musician—James Tew, Lyons Inn, g.
Edward Mounteney, Custom House, g.—Samuel Baldwin, Clements Inn, g., a
     Companion of this Society.
Thomas Spare, Clements Inn, g.—Same Samuel Baldwin.

1776

Nathaniel Allen, Clements Inn, g.—William Windale, Blackman Street, St Mary,
     Newington.
Andrew Parry, Clements Inn, g.—John Parry, Lincolns Inn, esquire.
Mordaunt Lawson Clennell, Clements Inn, g.—John Irving, Middle Temple, g.
Thomas Fossick, Clements Inn, g.—John Fossick, Butcher Row, cheesemonger.

Edward Yale,[1] Clements Inn, surgeon—George Norris, New Inn, g.
Samuel Greathead, Clements Inn, g.—John Marshall, St Clement Church Yard,
        stationer.
Thomas Eles, Clements Inn, g.—William Scarr, Lemon Court, Broad Street.
James Robert, Clements Inn, g.—Charles Robert, Clements Inn.
Joseph Hogan, Clements Inn, g.—Benjamin Wells, Staple Inn.

Mr Edward Bowman Pr.

Charles Grant, Clements Inn, g.—Peter Grant, New London Street, esquire.
Benjamin Tickell Green, Cross Street, Hatton Garden, g.—Edward Mounteney,
        a member.
Charles Seymour, Hind Court, Fleet Street, g.—William Woodfall, Dorset Street,
        painter.
Thomas Williams, Clements Inn, g.—Charles Shepard, Carey Street, g.
William Law Hamilton, Dorset Street, St Bridget, g.—Charles Seymour, a
        member.
Thomas James, Clements Inn, g.—Thomas Price, Fetter Lane, g.
William Brailsford, Portland Street, Cavendish Square, g.—Henry Shaw,[2] Garden
        Court, Temple, g.

1777

William Waterhouse, Clements Inn, g.—Edward Yale, a Companion of this
        Society.
Francis Blowers,[3] Clements Inn, surgeon—Edward Cannon, Snow Hill, g.
John Willie, Cornhill, painter—Thomas James, a Companion.
George Dandy, Printing House Yard, Black Friars—John Dixey Cornish, Printing
        House Yard, g.
William De Sanges, Wheeler Street, Spitalfields, esquire—Thomas Jones, South-
        ampton Street, Bloomsbury, g.
Benjamin Wells, Clements Inn, g.—Joseph Hogan, a Companion.
Hutton Wood, Red Lyon Square, g.—John Pacey, a Companion.
Michael Dorset, The Strand, esquire—Richard Hollist,[4] Middle Temple,
        esquire.
George Cater, Furnivalls Inn, g.—Simon Cater, High Street, St Mary le Bone.
Michael Hayman, New Inn, g.—John Moody, New Inn, g.
Thomas Metcalf, Chancery Lane, g.—Nathaniel Batten,[5] Inner Temple, esquire.
John Williamson,[6] purser of the London East India Man—Samuel Hooper,
        Ludgate Hill.

[1] Yale's name appears in a list of surgeons examined and approved in 1777, when his
address is given as Chandois Street.
[2] ? the Henry Shaw of the Middle Temple referred to (1777) in *I.T.R.*, V, 340.
[3] A note made available by the Royal College of Surgeons of England mentions
Blowers as "late surgeon, R.N., died, Aug. 5, 1818, *aet.* 78, buried at Rumburgh,
Suffolk".
[4] Second son of John Hollist of Lodsworth, Sussex: called to the bar at the Middle
Temple in 1771, treasurer in 1812.
[5] Admitted at the Inner Temple (*aet.* 32) 1777: *I.T.R.*, V, 344, 367.
[6] Purser in *London* (723 tons) in her first two voyages, May 1771 to July 1773 and
March 1776 to October 1777.

M

1778

Alexander Watt, Clements Inn, esquire—Charles Thomas, the Strand, hatter and hosier.

William Blenkhorn, Clements Inn, g.—John Welch, Clements Inn, a Companion.

Hildebrand Morley, late of Yarmouth, Norfolk, now Clements Inn, merchant—James Hebert, Fenchurch Street, mercer.

James Fenhoulet, Dean Street, Soho, surgeon—Joshua Jones Pritchard, a Companion.

George Chapman George, Lincolns Inn, g.—James Smith, Union Court, Holborn, g.

Thomas Barry, Clements Inn, g.—John Davenport, White Fryers, coal merchant.

Anthony Fay, Rotherhithe, esquire—Edward Clement, Rotherhithe, g.

Thomas Neville, Clements Inn, esquire—Nicholas Nugent, Duke Street, Manchester Square, esquire.

Henry Johnson, Clements Inn, g.—James Medlicott Flack, St Mary le Bone, John Knight, Hammersmith, g.

Charles Hutton,[1] Woolwich, esquire—Michael Saylor, Adam Street, Cavendish Square, esquire.

John Bowman, Clements Inn, g.—Francis Gillanders, Red Lyon Street, Clerkenwell, g.

1779

Robert Paterson, Clements Inn, g.—Michael Robinson,[2] Grays Inn, g.

Oliver James Murray, Clements Inn, esquire—Thomas Hughes, Little Wyld Street, g.

William Gatty, Clements Inn, g.—Francis Waters, Clements Inn, a Companion.

Rev. Charles Coote Spread, Clements Inn, g.—William Gapper, Pump Court Temple, g.

Mr Chessall principal.

William Cooke, Clements Inn, esquire—William Hawes, Paulsgrave Place, Strand, apothecary.

Thomas Fenton, Paulsgrave Place, Strand, g.—John Addison, Paulsgrave Place, g.

Arthur Smithson Dawes, son of the Rev. Arthur Dawes[3] of Mile End, clerk—the Rev. Arthur Dawes.

John Tate, Clements Inn, g.—John Pape, Bermondsey Street, Southwark, taylor.

George Clarkson, Clements Inn, g.—John Clarkson, Market Street, St James Market, chinaman.

[1] Hutton (1737–1823), son of a Newcastle colliery worker, opened a school of mathematics at Newcastle in 1764, having the future Lord Eldon among his pupils; professor of mathematics at the Royal Military Academy, Woolwich, from 1773 till his retirement in 1807; author of works on logarithms, mathematics, bridges, &c.: F.R.S. 1774 (Copley medallist and foreign secretary); friend of Baron Maseres—see *Royal Military Academy Records* (1851), pp. 29, 46–8, 69, 82, 85, 150–1, and *D.N.B.*

[2] Admitted at Gray's Inn in 1778.

[3] Son of William Dawes of Arborfield, Berks., rector of St Michael's, Cornhill, from 1784 till his death in 1793.

Stephen Brown, Crown Office, Inner Temple, g.—Richard Jones, Middle Temple,
    law stationer.
John Moody,[1] Clements Inn, g.—Michael Hayman, a Companion.

1780

Henry Smeetham, Clements Inn, g.—Dru Drury, Strand, silversmith.
Peter Marshall, Clements Inn, g.—Thomas Fossick, Clements Inn, g.
Richard Maw, Clements Inn, esquire—William Nelson, Strand, oilman.
John Burton, Dukes Court, Bow Street, g.—John Moody, a Companion.
John Buxton, Cursitor Street, g.—Abell Jenkins, Serle Street, Lincolns Inn
    Fields, g.
John Gubbins, Clements Inn, g.—John Port, Little Essex Street, St Clement
    Danes, glazier.
William Bishop, Temple, esquire—James Barnes, St Mary Axe.
Thomas White, Carey Street, g.—William Webb, Stanhope Street, g.
Thomas Francis Pritchard,[2] Clements Inn, esquire—Michael Hodgson, Temple,
    esquire.
George Mackay, Albion Place, Surrey, g.—Robert Shaw, a Companion.
James Gordon, Berry Court, St Mary Axe, merchant—Alexander Watt, esquire,
    a Companion.
Thomas Rogers, Inner Temple, g.—John James Pudney, Charter House Street, g.
James Kilner, Ship Yard, Temple Bar—John Atkinson, St James Market, cheese-
    monger.
William Platell, Clements Inn, esquire—George Hill, esquire, Companion.
Edward Lowndes, New Inn, esquire—William Nelson, Strand, oilman.
John Roe, Hemlock Court, Carey Street, g.—John Drawwater, Yeates Court,
    St Clements.
Edward Saxelbye, Ely Place, Holborn, g.—John Russell, Fetter Lane, baker.

1781

Nathaniel Austen, Clements Inn, g.—Alexander Bassett, a Companion.
Court Dewes,[3] Inner Temple, esquire—Francis Wheler,[4] Middle Temple, esquire.
Robert Savours, Clements Inn, g.—James Leach, Carey Street, taylor.
Robert Old, Wood Street, sugar refiner—William Old, Newport, Salop, esquire.
Frank Moore, Clements Inn, esquire, captain in the 11th Regiment of Dragoons—
    Joseph Green, New Inn, esquire.
Felix Clay, Threadneedle Street, broker—William Clay, Threadneedle Street,
    broker.
Thomas Johnson, Stanhope Street, St Clement Danes, g.—Christopher Metcalf,
    Wardour Street, Soho, cabinetmaker.
John Ashe, Arundle Street, g.—Robert Shaw, Clements Inn, g., a Companion.
Charles Shephard, Carey Street, g.—Charles Luxmoore, New Inn, g.

----

[1] See footnote to 1766 admissions above (another John Moody).

[2] A man with these names was admitted at the Inner Temple 1777/8: see *I.T.R.*, V, 360.

[3] See note to 1765 admissions above (another Court Dewes).

[4] Called to the bar at the Inner Temple in 1746, admitted to the Middle Temple in
1776, a bencher there in 1779: son of the Rev. William Wheler.

James Frith, Shephards Market, Mayfair, grocer—John Atkinson, St James,
    Westminster, cheesemonger.
Tobias Stapleton, Clements Inn, g.—Thomas Fenton, Clements Inn, a Companion.
Strethill Wright, Nether Knutsford, Chesh., g.—Edward Penny, Cheapside,
    grocer.
William Wilkins Terry, Clements Inn, g.—Thomas Wheatley, York Street,
    Covent Garden, mercer.

1782

John Welch, Clements Inn, g.—William Palmer, Clements Inn, a Companion.
John Eastabrooke,[1] the Hallswell, East India Man, g.—Thomas Hawkes, White
    Fryars, coal merchant.
Joseph Garnault, Bishopsgate Street, g.—Thomas Hawkes as above.
Richard Hodges, Custom House, g.—William Adams, Ludlow, mercer.
John Reed, Howard Street, St Clement Danes, coal merchant—Thomas Hawkes,
    White Fryars, coal merchant.
Anthony Chapman, Kensington Square, esquire—Joseph Graham, St Paul's
    Church Yard, upholsterer.
John Priestman, St Paul, Covent Garden, pawnbroker—William Brailsford, a
    Companion, as security for Mr Welch.

Mr Devon Prin[t]

Francis Todd, Clements Inn, g.—Nicholas Luff, Clare Market, butcher.
Hugh White, Clements Inn, g.—Mr John Allen, a Companion.
Walter Williams, Apothecaries Hall, g.—William Frodsham, Kingsgate Street,
    Holborn, watchmaker.
James Aickin,[2] Drury Lane Theatre, esquire—John Moody, a Companion.
James Perry[3], George Street, York Buildings, g.—John Fielding,[4] Paternoster
    Row, bookseller.
Meredith Vale, Brook Street, Holborn, g.—William Barfoot King, Salt Office.
Joseph Sparshott Loney, Bridge Yard, Tooley Street—Thomas Loney, Great
    Wild Street, Lincolns Inn Fields, g.

1783

Richard Jones, Middle Temple, g.—Henry Jones, Houndsditch, salesman.
Edward Barlow, Clements Inn, esquire—John Moody, Clements Inn.
Robert Maw, Clements Inn, esquire—Abdy Maw, St Martins in the Fields,
    esquire, Thomas Bullock, Knights, Herts., esquire.

---

[1] Third officer in *Earl of Lincoln* Dec. 1771 to July 1773: second officer in *Grenville*
April 1775 to April 1777: first officer in *Halsewell* (not Hallswell) March 1779 to Oct.
1781: captain in *London*, March 1783 to April 1785, Feb. 1786 to Nov. 1787, and April
1789 to Nov. 1790.

[2] An actor (died 1803), brother of Francis Aickin, also an actor (died 1805)—see
D.N.B. and p. lviii above.

[3] ? the journalist (1736–1821), originally a provincial actor, who edited the *Morning
Chronicle*—see *D.N.B.*

[4] Publisher of an edition of Johnson's *Dictionary*: see Boswell, *Life of Johnson*
(1734 edn.), IV, 421 n., 459.

John Presser, Cowley Street, Westminster, esquire—George Nelthorpe, King Street, Covent Garden, silk mercer.

John Gray Blair, Round Court, Strand, g.—William Richardson, Clare Street, Clare Market, cabinetmaker.

Henry Jackson, Lyons Inn, g.—James Down, Portland Street, g.

Benjamin Bourn, Cliffords Inn, g.—William Astill, Butcher Row, St Clement Danes, scalemaker.

James Hayward Shene, Grays Inn, g.—William Cardale, Grays Inn, g.

Francis Amyot, Cliffords Inn, g.—Charles Augier, Kensington.

Francis Grose,[1] Clements Inn, g.—George Ward, Inner Temple,[2] g.

Richard Reynolds, Clements Inn, esquire—John Reynolds, Great James Street, Bedford Row, esquire.

John Knight, Middle Temple, g.—John Dax, Cook's Court, Carey Street, g.

Abraham King, Middle Temple, g.—Christopher Metcalf, Wardour Street, Soho, cabinetmaker.

Richard Whalley Bridgeman,[3] Bartholomew Close, g.—Bolton Midson, Threadneedle Street, grocer.

Thomas Bish, Ludgate Hill, Lottery Office keeper—James Perry, a Companion.

Elbro Woodcock,[4] Lincolns Inn, esquire—Thomas Woodcock, Lincolns Inn.

1784

James Redit, Clements Inn, g.—George Hicks, Bishopgate Street, cheesemonger.

Huxley Sandon, Clements Inn, g.—Liscombe Price, New Inn, g.

George Buck, Clements Inn, g.—John Bowman, Clements Inn, a Companion.

Thomas Vinicomb, Adelphi, coal merchant—William Stronge, a Companion.

William Ely Cook, Clements Inn, g.—John Bowman, Clements Inn, a Companion.

Rev. Thomas Wigzell, Greenwich, Kent—George Wigzell, Greenwich, g.

Rev. William Williams, Vicar of Haslen, diocese of Worcester—Rev. John Hunt, Little Charles Street, St James's Square.

Hewett Cobb, Clements Inn, g.—Edward Bullock, Chidley Court, Pall Mall, esquire.

1785

Thomas Barrow,[5] Inner Temple, g.—Charles Nowell, Lincoln's Inn, g.

Richard Cheslyn, Chiswick, g.—Richard Cheslyn Creswell, Doctors Commons, g.

John Platt junior, Carey Street, g.—Jonathan Hayter, King Street, merchant.

Charles Heathcote, Lyons Inn, g.—Charles Sheppard, a Companion.

John Foulkes, Hide Street, St George, Bloomsbury, g.—John Barber, Hide Street, Bloomsbury, g.

[1] See note on another 'Francis Grose', p. 286 above.

[2] Admitted to the Inner Temple 1779/80—*I.T.R.*, V, 387.

[3] Attorney and writer on law (1761 ?–1820), clerk to the Grocers' Company—*D.N.B.*

[4] ? either Elbro or Thomas Woodcock was the "Mr Woodcock" whom Lincoln's Inn retained to act in the Inn's dispute with St Bartholomew's Hospital in 1751—*Black Books of L.I.*, III, 348. "Elborough Woodcock of Lincoln's Inn", when surety for an admittee at Staple Inn, is described as "one of the sworn clerks of the High Court of Chancery": see E. Williams, *Staple Inn* (1906), p. 172.

[5] Admitted to the Inner Temple 1781/2, called to the bar 1793, proposed for Reader to Clement's Inn 1796—*I.T.R.*, V, 427, 568, 602.

John West, Lincoln's Inn, g.—Charles Edward Beresford, Stamp Office, Lincolns Inn.
John Smith, Clements Inn, g.—Charles Pollock, Holywell Street, baker.

Mr Strong princ.
Mr Smith Steward from this time.

John Burrell, Clements Inn, g.—Stephen Brown, Clements Inn, g.
John Burton, Union Row, St Mary, Newington, g.—Robert Nugent, St Dunstan in the West, vintner.
Ashton Bertles, Middle Temple, g.—William Holdsworth, Clare Street, St Clement Danes, g.
Thomas Hutchinson, Clements Inn, g.—John Foulkes, Clements Inn, g.
John Hanson, Clements Inn, g.—Edward King, Serle Street, Lincolns Inn Fields, esquire.

1786

Alexander Hislop, Clements Inn, g.—John Sander, King Street, St Anne, Soho, cabinetmaker.
Thomas Danforth, Clements Inn, esquire—John Chalmers, New Inn, esquire.
Thomas Carter junior, Clements Inn, g.—Thomas Carter senior, Piccadilly, stationer.
William Streight, Clements Inn, g.—Joseph Allen junior, Furnival's Inn, g.
William Radcliffe, Middle Temple, esquire—William Gurdon, Stoney Stratford, Bucks.
Dennis McCarthy, Staples Inn, g.—James Perry, Clements Inn, g.
Romaine William Clarkson, Clements Inn, g.—George Clarkson, Clements Inn, g.
Thomas Handley, Clements Inn, g.—Henry Jackson, Clements Inn, g.

Mr Selbye Steward follow this vid. Sept.

Peter Still, Clements Inn, g.—William Strong, esquire, the then principal of said Society.
Henry Taylor, Clements Inn, g.—William Watts, Staple's Inn, g.
Thomas Hutton, Clements Inn, g.—Alexander Hislop, Clements Inn, g.
John Romaine, Clements Inn, g.—Thomas Touley, Size Lane, taylor.
Henry Chalcraft, Palsgrave Head Place, St Clement Danes, g.—William Holdsworth, Hollis Street, Clare Market, g.
Burtebant should come in here.

1787

William Joseph Dufour, Clements Inn, g.—Joshua Jones Prichard, Doctors Commons, g.
Robert Maundrell,[1] Inner Temple, esquire—Nathaniel Barton, Inner Temple, esquire.
Thomas Bradley, Clements Inn, g.—Thomas Vinicomb, Clements Inn, coal merchant.
William Jellico, Clements Inn, g.—Thomas Kennedy, Inner Temple, g.

---

[1] Admitted to the Inner Temple 1785, called to the bar 1791, proposed for Reader to Clifford's Inn 1794—*I.T.R.*, V, 484, 544, 578.

Thomas James, Clements Inn, g.—John Davidson, King Street, Covent Garden, tea dealer.

William Dawson, Clements Inn, g.—William Straight, Clements Inn, g.

Thomas Heslop, Grosvenor Place, St George, Hanover Square, g.—Thomas Taylor Railton, Cliffords Inn, g.

James Atkinson, Clements Inn, g.—John Johnson, Lincolns Inn, esquire.

Joseph Swaffield junior, Clements Inn, g.—Joseph Swaffield, Clements Inn, g.

Josiah Jowett, St Bartholomew the Less, merchant—William Owen, St George, Hanover Square, esquire.

John Davies, Clements Inn, g.—Thomas Lloyd, St Clement, g.

Henry Maundrell, Clements Inn, g.—Robert Maundrell, Inner Temple, esquire.

Henry Foley Price, Clements Inn, g.—Joseph Hodges, a Companion.

George Pyefinch, Clements Inn, g.—William Green, St Clement, Eastcheap, ironmonger.

William Pare, Clements Inn, g.—Robert Jaques, East Street, Red Lyon Square.

Edward Bullock, Clements Inn, g.—Hewett Cobb, Clements Inn, g.

Stephen Shorter, Clements Inn, g.—William Gyblott, Vere Street, Clare Market, goldbeater.

James Brooke, Hammersmith, esquire—Charles Wiseman, Bow Street, oilman.

James Yorke, Clements Inn, esquire—John Vernon, Lincolns Inn, g.

Richard Selby, Clements Inn, g.—Henry Jordan, Gloucester Street, Red Lyon Square, taylor.

31 May 1786 omitted and should have followed Mr Handleys.

Henry Dagge junior, Clements Inn, g.—Robert Watson, Milbank Street, Westminster, g.

James Fell, Clements Inn, g.—Anthony Hemming, New Basinghall Street, g.

Douglas Crunden, Clements Inn, merchant—John Martin, Lincolns Inn, esquire.

5 Apr. 1788 he should not come in this Term but to prevent the Loss of the Stamp [1] as James Lacey was inserted here who is only deemed a Holder of his Premises (tho' under Lease) and not a Member.

John Inskip,[2] London East Indiaman, of Clements Inn, g.—John Stride, St Clement Danes, g.

William Henry Duffield, Clements Inn, g.—John Gwinnell, Carter Lane, Doctors Commons, watchmaker.

Thomas Harvey, New Inn, g.—George Hall, Hammersmith, coal merchant.

1788

Thomas Bunn, Clements Inn, g.—Thomas Sheppard, Basinghall Street, factor.

Gabriel Buntebant,[3] Princes Street, St George, Hanover Square, pianoforte maker —Christopher Sieven, Princes Street, pianoforte maker.

This omitted 9 Dec. 1786.

[1] All parchments, &c., chargeable with stamp duty (see p. lix above) had to be stamped and marked before the document was written or engrossed (5 Will. & Mar. c. 21, s. 9).

[2] Second officer in the new *London* (758 tons, replacing her namesake—see note to p. 289 above—sunk in collision December 1778) Feb. 1786 to Nov. 1787.

[3] The name, thus printed in the St George's marriage register for 1771, appears as Buntebart for some ten years in the rate-books under Princes Street. A list of London pianoforte makers 1760–1851 in *The Pianoforte*, by R. E. M. Harding (1933), gives "Buntlebart, Gabriel, 1764–1795, 7 Princes Street".

William Masters, New End, Hampstead, g.—Thomas Pool, Hampstead, farmer.
Thomas Athorpe, Clements Inn, esquire—William Dawson, Clements Inn, g.
Aistroppe Stevin, Clements Inn, g.—William Dawson, Clements Inn, g.
William Wynn, Clements Inn, g.—John Foulkes, Clements Inn, g.
   Now Crunden comes in inserted 2 leaves back.

John Allen principal.

Robert Venables Hinde, Clements Inn, g.—Tobias Stapleton, attorney.
John Wolcot,[1] Great Newport Street, M.D.—James Perry, Clements Inn, g.
William Slann, Woodford, Essex, g.—Stephen Brown, Clements Inn, g.
Richard Allen, Clements Inn, g.—Henry Hall, Hackney, g.
William Harvey, Cook's Court, Carey Street, g.—William Dawson, Clements
   Inn, g.
John Brown, Clements Inn, g.—Richard Shortney, St Mary Axe.

1789

William Tinswood, Rathbone Place, g.—David Hewit, Millbank Street, West-
   minster, coal merchant.
Robert Bradshaw, Clements Inn, g.—Thomas Green, Grays Inn, g.
Rogers Heys, Preston, Lancs., g.—[No surety named.]
Charles Hart, Tax Office, Somerset Place, g.—Edward Dampier, Hampstead, g.
George Lister, Leeds (late of), merchant—Joseph Jowett, Keppel Court, Bartholo-
   mew Lane, merchant.
William Simpkins, Strand, g.—Thomas James, Clements Inn, g.
Joseph Hill, Southampton Court, St George, Bloomsbury, merchant—Daniel Hill,
   Southampton Court, surgeon.
John Foljambe junior, Rotherham, g.—William Dawson, Clements Inn, g.
Lewis Guery, Southampton Street, Westminster, clerk—Herbert Brace, Middle
   Temple, g.
Thomas Williams, Cursitor Street, Chancery Lane, g.—Daniel Charles Fabien,
   Half Moon Street, Piccadilly, g.
John Stanford Girdler, St Pancras, esquire—Thomas Williams, Drake Street, Red
   Lion Square, g.
Luke Hollester, East Street, Red Lion Square, g.—Mark Hollester, East Street, g.
John Webber,[2] Marsh Gate, Richmond, Surrey, captain in His Majesty's Marine
   Forces—Joseph Hill, Clements Inn, g.
John Lowe, Middle Temple, g.—Richard Stringer, Strand, druggist.
Joseph Wood Hussey, Middle Temple, g.—Thomas Phillips, Great Queen Street,
   Lincolns Inn Fields, g.
Robert Fleetwood, Somerset Place, g.—Richard Cook, Cook's Court, St Clement
   Danes, g.

[1] Wolcot (1738–1819), M.D. (Aberdeen) 1767, ordained deacon and priest 1769,
practised medicine in south-west England from 1773, moved to London 1776, and then
devoted himself to literature, publishing satires as "Peter Pindar": see *D.N.B.*
   [2] A subaltern (1759–62) during the Seven Years War in the frigates *Southampton*,
Surprise and *Blonde*, Webber served in North America (captain of marines in H.M.S.
Bristol 1777) in the West Indies and with the Channel Fleet, taking part in the second
relief of Gibraltar in 1781; afterwards on recruiting duty until the peace in 1783 when he
retired on half-pay; died 1794.

Thomas Palmer, Red Lyon Court, Fleet Street, g.—George Woolley, Red Lyon
     Court, taylor.
William Newby, Clements Inn, g.—James Burke, East Lane, Bermondsea.
David Evans Macdonnel, Brick Court, Middle Temple, g.—William Cook,
     Clements Inn, g.
George Atwick, Chapel Street, Mayfair, g.—James Hooper, New Bond Street,
     mercer.

1790

John Bursey, Auditors Office, Somerset Place, g.—Edgworth Moore, Auditors
     Office.
Edgworth Moore, Auditors Office—John Bursey, Auditors Office.
Thomas Kilner, Clements Inn, g.—John Jopson, Lincolns Inn, g.
Robert Parrey, Dulwich, esquire—Edward George, Bond Court, Walbrook, g.

1790 [1]

John Laurie, Crane Court, Fleet Street, surgeon—John Laver, Cliffords Inn, g.
Richard King, Grays Inn, g.—Thomas Norris, Essex Street, Strand, g.
John Butcher, Chancery Lane, g.—Benjamin Oakley, Stockwell Place, Surrey.
James Taylor, Castle Street, Holborn, g.—John Rooke,[2] Grays Inn, esquire.
Leonard Vassall,[3] Lincolns Inn, esquire—James Richard Baker, Boswell Court,
     St Clement Danes, esquire.
John Perrie Coffin,[4] Inner Temple, esquire—James Richard Baker as above.
Francis Hathway, Little St Thomas the Apostle, London, merchant—Thomas
     Bassi, Clements Inn.
John Browne, Barnards Inn, esquire—John Allen,[5] Grays Inn, esquire.
Wyndham Benjamin Radcliffe, Clements Inn, g.—John Dorrington, Milbank
     Row, Westminster, g.
William Blackstone, Red Lyon Street, Red Lyon Square, g.—Richard King, a
     Companion.
John Burrell, Clements Inn, g.—Stephen Brown, a Companion.

1791

Stretch Cowley Bromley, Hereford Street, Fitz Roy Chappell, Midd., g.—Robert
     Antony Bromley,[6] clerk.
Charles Dale, Basinghall Street, g.—David Sewell, Newgate Street, draper.
Francis Grant, Earlscourt, Cranbourn Street, g.—Robert Grant, bookseller.
Owen Phillips, Lincoln's Inn, esquire—William Veel, esquire.

[1] The second Admission Book (see pp. xi, liv) begins here.
[2] Of Standen, Herts., admitted at Gray's Inn in 1782.
[3] Called to the bar at Lincoln's Inn 1793—*Black Books of L.I.*, III, 241.
[4] Jonathan Perrie Coffin, admitted at the Inner Temple 1786/7 and called to the bar
1794, was proposed for Reader to Lyon's Inn 1798: see *I.T.R.*, V, 496, 584, 650.
[5] Second son of John Allen of Wheatley, Oxon.: admitted at Gray's Inn in 1784.
[6] Rector of St Mildred Poultry from 1775 till his death in 1806; also, towards the end
of his life, incumbent of St Bartholomew by the Exchange.

William Brooks, New Inn, g.—John Brookes, salesman.
James Carden,[1] Paper Buildings, Temple, g.—Matthew Wake, linen draper.
John Adolphus,[2] Rolls Buildings, Fetter Lane, g.—Thomas Wrightson, g.
Charles Morris, Clements Inn, g.—William Ridding, g.
William Ridding, Clements Inn, g.—Charles Morris, g.
Charles Mc Cormick,[3] St Mary Hall, Oxford, civilian—John Dent, 14 Webber
     Row, Black Friars, g.
Thomas Yeates the younger, Old Brompton, g.—Thomas Yeates the elder, 30
     Strand, g.
John Rose, Clements Inn, g.—Richard Stringer, the Strand, chymist and druggist.
John Ridgway, Clements Inn, g.—Richard Allen, Clements Inn.

Joseph Hodges esquire, principal.

James Nowland, The Auditors Office, Somerset Place, g.—Thomas Edlyne Tom-
     lins, Chester Place, Lambeth, esquire.
Thomas Edlyne Tomlins,[4] Chester Place, Lambeth—James Nowland as above.
William Gale, Houghton Street, St Clement Danes, g.—John Buxton, Broad
     Street, St James, g.
Philip Wynell Wynell Mayow, New Inn, g.—Mayow Wynell Mayow, Ely Place,
     Holborn, g.
Joseph Neeld, Norfolk Street, Strand, g.—John Bond, Hindon, Midd., esquire.
Thomas Kavanagh, Lincoln's Inn, esquire—J. H. Clarke, Inner Temple.
Hesketh Davis, Cornhill, g.—William Blew, Hylord Court, Crutched Friars, wine
     merchant.
Robert Macara,[5] The Ceres, East India Man, g.—James Cuthbert, Fleet Street,
     upholder.
Phineas Andrews, Prospect Place, Lambeth, g.—John Boxwell, Great Hermitage
     Street, Wapping, g.
William Shipton, Grays Inn, g.—Richard Bland, Raquet Court, Fleet Street, g.
Milliken Craig, Clements Inn, g.—Robert Macara, a Companion.

1792

Henry Parker, Clements Inn, g.—Charles Hart, the Tax Office, Somerset Place, g.
Henry Gregory, Clements Inn, g.—Hewett Cobb, a Companion.
John Brown, St Mary Street, Tottenham Court Road, g.—James Sivewright, 266
     Strand, hardwareman.
Richard Ireland, Furnivals Inn, g.—William Faviman, Furnivals Inn.

[1] Admitted at the Inner Temple 1786/7: see *I.T.R.*, V, 494, 496.
[2] Adolphus (1768–1845), historical writer, was admitted an attorney in 1790 and
called to the bar in 1807; he defended the Cato Street conspirators—see *D.N.B.*
[3] McCormick (1755?–1807), member of the Middle Temple, abandoned law for
literature: author of *History of England from the Death of George II to the Peace of 1763,
Memoirs of Edmund Burke*, &c.—see *D.N.B.*
[4] This can hardly be the Thomas Edlyne Tomlins (1762–1841), barrister of the Inner
Temple, called in 1782 and knighted in 1814, whose attendance to read at Clement's Inn
(1787), in place of Thomas Mott, was allowed to count despite the absence of the Principal
and Ancients—see *D.N.B.*, and *I.T.R.*, V, 431, 493, 501.
[5] Surgeon in *Ceres* (1180 tons) 1790–1, in *Valentine* (790 tons) 1792–3 and *King George*
(776 tons) 1794–5; purser in *Earl Talbot* (1200 tons) 1797–8 and *Lady Burges* (820 tons)
1800–1.

Samuel Denton, Beaufort Buildings, g.—George Gray, Stanhope Street, taylor.
Isaac Clementson, Beaufort Buildings, g.—George Gray above mentioned.
Thomas Dundas,[1] the Henry Dundas, East India ship—Richard Selby, a Companion.
Thomas Wyatt, Ford House, Wilts.—Peter Figes,[2] Southampton Row, Bloomsbury, g.
John Humphry Babb, Queen Square Place, Westminster—Thomas Lane, Canterbury, g.
John Guy, Middle Temple, g.—Thomas Symonds,[3] Inner Temple, g.
John Branston [entry not completed].
James Everingham, Clements Inn, g.—Samuel Hill, Deputy Controller of the Salt Office, esquire.
William Rawlins Edwards Bradley, New Castle Street, Strand, g.—[No surety named.]
James Reeves, 21 Lothbury, g.—Thomas Purcell, 9 Great New Street, Fetter Lane, glassman.
James Montagu Higginson, Southampton, esquire—William Turnbull,[4] Fenchurch Street, surgeon.
Owen Holmes, New Bridge Street—William Robins, Fleet Street, silversmith.
William Morrett, Goldsmith Street, St Brides, g.—Henry Fry, Mile End, Old Town, St Dunstan, Stepney, perfumer.

1793

James Houghton, Clements Inn, g.—Thomas Ward Blagrove, a Companion.
John Edwards, Clements Inn, g.—William Harvey, a Companion.
John Benbow,[5] Grays Inn, g.—William Ridding, a Companion.
John Ingelew, Stanwell, Middlesex, surveyor—James Graham, Lincolns Inn, esquire.
John Poulding Wright, Holborn Hill, g.—John Dalton, Oxford Street, surgeon.
Hesketh Davis, Cornhill, g.—Charles Chapman of the same place, shoemaker.
Thomas Brace, Middle Temple, esquire—John Peterson, Great Ormond Street, esquire.
Joseph Blunt, New Bridge Street, g.—Robert Blunt, Charing Cross, linendraper.
Isaac D'Israeli,[6] Broad Street Buildings, merchant—Benjamin D'Israeli of the same place, merchant.
George Newton, Yeatley, Hants., esquire—John Thorpe, Cold Bath Fields, plumber and glazier.
Robert Peterson, Belvedere Place, Surrey, g.—Henry Shiers, Rodney Row, Surrey.

[1] Second officer in *Warren Hastings* (763 tons) April 1787 to Sept. 1788: first officer in *Henry Dundas* (802 tons) March 1790 to Sept. 1791.

[2] A "Peter Figes esquire, attorney" appears in the London Directory 1805–7 as at 37 Norfolk Street, Strand.

[3] Admitted at the Inner Temple 1788/9, called to the bar 1795, proposed for reader to Clement's Inn 1798—*I.T.R.*, V, 522, 587, 630.

[4] Turnbull (1729?–1796), physician and writer on medicine, came to London in 1777 and was appointed to the Eastern Dispensary—*D.N.B.*

[5] Admitted at Gray's Inn in June 1792, the youngest son of John Benbow of Ribbesford, Worcs.

[6] Author (1766–1848), son of Benjamin D'Israeli, his surety: father of Lord Beaconsfield—*D.N.B.*

Robert Muddock, Cooks Court, Carey Street, g.—Richard Bernard Fisher, Middle
      Temple, esquire.
James Dewar,[1] Arundle Street, purser of the Warren Hastings, East Indiaman—
      James Watson of the same place, jeweller.

1794

Benjamin Bishop, Clements Inn, g.—John Bishop, Skinners Street, Bishopsgate
      Street, g.
Alexander Hale Strong,[2] Lincolns Inn, g.—William Strong of the same place,
      esquire.
John Humphries, Southampton Buildings, Midd., esquire—Hugh Leycester,
      Lincolns Inn, esquire.
Reverend John Brand,[3] M.A., rector of St Mary at Hill, London—John Topham,
      Grays Inn, esquire.
William Hughes, Carey Street, Lincolns Inn, g.—Edward Jones, Inner Temple
      Lane, g.
John Shearman, Bear Street, Leicester Square—John Moles, Chancery Lane,
      feather manufacturer.
William Davies, Bedford Court, Covent Garden, g.—George Carter, Bedford
      Street in the same parish, vintner.
Joseph Jones, the India House, London, g.—David Charles Collinge, Lincolns
      Inn, stationer.
John Hawes, Piccadilly, g.—Robert Howse, New Bond Street, tin plate worker.
John Littleney, Northumberland Street, Strand, g.—Atkinson Bush, Great
      Ormond Street, esquire.
James Poole,[4] Inner Temple, g.—George Poole, Palsgrave Place, g.

Matthew Chessall esquire principal.

Francis Bryer, Lyons Inn, g.—Henry Fuller of the same place, g.
Simon Hart Myers, Mark Lane, g.—Joseph Hart Myers,[5] John Street, America
      Square, M.D.
Charles Wyatt, Birmingham, merchant—Thomas Wyatt, New Inn, g.
John Day Blake, Cooks Court, Carey Street—Robert Blake of the same place, g.
John Larkham, The Excise Office, London—James Beeby of the same place, g.
William Marshall, Pickering, Yorks., g.—George Nicholl, Pall Mall, bookseller.
Jonathan Holmes, Lincolns Inn, g.—William Graham of the same place, g.
Charles Donald,[6] purser of the Fort William East India Man—Robert Donald,
      Ely Place, esquire.

[1] Purser for three voyages in *Warren Hastings* (763 tons), April 1787 to Sept. 1788,
May to October 1790 and July 1793 to Aug. 1794, and in *Earl St Vincent* (818 tons) March
1800 to June 1801.

[2] ? the member whose unsuccessful speculation is noted at p. lx above.

[3] Brand (1744–1806), rector of St Mary at Hill and St Mary Hubbard 1784, was
resident secretary to the Society of Antiquaries 1784–1806: see *D.N.B.*

[4] Admitted to the Inner Temple 1757/8, called to the bar 1764, proposed for Reader
to Lyon's Inn 1770, a bencher 1797—*I.T.R.*, V, 99, 172, 245, 612.

[5] M.D. 1770, physician to the Portuguese Hospital and the General Dispensary: died
in 1823.

[6] Purser in *Fort William* (798 tons) May 1793 to Sept. 1794.

James Colnett, Fleet Street, esquire—Henry Creed, Norfolk Street, esquire.
John Newhall Hepburn, Henrietta Street—Edward Powell, Red Lion Street,
    St George the Martyr.

1795

George Gordon, St Margaret Street, Westminster, g.—Humphrey Donaldson,
    Whitehall, esquire.
Philip Bradford, Bartlett Buildings, Holborn, g.—William Mullachy, Tavistock
    Street, hardwareman.
William Hewerdine, Crown Street, Westminster, esquire—George Gordon, g.,
    Companion.
William Hammond, Woodhouse, Salop, g.—Philip Bradford, g., Companion.
Jane Frith,[1] Sloane Street, Chelsea—Richard Atkinson, Jermyn Street, esquire.
William West, Leigh Street, Red Lyon Square, g.—William Machon, Elliotts
    Row, Newington, g.
George Arbuthnot, Navy Pay Office, Somerset Place, esquire—George Ross,
    Duke Street, Adelphi, esquire.
Henry Edward Hayman, Clements Inn, g.—Michael Hayman, g., Companion.
William Martin, St Pauls, Covent Garden, g.—George Gordon, g., Companion.
James Baker, Grays Inn, esquire—Joseph Miller, Bernards Inn, Holborn, esquire.
William Leacock, 17 Walbrook, Madeira merchant—John Steele Blackborow,
    Spa Fields, Clerkenwell, g.
Charles Hillyard, Symonds Inn, g.—Henry Parker, esquire, Companion.
Henry Humphries, Fleet Street, chymist and druggist—John Humphries, esquire,
    Companion.
Reverend Henry Garrioch Vernon,[2] rector of the parish church of St Clement
    Danes—George Lawrance, clerk of the said parish.
Thomas Beckett, Clements Inn, g.—James Donaldson, Bloomsbury Square,
    architect.

1796

William Collins, Middle Temple, g.—William Webb, Strand, upholsterer.
John Davies the younger, Clements Inn, g.—Robert Gatty, Cutlers Hall, Lon-
    don, g.
John Cliffe, Dukes Street, Lincolns Inn Fields, g.—Anthony Steventon, Castle
    Street, Holborn, esquire.
Thomas Delafare, Furnivals Inn, g.—John Hartley, Grays Inn, g.
Thomas Dobson, Furnivals Inn Court, g.—Charles Smith of the same place,
    citizen and pewterer.
Robert Lee, Clements Inn, g.—Thomas Fossick of the same place, g.
Joseph Sheppard Munden,[3] Kentish Town, g.—Hewett Cobb, Clements Inn, g.
Edward Griffith, Carnarvon, esquire—Thomas Ward, Lincolns Inn, esquire.

[1] See p. lviii above.
[2] Rector of St Clement Danes from 1795 to 1807 and thereafter of Great Bromley,
Essex, till his death in 1837: son of Bowater Vernon of Jamaica.
[3] Munden (1758–1832), a leading comedian in north-country theatres, came to
London 1790, acting at Covent Garden and (1813–24) Drury Lane: see *D.N.B.*

James Hall, Boswell Court, St Clement Danes, g.—William Ross of the same place, esquire.
Nathaniel Mason,[1] Stock Exchange, London, esquire—Harry Stoe, South Sea House, esquire.
Charles Holland, Chiswick, esquire—Thomas Holland of the same place, esquire.
John Hill, Pall Mall, g.—Luke Naylor of the same place, esquire.
Edward Gordon the younger,[2] Bank of England, esquire—Wentworth Malim, Cary Street, esquire.
Daniel Wilson Davison, Mansion House Street, g.—Henry Jones of the same place, esquire.
William Hodgson, Grocers Hall Court, g.—James Batty of the same place, g.

1797

Thomas Webb Ward, Clements Inn, g.—Joseph Ward, 324 Holborn, vendor of medicine.
John Manning, Castle Street, Midd., g.—Richard Chambers, Millman Street, Bedford Row, g.
John Allen the younger, Clements Inn, g.—John Allen the elder of the same place, g.
William Welch, Camberwell, g.—John Webb, a Companion.
John Gregson, 41 Paternoster Row, g.—Nathaniel Acheson, Ely Place, g.
Samuel Bachelor, 3 Tanfield Court, Temple, g.—George Rule of the same place, g.

1798

Charles Harrison, Great Surrey Street, Christchurch, Surrey, g.—William Henry Church, Chancery Lane, surgeon.
Charles Beckett, Great Queens Street, Lincolns Inn Fields, g.—William Beckett of the same place, sadlers ironmonger.

1799

Marmaduke Willis, Clements Inn, g.—James Willis, St James's Street, g.
Thomas Hurnall Shaw, Clements Inn, g.—Robert Shaw, Companion.

1800

Thomas Pitcher, Furnivals Inn, g.—William Allen, Inner Temple, g.
John Scriven, Clements Inn, g.—Charles Hillyard, Companion.

1801

Charles Hamilton, Clements Inn, g.—James Giffard, Shepherd Street, Oxford Street, g.

1802

John Wright, Chancery Lane, g.—Charles Hillyard, Companion.

[1] The Stock Exchange records, which begin in 1802, do not mention Mason, but they show Stoe, his surety, as having been a member from 1802 to 1816.
[2] Gordon entered the service of the Bank, on a salary of £50 a year, in 1784 (on the recommendation of Samuel Bosanquet, a director), quitting it in 1805.

1803

William Thompson, Essex Street, Strand, g.—Edward Nott esquire.

Thomas Rudall, Clements Inn, g.—Thomas Hutchinson, New Boswell Court, esquire.

Henry Llewellin the younger, Clements Inn—Henry Llewellin senior, Noble Street, Cheapside, water gilder.

Richard Teasdale, Chancery Lane, g.—Charles Hillyard, Companion.

William Broughton Flexney,[1] Chancery Lane, g.—Richard Teasdale, Companion.

John Carruthers the younger, Cheapside, g.—John Carruthers the elder, Cheapside, merchant.

Philip Thistlethwayte Strong, Great Ormond Street, g.—A. H. Strong esquire, an Ancient.

1804

James Dove, Blandford Street, Portman Square, g.—Robert Dove of the same place, g.

1808

Jonas Gregory,[2] Clements Inn, g.—Thomas Parker, Wood Street, Cheapside, g.

Thomas Moore Maydwell, Clements Inn, g.—Revd. William Morgan, Quebec Street, Midd., clerk.

Thomas Crosse, Clements Inn, g.—James Alexander, New Inn, esquire.

1809

Harry William Brewer, Clapham, g.—William Holship, North Cray, Kent, g.

William Francis Patterson, Newark, Notts., g.—James Hartley Patterson, Owens Row, Islington, lace manufacturer.

George Platel, Peterborough, g.—Alexander Forbes Gaskell, Holborn Court, Grays Inn, g.

Henry Hughes, late of Millman Street, Bedford Row but now of Clements Inn, g.— Christopher Lee, Lincolns Inn, g.

Matthew Richard Chessall, Norfolk Street, Strand, g.—William Fisher, Friday Street, Cheapside, g.

1810

Joseph Fowler, Basing Lane, Bread Street, g.—Lewis Wolfe, Manchester Buildings, Westminster, esquire.

Charles Devon, Red Lion Square, esquire—William Devon, esquire, one of the Antients of the Society.

---

[1] Flexney, entered in the King's Bench Roll Book of Attorneys in 1793, died in 1837 *aet*. 65. An obituary notice in the *Legal Observer* stated that he was formerly principal of Clement's Inn and that he had been appointed in 1798 secretary to the old Law Society (established in 1737), holding that office for 35 years. A son, Spencer Flexney, was called to the bar at Lincoln's Inn in 1828. See also the 1827 entries below.

[2] Shown in successive Law Lists as steward of Clement's Inn: see note to p. 308 below.

Thomas Adlington, Bedford Row, esquire—John Dax, Carey Street, esquire.
Joseph Neeld the younger, Norfolk Street, Strand, esquire—Robert Kerwan, Pall
　　　Mall, esquire.

1811

Henry North, Clements Inn, g.—William Tooke, Grays Inn Square, g.

1812

William Holship, Clements Inn, g.—[No surety named.]
Thomas Tayler, Clements Inn, g.—Samuel Hill, Braynes Row, Spa Fields, esquire.

1814

Robert Blake, Clements Inn, g.—Robert Blake senior, Cookes Court, g.
Richard Wise,[1] Crambourn near Truro, surgeon—Edwin Stevens, Camborne in
　　　the same county, g.
James Reilly, Clements Inn, g.—John Martin, Sloane Street, g.
Thomas Selby, Clements Inn, g.—[No surety named.]

1815

Alfred Umney, Clements Inn, g.—Stephen Howell Phillips, Norfolk Street.

1816

William Spence, Mark Lane, g.—John Spence of the same place, g.

1817

George Redaway, Strand, g.—Thomas Matthews Redaway of the same place,
　　　boot and shoe maker.

1818

James William Silk, New Road, near Euston Square, g.—Samuel Lock,[2] Farn-
　　　ham, Surrey, D.D.
William Harris Parker, New Boswell Court, Carey Street, g.—James Powell,
　　　Murchment Street, doctor of physic.

1819

William Thompson, Clements Inn, g.—Samuel Parsons, Red Lion Square,
　　　auctioneer and appraiser.
Thomas Rudhall, Clements Inn, g.—[No surety named.[3]]

　　[1] For Wise of Camborne (not Crambourn) see G. C. Boase and W. P. Courtney,
Bibliotheca Cornubiensis (1878), II, 898. His medical thesis (Edinburgh, 1825) is in the
Library of the Royal College of Surgeons of England.
　　[2] ? Samuel Locke (son of Thomas Locke of Taunton), Wadham College, D.D., 1808,
from 1816 rector of Hilgay, Norfolk; chaplain to the Duke of Kent; died 1849.
　　[3] Perhaps a re-admission: see the 1803 entry, p. 303 above.

1820

George Brace, Surrey Street, Strand, g.—Thomas Brace esquire, an Ancient.

William Nettlefold, Norfolk Street, Strand, g.—Isaac Clementson, Adelphi Terrace, Strand, esquire.

George Helder, Clements Inn, g.—[No surety named.]

Charles Comerford, Copthall Court, g.—Thomas Bartrum, St Mildred's Court, Poultry, g.

James Duncombe, Fleet Street, g.—Brandreth Duncombe of the same place, druggist.

1821

John Taylor, Walbrook, g.—George Taylor, Litchfield Street, Soho, timber merchant.

Henry Marchant, Clements Inn, g.—Henry Marchant the elder, Turnham Green, g.

1822

William Brenan, Clements Inn, g.—Charles Brenan, Cecil Street, Strand, g.

Willoughby McGhie, Clements Inn, g.—Vincent George Dowling, Queens Square, Bloomsbury, esquire.

Charles James Brown, Clements Inn, g.—Thomas Gray, 421 Strand, boot maker.

Alexander Jaques McCreery, Clements Inn, g.—Clement Prospère Arnand, Frith Street, Soho, vitriol manufacturer.

1823

Henry Frederick Tyler, Davies Street, Berkley Square, g.—John Rolls Whitner, Belvidere House, Lambeth, g.

Henry Rodolph Wigley, Essex Street, Strand, g.—Charles Wigley, Rayner Place, Chelsea, g.

Thomas Dyer Williams, Quality Court, Chancery Lane, g.—James Anderton, Lincolns Inn Fields, g.

William Hunter, Clements Inn, g.—Frederick Hunter, Upper North Place, Grays Inn Road, surgeon.

1824

William Chapman, Middle Temple Hall, g.—George Helder, Clements Inn, a Companion.

Thomas Ellis Adlington, The Exchequer Office, Inner Temple, g.—Thomas Adlington, Bedford Row, g.

James Turbutt Hall, New Boswell Court, g.—John Cressy Hale, Alfreton, Derbs., g.

1825

John Bruce, King's Parade, Chelsea, g.—George Bruce of the same place, g.

1826

William Henry Langley, Cliffords Inn, g.—Humphry Langley, Wellington, Som.,
    esquire.

1827

Thomas Brace the younger, Surrey Street, Strand, g.—Thomas Brace esquire, an
    Ancient.
Richard Flexney, Clements Inn, g.—William Broughton Flexney esquire, an
    Ancient.
Richard Jones, Old Walnut Tree Walk, Lambeth, g.—Charles Henry Rhodes,
    Chancery Lane, g.

1828

George Cobb, Clements Inn, g.—William Cobb, Apothecarys Hall, g.
William Smith, Carey Street, Lincolns Inn Fields, g.—Thomas James Smith,
    Carter Street, Walworth, g.
Thomas Edge, Essex Street, Strand, g.—Andrew Freeman, Beauford Row,
    Chelsea, g.
Thomas Sands Chapman, Essex Street, Strand, g.—Thomas Chapman, Henrietta
    Street, Brunswick Square, esquire.

1829

Josiah Pryce, Vauxhall Terrace, Lambeth, g.—George Richards, Panton Street,
    Haymarket, tailor.

1830

William John McBeath, Norfolk Street, Strand, g.—Mary McBeath of the same
    place, widow.
Thomas Gill, 1 Great Ormond Street, Queen Square, g.—Thomas Gill the younger,
    Great Hermitage Street, g.
Foster Edward Chell, Clements Inn, g.—[No surety named.]

1831

James Fowler, 73 St John Street, Clerkenwell, g.—John Fowler of the same place,
    tin plate manufacturer.
Antonine Dufaur, Melton Place, Euston Square, g.—[No surety named.]
Henry Dyte, 106 Strand, g.—Hannah Dyte of the same place, quill and pen
    manufacturer.

1832

Frederick Duncombe, Clements Inn, g.—Richard Bagshaw, Bridges Street, Covent
    Garden, news vendor.
Charles Paris Poole, Clements Inn, g.—John Minifie Poole, Culmstock, Devon, g.

1834

George Almen Hill, Snaresbrook, Essex, g.—William Pritchard, Princes Street, Leicester Square, engraver.
Pelham Maitland, Kensington, g.—Pelham Thomas Maitland of the same place, g.
William Quarles, 29 Haymarket, g.—Thomas Pearson the younger, Pump Court, Inner Temple, g.

1836

Richard William Webb, Clements Inn, g.—Richard James Webb, Lower Belgrave Street, Eaton Square, Pimlico, chemist.
Richard Hollier Atkinson, Clements Inn, g.—Margaret Atkinson, Lee Road, Blackheath, spinster.

1837

John Gregory, Clements Inn, g.—Jonas Gregory of the same place, g.
Henry Hall, New Boswell Court, g.—Cheslyn Hall, of the same place, g.
Stevens Wade Henslow, Clements Inn, g.—Hambly Knapp,[1] Haberdashers Hall.

1838

Charles John Whishaw, Grays Inn, g.—James Alexander Douglass of the same place, g.
James Alexander Douglass, Grays Inn, g.—Charles John Whishaw of the same place, g.
Cheslyn Hall, New Boswell Court, g.—Henry Hall of the same place, g.
Edward Blackmore, Mitre Court Chambers, g.—Bernard Senior of the same place, g.
John Watson Walmsley, Chancery Lane, g.—William Helder, Clements Inn, g.
David Jones Lee, Field Court, Grays Inn, g.—Charles John Whishaw, South Square, Grays Inn, g.
Samuel Piercy, 3 Crown Square, Southwark, g.—Charles John Whishaw, South Square, Grays Inn, g.
Thomas Bridges, King's Arms Yard, Coleman Street, g.—Charles John Whishaw, South Square, Grays Inn, g.
Thomas Lacy, Kings Arms Yard, Coleman Street, g.—Charles Paris Poole, Clements Inn, g.
Edward Wayman Wadeson, Godliman Street, Doctors Commons, proctor—Charles John Whishaw, South Square, Grays Inn, g.

1839

Campbell Wright Hobson, Raymond Buildings, Grays Inn, g.—William Henry Langley, John Street, Bedford Row, g.

[1] Contemporary Law Lists show Knapp as partner at 13 Clement's Inn with Henry Hughes, for whom see 1809 admissions above.

1840

Thomas William Flavell, 21 Bedford Row, g.—Charles John Whishaw, South
Square, Grays Inn, g.

1841

Edward Carven, 16 South Audley Street, g.—Samuel Dummer, 3 Kensington
Gore, g.

1842

Thomas Gregory,[1] 5 Upper Montagu Street, g.—John Gregory, 7 Harley Place
and New Road, Midd., g.
John Simpson, 5 Furnivals Inn, g.—Cheslyn Hall, 16 New Boswell Court, g.
Simon Rendall, Portman Place, esquire—Charles Rendall of the same place, g.

1852

John Tompsett, 68 Ebury Street, Pimlico, g.—William Winter Weller of the same
place, esquire.

1853

Henry Maddocks Daniel, 3 Leadenhall Street, g.—Nockalls Johnson Cottingham,[2]
Argyll Place, Regent Street, architect.
William Gregory, Clements Inn, g.—Jonas Gregory, Clements Inn, g.

1856

Laurence Foster Chapman, Richmond, Surrey, g.—William Chapman, Richmond,
esquire.
Robert Orridge,[3] Middle Temple, esquire—William Orridge, chemist and druggist.

1857

Henry Spence Fairfoot, Clements Inn, g.—Henry Webb of the same place, g.
Henry Webb, Clements Inn, g.—Henry Spence Fairfoot of the same place, g.
George William Hughes D'Aeth, Clements Inn—Henry Spence Fairfoot of the
same place, g.
Edward Hart Smith, Clements Inn, g.—Peter Tait Harbin of the same place, g.
Frederick Kidner Parkinson, Clements Inn, esquire—James Parkinson, 1 King
Street, St James's Square, esquire.

[1] Afterwards steward of the Inn for at least ten years, following his father who had so
served for thirty—see Thomas Gregory's evidence before the Royal Commission of 1854
on the Inns of Court and Chancery (Qq. 827, 857).
[2] Elder son (1823–54) of Lewis Nockalls Cottingham, architect; for both see *D.N.B.*
[3] Called to the bar at the Middle Temple 1853 (Norfolk circuit): he had chambers in
Brick Court: his name disappears from the Law List after 1865.

1858

Thomas Clark, Clements Inn, g.—Robert Clark, Clarence Place, Woolwich, B.A.

1861

Peter Tait Harbin, Clements Inn, g.—Edward Hart Smith of the same place, g.

1865

Henry Johnson, 10 New Square, Lincolns Inn—William Johnson, 160 Piccadilly,
    wine merchant.

1866

James Glenie Price,[1] 14 Clements Inn—Thomas Gregory, Clements Inn, g.
Charles John Mander,[2] 9 New Square, Lincolns Inn, g.—Robert Edward Diggles,
    The Grange, Twickenham, g.

1867

Henry Gibbon, 32 Great James Street, Bedford Row, g.—Patrick Marcellinus
    Leonard, Lincolns Inn, barrister-at-law.
John Francis White, 31 Guilford Street, Russell Square, g.—Richard Stephen
    Taylor, 3 Field Court, Grays Inn, g.
Richard Stephens Taylor, 3 Field Court, Grays Inn, g.—John Francis White,
    31 Guilford Street, Russell Square, g.

1868

Augustus Delanney Smith, 27 Great James Street, Bedford Row, g.—Henry
    Spence Fairfoot, 12 Clements Inn, g.

1869

John Kendall, 61 Carey Street, Lincolns Inn, g.—Henry Webb, 13 Clements Inn, g.

1871

Alfred John Wood, Richmond, Surrey, g.—William Chapman, Richmond, g.
William Hart Chamberlain, Clements Inn, g.—Peter Tait Harbin, Clements Inn, g.
Griffiths Smith, 15 Furnivalls Inn, g.—Francis Smith, Furnivalls Inn, g.

1875

John Cole Stogdon, Clements Inn, g.—Charles Needham Longcroft, Clements
    Inn, g.
Charles Needham Longcroft, Clements Inn, g.—John Cole Stogdon, Clements
    Inn, g.

[1] Called to the bar at the Middle Temple in 1846: his address in the Law List is at
first 14 Clement's Inn, afterwards Lincoln's Inn Fields. His name disappears from the
Law List after 1859.
    [2] Principal in 1880: see p. lii n. above.

1876

Thomas Lyon, Clements Inn, g.—Samuel Miles Benson, Clements Inn, g.
Edward Arthur Hughes, Clements Inn, g.—Arthur Kennedy, Clements Inn, g.

1879

Arthur Kennedy, Clements Inn, g.—Edward Arthur Hughes, Clements Inn, g.

1882

John Sydenham Francis, Clements Inn, g.—John Kendall, Union Bank Chambers,
     Carey Street, g.
Richard Stephens Taylor, 4 Field Court, Grays Inn, g.—Charles T. Fearon, 11
     New Inn, g.

1883

Mortimer Rooke, 13 Clements Inn—Thomas Henry Carew Hunt, 1 Lincolns Inn
     Fields, g.

INDEX OF PERSONS [1]

(Calendar years, shown in brackets, indicate the year of admission to the Inn.)

Abney, Robt (1705), 150, 183, 197, 268
Acheson, Nath., 302
Adam. *See* Till Adam
Adams:
  John, 285
  Mr, 56
  Thos (1768), 285
  Wm, 121
  — (Ludlow mercer), 292
Adderley, John (1741), 208, 277
Addison, John, 290
Adlington:
  Thos (1810), 304–5
  Thos Ellis (1824), 305
Adolphus, John (1791), 298
Agar, John, 186
Aickin:
  Fras, 292
  Jas (1782), lviii, 292
Aldey:
  Philadelphia, 188
  Ric. (1729), 183, 188, 274
  Roger: admitted (1712), 270; auditor,
    65, 68, 135–6, 173, 175; chambers,
    177, 188; deputy Principal, 194;
    pledge, 274; yard fencing, 40
Aldridge, Sam. (1668), 176, 256, 268
Aldus, Robt, 285
Aldwinckle, John (1705), 48, 268
Alexander, Jas, 303
Allen, J., 236, 250–1
  John (1764), 284, 286, 292, 296
  — (G.I.), 297, 302
  — jun. (1797), 302
  Joseph, 294
  Lewis (1715), 15–16, 99, 270
  Nath. (1776), 288
  Ric. (1788), 296, 293
  Robt, xxvii
  Thos (1766), 285
  Wm (1687), 264
  —, 302
Allix, Isaac (1766), 284
Allnutt:
  John, 288
  Martha, 64
  Zachariah (1677), 258–9
  — (1713), 62, 64, 270
Allsopp, Andrew, 286
Amiss, Edmund (1763), 283
Amyot, Fras (1783), 293
Anderton, Jas, 305

Andrews:
  Henry, 230
  Phineas (1791), 298
  Robt, 274
Aram, Thos (1662), 253–4
Arbuthnot, Geo. (1795), 301
Archer, Edw. (1658), 251, 256
Armiger, Gabriel (1669), 256
Arnane, Geo., 283
Arnand, Clement Prospère, 305
Arnold, Ric., 267
Arthur:
  John (1667), 256, 263
  — jun., 256
Asbridge:
  John (1762), 283
  — (1775), 288
Ashe:
  John (1745), 278
  — (1781), 291
Ashhurst, Wm Henry (1748), 279
Ashley, Marcus (1664), 254
Ashmore, Walter, 258
Astill, Wm, 293
Astry, Sam., 253
Athorpe:
  Laurence (1661), 252, 255
  Thos (1778), 296
Atkins:
  Jas, 287
  Robt, 271
Atkinson:
  Jas (1787), 295
  John (1766), 285, 291–2
  Margaret, 307
  Ric., 284
  —, 301
  — Hollies (1836), 307
  Sarah, 90
  Thos (1730), 275
  Wm (1709), 27, 56, 90, 269
Attweeke, 250
Atwell, Edw. (1682), 260
Atwick, Geo. (1789), 297
Atwood:
  John (1715), 182, 270, 275
  Wm (1731), 275
Augier, Chas, 293
Austen:
  Edw. (1727), 127, 131, 274
  Nath. (1781), 291
Ayland, May, 255

[1] The difficulty due to inconsistencies of spelling, and the problem of distinguishing between or identifying persons who bear the same names, will be borne in mind : see p. xl and note to p. 249 above.

Babb:
John Humphrey, 282
— — (1792), 299
Bach, Wm (1683), 261
Bachelor, Sam. (1797), 302
Bacon, Nicholas. *See* Denton–Bacon–
Cary report
Bagshaw:
Chas (1691), 52, 265, 267–9
Edw. (1683), 261
Henry (father of Edw.), 261
— (1689), 264
Nich., 237, 239
Ric., 306
Thos (1662), 237, 253, 259–61
Baird:
Jas., 287
Jos. (1765), 284
Baker:
Elias (1689), 264
Jas (1795), 301
— Ric., 297
Sampson (1685), 262
Walter, 280
Baldwin or Baldwyn:
Chas (1724), 119–20, 127, 273
Edwyn jun. (1663), 253
— sen., 253
Henry (1665), 254–5
Peter (1686), 263
Sam. (1775), 288
Stephen (1668), 256
Urian (1657), 250
Balgay, Henry, 252
Ball:
John (1658), 251
—, 285
Ric. (1667), 255
Ballam, Sam. Robt (1720), 272
Ballett:
Chas (1664), 254, 263
— jun. (1692), 265–6
Wm (1713), 56, 270
Bambridge:
Jas. (1738), 277
Thos, 277
Barber, John, 293
Barfoote, Jeremiah (1685), 262
Bargett, John (1663), 254
Barker, Peter Henry (1767), 285
Barlow, Edw. (1783), 292
Barnardiston:
Master, xxiv
Thos (Serjt), 186
Barneby, Sam. (1684), 261
Barnes:
Jas, 291
Wm (1709), 94, 108, 269
Barnwell, Thos (1662), 253
Baronneau, Fras (1768), 285
Barras, Joseph:
admitted (1719), 272; bond, 153;
chambers, 149; clerk, xl, 75; death,
132, 189, 193; payments to, 77, 80,
92–3, 97, 121; widow's claim, 141;
witness, 101
Barratt, Thos (1760), 282
Barre, Ric., 1
Barrow:
John (1763), 283
Thos (1785), 293
Barry, Thos (1778), 290
Bartlett, Wm, 286
Barton:
Nath., 294
Thos jun. (1680), 240, 260
— sen., 255, 260
Bartrum, Thos, 305
Barwell, Henry, 4
Baskervill, Jas. (1665), 255
Bassett, Alex. (1759), 282, 288, 291
Bassi, Thos, 297
Bateman:
Geo. (1700), 79, 267
Thos, xlvi
Baton, Ralph (1687), 264
Battam, John, 281
Batten, Nath., 289
Battersby, John (1716), 271
Batty, Jas., 302
Bayley, Thos, 155
Beach:
Robt, 251
Thos (1659), 51, 251, 253
Bearblock, John, 162
Bearcroft, Edw. (1680), 145, 260, 264
Beaumont, Master, xxiii
Beckett:
Chas (1798), 302
Thos (1795), 301
Wm, 302
Bedford, John, 288
Bedwell, Thos, 282
Beeby, Jas, 300
Beeding, John, 138
Bell, Posthumus (1705), 49, 133, 268
Bellamy, Wm, xxx
Bellinger, John (1694), 266
Belsire, Thos (1702), 267–8
Benbow, John (1793), 299
Benett or Bennet:
admitted (1714), 270; arrears, 35, 138:
auditor, 74, 151, 154; chambers,
187; pledge, 273, 276; subscription,
56
Benskyn, Edw., 286
Benson:
Hezekiah, 271
Jas (1717), 72, 271
Sam. Miles, 310
Wm, 93
Benton, Nath., 276
Beresford:
Chas Edwards (1763), 283, 294
Wm, 283
Berry, Thos (1721), 141, 272

Bertles, Ashton (1785), 294
Bewley:
 Ric. (1664), 254
 — (1709), 269; arrears, 33, 89, 153;
  bond, 194; chambers, 31–2, 128–9
Bidduck, John, 275
Biddulph, Edw. (1748), 212, 279
Bill, Chas, 279
Birch, John, 272
Bird, Wm, 258
Bish, Thos (1783), 293
Bishop:
 Benj. (1794), 300
 John, 300
 Wm (1780), 291
Bissell, Arthur (1730), 275
Blackborow, John Steele, 301
Blackmore, Edw. (1838), 307
Blackstone, Wm. (1790), 297
Blackwell:
 John (1714), 270; arrears, 54, 115, 125,
  133; auditor, 162, 165; chambers,
  134; executor, 145; pledge, 194, 271,
  274–5
 Joshua (1685), 262, 270; accounts,
  xxxvi, 34, 42, 59, 68, 74, 106; cham-
  bers, 134; death, 134; interest due to,
  63, 115; picture, xiv, lxiii, 104, 244;
  pledge, 264–6, 268–9, 273
 Rev. Thos, xxxvi, 107, 133, 153
Blagrove, Thos Ward, 299
Blair, John Gray (1783), 293
Blake:
 Anthony (1662), 253
 John Day (1794), 300
 Robt jun. (1814), 304
 — sen., 300, 304
Blakemore, John (1687), 53, 264–5
Bland:
 Ric., 298
 Thos (1773), 287
Blandew, John, 271
Blenkhorn, Wm (1778), 290
Blew, Wm, 298
Blount (see also Blunt):
 Chas, 252
Blowers, Fras (1777), 289
Blunt:
 Chas (1661), 252
 John, 252
 Joseph (1793), 299
 Robt, 299
Boddicoate, Jas, 280
Boid, Thos, 286
Bold, John, xlvi, 252, 258
Boley, John (1691), 265
Bolton, Wm, 288
Bolwell:
 Morgan (1662), 253, 261
 Thos, 237, 254
Bond:
 Geo. (1727), 142, 159, 183, 274
 John, 298

Bonell, Wm (1660), 252
Bonner, Sam, 206
Bootle, Edw. (Serjt), 186
Bosanquet, Sam., 302
Boswell, Jas, lix, 280, 284–5, 292
Bourn, Benj. (1783), 293
Bourne, Ric., 252
Bowler, John (1668), 148, 157, 177,
  256
Bowles, Chas (1715), 56, 94, 96, 270–3
Bowman:
 Edw. (1755), 281
 John (I.T.), 281
 — (1778), 290, 293
Bowness:
 Wm jun. (1736), 276
 — sen., 276
Boxwell, John, 298
Brace:
 Geo. (1820), 305
 Herbt, 296
 Thos (1793), 299, 305–6
 Thos jun. (1827), 306
Brackenbury:
 Chas (1715), 270; Ancient, 180–1;
  arrears, 54, 75, 119, 139, 153, 170,
  182; auditor, 191; chambers, 17;
  pledge, 271, 278
 Joseph, 265
 Thos (1690), 265
 — — (1742), 278
Bradford, Philip (1795), 301
Bradgate, Chris. (1656), 250
Bradley:
 Jas, 273
 Thos (1787), 294
 Wm Rawlins Edw. (1792), 299
Bradshaw:
 Geo., 276
 John, xxiii
 Robt (1789), 296
Brailsford, Wm (1776), 289, 292
Bramsford, Wm, 285
Bramston:
 John, 299
 Stephen (1704), 76, 103, 125, 150, 172,
  183, 190, 268
Bramwell, Lord, lxii
Brand, Rev. John (1794), 300
Bransby, Chas (1707), 21, 268–9
Brawne:
 Ann, xlix, 238–9
 Chas, 239
 Eliz, xlix, 239
 Ric., xlix
Brayfield, Mr, lv, 156
Brean, Wm, 276
Breedon:
 Elkanah (1674), 258
 Thos, 258
Brenan:
 Chas, 305
 Wm (1822), 305

Brereton:
Ric. (1702), 140, 267–8, 270
Theophilus, 267
Brewer, Harry Wm (1809), 303
Brewster:
Chris. (1716), 28, 52, 109, 118, 137,
271
John, 250
Sam (1656), 7, 10, 250, 254
— (1665), 84, 254, 259, 262, 265–6,
268
Brian (*see also* Bryan):
Joseph, 174–5, 195
Bridgeman, Ric. Whalley (1783), 293
Bridges:
Jas, ?49,105, 132, 171, 207
Thos (1720), 272
— (1838), 307
Briquett, John, 271
Bristowe, Wm, 282, 284
Brocklesby:
John (1691), 265
Ric., Dr (1765), lix, 284
Bromley:
Rev. Robt Antony, 297
Stretch Cowley (1791), 297
Brooke:
Jas (1787), 295
John (1667), 255
Brookes:
John, 298
Wm (1791), 298
Brooks & Dixon, xxxv
Brown (*see also* Browne):
Chas Jas (1822), 305
Isaac, 285
John (1738), 214, 276–7
— (1767), 285
— (1788), 296
— (1792), 298
Joseph, 282
Josiah (1758), 281
Owen, 287
Stephen (1779), 291, 294, 296–7
Thos, 281
Wm (Reader), 193
Browne:
Edw., 252, 255
John (1664), 254
— (1691), 265
— (1790), 297
Mr, 193, 195
Wm jun., xlvi
Brownsword, Roger (1729), 178, 185,
274
Bruce:
Geo., 305
John (1825), 305
Bruchfield, Sam., 283
Brufield, Thos (1721), 272
Brumstead, Thos, 252, 254
Bryan, Joseph (1733), 275
Bryer, Fras. (1794), 300

Buck:
Geo. (1784), 293
John (1686), 263
Thos, 254
Buckland, Wm, 272
Buckworth:
John, 275
Theophilus (1686), 263
Budgett:
Jas jun. (1746), 278
— sen., 278
John (1731), 167, 275
Bulcock, Thos (1731), 275
Bull, Stephen (1660), 252
Bulleme, John (1706), 268
Bullock:
Edw. (1787), 293, 295
Thos, 292
Bulstrode:
Edw. (1674), 90, 258
Sir Ric., 258
Whitelock, 258
Bunce, Thos, 273
Bunn, Thos (1788), 295
Buntebant or Buntlebart, Gabriel (1788),
295
Burdon, Henry (1735), 276
Burke, Jas, 297
Burman, Thos Wm, 275
Burnett, Thos (Serjt), 186
Burrard:
Paul (1674), 258–9, 260, 262
Thos, 258
Burrell:
John, 273
— (1785), 294
— (1790), 297
Thos (1722), 126, 129, 184, 273
Burrow, Chris., 281
Burrows, Wm, 273
Bursey, John (1790), 297
Burtebant. *See* Buntebant
Burton:
Geo., 275
Gilbert (1733), 185, 194, 275
John (1780), 291
— (1785), 294
Mr (taylor), xliii, 125
Bush, Atkinson, 300
Butcher, John (1790), 297
Butler, Beverley, 196
Butlyn, John (1664), 254
Buxton, John (1780), 291, 298
Byde, Ralph, 273
Byrd, Wm, 257, 260–1
Byrne, Redmond (1760), 282–3

Cadwallader, Jonathan, 275
Caldecot, John (1741), 277
Callowe or Callow:
(?), 250–1
John, 58, 265

Callowe or Callow—*continued*
  Thos (1669), 241, 257, 259
    — (1692): admitted, 265; chambers, 58–9, 69, 70; conference with New Inn, 242; death, 62; law charges, 17, 41; rent accounts, 35; steward or clerk, xiii, xl
  Wm: accounts, xxxvii; loan to Inn, 237–8; pledge, 253–5, 257
Calton, Ric., 89
Cam, Mr, 240
Campion, Wm (1766), 284–6
Cannon, Edw., 289
Cantelow:
  Sir John, l
  Sir Wm, l–li
Capper, Fras, 190
Cardale, Wm, 293
Carden, Jas (1791), 298
Carmalt, John (1745), 213, 278–9
Carrington, Jas, 278
Carrow, Robt (1707), 6, 83, 125, 149, 185, 269
Carruthers:
  John jun. (1803), 303
  — sen., 303
Carter:
  Edw., 260
  Geo. (1681), 260
  — (vintner), 300
  Laurence (1668), 5, 54, 109, 256
  — jun., 5, 216, 256, 266
  Nath. (1767), 285
  Thos (1699), 55, 95, 132, 266, 271
  — jun. (1786), 294
  — sen., 294
Carven, Edw. (1841), 308
Carvile, Mathew (1633):
  admitted, 260; Allnutt's bond, 62; arrears, 33, 79; chambers, 80, 149, 242; pledge, 263, 270
Cary Robert. *See* Denton–Bacon–Cary report
Caryll:
  Fras, 283
  Master, xxiii
Catchpole, John (1717), 271
Cater:
  Everard (1697), 265
  Geo. (1777), 289
  Simon, 289
Cave:
  Frances, 161–3
  Ric.: admitted (1731), 275; chambers, 161–3, 183, 192
Cawdron, Geo. (1683), 261
Chalcraft, Henry (1786), 294
Challis, Martin (1760), 282
Chalmers, John, 294
Chamberlain, Wm Hart (1871), 309
Chambers:
  Edw. (1669), 257
  Ric., 302
  Robt (1685), 262

Champante:
  Henry (1671), 257, 260
  — (1743), 278
Champernawne:
  Wm jun. (1687), 264
  — sen., 264
Chaplin, Thos (1694), 27, 78, 266
Chapman:
  Anthony (1782), 292
  Chas, 299
  Edw. jun. (1698), 266
  Laurence Foster (1856), 308
  Thos, 306
  — Sands (1828), 306
  Wm (1824), 305
  —, 308–9
Chapone:
  Hester, 280
  John (1753), xxxvi, lix, 280
Charnells, Thos (1666), 255
Cheales or Cheeles:
  John, 79, 202–3
  Ruth, 203
Cheble, John (1672), 258
Cheese, John (1688), 264
Cheeseborough, Wm, 279
Chell, Foster Edw. (1830), 306
Cheslyn, Ric. (1785), 293
Chessall or Chessell:
  Matthew (1757), 281, 283, 300
  — Ric. (1809), 303
Chetwynd, Wm, 212
Child:
  Benj. (1685), 262
  House of, xxxv
  Jas (1717), 118, 127, 150, 271
  Joseph, 150
  Sir Fras, xxxv
Chislet (?):
  Robt, 251
  Thos (1659), 251
Cholmley, Edw. (1659), 252
Christian, E. B. V., xx, lxi
Chumley, John (1738), 276–7
Church:
  Wm (1669), 257
  — Henry, 302
Churchill, Awnsham, 205
Clagett, Wiseman, 270
Clare, Earl of, xi, xlvii, xlix, li, 239
Clark (*see also* Clarke and Clerke):
  Robt, 309
  Thos (1745), 278
  — (1858), 309
Clarke:
  Giles, 4, 5
  J. H., 298
  John (1609), 256
  Robt, 283
  Sam., 212
Clarkson:
  Geo. (1779), 290, 294

Clarkson—*continued*
John, 290
Romaine Wm (1786), 294
Clay:
Felix (1781), 291
Wm, 291
Clement, Edw., 290
Clements:
Chas (1700), 267
Thos, 267
Clementson:
Isaac (1792), 299, 305
John (1759), 282
Clennell, Mordaunt Lawson (1776), 288
Clerke, Thos:
admitted (1695), 266; arrears, 10; chambers, 13–14, 116
Cliffe, John (1796), 301
Clifford, Lord, lxvii
Clifton, Wm. (1746), 214–5, 278
Clode, C. M., lxii
Cloton, Mr, 243
Cloudesley, Harry (1748), 217, 279
Coates, J., 250–1
John, 252, 254–5, 258–9
— (Newbury) (1669), 256
— (Peterborough), 259
Cobb:
Geo. (1828), 306
Hewitt (1784), 293, 295, 298, 301
Wm, 306
Cock:
Wm (1717), 52, 103, 117, 271
Mr (joiner), 140
Cocke, Anthony (1722), 98, 122, 201, 272
Cockcroft, Wm (1686), 263, 265
Coffin, John Perrie (1790), 297
Coke, Sir Edw., xix, xxix, lxi, 126
Coldham, G. J., lxvi
Coling, Joseph (1668), 256
Collett, Ric., 279
Colley, Thos (1717), 181, 271
Collinge, David Chas, 300
Collingwood, Antony (1667), 256
Collins:
Thos, 274
Wm (1796), 301
Collyer, Chas, 284
Colman, Fras, 282
Colnett:
Jas (1794), 301
Thos (1663), 253
Comerford, Chas (1820), 305
Complyn, Wm (1656), 250
Constable, Robt (1670), 257
Cook (*see also* Cooke):
Chris. (1677), 259
John, 260
Ric., 296
Wm Ely (1784), 293, 297
Cooke:
Fountain (1746), 278–9

Cooke—*continued*
Wm (1779), 290
(?), 214–15
Cookes:
Robt (1684), 261
Thos (1682), 260
Sir Thos, 260
Cooper:
Nicholas, lv, 18
Sam., 288
Wm (1774), 288
Coote:
Sam. jun. (1722), 273
— sen., 273
Cope, Thos (1663), 253
Coperthwaite, 251
Copley, 250
Corlet, Sam., 263
Cornish, John Dixey, 289
Cosyn, Cosyns or Cousins:
Edw. (1713), 33, 56, 150, 170, 270
Wm, 270
Cottingham:
Lewis Nockalls, 308
Nockalls Johnson, 308
Cotton:
Edw. (1687), 91, 264
Leonard (1718), 181, 271
Couchman, Nath. (1675), 259
Coupland, Geo., 247–8
Coventry, Lord Keeper, xxvi, 126
Coverly, Thos, 234
Covert, Nicholas (1663), 253, 256
Cowne, Robt, 270
Cox:
Chas, 4, 5
Jas (1752), 280
Mr, 43
Serjt, lxii
Craig, Milliken (1791), 298
Crashaw, Wm, 256
Crawford, John (1737), 214, 276
Crawley:
John (1766), 284
Wm, 284
Creed:
Chas, 276
Henry, 301
Cresswell:
Ric. Cheslyn, 293
Thos, 284
Crewe, Sir Randolph, viii, 126
Cripps, Thos (1658), 251
Crispin, Silver, 278
Croft, Ric., 275
Cromwell:
Ric. (1716), 56, 82, 123, 271
Wm, 271
Cropley, Luke (1658), 251
Crosley, John, 270
Crosse, Thos (1808), 303
Crosswell, Pollard (1689), 264
Crumpe, Chas, 274

Crunden, Douglas (1787), 295–6
Cruttenden, Joseph, 285
Cryer, Sam. (1668), 256
Cullingworth, Wm, 284
Curtis:
  Edw.: admitted (1704), 268; arrears, 26,
    53, 71, 102, 107, 115; chambers, 2,
    113, 187; pledge, 273
  Nicholas (1724), 273
  Noah, lv, 114, 149, 158, 182
  Robt (1735), 276
Cuthbert, Jas, 298

D'Aeth, Geo. Wm. Hughes (1857),
  308
Dagge, Henry jun. (1787), 295
Dalby, Geo. (1683), 30, 261
Dale, Chas (1791), 297
Dalton, John, 299
Dampier, Edw., 296
Dand:
  (?), 250
  John, xlvi, 254
Dandy, Geo. (1777), 289
Danforth, Thos. (1786), 294
Daniel, Henry Maddocks (1853), 308
Darley, Theodore (1737), 276–7
Dashwood, Ric., 199
Davenport:
  Geo. (1699), 56, 266–8
  John, 290
Davids:
  Geo., 279
  Wm (1755), 281
  — (1764), 284
Davidson, John, 295
Davies:
  Caleb (1767), 285
  Jenkin, 271
  John, bookbinder, 277
  — (1787), 295
  — jun. (1796), 301
  Ric. (1682), 260
  Thos (1762), 283
  Wm (1794), 300
Davis:
  Hesketh (1791), 249, 298
  — (1793), 249, 299
  Mr, 140
Davison, Dan. Wilson (1796), 302
Dawes: Arthur Smithson (1779),
  290
  Rev. Arthur, 290
  Wm, 290
Dawson, Wm (1787), 295–6
Day, Geo. (1686), 263
Dax, John, 293, 304
Deacon, Benj., 287
Degge, 250
Delafare, Thos (1796), 301
Delaport, Elias Philip, 279

Denman, Mr Justice, lxii
Dennett:
  (?), 250
  Ric., 252–3
Denshire, Geo.:
  admitted (1702), 267: arrears, 5; auditor,
    94, 96; chambers, 9, 10, 12, 21;
    reference to, of bill books, 61; and
    Fisk's arrears, 24
Dent:
  John, 298
  Robt, 268
Denton: Chas (1678), 259
  Sam. (1792), 299
  Thos. See Denton–Bacon–Cary report
Denton–Bacon–Cary report, xi, xv, xxii–
  xxiii, xxvii, xxxix, liv, lxi, 220
Desaguliers, John Theophilus, 274
De Sanges, Wm (1777), 289
Devaynes, Wm, 284
Devon:
  Chas (1810), 303
  Thos (1747), 279
  Wm (1759), 282
  — (1773), 246, 287, 303
Dew:
  Silett, 278
  Tomkyns (1745), 278
Dewar, Jas (1793), 300
Dewes:
  Bernard, 284
  Court (1765), 284
  — (1781), 291
  John: admitted (1718), 271; accounts,
    213, 215; Ancient, 180–1; auditor,
    94, 96, 151, 154; chambers, 157, 178;
    loan by, 209; Principal, 209, 216,
    278; relatives, 284
Diggles, Robt Edw., 309
Dignam, Wm, 285
Dilke, Wm, xlvi
D'Israeli:
  Benj., 299
  — (Ld Beaconsfield), lviii
  Isaac (1793), lviii, 299
Dixon:
  Mr (carpenter), 16
  Wm: admitted (1691), 265; arrears,
    22–3; chambers, 20–1, 92; trustee,
    4, 5
  — jun., 212
Dobbes:
  Thos (1656), xlvi, xlvii, 250
  — jun., 251
Dobson:
  Jas, 272
  John Jas: admitted (1721), 272; auditor,
    111–12; chambers, 83–4, 86; trustee,
    212
  Robt (1763), 283
  Thos (1796), 301
Dodd, Jas Solas, 280

Dodsworth:
  Mathew (1664), 254, 256–7
  Robt, xi
Dolling, Jas, 281
Donald:
  Chas (1794), 300
  Robt, 300
Donaldson:
  Andrew (1774), 288
  Humphry, 301
  Jas, 301
D'one:
  Chas (1685), 262
  Jane, 262
Dorrington, John, 297
Dorset, Michael (1777), 289
Dottin or Dottyn:
  Geo. 279
  Henry: admitted (1662), 253; pledge,
    254–6, 261, 263–5
  — jun.: admitted (1691), 265; arrears,
    120, 138, 164, 190; chambers, 8, 9,
    29, 60
Douglass, Jas Alex. (1838), 307
Dove:
  Jas (1804), 303
  Robt, 303
Dovey:
  John: admitted (1695), 266; accounts,
    111–12, 119, 129, 136; auditor, 15,
    34, 65, 68; Callow's bill, 17; chambers,
    24, 29–30, 180; fire insurance, 29,
    109; payments to, 27, 41, 49, 92;
    pledge, 269; Principal, 104, 273;
    property, 269
  — jun.: admitted (1724), 273; accounts,
    198, 201; Ancient, 192; chambers,
    113, 180; Keeling's bond, 193; loan
    by, 209–11; pledge, 275; proposed
    for Principal, 198; Principal, 195,
    277
  Walter, 212
Dowling:
  Alfred S., Serjt, xxvii
  Vincent Geo., 305
Down, Jas, 293
Downey, Philip (1666), 255
Downton, John (1721), 141, 272
D'Oyly:
  John, 275
  Shirley (1730), 174, 275
Draper, Ric. (Serjt), 186
Drawwater, John, 291
Druke, Thos, 285
Drury:
  Dru, 291
  Robt: admitted (1717), 271; auditor,
    74; bond up, 178; chambers, 32, 127
Duckett, Joseph (1682), 30, 260
Dudbridge, Joseph (1715), 13, 50, 270
Dudley:
  Robt (E. of Leicester), xxv
  Thos, 257

Dufaur or Dufour, Antonine (1831), 306
Duffeild:
  Huan (1664), 254
  Wm Henry (1787), 295
Duffy, Wm (1735), 276
Dufour. See Dufaur
Dummer:
  Edw., 266
  Sam., 308
Duncombe:
  Brandreth, 305
  Fredk (1832), 306
  Jas (1820), 305
Dundas, Thos (1792), 299
Dunmoll, Nicholas (1686), 263
Duthie, Archibald (1775), 288
Dutton, Gerard, 161
Duxon, Mr, 140
Dymoke:
  Chas, 259, 267
  — jun. (1700), 267
  Thos, lv, 69, 267
Dyson, Gravenor (1712), 10, 270
Dyte:
  Hannah, 306
  Henry (1831), 306

Earle, Jas (1660), 252
Eastabrook, John (1782), 292
Ebrall, Nath., 278
Eccles, Sam.:
  admitted (1710), 269; arrears, 64, 75,
    106, 156; chambers, 50; pledge, 270
Eden, Tobias (1663), 253, 256
Edge:
  Jas (1775), 288
  Ralph (1664), 237, 254, 256, 258
  Thos (1828), 306
  Wm (1667), 256
Edison, Nath. (1705), 33, 75, 268
Edwards:
  Henry, 274
  John (1793), 299
  Ric. 218, 227
  Saunders (1737), 193, 195, 276
  Sir Henry, 183
  Thos (1687), 264
Eede:
  Edmund (1664), 254
  — Dr, 263
  Fras, 254
Egleton, Robt (1671), 257–9
Ekins, John (Pr.), 239, 251, 258
Eldon, Lord, 290
Eldridge:
  Ambrose: admitted (1701), 267; audi-
    tor, 169; chambers, 2, 147; pledge,
    268; witness, 263
  Wm (1739), 277
Elers, Geo. (1743), 206, 217, 278
Eles, Thos (1776), 289
Elisha, Sam. (1729), 176, 194, 274
Ellam, Jas (1686), 263

Elliott, Ellyott or Elyott:
  John, 1
  Ric., 1
  Robt (1674), 258–60
  Wm, 1
Elly:
  Jas (1707), 26–7, 89, 269
  Ric., 89
Elmslie, John (1772), 287–8
Elton, C. I., lxiv
Elwick, John (1739), 277
Emerson, Michael, xlvi
Emes:
  John (1674), 258, 256
  Sam, 264
  Thos jun. (1698), 266
Erle, Sir Wm, lxii
Ervington, Thos (1662), 253
Esch:
  Winde Wm Van der (1752), 280
  Henry, 280
Etheredge, Geo. (1659), 251
Evans:
  Ann, 67
  Bernard (1719), 67–8, 149, 268, 272
  Mathew: admitted (1704), 268; auditor, 7; chambers, 38–9, 67, 145; death, 67; loan by, 117; pledge, 270–1; supervises works, xlvii; Tyson's chambers, 36
Everingham, Jas (1792), 299
Eyre (see also Eyres):
  Chas, 281
  John, 266
  Thos, 275
  Vincent, 274
Eyres (see also Eyre):
  Chas (1730), 155, 275

Fabian, Dan. Chas, 296
Fairfoot, Henry Spence (1857), lxiii, 308–9
Falkener:
  Lyon (1698), 42–3, 266
Farley, lx
Farr, Thos, 273
Farrer (see also Ferrar), Edw., 260
Farwell, Mr Justice, lxvi
Faviman, Wm, 298
Fay, Anthony (1778), 290
Fearon:
  Chas T., 310
  Joseph, 274
Feeler, Wm, 273
Feilder, Mr, 36
Fell, Jas (1787), 295
Fenhoulet, Jas (1778), 290
Fenn, Geo., 272
Fenton, Thos (1779), 290, 292
Ferrar (see also Farrer), Edw. (1667), 255–6, 258
Ferrour, Wm (1737), 276

Field, Mr, 240
Fielder. See Feilder
Fielding, John, 292
Fiennes, Edw., 241
Fifield:
  John jun. (1673), 258
  — sen., 258
Figes, Peter, 299
Firth:
  John, 279
  Ric. (1691), 265
Fish, Thos (1719), 272
Fisher:
  Edw. (1667), 255
  — (1685), 262
  Ric. Bernard, 300
  Wm, 303
Fiske:
  Sturgeon (1685), 23, 262
  Zachariah, 262
Fitzherbert, Wm, 5
Flack, Jas Medlicott (1766), 284, 290
Flamsteed, Wm (1668), 256
Flavell, Thos Wm (1840), 308
Fleetwood, Robt (1789), 296
Fleming, Ric., 277
Fletcher:
  John (1707), 18, 269
  Thos, 282
  Wm (1769), 286
Flexney:
  Ric. (1827), 306
  Spencer, 303
  Wm Broughton (1803), xxxviii, 303, 306
Floyer, Sam., 259
Fludd, John, 279
Foljambe, John jun. (1789), 296
Folkes (and see Foulkes):
  Henry, 282
  John (1785), 293
Ford:
  John, 212, 271
  Thos, xlvi, lii, 230
  — (1750), 279, 283
Forester, Alex., 188
Forster:
  Rev. Wm, 18, 62
  Sam., 188
Fortescue:
  Sir John, xviii–xix, xxi, l, lxi
  Thos, 274
Fortie, Alex. (1761), 283
Fossick:
  John, 288
  Thomas (1776), 288, 291, 301
  Mr, 247
Foster:
  Geo., 184
  John (1673), 258
  Michael, 186
  Rev. Wm, 18, 62
Foulkes (or Folkes), John (1785), 293–4, 296

Fowke:
  Anna, 152, 275
  Thos: admitted (1715), 270; auditor, 106; chambers, 20–2, 148, 151, 156
  — (1730), 275
Fowler:
  F. H., lxi
  Jas (1831), 306
  John, 306
  Joseph (1810), 303
  Roger (1657), 251
  Wm: admitted (1695), 266; auditor, 74, 126, 129, 169; bill books, 61; deputy Principal, 179; pledge, 273
Fox, Geo. (1661), 252
Foxcroft, Isaac (1657), 250
Fraine, John (1745), 213, 278
Francis, John Sydenham (1882), 310
Freeman:
  Andrew, 306
  Jonathan, 84–5
  Joseph (1748), 279
Fregleton, Wm (1691), 265
French, John (1759), 282
Frith:
  Jane (1795), lviii, 301
  Jas (1781), 292
Frodsham, Wm, 292
Fry, Henry, 299
Fryth:
  Edw., 252
  Harry (1660), 252
Fuller, Geo.:
  admitted (1694), 266; auditor, 55, 59, 106; bills, etc., referred to, 17, 36, 61, 83; chambers, 57, 112; Lamb Inn yard dispute, 65; loan by, 124; death, 112
  Henry, 300
  Mary, 112–13
Fullwood:
  Oliver (1686), 263
  Thos (1765), 284
Fyfield, Mr, 235

Gage, Ric. (1680), 260–1
Gale:
  John (1660), 255
  Wm (1791), 298
Gallaway, Robt (1772), 287
Gamall, Thos, 281
Gapper:
  Abraham (Serjt), 186
  Chas, 284
  Robt (1769), 286
  Wm (1770), 286, 290
Gardiner, Andrew (1680), 260–1
Gardner, John, 276
Garfoot, Mr, 242
Garlike, John (1665), 254
Garnault, Joseph (1782), 292
Garnett:
  Robt (1751), 280
  Wm (1657), 250

Garrard:
  Fras (1661), 252
  Joseph (1661), 252
  Thos, 272
Garry, 104
Gartnel, Remfry (1679), 22, 260
Gascoigne, Jas Cloberry (1747), 279
Gaskell, Alex. Forbes, 303
Gason, Wm (1738), 198, 201, 276
Gates, Ric. (1685), 262
Gatty:
  Robt, 301
  Wm (1779), 290
Gawler, Sam. (1763), 283
Geary:
  Jonas, 130
  Josiah (1663), 253, 262
George:
  Edw., 297
  Geo. Chapman (1778), 290
Gerard or Gerrard:
  Edw., xxxvi–xxxvii, xlix, 218, 237–9
  Fras, 218
Gery (bricklayer), 16
Gibbeson, Thos, 285
Gibbon, Henry (1867), 309
Gibbons:
  Fras, 274
  John: admitted (1699), 266; auditor, 7, 34, 42, 74, 119–20, 123, 127–8; bills, etc., referred to, 17, 36, 83; bond, 139; chambers, 131; death, 135; loan by, 66, 135
  Thos, 282
Gibson, Wm:
  admitted (1656), 250; loan by, 238–9; pledge, 254, 257, 259, 263
Giffard, Jas, 302
Gilbert, Jas (1689), 264
Giles, John (1659), 251–2, 255
Gill:
  Thos jun., 306
  — sen. (1830), 306
Gillanders, Fras, 290
Girdler:
  John Stanford (1789), 296
  Joseph, 281
  — (Serjt.), 281
Glenny, Geo. (1768), 285, 287–8
Glover, John, 281
Goddard, Thos (1692), 265
Godwyn, Wm (1665), 254
Gofton, Wm:
  admitted (1729), 274; appointed steward, xl, 172, 175; dismissed, 177
Goldan, Wm (1672), 257
Goldwire, Chris. (1703), 41, 267
Good, Ric. (1685), 262
Goodacre, Joseph:
  admitted (1722), 273; accounts, 207; Ancient, 192; arrears, 142; auditor, 135–6, 198, 201; Principal, 200
Goodlad, Ric., 277

Goodman:
　　Everard: admitted (1699), 266; auditor, 7, 65, 68, 137–8, 185; bills referred to, 36; chambers, 24, 117, 144, 204; death, 205; deputy Principal, 63; loan by, 66, 117; pledge, 271, 273
　　Sam. (1764), 284
Goodwin or Goodwyn:
　　Isaac (1730), 275
　　John (1665), 255
　　Thos (1747), 212, 279
Gordon:
　　Edw. jun. (1796), 302
　　Geo. (1795), 301
　　Jas (1780), 291
Gorham, Mr, 162
Gormey, Joseph (1666), 235
Gosnold:
　　Edmund, 252
　　Edw., 257
　　Geo., 257
　　Mr, 235
　　Ric. (1672), 258
Gouge, 104
Gould, John, 151, 273
Grace, John (1664), 254
Graham:
　　Jas, 299
　　Joseph, 292
　　Wm, 300
Gramer, Fras (1658), 251
Granger, Thos (1676), 259
Granom, Lewis Christian Austin (1749), 279, 282
Grant:
　　Chas (1776), 289
　　Fras (1791), 297
　　Peter, 289
　　Robt, 297
　　Sam. (1672), 257
Grantham, John, 248
Gray:
　　Geo., 299
　　Thos, 305
Grayhurst:
　　John (1707), 110, 268
　　Wm, 268
Greaves, John (1686), 263
Greathead, Sam. (1776), 289
Green (see also Greene):
　　Benj. (1760), 282
　　— Tickell (1776), 289
　　Fras (1741), 201, 216, 277
　　Geo. (1738), 277
　　— (1742), 277
　　— (1748), 279
　　John: admitted (1721), 272; Ancient, 180–1; auditor, 111–12, 135–6, 185, 198, 201, 217; declines Principalship, xv, 198; loan by, 209–11; pledge, 277
　　— (1742), 278–9, 231
　　Joseph, 291
　　Matthew, 144

Green—continued
　　Ric', 277
　　Thos, 296
　　Wm, 295
Greene or Grene (and see Green):
　　Geo. (1666), 255, 260
　　John (Principal), 236–7, 251, 254
　　— jun., 255–6
　　Sam. (1674), 258, 263
　　T., 251
　　Theophilus (1658), 251, 255
Gregge:
　　Fras (1683), 118, 261
　　John (1664), 254
　　Joseph (1680), 260–1
　　Ralph, xlvi, 250, 252, 254, 257
　　— jun. (1669), 257
　　Sam. (1664), 254
　　Thos (1676), 259–61
Gregory:
　　Henry: admitted (1718), 271; Ancient, 192; arrears, 105, 118, 128, 146, 159, 181; chambers, 64, 94, 147; loan by, 209–10; proposed for Principal, 198–9, 209
　　— (1792), 298
　　John (1837), 307–8
　　Jonas (1808), 303, 307–8
　　Thos (1842), lix, 308–9
　　Wm, (1853), 308
Gregson:
　　Geo. (1692), 265
　　Henry (1704), 3, 80, 268
　　John (1797), 302
Grene (see also Greene), John, 261
Grew, Geo., lv, 207
Grieves (see also Greaves), Geo. (1775), 288
Griffin:
　　Benj. (1734), lviii, 276
　　Rev. Benj., 276
Griffith, Edw. (1796), 301
Grose:
　　Fras (1771), 249, 286
　　— (1783), 249, 293
Grove, John (1727), 131, 274
Gubbins, John (1780), 291
Guery, Lewis (1789), 296
Guest, Nicholas (1693), 55, 266
Guilford, Lord Keeper, xxviii, liii
Gunter Henry (1743), 278
Gurdon, Wm, 294
Guy, John (1792), 299
Gwinnell, John, 295
Gwyne, Morgan (1717), 94, 102, 149, 181, 271
Gyblott, Wm, 295
Gyles, Dan. (1773), 287

Hadley, John, 203, 207
Haines (see also Hayne and Haynes), John, 285

Hale:
John Cressy, 305
— (fruiterer), xliii, 101
Sir Matthew, xix, 126
Halfhide, Geo. (1692), 265
Halfpenny, Thos, xi
Hall:
Cheslyn (1838), 307–8
Geo. 295
Henry, 296
— (1837), 307
— (deputy Reader), 209
Jas (1797), 302
— Turbutt (1824), 305
John (1693), 265
—, 276
Lancelot, 276
Matthew, 237, 239
Robt (1749), 279
Wm (1669), 256, 258
Hallier, Philip, 283
Halsted, Edw.:
admitted (1702), 267; auditor, 55, 60, 94, 96, 119–20, 123, 127–8, 135–6, 141–2; chambers, 25–6, 37–8, 80–2, 86, 91, 100, 112, 116, 119, 161, 163; clock subscription, 56; fire insurance, 108; fire-fighting apparatus, 140, loan by, 95, 132; pictures, viii, xiv, lxiii, 126, 245; pledge, 269; reference to, of—Barras's claim, 141, Carrow's debt, 83, Lamb Inn dispute, 65
Hamilton:
Chas (1801), 302
Wm Law (1776), 289
Hammond:
Thos (1755), 281
Wm (1795), 301
Hampson, R., xlix
Handley:
John (1704), 268
Ric. (1661), 252
Thos (1786), 294
Hannam:
John (1665), 254
— (1761), 282–3
Hanne:
Andrew, 276
John (1735), 276
Hansard, John (1658), 251
Hanson:
John (1785), 294
Robt (1763), 283
Hanwell, Shem (1677), 259, 263
Harbin, Peter Tait (1861), 308–9
Hardham, Wm (1685), 262
Harding, John (1724), 182, 273
Hardwicke:
Jas: admitted (1712), 270; arrears, 78, 106, 139; auditor, 151, 154; pledge, 274
Wm: admitted (1717), 271; arrears, 76, 143; bond up, 164

Harfeild, Edw. (1662), 253
Harfell, John (1667), 255
Harris:
Edw. (1687), 264
F., 251
Fras, 253, 257–8
Henry (1672), 258, 260
— jun., 258, 265, 268
John (Eydon) (1704), 20, 148, 174, 191, 268
— (Gt Missenden) (1715), 148, 270–1
— (King's Langley), 283
— (Worcs.) (1687), 264–5
Sam., 272
Thos (1686), 263
Harrison:
Andrew (1669), 256
Chas (1798), 302
Robt (1685), 263, 265
Timothy (1665), 254
Hart:
Chas (1789), 296, 298
Wm (1757), 281
Hartley, John, 301
Harvest:
Geo., 279
Wm, 279
Harvey:
Robt, 252
Thos (1787) [?lx], 295
Wm (1788), [?lx], 296, 299
Hathway, Fras (1790), 297
Hatsell, Geo., 278
Hatton:
Arthur (1658), 251
Edw., xxxi
Michael (1721), 131, 272
Sam., 272
Wm., 251
Haverkam, Coan, 286
Hawes:
John (1794), 300
Wm, 290
Hawford, John (1669), 242, 257, 259, 263–4, 266
Hawkes, Thos, 292
Hawkins, Wm (1672), 257
Hawte, Sir Wm, li
Hayes, Robt (1768), 285
Hayley, Thos (1721), 181, 272
Hayman:
Henry Edw. (1795), 301
Michael (1777), 289, 291, 301
Hayne (see also Haines and Haynes):
John (1657), 250, 258
— jun. (1682), 18, 44, 260, 263
Joseph: admitted (1717), 271; arrears, 76, 95, 171; chambers, 37, 47–8, 111, 172
Haynes (see also Hayne):
John (1705), 268
Robt, 268
Hayter, Jonathan, 293

Hayward, Wm (Serjt), 186
Healey, Geo., xlvi
Heath, Matthew (1663), 253
Heathcote:
  Chas (1785), 293
  Sam. (1685), 49, 102, 262
Hebden, John (1753), 280
Hebert, Jas, 290
Heckford:
  Sam. (1716), 270
  — (1722), 124, 127–8, 141–2, 273, 278
  Thos (1746), 208, 278
Helder:
  Geo. (1820), 305
  Wm, 307
Hemming, Anthony, 295
Hendy, Sam, 284
Henriques, David (1742), 277
Henry VII, lii
Henry VIII (and see Denton–Bacon–Cary report), xv, lii
Henslow, Stevens, Wade (1837), 307
Hepburn, John Newhall (1794), 301
Herne, Geo. (1764), 284
Heslop, Thos (1787), 295
Hester, Wm (1720), 149, 272
Hetherington, Philip Parry (1734), 276
Hewerdine, Wm (1795), 301
Hewit, David, 296
Hewitt, Thos (1769), 286
Heydon, Thos, 284
Heys, Rogers (1789), 296
Hicks, Geo., 293
Higgins:
  Rev. Thos, 283
  Thos, 283
Higginson, Jas Montagu (1792), 299
Hill:
  Dan., 296
  Geo. (1770), 286, 291
  — Almon (1834), 307
  John (1797), 302
  Joseph (1789), 296
  Sam., 299, 304
  Thos, 273
Hillier, John (1706), 51, 69, 268
Hillyard, Chas (1795), 301–3
Hinde:
  Ric. (1762), 283
  Robt Venables (1788), lvi, 296
Hinder, Thos, xliii, 40, 97, 119
Hinds, John, 276
Hislop, Alex. (1786), 294
Hitchcock, Ric. (1669), 256–7
Hoare:
  Edw. (1768), 285
  House of, xxxv
Hobbs, Wm, 281
Hobson:
  (?), 251
  Campbell Wright (1839), 307

Hodges:
  (?), 250
  Joseph (1764), 284, 295, 298
  Philip (New Inn), 11
  Ric. (1782), 292
Hodgkins, Chas (1689), 264
Hodgkis, John (1708), 72, 125, 269
Hodgson:
  Michael (1745), 278
  —, 291
  Ralph (1735), 195, 276
  Wm (1796), 302
Hodson, John, 272–3
Hogan, Joseph (1776), 289
Hogg, John (1722), 273
Holbech, Holbeche, Holbeach, Holbeech or Holbetch:
  Ambrose: Ancient, 231–2, 235; audit, 241; Kellett affair, xlviii, loan by, 238–9; Principal, 260
  — (Reader), xxx
  Chas (1674), 258
  Martin, xlvi, lii, 258
  Sam., 234
  Thos, Principal, 1635, xlvi, lii, 218
  — (1683), 261
Holden, Wm (1703), 20, 267
Holdsworth:
  Wm, 294
  Sir Wm, xvi
Holford, Peter, 212
Holland:
  Chas (1796), 302
  Thos, 302
Holles:
  Fras, li
  Sir John, li
  Sir Wm, li
Hollester:
  Luke (1789), 296
  Mark, 296
Hollis, Nicholas, 109, 143
Hollist:
  John, 289
  Ric., 289
Holloway, John, 241
Hollys, Gervas, xlvi
Holmes:
  Jonathan (1794), 300
  Owen (1792), 299
  Sam., 254
  Stephen, 173
Holship, Wm (1812), 303–4
Holwell, John Wm, 286
Honnor, Isaac (1727), 179, 274, 276
Hook, John, 272
Hoole, John (1768), lix, 285–6
Hooper, Edw. Giles:
  admitted (1705), 268; auditor, 34–5, 42 bond up, 139; chambers, 118, 127; loan by, 95
  Giles (1675), 241, 259–60

Hooper—*continued*
  Jas, 297
  Sam., 284, 289
Hooton, Edw. (1683), 261–2
Hope:
  Chas (1686), 263–6
  John: admitted (1717), 271; auditor, 65, 68; bond up, 93
Hopkins, Thos (1757), 281
Horne, Ric., 274
Horsman, Edw., 5
Horwell, Thos (1686), 263
Horwood, R., xliii–xliv
Hossack, Jas, 282
Hough:
  (?), 251
  John jun. (1658), 251
Houghton:
  Jas, 276
  Jas (1793), 299
Houlding, Nath., 270
Howe: Thos, 253
  Wm (1662), 253
Howse, Robt, 300
Huddleston, Baron, lxii
Hudleston, Ferdinando, 266
Hugbon, Wm (1768), 285
Hughes:
  Edw. Arthur (1876), 310
  Henry (1809), 303, 307
  Thos, 290
  Wm (1794), 300
Hull:
  Andrew (1665), 253
  — (1676), 259, 265
Hullock, John (Serjt), xxvii
Humberston, Mr, 174
Humphreys or Humphries:
  Henry (1795), 301
  Humphrey, 271
  John (1794), 300–1
  Thos: admitted (1716), 270; arrears, 99, 102, 105; chambers 23, 35, 98; pledge, 271
  Wm, 270
Hunt:
  John (1659), 251
  Rev. John, 295
  Joseph (1671), 97, 257–8, 268
  — jun.: admitted (1704), 268; arrears, 35–6, 90, 139, 172; chambers, 96–97
  Thos, 274
  — Henry Carew, liv, 310
Hunter:
  Fredk, 305
  Wm (1823), 305
Hurnell, John, 286
Hurst:
  John, 253
  Thos (1717), 136, 180–1, 210, 271
Hussey:
  Ignatius (1718), 76, 271

Hussey—*continued*
  Joseph Wood (1789), 296
  Thos (Serjt.), 186
Hutchins, Hassall, 287
Hutchinson:
  (?), 250
  Thos (1785), 294, 303
  Wm, 239, 251, 253, 256
Hutton:
  Chas (1778), 290
  Thos (1786), 294
Hyde:
  Humphrey (1717), 56, 111–13, 271
  Jas (1761), 282
Hyett:
  Benj. (1706), 268
  Chas, 268

Ingelow, John (1793), 299
Innys:
  Andrew (1693), 28, 164, 265–6, 269
  Martin (1693), 18, 105, 115, 165, 266
Inskip, John (1787), 295
Ireland, Ric. (1792), 298
Irving, John, 288
Ives:
  Fras (1660), 252
  Joseph, 287
Ivye, Geo. (1694), 266, 268

Jackson:
  Edw., 135
  Fras: admitted (1715), 270; arrears, 55, 112, 128, 130, 153, 172, 185; chambers, 12, 25
  Henry (1783), 293–4
  John (1685), 262
  — jun., 285
  Mr, 236
  Thos (1769), 285
  Wm (1723), 128, 181, 273
Jaffray, Henry (1771), 286
Jagoe, Edw. (1687), 263
James II, King, 241
James:
  Evan (1761), 282
  Robt jun., 285
  Sir Henry, A. G., lxiii
  Thos (1691), 265
  — (1776), 289
  — (1787), 295–6
Janney, John (1769), 285
Jaques:
  Edw. (1689), 264
  John, 268
  Robt, 295
Jeddere, Solomon, 278
Jefferies, Wm, xxx
Jeffrey:
  Barth., 273
  John (1686), 20, 263
Jefferys, Thos (1768), 285
Jellico, Wm (1787), 294

Jenkins:
  Abell, 287, 291
  John, 274
Jenner, Thos, xxxi
Jennings, David, 282
Jenyns, Jas, xxxi, 155
Jessel (M. R.), lxiv
Johnson:
  Edw. (1724), 124, 127–8, 139, 272–3
  Fras (1659), 251, 253
  Henry (1778), 290
  — (1865), 309
  John, 295
  Joseph, 152
  Matthew, 237, 239
  Maurice (1684), xlvii, 45, 66, 262–3
  — jun., 90, 262, 269
  Ric. (1732), 275
  Samuel, Dr, lix, 280, 285, 292
  Thos (1781), 291
  Warren (1737), 276
  Wm, 309
Jolland, Geo. jun. (1673), 43–4, 258, 263, 268
Jones:
  Edw. (1657), 250
  —, 300
  Geo., 284
  Henry (1664), 254
  — (1669), 257
  —: admitted (1721), 272; Ancient, 192; auditor, 151, 154, 193, 195, 206; loan by, 209–11; pledge, 273; proposed for Principal, 198–9
  — (Houndsditch), 292
  — (Mansion House St), 302
  Joseph (1794), 300
  Lewis (1721), 181, 272
  Ric. (1783), 291–2
  — (1827), 306
  Thos (Westminster), 282
  — (Bloomsbury), 289
  Wm, 282
Jopson, John, 297
Jordan, Henry, 295
Jorden, Humphrey (1731), 204, 275
Jowett:
  Joseph, 296
  Josiah (1787), 295
Judge, Jas (1705), 268

Kavanagh, Thos (1791), 298
Kecke, Sam., 250, 255
Keele, Thos (1685), 262
Keelinge or Kelynge:
  Ric.: admitted (1709), 269; arrears, 34, 77, 103, 124, 146, 173, 180–1, 193; retires, 193
  Thos (1719), 182, 272
Kellett:
  (?), 250
  Edw., xlix

Kellett—continued
  Fras, xi, xliv, 218, 257: dispute with Inn, xlvii–xlix, pledge, ? 250, 257
  Maurice, xlix
Kelynge. See Keelinge
Kemble, John, lvii
Kendall:
  Bernard (1656), liv, 250
  John (1869), 309–10
Kennedy:
  Arthur (1879), 310
  Thos, 294
Kentish, Fras, 276
Kerchivalli, Antony (1670), 257
Kerwan, Robt, 304
Kettleby:
  Ric. (1711), 270
  Robt Johnston (Serjt), 186
Keylway, Ric., xlvii
Kiddell, Henry, 284
Kidgell, John (1660), 252
Kilner:
  Jas (1780), 291
  Thos (1790), 297
Kinaston, Wm (1677), 259
King:
  Abraham (1783), 293
  Chas (1768), 285
  Degory (1715), 13, 270
  Edw., 294
  Harman, 51
  Jas, 284
  Ric. (1790), 297
  Wm Barfoot, 292
Kinsley, Wm, 279
Kirke:
  Robt jun. (1753), 280, 287
  — sen., 280
Kirwan. See Kerwan
Kitchin, Geo., 274
Knapp, Hambly, 307
Knight:
  John, 253
  —: admitted (1699), 266; auditor, 15, 34, 55, 59, 111–12; chambers, 6, 36–7, 47–8, 110, 134, 159; loan by, 66, 132; Seabrooke's accounts, 83
  — (Hammersmith), 290
  — (1783), 293
  Raleigh, 90
  Sarah, 132, 134, 160
Knighton, Ric. (1658), 251, 256
Knipe, Thos (1765), 284
Kniveton, Henry, 237
Knowler, John, 194
Knowles, Henry (1766), 285
Knype, Thos (1668), 256–7
Kynaston, Arthur (1708), 269

Lacey:
  Jas, 295
  Thos (1774), 288
Lacy, Thos (1838), 307

Lake:
Arthur (1677), 29, 241, 259, 262, 269
Chris.: admitted (1714), 270; arrears, 102, 125, 128, 140; Callow's bill, 17; chambers, 96–7; oversea, 140
Thos, 271
Lally, Jas, 274
Lamb, Jas, 285
Lambert, John (1760), 282
Lamborn, Jas, 276
Lamplugh, John (1700), 17, 50–1, 57–8, 267–8
Lan (?Lau), Christian (1752), 280, 282
Lancaster, Mathew (1731), 166, 275
Lander:
Chas, 282
Wm (1759), 282
Lane:
Edw., 259
Henry (1678), 259, 261, 264–5
James jun. (1658 and 1660), 251–3
John (1685), 262
Thos, 299
Wm (1661), 253
Langdale, Geo. (1752), 280–1
Langdon, Luke, 272
Langford:
Henry, 255
John (1666), 255
—, 280
— (murdered), xli
Langley:
Humphrey, 306
Leigh, lv, 128
Wm Henry (1826), 306–7
Langston:
Anthony, xlvii, 228–9
John (1669), 256
Peter, 256
Thos (1682), 260
Lannyng, Ric. (1671), 257
L'Archevesque, John (1760), 282
Larkham, John (1794), 300
Latimer, Jas, 272
Lau.   See Lan
Laurie, John (1790), 297
Laver, John, 297
Lawes, John, xlvii, 12–13, 15, 22, 25–6, 38, 66
Lawrance, Geo., 301
Lawrence, Robt (1669), 256
Lawson:
Henry (1680), 260
Jas (1734), 214–15, 276
Sir Wm, 260
Leach or Leech:
Geo. (1699), 266
Jas, 291
Wm, 132
Leacock, Wm (1795), 301
Leake or Leeke:
Robt (1664), 254–5, 257
Thos, 197

Lee:
Chris., 303
David Jones (1838), 307
Geo. (1685), 262
Dr John, lxii
Jonathan (1688), 264
Robt (1796), 301
Wm (1689), 264–5
— (1697), 266
Leech. See Leach
Leeke. See Leake
Legh, Thos (1684), 261, 263
Leicester, Earl of, xxv
Leigh:
Thos (1749), 279
Mr (butler), 240–1
Leonard, Patrick Marcellinus, 309
Lethbridge, Thos (1721), 141, 272
Letherland, John, 90
Lethieullier:
Pitt (1756), 281
Wm (1731), 167, 275
Leverland, Wm (1731), 194, 275
Levinge:
Fras (1658), 251
Thos, 251
Levis, Leuis or Lewis:
Maurice, 275
Ric. (1685), 262
Leycester, Hugh, 300
Limbrey:
Chas (1733), 173, 275
Ric. (1724), 147, 273
— jun., 275
Lindeman:
John (1770), 286
Wm (1763), 283, 286
Lister:
(?), 251
Geo. (1789), 296
Wm (1691), 265
Little, Wm (1675), 259
Littleney, John (1794), 300
Livett, John (1767), 285
Llewellin:
Henry jun. (1803), 303
— sen., 303
Lloyd:
Talbott (1692), 265
Thos (1732), 185, 275, 277
—, 295
Locke:
Sam., 304
Thos, 304
Loney:
Joseph Sparshott (1782), 292
Thos, 292
Long:
Giles (1772), 287
Henry Mynors (1769), 286
John (1771), 286
— Chas, 287
Thos, 283

Longcroft, Chas Needham (1875), 309
Longfellow, Mr, 202
Love, Andrew (1705), 94, 150, 178, 268
Lowe:
  John, 253
  — (1789), 296
Lowndes, Edw. (1780), 291
Lowth, Ric. (1683), 2, 3, 147, 253, 260, 268
Loyd, Henry (1739), 277
Luff, Nicholas, 292
Luke:
  Humphrey (1684), 261
  Sir Sam., 261
Lunel, John, 283
Lunn, Halmer (1671), 257
Luss, John, 234
Luxmoore, Chas, 291
Lye, Nath. (1707), 77, 269
Lynn, Geo., 253
Lyon, Thos (1876), 310
Lyster, Ric., 283
Lyte, Thos (1719), 181, 272

Macara, Robt (1791), 298
McBeath:
  Mary, 306
  Wm John (1830), 306
McCarthy, Dennis (1786), 294
Macclesfield, Lord, 4
McCormick, Chas (1791), 298
McCreery, Alex. Jaques (1822), 305
Macdonnel, David Evans (1789), 297
McGhie, Willoughby (1822), 305
Machon, Wm, 301
Mackay:
  Geo. (1780), 291
  John jun. (1727), 182, 189, 274
Mackdowall, Thos, 278
MacKinnon, Sir F. D., viii, xiv, xxvii
Madden, Jas (1754), 280
Madgwick, Thos (1723 and 1727), 118, 158, 249, 273–4
Maidwell. *See* Maydwell
Maitland:
  Frederic Wm, ix, xv, xxvii
  Pelham (1834), 307
  — Thos, 307
Malim, Wentworth, 302
Mallory, Fras (1691), 265
Manby:
  Edw. (1730), 152, 177, 275
  Robt, 275
Mander:
  Chas John (1866), lii, 309
  Thos (1731), 168, 275
Marlove, Joseph, 286
Manning, John (1797), 302
Mansfield:
  Isaac, 276
  Lord, xvi
  Timothy (1735), 276

Manwaring, Andrew (1677), 259
Marchant:
  Henry jun. (1821), 305
  — sen., 305
  Jarman, 276
Markeland, xi
Markwicke, Wm (1661), 252
Marriott, Will (1687), 92, 264
Marshall:
  John, 289
  Joseph, 287
  Mr, 189, 202
  Peter (1780), 291
  Ric., 276
  Wm (1794), 300
Martin:
  John, 295
  — (Sloane St), 304
  Robt, 284
  Thos (1766), 284
  Wm (1795), 301
Maseres, Baron, 290
Masfen, Jas (1762), 283
Maskell, Nicholas, 285
Mason:
  Jas, 281
  John, xlvi
  —: admitted (1730), 275; arrears, 175, 182, 188, 197; bond up, 197
  Nash: admitted (1726), 273; Ancient, 201; auditor, 173, 175, 207, 213; chambers, 204; deputy Principal, 216–17; executor, 205; loan by, 209–11; pledge, 275
  Nath. (1797), 302
  Robt (1760), 282
Masrey, Chas (1749), 279
Masterman:
  Henry (1705), 41, 164, 268
  — (1731), 275
  Stephen (1743), 278
Masters, Wm (1788), 296
Maugham, Robt, xxxi
Maundrell:
  Henry (1787), 295
  Robt (1787), 294–5
Maw:
  Abdy, 292
  Ric. (1780), 291
  Robt (1783), 292
Mawer, Thos, 275
May, John, 288
Maydwell:
  Godfrey, xlvi, 151, 232–3
  Thos Moore (1808), 303
Mayer, John, 283
Maynard, Wm (1685), 262
Mayow:
  Mayow-Wynell, 298
  Philip Wynell Wynell (1791), 298
Meakins, Thos (1663), 253
Mears, Wm, 274
Meighen, Ferdinando (1656), 250

Mence, Ric. (1709), 28, 53, 61, 117, 269
Merifield or Merrifield:
    Geo., xxxvii, 232–3, 234–6, 255
    Thos, 278
Metcalf:
    Chris., 291, 293
    Thos (1777), 289
Methuen, Robt, 285
Metingham, Sir John de, xvi
Middlemore, Ric. (1659), xiv, 240–1, 251, 254, 256
Middleton, Thos, lxi
Midson, Bolton, 293
Milbourne, Ralph (1668), 256
Millen, Wm John, 285
Miller:
    Humphrey, 121, 141
    Joseph, 301
    Thos (1728), 184, 274
    — (1747), 279, 280
Millington, John, 254
Mills:
    Fras, 272
    Wm (1742), 278
Milwarde:
    John (1657), 250, 255, 263
    Robt (1686), 44, 263–4
    Thos, 263
Mitchell, Thos (1770), 286
Moles, John, 300
Monger, Peter (1722), 94, 133
Moody:
    John (1766), lviii, 285
    — (1779), lviii, 291–2
Moore (see also More):
    Adrian, 69
    Edgworth (1790), 297
    Frank (1781), 291
    Jas, 272
    Robt (1684), 44, 89, 261
Mordaunt, John Wilkins (see also Wilkins) (1722), 273
More:
    Dagge, 286
    (?) Sir Thos, xxii
Morgan:
    Hugh (1747), 279
    Maurice, 281
    Rev. Wm., 303
Morley, Hildebrand (1778), 290
Morphy, Wm (1726), 165–6, 274
Morrett, Wm (1792), 299
Morris:
    Chas (1791), 298
    John, 274
    Stephen (1683), 261
    Thos, 284
    Wm (1717), 56, 271
Morse:
    Edw., 268
    Robt, 253–4
Mortimer, Thos (1772), 287

Morton, Jas, 279
Moseley, Arthur, 79
Mott, Thos, xxxi, 298
Motteram, Jas (1678), 259, 265
Mouteney, Edw. (1775), 288–9
Mowting, Jas (1685), 262
Moxon, Robt, 274
Moyle, 231
Mudd, John (1664), 254
Muddock, Robt (1793), 300
Mullachy, Wm, 301
Mulso, Hester, 280
Munday, John, 252
Munden, Joseph Sheppard (1796), lviii, 301
Mundy:
    Edw. (1708), 8, 92, 269
    Fras jun. (1708), 8, 92, 269
    — sen., 269
Murray, Oliver Jas (1779), 290
Muston, John (1656), 250
Myatt, Jas, 275
Myers:
    Joseph Hart, 300
    Simon Hart (1794), 300

Nares, Geo., 211
Naylor, Luke, 302
Neeld:
    Joseph (1791), 298
    — jun. (1810), 304
Nelson:
    Sam., 260
    Wm, 291
Nelthorpe:
    Geo., 293
    Henry (1717), 56, 77, 99, 271
Nettlefold, Wm (1820), 305
Nettleton, John (1710), 50, 269
Neville, Thos (1778), 290
Newby, Wm (1789/, 297
Newland or Newlands:
    John, 283
    Wm, 188
Newnham, Henry, 263
Newton:
    Geo. (1793), 299
    Wm, 275–6
Nicholas, Philip (1682), 260
Nicholl:
    Geo., 300
    Thos, 275
Nicholls or Nix:
    Thos (1664), 254
    — (1685), 262
Nicholson, Wm, 253
Nicoll, Joseph (1721), 158, 272
Noell:
    Edw. (1664), 254, 256
    Wm, 212
Norborn, Fras (1688), 264
Norcutt, Dan. (1774), 288

Norris:
  Geo., 289
  Thos, 297
North:
  Edw. (1686), 263
  Fras, xxviii, xxx
  Henry (1811), 304
  Hugh (1663), 253–4
  John, 109
  Roger, xxviii, xxx, liii, lv
  Sir Henry, 263
Norton:
  Jas (1734), 276
  Wm (1668), 256
Nott, Edw., 303
Nowell, Chas, 293
Nowland, Jas (1791), 298
Noyes:
  Peter (1672), 258
  Wm (1691), 265, 273
  — jun. (1724), 137, 148, 169, 173, 175, 273
Nugent:
  Nicholas, 290
  Robt, 294
Nuthall, Thos, 41, 267

Oakley, Benj., 297
Obrian, Wm, 173
Offley, Wm (1769), 286
Ogilby, John, xliii
Oglander, 251
Okeshott, Benj. (1662), 253
Old:
  Robt (1781), 291
  Wm, 291
Oldershaw, John (1676), 93, 259
Oldfield:
  Thos (1667), 256
  —, 284
Oldshaw (*see also* Oldershaw), 240
Orridge:
  Robt (1856), 308
  Wm, 308
Osbaldeston, John (1756), 281
Osborne:
  Benj. (1689), 264
  Geo. (1677), 259
  John, 269
Osgood:
  John (1734), 205, 276
  — (1757), 281
Owen:
  Edw. (1687), 70, 264
  Wm, 295

Pacey or Pacey:
  Henry (1706), 70, 268–9
  — Butler (1729), 172, 274, 281
  John (1657), 251
  — (1759), 281, 287–9
  Ric., 272
  Wm (1719), 70, 122, 272
Page, Ric., xlv

Pain, Edw. (1692), 265
Paley, Thos (1690), 264
Palmer:
  Benj. (1686), 260, 263
  Edw. jun. (1657), 250, 255, 257
  — sen., 250
  Geo. (1678), 260, 263
  Joseph, 278
  Thos (1670), 257
  — (1789), 297
  — (serjt), 183
  Wm (1770), 286, 292
Paltock:
  John, 273
  Robt (1722), lviii, 159, 273
Pape, John, 290
Papps, Geo., 287
Pardoe, Robt (1742), 277
Pare, Wm (1787), 295
Parke:
  Jas (1746), 208, 278–9
  Ric. (1714), 71, 145, 270
Parker:
  Geo., 274
  Henry (1792), 298, 301
  Joseph, 254
  Nicholas (1667), 256
  Sir Thos, L.C.J., 4, 5
  Thos, 255
  —, 267
  — (Serjt), 186
  — (1771), 286
  — (Wood St.), 303
  Wm (1669), 256, 264
  — Harris (1818), 304
Parkinson:
  Fredk Kidner (1857), 308
  Jas, 308
Parmire, John (1762), 283
Parrey, Robt (1790), 297
Parry:
  Andrew (1776), 288
  John, 288
Parsons, Sam., 304
Partridge, Jas (1658), 251
Paston, Edw. (1690), 264
Pate, Wm (1753), 280
Paterson, Robt (1779), 290
Patterson:
  Jas Hartley, 303
  Wm Fras (1809), 303
Pavey, Wm jun., (1719), 73, 97, 103, 272
Pawson, Sam., 284
Payn, John, xxiii
Peach:
  Edw. (1769), 286–7
  Geo., 163, 184
Peachey, Ric. (1668), 256
Pearse:
  Rev. Offspring (1771), 287
  Ric. (1690), 265
Pearson:
  Geo., 288

Pearson—*continued*
 Thos (1775), 288
 — jun., 307
Peart:
 G., 56
 John (1717), 135, 176, 194, 271
 Joshua (1733), 176, 179, 190, 275
 Robt: admitted (1707), 269; arrears, 54, 76, 135; chambers, 174, 176
Peckham:
 Thos (1666), 255
 — (1688), 264
Pegge:
 Chris., xlvi
 — (1661), 252
 Edw., 252
 Mr, 236
Peirce. *See* Pierce
Pelham:
 Humphrey: admitted (1715), 270; auditor, 55, 60; chambers, 13–14, 116; death, 128
 John, 128, 270
Peltier, Philip Elias (1731), 173, 275
Pennell, Wm (1661), 24, 252
Penny:
 Edw., 292
 John: admitted (1701), 267; accounts, xxxvi, 154, 162, 165, 169, 173, 175, 185, 191, 193, 195; auditor, 15, 34–5, 42, 82, 106, 111–12, 126, 129, 141–2; certifies Reading, xxxi, 155; chambers, 31; deputy Principal, 92; Dottin's compensation, 59; fire insurance, 158; loan by, 66, 94–5, 114, 136; murder, xiii, xli, 197, 267; payments by 55, 79; Principal, 137, 179, 267, 274; settles bills for pews, 130
Perkins, Thos:
 admitted (1741), 277; auditor, 198, 201; pledge, 278; steward, xl, 200
Perrott:
 Geo. (Reader), 216
 John (1749), 279
 Wm (1760), 282
Perry:
 Hugh, 230
 Jas (1782), 292–4, 296
Peters:
 Jas (1725), 141–2, 273
 John, 274
Peterson:
 John, 299
 Robt (1793), 299
Petre, Geo. (1729), 157, 169, 177–8, 274
Pettye, Mr, xi
Petyt, Wm, xxxvii, 241–2
Phelps, Wm (1747), 279
Philipps, Robt, 275
Phillipps:
 Erasmus (1769), 286
 Owen (1791), 297
 Sam. (1662), 253

Phillipps—*continued*
 Stephen Howell, 304
 Thos, 253
 —, 296
 Vaughan (1769), 286
Pick, Capell (1766), 285
Piddock, Thos (1685), 262
Pierce or Peirce, John (1723), 151, 273
Piercy, Sam. (1838), 307
Pigott:
 (?), xxii
 Ralph (1717), 56, 126, 132, 271
Pindar, Peter, lix, 296
Pitcher, Thos (1800), 302
Pitt:
 John (1753), 280
 Wm, 271
Platel or Platell:
 Geo. (1809), 303
 Wm (1780), 291
Platt, John jun. (1785), 293
Plaxton, Wm (1749), 279
Player, Sam. (1672), 258
Playter, Lionel, 272
Pleydell, John (1689), 264–6
Pococke, Ric. (1660), 252, 256
Pogson, John, 269
Polkett, John, 254
Pollard, Robt, 276
Pollen, Edw. (1725), 121, 155–6, 273
Pollexfen, John (1731), 184, 275
Pollock:
 Chas, 294
 Sir Fredk, xvi
Pool, Thos, 296
Poole:
 Chas Paris (1832), 306–7
 Geo., 300
 Jas (1794), 300
 — Minifie, 306
Popham, Stephen, 288
Port, John, 291
Potts:
 Joseph (1773), 287
 Wm, Capt, 287
Powell:
 Edw., 301
 Foster (1761), 249, 282, ?286
 — (1765), 249, 284, 286
 Jas, Dr, 304
 John (1658), 251
 Judge, lxiii, 126
 Mr (tools), 140
 Ric., xlix
Power, Thos, 17, 262, 264–5, 267–8
Powle, John (1694), 266
Powlett:
 Alice, 110
 Robt: admitted (1688), 264; arrears, 139; Callow's accounts, 35; chambers, 51, 57–8, 110; Dottin's compensation, 59; Lamb Inn Yard dispute, 65

Powlett—*continued*
 Thos (1724), 173, 273, 276–7
 Wm: admitted (1718), 271; Ancient, 180–1; auditor, 191; chambers, 110, 173; pledge, 273
Pratt, Thos, 197, 203
Prescott, Jas, xlvii, 232–3
Presser, John (1783), 293
Prevost or Provost, Peter (1747), 212, 279
Price:
 Henry Foley (1787), 295
 Jas Glenie (1866), xxxviii, 309
 John (1678), 260
 — (1741), 277
 Liscombe, 293
 Ric., 4, 5
 Robt (Serjt), 186
 Thos (1772), 287, 289
Prichard. *See* Pritchard
Priestman, John (1782), 292
Prigg, Sam., 270
Prince:
 John (1690), 265
 Sam. (Serjt), 186
Pritchard:
 John, 280
 — (1773), 287
 Joshua Jones (1770), 286, 288, 290, 294
 Thos Fras (1780), 291
 Wm, 307
Proutt, John (1739), 277
Provost. *See* Prevost
Prowse, Geo., 272
Pryce:
 Chas (1742), 278
 Josiah (1829), 306
Pryor:
 Thos, 30, 73, 82, 262
 Mr, 241
Pudney, John Jas, 291
Pulling, Serjt, lxii
Pulter, Wm (1683), 261
Purcell:
 Ric.: auditor, 7, 42, 162, 165; rent, 14
 Wm: admitted (1708), 269; auditor, 15, 34; chambers, 3, 149, ?243; dues, 62
Purnell, John (1688), 264
Purtell, Ric. (1684), 262
Pyefinch, Geo. (1787), 295

Quadring, Robt (1677), 259
Quaill, Jas (1735), 195, 276
Quarles, Wm (1834), 307

Radcliffe:
 Wm (1786), 294
 Wyndham Benj. (1790), 297
Raffyn, Wm (1657), 250
Railton, Thos Taylor, 295
Ramsby, John, 259
Rasen (*and see* Raysen), Geo. (1665), 254

Rawlins (*and see* Rawlyns):
 Benj., 270
 John (1661), 252
 Serjt, 253
Rawlinson, Wm, 274
Rawlyns, Sam. (1663), 253
Raymond, Wm jun. (1729), 274
Rayson (*and see* Rasen):
 Geo. 255–6
 Ric. (1665), 255
Read, Fras (1657), 250
Reading, Joseph, 281
Readinge, Geo., xlv
Redaway:
 Geo. (1817), 304
 Thos Matthew, 304
Redhead, John (1765), 284
Redit, Jas (1784), 293
Reed, John (1782), 292
Rees, Hopkin, 282
Reeve:
 Joseph, 281
 Wm (1685), 23–4, 262
Reeves:
 Jas (1792), 299
 Pelsant, 212
Reilly, Jas (1814), 304
Remen or Reman, Peter (1764), 283
Rendall:
 Chas, 308
 Simon (1842), 308
Reynolds:
 Fras, 273
 John, 293
 Ric. (1783), 293
Rhode, Casten, 288
Rhodes:
 Chas Henry, 306
 Derby, 162, 193
Ricard, Arthur jun. (1773), 287
Rich:
 Chris, 276, 281
 — Mosyer (1758), lviii, 281
 Edw. (1729), 178, 274
 John, 281
Richards:
 Geo., 306
 Lewis (1744), 278
 Wm (1661), 252, 254–5
Richardson:
 Thos (1666), 255
 Sir Thos, 126
 Wm, 293
Richmond, John (1705), 41, 268
Rickards:
 Arthur, 265
 Geo. (1691), 265
Ridding, Wm (1791), 298–9
Ridgway, John (1791), 298
Rigge, Wm (1779), 288
Ritson, Robt, 274
Roach. *See* Roch.

Robert:
  Chas, 289
  Jas (1776), 289
Roberts:
  Humphrey, 288
  Wm (1773), 287
Robins, Wm, 299
Robinson:
  Alex. (1688), 264
  Geo. (1753), 280
  John (1734), 276
  Michael, 290
  Paige (1683), 261
  Ric. 261–2, 264
  Sam. (1665), 255
  Thos, xlix
Robson, Dr R., lvi
Roch:
  Robt, 277–8, 281, 283
  Sam., 100, 280
Rochester, Robt (1735), 276
Rocque, John, xliii
Roe, John (1780), 291
Roebuck, Thos (1690), 264
Rogers:
  Ann, xlix, 238
  Frances, xlix, 238–9
  Henry, xxxv, 110
  Jas (1683), xlix, 261
  John, 256
  Mr (lecturer), 18
  Mrs, 238
  Thos (1699), 266, 268
  — (1780), 291
  Wm (1667), 255–6
Roland, John (1666), 255, 259, 262
Roles, Thos (1753), 279, 280
Rolt, Ric. (1753), 280
Romaine, John (1786), 294
Rooke:
  John, 297
  Mortimer, liv, 310
Rooks, Wm, 287
Room:
  Wm (1733), lvii, 196, 275
  — (1736), lvii, 181, 276
Roome, Thos, 279
Roper, Fras (1738), 189, 195, 276
Rose, John (1791), 298
Ross:
  Geo., 301
  Wm, 302
Rous:
  Fras (1683), 240, 261
  Jas, 240, 256, 259
  Thos, 261
Rowley:
  Thos, 273, 278
  — (1737), 276
Rowlin, Robt (1676), 259
Rowse (*see also* Rous), Jas (1661), 240, 253
Rudall or Rudhall, Thos (1803 and 1817),
    303–4

Rudge, Wm (1683), 261, 263–4, 266
Rule, Geo., 302
Russell:
  John, 291
  Sam. (1686), 263, 265
Ryan, Anthony (1740), 206, 214, 277
Ryley, John, 270

Sackfield, Anthony, 277
Sadler, Sam., 275
Salter, Ric., 272
Samuel:
  John, 287
  Ric. (1772), 287
Sandcroft, Chas, 275–6
Sander, John, 294
Sanderson, Geo., 284
Sandon, Huxley (1784), 293
Sandys:
  John (1722), 125, 128, 162, 272
  Miles (1684), 261
Saunders, Wm (1674), 258
Savage, John (1663), 254
Savours, Robt, (1781), 291
Saward, Michael (1666), 255
Saxby, Henry (1728), 178, 274
Saxelbye, Edw. (1780), 291
Saylor, Michael, 290
Scarr, Wm, 289
Scott:
  Jas (1722), 181, 272
  John (1687), 263–4
  Philip (1766), 284
Scrimshire:
  John, 250
  Wm (1657), 250
Scriven, John (1800), 302
Scroggs, Sir Wm, lxiii, 126
Seabrooke, Wm:
  admitted (1723), 273; accounts, 83;
    lease, 107–8; new buildings, xlvii,
    66–7, 83, 85–6, 107–8, 152
Seard, Wm (1661), 253
Secker, Edw. (1667), 256
Sedgwick, Sam., 286
Selby:
  Ric. (1787), 295, 299
  Thos (1814), 304
  Wm (Reader), 211
Selden, John, ix, xix, xxix
Sells, Thos, 152, 275
Senior, Bernard, 307
Serjeant, John (1656), 250
Serle, John (1673), 258
Settree:
  Jas, 286
  Joseph (1762), 249, 283, 285
  — (1770), 249, 286
Seward, Isaac (1685), 262
Sewell, David, 297
Seymour, Chas (1776), 289
Shallow, Robt, lvi

Shaw (*and see* Shawe):
  Henry, 289
  Robt (1771), 286, 291, 302
  Thos Hurnall (1799), 302
Shawe, Thos (1664), 254
Shearman, John (1794), 300
Sheldon, Hugh (1725), 122, 159, 273
Shelley, Tymothie (1658), 251
Shelton, Mr (Reader), 251
Shene, Jas Hayward (1783), 293
Shepard or Shepherd, Chas (1781), 289, 291, 293
Sheppard or Shepperd:
  Ric.: admitted (1717), 271; arrears, 76, 95, 111; bond, 158; chambers, 37, 47–8; death, 172
  Thos, 295
Shering, John (1775), 288
Sherman, John (1677), 259
Sherratt, Jas (1674), 19, 258, 260
Shiers, Henry, 299
Shipton, Wm (1791), 298
Shore, Patrick (1666), 255–6
Shorte, Darell (1707), 41, 269
Shorter, Stephen (1787), 295
Shortney, Ric., 296
Shuckburgh, John, lv, 276
Shuckforth:
  Thos, 122, 261
  — jun. (1713), 151, 270, 272
Sieven, Chris. 295
Silk, Jas Wm (1818), 304
Simpkins, Wm (1789), 296
Simpkinson, Roger, 285
Simpson:
  John (1842), 308
  Robt (1750), 279
Sitwell, Wm (1686), 263–4
Sivewright, Jas, 298
Skipper, Wm (1770), 286
Skrene, Wm (Serjt), xix
Skurray, Stephen, 273
Slack, John (1676), 259, 261–2
Slann, Wm (1788), 296
Sloper:
  (?), liv, 250
  Chas, 250
  Robt, 250, 259
  — (1690), 265
  Thos (1656), 250
  Walter, 250–1, 254, 256
Smart:
  Chas (1772), 287
  Sam. (1692), 265
Smeetham, Henry (1780), 291
Smith:
  Augustus Delanney (1868), 309
  Brightwell: admitted (1717), 271; auditor, 82, 126, 173, 175; bond up, 189; chambers, 77; clerk, xl, 132–3; pledge, 273, 275; represents Mrs Barras, 189; resigns, 172

Smith—*continued*
  Chas, 301
  Edw. Hart (1857), 308–9
  Fras, 309
  Griffiths (1871), 309
  Jas, 108–9, 269
  —, 290
  John (1732), 172, 189, 275
  — (1763), 283–4
  — (1771), 287
  — (1785), 294
  Laine, 271
  Mr, 185
  Sir Montagu, lxii
  Nath., 49
  Philip (1721), 105, 272
  —: admitted (1724), 273; arrears, 142, 154, 166, 178
  Sarah, 65
  Sir Thos, lvi
  Thos (Beaconsfield) (1670), 257–8
  — (Newbury) (1719), 176, 271
  — (Piccadilly), 285
  — Jas, 306
  Wm (1732), 275
  — (1828), 306
  — (shoemaker), 277
Smyth:
  Nath. (1684), 261
  Thos, 181, 258
  Wm (1740), 277
Snowden, Geo. (1774), 288
Somerset, Lord Protector, xxv
Southerton, John (1738), 276
Spare, Thos (1775), 288
Sparkes:
  Edw. (1710), 269
  Joseph, 269
Spread, Rev. Chas Coote (1779), 290
Squier, Mr (*and see* Squire), 256
Squire, Arthur:
  admitted (1678), 260; bond up, 93; chambers, xlvii, 46, 66; pledge, 262–4, 266; rating assessor, 241
Stacey, Mr, 242–3
Staffin, John, xlvi
Stafford:
  John (1728), 139, 274
  Wm (1759), 281
Stamford:
  Joseph (1676), 259
  Laurence, 263
Stampton, Fras, 256, 259
Stanley, Edw. (1767), 285
Stansby, John (1660), 252, 256
Stanton:
  Edw. jun. (1707), 40–1, 269
  — sen., 269
  Simon (1729), 141, 181, 274
Stapleton, Tobias (1781), lvi, 292, 296
Starling, Edw., 287

Statham:
    Sir John: admitted (1701), 267; arrears, 73; chambers, 45, 50; M.P., 267
    Thos (1674), 258, 262, 264–5, 267, 269
Staveley:
    Chris. (1685), 262
    Wm, 280
Stedman, John (1682), 250, 253
Steele, Wm, 286
Steggall, Thos (1717), 37, 40, 152, 271
Stephen, Sir Geo., xx
Stephens:
    Edw. (1688), 264, 266
    John (1769), 286
    Thos (Reader), 197
    Zachariah (1756), 281–2, 286
Stevens:
    Abraham, 280
    Ann, 174
    Edwin, 304
    Geo. 114
    Matthew, 174, 275
Steventon, Anthony, 301
Stevin, Aistroppe (1788), 296
Stewart, Jas, 283
Still, Peter (1786), 294
Stockton, John (1668), 256
Stoe, Harry, 302
Stogdon, John Cole (1875), 309
Stokes:
    John, 286
    Thos (1667), 255
    — (1688), 264
Stone:
    John, 288
    Thos (1663), 253–5, 257, 261
Straight or Streight, Wm (1786), 294
Stratford:
    Simon, 278
    Wm (1686), 71, 263–4
Stratton:
    Joseph (1726), 274
    —, 181
Stretehay, John (1676), 80, 259, 260
Stretton, Ric., xlv
Stride, John, 295
Stringer, Ric., 296, 298
Strong:
    Alex. Hale (1794), 300, 303
    Philip Thistlethwayte (1803), 303
    Wm (1761), 282–3, 286, 293–4
    — (Lincoln's Inn), 300
Stubbs:
    John (1681), 260
    — (1688), 264
    Walter: admitted (1709), 269; arrears, 34, 76, 103, 124, 146, 173, 180; bond up, 194
Stukeley, Adelard Squire (1729), 166, 176, 189, 274
Sturgeon:
    Ric. (1721), 272
    Thos, 285

Sturgis, Mr, lv, 43
Sturmy:
    (?), 251
    John (1669), 257, 259
    Thos: admitted (1658), 251; Kellett dispute, 218; payment to, 237; pledge, 257; Principal, xlviii, 259
Style:
    Philip, 259
    Wm (1677), 259, 262, 265
    —, liii
Styth, John, 278
Sulley, Dan. (1665), 255
Swaffield:
    Joseph jun. (1787), 295
    — sen., 295
Swainston:
    Ric., 285
    Wm (1766), 285
Swansby, John, 255
Swift:
    Ric. jun. (1719), 99, 272
    — sen., 271–2
    Thos (1719), 92–3, 99, 146, 271
Swindell, John (1670), 257
Symes, Andrew (1700), 267
Symonds, Thos, 299

Tadwell, John Samson (1774), 288
Tate:
    Bartholomew, 206
    John (1779), 290
Taubman:
    Thos (1725 and 1726), 121, 128, 249, 273–4
Tayler, Thos (1812), 304
Taylor:
    Dan., 288
    Geo., 305
    Henry (1786), 294
    Jas (1790), 297
    John (1821), 305
    Paul, 280
    Ric. Stephens (1867), vii, 309
    — (1882), vii, 310
    —, vii
    Robt (1701), 17, 267
    Sam. 256–7
    Thos (1656), 250
Teasdale:
    Benj. (1734), 276
    Ric. (1803), 303
Tekell, John, 285
Temple:
    Edw. (1687), 264
    family, xiv
Terry, Wm Wilkins (1781), 292
Tew, Jas, 288
Thacker, Chris., xlvi
Thackeray, W. M., lix
Thackrey, Robt (1773), 287
Thicknesse, Joseph (1675), 259
Thistlethwayte, Alex. (1763), 283

Thomas:
  Chas, 290
  David: admitted (1727), 274; Ancient,
    201; auditor, 191; loan by, 209–10;
    pledge, 276
  — jun. (1759), 282
  John (1772), 287
  — (1775), 288
  Wm, 282
Thompson:
  Thos, 272
  Wm (1803), 303
  — (1819), 304
Thorne, Prof. S. E., xvii, xxxi
Thornton:
  Benj. (1685), 262–3
  John, 253, 256
  Robt (1662), 253
Thorpe:
  John, 299
  Wm, 284
Tibson, David, xliii
Tichborne, John (1672), 134, 258
Tidmarsh, Ric. (1721), 149, 272
Tidy, John, xiv, 234
Tilden, Geo. (1690), 6, 32, 265
Till-Adam, John (1706), 88, 157, 268
Tinswood, Wm (1789), 296
Titterson, Wm (1749), 279
Todd:
  Fras (1782), 292
  Wm (1684), 262
Tomlins:
  Thos Edlyne (1791), 298
  — — (Inner Temple), xxxi
Tompset, John, 286
Tompsett, John (1852), 308
Tonstall, Barnabas (1667), 255–6
Tooke, Wm, 304
Tooth, Jas, 78
Topham, John, 300
Tothill, Bartholomew, 255
Touley, Thos, 294
Tout, Prof. T. F., xvii, xxi
Townrow, Sam. (1707), 21–2, 93, 181,
  268–9
Toy, Henry, 266
Trayton:
  Nath.: admitted (1684), 261; chambers,
    31–2; death, 31; pledge, 263
  —: admitted (1723), 272; Ancient, 192;
    auditor, 162, 165, 193, 195; chambers,
    134, 159; loan by, 209–11; Monger's
    bond, 133; Principal, 198–9; refuses
    office, 200
Trenchard, John, 241
Trevor, Thos (1721), 109, 272
Trimnell, Anne, 131, 135
Trollope, Messrs, lxiii
Trott, Baptist:
  admitted (1717), 271; arrears, 76, 95,
    111, 156, 171; chambers, 37, 47–8;
    death, 172

Truesdale:
  Thos (1673), 258, 261
  — (1708), 56, 71, 145, 269
Tufton, Thos:
  admitted (1713), 270; arrears, 125, 128;
    chambers, 156; clerk, xl, 62, 75;
    payments to, 64–5, 69, 71–3, 75–6;
    receipt, 89
Turkington, Geo. (1698), 266
Turnbull, Wm, 299
Turner:
  G. J., vii
  Geo. Sacvile (1738), 277
  John, 277
  Joseph Hatt (1770), 286
  Ric., 272
  Wm (1665), 254, 256
  — jun.: admitted (1713), 270; arrears,
    55, 71, 79, 106, 121, 125; enters Inner
    Temple, 146
Turney, Anthony, 277
Turston, Michael (1664), 254
Turton, Mr, 240
Tweedie, lxv
Twine, Edw. (1757), 115, 271
Tyler:
  Henry Fredk (1823), 305
  Ric. (1678), 259
  Sam., 259
Tyrer:
  John jun. (1662), 253
  Thos, 253
Tyson, Wm (1707), 36, 56, 105, 109, 269,
  271

Ullocke, Geo. (1684), 261
Umfrevile:
  Chas, 261
  Edw., 264
  —, 275
  Thos (1683), 261
Umney, Alfred (1815), 304
Unwin, Matthew jun. (1740), 277
Urlin or Urlyn, Simon (1669), 257–8, 264

Vale, Meredith (1782), 292
Van der Esch:
  Henry, 280
  Winde Wm (1752), 280
Vassall, Leonard (1790), 297
Vaughan:
  Geo., 266
  John (1775), 288
  Thos, 160–1
  Wm (1745), 278
Vaux:
  John (1729), 130, 170, 274
  Wm: admitted (1690), 265; arrears, 26,
    102, 115, 153; chambers, 130; pledge,
    265, 267, 272, 274
Veel, Wm, 297

Vernon:
  Bowater, 301
  Rev. Henry Garrioch (1795), 301
  John, 295
Vidal, Robt Studley (1766), 285
Vidler, P. A., lxv
Vinicomb, Thos (1784), 293–4
Vivian, John (1667), 256
Vower, Thos (1676), 259

Wadeson, Edw. Wayman (1838), 307
Wake, Mathew, 298
Wakeford, Geo. (1677), 259
Wakelin:
  Jonas (1717), 56, 158, 271
  Joseph, 181
Wakeman:
  Ric. (1662), 253–4
  Wm (1664), 254
Walcot:
  Elizabeth, 114
  Wm (1717), 32, 56, 76, 111, 113, 271
Walker:
  Benj. (1668), 256
  Chas. (1762), 283
  Edw.: admitted (1669), 257; bond up
    41; chamber, 134; pledge, 264, 268
  Fras, 276
  Humphrey (1660), 252–3
  Joseph (1722), 181, 273
  Walter (1663), 253
  Wm: admitted (1689), 264; arrears, 42,
    77; chambers, 78, 148, 174
Wall, Wm (1743), 278
Wallace:
  John, 288
  Peter (1774), 288
Wallett, John (1708), 131, 269
Walmsley, John Watson (1838), 307
Walrond, John jun. (1725), 273
Walter, Robt (1686), 263
Warcop, John, 283
Ward:
  Geo. (1685), 262
  — (1724), 131, 273
  —, 293
  Jos., 155, 173
  Joseph, 302
  Philip, 160
  Thos, 301
  — Webb (1797), 302
Warren, Mohun Cesar, 270
Washington, Ric. (1724), 273
Waterhous, Edw., xi, xviii–xix, xxiii,
  xxviii
Waterhouse, Wm (1777), 289
Waters:
  Fras (1767), 285, 290
  Sam., 272
Watkins:
  John (1730), 275
  Thos (1664), 249, 254

Watson:
  Henry (1674), 37, 152, 177, 258
  Jas, 300
  John (1664), 254
  Ric., 248
  Robt, 295
Watt, Alex. (1778), 290–1
Watts:
  Dan., 269
  Mr, 212
  Wm, 294
Way, Ric. (1758), 281
Webb:
  Dan. (1775), 287–8
  Edmund (1727), 128–9, 170–1, 274
  Henry (1857), 308–9
  John (1773), 287, 302
  Ric., 274
  — Jas, 307
  — Wm (1836), 307
  Wm (Stanhope St), 291
  — (Strand), 301
Webber, Capt John (1789), 296
Welch:
  John (1761), 282, 284, 286–7
  — jun. (1773), 287, 290
  — (1782), 292
  Wm (1797), 302
Weld, Ric. (1772), 287
Weldon, Philip (1772), 287
Wellard, Jegon (1765), 284
Weller, Wm Winter, 308
Welles, Sam. jun. (1685), 263, 267
Wells, Benj. (1777), 289
Werrey, Fras, 278
West:
  Edw., xlix
  John (1785), 294
  Wm (1764), 284
  — (1795), 301
Weston, John, 257
Westron, Geo., 278
Wharton, Lord, 257
Wheate, Geo., 179
Wheatly:
  Thos, 292
  Wm, 157, 177
Wheler:
  Fras, 291
  Rev. Wm, 291
Whiddon, Oliver (1685), 262
Whincop, Martha, 285
Whinyates, Chas (1683), 261, 264
Whishall, Jonathan jun., 272
Whishaw, Chas John (1838), 307–8
Whitaker:
  Alice, 156
  Henry, 152
Whitby, Nath. (1688), 264
Whitchurch, Ric., 277
White:
  B., 251
  Cornelius (1683), 261

White—*continued*
  Hugh (1782), 292
  John (1702), 19, 267, 270
  — (1709), 89, 150, 179, 269
  — Fras (1867), 309
  Ric. (1657), 250
  Thos (1780), 291
Whitfield, Thos, 245
Whiting, Henry, 290
Whitmore, John (1663), 252, 261
Whitner, John Rous, 305
Whitwell, Wm (1683), 260–2, 265, 267, 269
Wickham:
  Dan. (1690), 264
  Theodore (1705), 44, 268
Wigley:
  Chas, 305
  Henry Rodolph (1823), 305
Wigholm, Wm, 273
Wightwick, Chas (1739), 277
Wigzell:
  Atwood, 286
  Geo., 293
  Rev. Thos (1784), 293
Wilkins:
  John Mordant, 181
  Thos, xliii, 98–9
Wilkinson:
  Arthur (1775), 283
  Jas, 263
Willerton, Chas (1696), 266, 268
Willett, Henry (1689), 264
William III, 241
Williams:
  Reginald, 260
  Thos (1776), 289
  — (1789), 296
  — Dyer (1823), 305
  Walter (1782), 292
  Wm (1766), 284
  —, Rev. (1784), 293
Williamson:
  Geo. (1758), 281
  John (1777), 289
  Robt (1669), 256
Willie, John (1777), 289
Willis:
  Jas, 302
  Marmaduke (1799), 302
Wilsford, Ric. (1760), 282
Wilson:
  Alex, 285
  Henry (1661), 252
  Robt, 283
Windale, Wm, 288
Winde, Wm, 280
Winder:
  John (1750), 279
  Wm (1729), 182, 274, 279
Winford, Thos (1668), 256–7
Wingfield, Wm (1674), 258, 262–3, 265
Winter:
  Nehemiah (1774), 288

Winter—*continued*
  Ralph, 285
  — (1771), 286
Wintle, John (1707), 77, 269
Wirley:
  Humphrey, 253
  — jun. (1662), 253
Wise, Ric. (1814), 304
Wiseman, Chas, 295
Witham, Nath., 271
Wolcot, John (1788), lviii, 296
Woldich:
  John (1707), 10, 16, 269
  Wm, 269
Wolfe, Lewis, 303
Wolley, Thos, 255
Wolrich, xlvi
Wolsey, l
Wolstenholme, lxv
Wood (see also Woods):
  Alfred John (1871), 309
  Edw. (1761), 282
  Hatton (1777), 289
  John (1729), 181, 274
  Margaret, li
  Thos (1660), 252, 257
  — jun. (1670), 257
Woodcock:
  Elbro (1783), 293
  Thos, 293
Woodeson, Geo. (1671), 257
Woodfall, Wm, 289
Woodhouse, Fras (1687), 264
Woods:
  John, 234
  — (1674), 258
Woodward, Henry Wood (1762), 283
Woolley, Geo., 297
Worden, Geo. (1665), 255
Worgan:
  Jas (1751), 280
  John (1748), 279, 280
Worlidge, John (1685), 262
Worsley, Joseph, 277
Worth, Sam., 208
Wotton:
  Mathew, 277
  Thos (1742), 277
  Wm (1720), 80, 106, 121–2, 272
Wright:
  John (1802), 302
  — Poulding (1793), 299
  Strethill (1781), 292
  Thos (1685), 262
  — (1756), 281
  Wm (1683), 261
Wrightson:
  Michaell: admitted (1657), 250; ac-
    counts, xxxvi, 241; chambers, 8, 92;
    leases by 243–4; loans by, xxxvii, 84,
    238–9; pledge, 253; Principal, 8,
    260
  Thos, 298

Wyatt:
  Chas (1794), 300
  Edw.: admitted (1723), 273; Ancient, 201; auditor, 206; chambers, 156; pledge, 275
  Thos (1792), 299, 300
Wyche, Ric.:
  admitted (1705), 268; arrears, 28, 111, 121, 130, 147
Wynde:
  John, 286
  Sam. (1719), 138, 272
Wyne:
  Wm (1695), 266–7
  — (Serjt), 186
Wynell Mayow. *See* Mayow
Wynn, Wm (1788), 296
Wyther, John, 252

Yale, Edw. (1776), 289
Yarde:
  Ezekiel (1664), 254

Yarde—*continued*
  Gilbert (1664), 254
  Phillipe, 254
  Robt, 254
Yardley:
  Humphrey (1686), 263
  John (1660), 252
Yate, Joseph (1666), 255–6
Yates, Thos (1716), 115, 271
Yeal, Geo. (1689), 8, 264
Yeates:
  Thos jun. (1791), 298
  — sen., 298
York or Yorke:
  Edw., 276
  Jas (1787), 295
  John (1735), 214, 217, 276
Younge:
  Edw. (1705), 268
  Thos (1656), 250

Zachary, Thos (1762), 283

INDEX OF MATTERS

Abatement of dues, &c., xxxiii, 2, 240
Abjuration, Oath of, xxxviii, 192, 202, 214
Absent commons (*see also* Ancients;
    Arrears; Commons), xxxiii, 2
Abstract of deeds and writings, xi, xlix,
    lii, 141, 243
    of defaulters' bonds, xxxiii, 15
Accounts (*see also* Bills; Principal), 35
    (Callow's), 39 (Evans's), 83 (Sea-
    brooke's)
Actors admitted lviii, 276, 281, 292, 301
Admission Books (*see also* Admittances):
    Barnard's Inn, vii, lv
    Clement's Inn, viii, liv–lx, 249, 297
    Inner Temple, lv
    possible omissions or duplication, lv,
    249
    stamp duty, lix, 295
    Staple Inn, lv
Admittances (*see also* Admission Books):
    admission bond: amount, 218, 240;
    cancellation, xxxiv; duty to enter into,
    218, 225; surviving bonds, 250, 255
    building lease condition, xlv
    Christmas payment after admission, 218
    commons. *See* Commons
    fee, 125, 218
    general or special, liv, 218
    Inns of Chancery, entry from, xxiv,
    xxix
    rate of admissions, lvii, lix
    requirement of admission: generally,
        xlii, 232, 235;
        particular cases: Biddulph, Provost,
        Watt and Goodwin, 212–13;
        Longfellow, 202
        Monger, 94, 272;
        Obrian and Limbrey, 173, 275;
        Parke, Heckford, and Worth, 208,
        278;
        Roper and Marshall, 189, 202, 276;
        Trott, Haynes and Shepherd, 37, 48
Advances:
    for rebuilding Hall, l, 3–5, 48, 118; for
    rebuilding No. 14, 209–11
    individuals' loans: Blackwell's, 63,
    115–16; Brewster's 109; Carter's, 54,
    132; Dovey's, 65–6, 94, 110; Evans's,
    117; Fuller's, 124; Gibbon's, 135;
    Goodman's, 117; Gregg's, 118;
    Knight's and Halsted's, 132; Wright-
    son's, 84, 237–8
Advertisements forbidden, lix, 246
Allegiance, Oath of, xxxviii, 181, 192,
    202, 214
Amicable Contributionship, 29, 108

Ancient amity of Inner Temple:
    with Gray's Inn, xxvii
    with Clement's, Clifford's and Lyon's
    Inns, xxv
Ancient lights, xiv, xlii, 12, 100, 242, 245,
    247–8
Ancients:
    approve choice of Principal, xxxvii, 137,
    179, 190
    calling up to Ancients' table, xiii,
    xxxvii, 180–1, 192, 201, 214
    choice of, 226
    collecting arrears, xxxiii
    commons free, xxxiii, lx, 205, 245, 246
    excused absent commons, 5, 205, 245
    privilege as to chambers, xlvi, liv, 225
    seats in church, 14
    title dropped (Barnard's Inn), lxv
Angel Inn, xviii, xliv, 167, 247–8
Antiquaries, Society of, 262, 300
Apprenticii, xvi, xx, xxi
Arrears (*see also* Commons; Padlocking):
    abatement, xxxiii, 2, 240
    accounting and collection xxxii–xxxiv
    bill books examined, 61
    bonds put in suit, xxxiv, 237
    chambers forfeited for non-payment,
    232
    distraint ordered, 121, 141
    insolvent defaulters, 181
    payment: as Principal prescribes, 232;
    on return to commons, 223
Ascension Day, xiv, 246
Assignments. *See* Chambers
Attorney General and sale of Chancery
    Inns, lxiii, lxvi
Attorney, power of, xv
Attorneys (*see also* Solicitors):
    driven from Inns of Court, xx, lvii
    excused attending moots, 220
    "gentlemen", lvi, 249
    must join Inn and produce certificate,
    xxxiii, lvii
    must keep commons, lvii
    occupy Inns of Chancery, xviii, xx
    social status, xx, lvi
    statutory regulation, xiii
Auctions in chamber forbidden, lix
Audit of Principal's accounts (*see* Prin-
    cipal), xxxv–xxxvi

Babies "dropt", xiv, xli
Bailiffs' fees, xxxiv, 41
Banks:
    Bank of England, lviii, 302
    Inns' use of, xxxv

Bar:
    call to the, xvi, xix, xxix, xxx, 220
    place of, in Hall, 220
    See also Barristers
Barnard's Inn (*see also* Inns of Chancery;
    Legal Inns; Pictures):
    Admission Books, vii
    admissions to, lv, lx
    Ascension Day closing, xiv
    banking, xxxv
    economies, lxiv
    "grand company", xiv, lxv
    "grave company", xiv
    Gray's Inn hospitality, xxvi–xxvii
    last years, lxiv–lxv
    mooting discontinued, xxxi
    not at call of Serjeants, 187
Barristers (*see also* Bar; Counsel):
    in Inns of Chancery, xix, xxix
    in Inns of Court, xvi, xix
    inner and outer, xix, 220
    mooting, 220
Beating:
    butler or cook, 221, 240
    fellow-Companion, 221
Bills:
    bill books examined, 61
    bills of bricklayer, 16–17, 162; car-
        penter, 16–17; roof repairer, 234;
        smith, 36
    law charges, 17, 41
Boar's Head deeds, xi
Bonds (*see also* Admission Bonds):
    abstracting, xxxiii, 15
    butler's, xl, 246
    steward's xxxix, 200
    suing on, xxxiv, 105, 128, 237
Book of Entries, 218
Books, l, 252
Borrowing. *See* Advances
Bowling green, 230
Building leases:
    covenants, xlv
    examples, xxxv, xlv–xlvii
    Kellett's case, xlvii
Buildings (*see also* Ancient lights; Build-
    ing leases; Chambers; Fire; Hall):
    cost of repairs, lxiv
    cross building, 235
    finance, xxxv
    named after builders, xliv, xlvii
    restrictions, xlv, xlvi, 230
    Seabrooke's undertaking, 66, 85
    supervision: by Evans, 39, 50; by Sea-
        brooke, xlvii, 107, 152
    timber building, xlvii, 46
Burdens, persons with, 239
Burials, xxvi, l
Buttery, 221, 229
Butler (*see also* Porter: Servants):
    bond, xl, 246
    duties, xli, 222, 223, 229

Butler—*continued*
    pay, xl, 246
    protection, xiv, liii, 221, 240
Calendar (old and new style), 9
Cancellarie hospucia, xviii
Case-putting, xxviii, 219
Cellar-book (lost), viii, lx
Certificates of having mooted, xix, xxiv,
    xxix
    of membership of Inns of Chancery,
        xx, xxiv, xxix
    on joining Inn of Court, 61, 76, 93, 99,
        103
    proving attorney's membership of Inn,
        lvii
Chamber-pots, emptying, 236
Chambers (*see also* Buildings):
    absentees', shutting up, 222
    admission to by Principal, 221
    assignments, how far restricted, xlii–xliii,
        57, 144, 160
    coal hole, 51, 58, 69
    cost of building, xxxv
    covenants, xlii, xlv, 246
    "coving", 32
    dust hole, 100
    Earl of Clare's rights, li
    fencing between yards, 40
    grants in reversion, xliii, 235, 242
    House chambers, 236
    joining two sets, 178
    location, xliii
    occupant must be member of Inn. *See*
        Admittances
    padlocked up. *See* Padlocking
    plural holdings (double dues), xliii, 31,
        178, 181
    roof repairs, 234
    students' chambers, xx, 226
    "studies", xlv
    transfer, xiii, xlii
    vacating on joining Inn of Court, xx,
        203
    walls, no breaking of, 246
Chancery actions, xv, li, lxvi, 218
Chancery clerks, xxi
Chancery, Inns of. *See* Inns of Chancery
Charitable trusts, lxii–lxvii
Charity Commissioners, lxiii, lxv
Chester or Strand Inn. *See* Strand Inn
Children "dropt", xiv, xli
Child's Bank, xxxv
Christmas revels, liii, 218–19
Church attendance (*see also* St Clement
    Danes), 222, 229
Civil war, effect of, xxx
Clare, Earl of:
    chambers reserved for, li
    conveyance to Kellett, xliv, xlvii, xlix–l,
        239
    Holles family, li
    title to Inn, xlix, l, li

Clement's Inn (*see also* Ancients; Arrears; Butler; Constitutions and Orders; Inns of Chancery; Legal Inns; Pictures; Servants; Steward):
admission to. *See* Admission Books; Admittances.
admission to Inns of Court from, xxiv, 223
attached to Inner Temple, xxii
barristers at, xix, lx, 221
Black Boy statue, viii, lxiii
buildings and chambers. *See* Building Leases; Buildings; Chambers
cellar book, viii, lx
certificates of membership and mooting, xxiv, xxix
church. *See* St Clement Danes
"Clement's Inn prize", lxiv
Clifford's Inn precedence dispute, xvii
courts and staircases, xliii–xlv
early history, 1
feoffees, xv
finance, xxxv
Fortescue a feoffee, xviii
hospicium for men of the law, 1, 218, 232
last years, lxiii
laymen joining, lvii
members: leaving off practice, lvii; list of, viii, xv, 87, 249; numbers of, xv, lix, lx. *See also* Companions
mooting, xxxi
New Inn, disputes with, 11–12, 242, 244
offences at, liii–liv
Principals: admitted to Inner Temple, xxiii; elections, audit of accounts, &c. *See* Principal
Readers from Inner Temple: nomination, xxiii, xxx–xxxii; payment by, xxxii; Pension Book record. *See* Readers at Inns of Chancery
Readership prized by Inner Temple, xxv
reading neglected, xxxii
sale, lxiii, lxiv
Serjeants, attendance at call of, xiv, 186
site, xliii, 1
Taylor papers, vii, viii, xi
title to Inn, xlvii, 1, 141, 143
unincorporated, xv
vanished relics, viii, xxxvi, lx, lxiii, 126
Clement's Lane, xliv, xlv, 163–4, 183, 245
Clement's Well, 219
Clergy, xvi, lviii
Clerks: clerk or steward. *See* Steward:
clerks of Chancery, xxi
clerks of court, lvii, 220
clerk to a Counsel, xxxiv, 181
masters responsible for clerks' conduct, 236
new Serjeants' clerks, 187
Clifford's Inn (*see also* Legal Inns; Inns of Chancery):
attached to Inner Temple, xxii

Clifford's Inn—*continued*
barristers at, xix
certificates of exercises performed, xxix
disputed precedence, xvii
ceremonial at call of Serjeants, 187
"dropt" babies, xiv
fine for absence from reading of writ, xxvii
gratis admission at Inner Temple, xxiv
Minute Books, vii, xiv
offence of challenging Principal, 222
Principal's accounts and tenure of office, xxxvi, 227
Serjeant from, xix
statutes and ordinances, lii, liii, liv
steward, xxxix
Clock, xiii, 56, 244
Commons:
attorneys and clerks to keep, lvii
commoners' roll, 219
compositions for, 240
dues and arrears, xvii, xxxii–xxxiii, 219, 240
duty to be in, 222, 224–5, 228, 229
in issuable terms, xxxiii, 138
liability suspended, 16, 23, 27
misconduct when out of, 223
notice of absence from, 240
putting out of, xxxii, 181, 220
separate dues for several chambers, xliii, 31, 180
servants in commons, 224
vacation payments, 219
Companions (*and see* Ancients):
disturbing fellow-Companions, 223
limited powers, xiv, xxxvii
numbers, xv, lx
subscriptions, 56, 87
Constitutions and orders:
code, 218
dating, liii
fines and forfeitures under, lii
mooting, revels, &c., xix, liii
statutes, power to frame, 223
subject-index, lii
text and reprint, viii, xi, lii, 218
three versions, li, 218, 232
Corporation (King's law students), xv, liv
Council of Legal Education, lxiv
Counsel:
advising on mortgage, 5
attending call of Serjeants, 187
clerk to a Counsel, xxxiv, 181
see also Barristers
Court:
accomplishments, xx–xxi
court hand, xxi, xl, lv
"Inns of Court", xx
Court of Probate Act, 1857, lxii
Covenants, xlii, 31, 180, 246–7
"Coving", 32
Cross building, 235
Custom service, member joining, xxxiv, 20

Davy's Inn. *See* Thavies Inn
Denton–Bacon–Cary report, xi, xv, xxii, xxvii, xxxix, liv, lxi, 220
Deversoria, xvii, xx
Distraint. *See* Arrears
Distributions, Statute of, 179
Doctors' Commons, lxii
Doors. *See* Gates
"Dropt" children, xiv, xli
Dues (*see also* Arrears; Commons; Pensions), xxxii
 double duties order, xliii, 31, 178, 180

Early Holborn and the Legal Quarter of London, viii, xi, 1
East Indiamen, lviii, 289, 292, 295, 298–9, 300
Ecclesiastical Commissioners, lxiv
"Esquire", lvi
Essoins, 240
Excise Office, lviii
Exercises of learning (*see also* Mooting), xxvii–xxxii
 case-putting, xxvii, xxviii, 219
 evidence in Constitutions and Orders, xxvii
 imparlance, xxviii
 moots (quashing, failing, &c.), xxvii
 Readings. *See* Readers at Inns of Chancery
Expulsion:
 defaulters, 232
 Kellett, xlviii
 steward cheating the House, 224
 striking off padlocks, 237
Extra-parochial status, xiv, xxxviii, 242

Feoffees, xv, xviii
Finance of Clement's Inn, xxxv–xxxvii
 Principal: accounts of. *See* Principal; handing over balance to successor, 237
Fines, lii
Fire:
 fire plug, 50
 insurance, xv, 29, 108
 safety apparatus, &c., xiv, xli, 140, 245
Firearms, discharge of, liv
Fleet Prison, member in, xxxiv, 90
Foregate. *See* Gates
Fornication, 221
"Fountain" (Clement's Inn), 219
French language, xxviii, lii, liii, 218
Furnival's Inn (*see also* Inns of Chancery; Legal Inns):
 acquired by Lincoln's Inn, xxii
 admissions, decline of, lvi, lx
 barristers at, xix
 call of Serjeants, attending, 187
 challenge of Principal's election, xxii
 Christmas revels, liii
 early records, vii
 funeral attendance, xxvi

Furnival's Inn—*continued*
 mooting discontinued, xxxi
 orders and statutes, lii
 Principal admitted at Lincoln's Inn, xxiii
 Reader in 1408, xxiii
 record of pledges, lv
 steward, xxxix

Games, unlawful, liii, 221
Garden:
 damaging plants, &c., 221
 rails, replaced, 157
Gardener, xiv, xli, 234, 246
Gates:
 butler to shut, 223
 Clare Market gate, 104, 109, 143
 fore-gate: new, 98; re-building, 94
 "gate stead", 94
 Horseshoe Court, xliv, 246
 keys, 107, 143
 locking at night, 223, 228
 scaling walls, 223
"Gentleman", lvi, lvii, 249
Gentlemen Practisers, Society of, xiii
Goldsmith banker, xxxv, 110
Gown:
 porter's, xiii, 56
 wearing in Hall, 222
Grand Company, xiv, xxxvii, lxv, 226, 228
Grand Council, 223, 224
"Gray" family, xiv
Gray's Inn (*see also* Inns of Court; Legal Inns):
 "ancient amity" with Inner Temple, xxvii
 banking arrangements, xxxv
 Barnard's and Staple Inns attached to, xxii
 Clement's Inn men joining, 51, 76
 early history, xvii
 hospitality to Inns of Chancery, xxvi–xxvii
 index to orders, lii
 offences at, liv
 "pensions" at, vii; records of, xiii
 steward, xxxix
 Treasurer accounting, xxxvi

Hall:
 behaviour in, 222
 clock for, xiii, 56
 cloths laid in, 229
 fire insurance, 29, 109, 158
 new buildings near, 32, 37
 paving of way near, 22
 reconstruction: xxxiii, 1, 3–5; audit postponed during, 24; commons suspended during, 16, 23, 27; damage to adjoining chambers, 29, 59; financing, xxxv, 1, 3–5, 48, 118; supervised by Evans, 39
 site, xliv, 1, 4, 100–1

Hand-in-Hand Fire Office, 29, 158
Handwriting, xiii, xl, lv
Head, covering, in Hall, 222–3
Hearth money, 240
Home Secretary, lxv
Horseshoe Court, xiv, xliv, 246
Hospicia, xvii, xviii, xx–xxi
House chamber, 236
House of office:
  duty to clean, xlii, 203
  levy for repair, xxxv, 233–4
  tenant's right to use, 166–8
  watchmen to visit, xli, 202
"Housekeeper", xxxiv, 33

Imparlance, xxviii
Infamy, conduct causing, 223
Infant members, xlii, 70–1
"Inn", meaning of, xvii
Inner Temple (*see also* Inns of Court;
  Legal Inns; Temple):
  Admission Books, liv
  admissions from Inns of Chancery,
    xxiv, 61, 146
  admittance and pledges, lv
  certificates of performance of learning,
    xxiv, xxix
  choice of Reader of Inns of Chancery,
    xxiii
  committee on mooting, xxix
  dispute with Middle Temple over
    Lyon's Inn, xxv
  imparlance at, xxviii
  index to orders, lii
  Inns of Chancery belonging to (*and
    see* Clement's Inn; Clifford's Inn;
    Lyon's Inn), xxii
  Kellett affair referred to, xlviii
  mooting, &c., in, xxvii
  "parliaments", vii
  petty moots required, xxx
  practice as to assignments followed, 244
  precedence, dispute over, xxvi
  sale of Clifford's Inn, action on, lxvi–
    lxvii
  tax assessment, 241
  threatened secession from, xv
  trading forbidden, xli
  under-Treasurer, xxxix, xl
Inns of Chancery (*see also* Legal Inns):
  attached to Inns of Court, xxii
  attorneys driven back to, xx
  attorneys or solicitors occupy, lvi
  barristers in, xix, xxix
  decline of mooting, xxxi
  Defence Fund, lxv
  juvenes in, xviii
  last years of, lxi–lxvii
  list of, xviii, xxii
  minora hospicia, xviii
  Readers sent to, xxiii, xxv
  subordinate to Inns of Court, xxii
  university, project of legal, lxi, lxiv

Inns of Court (*see also* Gray's Inn; Inner
  Temple; Lincoln's Inn; Middle
  Temple; *and see* Legal Inns):
  attachment of Inns of Chancery, xxii,
    xxv
  attorneys excluded from, xx
  majora hospicia, xviii
  name, explanation of, xx–xxi
  number of members, xviii
  origins, xvi
  Readers sent from, to Inns of Chancery,
    xxii, xxiii
  supervision of Inns of Chancery, xxii
Insolvent defaulters, 181
Interest:
  general directive to pay, xxxv, 143, 160
  on individuals' loans. *See* Advances
  on loans: for rebuilding Hall, 4, 5, 48,
    118; for rebuilding No. 14, 209–11
  release by Blackwell, 115–16

Johnsoniana, lix, 280, 284–5
Joiner's room, 143
Judicature Act, lxii

Kellett dispute, xlvii, 218, 238
"Kentish men" (Clifford's Inn), lxvi
King's tax (*see also* Taxes), 177
Kitchen:
  cellar, 38
  cook not to be disturbed, 221
  New River water for, 50
  re-building, xxxv, 232–3
  vessels not to be removed, 222

Lamb gate, li
Lamb Inn, xliv, 65, 100, 243, 244
Land tax (*and see* Taxes):
  Gofton's default, xl, 177
  parish authority resisted, 242
Latin, lii, lv, 218
Law courts:
  at Westminster, xvi
  in Strand, lxiv
Law schools excluded from City, xvi
Law Society, xxxi, lxi, lxiii–lxiv, lxvi, 303
Laymen admitted to Inn, lvii
Learning:
  conduct prejudicial to, 222, 224
  exercises of, xxvii
  Vacations, xvii
Leases:
  Book of, 141, 243
  building. *See* Building leases
  covenants in, xlii, xlv, 246
  lessee for another person, 245
  Wrightson's, 243
  see also Chambers
Lector. See Readers
Lecturers. *See* St Clement Danes
Legal education (*see also* Exercises of
  learning; Mooting; Students):
  charitable purpose, lxii–lxvii

Legal education—*continued*
 Inns' function, xvi–xix, xxii, xxvii–xxxii, lxi–lxii, lxiv, lxvii
 Readers' responsibility, xxv
 Select Committee on, xxxi
Legal Inns (*see also* Inns of Chancery; Inns of Court):
 accommodation in, xx
 Denton–Bacon–Cary report, xi, xv, xxii, xxvii, xxxix, liv, lxi, 220
 extra-parochial and privileged places, xiv, xxxviii, 243
 hospicia majora and *minora*, xvii;
 not incorporated, xv, xvii
 numbers in, xviii
 origins obscure, xvi–xvii
 property held in trust, xv
Lent and Autumn Readers, xvii
Limitations, Statute of, 190
"Lincoln" family, xiv
Lincoln, Dean and Chapter of, lxiv
Lincoln's Inn (*see also* Inns of Court; Legal Inns):
 acquires Inns of Chancery, xxii
 attachment of Furnival's and Davy's Inns, xxii–xxiii
 banking, xxxv
 Clement's Inn men joining, xxxiii, 22, 93
 committee on mooting, xxix
 early records, xvii
 Fortescue a governor, xviii
 Furnival's Inn Principal admitted, xxiii
 index to orders, lii
 litigation, 277, 293
 steward's fees, xxxix
Lincolnshire, lvi
Literary admittees, lviii–lix
London:
 building restrictions, xlv–xlvi, 230
 householders in, xxxiv
 law schools vanished from City, xvi
 Lord Mayor and lawyers, xvi
 New Inn and L.C.C., lxvi
Lyon's Inn (*see also* Inns of Chancery; Legal Inns):
 acquired by Inner Temple, xxii, xxv
 choice of Reader, xxiii
 demolition, lxi
 gratis admission at Inner Temple, xxiv
 Middle Temple asks for, xxv
 mooting at, xxix, xxxi
 last years, lxi
 rent, 4
 Serjeants, attending call of, xxvi, 187

Map, Horwood's (frontispiece), xliii
Marshal marks, lii, liii, 218–19
Mercers' Company, lxv
Middle Temple (*see also* Inns of Court; Legal Inns; Temple):
 acquires New Inn, xxii
 admissions to, xxiv

Middle Temple—*continued*
 attachment of New and Strand Inns, xxii
 attempt to obtain Lyon's Inn, xxv
 Clement's Inn men joining, xxiv, 99, 103, 184
 Furnival's Inn MS., vii
 New Inn compensation, lxvi
 seniority dispute, xxvi
 Serjeants, ceremonial at call of, xxvi, 186
Minora hospicia, xviii
Minors, xlii, 70–1
Mooting:
 at Clement's Inn in vacation, xvii, 220
 at Inns of Chancery, xxxi
 at Lyon's Inn, xxix
 duty to moot, 224
 exercises of learning, xxvii–xxxii
 fine for absence, 220, 224
 "quashing" moot, xxviii, 220
Mortgage:
 of Barnard's Inn, lxv
 Clement's Inn, xxxv, 4–5, 109, 114, 211–212
 Staple Inn, lxiii
Murders, xiii, xli, 197, 267

Natura Brevium, reading from, liii, 220
Necessary house. *See* House of office
New Inn:
 attached to Middle Temple, xxii
 disputes with Clement's Inn over: ancient lights, 242; garden gate, xiv, 11–12, 244
 Elyott, Serjt, Reader of, l
 last years, lxvi
 L.C.C. acquires, lxvi
 Serjeants, attending call of, 187
New River water, 50
Noble pensioners, liii, 222, 226
Nomine poenae, 222
Nuisance, complaints of:
 Ford's proposed building, 230
 Lamb Inn horsepond, 243

Oaths:
 admittees', xi
 Ancients, xxxviii, 181, 192, 202, 214
Orders. *See* Constitutions and orders; Statutes and ordinances

Padlocking:
 House chamber wrongly occupied, 236
 new locks ordered, 240
 non-members' chambers, xlii, 94, 173, 179, 202, 208, 212–13
 offence of striking off lock, 236, 240
 rent defaulter's chamber, 94, 102, 241
 warrant against offenders, xxxiv, 240
Palings, 17, 40
Panniermen, xlii
Paving way through courts, 22

Pendennis, lix
Pension:
  (i) *governing body of Inn*, vii
      constitution (*see also* Ancients;
        Principal), xiv, xxxvii
      duty to attend, 224
      meetings and business, xiv, 124
      no quorum, xiv
  (ii) *periodical payment:*
      amount, xxxiii, 2
      no abatement, xxxiii, 240
      Principal excused, 228
      separate liability for additional
        chambers, xliii, 31, 178, 180, 244
      suspended (no Roll), 16, 23, 27
Pension Book:
  Clement's Inn MS., vii
  clerical errors, xiii, xl, 68, 107, 118,
    135, 141, 170, 176, 182
  supplementary extracts, viii, xi, 227, 239
  text, 1
Pews. *See* St Clement Danes
Pictures:
  Barnard's Inn, lxiii, lxv
  Clement's Inn: Blackwell's portrait,
    xiv, lxiii, 104, 244; Crewe's portrait,
    viii, 126; Halsted's gift, viii, xiv, lxiii,
    126, 244;
  sale, lxiii
  Serjeant's Inn, lxiii
Pledge or surety, xxxii, liv, lv, 249
Porters (*see also* Servants):
  appointments, 203
  attorneys' addresses left with porter,
    lvii
  butler and head porter, xl, xli, 203
  "Clare Market gate" (back gate), xli,
    104, 109, 143
  duties, xli–xlii, 202–3, 223, 228
  fore-gate, xl, 109, 203
  gown and staff, xiii, 56
  lodge, xxxv, 143
  officiating porter, 144
  "porters' rolls", xxxiii
  rent reduced, 202
  wife's services, 203
Praetor, xvii
Precedence:
  among members of the Inn, 246, 279,
    282, 295
  between Inns, xxvi
Principal:
  accounts audited, 7 (Brewster); 34, 42,
    59, 68, 74, 82, 96, 106, 116 (Black-
    well); 111, 120, 127, 129, 136, 142
    (Dovey); 154, 165, 169, 185,
    191 (Penny); 213–15 (Dewes); 241
    (Wrightson)
  choosing of, xxxvi, 227, 231
  contradicting, 222
  duty to accompany at revels, 223
  excused pension, 228
  financial functions, xxxv–xxxvi

Principal—*continued*
  Edwards retires, 227
  election, xxxvii, 122–3 (Dovey); 137,
    179, 190 (Penny); 195 (Dovey); 198–
    200 (Green, Trayton and Goodacre);
    207, 209, 216 (Dewes)
  gift to outgoing, xiv
  handing over balance, 237
  not to demand allowance, 224
  not to take less from debtor, 225
  period of office, 227, 231
  refusal to serve, xv, 198, 200, 228
  seat in church, 14
  students' chambers, 226
  title: of "Principal", xxi; stopped at
    Barnard's Inn, lxv
  vote at appointment of officers, &c., 226
  voting for Principal, xiv–xv
Prosecution of bond. *See* Bond
Prudential Assurance, lxiii, lxv
Public houses, frequenting, 221
"Put-case", xxviii, 219
"Putting extra", 67, 252, 254, 255, 258,
  260

Railings, 17, 40
Readers at Inns of Court:
  payments by, xxx
Readers at Inns of Chancery:
  admonitions to, xxviii–xxix
  choosing of, xxiii, xxx–xxxii
  certificate of Reading performed, xxx
  functions, xxv, xxxii
  Pension Book records of Readings: 155
    (Jenyns); 160 (Ward); 168 (New-
    lands); 179 (Wheate); 183 (Parker);
    188 (Forester); 190 (Capper); 193
    (Brown); 194 (Knowler); 196 (But-
    ler); 197 (Stephens); 199 (?); 205
    Churchill; 206 (Bonner)
  Reader's privileges for students, xxv,
    251, 253, 255
  Readership prized by Inner Temple, xxv
  refusing or failing to read, xxix, xxx
  students from Inner Temple accom-
    pany, xxviii, 155, 160–1
  topics, xxxi
  vacation Readings, 220
Regnal year, lv
Rent:
  abatement decisions, 139, 234, 244
  accounts, 35
  scales, 226, 228
Repastor, xxxiii, 242
Reporting, exercise of, 220
Revels, liii, 219, 222, 223
Royal Commission:
  of 1854, xi, xxxi, xxxii, l, lix, lx, lxii,
    lxiv
  on City Companies, lxiv
Royal Mint, 280
Royal nobles, liii, 218, 219

Rolls:
  attorneys' roll, lvii, 303
  commoners' roll, 219
  duplication of rolls, 225
  pension rolls, 16, 23, 27
  servants' (or porters') rolls, xxxiii, 43
  striking off insolvent debtors, 181

Sacrament, duty to receive, 229
St Clement Danes:
  absence from church (fine), 222
  contributions from Clement's Inn: for
    beautifying and organ repair, 243;
    church and steeple repairs, 87–8, 244;
    rectors and lecturers, xiii, xxxvi, 18,
    62, 107, 109, 153; re-lining of pews,
    130, 244
  Dr Johnson at, lix
  fore-gate opposite, xliv
  seats reserved for Inn, xli, l, 14, 244
St Mary's Inn, xviii
Select Committee (House of Commons),
  xxxi
Serjeants at Law (see also Serjeants' Inn):
  call ceremony, xiv, xxvi, xlii, 186
  Clifford's Inn, Serjeant from, xix
  Judicature Act effect, lxii
Serjeant's Inn:
  Chancery Lane site sold, lxii, lxiv
  Fleet Street site, lxii
  not founded for legal education, xvi,
    lxii
  pictures, lxiii
Servants (see also Butler; Porter; Watchmen):
  appointment by Principal, 221, 237
  beating or displacing, 221, 240
  Clement's Inn establishment, xl
  masters' responsibility, 228, 236
  permitted to be in chambers, 232
  salaries increased, 246
  seats in church, 14
  servants in commons, 224
  servants' (or porters') rolls, xxxiii, 43
"Shepherd's Inn", lix
Sheriffs' fees, xxxiv, 41
Shops:
  fruiterer's, 101
  stationer's, 98
  vintner's, 40, 97, 119
  watch distrained for shop rate, 242
Six Clerks' Office, lviii
Solicitors (see also Attorneys; Law
  Society):
  dining club, lx
  "gentlemen", lvi
  ordered to join an Inn, xxxiii, lvii
  social status, xx, lvi
Spalding Gentlemen's Society, 262
Staff for back-gate porter, 56
Stair-cases:
  position, xliii–xlv
  re-numbered, xlv, 168

Stamp duty, lix, 295
Staple Inn (see also Inns of Chancery;
  Legal Inns):
  admissions, lv
  attached to Gray's Inn, xxii, xxvi
  call of Serjeant from Gray's Inn, xxvi
  last years, lxiii
  mooting discontinued, xxxi
  sale, lxii–lxiv
Statutes and ordinances:
  power to make, 223
  Principal to read, 224
  see also Constitutions and orders
Steward (or clerk):
  appointments at Clement's Inn, xl; 62
    (Tufton vice Callow); 75, 153, 159
    (Barras); 132 (Brightwell Smith);
    172, 177 (Gofton); 199–200 (Perkins)
  answerable for profit, 210
  attends at times of eating and learning,
    219
  collection of dues, xxxv
  fine: for not serving, 219; for super-
    fluous expense, 219
  law case put to, 219
  office and duties, xxxix
  shows roll of commoners, 219
  weekly tenure, 219
Stock of the House, xxxv, 225, 246
Stock Exchange, 302
Strand (or Chester) Inn:
  attached to Middle Temple, xxii
  demolished, xxv
Strand Hotel Company, lxi
"Strangers" (see also Admittances), 235
Students:
  chambers for xx, liii, 226
  clerks of Chancery, xxi
  exercises of learning, 226
  no distractions of, 230
"Studies", xlv
Subscriptions. See Advances; Companions; St. Clement Danes
Supremacy, Oath of, xxxviii, 181, 192, 202,
  214
Surety. See Pledge

Talbot alehouse, xlv, 91, 161–4, 184, 193
Taxes (see also Land tax; Stamp duty):
  Clement's Inn and members' arrears,
    xxxiv, 2, 10
  Gofton's default, 177
  Inner Temple, assessment, 241
  "King's tax", 2, 177
Taylor papers (in P.R.O.), vii, viii, xi, li, 249
Temple (see also Inner Temple, Legal
  Inns; Middle Temple):
  disputed seniority between Inner and
    Middle, xxvi
  "dropt" children, xiv
  how founded, xviii
  Temple Bar, xxiii, 230
  "Temple" family, xiv

Terms, admissions recorded by, 249
  attorneys in town during, xviii
  "issuable", xxxiii, 138
  length of, xvii
  members' absence during, xxxiii
Thavie's (or Davy's) Inn (*see also* Inns of Chancery, Legal Inns):
  attendance at call of Serjeants, 187
  barristers at, xix
  linked to and acquired by Lincoln's Inn, xxii
  Principal from Inner Temple, xxiv
  two Temples perhaps founded from, xviii
Theatrical associations, lviii, 276, 281, 292, 301
Trades:
  shops in Clement's Inn, xliii
  trading advertisements, lix, 246
Treasons, disclosure of, xxxviii
Trover, 242
Trusts:
  Inns held by trustees, xv, 4, 109–10, 114, 238
  sale as breach of trust, lxiii, lxiv, lxvi
  trust for sale (Barnard's Inn), lxiv
  trustee for deceased member, 135
Turnspits, xlii

Under-Treasurer (Inner Temple), xxxix
University:
  medieval, xvi
  project of legal, lxi, lxiv
  students from, xix

Vacations:
  dues during, xvii, 219
  Learning Vacations, xvii
  lectures and moots, 220, 226
  readings, 227
Visus in villa, 222
Voting, 226

Wagers amongst Ancients, lx
Wainscotting, &c. *See* Chambers
Warrant, Chief Justice's, 240
Warwickshire, lvi
Washpots, xlii
Watchmen:
  appointment, xli, 197, 203
  duties, xli, 202
  fine for neglect, 207
  keeping premises clean, xlii
Water:
  supply, 50
  throwing out of windows, 236
Weapon, thrusting, 221
Westminster:
  Court of C.P. at, xvi
  householders in, xxxiv
  Serjeant's procession to, xxvi, 186
Windows. *See* Ancient Lights
Wine, lx
Wives, members', xxxiv, 222, 225
Women:
  in the Inn, lviii, 221, 301
  pledges, 262, 275, 278, 306, 307
Words, disquieting or annoying, 221
Workmen. *See* Buildings
Works and Buildings, H.M. Commrs of, lxiii
Writing (*see also* Court hand):
  writings to be abstracted into Book of Leases, 141, 243
Writs:
  daily reading, xxvii, liii, 220
  Natura brevium, 220
  nuisance (Ford's case), 230
  study of, xxi
  trover and conversion, 242

Yards:
  Angel Inn, 247–8
  fencing (between chambers), 40
  Lamb Inn, 65

Copies of *Publications, List of Members and Rules*, current to January 1959, can be
obtained on application to the Secretary of the Society at the Institute of Advanced
Legal Studies, 25 Russell Square, London, W.C.1.

THE FOLLOWING VOLUMES ARE NOW IN THE PRESS (April, 1960):—

Lord Nottingham's Chancery Cases. Vol. II. Edited by Mr. D. E. C. YALE, Fellow
of Christ's College, Cambridge.

Early Register of Writs. Edited by Dr. ELSA DE HAAS, Brooklyn College.

Year Book Series. Year Books of 12 Edward II (1319). Edited from sundry MSS. by
Professor J. P. COLLAS. Part Easter Term and Trinity Term.

Readings at the Inns of Court in the 15th Century. Vol. II, *Moot Cases.* Edited by
Professor S. E. THORNE, Professor of Legal History, Harvard University.

Doctor and Student by CHRISTOPHER ST. GERMAIN. Edited by Professor T. F. T.
PLUCKNETT, F.B.A.

Glossary of Law-French. Compiled by the late Miss ELSIE SHANKS and Professor
T. F. T. PLUCKNETT, F.B.A.

*A General Guide to the Society's publications, with a detailed and indexed summary of
the contents of the introduction.* By Dr. A. K. R. KIRALFY, Reader in Law, and GARETH
JONES, Lecturer in Law, King's College, University of London.

THE FOLLOWING VOLUMES ARE IN PREPARATION:—

Pleas before the King or his Justices, 1203–1212. Edited by Lady STENTON, F.B.A.

Year Book Series. Year Books of 14 Edward II. Edited by Dr. S. J. STOLJAR and by
Professor T. F. T. PLUCKNETT, F.B.A.

The Eyre of London, 14 Edward II. Edited by Professor HELEN CAM, C.B.E., F.B.A.

Pleas in Ecclesiastical Courts, from MSS. in Canterbury Cathedral. Edited by Professor
NORMA ADAMS, Mount Holyoke College, Mass.

Fleta. Vol. I. Introduction, Commentary and Index. Vol. III. Books 3 and 4.
Vol. IV. Books 5 and 6. Edited by H. G. RICHARDSON, F.B.A. and Professor
G. O. SAYLES, D.Litt., of the University of Aberdeen.

Decrees and Cases in the Court of Wards and Liveries. Edited by Mr. H. E. BELL,
Fellow of New College, Oxford.

Novae Narrationes. Edited by the late Miss ELSIE SHANKS and Mr. S. F. C. MILSOM,
Fellow of New College, Oxford.

The Fine of Lands. Edited by Mr. H. G. RICHARDSON, F.B.A.

Novum Formulare Anglicanum. Edited by Professor V. H. GALBRAITH, F.B.A., Emeritus
Professor of Modern History in the University of Oxford.

A New Placita Anglo-Normannica. Edited by Dr. R. C. VAN CAENEGEM, University of
Ghent.

Select Cases in the Court of King's Bench. Vol. VI. Edward III: 1341–1377. Edited
by Professor G. O. SAYLES, D.Litt., of the University of Aberdeen.

Maitland's Collected Papers. 2 vols. Edited with bibliographical notes by Professor
S. E. THORNE, Professor of Legal History, Harvard University.